D1175193

The Challenge of Affluence

The Challenge of Affluence

Self-Control and Well-Being in the United States and Britain since 1950

Avner Offer

OXFORD
UNIVERSITY PRESS

OXFORD

UNIVERSITY PRESS

Great Clarendon Street, Oxford OX2 6DP

Oxford University Press is a department of the University of Oxford.
It furthers the University's objective of excellence in research, scholarship,
and education by publishing worldwide in

Oxford New York

Auckland Cape Town Dar es Salaam Hong Kong Karachi
Kuala Lumpur Madrid Melbourne Mexico City Nairobi
New Delhi Shanghai Taipei Toronto

With offices in

Argentina Austria Brazil Chile Czech Republic France Greece
Guatemala Hungary Italy Japan Poland Portugal Singapore
South Korea Switzerland Thailand Turkey Ukraine Vietnam

Oxford is a registered trade mark of Oxford University Press
in the UK and in certain other countries

Published in the United States
by Oxford University Press Inc., New York

© Avner Offer 2006

The moral rights of the author have been asserted
Database right Oxford University Press (maker)

First published 2006

All rights reserved. No part of this publication may be reproduced,
stored in a retrieval system, or transmitted, in any form or by any means,
without the prior permission in writing of Oxford University Press,
or as expressly permitted by law, or under terms agreed with the appropriate
reprographics rights organization. Enquiries concerning reproduction
outside the scope of the above should be sent to the Rights Department,
Oxford University Press, at the address above

You must not circulate this book in any other binding or cover
and you must impose the same condition on any acquirer

British Library Cataloguing in Publication Data

Data available

Library of Congress Cataloging in Publication Data

Data available

Typeset by Newgen Imaging Systems (P) Ltd., Chennai, India
Printed in Great Britain
on acid-free paper by
Biddles Ltd., King's Lynn, Norfolk

ISBN 0–19–820853–7   978–0–19–820853–2

10 9 8 7 6 5 4

For Leah, again

Only a very small part of the art of being happy is an exact science
Stendhal, *Love* (1822)

Preface

Resources and cravings do not map precisely on to well-being. Back in the eighteenth century, Adam Smith asked, 'What are the advantages which we propose to gain by that great purpose of human life which we call bettering our condition?'[1] In the 1980s, the answer was often that 'greed is good'. That notion was the spur for my inquiry. It was brashly counter-intuitive, but why? Over the last two decades, a new understanding began to emerge, especially from psychology and economics, that what we want and choose can often fail to deliver, and can even be counter-productive. It might be paraphrased (brutally) by asking 'what is greed good for?' This understanding is the work of many inquiries and disciplines. My effort here is to extrapolate it to the personal dynamics of affluence during the last six decades, in the United States and Britain.

The argument is that affluence is driven by novelty, and that novelty unsettles. It is summarized in a brief introduction. The chapters connect with common experience at many points: how to evaluate well-being; the dilemmas and rewards of choice, reciprocity, and trust; the impact of advertising, eating, appliances, and automobiles; the prizes and penalties of personal appearance, of social status, of love, of parenthood, and of separation. I conclude with summaries of findings, and with some larger reflections. The book navigates the vast river of social-science research, both old and new. For its primary sources, it draws on archives, on statistical sources, and on magazines and books from the times and places it studies.

Modern universities are typical products of affluence, but also provide a haven where truth can be pursued. Thanks to those I have worked in, Oxford primarily, and before that the Australian National, and York in England. Nuffield College provided challenge and companionship, and the relentless bustle of current thinking. It was a joy to be there. All Souls College is equally friendly, but tuned to longer cycles of experience. My Oxford colleagues in economic and social history have helped in various

---

[1] Smith, *Moral Sentiments*, Bk 1, ch. ii.l, p. 50.

ways, and have stood in during sabbaticals. Visiting fellowships at Duke, Rutgers, and New York Universities gave observation posts on American society. Especially warm thanks to Victoria de Grazia and to Tony Judt, my academic hosts in New Jersey and New York. Among archivists, I am grateful for hospitality and help to the late Michael Cudlipp and to Margaret Rose at the History of Advertising Trust, to Elaine Gartrell McGeorge at Duke University, to Darleen Flaherty at the Ford Industrial Archives at Dearborn, Michigan, to the Henry Ford museum and archives in the same town, and to the late Mark Abrams, for the generous loan of personal papers on advertising and market research. The Leverhulme Foundation, Oxford University, Nuffield, and All Souls also gave financial support.

Over more than a decade, my graduate course on 'the challenge of affluence' enrolled able students from the four corners of the earth. Of their dissertations, those of Bryan Leach, Sara Franks, Michael Hicks, Joo Lee Lim, Joyce Liu, Shinobu Majima, Craig Mullaney, Raphael Schapiro, and Christine Whelan are acknowledged here. Harold Carter was an incisive commentator in those classes. Over the years, a succession of research assistants have each made distinctive contributions and comments. I include their names here among the many friends and colleagues who have generously made time to read separate chapters (sometimes many more than one) or to make helpful criticism. The list is long, and comes with apologies for any oversights: Rebecca Abrams, Robert Allen, Tony Atkinson, Eleni Bantinaki, Katerina Bantinaki, Yoram Barzel, Joanna Bourke, Sue Bowden, Gavin Cameron, Harold Carter, Annie Chan, Tak Wing Chan Jerry Cohen, Lynn Cooke, Paul David, Chris Davis, Eleni Delivani, Nicholas Dimsdale, Juliet Dowsett, David Engerman, the late Charles Feinstein, James Foreman-Peck, Robert Frank, Diego Gambetta, David Garrard, Jay Gershuny, Joshua Getzler, Flora Gill, David Halpern, Irit Harchol, José Harris, Maïa-Laura Ibsen, Harriet Jackson, Heather Joshi, Daniel Kahneman, Pramila Krishnan, Robert Lane, Tim Leunig, Christian List, Ian Little, Ofra Magidor, Robin Mason, Katharine Massam, Siobhan McAndrew, Mara Meacci, John Muellbauer, Sharon Musher, Shepley Orr, Andrew Oswald, Derek Parfit, Joy Parr, Matthew Polisson, John Robinson, Raphael Schapiro, Hetan Shah, Todd Shaiman, Martin Spät, Peter Temin, J.L.H. Thomas, Mark Thomas, Julia Twigg, Hans-Joachim Voth, Christine Whelan, and Jay Winter. An earlier version of Chapter 8 was initially published jointly as an article with Prof. Sue Bowden. Four other previously published papers have also been rewritten and updated. Along the way, editors and referees were usually helpful and reasonable, and sometimes not. Blame me alone for anything shoddy or wrong.

My tentative intuitions were encouraged by George Ainslie, initially through his tour-de-force *Picoeconomics* (1992), and later in personal meetings. Other inspiration was provided by Jon Elster, in his *Ulysses and the Sirens* (1979) and a sequence of equally elegant books. Daniel Kahneman, David Laibson, George Loewenstein, and Andrew Oswald were also important influences. As with previous efforts, my wife Leah has supported me throughout, and has enlarged my vision with her subtle conception of well-being, derived from the teachings of South Asian philosophies. Thanks to my son and daughter too, whose own lives are sources of happiness and reflection to me. The book has taken long to write, and is still not quite finished. But it is ample enough for now. Please come in. Samuel Madden, a friend of Dr Johnson, said that in an orchard 'there should be enough to eat, enough to lay up, enough to be stolen, and enough to rot upon the ground.'[2] I feel that way about this book. Make it yours as well.

Avner Offer

Oxford
March 2005

[2] Dr Samuel Madden, cited in Boswell, *Life of Johnson*, 296.

Acknowledgements

For permission to reproduce illustrations, I am grateful as follows: Figure 6.1 is reproduced with kind permission of Unilever plc. Figures 6.2 and 11.6 are reproduced with permission from the Hartman Center, Rare Book, Manuscript and Special Collections Library, Duke University, and also from the Ford Motor Company. The Ford Motor Company has also granted kind permission to reproduce Figure 9.1. Figure 9.2 is reprinted with permission from the American Society of Automotive Engineers, from SAE Paper 620236 © 1962 SAE International. Figure 12.3 is reprinted with permission from Simon and Schuster Inc. Earlier versions of some chapters have appeared in the following publications: Chapter 2 in Paul A. David and Mark Thomas (eds.), *The Economic Future in Historical Perspective* (Oxford: Oxford University Press for the British Academy, 2003), ch. 12. Chapter 5 is based on 'Between the Gift and the Market: The Economy of Regard', *Economic History Review*, 50,3 (1997); Chapter 6 is derived from A. Offer (ed.), *In Pursuit of the Quality of Life* (Oxford: Oxford University Press, 1996), ch. 10. Chapter 7 is based on 'Body Weight and Self-Control in the United States and Britain since the 1950s', *Social History of Medicine*, 14,1 (2001). Chapter 8 is developed from 'Household Appliances and the Use of Time: The United States and Britain since the 1920s', *Economic History Review*, 47,4 (1994), like Chapter 5 with permission from the Economic History Society. Chapters 9 and 10 incorporate some material which first appeared in K. Bruland and P. K. O'Brien (eds.), *From Family Firms to Corporate Capitalism* (Oxford: Oxford University Press, 1998), ch. 12. Apologies to any owners of copyright whom I have inadvertently overlooked or have failed to trace.

Contents

List of Figures

List of Tables

List of Abbreviations

AA	Advertising Association
BBC	British Broadcasting Corporation. Britain's tax-funded public broadcasting agency
BLS	Bureau of Labor Statistics
BMI	Body Mass Index (BMI = weight (kg) / height^2 (cm))
Cmnd. (or Cmd.)	Serial number in House of Commons papers (See 'PP' below)
EAW	Economic Aspects of Welfare. An index developed in Zolotas, *Economic Growth*
ESI	Economic Security Index
FIA	Ford Industrial Archives (Dearborn, Mich)
FTC	Federal Trade Commission. An American regulatory agency, involved *inter alia* in the regulation of advertising
GCI	Gross Community Income, Australia (from Snooks, *Portrait of the Family*). An extended accounting measure of national income which includes household production
GDP	Gross Domestic Product. An element of SNA (see below). Estimate of annual output excluding depreciation and property income from abroad
GNP	Gross National Product. An element of SNA (see below). Estimate of annual output including property income from abroad
GPI	General Progress Indicator (Cobb et al., *General Progress Indicator*)
HAT	History of Advertising Trust, located in Raveningham, Norfolk, UK
Hartman Center	John W. Hartman Center for Sales, Advertising and Marketing History, Rare Book, Manuscript, and Special Collections Library, Duke University
HDI	Human Development Index, endorsed by the United Nations
ILO	International Labour Organization
IPUMS	IPUMS consists of high-precision samples of historical (and current) American censuses. The official citation is Steven

	Ruggles, Matthew Sobek, Trent Alexander, Catherine A. Fitch, Ronald Goeken, Patricia Kelly Hall, Miriam King, and Chad Ronnander, *Integrated Public Use Microdata Series: Version 3.0* (machine-readable database). Minneapolis: Minnesota Population Center (producer and distributor), 2004. **www.ipums.org**
ISEW	Index of Sustainable Economic Welfare. Introduced by Daly and Cobb, *Common Good*
JAMA	*Journal of the American Medical Association*
JWT	J. Walter Thompson. The leading advertising agency in the United States up to the 1980s. United States archives are kept in the Hartman Center, Duke University Library. A collection of the London office papers is in History of Advertising Trust archive at the Raveningham Centre, Raveningham, Norfolk
MDP	Measure of Domestic Progress. A measure of welfare developed by Tim Jackson in the UK
MEW	Measure of Economic Welfare. Proposed by Nordhaus and Tobin, 'Is Growth Obsolete?'
NADA	National Automobiles Dealers Assocation (USA)
NNP	Net National Product. An element of SNA (see below). Estimate of annual output including property income from abroad, and taking account of the depreciation of capital
NRR	Non-renewable resources
OECD	Organization for Economic Cooperation and Development
OLS	Ordinary Least Squares. A method of applying the best-fit linear trend to statistical data
ONS	United Kingdom Office of National Statistics
PP	Parliamentary Papers. The item is part of British government publications in the House of Commons series of parliamentary papers. 'Cmnd. or Cmd.' [q.v.] number gives the serial number
PPP	Purchasing Power Parity. An exchange rate at which it is possible to purchase the same amount of goods in two different currencies
PQLI	Physical Quality of Life Index. Introduced by Morris David Morris
SEI	Socio-economic index. A measure of occupational ranking based on a combination of education and income. In this book, primarily the index devised by Otis Dudley Duncan
SEP	*Saturday Evening Post*
SNA	System of National Accounts (estimates of National Income, Output and Expenditure)

List of Abbreviations

SUV	Sports Utility Vehicle
SWB	'subjective well-being'. A response (on a linear scale) to a survey question about the subjective sense of happiness or well-being
TISA	Total Income System of Accounts
USDA	United States Department of Agriculture
WHO	World Health Organization

1

Introduction

'The test of your generation will not be how well you stood up under adversity, but how well you endured prosperity'

(Robert McNamara, General Manager of the
Ford Division, Ford Motor Company; commencement speech
at the University of Alabama, 29 May 1955)[1]

Impatience

Affluence breeds impatience, and impatience undermines well-being. This is the core of my argument. For detail and evidence, go directly to the chapters; for implications, to the conclusion, which also has chapter summaries.

Since the Second World War, the markets of Western Europe and the United States have delivered a flow of novel and compelling opportunities, services, and goods. North America and Western Europe are about three times as rich as they were in 1950. I call that affluence. But abundance and novelty cause harm as well. They displace and devalue the stock of pre-existing possessions, virtues, relations, and values. Enticing rewards have mutated into unwelcome consequences. 'I'd walk a mile for a Camel' declared an early cigarette ad. By 1955, some three-quarters of men in Britain were smoking, and 40 per cent of women.[2] From the emergence of cheap cigarettes early in the century, five or six decades had to go by before it emerged that smoking is easy to start, hard to give up, and kills prematurely and painfully. For decades the pleasures of smoking screened out the

---

[1] Ford Industrial Archives (henceforth FIA), AR-20–46, Speeches.
[2] In the USA, half the men and a quarter of the women. Nicolaides-Bouman, *International Smoking Statistics*, tables 21.4.1–2.

potential damage to health. But tobacco continues to be indulged in by smokers, and defended by vendors. It exemplifies a pervasive dilemma: how to balance immediate desires against the interests of the future?

During the economic 'golden age' of the 1950s and 1960s there was work for all, better food, housing, clothing, entertainment, education, health; upwards mobility, more choice and freedom for women, easier travel and migration, a more inclusive society, more open to outsiders and to aliens. Progress persisted more fitfully during the 1980s and 1990s, and its benefits did not reach so far down, but people live seven or eight years longer than they did after the Second World War.

On the dark side, in the United States, more than 2 million people are in prison, about one adult male in fifty (one out of ten of black men between 25 and 29). Except for homicide, Britain has overtaken the United States in most types of crime. Other disorders abound: family breakdown, addiction, stress, road and landscape congestion, obesity, poverty, denial of health care, mental disorder, violence, economic fraud, and insecurity. Social critics warn that communities are unraveling and 'social capital' dissipating, interpersonal trust is declining, subjective well-being is stagnant, and most social institutions, business and government, but also science and the media, are held in lower repute.

The paradox of affluence and its challenge is that the flow of new rewards can undermine the capacity to enjoy them. All experiences are ultimately in the mind. They all demand attention and time. Attention can be taken as the universal currency of well-being. At any given moment, we can 'consume' it, by focusing on one or more pleasant or enjoyable activities. Or we can 'invest' in some activity which holds out the promise of more satisfaction in the future. A young student ponders whether to spend the evening revising at her desk, or to go out with friends. Call her Emma. Better marks mean better prospects, but dancing and drink are attractive too. How much to sacrifice tonight for a remote future? When to stop having fun, but also, when to stop being serious?

It makes it easier that many decisions are already made for her: examination dates are fixed, teachers, parents, friends, all have their expectations, she has expectations too, and can imagine what success and failure might bring. Education sets up a sequence of deadlines, rules, norms, rites of passage, 'bright lines' for failure and success, that help to allocate attention appropriately, and punish her if she doesn't. Her parents have given her, over many years, a great deal of attention. Nameless taxpayers, many not even parents themselves, have sacrificed something they wanted more (a longer holiday, a better car?) to make it possible for her to study. These conventions, expectations, and institutions have built up gradually over decades and centuries, to form a stock of equipment available to deal with her problem. Call them 'commitment devices', or 'commitment technologies', which she leans on in devising her own 'commitment strategies'.

Well-being is not measured merely in terms of the abundance of goods and services. It requires a sustainable balance between the present and the future. This also requires a personal capacity for commitment. Call this capacity 'prudence'. Prudence is not easy. It takes an effort for Emma, although she can draw on a long course of socialization, on exposure to other people, and on the disciplines of institutions. The resources and strategies of self-control, both cognitive and social, take time to develop. When they persist, they form durable cultures and norms.

The opposite of prudence, imprudence, is also pervasive, but nevertheless presents a puzzle to social scientists. If people know their own interests, why should they make self-defeating choices? When choices imply adverse consequences, they are called 'time inconsistent'. More colloquially, I call them 'myopic choice'. Myopia implies that it is possible to do better by resisting something that looks good. The persistence of myopia suggests that choice can be fallible.

Freedom of choice ranks very high among the values of consumer societies, but even liberal societies do not entirely trust our capacity to choose wisely, and do not rely on self-interest alone to guide us. Individual choice is restricted by statute and regulation. It is also circumscribed by a web of voluntary constraint, of prior obligation to families, and children, to lovers, spouses, and friends, to colleagues and employers, to religion and nation. Even in a free society, the notion of 'freedom' is elusive, or (in view of the legitimate, binding, moral force of obligation), occasionally pernicious. But in the absence of all of these bonds, the task of self-control would be even more difficult than it is.

The strongest form of myopia is addiction. Addicts regret their craving, but find it difficult to stop. They are locked into a cycle of myopic choices. Society's response is often driven by despair and even brutality: addicts are punished as criminals. But the cravings are strong enough to defy legal sanctions. They drive relentless and painful cycles of offending and punishment. Addiction shows how choice is fallible.

Here is a hypothesis about prudence: if self-control is difficult to achieve, if it is easier for those with education, assets, and access to institutions like banks and insurance companies, then the well-off are in a better position to achieve it than those who are not. The better-off have more to invest to begin with, and more to gain. But that does not mean that prudence will increase when society as a whole becomes more affluent. At any given point in time (for economists 'in the cross-section'; for historians, 'synchronically'), the capacity and exercise of self-control increases with social standing and wealth. But with the passage of historical time ('diachronically'), and as affluence has risen overall, the capacity for commitment and for prudence has declined. Prudence has built up affluence, but affluence undermines prudence. What accounts for this reversal is myopic choice. The strategies of self-control take time to discover, develop, learn, and teach. Affluence is a relentless flow of new and cheaper opportunities. If these rewards arrive faster than the disciplines of prudence can form, then self-control will decline with affluence: even the affluent will become less prudent (a fringe at the top might lose control altogether). Commitment strategies take time and effort to devise and to learn. Under the impact of affluence, they become obsolete. The rewards of affluence produce the disorders of affluence.

Affluence as a natural experiment

Rational choice

The challenge of affluence to well-being unfolds over time. Affluence developed in history. Economics treats choice as a judgement about the future. In making her choice on whether to stay in or go out, Emma anticipates the pleasures that await her tonight (and some probability of disappointment), and she can also place a value on the academic success that she may forgo. The future is worth so much for her, and its value is worked out by means of an implicit or explicit 'discount rate': distant payouts are diminished (as if by optical foreshortening) at a given rate per unit of time, when compared with other claims on her immediate attention. Economists assume that Emma makes her decision to revise or to go out so as to maximize the 'discounted present value' of benefits over time, or in their term, to 'optimize'.

In fact (as some economists acknowledge), optimizing is not so easy. In order to compare rewards with each other, say those facing Emma tonight, of immediate conviviality as against future academic success, they have to be converted into a common unit of measurement, say 'dollars' or 'pounds'. Economists find such choices interesting because they can calculate an optimal, maximizing equilibrium in conditions of scarcity ('constrained optimization'). This gives the profession a credible role in advising what choices to make. Given that choice is difficult, this role is meaningful and prestigious, even when the advice is less than perfect. In fact it is always less than perfect (unless by chance), because for this procedure to work, some stringent conditions have to be met. Emma must know her own preferences, and how they rank; must be confident that if she chooses to go out, she will not regret it tomorrow morning. She must know the payoffs for academic distinction, that she will like them, that she will be around to have them, that the world will have a use for her skills, that her vision of the future will not change, that some completely unforeseen factor or event (an earthquake, war, air crash, stock market collapse, mental illness, cancer) will not sideline her prudent choice. These are also reasons why choice is fallible.

Intractable dilemmas

In contrast, historians often approach choice not in terms of optimizing, but as intractable dilemmas.[3] They implicitly assume that conditions for optimizing are rarely ever met. This is not a method they formally subscribe to—historians do not reflect very much about what they do. The historian follows a historical actor who is grappling with intractable choices. Will the statesman decide for peace or war? Will the cabinet tax or spend? When advantage is in conflict with ethics, when obligation conflicts with pleasure, what choice to make? Unlike economists, who reach for 'constrained optimization', what historians find interesting are dilemmas which neither equations nor intuitions can easily resolve. But however vexing for historical actors, however intractable to calculation, dilemmas eventually get resolved. History sees to that. This gives rise to some of the more limited social usefulness of historians. Not that solutions are transferable, but simply that history shows that they exist, and what they have consisted of: how stories end. That is fascinating, if not strictly useful. So historians are paid less than economists—but they still get paid. But which of the two models is the more realistic? The optimizing model that is impossible to solve? Or the intractable dilemma that is actually resolved? A social-science historian might seek to discover, retrospectively, how choices have actually been made. That is essentially how economics and history are combined in this book.

---

[3] Intractable dilemmas have been studied by philosophers, e.g. Levi, *Hard Choices*; Morton, *Disasters and Dilemmas*.

Even Emma's choice is not necessarily trivial. If she consistently prefers the student bar to the open book, then her small choices gradually add up to a big one. A single choice is trivial, but when repeated persistently, can make the difference between failure and success. Multiplied many times, it can form patterns of diligence or decadence at the aggregate level of society.

Take a couple (call them Allan and Ellen), in a constant state of vexation with each other. Should they stay together ('for the sake of the children'), or split up in pursuit of some fresh start, of dignity and freedom? This is another daily dilemma which, when multiplied in the millions, can generate a large social pattern. There are many considerations to ponder, some of them unadmitted and inadmissible, many wills and desires to square. When society changes, making it easier, for example, for mothers to be self-supporting, the shift of individual choices can be detected at the aggregate level. But still, for Ellen, no 'economically optimizing' decision is available: too much is unknown. It is impossible to know whether the 'best' choice has been made, even in retrospect, or what the best choice might have been. The methodological and practical inability to square the claims of the children with those of parents are another demonstration of how choice is fallible.

Similar decisions add up to existential dilemmas for global society. In the first half of the twentieth century, statesmen pondered whether to go to war, or to keep their powder dry. The deaths of millions were signed and sealed in closed rooms. Grand dilemmas continue to unfold. Some of the world's most abundant fisheries have dwindled. Climate change presents societies with an intergenerational dilemma: procrastination is already in full flood, but the consequences are not yet in. Sir Martin Rees, Professor of Cosmology and Astrophysics, and Master of Trinity College, Cambridge (note the authority cues) gives present human civilization no more than a 50 per cent chance of surviving the current century, in his recent book *Our Final Century*. Most of the risk is made by man. Are we closer to the beginning of history, or to its end? We may not wither in the next hundred years, but if we do, it will be because of decisions that appeared correct to those who made them.

Affluence, by throwing up new opportunities, requires more frequent choices. That is another reason to think of affluence in terms of history. In recent years, economics (and other social sciences) has increasingly accepted that mechanical optimization within budget constraints fails to capture the complexity of decisions, especially when they interact with the choices of other persons. Whatever people end up doing is not informed entirely by foresight, calculation, and a purpose, but is often impulsive, accidental, indeterminate, and therefore not entirely predictable. Instead of rational foresight, there is a turn to experiment and observation. Several methods are used: in computer simulations, artificial agents are endowed with a set of capabilities, and sent out to interact with others in a virtual environment, often with millions of repetitions. Structured, simple experiments discover what choices people are inclined to make in the artificial conditions of a psychological lab. Social sciences are also paying more attention to the 'natural experiments' of history, looking at how real people have ended up resolving real dilemmas. Affluence is a 'natural experiment' of this type.

USA vs. UK

An experiment requires a 'control', a similar group that is left unaffected by the explanation being canvassed. We get this by comparing the experience of affluence in the United States and Britain. The two societies share a similar language, a similar past, and many institutions that are superficially or deeply similar. If affluence is measured simply by average income per head, the United States has led Britain by about one generation (twenty to thirty years) throughout the period. This provides a simple 'natural experiment': if behaviour is driven by affluence alone, then we might expect Britain to converge on the United States with a lag of about that length of time. If, on the other hand, Britain had a distinctive identity, and different set of norms, then it would make its own distinctive choices.

Convergence is a test of the power of 'affluence' as an explanatory variable. Nor is it necessary to wait twenty-five years. Responses to affluence can be handed over and learned, in which case, convergence will happen more quickly. When it hasn't taken place, then it is possible to be more precise about the distinctive attributes of the two societies.

The great transition

Our decades fall into two parts, with a turn in the 1970s. This turn occurs in many seemingly unrelated domains, and suggests an underlying dynamic that is common to all. The great collective institutions of the Second World War lingered on afterwards. Taxes remained high, and a large public sector, with electoral support, constructed a social infrastructure of roads, schools, hospitals, social insurance, and state pensions. National purpose consolidated around the Cold War. Towards the end of the 1960s, attitudes began a slow shift away from the common welfare and public service as sources of well-being, and towards private benefits. That 'great transition' is an ideological and institutional upheaval which is still unfolding, unevenly and not without resistance, across the globe. It is still rather poorly understood, and has not been adequately explained in terms of economic and social fundamentals. From our vantage point it appears that 'the great transition' has been driven (in part at least) by the dynamic of affluence.

Partly this convergence was a consequence of deliberate choices, by con-sumers, voters, politicians experts, and academics. The market is the source of novelty, individual choice, and compelling reward. Institutions, on the other hand, act to restrain, and focus attention on larger and longer commitments. They embody behavioural norms, and act as commitment devices, helping individuals to find an equilibrium between the present and the future, giving them clues about 'when to stop'. Like parents at the private level, governments have the power to compel, and are positioned to enforce social commitment. Elections aggregated individual preferences and sent a signal to politicians that it was acceptable to withdraw from long-term commitments like the welfare state. The choice to 'go private', which is widely perceived as a driver of affluence, is perhaps one of the consequences of affluence.[4]

Women and men

For men, the notion of 'freedom' from obligation seems to come naturally. Robinson Crusoe was male. Women have traditionally invested a great deal more time and emotion in dependent others, primarily in pregnancy and child-rearing. This difference presents women with another intractable dilemma: how much of their own freedom and private aspirations to sacri-fice for the sake of family, at a time of broadening opportunities for indi-viduals. If the measure of affluence is the well-being that it generates, this is the central 'natural experiment' of affluent societies since the 1960s, and one that is also still unfolding. In surveys, on the average, men and women declare themselves satisfied with life in almost equal measure. This sug-gests a reasonable measure of balance between the genders, which is one of the agreeable findings of this study. But the opportunities forgone made children more costly for women. In consequence, fewer were born. Children and youth have shown increasing symptoms of anxiety, stress,

---

[4] Explored tentatively in Offer, *Public Sector*.

mental disorder, even suicide. At the same time, affluence was extending life expectation. Fewer dependent children and young people, but more non-working dependent older ones: that is a central dilemma of affluence which is still unresolved. The generations that were at childbearing ages after the 1960s reduced their investment in children. A future is approaching in which these men and women will live to an older age than their parents, when they will once again probe the strength of social obligation, this time as dependants.

Issues and domains

Affluence is driven by desires. It is the way the economy responds to human wants. In the absence of material scarcity, how would human nature express itself? Abundance provides a mirror for human nature. History lays out an endlessly complex kaleidoscope of cultures, languages, customs, ways of living. But the rich diversity of any language, for example, can be reduced to a limited set of vowels and consonants, and to twenty-something letters. Likewise, I assume that there is only a small number of primitives that drive the complexity of affluence. Jeremy Bentham reduced human motivation to pleasure and pain. Paul Ekman shows that a small range of facial expressions is universally understood.[5] Brown describes a 'universal people', with attributes that every human society appears to share:[6] a partial list consists of language, communication, sexual attraction, individuality, tools, communities, social parenthood, inequality, division of labour, governance, cooperation, morality, knowledge, ritual, music, art. It might be possible to reduce this list even further, to a core of universal drives. For satisfaction, balance is the key: homeostasis, equilibrium, set-points, not too much, not too little. Not too cold and not too hot, not too wet and not too dry, not too hungry, but not bloated, not too dark and not too bright, and so on. And confidence in the ability to secure all of this. Second to this is the need for human regard: for acknowledgement, attention, acceptance, respect, reputation, status, power, intimacy, love, friendship, kinship, sociability. A sense of justice, of dignity, of fairness, of defiance. A quest for understanding, order, and beauty. Too little stimulation gives rise to desire for novelty; too much, and habituation sets in, and swamps the capacity of drives to deliver satisfaction. Ultimately, all rewards are in the mind. In studying affluence, it is

[5] Ekman, *Emotions Revealed.*   [6] Brown, *Human Universals*, ch. 6.

necessary to keep the mind in mind, to stay connected to the psychic level at which well-being is ultimately experienced.

As affluence unfolds, the historian is faced with a 'when to stop', or 'Forth Bridge' dilemma. By the time you are painting the northern end, the southern one is rusting again. You might have captured the logic of a particular dilemma, but history has moved on. I forgo an overarching narrative, and stick with cases. This provides a richness of texture and breadth of example which cannot be sustained over broad issues and long periods. If these cases capture an essential regularity, then subsequent developments provide 'out of sample' tests of understanding. The dynamics of car design competition in the 1950s foreshadowed a good deal of what has happened since, and will probably happen again. The spillover from commercial advertising into politics during the 1970s anticipated the deceit and 'spin' of politics during the 1990s. The outcomes of one dilemma enter the initial conditions of the next one. This is difficult to capture with any richness in the standard social-science models of cause and effect, hence the combination here of history and social science. This is intended as a contribution to both.

The book is made up of three parts. The first is conceptual—how to think about affluence, well-being, and self-control. The second part moves into the market place: it considers the dynamics of personal choice in the space of commodities. The third is about the rewards and penalties of social relations, primarily of social standing and of heterosexual attachment. This is not all-encompassing, but was judged, at this point, to be enough. Originally I planned a fourth section, on social choice: issues like crime and punishment, housing, urban layout, social movements, leisure, and most importantly, public goods and government. In the end, stamina did not live up to ambition. I hope to deal with some of this in subsequent work.

In Part I, Chapter 2 considers how the resources of well-being are conventionally evaluated, and in particular, the impact of economic resources on subjective and social well-being. Chapters 3 and 4 consider the psychic challenges of reconciling a variety of wants and desires at different time ranges. The fallibility of choice is traced to this problem. It is this difficulty which legitimizes (empirically) external regulation and social paternalism. Reciprocity, the main source of rewards outside the market, is investigated in Chapter 5. It generates mutual 'regard', which is among the most highly valued of satisfactions, and cannot be authenticated reliably in the market. This accounts for its pervasive (but underestimated) persistence as a form of exchange.

Part II considers the satisfactions delivered by means of market commodities. Chapter 6 shows how advertising balances its dependence on expectations of honesty, with the temptation to deceive. In Chapter 7, eating presents a straightforward conflict between the satisfaction of appetites and the consequences for physical appearance and health. Affluence has tipped the balance away from self-control and towards rising obesity. Chapters 8–10 investigate the hedonic dynamics of anticipation and habituation. Household appliances are analysed in Chapter 8, and automobiles in Chapters 9 and 10.

Part III is about the satisfactions provided by other people. Chapter 11 deals with the rewards of status, with the advantages of ranking over other people. Chapter 12 deals with its obverse, with the psychic, economic, and health costs of status 'complaints', of ranking below other people. Chapter 13 deals with the intractable dilemmas of love under affluence, and Chapter 14 mostly traces their costs: how greater freedom for adults has been paid for most heavily by children. The conclusion recapitulates with chapter summaries, and some general implications and reflections.

Hence, the argument is not packaged into some grand multivariate statistical test, in the style that is currently fashionable in some of the social sciences. There is no single 'dependent variable' to explain. Instead, there is a variety of quantitative and descriptive tests for local arguments where appropriate and possible. Textual sources and numbers have been pulled in from public, open, printed, and electronic sources, and unique documents come from several different archives. I have woven the argument from the whole range of evidence: this is both social science and history.

I conclude by repeating my basic insight: affluence is a challenge because choice is fallible. Every choice affects the future, and it is difficult to bring objectives at different time ranges into agreement. To cope with choices, societies have evolved a variety of solutions (from the individual point of view, they can be regarded as 'commitment devices'), which provide guidance about the right choices to make. Think (in order of their time range) of table manners, education, mortgages, marriages, pensions.

But the flow of novelty under affluence undermines existing commitment conventions. It diverts attention to untested new rewards, and replaces working arrangements with untried ones. The challenge of affluence is coping with novelty. Novelty will continue, at an ever faster pace. Understanding this challenge is necessary to coping with it. I hope to contribute to that understanding.

Part I

Evaluating Affluence

2

Economic Welfare Measurement and Human Well-Being

'The richer a country becomes, the less need it has to be ruled by economic thinking.'

Charles Carter, *Wealth* (1968), 168

In economics, the craving for commodities is generally viewed as insatiable.[1] But in 1976, Richard Easterlin asked provocatively, 'Does Economic Growth Improve the Human Lot?'[2] Thirty years later, the emerging answer has to be read as 'not always', or 'it depends'. In particular, the human value of economic growth appears to be historically contingent, and to decline with the growth of affluence.

In 1953, a standard System of National Accounts (SNA) was adopted by the United Nations.[3] Its rapid acceptance facilitated international and intertemporal comparisons, and generated a competitive preoccupation with economic growth, which continues among economists and economic historians to the present day. Extended into the past, it allowed the measurement of modern economic growth back to its beginnings. The primary purpose of the SNA was not to monitor human welfare, but to provide an efficient measure of cyclical changes in total economic activity. In that role it is an enduring success. As a measure of human welfare it is more problematic. Nevertheless, during the 1950s and the 1960s, the output measure of Gross Domestic Product per head (GDP), or its annual rate of change, became a normative benchmark for economic and even social performance, the higher the better.[4]

[1] Hausman, *Science of Economics*, 30–2.   [2] Easterlin, 'Economic Growth'.
[3] Studenski, *Income of Nations*, 154–5; United Nations, *System of National Accounts*.
[4] Net National Product (NNP), would be more appropriate, but is not generally invoked as a measure of welfare. The prioritizing of economic growth in post-war America is surveyed in Collins, *More*.

But the post-war 'golden age' of 1950 to 1970 had barely taken off when the welfare value of economic growth began to be queried.[5] Books like John K. Galbraith's *The Affluent Society*, Vance O. Packard's *The Waste Makers*, David Riesman's *Abundance for What?*, and E. J. Mishan's *The Costs of Economic Growth* sold well in the late 1950s and early 1960s. They were followed by the anti-materialist 'counter-culture' of the 1960s, and the anti-growth environmentalism of the 1970s. The discipline of economic history was also affected. In Britain, the 'pessimists' in the 'standard of living' debate argued that material improvement during the industrial revolution was compatible with a decline in well-being.[6] In the United States, *Time on the Cross* by Fogel and Engerman described an efficient ante-bellum economy relying on the human degradation of slavery.

The debate on economic growth is usually regarded as an expression of conflicting values. But it might also be the case that the sources of human welfare are historically contingent. As the two decades of the post-war age (*c.*1950–1970) came to an end, attention began to shift towards the costs of affluence, ecological, social, and psychic. In the poorest of countries, priority was claimed for a set of basic needs over the sacrifices necessary for maximizing GDP. Hence, from the late 1960s onwards, the quest for alternatives to GDP as measures of welfare.

'Alternative' measurements of welfare have followed three approaches. The first involved 'extending' the national accounts, to incorporate non-market goods and services, and to eliminate detrimental components. A second approach identified social norms, and evaluated their satisfaction by means of 'social indicators'. A third approach has targeted mental states directly, with surveys of reported subjective well-being, and research on the dynamics of hedonic experience. Cumulatively, these three approaches suggest that the pursuit of welfare is not always satisfied by economic growth alone, and may require different measures at different times.

Extended accounts

The micro-economic foundations of the SNA are insecure. The obstacles to the measurement of economic welfare at the micro-level are formidable. Much of the difficulty arises from the problem of disaggregation from market prices and quantities to household and to individual

---

[5] Kapp, *Social Costs*; Horowitz, *Anxieties of Affluence*, ch. 3.
[6] Feinstein, 'Pessimism Perpetuated'.

consumption.[7] Adding up welfare upwards from individuals and households to the level of society is even less tractable. As Amartya Sen puts it, 'personal real income theory translates readily into the theory of real national income [only] if the nation is viewed as a person.'[8] This 'welfarist' position, he says, is 'not outrageously realistic'. Since the nation is not a single person, a higher level of GNP might fail to deliver more 'welfare', even in a narrow utilitarian sense.

In the face of such doubts, the pervasive use of GDP per head as a social welfare measure is a puzzle. The assumption that society is a unitary actor does help to sidestep some intractable problems: the difficulty of making interpersonal and intertemporal comparisons of welfare, of taking account of inequality, of compensating losers for Pareto improvements, and of evading Arrow's impossibility theorem. One explanation might be an assumption that underneath we are all pretty much the same, and share a repertoire of innate needs.[9] When GDP is defended as a measure of welfare, it is on pragmatic grounds, by pointing to positive correlations, often implicit ones, with social indicators such as health, life expectation, and education.[10] The unitary actor assumption is useful for international comparisons. And sometimes there is an a priori preference from doctrine or self-interest for market-friendly policies that can be justified as maximizing GDP.

Unlike the SNA, systems of 'extended accounts' are mostly designed to measure welfare. They start out with the SNA core, and make adjustments on consumption and capital accounts: they typically eliminate some commodities and services which are seen not as final goods in themselves, but as 'regrettable necessities'. Finally, they impute a value to sources of welfare from outside the market. Early estimates were produced in the late 1960s, by Kendrick and Sametz.[11] Nordhaus and Tobin's 'Measure of Economic Welfare' (MEW) of 1972 was very influential.[12] This measure eliminated 'regrettables', such as commuting, police, sanitation, road maintenance, defence, and the disamenities of urban life from total output. On the positive side, Nordhaus and Tobin imputed values for household production, and for time available for leisure.

Extended accounting of this and similar kinds has continued into the 1980s and the 1990s, and has included estimates for the United States,

---

[7] Slesnick, 'Empirical Approaches'.   [8] Sen, 'Welfare', 36.

[9] Stigler and Becker, '*De Gustibus*', 76–7; Diener and Suh, 'Measuring Quality', 445–6.

[10] Abramovitz, 'Retreat'; Dasgupta, *Inquiry*; Olson and Landsberg, *No-Growth Society*; Lebergott, *Pursuing Happiness*; Beckerman, *Defence*.

[11] Kendrick, 'Studies'; Sametz, 'Measurement'.

[12] Nordhaus and Tobin, 'Is Growth Obsolete?'

Britain, Europe, and Australia.[13] Some of these contained retrospective historical accounts, going back to 1950 for Britain, 1869 for the United States, and all the way to 1788 for Australia.[14] These indices indicate that extended welfare has been positively correlated with GNP over the long run, though the actual growth rates have differed.[15]

The most striking implication is that more welfare is derived from non-market than from market activities. Typically the imputed value of leisure equals or exceeds the value of GDP, and household production adds another 25 to 45 per cent. About two-thirds of output arises outside the market. This dominance of non-commodities casts doubt on the 'welfarist' assumption that all well-being can be priced. Leisure and housework dominate the index, and are relatively slow to change. Hence, the summary indicators are not much use for monitoring cyclical fluctuations.

Extended accounting relies heavily on the allocation of time. There is also a strand of research which takes time use as the measure of welfare. This lends itself both to micro and to macro applications.[16] Gershuny has worked towards an encompassing system of accounting based on time use, with a wide international coverage, and going back to the early 1960s.[17]

The concept of sustainable consumption goes back to Hicks, who defined it as the maximum value of consumption which would leave the individual afterwards as well off as before.[18] In their study of 1972, Nordhaus and Tobin attempted to estimate 'sustainable' welfare, which they took as consumption plus net investment.[19] They admitted the need to deduct the depletion of non-renewable natural resources. This had been anticipated by Kapp in 1950, and several estimates were produced during the 1970s.[20] Weitzman provided theoretical underpinning: national product net of asset depletion also described the discounted sustainable productive potential of the economy.[21]

A more normative and radical approach was pioneered by Zolotas in 1981. He incorporated pollution and natural resource depletion into a set of extended accounts for the United States for the period 1950 to 1975,

---

[13] Kendrick, 'Studies'; Zolotas, *Economic Growth*; Eisner, *Total Incomes*; Nordhaus, 'Reflections'; Beckerman, 'Comparable Growth'; Crafts, 'Thatcher Experiment'; Snooks, *Portrait*.

[14] Crafts, 'Thatcher Experiment'; Eisner, *Total Incomes*; Sametz, 'Measurement'; Snooks, *Portrait*.

[15] Nordhaus, 'Reflections'.

[16] Juster and Stafford, *Time*; Gershuny and Halpin, 'Time Use'; Robinson and Godbey, *Time for Life*; Schor, *Overworked American*.   [17] Gershuny, *Changing Times*.

[18] Hicks, *Value*, 172.   [19] Nordhaus and Tobin, 'Is Growth Obsolete?'

[20] Kapp, *Social Costs*; Kneese et al., *Economics*; Drechsler, 'Problems'; Meyer, 'Greening'.

[21] Weitzman, 'Welfare Significance'.

and also imputed shadow costs to some social detriments.[22] His index of the economic aspects of welfare (EAW) rose progressively more slowly than GNP. A time would come, a generation hence, when an increment of economic growth would produce no welfare at all. This was a systemic feature: 'beyond a certain point, economic growth may cease to promote social welfare. In fact, it would appear that, when an industrial society reaches an advanced state of affluence, the rate of increase in social welfare drops below the rate of economic growth, and tends ultimately to become negative.'[23]

Concern over the detriments of inequality has motivated a good deal of the effort to devise measures of welfare.[24] Atkinson's influential index provided a measure for evaluating the effect of income inequality on welfare, which could be adjusted to the amount of inequality tolerated (or desired).[25] This adjustment has been applied to extended accounts several times.[26]

After a hiatus in the 1980s, Daly and Cobb continued to develop the Zolotas model: they incorporated inequality (based on Gini coefficients) into a new measure, the Index of Sustainable Economic Welfare (ISEW).[27] This had the effect of depressing the index: inequality has worsened since the 1970s, and it offset the benefits of economic growth.[28] The principle of 'sustainability' in the rubric referred primarily to the depletion of non-renewable resources. Daly and Cobb also removed the imputation for leisure time, on the grounds that it dominated the index and was conceptually unsound. It was this item mainly that had tended to offset the increase in inequality in less radical accounting exercises.[29] While GNP continued to grow, the American ISEW declined overall by about 25 per cent between the 1975 and 1990, and the British one by almost 50 per cent during the same period.[30] Later versions (Figure 2.1) show smaller declines.[31] The innovation has caught on, and ISEW measures are available for Australia, Austria, Chile, Germany, Italy, the Netherlands, Sweden, the UK, and the USA.[32] All except Italy record ISEW growth until the 1970s, with stagnation or decline afterwards. ISEW is explicitly normative, where

[22] Advertising, commuting, and 'corrective' spending on health and education. Crime and divorce were also considered as bads, but kept out of the accounts.

[23] Zolotas, *Economic Growth*, 1.

[24] Another has been the measurement of household consumption; see Slesnick, 'Empirical Approaches'. [25] Atkinson, 'Measurement'.

[26] Beckerman, 'Comparable Growth'; Crafts, *Economic Decline*, 58–60; Jackson et al., *Economic Welfare*. [27] Daly et al., *Common Good*.

[28] Crafts, *Economic Decline*, 58–60.

[29] Daly et al., *Common Good*, 412–13; Crafts, *Economic Decline*, compare table 4, 20 and table 17, 59. [30] Cobb et al., *Progress Indicator*; Jackson and Marks, *Economic Welfare*.

[31] e.g. the latest revision of the British estimates by Tim Jackson, in New Economics Foundation, 'Chasing Progress'. [32] Friends of the Earth, website.

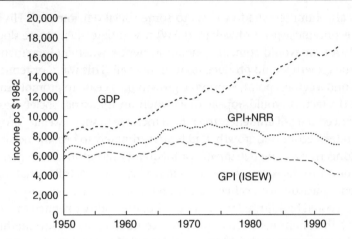

Fig. 2.1. GDP and Index of Sustainable Economic Welfare USA, 1950–1995

Notes: GPI = General Progress Indicator, equal to ISEW = Index of Sustainable Economic Welfare. 1982 prices.
NRR = Non-renewable resources.

Sources: Cobb et al., *Genuine Progress Indicator*, table 2, pp. 40–1.

the SNA is only so implicitly. An American variant, the 'Genuine Progress Indicator', is bolder still, and introduces imputations for divorce and crime.[33] For all their defects, these measures (like the SNA) are effective ways to express a normative position on economic change. Kenneth Arrow, Partha Dasgupta, and nine other economists have recently asked 'Are We Consuming Too Much?' They find, provisionally, that consumption may be too high on the 'maximize present value' criterion, and that several nations, especially poor ones, do not invest enough to offset the depletion of natural capital.[34]

If we regard society as a unitary actor, then according to the ISEW, the growth in economic activity since the mid-1970s has been producing a *reduction* in aggregate welfare. Since the 1970s, from this perspective, the pursuit of further growth has been irrational. It is only myopia and habit which allow it to continue in the face of negative welfare returns. The problems of aggregation should be borne in mind, and the imputation of environmental depletion is open to criticism. For Britain, in the latest version, known as MDP (measure of domestic progress), the mid-1970s inflection point remains even without this imputation, though progress has recovered a little since the mid-1990s.[35]

[33] Cobb et al., *Genuine Progress*.   [34] Arrow et al., 'Consuming Too Much?', 167.
[35] Jackson, 'Chasing Progress'.

Extended accounting is approaching official recognition. Following two decades of research and consultation, in a recent revision of the SNA the United Nations introduced guidelines for an optional set of 'satellite' environmental accounts, designed to integrate with the main core SNA.[36] 'Sustainability' has become a normative public policy objective in the UK.[37] This perspective of diminishing returns to economic growth is also captured in a different research programme, the measurement of normative social indicators.

Social indicators

An abiding idea is that access to certain goods constitutes a precondition of welfare. Early examples in Britain were the Poor Law, compulsory primary education, and B. S. Rowntree's 'Poverty Line' of 1901. In the 1960s and early 1970s this approach re-emerged as the 'social indicators' movement. This was also inspired by the idea that real welfare was not captured by the SNA indicators.[38] Typically the goods in question consisted of nutrition, housing, education, health and life expectations, environmental quality, crime, and poverty levels. They might also include such objectives as the freedoms of movement, expression, and political organization. Implicit in social indicators is some notion of adequacy: there is too little of some things, such as nutrition, housing, or education; or too much of others, such as poverty, inequality, or crime. Social indicators are rarely scaled in the metric of money, or set within an accounting framework.

A United Nations committee engaged with the problems of measuring 'levels of living' in 1954, and identified a set of twelve domains.[39] A flow of academic research built up during the 1960s, and by the early 1970s, several leading countries and international bodies had published one-off or serial collections of social indicators.[40] This enterprise has not abated. Social indicators relied implicitly on a social-democratic consensus, with an egalitarian bias and a quest for social inclusion, as in the Scandinavian 'level of living' surveys.[41] But there was a lag between impulse and execution, and by the time social indicators were delivered, the impetus of social democracy was spent. Priorities for social expenditure had already been set

[36] Meyer, 'Greening'.
[37] Great Britain, Department of Environment, *Sustainable Development; Sustainability Counts; A Better Quality of Life.*   [38] Bauer, *Social Indicators.*
[39] UN, 'International Definition'.   [40] Terleckyj, *Quality of Life*, 3–4, nn. 1–6.
[41] Nordic Council, *Living and Inequality.*

in the 'golden age' period of expansion and the 1970s were a period of fiscal retrenchment. Social consensus swung away from equality and towards competition, from the left towards the right. The absence of a coherent accounting framework was another disadvantage.

In developing countries, deprivation was not relative but absolute. In the 1970s a 'basic needs' movement identified a bundle of goods that might claim priority over economic growth.[42] Morris argued that if encompassing was beyond reach, there was a virtue in parsimony. He introduced an unweighted 'Physical Quality of Life Index' (PQLI), made up of infant mortality, literacy, and life expectation at age 1, as a single measure of welfare.[43] Economic historians adopted the same principle by taking anthropometric measures, primarily heights, as a welfare index.[44]

What followed shows how social indicators not only depend on norms, but could also help to create them. The focus on basic needs came into conflict in the 1980s with the World Bank/IMF 'structural adjustment' policy, and with the increasing market orientation within development economics. The results of these programmes have been mixed, but the impression was that costs fell often disproportionately on the poor. In the late 1980s, dissatisfaction with the 'structural adjustment' programme inspired the creation of a new social indicator, the Human Development Index (HDI).[45] This is made up of income per head, life expectation at birth, and an education indicator, expressed in a single figure between 0 and 1. It has gained wide acceptance, and may have played some role in the partial retreat of the World Bank, and its acknowledgement of poverty as a policy objective.[46] Morris's updated index of 1996, which covered a longer time span, also exposed the ambiguity of the links between growth and welfare.[47]

It is interesting to compare HDI and GNP with Sen's 'capabilities' approach, which has attracted a great deal of discussion. Sen moved from an axiomatic 'welfarist' position to the view that income alone does not satisfactorily capture welfare. In keeping with liberal values, he has not privileged any particular good. Even under indigence it was necessary to respect individual priorities.[48] Well-being consists in having the 'capabilities' with which to achieve valuable 'functionings'. Both of these categories extend beyond the purely economic. Sen has not embodied his approach

---

[42] Miles, *Human Development*, 153–6.   [43] Morris, *Measuring the Condition*.
[44] Floud et al., *Nutritional Status*; Fogel, 'Economic Growth'.
[45] Desai, 'Human Development'.
[46] World Bank, *Poverty Reduction*; Narayan et al., *Voices of the Poor*. On the quest for alternatives to 'structural adjustment', Mallaby, *World's Banker*.   [47] Morris, *Measuring*.
[48] Sen, 'Capability'.

in any metrics, but it has influenced the Human Development Index. 'Alternative' approaches, especially Sen's capability/functioning approach, and the various 'sustainability' measures are congruent to some extent with non-utilitarian ethical frameworks—Bhuddist, Hindu, Jewish, Greek, Christian, 'Enlightenment', Romantic—which teach that acquisitiveness may be self-defeating, and which highlight other welfare criteria: virtue, stoicism, altruism, approbation, self-realization.

The most compelling justification for the SNA as a measure of welfare is its correlation with social indicators which enjoy normative consensus as 'good things'. Hence, it is instructive to test the claims that this correlation exists. What such tests indicate is that the correlation is strong under conditions of indigence, but loses its power at surprisingly low levels of real income. In Figure 2.2, three such indicators are plotted against income per head. These are Morris's Physical Quality of Life Index (3 indicators), Estes' Index of Social Progress (36 indicators in 10 subgroups), and Slottje's Multidimensional Quality of Life Index.[49] All three suggest a strong abatement of welfare returns to income at around $2,500–3,000 US in 1981 prices. A logarithmic curve provides the best fit. The HDI already incorporates such a turning point in its premisses, by including income per head in its arguments, with a lower value placed on incomes higher than the whole-sample average.

Visual examination shows that some countries achieve very high levels of welfare indicators on very low incomes, and that others persist in low welfare indicators on high incomes. These three exercises in social indicators research echo the 'extended accounting' findings of a curvilinear relation between income and welfare.

These data are cross-sections at one point in time. Similar patterns also appear to obtain over the long term. The contribution of economic growth to welfare may have been underestimated for the earlier periods of economic development, as has been noted by Crafts.[50] It follows that its contribution to welfare may be overestimated for the period of affluence. This is suggested by some very crude measures in Table 2.1. This table takes two measures of welfare, (a) an ad hoc welfare index made up of percentage school enrolment and life expectation,[51] and (b) the Human Development Index. For both measures, the corresponding purchasing power of a 1990 dollar and the income elasticity (in 1990 dollars) are calculated over the period 1870 to 1973. In all the four countries followed, there is a downwards

---

[49] Morris, *Measuring*; Estes, *Social Progress*; Slottje, *Quality of Life*.
[50] Crafts, 'Human Development Index'.
[51] A more reliable measure than notional literacy, which peaks early.

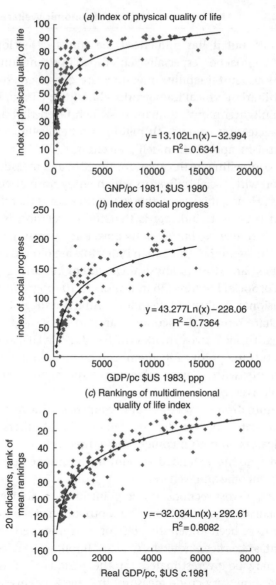

Fig. 2.2. Social indicators and income per head, 1981, 1983 (selected countries)

Notes:

(*a*) Simple average of indices of infant mortality, literacy, and life expectation at age 1.

(*b*) Average of normalized indices of 10 domains, based on 36 indicators. The domains are: education, health, women's status, defence effort, economics, demography, geographic, participation, culture, and welfare effort.

(*c*) Index of 20 indicators for: political rights, civil liberty, household size, militarism, energy consumption, female and children labour participation rates, roads, telephones, life expectancy, infant mortality, medical services, nutrition, literacy, media access, GDP. Rank of mean rankings.

Sources:

(*a*) Morris, *Measuring the Changing Quality*.

(*b*) Estes, *Trends in World Social Development*, table A2, pp. 186–8.

(*c*) Slottje et al., *Measuring the Quality of Life*, table A. 2.2, pp. 96–9.

Table 2.1. Measures of the relation of welfare to income per head, c.1870–1973

	UK	USA	France	Germany
(a) Welfare units per 1990 dollar of GDP per head, 1870–1973				
1870	1.2	1.8	2.2	2.0
1913	1.0	1.0	1.5	1.2
1950	0.9	0.7	1.1	1.5
1973	0.6	0.5	0.5	0.5
(b) HDI* per 1990 dollar of GDP per head, 1870–1973				
1870	1.1	1.5	1.7	1.7
1913	1.0	0.9	1.3	1.2
1950	0.9	0.7	1.1	1.4
1973	0.6	0.5	0.6	0.6
(c) Income Elasticity of Welfare Index				
1870–1913	0.5	0.3	0.4	0.3
1913–1950	0.7	0.3	0.2	0.9
1950–1973	0.3	0.1	0.1	0.1
(d) Income Elasticity of HDI*				
1870–1913	0.7	0.4	0.6	0.5
1913–1950	0.8	0.6	0.6	2.2
1950–1973	0.3	0.3	0.3	0.2

Notes: Welfare index is made up of % school enrolment + life expectation / 2. HDI* is the Human Development Index, with the income element untruncated. Index units multiplied by 100. The indices are bounded variables but are well short of the maxima even in 1973.

Source: Calculated from Crafts, 'Human Development Index'.

trend in the welfare purchasing power of income over time, although the income elasticity of welfare tends to peak in the interwar years.[52] In brief, then, dollars deliver diminishing returns in simple welfare measures over time, as well as in the cross-section.

It could be argued that the simple development indices are misleading, in that the measures used are exhausted under affluence. Measures like HDI and PQLI are oriented strongly towards the priorities of indigence. The most extensive social indicators study so far puts this possibility to the test.[53] Easterly used a panel dataset of eighty-one indicators covering up to four time periods (1960, 1970, 1980, and 1990), in seven domains.[54] Each of these indicators was regressed on income per head, with fixed time effects. The criterion for robustness was an impact on the quality of life indicator that was significant, positive, and stronger than exogenous

[52] Income elasticity of welfare—how fast welfare increases when income rises.
[53] Easterly, 'Life during Growth'.
[54] (1) Rights and democracy, (2) political stability and war, (3) education, (4) health, (5) transport and communication, (6) inequality, and (7) 'bads'.

shifts. Exogenous shifts capture the effect of global socio-economic progress which may arise from the diffusion of knowledge or of norms. Three methods were used. In the first, all data were pooled, and only time effects were controlled for in the regression. Thirty-two out of eighty-one indicators passed this test. When country fixed effects were added, the number of robust indicators fell to ten. With a first-differences IV estimator to establish causal effects, only 6 indicators survived out of 69. Three variables alone passed all three tests: calories per head, protein per head, and telephones per head. The first two, however, are known to be problematic once adequacy has been reached.[55] This comprehensive study confirms that the relationship of well-being and income per head is weak, both in cross-section and over time.

Association between health and economic status has long been observed within countries.[56] It is not entirely clear how much ill-being arises simply from material deprivation, and how much from the psychic costs of exclusion. There are good descriptive indicators of inequality, such as the Poverty Line, the Lorenz Curve, the Gini Coefficient, Atkinson's index, and P-alpha. What is lacking are standard, simple, social indicators of the *consequences* of inequality for affluent societies, an index of deprivation and detriment similar perhaps to the PQLI or HDI. Such indices are currently under construction.[57] It is also possible, of course, that causation is not exclusively from low status/income to poor health, but also the other way round, from poor health to low status/income.

'There is no wealth but life', wrote John Ruskin. The most telling corollary of affluence is the large extension of life expectation. In Britain, for example, a woman aged 15 in 1990 could expect to live seventeen years longer than if it was 1900.[58] Incorporating life expectation (and health) into extended accounts has the effect of raising the level of measured welfare very substantially, and 'would double the rate of growth in the recent past'.[59] As with other elements of 'extended accounting', non-market goods (life expectation is not directly up for sale) overshadow goods and services as sources of welfare. Whereas income growth increases life expectation over time, higher wealth does not guarantee longer lives in the cross-section, when countries are compared for income and longevity. The United States,

[55] Chapter 7, below.

[56] Black et al., *Black Report*; Marmot, 'Social Differences'; Smith, 'Healthy Bodies'; Wilkinson, 'The Epidemiological Transition'. In detail, Ch. 12 below.

[57] Noble et al., 'Measuring Multiple Deprivation'.

[58] Charlton and Murphy, 'Monitoring Health', table 3.7, 27. Using 'period' method.

[59] Nordhaus, 'Health of Nations' (1998); 'New Directions'; 'Health of Nations' (2002); quote from Crafts, *Relative Economic Performance*, 50.

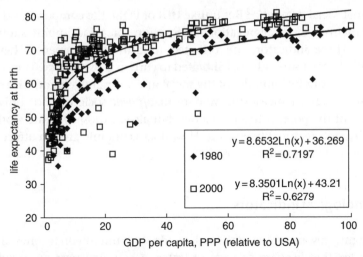

Fig. 2.3. Life expectancy at birth, 1980 (173 countries), 2000 (191 countries)

Source: World Bank, *World Development Indicators* (2003). Accessed online via the Economic and Social Data Service International, through the Oxford University subscription.

spends a much higher share of GDP on health care (about 14 per cent) than any other country, and since it is usually the very richest country, as well, it outspends everyone per head absolutely by far. Despite its wealth and heavy outlays, the United States has delivered poor life expectation for its wealth. In 1980, it ranked sixteenth, and in 2000 it ranked twenty-seventh, behind e.g. Greece and Costa Rica.[60] That suggests strongly that the simple income per head measure needs to be unbundled much further before it can say anything significant about health. Figure 2.3 demonstrates this graphically. It compares life expectation and income per head in a large array of countries in 1980 and in 2000. In both years, United States levels of longevity could be obtained at about one-fifth of the level of income. Life expectation increased, but it increased across the board, and the declining R-squared suggests that the link between life expectation and income per head had weakened considerably. What seems to be at work is the diffusion of knowledge rather than of simple economic growth, but the data do not provide a clue as to what the knowledge is and where it diffuses from.

The HDI has the prestige of UN approval, is widely used and quoted, and has also been used retrospectively, for historical evaluation.[61] The United Nations has now also laid down a standard for a fifteen-item 'minimum

[60] Figure 2.3, and the underlying sources.
[61] Costa and Steckel, 'Trends in Health'; Crafts, *Economic Decline* and 'Development Index'.

national social data set'.[62] But unlike HDI or PQLI, the components do not lend themselves to aggregation, indexation, or a focal-point summary figure. These indicators are oriented towards development. They are essentially catch-up indices, calibrated to current best practice. They fail to address the original impulse of the social indicators movement, which was finding a way of measuring welfare in *affluent* societies; not only the welfare of the poor in those societies, but also of those who are working, healthy, and reasonably well off. How does economic growth affect such people, and is it worth the cost?[63]

Psychological indicators

Economic resources are not final goods, but intermediate ones. Pigou conceded that 'welfare consists of states of consciousness only and not material things', and Irving Fisher wrote, 'human beings are ever striving to control the stream of their psychic life by appropriating and utilizing the materials and forces of nature'.[64] From this viewpoint, to understand the economy, more needs to be known about the mind. Psychological approaches attempt to reach directly into the experience of welfare. They test the validity of the national accounting measure of welfare in two ways: 'static' measures estimate the correlation between SNA goods and psychological indicators of well-being. 'Dynamic' approaches probe deeper into the hedonics of satisfaction.[65]

Like 'human development', the static 'happiness' approach has also produced a measurement standard. This constitutes survey data on responses to a simple question about current subjective well-being on a bounded ordinal scale (1–3, 1–5, 1–7, or 1–10). One variant is the following survey question: 'Taking one thing with another, how would you describe your feeling today? Very satisfied, quite satisfied or not so satisfied?' The response to questions of this kind is known as 'subjective well-being' (SWB). The stock of surveys of this kind is very large. Some time series go back as far as the 1940s.[66] The indicator is crude, but this is not necessarily a defect. Empirical validity is robust.[67] A common theme in this literature is that

---

[62] UN, 'Social Statistics'.

[63] Van Praag and Ferrer-i-Carbonell, *Happiness Quantified*, is a comprehensive monograph offering a consistent theoretical and empirical approach to the study of choice and satisfaction. It appeared too late to be considered in this book, but requires close attention.

[64] Pigou, *Economics of Welfare*, 10; Fisher, *Interest*, 3.

[65] Kahneman et al., *Hedonic Psychology*.   [66] Veenhoven, *Database*.

[67] Veenhoven, 'Satisfaction Research'; Diener and Suh, 'Differences'.

levels of reported well-being are remarkably high in affluent societies. Those describing themselves as unhappy or very unhappy are typically fewer than 15 per cent.[68]

Easterlin originally highlighted the absence of relation between country income levels and SWB.[69] This was challenged by Veenhoven, who identified a curvilinear relation, rather like the social indicators in Figure 2.2.[70] A subsequent comparison of countries was carried out by Diener et al. (Figure 2.4a).[71] They found that SWB rose moderately but significantly with income, with a large variance, of which 37 per cent was explained. Subsequent analysis of the same data indicated an inflection point at the 75th percentile: above that level, income did not provide any increment to subjective well-being.[72] My own study of 40 countries (reported in Chapter 12) suggests that when social ranking is controlled for, absolute levels of income provide virtually no increment in subjective well-being.[73] But any positive relation found in cross-sections does not establish change over time. In fact, for the United States, France, and Japan, SWB has changed hardly at all since 1946, over a period in which real incomes per head have more than doubled (Figure 2.4b).[74]

This result has been confirmed by surveys of SWB at the individual level. SWB has been correlated with an array of socio-economic determinants and domains. This approach was first applied in cross-section on an American national sample in the early 1970s.[75] The predictive power of each individual determinant of global well-being was low, and even all of them together accounted for only about half of the variance. Income on its own counted little for happiness, and the relation is again curvilinear: the effect was strongest at lower incomes. The positive effect of income is stronger in cross-section than over time. A large longitudinal study in the United States found a very modest relation of income to well-being ($r = 0.12$), with a curvilinear form, flattening out at about $6,000–8,000 (1971 to 1975).[76] Interestingly, a rise of income over time for particular individuals produced no improvement at all in well-being. Among the determinants of SWB, the quality of relationships, of leisure, and of work experience counted considerably more for aggregate well-being than

---

[68] Veenhoven, 'Study', table 2, 26.   [69] Easterlin, 'Does Economic Growth?'
[70] Veenhoven, 'Is Happiness Relative?'   [71] Diener et al., 'Factors Predicting'.
[72] Diener and Suh, 'Differences,' fig. 22.1.   [73] Table 12.1, Ch. 12 below.
[74] Diener et al., 'Income and Subjective Well-Being'; 'Predicting Subjective Well-Being'; Diener and Suh, 'Quality of Life'; Blanchflower and Oswald, 'Well-Being'.
[75] Campbell et al., *Quality of American Life*.
[76] Diener et al., 'Income and Subjective Well-Being'.

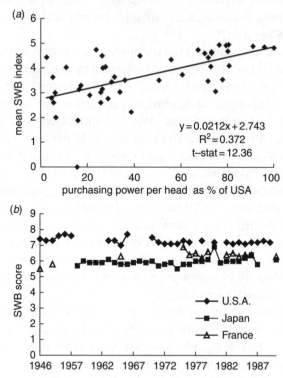

Fig. 2.4. Subjective well-being, income and time (selected countries)
(*a*) SWB and income, cross-section, early 1990s.
(*b*) SWB over time, USA, France, Japan.
Scale 0 to 10. 5 is neutral midpoint.

Sources:
(*a*) Diener et al., 'Factors Predicting', table 1, p. 856.
(*b*) Diener and Suh, 'Measuring Quality of Life', table 1, p. 211.

income and consumption measures.[77] Materialism, a preoccupation with economic well-being, was negatively correlated with SWB, and especially so in those who believed that more money would make one happier.[78]

The determinants of SWB have more recently been investigated on very large samples over time, in both the United States and in Europe.[79] The

[77] Campbell et al., *Quality of American Life*, 80; Levy and Guttman, 'Multivariate Structure'; Argyle, 'Causes and Correlates', 356–9; Headey and Wearing, *Understanding Happiness*, 78–9.

[78] Ahuvia and Friedman, 'Macromarketing Model', 154, 161. Materialism is further discussed below, Ch. 14. See also Kasser, *High Price of Materialism*; Kasser et al., *Psychology and Consumer Culture*.

[79] Di Tella et al., 'Macroeconomics of Happiness'; Blanchflower and Oswald, 'Well-Being'.

findings are consistent with previous ones. SWB varied little over time. Absolute income counted for little but relative income (that is position in the ladder of earnings) had significant influence on well-being, from the second quartile upwards. Misery, that is strong negative divergences from the reference case (white, married, female, employed), is caused primarily by three conditions: non-white race, unemployment, and non-marriage. There were also a number of consistent but weaker effects, such as age (U-shaped). Gender made no difference. In the European sample there were also very strong country effects. The magnitude of the coefficients is remarkably similar from one large sample to another, which indicates that however crude SWB is as a measure of well-being, its components are surprisingly robust. Table 2.2 is typical.

The positive cross-sectional correlation of income and SWB *within* countries has long suggested a link from static to dynamic approaches, and

Table 2.2. Happiness in the United States (ordered probit), 1972–1994

Variable	Coefficient	Standard error
Unemployed	−0.379	0.041
Self-employed	0.074	0.023
Male	−0.125	0.016
Age	−0.021	0.003
Age squared	2.77E–04	3.00E–05
Education:		
High school	0.091	0.019
Associate/Junior college	0.123	0.04
Bachelor's	0.172	0.027
Graduate	0.188	0.035
Marital status:		
Married	0.38	0.026
Divorced	−0.085	0.032
Separated	−0.241	0.046
Widowed	−0.191	0.037
No. of children:		
1	−0.112	0.025
2	−0.074	0.024
3 or more	−0.119	0.024
Income quartiles:		
Second	0.161	0.022
Third	0.279	0.023
Fourth (highest)	0.398	0.025
Retired	0.036	0.031
School	0.176	0.055
At home	0.005	0.023
Other	−0.227	0.067

N = 26,668, Dependent variable = Reported Happiness on a three-point scale

Source: Di Tella et al., 'Macroeconomics of Happiness', table 3, p. 20.

to the 'relative income hypothesis', which states that what counts is not absolute income, but relativities.[80] From this point of view, even a large rise in income will leave no impact on well-being, if distribution is unchanged. For example, the large rise in American, French, and Japanese incomes since the war has hardly changed their SWB scores (Figure 2.4b). The reason for this, it is argued, is that as incomes increase, so do consumption norms.[81] Consumers become habituated to new levels of consumption. Scitovsky reviewed psychological research on arousal and habituation to probe the dynamics of diminishing returns,[82] and questioned whether American acquisitiveness was in fact increasing welfare. The Dutch 'Leyden Approach' to welfare research has also found that the welfare increment declines substantially as income increases. Earning norms drift up with income, though not all the way.[83] A more vivid metaphor, which applies to all three measurement approaches to welfare, is the 'hedonic treadmill': income has to rise in order to sustain satisfaction at a constant level.[84]

The World Values Survey permits a cross-sectional test of the importance of the effect on subjective well-being of relative and absolute income. Figure 2.4 indicates that in the cross-section absolute income is quite highly correlated with subjective well-being scores. But the same dataset also makes it possible to distinguish whether it is relative or absolute income that produces well-being. The first three waves of this survey (in the early 1980s, and early and mid-1990s, covering forty-six countries in all) record both relative and absolute income levels. The effect of income on subjective well-being was analysed in regressions with a very large sample of 87,806 observations, which included a maximum of 38 variables (some of them sub-categories). It was found that both absolute and relative income delivered strongly diminishing returns of well-being. Taking relative incomes first, for an individual to move from the fourth to the fifth income decile raised well-being by 0.11 units, but from the ninth to the tenth, only 0.02 units, although in absolute terms the latter was the much larger increase. Comparing absolute income internationally, a 10 per cent increase in per capita incomes at half the US level would increase average individual well-being by only 0.0003 of the same units, while net gains

[80] Duesenberry, *Consumer Behavior*; Hirsch, *Limits to Growth*. The effect of relative income on well-being is investigated empirically in Ch. 12 below. See Table 12.1.
[81] Easterlin, 'Raising the Incomes'. [82] Scitovsky, *Joyless Economy*.
[83] Van Praag and Frijters, 'Measurement of Welfare'; an advanced statement of the 'Leyden School' approach is in van Praag and Ferrer-I-Carbonell, *Happiness Quantified*.
[84] Coleman et al., *Social Standing*, ch. 17; but see Diener et al., 'Income and Subjective Well-Being'; 'Predicting Subjective Well-Being'.

became zero before US levels were achieved.[85] The income measure here is not entirely robust. My own analysis of the fourth wave (Table 12.1 below) supports this interpretation. Although absolute income (and educational levels as well) have little effect on subjective well-being, the richer countries are nevertheless happier. The reason, says Helliwell, is that 'those who have the highest levels of subjective well-being are not those who live in the richest countries, but those who live where social and political institutions are effective, where mutual trust is high, and corruption is low'.[86]

The low responsiveness of well-being to income under affluence may arise because people are simply born happy or unhappy, and most are happy already. Longitudinal studies indicate that personality is a strong predictor of SWB.[87] One review concludes that happiness is more a trait than a state.[88] A study of separated identical twins suggests that neither social and economic status, educational attainment, family income, marital status, nor religious commitment could account for more than 3 per cent of the variance in 'happiness'. About half the variance was associated with genetic variation. Subsequent retesting suggested that about 80 per cent of the stable element in well-being was heritable.[89]

Culture provides another element of stability. Affluent industrial societies with similar levels of income per head report very different levels of subjective well-being, with a gradient coming down from the Nordic countries, which have very high levels, the English-speaking countries at an intermediate level, the Catholic middle and south of Europe lower still, and Japan lowest of all.[90] Inglehart regards this gradient as representing an adaptation or adjustment to affluence. He classifies societies on two value orientation dimensions, the pursuit of economic security and deference to traditional authority. As societies become more affluent, they move gradually away from both. This implies that the experience of affluence reduces concerns about economic security, and that culture adapts, albeit slowly, to changes in economic endowment.[91]

In affluent societies, culture appears to affect SWB more strongly than income. Japan and Australia had comparable incomes per head in the early 1990s but Australia scored an SWB of 1.02 (mean of 60 countries at 0), with Japan at the other end of the affluent country distribution, at 0.86. Once controlled for 'individualism', the correlation of income and SWB disappeared.[92]

[85] Helliwell, 'How's Life?' (2000), 13–15.   [86] Helliwell, 'How's Life' (2003), 355.
[87] Headey and Wearing, *Understanding Happiness*, 84–5.   [88] Stones et al., 'Happiness'.
[89] Lykken and Tellegen, 'Happiness'; Stones et al., 'Happiness', 135.
[90] Inglehart et al., *Human Values*, table V18.   [91] Inglehart, *Modernization*, ch. 3.
[92] Diener et al., 'Factors Predicting', 860–2.

33

This suggests that the hedonic ideal of individual welfare, utility, or happiness might be an ethnocentric cultural construct that is peculiarly Nordic, Anglo-Saxon, or Protestant. European surveys of SWB over time have produced very large country coefficients.[93] The long-term persistence of SWB scores in particular countries even brings to mind the concept of 'national character'.

An early inspiration of the social indicators movement was the 1960s 'rediscovery of poverty', which redefined it as a relative rather than absolute form of deprivation. Easterlin has hypothesized that expectations are formed by comparisons with parents, and that demographic cycles mean that (in the United States, at least, since the Second World War), different cohorts have had different expectations.[94] Satisfaction has moved pro-cyclically for young adults, with those of the 'golden age' exceeding their own modest expectations, while the successor 'baby boom' having its higher expectations disappointed. A related perspective is Inglehart's long-standing study of 'post-materialism'. The argument here is that the post-war cohorts have shifted their preferences from economic to non-economic rewards, as a result of their experience of economic security.[95]

A different psychological approach is to investigate the hedonic dynamics of satisfaction. In welfare economics, it is assumed axiomatically that the consumer is well informed, self-aware, consistent, and acquisitive. These assumptions are necessary if 'revealed preference' is to equal welfare.[96] Other approaches do not have such confidence in the cognitive abilities of the consumer. That individual choice might fail to maximize welfare is an old but neglected theme in welfare discourse. The Victorians distinguished between the deserving poor, who had suffered from adversity, and the feckless and undeserving, who had brought about their own misfortune. B. S. Rowntree made a distinction between 'primary poverty', which was caused by the shortfall of subsistence resources, and 'secondary poverty', caused by impulsive consumption and poor resource management.[97] This is brought out by the difference between a 'social indicator' poverty line, which focuses on normative consumption, and a money metric one, which merely measures access to resources. Economists committed to rational choice might regard 'secondary poverty' as reflecting legitimate lifestyle choices.[98]

---

[93] Di Tella et al., 'The Macroeconomics of Happiness'.   [94] Easterlin, *Birth and Fortune.*
[95] Inglehart, *Modernization.*   [96] Sen, 'Income Comparisons'.
[97] Rowntree, *Poverty*, ch. 5.   [98] Hagenaars et al., 'Patterns of Poverty', 26.

Empirical research into the determinants of choice queries the empirical validity of the axioms of rationality. This is not very damaging to SNA welfare measures, since, as we have seen, their micro-foundations are already insecure. These lines of research have not so far provided direct measures of the validity of welfare aggregation, but rather implicitly query the premisses of consumer sovereignty. This effort has highlighted a sequence of systematic and recurrent deviations from normative optimizing choice behaviour.[99] The most robust ones appear to be 'loss aversion', the asymmetrically higher valuation of losses than gains, and the related 'endowment effect' by which goods acquire additional value simply by virtue of possession. If correct, these findings cast further doubt on the possibility of compensating losers, and on the notion of 'opportunity cost'. Research in the hedonics of satisfaction continues. It stresses that satisfaction depends on habituation, anchoring, contrast, and temporal effects; that the experience of satisfaction varies with time, and changes between decision, experience, and retrospection.[100] The following chapters (3 and 4) investigate the pervasive cognitive biases of time-inconsistency and myopia.

Under affluence SWB appears buoyant and quite stable, and responds quite sluggishly to economic indicators, both stagnation and growth. It is poorly correlated with income in affluent societies, and highly correlated in poor countries, confirming the diminishing returns to income detected in social indicators research.[101] Both extended accounting and static psychological indicators suggest that well-being is derived to a great extent *outside* the market, from human relations in the workplace, the family, and from other forms of attachment. The psychic payoff of rising absolute income is small, but gains from relative income are considerable. There are high levels of satisfaction with stable attributes such as personality, gender, and nationality. Stability and habituation appear to promote well-being.

This also suggests that novelty may undermine it. New rewards are compelling, while their costs are not yet known. Economic competition is driven by novelty and innovation, which stimulate myopic rather than informed choices. In the absence of prior experience, new forms of stimulation are highly compelling. Innovation devalues existing prudential conventions and norms, and is to that extent destructive of existing psychic and social capital. Diener found that SWB is inversely related to the pace of economic growth.[102] Cheap alcohol, drugs, tobacco, and fast

[99] Rabin, 'Psychology'.   [100] Kahneman, 'Objective Happiness', 14–21.
[101] Veenhoven, 'Satisfaction Research', 25.
[102] Diener et al., 'Income and Subjective Well-Being'; 'Predicting Subjective Well-Being'.

food are all innovations which it has taken society decades to adjust to and cope with.

Conclusion

'Alternative' measures of welfare provide a great variety of indicators, in cross-section and over time, international, intra-national, and individual. One reason why we need so many different indicators is that no single one maps very precisely on to human welfare. That different measures are incommensurate with each other is something that we need to accept. One common pattern that emerges is that the relation of economic welfare and human welfare is historically contingent. Many measures suggest a curvilinear (non-linear) relationship. Using extended accounting and social indicators, international comparisons suggest a historical cycle of two periods. In the first, economic growth provides high welfare payoffs, as basic deprivations are remedied and basic needs are satisfied. In the second phase, GDP goods provide diminishing, steady, or even negative returns, depending on the measure used. This pattern can be fitted to different non-linear (knee-shaped) curves. A logistic (s-shaped) curve model was first proposed by Xenophon Zolotas in 1981. He described three phases in the relation of income and welfare—of privation, steady improvements and declining ones, respectively.[103] More graphic metaphors might be the economy of deprivation and the economy of satiation; or the economy of pain followed by the economy of pleasure. For social indicators the logarithmic curve relation of welfare to income provides a good fit. The three studies presented in Figure 2.2, as well as the HDI, all have in common the initial steep rise, followed by an increasingly flat trajectory.

Subjective individual welfare also follows a similar log-normal or power curve response to economic welfare.[104] The cross-sectional international comparative relation of subjective well-being with income is positive, linear, and fairly weak; it almost disappears when controlled for relative income. The temporal relation for individual countries is almost completely flat. This is consistent with low psychic welfare returns to rising economic growth, the classic 'hedonic treadmill'.

If it is true that GDP goods and services have delivered and are delivering diminishing welfare returns, the question is 'Why?' It is premature to

[103] Zolotas, *Economic Growth*, fig. 1, 16.
[104] Kahneman, 'Objective Happiness', 17; van Praag and Frijters, 'Measurement', 419–20.

attempt to answer it here, but a few observations might be ventured. Both ecological and psychological approaches have one notion in common, namely that affluence produces congestion. In both cases, the affluent economy produces more than it can absorb. The ecology cannot absorb the extra energy, the extra traffic, the extra pollution, without incurring costs that equal or exceed the benefits. Likewise, the abundance of psychic reward under affluence leads to satiation and habituation. These are simple-minded metaphors that require further development.

But policy cannot wait. Alternative accounting of welfare is pragmatically motivated, and even at this stage, it has some implications for policy:

(a) In the most advanced economies, the increased supply of GDP goods and services is not the highest priority.

(b) For policy to find a coherent focus, it requires a better understanding of hedonic dynamics.

High levels of well-being are already pervasive, and it is evidently difficult to improve them much further by raising incomes overall. What is needed is a more systematic targeting of *ill-being*, its determinants, and the economic costs of its amelioration, to make the reduction of ill-being the focus of international competition: of such things as life expectation, material deprivation, the prevalence of crime and the severity of punishment, ethnic, social, and political exclusion and repression, family structure and break-down, mental health, suicide, morbidity, education, quality of working life, job security, access to health care, urban congestion and sprawl, and perhaps also of the quality of personal and social interaction.[105] It might be more useful to shift the focus of measurement from happiness to unhappiness. There is a view that ill-being does not belong on the same dimension as well-being.[106] 'Prospect theory' argues that losses are more acutely experienced than gains. Unemployment and discrimination have a more powerful effect on well-being than material gains.[107] It may be easier to reach consensus about welfare 'bads' than about welfare goods.

This does not mean that GNP goods have lost their relevance permanently. A society dependent on exponential growth for a stable experience of well-being might suffer badly if growth is withdrawn. Many societies have yet to arrive at that state of abundance, and can still anticipate large welfare returns to growth. A shift away from GDP goods towards leisure or short-term gratification might eventually return us to the economy of

[105] Doyal and Gough, *Human Need*.

[106] Bradburn, *Psychological Well-Being*; Diener and Emmons, 'Positive and Negative Affect'.

[107] Campbell et al., *Quality*, fig. 2-5, 52–3; Blanchflower and Oswald, 'Well-Being', 20.

pain. Longer life expectation, high dependency rates, and shorter working lives suggest that material scarcity could be a problem in the future as much as in the past. In other words, we should recognize the possibility that the determinants of human well-being are themselves historically contingent.

3

Passions and Interests: Self-Control and Well-Being

'Reason is, and ought only to be the slave of the passions, and can never pretend to any other office than to serve and obey them.'

David Hume, *A Treatise of Human Nature* (1739–40),
Bk. II, pt. iii, sect. 3

For a young woman of 20, life expectation in Britain today is 81, and 76 for a man.[1] Most people can expect to live for a decade or two after withdrawing from work. By setting aside and investing, say, one-fifth of their incomes, they might be reasonably confident of providing for retirement. But even the most cognitively sophisticated do not attempt this task unaided. Academics in Britain submit voluntarily to mandatory payroll pension deductions, which amount to more than 20 per cent of their pay overall.[2] In the United States, the sum of (mandatory) employer and employee old age, Medicare, and other social security contributions is more than 18 per cent.[3] By the early 1970s, nearly everyone in Britain was compelled to save, by means of state and employer payroll deductions, some of them by stealth.[4] When saving voluntarily, people have also typically placed assets beyond their own reach, in illiquid houses, insurance, or pension accounts.

This discipline sometimes failed to deliver: state pensions have withered, employers have closed their pension schemes, private pensions were mis-sold or mismanaged, while lenders encouraged homeowners to borrow against their equity and even their pensions. With saving becoming more

---

[1] UK, ONS, *Health Statistics Quarterly*, Table 5.1, 25 Feb. 2004. **www.statistics.gov.uk/ statbase/Expodata/Spreadsheets/ D7628.csv**.

[2] Six per cent deduction, 14 per cent employer contribution. A further 'national insurance' deduction gives rise to a small state pension entitlement. Deferred taxation adds to the incentives.   [3] Below a pay ceiling. Mulligan, 'Flat Tax'.

[4] Which is what employer pension contributions amount to.

discretionary, young people do not save enough, and for large minorities, savings are insufficient or non-existent.[5] To close the gap, providers say, 53 per cent more savings are needed in the UK.[6] It is difficult to look in the future. And yet old age will come to be as real as youth is today.

Modern consumption theory assumes that rational consumers (by definition) make choices that are well informed, far-sighted, and prudent. An attribute of rational choice is *consistency*, namely that if *a* is preferred over *b* then *b* cannot be preferred over *a*. Consumers reveal their preferences by means of market choices, and market choices correspond to their well-being (or 'welfare').[7] Taking account of the expected value of lifetime wealth, they maximize welfare by smoothing consumption over the life cycle.[8] An 'invisible hand' then acts to aggregate individual choices to maximize the economic welfare of society.

A great deal is at stake in this model. The primacy of 'revealed preference' as the source of well-being is the conceptual underpinning of liberal society. This doctrine regards the free exercise of market choice as not only economically efficient, but also as a vital human aspiration, suggesting that both social virtue and personal dignity depend on it. Even Amartya Sen, who is second to none in his sensitivity to deprivation and indigence, endows market participation with a human significance quite independent of its instrumental value.[9] Milton Friedman's credo is 'free to choose':

The possibility of co-ordination through voluntary co-operation rests on the elementary—yet frequently denied—proposition that both parties to an economic transaction benefit from it, *provided the transaction is bi-laterally voluntary and informed*.

Exchange can therefore bring about co-ordination without coercion. A working model of a society organized through voluntary exchange is a *free private enterprise exchange economy*—what we have been calling competitive capitalism.[10]

The key assumption is that choice is both *voluntary* and *informed*.

The methods (and failures) of providing for old age suggest that the model is not perfect: that in western affluent societies, most people might not have saved if they had not been forced to. That suggests choice can be *time inconsistent*, or 'myopic'. Priorities for the present (consumption) are

---

[5] Summary findings on savings in the USA, Laibson et al., 'Self-Control and Saving', tables 6–8, pp. 137–9.

[6] Oliver Wyman & Co., 'Future Regulation of UK Savings'; King, 'No Nest Egg'; for the USA, Farkas and Johnson, *Miles to Go*.   [7] Criticism in Burrows, 'Patronising Paternalism', 544–9.

[8] Deaton, *Understanding Consumption*, ch. 1; Lord, *Household Dynamics*, ch. 1.

[9] Sen, *Development as Freedom*, 25–30.

[10] Friedman, *Capitalism and Freedom*, ch. 1, p. 13 (emphases in original).

in conflict with priorities for the future (saving). Time inconsistency means that the wish to be virtuous tomorrow may not be sustained when tomorrow arrives. If the myopic consumer is 'naïve', he will make a resolution for the future, and simply fail to keep it. If he is 'sophisticated', he knows that he will be as self-indulgent tomorrow as today. External compulsion solves his problem of self-control. Time inconsistency raises the possibility that individual choice may not be sufficiently reliable as the source of personal well-being, and that freedom of choice is not a secure foundation for social well-being.

Here is a list of some self-defeating choices:

- Late to school/truancy/dropping out.
- Smoking/drink-driving/drug addiction.
- Overeating/dieting/eating disorders.
- Gambling.
- Unwanted pregnancy/abortion/marital discord/divorce.
- Marital infidelity.
- Crime.
- Urban/suburban sprawl, congested roads.
- Politicians' campaign promises.
- Chronic budget deficits.
- Undersaving.
- War.

But time-consistency problems are also resolved successfully:

- Punctuality.
- Temperance.
- Saving.
- Investment.
- Homeownership.
- Insurance.
- Education.
- Urban parks, green belts, national parks.
- Vibrant, attractive, liveable cities.
- Abiding friendship, enduring love.
- Stable families.
- Balanced budgets.
- Truthful politicians.
- Secure old age.
- Rule of Law.
- Peace.

David Hume wrote, 'There is no quality in human nature, which causes more fatal errors in our conduct, than that which leads us to prefer whatever is present to the distant and remote.'[11] Striking a balance between immediate and remote satisfactions is a problem as old as civilization. Indeed, civilization may be regarded as a solution. Moralists have traditionally privileged prudence over gratification. In religion, temptation is sin. No such judgement is intended here. Gratification eternally postponed is futile.

At the other extreme, affluence is seen as simply a matter of 'it's getting better all the time'.[12] But good choices are not a trivial issue of maximizing preferences in conditions of affluence. For the unaided individual, inconsistent preferences give rise to intractable dilemmas. Myopic choice is pervasive, but in spite of large conceptual breakthroughs, understanding is still in flux.[13]

Time inconsistency and discounting

For an individual, from the point of view of the present, an asset delivered tomorrow is worth less than its value today. The value today of a future benefit is calculated by discounting it *at a constant rate* for every period of time. At a 5 per cent discount *rate*, an asset worth unity now is worth only 0.95 if it is expected to be delivered in $t + 1$, 0.902 in $t + 2$, 0.857 in $t + 3$, etc. (the fraction is the discount *factor* at time t). This is 'exponential discounting'.[14] If it is the only good (or all goods, i.e. 'utility'), then the discount rate represents a 'rate of time preference' for the present over the future. The higher the rate, the less a given future benefit is worth today. To maximize a person's well-being only requires markets in which choices are reliably delivered. Between two rewards, at any given point in time, the 'exponential' discounter always makes the same choice, whether delivery is today or tomorrow. At her chosen discount rate, she is also indifferent between the present and the future. That is the sense in which exponential discounting is *time consistent*. Expected utility theory (which embodies exponential discounting) is hegemonic in economic analysis.[15]

---

[11] Hume, *Treatise of Human Nature*, Bk. III, pt. ii, section vii.

[12] Moore and Simon, *It's Getting Better*; Lebergott, *Pursuing Happiness*.

[13] What follows is not comprehensive. For surveys, see Loewenstein and Elster, *Choice over Time*; Elster, *Ulysses Unbound*; Ainslie, *Breakdown of Will*; Loewenstein et al., *Time and Decision*.

[14] A brief account in Frederick et al., 'Time Discounting', 355–60. More detail, Schoemaker, 'The Expected Utility Model'.

[15] Schoemaker, 'Expected Utility Model'; Frederick et al., 'Time Discounting', 351–9; Price, *Time, Discounting and Value* is thoughtful, mostly non-technical, and very informative.

But it is often wrong. People indulge in hedonic gratification, even at a large cost in the future. Conversely, they will also commit to benefits so remote (like a slow-growing tree), that an exponential discounter would value them at zero. This type of behaviour is captured by an alternative model, of 'hyperbolic discounting'. In this model, the future is discounted not at a constant rate, but at a varying one, usually a declining one. Between the present and the immediate future, value is discounted at a high rate, but for more remote future payoffs, the discount curve levels off. Given a immediately, the hyperbolic discounter will go for it, rather than wait for the larger b. But if delivery is delayed, she prefers the large b over the small a. Depending on *when* the payoff occurs, she prefers either a or b. The hyperbolic discounter is *inconsistent*. This dilemma has always been known, but its recent rediscovery in economics and psychology (some fifty years ago) has recently made it more salient.[16]

The 'rational' and 'inconsistent' approaches to intertemporal choice can each be described in terms of simple mathematical models.[17] In exponential discounting, the current value of a future benefit is calculated by

$$V = \frac{B_t}{(1 + r)^t}$$

V is the current value of benefit B at time t. r (<1) is the discount rate in each period. Value declines at a constant percentage from one period to another.

In hyperbolic discounting, present value is inversely related only to time. In a very simple form, the equation describing hyperbolic discounting is:

$$V = \frac{B_t}{(1 + kt)}$$

Where V is again the present value, B is the benefit at time t, k is a constant which expresses the intensity of time preference, and t is the number of time units. 1 is added to kt to prevent V from rising to infinity at $t = 0$, when there is no delay. Value declines with time, not at a constant rate, but at a declining rate, more steeply at the start, and more slowly thereafter.

Figure 3.1 represents the two equations, at (*a*) short and (*b*) long delays. For exponential discounting, the discount rate has been set at 0.15 (15%). For hyperbolic discounting, the constant (k) has been set to 1. The two

---

[16] Fredrick et al., 'Time Discounting', 366–8; Chung and Herrnstein, 'Relative and Absolute'; Ainslie, 'Specious Reward'.

[17] There are several different representations of both approaches. I present the simplest.

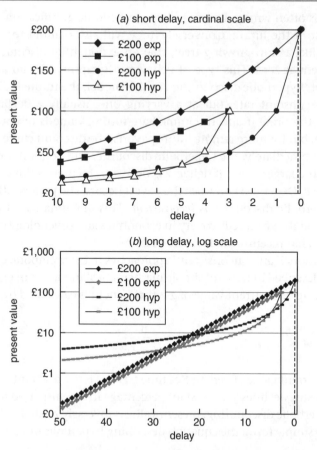

Fig. 3.1. Exponential and hyperbolical discounting of £100 and £200 at different delays

Note: Exponential discount rate = 0.15, $k = 1$.

models, exponential and hyperbolic discounting, are 'ideal types', which capture some of the attributes of real choices. Figure 3.1(*a*) shows the present value of two assets, worth £200 and £100 respectively, at delays of $t = 10$ (broken vertical line) and $t = 7$ (solid vertical line) respectively. The top two curves are the exponential discounting curves, the bottom two are the hyperbolic discounting ones.

Exponential discounting describes the values at which the owner is indifferent between immediate and delayed possession. The discount rate ($r = 0.15$) determines the slope, and expresses the intensity of the hedonic preference. The large reward is always preferred to the smaller one. Under hyperbolic discounting, however, there is a cross-over point at $t = 5$, when the smaller reward becomes more compelling. Value rises at a faster rate as delivery approaches. Exponential discounting can be highly myopic without being inconsistent. When the discount rate is very high (as with addicts) a small reward now might still be preferable to a large one later. Nor is it always the case that hyperbolic discounting is the more myopic. When delays are long (Figure 3.1(b)), hyperbolic discounting crosses over, and places a positive value on very distant rewards, which would decline down to nothing under exponential discounting.

Some writers regard exponential discounting as representing normative rationality: hyperbolic discounting is inferior. 'Mr Exponential could buy Ms. Hyperbolic's winter coat cheaply every spring', and sell it back to her at a high price next winter.[18] Others deny this, and find arguments from evolutionary theory and animal behaviour, from logic, or from imperfect information, to reconcile hyperbolic discounting with rationality.[19] On one view there is no substantive difference between the two discounting models as descriptions of choice,[20] or that the preferences of the hyperbolic discounter should be respected, and that they exclude an external viewpoint which would allow an 'objective' choice.[21] One enduring view even regards discounting as unjustified, given that both present and future are equally real, and takes the appropriate time preference to be zero.[22]

Discounting is real, but it does not necessarily represent an overarching psychological 'time preference' for the present over the future. There are other reasons to discount: (a) delivery is uncertain: death might intervene; (b) diminishing marginal utility: as the subject becomes wealthier, he may value the reward less; (c) the unit of delivery is not the same as the unit of calculation, e.g. due to inflation; (d) incompleteness of options, due to proliferation of outcomes with time, including some not available when choices were made; (e) unstable preferences due to habits building up, heightened (or diminished) anticipation, temporary impulses, infatuations or repulsions, or life-cycle unfolding of preferences and tastes; (f) cognitive biases, e.g. small sums are discounted more than large ones, gains more than losses, preferences for rising rather than smooth incomes, or, indeed, hyperbolic discounting itself;[23] (g) exponential discounting assumes that

[18] Ainslie, *Breakdown of Will*, 30–1. Mulligan, 'Logical Economist'; Laibson, 'Life-Cycle Consumption'.

[19] Kacelnick, 'Evolution of Patience'; Read, 'Subadditive Intertemporal Choice'; Fernandez Villaverde and Mukherji, 'Can We Really Observe?'

[20] Rubinstein, 'Economics and Psychology'. The 'quasi-hyperbolic' model used by Laibson and others is an exponential curve starting at time 1 rather than time 0.

[21] Schelling, 'Self-Command in Practice'.

[22] Survey in Price, *Time, Discounting and Value*, ch. 7.

[23] Ibid. 103–14; also Frederick et al., 'Time Discounting', 363–4, 380–4; Frank, 'Wages, Seniority'.

putative revenues are reinvested at a constant rate of return, but if revenues are not financial, they cannot be reinvested.[24]

If discounting is not an overarching rate of substitution between different periods of time, but is attached to particular goods, then time inconsistency arises again. In practice, different goods are often associated with different discount rates. Think of them as different half-lives, from the very short to the very long. Perishable goods are more compelling than durable ones. If not consumed, they are lost. Passions do not keep well in storage. Novelty depreciates by definition. Empirical studies show a wide range of discount rates, and these are already averages over heterogeneous individuals, heterogeneous goods, heterogeneous attributes, and heterogeneous time horizons. No evidence of uniformity there.[25] For example, when time preferences for health are examined (e.g. as between prevention and cure) 'decision makers apparently do not have a consistent time preference trait that can be measured or manipulated in one setting and used to predict or influence health behaviour in another'.[26]

When governments make investments, they do not use a single time preference. Different discount rates for different payoffs at different time horizons are broadly accepted policy practice. In the United States, different agencies use different discount rates, depending on the project and the time horizon expected.[27] This is unavoidable, since typical market rates of return exclude projects beyond twenty to thirty years. Since its introduction in the 1960s, the UK government 'test discount rate' has varied at different times between 8 per cent and 3.5 per cent real.[28] Of the latter, only a small proportion (between 0 and 0.5 percentage points) represented pure time preference. The British Forestry Commission used discount rates ranging between 1 and 10 per cent at the same time for different types of activities.[29] For longer-term discounting, the UK Treasury has recently accepted a declining discount rate, falling down to 1 per cent at a time horizon of 301 years. Since only exponential discounting is time consistent, government choice (like that of private individuals) is also prone to the dilemmas of time inconsistency.[30]

[24] Price, *Time, Discounting, and Value*, ch. 6.
[25] Frederick et al., 'Time Discounting', 377–80; Price, *Time, Discounting and Value*, 100; Soman, 'Effect of Time Delay'.   [26] Chapman, 'Time Discounting', 413.
[27] Price, *Time, Discounting and Value*, 118; Henderson and Bateman, 'Empirical and Public Choice Evidence'; Bazelon and Smetters, 'Discounting inside the Washington D.C. Beltway'.
[28] Unpublished work by Martin Chick; Great Britain, HM Treasury, 'The Test Discount Rate'; Spackman, 'Discount Rates'; Great Britain, HM Treasury, *Green Book*, 1997, 2003; Great Britain, 'A Social Time-Preference Rate'.   [29] Price, *Time, Discounting and Value*, 118.
[30] Hepburn, 'Hyperbolic Discounting'.

Ainslie, an imaginative and inspiring pioneer of hyperbolic discounting, first observed it in pigeons, and assumes that 'hyperbolic discounting' comes naturally: it is the innate mode of perceiving time. In physiology and psychology, a widely accepted principle is that the intensity of sensual experiences declines with distance (the Weber–Fechner rule).[31] From this point of view, both the past and the future recede just as steeply.[32] Consistent with this view, the past is not available in its totality—experience selects out of 'peak' and terminal experiences—which is consistent with a retrospective Weber–Fechner rule.[33] Remorse about large expenditures declines as they recede into the past.[34] The atrophy of the past means that it is difficult to learn from experience.[35]

The hyperbolic discounting curve is at best a description, not an explanation. Instead of being a particularly skewed version of foresight, the privileging of the present can also be conceptualized as the immediate response to innate, 'visceral' emotions of irresistible desire, shame, or anger, to external provocation or stimulation.[36] In one research programme, children were offered a choice between one sweet immediately, or two with a short delay. A minority of children were able to choose delayed rewards, mostly by controlling the internal visualization of enticing images. In subsequent life courses the prudent children had more success-ful careers.[37] Another approach to visualization implies a (Weber–Fechner) perceptual gradient, arguing that 'The greater the temporal distance from future events, the more likely are the events to be represented in terms of a few abstract and essential features (high-level construals), rather than in terms of more concrete and superficial features (low-level construals).'[38] Desires can be classified as being 'hot' or 'cold'—immediate and pressing, or long-sighted, capable of calculation and delay, and more rewarding objectively.[39] The mere passage of time can lower the temperature of desire. This is captured by the common advice to 'sleep on' a decision, and by the 'cooling off' periods which permit withdrawal from consumer contracts. There is some progress in identifying the physiological, brain location, and biochemical attributes of impatient preferences.[40]

[31] Ainslie, *Breakdown of Will*, 35; Poulton, *Quantifying Judgements*. There is some debate about the appropriate model, whether logarithmic or power-law.

[32] Price, *Time, Discounting, and Value*, 114–15; Pigou, *Economics of Welfare*, Pt. I, ch. 2, par. 3, p. 25.

[33] Kahneman, 'Experienced Utility'. On retrospective evaluation, see Ariely and Carmon, 'Summary Assessment'.   [34] Heath and Fennema, 'Mental Depreciation'.

[35] Kahneman, 'New Challenges'.   [36] Loewenstein, 'Out of Control'.

[37] Mischel et al., 'Delay of Gratification'; Shoda et al., 'Predicting Adolescent Competencies'.

[38] Liberman and Trope, 'Construal Level Theory', 236.

[39] Mischel et al., 'Sustaining Delay of Gratification'.

[40] Manuck et al., 'Neurobiology of Intertemporal Choice'.

If the present is compelling, then commitment to the future is difficult. Choice is genuinely intractable—rather like those forbidden 'interpersonal comparisons of welfare' in orthodox welfare economics. Rewards at different time horizons can be compared to different interests of the same person. Time inconsistency is an expression of a 'divided self', of preferring, for example, indulgence for the immediate self, and prudence for the future one.[41] But prudence in the future is likely to be rejected when that future arrives. The long-term, 'cold' interest would like to find a strategy to lock the immediate, 'hot' interest into the long-term priority. Commitment might be seen as a bargain between two interests, each mobilizing their resources to achieve the best outcome for both.

This bargain is managed in two ways, *intrinsic* and *social*. Intrinsic mental commitment is a promise enforced by means of psychic self-disciplines, such as control of attention, clear behavioural rules, and 'bright lines' that make it easier to define the objective and achieve it.[42] 'Attention control' involves avoiding exposure to the reward, as when a glutton keeps the home clear of chocolate. Another psychic strategy is 'personal rules', e.g. 'no eating between meals'. Successful strategies provide 'bright lines', e.g. in the case of the glutton, a clear definition of what constitutes a 'meal', and closing of any 'loopholes' that lie beyond this boundary. An effective strategy is giving psychic 'hostages', (or placing 'side-bets'), by specifying in advance a high penalty for failure. A lapse then not only defeats the objective, but also damages self-credibility and self-esteem. Conversely, however, persistent failure, can lead to lasting harm to self-esteem.[43]

Social methods of commitment rely for enforcement on third parties. In a recent experiment, students produced better work against self-imposed deadlines than with no deadlines, but the best work was produced with deadlines that were imposed from the outside.[44] In contracts like insurance, mortgages, deposit accounts, and pension plans, compliance is monitored impersonally, and lapses are punished by loss. Money and contracts provide a set of 'bright lines'. Informal but binding social pressures are also effective: Alcoholics Anonymous and Weight Watchers combine intra- and interpersonal commitment. In the case of celebrities, the transgression of marriage by extra-marital affairs, for example, is punished at a heavy cost in money and shame.

---

[41] This framing of the problem dates back to the originator of modern discussion, Strotz, 'Myopia and Inconsistency'.

[42] Ainslie, *Picoeconomics*, 133–5; Schelling, 'Intimate Contest for Self-Command'; Schelling, 'Self-Command in Practice'; Rabin, 'Moral Preferences'.

[43] e.g. Green, *Diary of a Housewife*.

[44] Ariely and Wertenbroch, 'Procrastination, Deadlines, and Performance'.

Tried-and-tested commitment strategies, whether psychic or social, might be described as 'commitment technologies', or 'commitment devices'.[45] Numbers, the calendar, time—are all commitment devices.[46] The Sabbath rest day controls the compulsion to work. The mechanical clock was initially a public, interpersonal commitment device, then a private, intra-personal one; alarm clocks help with the micro-commitment problem of getting up, the snooze control with the pico-commitment problem of ignoring the alarm.

Commitment technologies underpin the capacity to undertake a sustained task. They arise in history, evolve, do useful work, and decline. The right to mint or print money has always given rise to the temptation of excess. The nineteenth-century gold standard was a commitment technology, which broke down under the compelling immediacy of war. The doctrines and practices of central banking have evolved over two centuries, converging recently on the device of an independent central bank. Exponential discounting is a financial commitment technology. The cost of medical care under the traditional American 'fee for service', paid to the doctor up front by the sick patient at the point of need, is higher than where medical fees are determined in advance by healthy administrators, as under the British Health Service, or American Health Maintenance Organizations (HMO). The heavy investment in advertising and branding (more than 2 per cent of national income in the United States) is an effect-ive way of locking consumers into consumption habits, and of solving the intractable problem of consumer choice in conditions of abundance.[47] Coca-Cola or Chevrolet have been as much of a commitment, as much a part of the fabric of American life, as churchgoing.

Statutory law restricts the range of choice in advance, for rulers and subjects alike. Constitutions bind legislators, to protect long-term prefer-ences against temporary advantage (or to lock in temporary advantage into the future). The building-blocks of society can be seen as clusters of intertemporal strategies and technologies. Personality, class, family, culture, ideology, policy, national character: all of them constitute sets of priorities at different ranges of time. All of them constrain the freedom of choice.

For the individual, society helps to achieve self-control. For society, an individual's failure to commit constitutes a nuisance. The criminal, the truant, the latecomer impose costs ('externalities') on other people. A failure to cooperate hurts not only the defector, but also those who might have

---

[45] The terms are current in monetary economics. See also Brocas et al., 'Commitment Devices'.   [46] Zerubavel, *Hidden Rhythms*.
[47] The consequences are discussed in more detail below, Chapter 6.

gained from his cooperation. Typically, commitment technologies are not devised by individuals seeking to control their own vices, but by social agencies controlling the vices of others. By analogy, a psychic myopic equilibrium such as addiction is deemed to be an 'internality', an inconsistency which consumers inflict on themselves.[48]

Equilibrium must always be found, if only by default, but the dilemma is not easily tractable. In his poem 'A Feaver' John Donne says to the woman, his lover,

> I had rather owner bee
> Of thee one houre, than all else ever.[49]

But when 'one houre' is over, and 'ever' arrives, is the deal still going to look so good? Of the two interests, the 'hot' and the 'cold' ones, 'the question, which is the authentic one, may define the problem wrong. Both selves can be authentic... the problem seems to be distributive, not of identification.' Is an hour of extreme pleasure worth more than the rest of life? 'The conclusion that I reach', says Thomas Schelling, 'is that I do not know, not for you and not for me.'[50]

It is possible to overcommit.[51] Anorexia/bulimia, vows of celibacy, teetotalism, and the pursuit of honour, are examples of overcommitment. In late Victorian Europe, an insult required an upper-class person to 'demand satisfaction' by means of a duel. This may have restored social approbation in the present, but at the cost of a high-risk gamble on injury or death shortly afterwards.[52] Ainslie calls these forms of excessive commitment 'compulsions'.[53]

A straightforward measure of prudence is saving. A hyperbolic saver wants to spend now and to save later. But when 'later' arrives, he wants to spend again. With a perfect (and costless) commitment technology, he would precisely match the saving level of an exponential saver. If a commitment technology is available at reasonable cost, he will try to lock his savings for release in the future. Society abounds with commitment devices and technologies, so it is not easy to characterize saving behaviour as either exponential or hyperbolic. Laibson has carried out simulations in which both exponential and hyperbolic models of saving are calibrated to

---

[48] O'Donoghue and Rabin, 'Addiction and Self-Control', 171, 176; Loewenstein and Elster, *Choice over Time*, p. xxi; Herrnstein et al., 'Utility Maximization'.

[49] John Donne, 'A Feaver', in Donne, *Selection*.

[50] Schelling, 'Self-Command in Practice', 9. He uses an example of a man who is forced to undergo a painful procedure in order to save his life.

[51] Ameriks et al., 'Measuring Self-Control'.

[52] Offer, 'Going to War: A Matter of Honor?'

[53] Ainslie, *Breakdown of Will*, 50–1; in earlier work he calls them 'sell-outs'.

match observed savings behaviour. These simulations suggest that hyperbolic discounters can be quite successful in putting off consumption. But since commitment is not perfect, the simulated hyperbolic discounter falls short (about as much as the real saver claims to fall short of his own targets). In one of these simulations, the shortfall from optimizing exponential saving level models is estimated at almost a year's income.[54] While an exponential discounter would smooth consumption over the lifetime, a hyperbolic one would spend some of the expected increase in income when it occurs. The actual increase of spending of expected income matches the hyperbolic model.[55]

In terms of the gap between consumption and income, there is not much to choose between the two models. But on other attributes, a difference emerges. The hyperbolic discounter is predicted to have low liquid assets (because of splurging and under-commitment), and also high credit card debts. Simulations confirm this pattern. In fact, behaviour is even more 'hyperbolic' than simulations suggest. In the USA in c.1980–1992, only about 10 per cent of assets were held in liquid form (as against simulations of 50 per cent (exponential) and 39 per cent (hyperbolic)). And credit card debts at an average $5,000 per household are more than five times as high as exponential discounting would predict.[56]

To summarize the argument so far, if myopia is natural, and time consistency is desired, then achieving it requires a cognitive and psychic effort, and access to social commitment technologies is costly. As Adam Smith put it, commitment required two separate attributes, both of them scarce, namely 'reason' and 'self-command'.

The qualities most useful to ourselves are, first of all, superior reason and understanding, by which we are capable of discerning the remote consequences of all our actions, and of foreseeing the advantage or detriment which is likely to result from them: and secondly, self-command, by which we are enabled to abstain from present pleasure or to endure present pain, in order to obtain a greater pleasure or to avoid a greater pain in some future time. In the union of those two qualities consists the virtue of prudence, of all the virtues that which is most useful to the individual.[57]

Far from being costless (as assumed in standard consumption theory), overcoming time inconsistency is difficult, and carries a heavy psychic and social transaction cost.[58] For example, the private pension accounts managed

---

[54] Laibson, 'Life-Cycle Consumption', 868–70.
[55] Angeletos et al., 'Hyperbolic Consumption Model', 534–5.   [56] Ibid, 531–3.
[57] Smith, *Moral Sentiments*, Pt. IV, ch. 2, par. 6, p. 189.
[58] The cost of commitment is explicitly modelled in Gul and Pesendorfer, 'Temptation and Self-Control'.

by financial institutions typically incur an annual management fee of more than 1 per cent, and these fees can claim a third or more of savers' contributions.[59] Delaying consumption incurs an additional commitment cost which reduces the ultimate value of the postponed benefit. This, by the way, provides yet another reason for discounting.

Prudence and social position

If commitment technology is costly, it is more readily available to those who are better off. How costly? Well, precisely $149.95. That is the price of *ESPlanner™*, 'a unique patented financial planning software package based on the life-cycle model of saving'. This is the same lifetime consumption smoothing that rational consumers are supposed to be doing costlessly, but as the authors explain, 'Solving the problem of both maximizing and smoothing your household's living standard over time and across survival contingencies is not easy. *ESPlanner* uses a patented dynamic programming method to solve this problem.' It took a decade to develop.[60] This underlines the point: commitment is both difficult and expensive. The authors are senior professors, access sets a high cognitive threshold, and it is just a tool. Willpower is not included. And what did people do before it was invented?

The capacity for commitment is built up by education. Like a muscle, it can be trained and strengthened (and also exhausted by use).[61] Larger financial savings are achieved with a college or postgraduate education.[62] Discount rates are highest for high-school dropouts, decline sharply in high-school graduates, and are lowest among college graduates.[63] Comparing one group with another (and not specific individuals), we shall argue that, at any given point in historical time, those who are better off are likely to show more capacity for self-control. Prudence is essentially a bourgeois attitude. Not the very rich, who are secure in their assets, nor the very poor, who have little long-term prospect of gain. This bourgeois virtue is underpinned by the infrastructure of legal and financial institutions, and by the 'bright lines' of bourgeois virtue, namely money.

---

[59] Offer, *Public Sector*, p. 3, n. 11; Kotlikoff and Burns, *Coming Generational Storm*, table 8.1, p. 199.   [60] Economic Security Planning, *ESPlanner™*, 2, 5.

[61] Baumeister and Vohs, 'Willpower, Choice'.

[62] Lord, *Household Dynamics*, fig. 1.9, p. 26; Gourinchas and Parker, 'Consumption over the Life Cycle', fig. 3, p. 68; table IV, p. 77.

[63] Laibson et al., 'Self-Control and Saving', table 4, p. 121.

For the classical economists of the eighteenth century, prudence and thrift were necessary in order to accumulate wealth. But wealth gave rise to temptation, temptation to indulgence, and indulgence ate up the wealth.[64] Affluence instigates a conflict between passion and reason. At the end of the eighteenth century, Malthus thought that sexual desire would keep the population growing as fast as the economy, and keep most people down to the level of poverty. To escape this trap, it was necessary to bring the urges of sexual attraction under control. The idea that restraint is necessary for wealth to accumulate was a staple of Victorian morality, and resonates through Victorian economic thought, from John Rae's condemnation of improvidence, through Nassau Senior's 'abstinence', Jevons's 'foresight', and Böhm-Bawerk's 'waiting'. Max Weber's prudential 'Protestant Ethic' is linked in the same way with the 'spirit of capitalism'.[65] Recently, Becker and Mulligan have once again argued that wealth induces self-control.[66]

Conversely, improvidence was associated with the poor.[67] For Irving Fisher this fecklessness was partly rational: 'a small income, other things being equal, tends to produce a high rate of impatience, partly from the thought that provision for the present is necessary ... and partly from lack of foresight and self-control.'[68] Post-war American social science described lower-class behaviour in America as 'impulse following' rather than 'impulse renunciation', though it was not clear whether poverty arose from excessive desires, or whether people yielded to desire because they were poor. During the last fifteen years, myopia and poor self-control have been implicated in an influential theory of crime.[69]

The extent of 'hand to mouth' living can be estimated by measuring liquidity constraints at different levels of education and age. Liquidity constraint (i.e. absence of ready assets) declines substantially as education rises. One interpretation is that education provides a stronger capacity for psychic self-control, and hence less reliance on external self-commitment devices. Consumption surveys indicate much higher levels of 'hand to mouth' consumption than either exponential or hyperbolic models suggest, but the hyperbolic model comes closer to reality, and reality is much less prudent even than the hyperbolic model.[70] Surveys also indicate that the presence of illiquid savings plans would increase retirement savings

---

[64] Smith, *Wealth of Nations*, Bk. II, ch. iii.   [65] Loewenstein, 'Rise and Fall'.

[66] Becker and Mulligan, 'Endogenous Determination of Time Preference', 738–46, 750–3.

[67] Johnson, *Saving and Spending*, ch. 7.   [68] Fisher, *Theory of Interest*, 73.

[69] Miller et al., 'Poverty and Self-Indulgence', quoting Lysgaard, 'Social Stratification', 142; Davis, *Social Class*. More recent evidence, Lawrance, 'Poverty and the Rate of Time Preference', 54–5, and references therein; Goffredson and Hirschi, *General Theory of Crime*.

[70] Laibson et al., 'Self-Control and Saving', 132–9.

considerably.[71] For all its complexity, this work is tentative and incomplete. In particular, although it deals with life-cycle decisions, it does not attempt to identify changing consumption patterns over time. Nevertheless, it suggests that a college education, at least, is conducive to higher levels of self-control, though that is facilitated by higher incomes and presumably greater security.

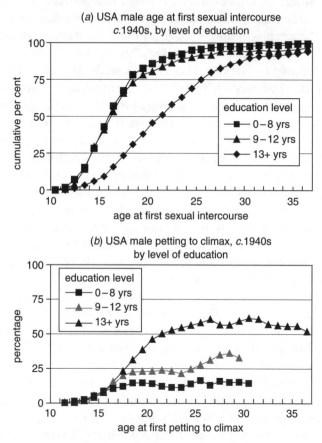

Fig. 3.2. Male sexual initiation, USA *c.*1940s

(*a*) Age at first intercourse, white men, United States, 1938–47 by educational level
Source: Kinsey et al., *Sexual Behaviour in the Human Male*, table 137, p. 566, n = 4,148.

(*b*) Premarital petting to climax, white men, by educational level, United States, 1938–1947
Source: Ibid., table 135, p. 536, n = 2, 304. The curves are not truly cumulative: they dip because sample sizes declined with age.

[71] Laibson et al., 'Self-Control and Saving', 171.

The relation between financial prudence and education is replicated at the micro-level in the case of sexual prudence. Like consumption, only more so, sexuality offers intense, compelling, and immediate pleasures. Several different time scales are involved: the brief and intense cycle of arousal, climax, and deflation, the extended ritual of courtship, the unfolding of a relationship, the making of a family, and its possible unmaking. The costs of gratification and commitment have to be set against opportunities forgone.

Contraception is a challenge for commitment. Kinsey's work on American sexuality in the 1940s provides an example of the difference that cognitive resources, education, and prospects could make.[72] Figure 3.2 plots the age of first sexual intercourse against final level of education. Figure 3.2(a) indicates that educational prudence and sexual prudence were strongly associated. Men who aspired to and went on to college kept their sexual appetites under tight control. At age 21, they were five years behind their grade-school contemporaries (as a group), and half the college students were still virgins. Figure 3.2(b) indicates that college graduates developed the commitment technology of 'petting to climax', in order to avoid penetration and pregnancy.[73]

Time inconsistency suggests why saving and sexuality might each be a problem. Consistency is costly. For both saving and sex, education and income help to cope with the challenge of choice. What is the nature of that challenge?

Pacing reward under affluence

For Ainslie, the ultimate reward of commitment is the optimal flow of psychic satisfactions.[74] Time-inconsistent preferences become particularly troublesome under affluence: subsistence no longer has priority, and most rewards are psychic ones. Novelty, by definition, depreciates very rapidly. Physiological drives are easily swamped by an excess of reward. They are saturated by habituation. Disco music, for example, can cause permanent hearing loss.[75] Eating stimulates, then deflates appetite. The Wundt curve (Figure 3.3), dating back to the nineteenth century, describes a stylized empirical relation between stimulation and satisfaction.

---

[72] Kinsey, *Human Male*. Kinsey's sampling was non-random, but did present reliably the two extremes of white American educational endowment.

[73] See e.g. Greene, *Sex and the College Girl*, ch. 5.   [74] Ainslie, *Picoeconomics*, ch. 9.

[75] Curry, 'Guarding against Hearing Loss'.

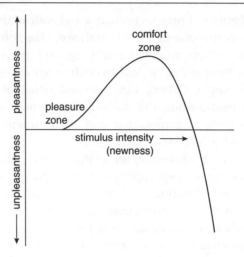

Fig. 3.3. The Wundt curve
Source: Scitovsky, *Joyless Economy*, 35.

On the Wundt curve, less is more. At low levels of stimulation returns are increasing, whereas high levels of stimulation deliver decreasing returns. Take the example of temperature, perhaps of water in a bath. At the bottom of the curve, when stimulation (temperature) is low, every increment produces increasing pleasure, i.e. 'productivity' in terms of satisfaction is increasing. Scitovsky calls this the 'pleasure zone'. After the inflection point is passed, diminishing returns (habituation) set in.[76] It is possible to maintain the rate of growth of satisfaction, but only by raising stimulation (temperature) at an accelerating rate, and even that has its limits. Satisfaction eventually levels off at a physiological ceiling of habituation that Scitovsky calls the 'comfort zone', where more stimulation produces no further satisfaction. 'Up to a point, more is more; beyond that point, more is less.'[77] There is nowhere to go but downwards. But there is another option: to scale back stimulation deliberately, and maintain it permanently at the lower level of increasing returns. At that level, every additional increment of stimulation provides *increasing* satisfaction. In terms of time preference, raising consumption in the comfort zone implies a rising discount rate; while slowing it back into the 'pleasure zone' implies a reduction of the discount rate.

Ainslie has a similar argument. Under affluence, the basic drives are easy to swamp cheaply with short-term rewards. Food and alcohol both get

---

[76] Scitovsky, *Joyless Economy*, ch. 4.   [77] Elster, *Ulysses Unbound*, 263.

cheaper. In conditions of plenty, the problem is not to maximize the flow of rewards, but to keep them under control, not to maximize consumption, but to pace it.[78] Scarcity itself becomes scarce. As wealth rises, social conventions like table manners, family meals, or courting rituals have evolved (as commitment devices) to slow the pace of rewards down to more optimal levels.

Ainslie states provocatively that 'the main value of other people is to pace one's own self-reward'.[79] In the nineteenth century, young middle-class people of the opposite sexes could only meet in the presence of a chaperone, thus keeping sensuality buttoned up and scarce. The German distinction between the formal 'Sie' and the familiar 'du' acts to pace social interaction. Scitovsky wrote that novelty is the most stimulating and the most pleasant when it provides surprise, conflict, incongruity, 'cognitive disssonance', deviation, or divergence beween expectation and experience. Quite apart from their function as 'enforcers' in self-control agreements, 'other people' help to pace social interaction, and also provide a source of surprise and novelty, which protects from habituation and keeps up arousal levels. That is also a function of literature and art, to amplify that variety, and generate unpredictability. In that sense, a good life might also be regarded as a creative 'work of art'. 'People use reality mainly for aesthetic purposes, that is, for entertainment, in the broad sense of the word,' writes Ainslie.[80] Irving Fisher, the great American economist, said that 'human beings are ever striving to control the stream of their psychic life by appropriating and utilizing the materials and forces of nature.'[81] Artists achieve more by accepting the constraints of medium and style.[82]

In the face of plenty, the better-off increase their satisfaction by slowing down. Costly goods, by virtue of their scarcity, perform the function of pacing consumption in conditions of abundance. Very expensive wines cannot be savoured frequently, expensive cars cannot be kept new all the time. Status is satisfying because it is scarce: only few can be at the top. As Ainslie points out, the web of social relations, the conventions of social interaction, the obligations of reciprocity and kinship, the structures of social hierarchy, place an obstacle between people and their desires, and so act to keep an edge on those desires.

From this perspective, well-being is the consequence of a succession of intertemporal compromises. The task is not always to defer gratification,

---

[78] Empirical research on self-rationing, see Wertenbroch, 'Self-Rationing', 500–11.
[79] Ainslie, *Picoeconomics*, 296.   [80] Ibid. 304.   [81] Fisher, *Theory of Interest*, 3–4.
[82] On self-constraint in art, Elster, *Ulysses Unbound*, ch. 3.

but to devise a cycle in which self-control in the present is rewarded with the payoffs from self-denial in the past, combined with controlled concessions to current cravings. Unlike 'exponential discounting', it cannot be assigned to a computer. The *quality* of payoffs and their probabilities are imperfectly known. There is room for error, excessive restraint, undercommitment, overcommitment, or excessive indulgence, none of which can be judged with finality except in retrospect, and not reliably even then. The European bourgeois conception of the good life, a complex combination of restraint and gratification, of commitment and hedonism, might be seen as another bourgeois virtue.[83] The calendar of workdays alternating with rest days and festivals is another example of an evolved (and evolving) social equilibrium between gratification and prudence. It has changed substantially over time, and has been mostly swept away by the salience of consumption, so that every day can now be a working day—but in terms of consumption, every day is now a feast as well.

---

[83] This was Scitovsky's view. Needless to say, it excluded most of the population, and affected men and women differently.

4

Choice: Myopic and Rational

Affluence affects prudence

If the affluent are likely to be more prudent, it does not follow that prudence increases with affluence. Prudence can decline with affluence, if (*a*) growing wealth diminishes the *incentive* for prudence or (*b*) growing wealth diminishes the *capacity* for prudence.

If people anticipate becoming wealthier anyway through the process of economic growth, that reduces their incentive to make a sacrifice now, when they are poorer, for the sake of a future when they are going to be rich (diminishing intertemporal marginal rate of substitution). Furthermore, if a dollar returns more satisfaction to the poor than to the wealthy, then in a growing economy an additional dollar of consumption now is more satisfying than an additional dollar in the future (diminishing marginal utility of consumption). The elasticity of the marginal utility of consumption measures the percentage rate at which the marginal utility falls for every percentage increase in consumption. It is normally assumed that this figure is positive, but that it falls as consumption increases. There is empirical support for diminishing marginal utility of consumption. In affluent societies, for every increment of economic output, the marginal increment of utility is progressively smaller. Current estimates place this elasticity in a range of 0.8 to 1.5 for the UK.[1] Other methods indicate a somewhat wider range over several different countries (*c*.0.4 to 2.8).[2] Declining marginal utility of consumption is also suggested by our own plots and tables of welfare indicators against income per head.[3] Under affluence (i.e. near the top of the Wundt curve), it requires a great deal of additional income to deliver even a small increase of welfare.[4]

[1] Pearce and Ulph, 'Social Discount Rate', 275–82.
[2] Price, *Time, Discounting and Value*, 231–3.   [3] Ch. 2 above, Fig. 2.2, Table 2.1.
[4] See also Helliwell, as cited Ch. 2 above, n. 85; Pearce and Ulph, 'Social Discount Rate', 281.

Diminishing marginal utility of consumption may be attractive as an overarching explanation for the decline of prudence under affluence. But it does not quite square with the facts. For the majority in the United States (and for medium- and low-skilled male workers), between the 1970s and the mid-1990s incomes have stagnated, not risen.[5] Yet it was precisely in this period, since the 1970s, that many 'commitment technologies' began to break down, most visibly in family dissolution and rising crime.[6] Moreover, those affected most strongly were those who fared the worst, who experienced little or no material increase, namely the blacks and poor whites at the bottom of the social scale. The first argument, that prudence declines due to the anticipation of greater wealth, has some persuasiveness, but cannot stand on its own.

Another reason for the decline of prudence is that under affluence, commitment devices, the conventions and technologies of self-control, are challenged and offset by hedonic technologies, that offer ever-cheaper rewards: 'knowledge of how to speed the availability of reward has outdistanced knowledge about how to delay it. Recent developments in technology have served our short-term interests better than our long-term interests.'[7]

Technologies of commitment take time to develop and diffuse. They have evolved to cope with enduring problems. Calendars are stable, constitutions change slowly, the common law evolves gradually 'from precedent to precedent'. Under affluence, the flow of novelty undermines those who lack the capacity to cope with its compelling attractions. A compelling reward appears, like cigarettes, fast cars, or fast food. If there is a risk of long-term harm, it is invisible initially. The institutions and techniques of self-control, the conventions of pacing, have yet to be developed. Before motor cars, there was no speeding. Traffic rules, traffic signs, traffic lights, and motoring offences emerged later, together with appropriate insurance. Like the railways before them, the diffusion of motor cars generated a race between the hedonic technologies of speed and the prudential technologies of safety.

Temperance campaigns culminated in total prohibition of alcohol for more than a decade in the USA in the 1920s, and its strict regulation in Britain. Cigarettes have gone through a complete cycle from pervasive acceptance to legal proscription. In the post-war years, hard drugs were suppressed, but consumption continued. After two decades of rapid

---

[5] Ch. 11, below, Figure 11.4.   [6] Fukuyama, *Great Disruption*.
[7] Ainslie, *Picoeconomics*, 296.

criminalization of drug use, something is bringing crime rates down: most probably a combination of severe punishment and more effective individual coping with the challenge of compelling drugs, either by avoidance, or by avoiding capture.[8]

The dynamics of self-control are also usefully explored at the micro-level by the example of sex, at the macro-level by the example of saving.

Sexuality

The timeline of sexual initiation in Britain provides a comparison of prudential time lags with the United States. Britain, the less affluent society, demonstrated more prudence on this dimension, a prudence that itself had been formed during the demographic transition in Britain to low birth rates.[9]

University graduates were rare in Britain, but English 'sixth-formers' (comparable to American high-school seniors) were more restrained even than American college students of a generation before. At age 20 in the 1960s, their sexual initiation lagged three years behind American college students of the 1940s. Partly this is due to the inclusion of women in the British group, but the male–female difference only accounts for a little more than a year at these ages, in both Britain and the United States. These

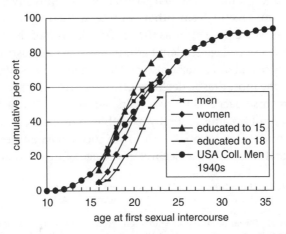

Fig. 4.1. Age at first intercourse, England 1969, by gender and educational level

Source: Gorer, *Sex & Marriage in England*, table 20, pp. 274–5. n = 1987 (total interviewed). American data from Fig. 3.3, above.

[8] Rosenfeld, 'Unsolved Crime Decline'. [9] Szreter, *Fertility, Class, and Gender*, ch. 8.

statistics reinforce other impressions of much more restraint in courting practices in Britain compared with the United States.[10]

The Kinsey reports from the 1940s indicated that in the USA, as affluence increased over time, sexual activity began earlier with each successive cohort. Fourteen per cent of women born before 1900 had premarital intercourse by the age of 25, compared with 39 per cent of those born a decade-plus later.[11] For men, an intergenerational reduction in the age of first intercourse registered quite strongly for primary-school-only males, but the age remained almost constant for college graduates.[12] In a mainly middle-class and married American sample, of those aged below 35 in 1970, 74 per cent had had some sexual experience before marriage, of those aged between 35 and 64, 56 per cent, and of those over 64, only 44 per cent.[13]

More recent surveys of sexual behaviour confirm that age at first sexual intercourse was inversely (and strongly) related to levels of education. This pattern has persisted, though the differences have narrowed.[14] Sexual restraint in Britain has continued to erode, and converged down to American levels. In the past four decades, median age at first heterosexual intercourse fell from 21 to 17 for women, and from 20 to 17 for men, and a sizeable minority were now sexually active before the age of 16.[15] The typical American has the first experience of sexual intercourse at 16–17, and this threshold has fallen with each cohort.[16] Sexual initiative and activity rose from older to the younger cohorts: age at first intercourse, premarital sex, and number of sexual partners.[17] This only gives a statistical gloss to the impression from other sources about the spread of sexual permissiveness since the 1940s, as the open hedonism of the 1960s undermined the prudent college-student pattern of sexual liberalism described by Kinsey.[18] Early sexual intercourse also predicted a higher risk of divorce.[19]

In Britain, the most drastic decline occurred during the 1950s, when age at first intercourse declined by two years, almost two decades before the contraceptive pill became generally available to unmarried women. Early intercourse was still associated with lower social class and education. In the United States as well, the decline in the age of first sexual intercourse

---

[10] Gillis, *For Better*; Humphries, *Secret World*; Schofield, *Sexual Behaviour*, 248.

[11] Kinsey, *Female*, table 83, p. 339.   [12] Kinsey, *Male*, 396–417.

[13] Klassen, *Sex and Morality*, 141.

[14] Wellings et al., *Sexual Behaviour in Britain*, ch. 2; Laumann et al., *Social Organization of Sexuality*, section 9.1.   [15] Wellings et al., *Sexual Behaviour in Britain*, 106, 73.

[16] Rheinisch, *Kinsey Institute New Report*, 6; Laumann et al., *Social Organization*, 326; Smith, 'American Sexual Behavior', table 1.

[17] Wellings et al., *Sexual Behavior*, tables 2.4, 3.1, fig. 3.3; Laumann et al., *Social Organization*, sections 5.2–5.4, 9.1.   [18] D'Emilio and Freedman, *Intimate Matters*, 301–9.

[19] Cameron, 'Economic Model', 313.

over the last forty years has been slow, with little evidence of a discrete 'sexual revolution'.[20]

Americans remain more affluent than the British, and (consistent with our model), more impulsive as well, at least as far as sexual behaviour is concerned. A good deal of evidence indicates that women and men do not manage contraception very effectively. By far the most popular form of contraception in the United States is sterilization, used by 51 per cent of married persons, and 13 per cent of singletons. This is a rather drastic 'commitment technology', which ditches discretion, permits no second thoughts, and locks in the future.[21] In the UK, surgical contraception among married and cohabiting couples is less than half that rate, and it is even lower in continental Europe.[22] No one has sexual intercourse intending an abortion, so the abortion rate is also a measure of self-control. In the late 1980s, the rate of abortions to all pregnancies in the United States was 0.286, while in England and Wales it was 0.186. The rate of abortion per 1,000 women was 27.3 and 14.2 in the two countries respectively.[23] For teenage pregnancy, abortion, and birth rates, the American level was roughly twice as high.[24] Another indication is the course of the AIDS epidemic. Controlling for population size, the United States has had five adult cases of AIDS for every case in the United Kingdom.[25]

Saving

Sexuality challenges prudence at the level of micro-decisions. At the macro-level, the decline of prudence under affluence appears to be demonstrated in household savings. In the United States and Britain, and especially during the 1990s, household discretionary savings have declined down to very low levels, and this decline has given rise to some alarm about overconsumption and undersaving.[26] But the national accounts measures of household savings are somewhat misleading. What they measure is simply the difference between income after taxes and consumption. This statistic in itself does not adequately measure whether households (in the aggregate) are putting aside enough for unemployment and ill-health, and for

[20] Wellings et al., *Sexual Behaviour*, 73, 80–1; Laumann, *Social Organization*, 323–4.

[21] Morgan, 'Modern American Fertility', table 5, p. 51.

[22] Frith, 'Britons pick Sterilisation'.

[23] Women aged 15–44. United States, *Statistical Abstract of the United States*; UK, *Population Trends*.   [24] Morgan, 'Modern American Fertility', table 6, p. 53, fig. 9, p. 31.

[25] Joint United Nations, *Aids Epidemic 2002*, table, p. 198.

[26] Hatsopoulos et al., *Overconsumption*; Poterba, *Public Policies*.

the cost of retirement and the desire to bequeath. For these purposes, there are other assets which ought to be counted, namely education and skills (human capital), financial wealth, durables including housing, and non-discretionary benefits like social security pension entitlements. From the point of view of the economy as a whole, household saving is not a measure of the ability to sustain the social rate of consumption or the capital base.[27]

Only a minority share of saving is undertaken by individuals: most is done by business and government. But since business is owned by individuals, and governments act as agents for individuals, the line between household and social savings is more significant for understanding the incentives to save, than for its effect on social and economic performance. Household savings indicate what proportion of income is withdrawn from consumption through the discretionary decision of households. Gross national savings indicate how much saving is undertaken by society overall. The relation between the two suggests the extent to which households rely on impersonal commitment technologies to achieve savings, and what levels of saving society achieves. It is not a measure of the efficiency in which savings are converted into investment, which is a separate issue.

Figure 4.2 compares household and social savings, in four groups of countries: Japan (representing the industrialized countries in East Asia), a sample of European countries (Belgium, France, Netherlands, West Germany), 'Anglo', i.e. the main English-speaking countries (Australia, Canada, the United Kingdom, and the United States), and Scandinavia (Denmark, Norway, Sweden). Comparative data have been collected by the World Bank Savings project.[28]

Looking at household savings rates first, what counts here is not trends but levels. Each cluster follows a distinctive pattern. Highest levels of discretionary household savings are in Japan. In the absence of effective social commitment technologies (in the form of employer and state pensions, as well as mortgage lending), households have had to rely on their own commitment resources, and have saved at very high levels. Korea follows a similar pattern, with a lag of several years. Strong family and social bonds reinforce the capacity for household commitment. National savings rates are also very high, suggesting that household savings capacity is a complement rather than a substitute for the capacity of firms (and government) to save.

[27] Gale and Sabelhaus, 'Household Saving Rate'.
[28] Loayza et al., 'World Saving Data Base'.

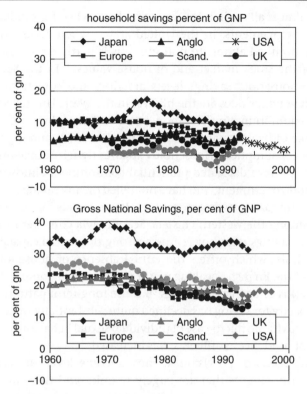

Fig. 4.2. Household and national savings, *c.*1960–1992

Note: Anglo: English-speaking countries—Australia, Canada, United States, UK.

Sources: World Bank Savings Project: **www.worldbank.org/research/projects/savings/ policies.htm**; **www.worldbank.org/research/projects/savings/data.htm**

European countries have sustained household savings at a high level as well. Since Europeans also have large illiquid state pension entitlements, that suggests a capacity to exercise prudence over personal resources. The high level of household savings suggests either difficulties of borrowing, a prudent desire to diversify savings risk away from dependence on government, or perhaps a greater cultural capacity for prudence. In the English-speaking countries, household savings levels are lower. These countries have several distinctive attributes: mandatory state and employer pension systems, high levels of house ownership, liberal credit markets (since the 1980s), and considerable inequality of wealth. Discretionary saving in the USA is largely done by the rich.[29] In these circumstances, most households

[29] Bosworth et al., 'The Decline in Saving'; Gokhale et al., 'Understanding the Postwar Decline'.

consume almost all of their incomes, and have relied for prudence largely on social arrangements. In the United States, where household savings rates have declined almost to nothing, this is partly compensated for by the rise of the stock market and of house values.[30] In the Scandinavian countries, household savings levels are tiny, and sometimes negative, while social savings rates are the highest in the West. This reflects another prudence equilibrium: in these more equal societies, there are fewer ultra-rich capable of heavy saving, as there are in the USA, and high tax levels encourage consumption. Households apparently felt sufficiently trusting and secure to have delegated prudential commitment almost entirely to business and government, and have not relied on any savings of their own.

Shifting the gaze to aggregate savings, Japan stands highest in a class of its own. Among the western clusters, Scandinavia consistently maintains the highest savings rates, suggesting a strong prudential capacity for society as a whole, which offsets the virtual absence of household savings. Europe and the English-speaking world are lower, but comparable to each other in terms of aggregate savings. But the long-term pattern is that the overall capacity for saving has declined quite substantially since the 1960s, suggesting (as in the micro-case of individual sexual behaviour), a declining capacity for prudence as affluence has increased.

Adequate levels of provision at most income levels are achieved by means of entitlements that are largely illiquid, and therefore protected from the myopic saver. The construction of these savings technologies, most of them underpinned by large tax incentives, or by outright compulsion, is a feature of advanced consumer societies, and has gone to the greatest extreme in the Scandinavian countries. How robust it is to the ageing of society, to market volatility, and to political contention, is an important question. The very high household savings rates in the newly industrialized East Asian societies suggest that where social pooling commitment technologies are underdeveloped, people have to rely largely on their own discretionary savings, i.e. on small-scale commitment devices at the family and even personal levels.

The low levels of household savings in the English-speaking countries indicate that these affluent societies have reduced their reliance on discretionary savings, and instead have relied increasingly on society, by means of commitment technologies, to do their saving for them. Whether household savings are adequate (given the existence of social assets) is difficult to resolve. Simulations indicate that on more or less plausible assumptions,

---

[30] Gale and Sabelhaus, 'Household Saving Rate'.

household saving at the median saver level is adequate to maintain current patterns of intertemporal consumption.[31] But the probability of bad luck, the prospect of low household saving rates, declining social savings rates, and uncertainties about the robustness of business and social institutions, justify some concern both about the adequacy of intertemporal provision, and about its social distribution. These trends are not fully understood, nor is it very meaningful to aggregate savings rates over very unequal societies. Nevertheless, at this crude level, trends in the household saving rate may be related to the issues of prudence and commitment technologies. Cohort studies suggest that the emergence of credible state social security has acted to reduce personal savings rates in the United States, and presumably in Britain as well.[32] In continental Europe, social security levels are higher, and presumably just as secure, and yet personal saving rates are higher, suggesting stronger prudential motives, and a prudential diversification of risk. In East Asia credible social commitment is undeveloped, and hence the large commitment effort within the household.

Other reasons given for the precipitate decline in household savings in the English-speaking countries are the rise in personal wealth, mainly housing and financial assets, which increased during the 1980s and 1990s almost inversely to the decline of household savings.[33] This is not entirely an adequate explanation. Financial assets are highly concentrated at the top end of society, and about half the population have none at all. About one-third of households have no housing equity either. In spite of higher levels of income per head, compared e.g. to the newly developing countries, middle- and low-income earners in the United States and Britain have very low household savings rates. This is not totally imprudent: they rely implicitly on the robustness of social safety nets.

Commitment to saving depends on the technologies available. For example, whether people enrol in voluntary pension schemes depends a great deal on whether they are only permitted to opt out (which leads to high participation) or required to opt in (which leads to low participation).[34]

Before the 1980s, savers relied on the commitment technologies of illiquid savings, whether in pension entitlements, insurance, or house purchase. Deregulation of personal credit in the United States (and Britain) was accompanied by a sustained decline in saving rates. Liberalization of lending during the 1980s has undermined these technologies, by making

---

[31] Sabelhaus and Pence, 'Household Saving'; Engen et al., 'Adequacy of Household Saving'.
[32] Gokhale et al., 'Understanding the Postwar Decline'.
[33] Verma and Lichtenstein, 'Declining Personal Saving Rate'.
[34] Thaler and Sunstein, 'Libertarian Paternalism', 176–7.

it easier to borrow against illiquid savings, e.g. by withdrawing housing equity. Some predatory lenders have been targeting the collateral.[35] One of the consequences was a ninefold increase in personal bankruptcy rates since the 1970s, a social disaster comparable in scope and magnitude to the rise in obesity (Ch. 7 below) and in prison populations.[36]

Choice again: rational, myopic, and regulated

In economics, it is implicitly assumed that the unfettered choice of individuals adds up to maximize the welfare of society. This 'invisible hand' assumption is the core doctrine of the discipline, but it had long remained just an article of faith. Over the last seventy years, the quest to pin down this holy grail was intensified.

One basic difficulty was how to add up the subjective preferences of heterogeneous different consumers. In the 1930s, it was agreed that they could not be aggregated, and that interpersonal comparisons could not be made. The concept of utility was sidelined out of consumer behaviour and welfare economics.[37] Instead of a mentalistic view of utility, actual dollar choices of consumers ('revealed preferences') were used to construct demand curves. In the early 1950s, Arrow's 'impossibility theorem' suggested, on the face of it, that the 'invisible hand' could not transform individual choice into social optimality. Later in the 1950s Arrow and Debreu came closest to formalizing the invisible hand in their two theorems of welfare economics. These showed that any general equilibrium (i.e. an idealized, encompassing market) could produce a distribution of income that was Pareto Optimal (i.e. left everyone the same or better off), given some initial distribution of endowments. Modigliani's 'life-cycle consumption' hypothesis assumed that consumers rationally allocated their expected resources so as to smooth consumption over the life cycle. In the 1970s the 'rational expectations' doctrine argued that individual agents would anticipate and offset any attempt to regulate the economy. After more than half a century of theoretical activity, the invisible hand and the optimality of markets is underpinned in economics by formidably technical, theoretical constructions. But it all depends on severe abstraction. In reality the invisible hand remains what it was to begin with, an article of faith. At the core of it is belief in the rational, consistent consumer. There

[35] Laibson et al., 'Self-Control and Saving for Retirement'; Warren and Tyagi, *Two-Income Trap*. [36] Below, Ch. 12, nn. 106–7.
[37] Meeks, 'Utility in Economics'.

remains some doubt even as to whether the abstractions of general equilibrium and its optimality theorems are 'computable', i.e. whether they are mathematically tractable.[38] Simon's concept of 'bounded rationality' captures the same difficulty more pragmatically: even if the options were all knowable, ranking them is beyond human cognitive capacity.

The market order was only efficient and just if buyers and sellers reliably and consistently knew what they wanted. In the words of Friedman, already quoted, *'provided the transaction is bi-laterally voluntary and informed'*. 'Informed' in this context means that the consumer knows her own mind, knows her own good, and knows the options available to her. 'Voluntary' in this context means that she is aware of all her motives.[39]

The ubiquity of inconsistent preferences has placed these assumptions in doubt. Experiments and attitude surveys indicate that the immediate present is disproportionately compelling, and that the mere passage of time can cause preferences to be altered or even reversed. Rationality requires that consumers should be consistent, so these observations undermine the assumption that choice is reliable. That choice could be inconsistent was shown early on in the experimental paradoxes of Allais and Ellsberg. Since then, many empirical findings have found against the assumptions of rational consumer theory.[40] Kahneman and Tversky have shown that choice is biased in other important ways: losses are experienced more intensely than gains of the same magnitude, and the asymmetry is too large to be accommodated by the standard economic assumption of diminishing returns.[41] Another bias is 'framing'—choice is affected by the context in which it is presented. Consumers do not reason probabilistically and make consistent errors. Instead, they follow various rules of thumb, 'heuristics', although such heuristics can be efficient, in the sense that they may economize on information.[42] Rewards are evaluated differently in anticipation, while being experienced, and in retrospect.[43] This made it difficult to learn from experience. In behavioural experiments, subjects agreed to cooperate and share much more than rational consumer theory predicts. The range of choices increases the cognitive burden and the stress on individuals, especially when it is difficult to find reasons to differentiate among them.[44]

---

[38] Velupillai, *Computable Economics*; Mirowski, *Machine Dreams*.

[39] See O'Donoghue and Rabin, 'Self-Awareness'.

[40] Hogarth, *Judgement and Choice*; Hogarth and Reder, *Rational Choice*, esp. papers in pp. 1–100.

[41] Kahneman, 'Psychological Perspective'; Rabin, 'Diminishing Marginal Utility'.

[42] Gigernzer, *Simple Heuristics*.

[43] Kahneman, 'Objective Happiness'; id., 'Experienced Utility'.

[44] Schwartz, *Paradox of Choice*.

Investment in advertising, amounting at times to more than 2 per cent of GDP, indicates that consumers respond to external suggestion, much of which cannot be regarded as pure information.[45] In marketing, where real money is at stake, there is no single paradigm of consumer choice, and many competing understandings are in contention.[46] The thrust of empirical work since the 1960s in a variety of approaches is that the rational consumer is a fiction, and that choice is often fallible. The choices people make do not always accord with what, from a different temporal viewpoint, they would judge as being good for themselves.

To repeat, a great deal is at stake here: at a technical level, the assumption of consistency in choice, which is a pillar of economic analysis. At the level of ideology, the justification of market outcomes as being both efficient and equitable. At the political level, the bias in favour of deregulation, privatization, and low taxes. One response of consumer theorists was simply to brush off these criticisms.[47] Several writers have constructed models which attempt to resolve the problem mathematically.[48] Theories that postulate temporary 'hot' emotional influences which deflect choice off course, leave rationality in place as a model of 'cool' decision making, which is presumably appropriate to social choice.[49]

Friedman's Chicago first anticipated, then subsequently acknowledged the challenge, with a clever alternative, which is designed to save the notion of consumer rationality and consistency. Two such models attempt to capture the key attribute of hyperbolic discounting, namely the variable rate of time preference, high to begin with, and low at long delays. The purpose is to reconcile addictive behaviour with time consistency.[50] Both approaches deal with the problem by making time preference a function of prior accumulation or endowment. The first is the theory of rational addiction.[51] The crucial assumption is again a temporal one, but one that looks backwards rather than forwards. Consumer choice is influenced not only by relative prices, but also by the investment in past consumption, which has built up a stock of appetites: a larger stock of past consumption raises the marginal utility of current consumption. Accumulated 'consumption

---

[45] Ch. 6 below. O'Shaughnessy, *Why People Buy;* id., *Explaining Buyer Behavior.*

[46] O'Shaughnessy, *Explaining Buyer Behavior.*   [47] Lord, *Household Dynamics*, 34, n. 4.

[48] Orphanides and Zervos, 'Rational Addiction'; id., 'Myopia and Addictive Behaviour'.

[49] Mischel et al., 'Sustaining Delay'; Baumeister and Vohs, 'Willpower, Choice'. This is also implicit in quasi-hyperbolic discount curves, in which all but the first period are modelled exponentially.

[50] 'The presence or lack of "preference reversals" is the important distinction in any formulation.' (Mulligan, 'Logical Economist'.)

[51] Stigler and Becker, '*De Gustibus*'; Becker and Murphy, 'Rational Addiction'; Becker et al., 'Rational Addiction'.

capital', or 'habit', affects immediate responses, so that withdrawal becomes costly in the amount already consumed, rather in the manner observed towards the 'comfort zone' of the Wundt curve. Discount rates are high, so the benefits of withdrawal are beyond the horizon, and the pains of withdrawal are avoided by increasing consumption today. The rationality of such addicts is said to be confirmed by the fact that they remain price sensitive.[52]

The second response is a theory of 'endogenous time preference'.[53] It acknowledges that commitment, or prudence, is costly. If delayed rewards can be made sufficiently vivid, it is worth investing in them; and it is worth investing in raising awareness of future rewards. The commitment devices and technologies are similar to those invoked by Ainslie, namely control of attention, and education. 'The rich' are more likely to invest in commitment, because they have the means to do so, because that investment allows them to perceive the future more clearly, and because the rich have more to lose. They are motivated and able to invest in order to reduce their discount rates.

By accepting the 'rationality' of high discount rates, 'rational addiction' theory defines away much of the problem that needs to be explained. Otherwise, the test of price responsiveness is hardly a refutation of cognitive-bias theories of behaviour. Such theories do not assume that consumers, even addicted ones, would ignore prices altogether. Crucial experiments between rival theories are rare, but in the area of self-control, one has recently come up. In Canada, tobacco taxes were increased in some provinces but not others. A survey has shown that where taxes rose, the subjective well-being of smokers has risen as well. Had they been 'rational addicts', the increase of price should have reduced their perceived well-being. That their satisfaction actually increased suggests that (as smokers often aver) smoking was a choice they regretted, and that they welcomed higher taxes as an aid to self-control.[54] Another set of data, on the anticipation of tobacco tax increases by smokers in American states, showed that preferences with respect to smoking were time inconsistent, with individuals both not recognizing the true difficulty of quitting and searching for self-control devices to help them quit.[55]

---

[52] 'Sarcastically, the test amounts to asking whether smoking falls when prices are increased the next year' (Gruber and Köszegi, 'Is Addiction "Rational"?', 1265).

[53] Becker and Mulligan, 'Endogenous Time Preference'.

[54] Gruber and Mullainathan, 'Do Cigarette Taxes Make Smokers Happier?'

[55] Gruber and Köszegi, 'Is Addiction "Rational"?'

For all the sophistication of discount modelling, it is not psychologically grounded.[56] It takes the mind as a black box, and does not presume to say how discounting really works. In fact these models are also experimentally insecure, not always finding decisively in favour of one model or the other.[57] If Ainslie's rich psychological speculations are perhaps beyond falsification, the premisses of Rational Choice are equally speculative. We are nevertheless left with a clear pattern: a multitude of observations and intuitions give rise to time inconsistency, and an excessive preference for the present, which can be overcome by commitment.

If people do a good job in making decisions, then there is no reason for any social intervention beyond perhaps updating information. If choice is known to be fallible, and shown to be so, then there is a case for social cooperation in making decisions, not only in acquiring information and understanding it, but (in what Smith realized was a separate problem), in mobilizing the will to act on that choice. That nannies are sometimes good for children is rarely in question. The 'nanny state', however, has a bad press. But if consumers are fallible, then grown-ups can also do with some guidance occasionally. A few economists are coming round to this view, and accepting that well-designed interventions can raise the level of well-being.[58] The drinker's judgement of his fitness to drive deteriorates with each additional glass. Paternalism protects both the driver and the public. Likewise, the pervasive use of goods in kind for redistribution. In Britain, 'housing benefit' is a common welfare entitlement, which is earmarked exclusively for housing. In the United States the food stamp entitlement is likewise not fungible. This protects the indigent from themselves. In both countries free education and health care provide commitment crutches for the middle classes as well.

Outside economics, that is plain common sense. But it presents a challenge to those who believe that choice is sacred: those with freedom have chosen to be unfree. For pure liberals to argue that people are misguided in choosing to be regulated, is self-contradictory: it rejects the choices that the people have exercised freely. In fact, scaling up from individual to social choice is fraught with difficulty.[59] In the United States, restriction of

[56] Rubinstein, 'Economics and Psychology'; Price, *Time, Discounting and Value*; Loewenstein et al., *Time and Decision*, contains several suggestive explorations; Ainslie's brilliant speculations (in *Picoeconomics*) are highly suggestive, but do not require the mathematical model.

[57] Rubinstein, 'Economics and Psychology'; Fernandez Villaverde and Mukherji, 'Can We Really Observe?'; Cairns and van der Pol, 'Saving Future Lives'; but see id., 'Valuing Future Benefits'.

[58] Burrows, 'Patronising Paternalism'; Thaler and Sunstein, 'Libertarian Paternalism'; O'Donoghue and Rabin, 'Studying Optimal Paternalism'.

[59] Elster, *Ulysses Unbound*, ch. 2.

choice is part of the conservative repertoire: balanced budget constitutional mandates, designed to protect voters against themselves, were implemented in most American states, and only failed in the United States Senate by a single vote in 1995. Such strong pre-commitment, with its admission of time inconsistency, undermines Friedman's insistence on freedom of choice, which depends on time-consistency for its identification of choice with welfare.

When Friedman was defending freedom of choice, he suggested that the alternative was tyranny. But that was disingenuous. The fact remains that in liberal societies, and under democratic government, people on the whole choose to delegate or surrender a great deal of discretion to public and private institutions. That is also demonstrated in saving behaviour.

As the USA and Britain have grown wealthier and more democratic over the last century, intervention and regulation have increased. Much of it accepts implicitly that what people might want to choose is bad for them, and that they should not be allowed to have it. There are three levels of paternalism: exhortation, inducement (by means of taxation or pricing), and compulsion. The freedom of private individuals to buy and consume hard drugs is restricted by means of a repressive police and prison apparatus that keeps about a million people in prison in the United States and sustains a large global industry that operates entirely outside the law. Apart from a few libertarians, this repression is supported even more strongly on the political right than on the left. That serves as evidence that democratic, liberal states have only limited trust in people's choices, and are willing to intervene in order to change them. A theory that aligns unfettered choice with maximizing welfare would find such regulation difficult to justify.

If one accepts that cognitive bias makes choice and self-control both difficult and fallible, then the normative issue is not whether intervention is ever justified, but how much, in what form, and when. History can monitor the positive extent of intervention, cooperation, and consensus, that individuals have been willing to accept in order to gain some control over compelling appetites. History can evaluate how difficult the problem of choice really is, and what forms it takes. Paternalism is often the voter's revealed preference, and the historian, at least, should treat it with respect.

Conclusion

Choice is inconsistent, and finding a good equilibrium is a dilemma. To escape the compelling immediacy of the present, it is necessary to lock in the future, by means of 'commitment technologies'. These are costly. As an array of internal disciplines, they take time to build up by means of education and experience. As a set of external disciplines, they are enforced by means of social norms, conventions, reputation and shame, or by legally binding contracts. Even if we valued the future equally with the present (as some writers recommend), locking in the future incurs a cost (the 'commitment technology') that consuming in the present does not. That in itself would provide a reason for discounting.

At any point in time, self-control is positively associated with social position and wealth. The better-off have more cognitive, material, and social resources, and are better equipped to attempt a rational allocation of satisfaction over time. But taking affluent societies as a whole, there is a tendency for prudence to decline with affluence. One reason is that affluence delivers diminishing returns. Another is that under affluence, the environment changes faster than commitment strategies can keep up with it. Adaptive technologies take time to form. If a problem persists for long enough society will eventually find the means to cope, the better-off first, then the rest of society. This can be likened to an evolutionary process: society gradually adapts into greater fitness with its environment. But when environments change, existing adaptations become obsolete. In a world of constant change, individuals and institutions are likely to be permanently out of kilter with the environment, and it should be no surprise to find novel pathologies emerging repeatedly. Under affluence, novelty tends to produce a bias towards short-term rewards, towards individualism, hedonism, narcissism, and disorientation.

Market competition promotes myopic bias. It promotes hedonism over other forms of satisfaction, since hedonic reward is easier to identify, package, and sell. It promotes individualism, since that reduces the costly and time-consuming need to negotiate and compromise with others, and to contract with the future. Individualism and hedonism combined give rise to narcissism, an obsessive interest in the self. And hedonistic, individualistic and jaded consumers will, in their turn, make more eager consumers for the next twist in immediate gratification. The compelling products of innovation raise the psychic cost of investing in long-term rewards. Innovation also creates an ambience in which the uncertainty and instability of tastes makes it more difficult to invest in consumption and pacing skills that might only deliver in the longer run. Popular culture is not bad: nor is high culture necessarily better. But the proliferation of cheap rewards makes those rewards that need an investment of patience and time that much more difficult and expensive to achieve.

5

The Economy of Regard

The original insight of economics is contained in Adam Smith's account of the efficiency of an impersonal market, in which every individual seeks his own advantage, with no regard for the welfare of others. Karl Polanyi posited a 'Great Transformation', from socially embedded reciprocity to impersonal price-driven market exchange, which he saw as culminating in late eighteenth-century Britain.[1] This trajectory is disputed by writers who identify pervasive market exchange in antiquity, the early Middle Ages, and pre-modern Africa.[2]

What is less noted is the persistence of non-market exchange into modern times. Goods and services continue to be transferred without the benefit of markets or prices, to be exchanged as gifts. There are unilateral transfers in the form of organ donations, charity contributions, and bequests. There is an important non-profit sector, providing 4 and 7 per cent of employment in Britain and the United States respectively in the 1990s.[3] Most non-market exchange, however, takes place in a context of *reciprocity*. Foremost is exchange within the household. But reciprocity also motivates much retail purchasing. It abounds at work, it affects management, agriculture, marketing, entrepreneurship, and politics. It mobilizes resources for growth, and is also implicated in corruption and crime. The persistence of non-market exchange on such a scale indicates that reciprocity may be, if not always 'efficient' in the formal sense, at the very least a viable alternative to the market system. This preference, it is argued here, arises out of the intrinsic benefits of social and personal interaction, from the satisfactions of *regard*. Prices facilitate exchange when information is scarce and coordination difficult, when goods are standardized and cheap. The

---

[1] Polanyi, *Great Transformation*; also Polanyi, 'Economy as Instituted Process'.
[2] Anderson and Latham, *Market in History*.
[3] Rose-Ackerman, 'Altruism, Nonprofits', 705.

market works best when the efficiency of production runs ahead of the efficiency of cognition and communication. Markets economize on costly information. That was Friedrich Hayek's key insight.[4] Conversely, reciprocal exchange is preferred when trade involves a personal interaction, and when goods or services are unique, expensive, or have many dimensions of quality. This chapter examines the dynamics of reciprocity. It indicates why and to what extent 'the Great Transformation' into market exchange remains incomplete, and why, in some areas, it has even retreated.

The dynamic of reciprocity

Accounts of gift exchange abound in the literatures of anthropology and development. Mauss analysed the *potlatch*, a periodic feast of Indian tribes in the Pacific Northwest, as a status competition in generosity and waste.[5] Malinowski described a regular cycle of hazardous sea voyages (the *kula* ring), undertaken by Trobriand islanders in the Pacific to exchange in decorative sea shells, whose value was purely symbolic.[6]

From the ethnographic record, the following pattern emerges. Exchange begins with a transfer, for which reciprocity is expected. Reciprocity is usually *delayed*. Both the *value* of the reciprocal gesture and its *timing* are left to discretion, although expectations are often informed by convention and custom. When the exchange is completed, a new sequence can begin. Take the practice of hospitality. The middle-class exchange of dinner invitations, and the wine, chocolate, or flowers that accompany them, are an example of *delayed* reciprocity. Reciprocity can also be *indirect*, with no return from the beneficiary (who may be unknown), but a credit lodged with the community, to be reciprocated at some other time and place. Unconditional hospitality to total strangers has been the norm in many parts of the Mediterranean, Arab, Iranian, and Indian worlds.[7]

In neoclassical market exchanges personal acquaintance is immaterial. The gains from trade are all the gains there are. Every sale is simultaneously a purchase. Any delay is paid for with interest. In contrast, in the gift exchange, price is indeterminate. 'Delivery' and 'payment' are separated by the exercise of discretion and the passage of time. Over and above the

---

[4] Hayek, 'Use of Knowledge'.　　[5] Mauss, *Gift*.　　[6] Malinowski, *Argonauts*.
[7] Abraham's welcome to the angels, Genesis 18; rural Greece today, du Boulay, 'Strangers and Gifts'; Iran, Simpson-Herbert, 'Hospitality in Iranian Society'; Yemen, Gingrich, 'Is Wa Milh: Brot und Salz'; India, Khare, 'Indian Hospitality'; discussion, Pitt-Rivers, 'Stranger, Guest and Hostile Host'.

material gains from trade, something else is also acquired. Exchange is not only an economic transaction, it is also a good in itself, a 'process benefit',[8] usually in the form of a personal interaction or relationship.

Personal interaction ranks very high among the sources of well-being.[9] It can take many forms: acknowledgement, attention, acceptance, respect, reputation, status, power, intimacy, love, friendship, kinship, sociability, conviviality. To wrap it all into one term, interaction is driven by the grant and pursuit of *regard*. In *The Theory of Moral Sentiments*, Adam Smith described the purpose of economic activity as the acquisition of regard.

What is the end of avarice and ambition, of the pursuit of wealth, of power, and preheminence? Is it to supply the necessities of nature? The wages of the meanest labourer can supply them . . . what are the advantages which we propose to gain by that great purpose of human life which we call bettering our condition? To be observed, to be attended to, to be taken notice of with sympathy, complacency, and approbation, are all the advantages which we can propose to derive from it.[10]

The propensity for 'sympathy' which dominates *The Theory of Moral Sentiments* performs the same role, in motivating gift exchange, as the propensity to 'truck, barter and exchange' performs for the market economy.

What is the relation between 'gift' and 'regard'? Regard is an attitude of approbation. It needs to be *communicated*. The gift embodies that communication and carries the signal. Trade in regard is vital: self-regard is difficult to sustain without external confirmation. The gift can be dear or cheap, substantive or symbolic. It is not costless. At the very least, 'regard' is a grant of attention, and attention is a scarce resource.[11] The capacity for regard is constrained by the limited endowment of time and psychic energy. Withholding regard signifies indifference and rejection. Ostracism, the silent treatment, 'Sending to Coventry' or solitary confinement, are among the harshest of punishments.[12] 'Compared with the contempt of mankind, all other evils are easily supported,' wrote Adam Smith.[13] This concept of 'regard' contains, but is different from, the concept of 'esteem', recently introduced by Brennan and Pettit. 'Esteem' is impersonal and objective, 'regard' is personal and subjective.[14]

Gift exchange has two benefits: the gains from trade, and the satisfactions of regard. The efficiency attributes of the economy of regard arise from

[8] Gershuny and Halpin, 'Time Use, Quality of Life and Process Benefits'.
[9] Argyle, 'Subjective Well-Being', describes experimental and survey data.
[10] Smith, *Moral Sentiments*, Bk. I, ch. ii.1, p. 50   [11] Gifford, 'Entrepreneurial Attention'.
[12] In marital contexts, Gottman and Levenson, 'Social Psychophysiology of Marriage', 184–5; Komarovsky, *Blue-Collar Marriage*, chs. 6–7; Hite, *Hite Report: Women and Love*, 15–26; Rubin, *Worlds of Pain*, 115–25.   [13] Smith, *Moral Sentiments*, 61.
[14] Brennan and Pettit, *Economy of Esteem*, 16–21.

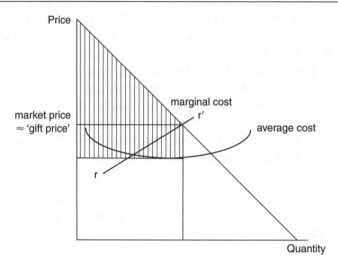

Fig. 5.1. Gift exchange as perfect price discrimination
Note: rr' is the marginal cost curve.

their combination. This is suggested by analogy with the economic model of perfect price discrimination under monopoly.[15] In this model, the supplier is able to charge each buyer as much as, and no less than, that individual buyer is willing to pay, or in other words, not the uniform market price, but a personal price corresponding to that buyer's position on the demand curve. For each buyer, the exchange value equals the use value. Since the price is not set at the margin, there is no surplus for consumers inside the margin. All the surplus goes to the seller. Under perfect price discrimination, both total output and surplus are the same as in the competitive market, i.e. production is as efficient as under competition.

For this to happen, two conditions must be satisfied: the monopolist must know each buyer's maximum price, and there can be no arbitrage: buyers cannot trade with each other. These conditions are rarely met in an impersonal market economy, but they are commonplace in reciprocal exchange. Every provider is a monopolist of her own regard. No one else can supply it. Hence it cannot be traded among recipients. To divine the buyer's maximum price is more difficult. Like a seller in market exchange, the giver of gifts needs to evaluate her counterparty's preferences by means of external cues. Like the market vendor, the gift giver has an interest in

---

[15] Suggested to me by Robert Allen; Frank, *Microeconomics and Behavior*, 393–5. Slightly more extended discussion, Offer, 'Gift and Market', 452–3.

getting it right. Like the market vendor, she can get it wrong. But when the face-to-face interaction is repeated, there is an opportunity to tune the transfer more precisely to the counterparty's needs. This counterparty cannot trade this regard with anyone else: he can only reciprocate with the original provider.

Under perfect price discrimination, all the surplus goes to the monopolistic seller. In reciprocal exchange, however, the first mover acquires a credit, and when reciprocity begins, the two parties take the surplus alternately. In the long term, therefore, the exchange value will approximate not to the recipient's use value (their position on the demand curve) but to the market value.[16] This outcome suggests that reciprocity can be an efficient means of exchanging goods and services, that it has the property of allocative efficiency. The initial gift may be driven by an impulse of regard, by the desire to elicit regard, or by both. The fear of losing regard provides a strong incentive to continue. Repetition is self-enforcing. The penalty for defection is exclusion.

In a study of dating in the USA, some gifts sustained the bond, but others led to misunderstanding, disappointment, and unwelcome obligations.[17] But equilibria are reasonable. In two studies, Waldfogel found that the cost of gifts to the givers (excluding the element of regard) was about 10 per cent more than the compensation that recipients would require to give them up. Others have found that gifts were valued more highly than cost, and Waldfogel himself stresses that the value of *receiving* a gift will exceed the tradeable value of the gift itself.[18]

Experienced partners can form a judgement on preferences, trustworthiness, and credibility.[19] Trust itself resembles a gift: a unilateral transfer with the expectation, but no certainty, of reciprocity. Regard provides a powerful incentive for trust, and trust is efficient: it economizes on the 'transaction costs' of monitoring, compliance, and enforcement.[20] The concept of 'transaction cost' is familiar. Regard may be seen as a 'transaction benefit'.

In one respect, the economy of regard pervades all human interaction. Language is a vehicle of regard, and conversation is a gift economy, loaded with cues of acceptance or disdain.[21] The normal pleasantries, 'please', 'thank you', 'g'day', are all statements of regard, their withholding a hint of rejection. Beyond language, non-verbal cues communicate intensities

---

[16] Figure 5.1, above.   [17] Belk and Coon, 'Can't Buy Me Love'.
[18] Reviews in Waldfogel, 'Deadweight Loss of Christmas'; Solnick and Hemenway, 'Deadweight Loss of Christmas'.   [19] Frank, *Passions within Reason*.
[20] A pioneer study in this vein is Ben-Porath, 'The F-Connection'.
[21] Lojkine, 'Valeur, valeur d'usage et valeur symbolique'; Dunbar, *Grooming, Gossip*.

and qualities of regard; the smile, like scores of other gestures, is universally understood.[22]

Real regard is typically not for sale. There is widespread reluctance to use money as a gift. Some goods are devalued if paid for in cash: a lover's devotion, a friend's companionship. Trollope's Phineas Finn, a handsome and penniless political adventurer in Victorian London, says to Madame Goesler, his admirer and potential benefactor, 'No;—presents of money are always bad. They stain and load the spirit and break the heart.'[23] Other goods are enhanced if given voluntarily: a temporary loan, expert opinion, a cooked meal, used clothing. The retail boom at Christmas is almost entirely based on this reluctance to use cash directly in gift exchange.[24] Often, the convenience of money makes it the preferred medium for a gift. In this case money is often 'disguised', in elaborate gift wrapping, as in the Chinese New Year, or even in a plain envelope. Money is also personalized by 'earmarking', which constrains its fungibility. Book tokens and department store certificates endow money with the semblance of a gift.[25] When money is given, its transfer is circumscribed by strict rules. In 'Middletown', Indiana, in 1978, money transfers at Christmas were only used as a gift from senior to junior kin, and very rarely in any other way.[26]

Why is money so persistently avoided? To have value, regard must be authentic, i.e. unforced. Hence, in reciprocal exchange, discretion is not only allowed, but is actually required. A money gift is impersonal: too much like a wage.[27] Cash is fungible and faceless. In business, the vendor's regard for *customers* is often perceived as inauthentic, as a *pseudo-regard*.[28] The customers have reason to suspect it doesn't matter precisely who they are. A gift, on the other hand, is personalized. Even when obtained from the market, it provides evidence of an effort to gratify a particular individual. It conveys a signal that is unique to giver, receiver, or both. The personalization of gifts, with its evidence of caring, serves to authenticate the regard signal.[29] A gift without regard would be a bribe.

Reciprocity is not all pleasure: like the market, it produces 'bads' as well as goods. Giving gives rise to obligation, in other words, a *debt*: the giver

---

[22] Ekman, *Emotion and the Human Face*; Ekman, *Telling Lies*.

[23] Trollope, *Phineas Finn*, 319. But he relied on a regular allowance from his father.

[24] Burgoyne and Roth, 'Constraints on the Use of Money'; Belk and Coon, 'Can't Buy Me Love'; Cameron, 'Unacceptability of Money'; Gonul, 'Is Money an Acceptable Gift?'; Waldfogel, 'Deadweight Loss of Christmas'; Webley et al., 'Unacceptability of Money'; Webley and Wilson, 'Social Relations and Unacceptability of Money'; Webley and Lea, 'Partial Unacceptability of Money'. [25] Zelizer, *Social Meaning of Money*, ch. 3.

[26] Caplow, 'Rule Enforcement', 1315. [27] Zelizer, *Social Meaning of Money*, 91–9.

[28] Hochschild, *Managed Heart*.

[29] Inspired by discussion with Diego Gambetta; Carrier, *Gifts and Commodities*, ch. 8.

notches up an emotional and material credit, in the form of a bond on the recipient. The term *bond* will be used to signify a repeated exchange of regard. It applies here in three senses. Like a financial bond, it has some features of a contractual obligation. Like the human bond, it is an emotional link. The term bond is also used in the sense of a fetter, as a form of oppression: 'With gifts you make slaves,' an Alaskan Inuk is reported as saying.[30] Competitive exchange in which gifts are reciprocated with a premium can drive the weaker party into permanent subordination.[31]

The obligation to reciprocate is typically a burden, which can only be relieved by means of a return gift. Asking for help is psychologically difficult,[32] and so is the obligation to reciprocate.[33] Excessive intimacy can be stressful. A gift without reciprocity vexes both giver and receiver, as in beggary, or some forms of religious almsgiving, like the unilateral donations of *dana* in Benares, India.[34] The gift signal can be rejected or misconstrued. Instead of a benign cycle of exchange, we get a spiral of insult, hate, and retribution, which may be difficult to break. Pathological gift cycles are expressed in such historical institutions as the duel, the blood feud, and the crime of passion. A modern equivalent is the painful spiral that leads on to divorce. The anonymity of the market confers an immunity from such bonds, it 'economizes on love'.[35]

Where does regard come from? Computer tournaments suggest that positive regard confers an evolutionary advantage, that 'nice' is better than 'nasty'.[36] Regard promotes sociability, and sociability facilitates cooperation. It breaks the deadlock of prisoner's dilemma with a norm of first-mover cooperation. 'Reciprocal altruism' is widely observed in animal species, and is supposed to confer genetic benefits. It is easy to imagine the capacity for regard as being selected in human evolution for its survival benefits.[37] Hunting-gathering involves foraging over large areas, with occasional large windfalls (e.g. a large mammal), which are more than a single hunter could either capture or consume. Regard promotes sharing. Ache households of Eastern Paraguay, for example, derive more than 70 per cent of their food through sharing with others, and those who provide more than their share gain prestige.[38] It is reasonable to assume that the capacity for regard, like the capacity for language, is innate, even if the forms that it

---

[30] Kelly, *Foraging Spectrum*, 167.   [31] Mauss, *Gift*, 37.
[32] Krishnan, 'Recipient Need'.
[33] Farber, 'Limiting Reciprocity'; Bourdieu, 'Modes de Domination'.
[34] Gmelch and Gmelch, 'Begging in Dublin', 450–2; Parry, 'Moral Perils of Exchange'.
[35] Robertson, *What Does the Economist Economize?*
[36] Axelrod, *Evolution of Co-operation*. These are his terms.
[37] Trivers, *Social Evolution*, ch. 15, esp. pp. 386–9.   [38] Kelly, *Foraging Spectrum*, ch. 5.

takes are culturally specific.[39] On this interpretation regard arises from an innate propensity which we wish to satisfy by means of giving and receiving. The positive emotions (unlike the negative ones) are easy to fake.[40] The ability to fake regard facilitates gift exchange, but it also places a premium on material authentication, i.e. on gifts.

Even unilateral or asymmetric transfers are not entirely disinterested. The giver hopes for regard from the younger generation; or aspires to a lasting reputation. Such transfers may also have insurance attributes: by treating others with consideration, we uphold a norm of mutual support. But the existence of 'pure gifts', e.g. in the case of 'giving by stealth', confirms the existence of a positive impulse of regard.[41] The existence of such an impulse is necessary to endow the gift exchange with credibility.

Gift exchange is not easy to model.[42] As in repetitive bargaining generally, there is no unique equilibrium, although the outcome ought to reflect the 'terms of trade', the prior endowment of the two parties and their consequent 'bargaining power'.[43] These 'terms of trade' can be steeply asymmetric. One difficulty in modelling is that regard is intangible, and hence the 'visible' terms of trade in commodities may fail to capture the 'real' terms of trade, including regard. There is no reason why a *single* exchange should be Pareto optimal, although repetitive reciprocity ought, like its market analogue, to converge onto a contract curve. At the same time, the casual evidence for regard motivation is pervasive and compelling. It is supplemented by the experience of non-cooperative game playing in experimental economics. Prior face-to-face interaction, even very brief, will incline participants towards more cooperative strategies. This is not predicted by axiomatic game theory.[44] Other evidence comes from 'ultimatum' games, in which pairs of players are invited to divide a sum of money between them. The first player has to offer a share to the second player. If the offer is rejected, the money is forfeited. Game theory predicts that any offer ought to be accepted, as being better than nothing. In actual play, offers of less than 20 per cent tend to be rejected, the average division hovers around one-third, and many players offer 50 per cent. While high share

[39] Pinker, *Language Instinct*, 412–15; Brown, *Human Universals*; Cosmides and Tooby, 'Cognitive Adaptations'; Lojkine, 'Valeur, valeur d'usage et valeur symbolique'.

[40] Ekman, *Telling Lies*, 36, 86, 126. Happiness is a positive emotion, anger a negative one.

[41] Collard, *Altruism and Economy*; Zamagni, *Economics of Altruism*; Stark, *Altruism and Beyond*; McLean and Poulton, 'Good Blood, Bad Blood'. But if this impulse is satisfying, can it be devoid of self-interest?

[42] See e.g. Smith and Boyd, 'Risk and Reciprocity'; Dasgupta, *Inquiry into Well-Being*, 324–42; Hollander, 'Social Exchange Approach'; for various models, Landa, *Trust, Ethnicity and Identity*; Molm, *Coercive Power*.   [43] See e.g. Kreps, *Course in Microeconomic Theory*, ch. 15.

[44] A list of references in Ostrom et al., *Rules, Games*, 149.

offers cannot be interpreted exclusively as fear of rejection (they are usually described as a preference for fairness), the rejection of low shares is consistent with avoidance of insult.[45] Face-to-face appeals also improve the response for charity appeals, street beggars, and hunter-gatherers.[46] Most recently reciprocity is being modelled primarily in terms of fairness perceptions, in which actors (either in theory or in experimental settings), respond to positive and negative gestures in kind.[47]

Here are the features of the gift so far:

a. A voluntary transfer.
b. An expectation of reciprocity.
c. Reciprocity is notionally open to discretion as to value and time.
d. Is motivated by a desire for regard, over and above any gains from trade.
e. Regard communicated by gift.
f. Personalized gift authenticates regard.
g. Hence avoidance of money. Gift is unpriced, often unpriceable.
h. Establishes repetitive, self-enforcing bond, which facilitates trade.

Reciprocity has held or even extended its sway in several substantial domains during the period of modern economic growth.

Family and household

Direct and indirect reciprocity pervaded pre-industrial societies. In pastoral and agrarian settings, it was used to reduce the variance of food supplies, to allocate resources over time, and to share risks.[48] It also expressed inequalities in social position and power. Fiske distinguishes three types of non-market exchange.[49] Extrapolating from his model, *communal sharing* is the joint exploitation of a resource, as often practised in foraging. In *authority ranking*, distribution is governed by rank: relations are paternal and exchanges are asymmetric. This is often a form of indirect reciprocity. Elders, chiefs, or landowners collect tribute, which enforces a level of production

[45] e.g. Thaler, *Winner's Curse*, ch. 3; Frank, *Passions within Reason*, 170–4. Outcomes are affected by occupational and ethnic background. A survey, Roth, 'Bargaining Experiments', section I, pp. 253–92.
[46] Freeman, 'Give to Charity?'; Peterson, 'Demand Sharing'; Gmelch and Gmelch, 'Begging in Dublin'.
[47] Falk and Fischbacher, 'Theory of Reciprocity'; Fehr and Gächter, 'Fairness and Retaliation'; Fehr and Fischbacher, 'Social Preferences'.
[48] e.g. Cashdan, *Risk and Uncertainty*; Finley, *Ancient Economy*, 150–2; Reynolds, *Kingdoms and Communities*, 148–54.   [49] Fiske, 'Relativity within Moose ("Mossi") Culture'.

substantially above subsistence. Authority and prestige are then underpinned by displays of generosity. The inability to reciprocate perpetuates subordination.[50] *Equality matching* is an exchange between equals.

In pre-industrial societies, the intensity of obligation is related to kinship.[51] The family can provide good protection at lower cost than capital markets, because of the low risk of default.[52] Default is minimized by the value placed on family regard and the ability of parents to control bequests.[53] The family retains a grip over migrants, who send remittances for long periods of time. 'Remittances are of a gigantic magnitude', as a source of foreign exchange in several large countries, including Pakistan, Egypt, Turkey, Portugal, and Yugoslavia.[54] Beyond the nuclear family, gifting fulfils some of the functions of insurance, financial, and welfare systems. Relatives, friends, and neighbours lend their support both for investment and in adversity. In Asian mercantile families a successful entrepreneur was often obliged to share with large numbers of relatives, and similar assumptions were sometimes implicit in relations within Jewish families in Eastern Europe.[55]

Families remain the wellspring of regard. They are held together by two intense bonds: between spouses and between the generations. In pre-industrial societies family formation was preceded by exchanges of dowry or brideprice, which played a variety of roles in reciprocity webs.[56] Such transfers came with the key for sexual exchange. Modern family formation is more discretionary, and hence conforms more closely to our voluntary model of gift exchange. In modern courting and romantic attachment, the road to intimacy is a spiral of mutual self-disclosure, an exchange of information and gifts.[57] It leads to erotic interaction, a potent form of bonding. Sexual exchange used to be a prime incentive for marriage, and it remains the case that marriage partners have it much more frequently than those living alone.[58]

In pre-industrial agrarian and craft societies, household production accounted for the vast bulk of output. Domestic food production fell sharply as a share of output, but the household economy remains very

[50] e.g. the jajmani caste system in India, Dasgupta, *Well-Being and Destitution*, 237.
[51] Sahlins, *Stone Age Economics*; Lucas and Stark, 'Motivations to Remit'.
[52] Kotlikoff and Spivak, 'Family as an Incomplete Annuities Market'.
[53] Bernheim et al., 'Strategic Bequest Motive'.   [54] Stark, *Altruism and Beyond*, 89.
[55] Hwang, 'Face and Favor', 950; Bellow, 'The Old System'.
[56] Dixit, 'Bride-Price and Dowry'; Gregory, *Gifts and Commodities*, 63–7.
[57] Rubin, 'Lovers and Other Strangers'; Altman, 'Reciprocity of Interpersonal Exchange'; Belk and Coon, 'Can't Buy Me Love'.
[58] Humphries, *Secret World of Sex*, 32–4 and ch. 4; Michael et al., *Sex in America*, ch. 6. On mating, see Ch. 13 below.

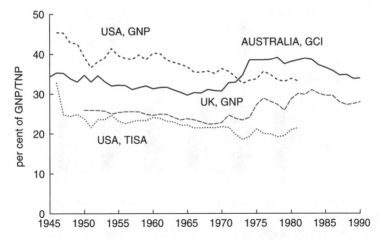

Fig. 5.2. Household production as percentage of national product

Sources: USA GNP, in Eisner, *Total Incomes System*, table A.15, p. 73. Australia GCI, in Snooks, *Portrait of the Family*, table 7.2, p. 167. UK GNP, in Jackson and Marks, *Sustainable Economic Welfare*, Appendix A, pp. 39–42. USA, TISA, in Eisner, *Total Incomes System*, table A.15, p. 73.

substantial today. Its scale is captured by 'extended national accounts', which incorporate household production in national output. Domestic labour is assigned a notional wage extrapolated from women's paid labour. The use of shadow wages is reasonable. It is this, at the margin, that women sacrifice when deciding to stay at home. In these estimates, household labour amounts to between one-quarter to more than one-third of national product (Figure 5.2). The level fluctuates a little, and has some cyclical components (it moves inversely with the market economy). In Australia, for example, household production has remained a high proportion of the economy over two centuries, producing an average of 36 per cent of 'Gross Community Income' (i.e. the sum of market and household income) for the whole period 1860 to 1990, with only a very slight decline from 38 to 35 per cent (exponential trend) over the whole period.[59] American and British estimates are lower. Household production is very labour intensive. An input–output analysis in Australia in 1975–6 indicates that 70 per cent of household inputs are represented by labour, another 22 per cent by materials and energy, and only 8 per cent by equipment and housing.[60] Although household production continues to be labour intensive, its

---

[59] Snooks, *Portrait of the Family*, 17, and table 7.2, pp. 166–7.
[60] Ironmonger, *Households Work*, table 2.3, p. 30.

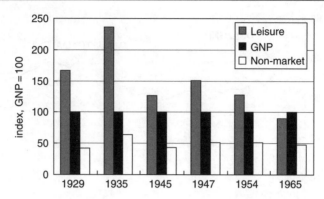

Fig. 5.3. Leisure, GNP, and non-market activities, USA 1929–1965, in actual or imputed 1958 dollars

Note: GNP held constant at 100.

Source: Nordhaus and Tobin, 'Is Growth Obsolete?', table A.17, p. 415.

output remains (like many other services) a superior good. It remains in demand, and can maintain or sometimes increase its share of national output under affluence.

Shifting our gaze from women to men, history presents a positive shift away from the market and into the household. Typical male working hours have fallen drastically since the nineteenth century; from 65 hours a week for average full-time work in Britain in 1856, to 42 hours in 1973.[61] Most of this time has been transferred into the home. Nordhaus and Tobin have attempted to impute a value to leisure time (and non-market activity) in their set of extended national accounts (Figure 5.3). If a price is placed on free time, this value dominates the flow of welfare. In Figure 5.3, leisure has contracted in comparison with GNP since the 1930s. Part of the effect is cyclical, representing the shift to full employment between the 1930s and the 1960s. On the other hand, 'non-market activities' (mostly house-work) have generally kept up with the growth of GNP, rising from 42 per cent in 1929, to 48 per cent in 1965. These two sets of data give some sense of the shifting boundaries of the gift economy. In terms of time alone the shift out of market work has continued for men in the last two decades, while women's participation has increased in some countries, and remained stable in others.[62] All in all, time spent in paid employment in a twenty-country 'world' between the 1960s and the present, for women as well as men, amounted to less than 21 per cent of the total time available.

[61] Matthews et al., *British Economic Growth*, table D.1, p. 566.
[62] Gershuny, *Changing Times*, ch. 5. More on USA trends in Fig. 11.4 and in Ch. 13 below.

Almost four-fifths of the time available was spent *outside* paid work, in various forms of social interaction, in domestic work, or alone.[63]

A massive asymmetry arises from the gift of life itself. Children are another good whose provision has shifted *out* of the market and into the gift economy. In pre-industrial and early industrial societies, children were able to bring in a current income, and were counted on for support in hardship and in old age. The demographic transition is associated with children losing their economic value and gaining a large affective value. They become economically worthless, but emotionally priceless.[64] Child-rearing can extend into three decades, and places heavy demands on mental energy and time. Attempts have been made to measure the money cost of children. The magnitudes are staggering. For Britain, the estimated cost in earnings forgone for an average woman with two children came to £202,500 in 1990 prices, approximately 46 per cent of her potential life-time earnings. It was made up of earnings forgone while out of employment, while working shorter hours, and at lower rates of pay.[65] The direct costs added another £50,000 or so. In the United States the earnings forgone appear to be lower, but the direct costs higher, as less time was taken off work, and more spent on childcare.[66] Just the capitalized child-rearing costs (excluding domestic labour) in the United States were estimated as representing 11 per cent of the total private capital stock in 1929, and 6.5 per cent in 1969.[67] The gift of life is only a modest addition to the macroeconomic measures of the household economy since most of it is already counted in household production. Parental care is an unmeasured but vital input into human capital, and determines the ability to participate in the economy and society. When marriages break down, the probability of educational, behavioural, and emotional disorders is doubled, even after controlling for socio-economic factors.[68] This is not an argument against divorce, but an indication of the cost of inadequate parenting.

Another parental asymmetry arises from intergenerational transfers and bequests. From the point of view of the economic model of lifetime consumption (or 'permanent income'), bequests are an anomaly. Self-interest ends at death.[69] 'Strategic bequest' theory interprets the prospect of bequest

[63] Gershuny, *Changing Times*, table 7.1; 28 per cent for men, 14 per cent for women (tables 7.2–7.3).   [64] Zelizer, *Priceless Child*, 209.

[65] Joshi, 'Cost of Caring', 121.   [66] Joshi, 'Cash Opportunity Costs of Childbearing', 58.

[67] Kendrick et al., *Total Capital*, table B-29, pp. 222–3. On the cost of children, see also below Ch. 11, n.101, Ch.13, n.102.

[68] Zill et al., 'Long-Term Effects of Divorce'; McLanahan and Bumpass, 'Intergenerational Consequences'; Wallerstein, 'Long-Term Effect of Divorce'. More in Ch. 14 below.

[69] As e.g. in the lifetime consumption theory of Modigliani and Brumberg; see Kotlikoff, 'Intergenerational Transfers'.

as a form of bond, which is designed to elicit regard from offspring.[70] One study estimated that bequests could account for between 15 and 70 per cent of net wealth in the USA; another estimates intended transfers as accounting for at least 20 per cent of net worth, and possibly much more; a third, using a different methodology, has found the range to be between 25 and 40 per cent in the USA and Japan.[71] Kotlikoff argues that all intergenerational transfers taken together (beyond the age of 18), including parental payments for higher education, account for about 80 per cent of assets in the USA.[72] Likewise, a good deal of life insurance cover may be regarded as reciprocal or altruistic transfers.[73]

How do offspring reciprocate? Across the life course, parents and children engage in constant interaction. In return for care and attention, children provide parents with status, a sense of worth, and sheer pleasure.[74] But in North America, at least, intergenerational reciprocity is asymmetrical, and offspring receive more in financial, household, and emotional aid than they return.[75] At the macro-level, this asymmetry may be seen as an instance of delayed or indirect reciprocity. It is estimated that 60 per cent of workers and 70 per cent of old people in the world in the 1990s still relied exclusively on family support for social security.[76] In advanced societies, money transfers from the young to the old dwindle down almost to nothing, which is remarkable in view of the large investments of the old in the young.[77]

But offspring and kin nevertheless reciprocate on a massive scale, not directly in money, but by caring for the old, the infirm, and the disabled. In the United States, about two-thirds of households maintain some form of reciprocal intergenerational assistance.[78] In Britain in 1985, about one adult in seven (some 6 million people) was providing unpaid care, and about one in five households contained a carer. About 3 per cent of British adults (1.4 million) devoted at least twenty hours per week to caring and 8 per cent carried the main responsibility for looking after someone.[79] Obligations arose, and were discharged, in a complex web of personal

---

[70] Bernheim et al., 'Strategic Bequest Motive'.

[71] Kotlikoff and Summers, 'Role of Intergenerational Transfers'; Barthold and Ito, *Bequest Taxes and Accumulation*.

[72] Kotlikoff, 'Intergenerational Transfers'.

[73] Zelizer, *Morals and Markets*; Bernheim, 'How Strong are Bequest Motives?'; Rossi and Rossi, *Human Bonding*, ch. 10.

[74] Rossi and Rossi, *Human Bonding*. In the words of Rebecca Abrams, personal communication.

[75] Kulis, 'Locus of Reciprocity'; Osborn and Williams, 'Patterns of Exchanges'; Spitze and Logan, 'Helping as a Component'; Caplow, 'Rule Enforcement ', 1316.

[76] World Bank, *Averting the Old Age Crisis*, 49.   [77] Ibid., table 2.3, p. 63.

[78] Kulis, 'Locus of Reciprocity', figs. 1–2, pp. 489–90.   [79] Green, *Informal Carers*, 1.

reciprocity, in which intensity of kinship was only one factor, and less important than the quality of previous interactions.[80] Indeed, caring extended well beyond the family circle: about 24 per cent of those cared for were friends or neighbours.[81] Based on local authority pay rates (of £7 per hour in 1989), the market value of caring provided by unpaid carers came to £39.1 billion in 1992, or about 7.5 per cent of national income in that year. Of the time that this represents, 83 per cent was spent on caring for the aged, for persons older than 65.[82] In total, this was almost four times as much as joint private and public expenditure for long-term care, and about the same as the total spent on the National Health Services.[83]

Labour markets

Discretion at work involves an element of gifting. When intensity and quality of effort are difficult to observe, they are to that extent discretionary, and need to be acknowledged reciprocally.

In managing their workers, American executives have oscillated between two approaches, 'hard' and 'soft'. To achieve scale economies with poorly educated immigrants, they turned to strict discipline and time management, attempting to isolate the worker and to depersonalize the working environment. Application fell short of the ideal even in Detroit,[84] and proved impossible to implement fully in more cohesive environments, such as Britain and Japan. An alternative tradition has advocated the carrot of regard, from the paternalism of the late Victorian period, to the 'human potential' approach of the 1920s and up to the recent years, in which management gurus have preached 'empowerment' in the workplace.[85] Even the largest multinational corporation, even the largest factory, is made up of small groups, in the paintshop, on the assembly line, or in the boardroom. In face-to-face settings, the economy of regard kicks in. It has long been a powerful element in the solidarity culture of restricted effort in Britain. In the last two decades, it is increasingly being harnessed in the service of productivity: starting with 'quality circles', and moving on to 'team production', a more recent buzzword.[86] In Japanese industrial

---

[80] Finch and Mason, *Negotiating Family Responsibilities*; Twigg, *Carers*; Finch, 'Quality of Relationships in Families'; Rossi and Rossi, *Human Bonding*.

[81] Calculated from Green, *Informal Carers*, table 2.3, p. 8.

[82] Laing, *Financing Long-Term Care*, table 3, p. 39.

[83] Ibid.; Great Britain, Dept of Health, *Health and Personal Social Services 1994*, table 7.2, p. 111. (data for England, extrapolated to the UK).   [84] Mathewson, *Restriction of Output*.

[85] Waring, *Taylorism Transformed*.

[86] e.g. Gmelch and Miskin, *Productivity Teams*; Wellins et al., *Empowered Teams*.

culture, it is underpinned by a gift economy of secure employment and overt rituals of mutual obligation between worker and corporation.[87]

From a different perspective, the 'New Institutional Economics' accepts that contractual obligations are difficult to specify completely in advance.[88] One implication (rejected, however, by Williamson) is that contracts rely on reciprocal good will for their application. Keynesian economists have applied the idea to labour markets: Akerlof has explained the persistence of wages above market-clearing levels as evidence of implicit contracts, of a gift relation between employers and workers. Where effort and quality are difficult to monitor, workers give effort and commitment voluntarily in return for levels of pay and regard that exceed market-clearing levels.[89] Effort is difficult to monitor, and Holmstrom and Milgrom detect elements of discretionary gift economy in *any* fixed wage.[90]

In the professional sphere, academic tenure is a gift of lifetime income, usually by a group of peers, subject only to minimal contractual obligations. The recipient has discretion to repay the gift in the time and quality of her choosing. Some fail to honour the deal. What keeps the others honest are the bonds of regard. There used to be little systematic monitoring, but the professor was under scrutiny by her immediate colleagues, and also in the 'invisible college' of far-flung peers, where reputations are made and maintained. Another form of obligation arose between teacher and students; indeed, the conflicting demands of these two bonds are often difficult to resolve. Analogous regard incentives are to be found in most professions.[91] A great deal of evidence (both experimental and historical) has accumulated to show that money crowds out virtue. When the incentives of peer approbation are replaced by cash, the quality and quantity of performance suffers. Economists and psychologists call these non-cash incentives 'intrinsic motivation', but they constitute clear evidence of the power of regard.[92]

Agriculture

Farming remains an extension of the household form of production. In the long term, it has largely resisted the economies of scale offered by the

[87] e.g. Hampden-Turner and Tompenaars, *Seven Cultures of Capitalism*, ch. 8.
[88] Williamson, *Economic Institutions of Capitalism*.
[89] Akerlof, 'Labor Contracts as Partial Gift Exchange'.
[90] Holmstrom and Milgrom, 'Multitask Principal-Agent Analyses'.
[91] Not discussed here for lack of space.
[92] Deci et al., 'Meta-analytic Review'; Frey, *Not Just for the Money*; Gneezy and Rustichini, 'Pay Enough or Don't Pay'.

labour market. Pre-modern agriculture often used communal forms of management. After the transition to capitalism, agriculture continues, in the most advanced countries, to be dominated by family farms, with a little hired help.[93] In the United States, 86 per cent of agricultural units were organized as 'family farms' in 1997, and family farming dominates agriculture in North America up to the present.[94] Individual farm acreage has increased with better technology, and the number of farms and farmers has declined, but farmwork is still largely a family (or very small business) affair: the ratio of self-employed and family to paid workers in United States agriculture was 2.7 in 1960, and still 1.8 in 1985.[95]

Except for the seasonal peaks, there are few economies of scale for labour in agriculture. On the family farm the face-to-face methods of household work allocation are used for market production. In the early modern period and in some places in Britain up to the twentieth century, farmworkers were taken into the household, on annual engagements that left considerable scope for discretionary effort and reciprocity.[96] The typical hired hand in North American family farming was also a boarder. The earlier trend towards large farms, which developed in European agriculture during the high-farming/high-prices period up to 1870, was reversed during the subsequent quarter-century of depression, when farmers found it more difficult to bid in the labour market, and drew increasingly on family workers.[97] From the 1870s to the 1890s, family farmers in North America, Germany, France, Scandinavia, and the Low Countries had to cope with falling prices. In many countries, they turned to cooperation. On their farmsteads, they applied the incentives of regard, and reverted to family labour (one should not idealize these bonds, which often weighed heavily on wives and offspring). In staying on the farm, they sacrificed income for dignity. Their product, however, had to be sold for cash in impersonal markets.[98] As Richard Hofstadter argues, that is what accounts for the particular moral vehemence of agrarian pressure groups, their conviction of virtue, their sense of outrage.[99] Agrarians laid moral claims on the rest of society which continued to resonate even after the agrarian upturn.[100] They are exemplified in the persistence of the Common Agricultural Policy

[93] Offer, *Agrarian Interpretation*, 110–16; Allen and Lueck, *Nature of the Farm*.
[94] Allen and Leuck, ibid., 23–4.
[95] United States Bureau of Census, *Statistical Abstract 1989*, table no. 1075, p. 626.
[96] Kussmaul, *Servants in Husbandry*; Chaunce, *Amongst Farm Horses*.
[97] Koning, *Failure of Agrarian Capitalism*.   [98] Ibid.; Offer, *Agrarian Interpretation*, ch. 8.
[99] Hofstadter, *Age of Reform*, 46–7.
[100] Offer, *Agrarian Interpretation*, ch. 11, esp. pp. 151–2; pp. 381–2.

in Europe and farm support programmes in North America, despite their familiar abuses.[101]

Selling

Gifting and reciprocity need to ascertain the counterparty's preferences from the outside. That is also the basic problem of selling. There is an overlap between the two forms of exchange, and regard pervades the market.

Some goods are useful only or mainly as gifts. Greeting cards are one example, gift-wrappers, toys, flowers, and wedding rings are others. Davis has estimated the scale of all retail purchases for gift giving at approximately 4.3 per cent of consumer expenditure in Britain in 1968.[102] The year and the life cycle are punctuated by gifting occasions, by birthdays, weddings, and holidays. Durable goods retailing has a large peak at Christmas. In 1990, American households spent an average of $770 on Christmas purchases, $72 billion altogether, about 1.9 per cent of total consumer expenditure.[103] In 'Middletown' in 1978, 39.5 Christmas gifts were inventoried for each respondent, and the celebrations accounted for about 4 per cent of total annual expenditures.[104]

Advertising attempts to apply mass production to personal suasion. Marketers strive to endow their goods with a 'personality', by means of branding. An ad can simulate a smile and reproduce it by the million. American magazine advertising between the 1940s and the 1960s usually incorporated an element of direct interpersonal appeal, in the form of 'endorsement', which is ubiquitous in that period in various forms. Price information was almost never included. This simulated regard was designed to bypass the filter of reason, in order to create an obligation to purchase in the customer's mind.[105] Tupperware, Avon, and Ann Summers recruit women to draw on their social networks and convene house parties, where the conventions of female reciprocity are invoked to sell plastic crockery, cosmetics, or sexual accessories. In the last two decades marketing has increasingly aimed to escape 'the law of one price', to discriminate among different market segments, in order to push prices up the demand curve.[106] As information becomes cheaper, marketers attempt to personalize

---

[101] Koning, *Failure of Agrarian Capitalism.*
[102] Davis, 'Gifts and the UK Economy', 412–13.
[103] Solow, 'Is it Really the Thought that Counts?', 506–7.
[104] Caplow, 'Rule Enforcement', 1307; also Miller, *Unwrapping Christmas.*
[105] Ch. 6 below.   [106] Gunter and Farnham, *Consumer Profiles.*

their appeal, and to collect information about individual clients in so-called 'database marketing'. The goal is to target promotions at the smallest possible market niche—the individual—in order to simulate a personal relationship between sellers and buyers. Customers are increasingly exposed to personalized birthday letters and sales pitches cunningly disguised as personal communications.[107]

Advertising has accounted for 2 to 3 per cent of GDP in the United States since the 1920s. But this kind of simulated intimacy, however vivid, is no substitute for interpersonal persuasion. When selling at fixed prices to anonymous consumers, advertising is chosen. When selling high-value goods to individuals, personal bonding is preferred. Table 5.1 compares advertising and personal selling costs for department stores, wholesalers, and manufacturers in the USA during the 1930s. Even at the retail level, outlays on personal selling were almost double those on advertising. At the wholesale and producer goods level, selling costs remained high, but the vast bulk of the marketing effort was devoted to personal selling, in face-to-face interactions.

The common perception is that retail customers are open to manipulation, while business-to-business trading is pure calculation. It appears, however, that interbusiness trading involved a massive effort of interpersonal persuasion. Department stores and consumer goods manufacturers spent more than twice as much on personal selling as on advertising. Producer

Table 5.1. Advertising and personal selling costs in retail, wholesale, and manufacturing, USA, 1930s

	Mean percentage of sales				
	Advertising and sales promotion (1)	Personal selling (2)	Total marketing expenditure (3)	Number of observations (4)	Year
Retail				size classes	
Dept. stores	4.6	9.3	13.9	9	1935
Wholesale				sectors	
Profitable	1.5	6.9	8.4	32	1934
Unprofitable	0.8	8.6	9.4	32	1934
Manufacturing				industries	
Consumer goods	5.8	11.4	17.2	19	1931
Producer goods	2.3	10.1	12.4	10	1931

Note: Means of data columns.

Source: Borden, *Economic Effects of Advertising*, tables 6, 7, 8, pp. 63, 65, 67.

[107] Anon., 'Database Marketing'; personal experience.

goods manufacturers spent a little less on sales overall, but devoted more than five times as much to personal selling as to advertising.[108]

Any difference in quality, delivery, service etc. can be competed away by the price, which theory says will be shaved of all profit. Hence the only remaining source of market advantage could well be the quality of regard. The impression that personal interaction was vital to business is reinforced by the finding that almost half of American GNP (in 1970) could be described as transaction costs, i.e. as the measured extent of the divergence from the ideal of costless transactions. Of this, 55 per cent was incurred between firms.[109] The proportion of sales workers in the American labour force rose from 4 per cent in 1900 to 7.5 per cent in 1970, and up to 12 per cent in 2000. In Britain it was 9.5 per cent in 1961, and 8.8 per cent in 1981.[110] On this measure as well, the impersonal market has not retreated.

Bonding for sales purposes is known as 'relationship selling'.[111] A stockbroker explains in a company instructional video, 'I could be the best stock-picker in the world, but if I don't establish a relationship, the client won't stick with me . . .'[112] A year-long participant-observer of a Xerox sales office in Cleveland, Ohio, in the 1990s describes how intensely corporations rely on bonding to capture and hold their business customers, as several quotes will illustrate:

It's a friendship. The more routine the business becomes, the less it threatens the friendship, and the more solid the friendship, the more Diane can expect business as a matter of routine . . . [113]

It's a salesman's favorite tone, a way of establishing a sense of almost illicit familiarity, a way of making the listener feel privileged and special.[114]

A salesman needs nothing less than to be loved by everyone, so he's haunted by the specter of failure as a personal rejection, a sort of unrequited love.[115]

Sales was pressing the flesh. The act of trust, of partnership, of friendly congress.[116]

No one was immune to affection, calculated or otherwise.[117]

The toughest customers would ask for more information until they got it . . . but most customers wanted to preserve their friendly relationship with the salesman. . . . They valued the relationship as much as they valued the particulars of a given deal.[118]

---

[108] 1931, however, was not a normal year.
[109] Wallis and North, 'Transaction Costs', 654–5.
[110] Ibid., table 3.1, p. 106; Friedman, *Birth of a Salesman*, 260; Mitchell, *British Historical Statistics*, table 'Labour force 2.', p. 107; Great Britain, Office of Population, Censuses and Surveys, *Census 1981*, table 12, p. 52.   [111] Levitt, *Marketing Imagination*, ch. 6.
[112] Shorris, *Nation of Salesmen*, 308.   [113] Dorsey, *The Force*, 45.   [114] Ibid. 92.
[115] Ibid. 179.   [116] Ibid. 204.   [117] Ibid. 121.   [118] Ibid. 204.

A standard negotiating fixture in commerce is the 'business lunch', which uses the gift-exchange trappings of food and hospitality to create an emotional setting for trade. That part of the hospitality industry which does not cater primarily to courtship, kinship, or friendship relies on the businessman, travelling in pursuit of the *personal* contact.

Personal obligation can drive consumer preferences. In 1965, of American car buyers giving the prime reason for choosing a particular dealer, 11.9 per cent of new-car owners cited 'personal relationship'; for used-car owners the level was higher at 12.7–15.2 per cent, and another 5 per cent cited positive dealer attitude or reputation. Earlier surveys found comparable results.[119]

The mix of regard and of salesmanship is uneasy. Many employees, like the Xerox salespeople, have found fulfilment in genuine exchanges of regard, using time and goods provided by their employer. But because money is involved, authenticity is suspect, it is *pseudo-regard*. Rapport with customers is often driven, back at the office, by output quotas as relentless as any in the old Soviet Union (with similar techniques of emotional terror and account massaging).[120] In the web of commerce, every human bond is open to betrayal. That, at any rate, is the theme of a vein of critical writing, from Arthur Miller's *Death of a Salesman*, through to Saul Bellow's *Seize the Day*, to such documentaries as Dorsey's *The Force*, and a cover story in *Business Week*.[121]

Entrepreneurship

Entrepreneurship cannot be taught, or many more would succeed. It begins with an untried concept, and depends on the ability to inspire trust: to attract reciprocal transfers from investors, lenders, suppliers, and customers.[122] Hence, it is often those entrepreneurs who understand the gift economy who are most likely to succeed in the market economy. But success may also require a ruthless readiness to disown the obligations of regard.[123] The same applies to the practice of politics: a field too vast to more than mention here.

A common identity can substitute for face-to-face relations. Jewish Maghribi traders in the eleventh-century Mediterranean had enough in

---

[119] *Look, Automobile and Tire Survey* (1965), 31, 43; ibid. (1958), 36; United States, *Automobile Price Labeling, Hearings*, 56–60.   [120] Dorsey, *The Force*, passim.
[121] Miller, *Death of a Salesman*; Bellow, *Seize the Day*; Dorsey, *The Force*; Maremont, 'Blind Ambition'.   [122] Starr and McMillan, 'Entrepreneurship, Resource Cooptation'.
[123] Choi, *Paradigms and Conventions*, ch. 7.

common to establish a high probability of trustworthiness: their communal culture made the penalty of exclusion all the more painful.[124] Similar bonds have facilitated the formation of other commercial communities: the Quakers in Britain, the Parsis in India, the overseas Chinese.[125] The diamond trade in Israel, one of its three world centres, relies on informal handshake contracts, sealed by the blessing 'Mazal Ubracha' (luck and bounty), and is dominated by Orthodox Jews. Business credit is essentially a form of delayed reciprocity. In its first century, British industrialization relied primarily on funds raised locally from family, friends, and business contacts, who based their trust on personal knowledge.[126] The family firm or the partnership were typical forms of ownership. They remained so until the scale of economic projects (such as the railways and overseas enterprises) exceeded the resources of personal networks.

Asian entrepreneurs, especially the overseas Chinese, make extensive use of family and gift reciprocity. Chinese culture subscribes to *guanxi*, a set of norms of reciprocity and gifting which promotes trust among initiates and excludes others. In the People's Republic *guanxi* was necessary to obtain goods and services. Overseas Chinese had the cultural equipment to connect into these pre-existing webs, often by going back to their village or town of origin, and taking on a local partner. In the absence of secure property rights in the People's Republic, reciprocity fulfils a similar function of making trade and investment possible.[127] Hence, more than two-thirds of China's massive exports to the United States used to be routed through Hong Kong.[128]

Corruption

Loyalty and reciprocity can be used effectively for anti-social ends. Italy has its Cosa Nostra, the Chinese their Triads. A Russian Mafia, with deep roots in the past, is in the process of re-emerging.[129] Small groups collude

[124] Greif, 'Reputation and Coalitions in Medieval Trade'.
[125] Landa, *Trust, Ethnicity and Identity*, chs. 5–6.
[126] Neal, 'Finance of Business during the Industrial Revolution', 152, 155; McCloskey, '1780–1860: A Survey', 270.
[127] Gold et al., *Social Connections in China*; Hwang, 'Face and Favor: The Chinese Power Game'; Smart and Smart, 'Personal Relations and Divergent Economies'; Smart, 'Gifts, Bribes, and Guanxi'; Yang, 'The Gift Economy and State Power in China'; id., *Gifts, Favors and Banquets*; also Landa, *Trust, Ethnicity, and Identity*, ch. 5.
[128] *The Economist*, 'China: The Numbers Game'.
[129] Booth, *The Triads*; Murray and Baoqi, *Origins of Tiandihui*; Varese, *The Russian Mafia*.

more effectively than large ones.[130] Reciprocal communities of businessmen, professionals, and workers often organize for rent seeking. A strong gift economy can crowd out the market if exchange depends entirely on reciprocal inclusion.[131] This is a strong argument for liberalism, for the *impersonality* of the market, the law, the public service, and the vote. Some forms of gifting are used to subvert the 'rules of the game'. Even law-abiding societies, with a tradition of public integrity, are not immune to 'old boy networks'. Illegal gift economies subvert the effectiveness of government; sometimes due to a general ethos of reciprocity (known as 'protektsia' in Eastern Europe and Israel), or the activities of organized crime. But corruption can also be beneficial. Like the market economy, the planned economy in Eastern Europe also depended on an extensive network of 'fixers', who acted as brokers in a gift economy ('blat') mediated by their access to resources, relationships, and reputations.[132]

Implications and conclusions

The boundaries of the market and regard economy shift in response to technological changes in the efficiency of communication.[133] Some gifts, like romantic love and 'the gift of life', are provided only, or almost entirely, within the gift economy. Other goods (like insurance) can be provided with or without regard. Since the demand for regard is beyond the capacity of authentic gifting alone to satisfy, there is an opportunity for salesmanship to make use of pseudo-regard for the purpose of price discrimination, to charge some customers at higher (personalized) rates.

When market productivity increases, the relative share of the market will expand. This, in general, corresponds with the historical 'Great Transformation' from pre-industrial to more market-oriented societies. A more recent instance is the growth of the welfare state, where social insurance has shifted outwards from regard-intensive family and community obligations, to mutual societies which still require an investment of regard, and finally to impersonal tax systems and insurance markets.

It is, however, possible for the economy of regard to expand its share as well, in consequence of technological change. Transport development has facilitated migrant remittance transfers. Telecommunication has extended

---

[130] Olson, *Rise and Decline of Nations*.   [131] Kranton, 'Reciprocal Exchange'.
[132] Grossman, 'The "Second Economy" of the USSR'; id., 'The "Shadow Economy" '; Ledeneva, *Russia's Economy of Favours*; Lovell et al., *Bribery and Blat*, chs. 9–10.
[133] Offer, 'Between Gift and Market', 469–71, esp. figure 4.

the reach of both families and entrepreneurs. The shift from Taylorism to teams in the workplace, assisted by cheap computing power, has reinstated artisans in corporate factories. The relative shares of the gift and market exchange are governed by their respective technologies. They are determined dynamically over time by the cost of communication relative to the cost of time, i.e. by the growth of productivity in regard, and in the market forms of exchange.

The economy of regard operates wherever incentives are affected by personal relations. Its core is in the household, but it extends whenever people work in small groups or negotiate face to face. Gift exchange is sensitive to the cost of information and the cost of time. As market incomes rise, so does the cost of time. On the other hand, the cost of information is declining. These trends work in opposite directions. As the cost of time increases, regard-intensive exchanges like childcare become more expensive. Men, for a long time, have traded working hours for more time at home, with the exception of workers in the higher professional and managerial occupations, who have sought regard in the workplace. This choice was even starker for women, and those who have had the best careers have forgone children and often marriage as well.[134] For women, market work provides additional choice and a new measure of regard. But the redirection of regard (by both men and women) is also creating a wake of social consequences, ranging from marriage breakdown at the personal end, to the fiscal crisis of the welfare state at the societal one.

Regard is difficult to measure because the yardstick of price is explicitly rejected. When regard and goods are traded together, 'revealed preferences' will therefore not measure accurately the welfare produced. It is therefore necessary to look for other indicators, to decipher the cues and language of regard. Otherwise, when making policy, there is an inclination to maximize only what is measurable, thus falling short of real optimality.[135] This failure is a feature of public policy: individuals are less likely to succumb in their private affairs, since regard is a compelling part of their preferences. In public services, there has been a strong movement towards simulated market forms of provision. In neglecting the economy of regard, these policies may fall well short of their objectives, because (*a*) quantitative measures are often unable to capture quality, which is more easily monitored in face-to-face interaction with peers and clients, (*b*) quantitative sanctions replace approbation with fear, and informal monitoring with

---

[134] Joshi, 'Combining Employment with Child-rearing'; Ch. 13 below.
[135] Holmstrom and Milgrom, 'Multitask Principal-Agent Analyses'.

costly evaluation, and lead to neglect of unmeasured but vital tasks, and (c) there are unmeasured losses of regard, goodwill, and trust. Regard is a good in its own right, quite apart from its instrumental value, especially where personal interaction pervades, as in education and medical care.

In the market sector, transactions legitimized by market impartiality, and justified as market clearing, may actually be driven by pseudo-regard. One suspect is the rise of executive pay in the United States and Britain, which has reached such multiples of average earnings that have alarmed even *Business Week*. Remuneration bears little relation to economic performance, and is influenced by the reciprocal gifting motives of compensation committee members.[136]

Decades after integration into the market economy, the *kula* and the *potlatch* have persisted in the South Seas and on the Pacific Coast, absorbing ever larger resources in line with increased affluence.[137] Likewise, a variety of reciprocal interactions persist into the modern world and cover a large proportion of the exchange of goods and services. This peculiar form of exchange, with its personalized gift and discretionary delay, is required to authenticate regard. It motivates gains from trade in ways that are similar to the market. It persists, however, because regard is an abiding need, perhaps 'wired in', which impersonal markets are poorly equipped to gratify.

[136] Byrne et al., 'That Eye-Popping Executive Pay'; Anon, 'Executive Pay: The Party Ain't over Yet'; Bynre et al., 'Executive Pay: Compensation at the Top is out of Control'; Crystal, *In Search of Excess*. [137] Gregory, 'Gifts', 527.

Part II

In the Market Place

6

The Mask of Intimacy: Advertising and the Quality of Life[1]

When the motor car began to diffuse in Britain in the early 1920s, oil companies erected roadside signs and billboards with little regard for the rural landscape. But soon after, in response to public outcry, the advertisers withdrew the signs from the countryside, not only in Britain, but across most of Europe (though not in the United States).[2]

If signs in a country meadow can lower the quality of the natural environment, the marketing message can have a similar effect on the interpersonal environment. Interpersonal relations form the core of subjective well-being. The web of social interactions is one of the main sources of satisfaction, and thus a key element in the quality of life.[3] Marketing and advertising affect the quality of interpersonal relations, because they *have* to intrude into the interpersonal domain. In consequence, like several other forms of environmental degradation, advertising came under public scrutiny between the 1950s and the 1970s, and the chapter concludes with an assessment of how it was regulated and restrained.

Advertising enhances the quality of life. It engages the senses, stimulates novelty, broadens the range of experience and choice. It makes townscapes, newspapers, magazines, and television more lively and colourful than they might otherwise be. It presents information about products and services. It commits suppliers to consistent standards of quality. It pays for a good part of the media, and underwrites sporting and cultural activity. Would we wish to be without advertising? The memory of grey cities in Eastern Europe under communism suggests that we would miss it. For

[1] Thanks to the History of Advertising Trust, the Hartman Center at Duke University Library, the Ford Motor Company, and the Henry Ford Museum in Dearborn, Michigan, for generous access to their archival collections, cited in this chapter.
[2] Brown, 'Cultivating a "Green" Image'.   [3] Chs. 2 and 5, above.

purveyors of such benefits, advertisers have been curiously defensive and insecure.[4] There is a widespread sense that advertising is a mixed blessing. It has been under continuous attack for most of the last century.[5] Critics assail it in two different ways: it promotes the wrong kinds of goods, and is also a bad in itself.

Good and bad goods. Almost everyone agrees that illegal narcotic drugs should not be advertised, and racial and religious abuse is also banned, but there is less accord on alcohol and tobacco. Some critics claim that advertising promotes spurious wants. J. K. Galbraith, for example, used to argue that it diverts outlays from public and communal goods towards private ones.[6]

A bad in itself. We have argued that choice is intractable (Chs. 3–4 above). To solve the problem of choice, people fall back on established social conventions and institutions. Advertising invests in creating habits and loyalties (for example, to brands) that transcend price comparison and calculation. Like other commitment technologies, it is expensive, typically deploying between 1 and more than 2 per cent of national income. But the harm may be greater than the cost of the money spent.

Advertising, it is argued, supports the spurious differentiation of identical goods, and thus makes them more expensive. In 1992 American food companies launched 11,500 new products, many of them copies of existing brands.[7] Advertising, it is said, undermines rational choice: it conveys seductive but misleading information, making it harder to compare quality and prices. Let us pay for novelty and stimulation directly, critics argue, rather than through this indiscriminate and indirect tax. Some economists argue that the use of advertising to establish a market presence raises barriers to entry. It stifles innovation and entrenches monopoly.[8] Scholars and laypersons have blamed it for degrading

---

[4] e.g. O'Toole, *Trouble with Advertising*; Bullmore, *Advertising Association Handbook*.

[5] Extensive (but not exhaustive) survey, Pollay, 'Distorted Mirror'; cogently in e.g. Whitehead, 'Advertising'; more recently, Preston, *Tangled Web*; Lears, *Fables of Abundance*; Lasn, *Culture Jam* and his magazine *Adbusters*; De Graaf, *Affluenza*. Some prominent book-length critiques are Chase and Schlink, *Your Money's Worth*; Schlink and Kallet, *100,000,000 Guinea Pigs*; Thompson, *Voice of Civilisation*; Packard, *Hidden Persuaders*; Seldin, *Golden Fleece*; Baker, *Permissible Lie*; Wight, *The Day the Pigs Refused*; Preston, *Great American Blow-up*; Ewen, *Captains of Consciousness*; Schudson, *Advertising*; Marchand, *Advertising and the American Dream*; Leiss et al., *Social Communication in Advertising*. A comprehensive earlier bibliography of advertising is in Pollay, *Information Sources*.   [6] Galbraith, *Affluent Society*, 133–5.

[7] Giles, 'Indigestion', 8.

[8] Borden, *Economic Effects*; Kaldor, 'Economic Aspects'. Other economists dispute this reasoning. A survey of the arguments, from a point of view favourable to advertising, can be found in Bullmore and Waterson, *AA Handbook*, part 5; Ekelund and Saurman, *Advertising and Market Process*; also Becker and Murphy, 'Simple Theory of Advertising'; most extensively, Sutton, *Sunk Costs*.

women with its use of sex.[9] Environmentalists and urbanists deplore its visual impact.[10]

Here, in a paragraph, is my own argument. Advertising seeks to capture a jaded and wary consumer. In order to persuade, it needs to be credible, to establish trust. Credibility, however, is not easy: few products or services are remarkably superior to the competition. There is a temptation to stray from the literal truth, which makes the achievement of credibility more difficult still. The more credible advertising becomes overall, the higher its standards of truthfulness, the more tempting it is to mislead. Formally, the dominant strategy for an individual advertiser is to mislead. But if everyone follows this strategy, credibility overall is destroyed. Discourse becomes less truthful than any single actor would wish. This is a market failure known as 'the tragedy of the commons': every grazier believes that just one additional cow on the common will hardly be noticed. When each of them grazes only one more cow, the common is soon ravaged. The 'commons' in this case are credibility and trust. We end up with less than we would like. Hence advertising becomes less useful than it might be, for the public of course, but also for those who pay for it.

Misleading advertising may also be creating spillovers for society as a whole, undermining credibility not only in the discourse of marketing, but also in other interactions: political, social, personal. Trust depends on truthfulness; it is necessary for effective leadership, and it underpins coordination and cooperation at every level of economic and social life. Without trust, personal interaction is unsafe, and requires caution, monitoring, and enforcement. Society has recognized these hazards, and has acted historically to counter them in several ways: by means of conceptual analysis, of economic, social, and cultural critiques; it has mobilized voluntary action to resist the contamination of the public domain. This has led to legislation, regulation, and control, which may differ from one country to another, but are nowhere completely absent. Finally, people change their lifestyles and consumption patterns to take account of the contamination of the common, to limit the damage, or to respond to it.

Selling intimacy

In a business or retail exchange, both parties enter the transaction with the expectation of gain. Since both stand to benefit, there is scope for dividing

[9] e.g. Haug, *Commodity Aesthetics*; Bartos, *Marketing to Women*, ch. 20.
[10] e.g. Tunnard and Pushkarev, *Man-Made America*; Brown, 'Cultivating a "Green" Image'.

the gain in different ways. A market exchange, while capable of benefiting both sides, also has an adversarial undertone. Many people experience it as stressful.[11] Information can narrow down the scope for disagreement: if both sides are well informed about quality, cost, and each others' preferences, the potential for friction is smaller. In retail environments, however, it is typical for information to be distributed asymmetrically. An experienced vendor knows more about cost and quality than the casual buyer. The vendor has a choice of pricing strategies to maximize returns. One device is 'price discrimination', pricing goods higher than marginal cost in the hope of capturing intra-marginal buyers, and letting others earn their surplus by means of bargaining or search. Hence, list prices tend to be higher than 'street prices'. In the motor industry, list prices used to be known as the 'vicar's wife' price: she is unlikely to haggle, and has to pay a premium.[12] The buyer might well suspect that a better deal could be obtained, but often lacks the resources to bargain effectively or to investigate the options.

Over and above legitimate price discrimination, fraud and sharp dealing appear to be endemic in retail trading, especially with regard to advertised and actual prices.[13] A common device is the mark-up/mark-down gambit. Prices are sometimes marked up for brief periods of time, so that they can then be marked down for a deceptive 'sale'. The 'sale' gambit is universal but price reductions do not always follow. Sometimes they even rise. Another gambit is 'bait and switch', in which a store has the goods, but tries to switch the customer to something more expensive. Or the shop may have limited quantities, insufficient to meet demand; sometimes it never actually has the advertised goods at all.[14]

This is acknowledged in advertising itself. There is a genre which acknowledges that opportunism is rampant, but which then claims honesty in its particular case. An ad in a computer magazine announces candidly 'SOME ADVERTISERS WILL SELL YOU ANYTHING: Most computer suppliers sell first and ask questions later.' A mail order catalogue states, 'We price our products fairly and honestly. We do not, have not, and will not participate in the common retailing practice of inflating markups to set up a future phony sale.'[15]

Buyers may be eager, but they are wary as well. The problem for advertisers is to dispel their inhibitions. Several approaches are commonly used.

---

[11] Frey, 'Economists Favour the Price System'.   [12] Letter, *The Times*, 10 Jan. 1994.
[13] Blumberg, *Predatory Society*; Shorris, *Nation of Salesmen*; Yang and Stern, 'Call them "Scammers"'.   [14] Blumberg, *Predatory Society*, 32–40.
[15] *Personal Computer World* (Mar. 1994), after p. 509; *Land's End Direct Merchants* (Spring 1994), magazine insert.

One is a straightforward presentation of product merits, the 'value' approach. It was pioneered by David Ogilvy, whose 1950s ads spelled out product attributes in big chunks of small print. Another example is the two-page spread prepared by J. Walter Thompson agency for the launch of the Ford Falcon compact car in 1959, headed with a signed statement by Henry Ford II (the company president), and followed by a long sequence of factual questions and answers, and small informative sketches.[16] Even such factual advertisements rarely contained price information. They are more common in trade periodicals, and tend to be rare in consumer-oriented ones.

On the whole, however, value-oriented advertising is uncommon. Much more popular is 'appetite appeal'. A famous advertisement for 'Life-savers' shows a colourful array of the tinted, transparent, ring-shaped sweets laid out on a magazine page, over the slogan, 'please do not lick this page!'[17] 'Letters from parents followed the appearance of this ad, informing the client that they had caught their children actually licking the page.'[18] Advertising can make goods appear to be succulently tempting: a single, big, yellow peanut, shining with oil and sprinkled with salt, appears over the following copy: 'Something no one ever ate...Just one Planters Cocktail Peanut! No one we know of ever stopped after eating only one Planters Cocktail Peanut.'[19] Both ads use verbal and visual cues in order to get the juices flowing, to evoke the visceral attributes of sweetness and saltiness. Food in particular lends itself to sensual appeal, but this is also found in ads for cars and for travel.

A shiny blue Rover Metro Tahiti Special, incongruously parked on a palm-fringed tropical beach, appeals to two appetites at once, for waxed and polished metal, and for sun and surf. It uses another common marketing device. The headline says 'Just £99* PER MONTH'.[20] Psychologists call this device 'anchoring', a mental process of rounding-down which brings the perceived price down to the next-lower reference point (perhaps in this case £90?) on the mental scale.[21] The price is entirely contrived: the asterisk refers to a table of small print from which it is possible to work out that the monthly payment covers only 20.6 per cent of the full cost of the

---

[16] Ogilvy, *Confessions*; 'The first official facts about the new size Ford for 1960', *Life*, 28 Sept. 1959, ad. no. 4925, JWT Papers, Hartman Center, Duke University Library.

[17] e.g. *Saturday Evening Post* (30 Jan. 1960), 62 (henceforth *SEP*).

[18] Schofield, *Top Copy Writers*, 22.

[19] JWT archives, Hartman Center, Duke University, ad. no. 13433, for *Life*, 16 Feb. 1962.

[20] From *Radio Times*, 1994 (date uncertain), in possession of the author.

[21] On the psychology of anchoring, see Tversky and Kahneman, 'Judgment under Uncertainty'.

car. Like the picture, the price is too good to be true.[22] Often the word 'only' precedes the price, to achieve another anchoring effect. In this case, the word used is 'just'. The practice of setting a price a fraction short of the next perceptual step is universal. A letter in *The Times* proposed that the next coin to be minted should be for a value of 99 pence.[23] A very common 'anchoring' device, is the separate quotation of price (in large figures) and Value Added Tax (in smaller ones).[24] Like 'appetite appeal', anchoring also bypasses the filter of reason. The tactic is transparent, we understand how it works, and yet it is hard to resist.

Another method, which also seeks to reach visceral sources of motivation, is puffery. 'The Greatest Show on Earth!' (Barnum & Bailey); 'The World's Greatest Newspaper' (Chicago Tribune); 'Nothing acts faster than Anadin'; 'Hands that do dishes can feel as soft as your face' (Fairy Liquid)—these are examples of puffery.[25] Many more follow further below, taken from American magazines of the 1950s and the 1960s. The definition of a 'puff' is a claim that is impossible to validate, and which no reasonable person would believe.[26]

'Puffs' are manifestly untrue, and yet the law does not regard them as deceptive, since no reasonable person would believe them. Kool cigarettes, for example, are 'measurably long... immeasurably cool'; immeasurably indeed. Sometimes the puff is in the name of the product, e.g. 'Wonder Bread', or, indeed the 'Rover Metro Tahiti Special'—each element in its name conveying exaggerated pretensions for what is no more than an ordinary subcompact car.[27] Puffs are ubiquitous; every newspaper, every television commercial, is full of statements which are not intended to be taken literally. Why then are they used? To the extent that advertising forms a pre-commitment to quality, puffs reinforce that commitment. Maybe it does not 'wash whiter than white', but at least we can rely on mere whiteness. Large numbers of people do regard puffs as being literally true. In one test, Alcoa's claim that 'Today, aluminium is something else' was appraised as completely true by 47 per cent, and partly true by 36 per cent of those questioned.[28] Tests of advertising comprehension indicate that typically between 30 and 35 per cent of television viewers and press

---

[22] Cash price, £7,553; deposit £2,544; deal covers two years, at 6,000 miles a year; final payment £3,300; credit charge £702; miscellaneous charges £47. The picture is also quite obviously a studio collage.   [23] *The Times* (10 Jan. 1994).

[24] Office of Fair Trade, 'VAT Exclusive Prices', Reference to the Consumer Protection Advisory Committee by the Director General of Fair Trading, (1977), Dossier 17/4; Advertising Association Papers (henceforth AA), History of Advertising Trust, 11/15/4.

[25] Preston, *Great American Blow-up*, 18–19; Wight, *Day the Pigs Refused*, 68.

[26] Preston, *Great American Blow-up*, 3.

[27] These examples are taken from Preston, ibid. 18–19.   [28] Ibid. 29.

media readers either understand advertising messages incorrectly, or fail to comprehend them altogether.[29] Puffs, like anchoring, are effective even when known to be untrue. What else could account for their widespread use? Hence the legal attitude is misconceived: it applies the test of reason to claims that are designed to bypass the filter of reason.[30] Decisive evidence for the effectiveness of puffs is how ubiquitous they are. Whether effective or not, advertisers cannot afford not to use them, for fear of losing ground to the competition. If truthfulness is a public good, then puffs are an example of the 'tragedy of the commons', which no competitor feels they can avoid, for fear of losing out.

The more truthful marketing discourse is, the more tempting it is for any single advertiser to dissimulate or deceive. To control this hazard, misleading advertising is banned or regulated in most countries, though the systems of regulation vary.[31] These constraints are quite weak and tolerate a good deal of puffery. There is also a grey area between puffs and misleading claims, which advertisers can try to exploit. Advertisers claim that regulations have pushed them away from deception and into puffery.[32] As Dorothy Sayers (crimewriter and copywriter) wrote, 'Plain lies are dangerous. The only weapons left are the *suggestio falsi* and the *suppressio veri*.'[33]

In Britain, advertising is constrained by more than eighty statutes, it is regulated by a voluntary body (the Advertising Standards Authority) and is also policed by the media. Nevertheless, the incidence of misleading claims is quite high. A sample of ads taken by the government Office of Fair Trading in March 1978 revealed that 13 per cent of advertisements in national newspapers and magazines failed to comply with the ASA code; 17 per cent of display ads larger than a quarter-page, 12 per cent of retail ads, and 29 per cent of mail order advertisements.[34] Of 2,993 advertisements sampled, 315 (10.5 per cent) were considered to have breached the code (Table 6.1).[35]

To dispel the wariness of buyers, sellers resorted to a repertoire of gambits: value claims, price manipulation, honesty ploys, appetite appeal, anchoring, puffery, dissimulation. The challenge for advertising was to

[29] Jacoby and Hoyer, 'Viewer Miscomprehension'; id. 'Comprehension/Miscomprehension of Print'; id., 'Miscomprehension of Mass-Media Advertising'.
[30] Preston, *Great American Blow-up*; id., *Tangled Web*.
[31] Braun, 'Unfair Competition'; Wagner, *Federal Trade Commission*; Neelankavil, *Advertising Self-Regulation*; Boddewyn, *Global Perspectives*.
[32] Ogilvy, *Confessions*, 155; Preston, *Great American Blow-up*, 259.
[33] Ogilvy, *Confessions*, 155; see Borden, *Economic Effects*, 810.
[34] Borrie, 'UK Self-Regulatory System', ch. 3.   [35] Ibid., table 1, 14–15.

Table 6.1. Breaches of Advertising Standards Authority Code, May 1978

Type of breach	Number	%
1. Truthful presentation of product or company.	47	15
2. Bargain offer claims or prices.	107	34
3. Use of Testimonials.	10	3
4. Use of word "Guarantee".	39	12
5. Medical products.	15	5
6. Absence of specified information	77	24
7. No substantiation provided.	20	6
Total in breach	315	100
Total number of ads	2,993	

Source: Borrie, 'Review of the UK Self-Regulatory System of Advertising Control', table 1, pp. 14–15.

overcome this mistrust, which arose at the adversarial interface of buyer and seller.

Dispelling suspicion

The efficient solution was to establish trust between buyer and seller. Trust turns adversaries into cooperators. It enables the buyer to accept the seller's claim at face value. For the buyer, it reduces uncertainty, and the effort of monitoring and enforcement. It helps to overcome the reluctance to buy. Some people find conflict stressful, and will pay a premium to avoid it.

Given that trust can be efficient as well as agreeable, it has attracted a good deal of analytical and empirical attention.[36] In any single encounter, it pays to take advantage of a trusting protagonist. If the encounters are to be repeated, however, defection will be punished by the withdrawal of trust. As further encounters take place, the experience of trustworthiness builds up into a reputation, into a stock of goodwill. Repetition and reputation, then, are necessary in order to reap the benefits of cooperation. 'Your...dealer counts on your continued business week after week, month after month' says a car battery ad.[37] A 'candid statement on the car owner's problems' (of dubious candour) stated that 'the essential industry need today is for increased confidence and trust between serviceman and

[36] Axelrod, *Evolution of Co-operation*; Taylor, *Possibility of Cooperation*; Gambetta, *Trust*; Ostrom, *Governing the Commons*; Bromley, *Environment and Economy*; Cook, *Trust in Society*; Braithwaite and Levi, *Trust and Governance*.
[37] For Atlas Batteries, *SEP*, 28 Sept. 1957. Not particularly appropriate for a durable.

car owner.'[38] 'The man from Nationwide is on your side.'[39] Salesmanship was partly a matter of winning trust.[40]

Repetition and reputation occur naturally in a face-to-face relationship. Indeed, in this respect advertising is a second-best. Research in the 1930s found that although advertising had already reached a level of about 3 per cent of GDP, for most sectors personal selling costs were 'several times as large' as advertising and promotion costs. A compelling face-to-face interaction with a salesperson was conducive to selling.[41]

Each face is unique and individual. Facial expressions are a pre-verbal form of communication, recognized by babies from the age of a few weeks. A smile, a frown, a scowl, are universal messages, which carry the same meaning in all cultures.[42] The eye's ability to make finely graded qualitative distinctions among different facial expressions is exploited in Chernoff faces, which statisticians use to represent a large spectrum of information using only the curvature and size of the mouth, the length of the nose, the size of the eyes, and the shape of the face. These reduce well, maintaining legibility even with individual areas of 0.05 square inch.[43] The simple smile is the easiest expression to recognize: it can be seen from further away (up to 300 feet) and with briefer exposure, than any other expression. People enjoy looking at most smiles and will reciprocate them even when shown in a photograph.[44] Smiles elicit cooperation, and men respond particularly well (in this respect) to women's smiles.[45] Subliminal presentation of happy faces increased the willingness to pay for a fruit drink.[46]

Facial expressions convey attitudes much better and more concisely than words. They provide an immediate insight into mental states. A smile conveys acceptance, approbation, ease. Non-verbal signals communicate a friendly attitude: proximity, orientation, gaze, facial expression (more smiling), gestures (head nods, lively movements), posture (open with arms stretched towards the other rather than arms on hips or folded)—all of these are cues of acceptance. And confidence of acceptance is the basis of trust. An intriguing idea is that emotive experience has a functional basis. Strong emotions are expressed in the face and in other non-verbal gestures. Such expressions allow individuals to make a good estimate of

[38] For Carter Carburetors, *SEP*, 28 Sept. 1957.
[39] Nationwide Insurance, *Life*, 20 May 1966, 126.
[40] Ch. 5 above; Friedman, *Birth of a Salesman*, 61, 102.
[41] Borden, *Economic Effects*, 61–8 (p. 68 cited), and table 106, p. 444. Also Table 5.1 above.
[42] Ekman *Telling Lies*, 16; Brown, *Human Universals*, 112.
[43] Tufte, *Visual Display*, 96, 142.   [44] Ekman, *Telling Lies*, 145.
[45] Scharlemann et al., 'Value of a Smile'.   [46] Berridge, 'Irrational Pursuits', 19–21.

the trustworthiness of others. The selection of trustworthy partners for cooperative ventures has a survival value, and is thus likely to have been selected by an evolutionary process. The emotions facilitate the creation of trust. They can do so because facial expressions are difficult to fake.[47] It is interesting, however, that it is only the negative emotions (and non-facial cues) that are difficult to fake. False bonhomie is easy to simulate. Most people are confident in their ability to detect it, but in fact do not seem to do so at a rate that is better than chance.[48]

Advertising aims to simulate trust. 'Ayer has a way of creating intimacy with its client's customers... They believe you need to find a way to touch people.'[49] 'Ads Are Like People' was the title of a presentation at J. Walter Thompson's creative forum in July 1966:

People feel a kinship, a sympathy, an identity with other people... other human beings. They do not feel this for a large, impersonal, bloodless corporation.

It stands to reason then, that if an ad can have a warm, human personality, if it can share unashamed, genuine emotion with the viewer, it can set up a feeling of understanding and affection that can be a real asset to an advertiser just as it can for a person.[50]

Another presentation made a similar point: 'Products whose advertising lacks sincerity fail for the same reason insincere people fail. Other people do not trust them.'[51] Advertising simulates the emotional cues of closeness and intimacy, and the cues of non-verbal communication; in particular, it projects a great many faces. This is what I call 'the mask of intimacy'. A wink, for example, is a concise arrow of intimacy, a one-bit affirmation. There she is, 'The sassy one from Canada Dry', a fetching woman in her twenties, winking at the reader with the puff, 'You'll come up a winner with Wink' (a soft drink).[52] This was probably too brassy, since winks are not in common use, and the soft drink has not survived.

To simulate interpersonal relationship, the prime device in advertising is the testimonial. Often what this means is simply to project a face (Figure 6.1). A statement coming from a friendly face is accorded a friendly reception. Testimonials fall into several groups. One is the expert testimonial. A series of classical experiments by the psychologist Stanley Milgram suggested that a majority of ordinary Americans would cast aside

[47] Frank, *Passions within Reason*, chs. 5–6.   [48] Ekman, *Telling Lies*, 35, 48, 86.

[49] Anon., 'Ayer at 125', p. A–6.

[50] Chip Meads, 'Ads Are Like People', JWT, Creative Forum no. 2, July 1966, fo. 3; Speeches and Writings, Creative Forum Papers, JWT papers, Hartman Center, Duke University.

[51] Robert Westerfield, 'Style in Advertising' (29 Dec. 1966), Speeches and Writings, Creative Forum Papers no. 11, JWT papers, Hartman Center, Duke University.

[52] Canada Dry, *Life* (20 May 1966), inside back cover.

The smile that wins is the Pepsodent Smile!

Patricia Wolcott, Young Matron, made Little Theater history in Scarsdale, N. Y., recently when she was awarded the leading rôle in the Fort Hill Players' production, "Years Ago." A newcomer to the amateur stage, she stole the show during tryouts for the part of the beautiful heroine . . . and her subsequent performance won the acclaim of the community. But Patricia's favorite role is wife and mother. She's married to her high school sweetheart . . . has a two year old daughter. Patricia's smile, so dazzling behind the footlights, is sparkling in real life, too. It's a Pepsodent Smile! "I've always depended on Pepsodent Tooth Paste to keep my teeth bright," she says. "Besides, I love its taste!"

Wins 3 to 1
over any other tooth paste!

Fig. 6.1. 'The smile that wins'
Source: Better Homes and Gardens (Sept. 1948), 7.

their self-proclaimed ethical values in obedience to men in white coats.[53] Hence doctors were often recruited to provide testimonials. 'Doctors Warn You: "Harsh toilet papers are dangerous".' It sounds like a joke, but is taken from a real ad.[54] The classic instance was J. Walter Thompson's campaign which established Fleischmann's Yeast as a health food, using medical testimonials. The product had no genuine health benefits, so American doctors were barred from promoting it by professional ethics. The agency recruited European doctors instead.[55] Doctors testified widely to the

[53] Milgram, *Obedience to Authority*, esp. ch. 3.
[54] Scott Paper Company, *Good Housekeeping* (Apr. 1928), 177. Copy in JWT, Wallace Elton Papers, Oversize 4, Hartman Center, Duke University.
[55] 'George Butler Remembers', JWT archives, London 1925–62, Hartman Center, Duke University; Levenstein, *Revolution at the Table*, 153, 159, 197–8.

benefits of cigarettes.[56] When testimonies could not be had, a white-coated figure would suffice.[57] Celebrities offered another class of testimonial. Ed Sullivan, the popular broadcaster, proclaimed 'Chesterfield is best for YOU!' For good measure, he also reported 'scientific evidence' from a medical specialist, observing 'no adverse effects...from smoking Chesterfield'.[58] David Ogilvy paid the President's widow Eleanor Roosevelt $35,000 to tell television viewers that 'the new Good Luck margarine really tastes delicious'.[59] If trust is based on reputation, then with celebrity endorsement, the advertiser buys a ready-made reputation to associate with the product.

Even more common, and certainly cheaper, is the ordinary testimonial. A Sylvania Television ad ('Halolight: The Frame of Light That's Kinder to your Eyes') is framed by eighteen passport-type photos of named 'ordinary' people, from locations all over the country, each providing a rather implausible personal testimonial (e.g. 'Day or night, HALOLIGHT makes the Sylvania picture wonderfully clear and restful to watch').[60] Such testimonials were often bogus.[61] Others were acquired as entries in prize competitions. Testimonialists received substantial sums, e.g. $25 in 1931, rather more than a weekly manual wage.[62] The face of 'Betty Crocker' ('I guarantee a perfect* cake every time you bake'), was invented, her fictional character part of the 'personality' of the brand.[63] Even more common is the anonymous endorsement, a nameless face, in colour or black and white, in photograph, painting or drawing, gazing intently and candidly at the viewer and communicating a friendly message. Sometimes, in radio or television, it is merely a disembodied voice. Often, when the appeal takes some other form, a face or facelet is thrown in as well. Advertisers call this 'touching all bases'.[64]

Faces are ubiquitous in the advertising of the 1940s and the 1950s. A convenience sample of 1,128 ads between 1946 and 1966 indicates that about two-thirds of display ads in general circulation and women's

---

[56] Pollay, 'Promotion and Policy', 5; id., 'Chronological Notes on the Promotion of Cigarettes', 3, 7.   [57] Viceroy ad, Schofield, *Top Copy Writers*, 95.

[58] *SEP*, 7 Feb. 1953, back cover.   [59] Ogilvy, *Ogilvy on Advertising*, 109.

[60] *SEP*, 7 Feb. 1953, p. 106.

[61] e.g. paper by F. A. Bell, 'Legal Pitfalls' (11 Oct. 1934), describing two instances indicating routine use of bogus testimonials, JWT Staff Meetings, box 6/4, Hartman Center, Duke University.

[62] Letter to Arthur Ritter from JWT, 2 Dec. 1931, JWT Inactive Accounts, box 18, History of Fleischmann Yeast Account, JWT papers, Hartman Center, Duke University.

[63] General Mills ad, *Ladies Home Journal* (Feb. 1956), 45. The small print reads '*PERFECT? Yes, we DO mean perfect,' followed by a money-back guarantee.

[64] e.g., ad for One-Dollar Book Club, *Ladies Home Journal* (Feb. 1956), 9; Seldin, *Golden Fleece*, 185.

magazines used 'face-appeal' as a basic form of endorsement. This theme of trust runs right through advertising literature. And yet, for all the resources at its command, advertising has little awareness of its own methods: a speaker at a J. Walter Thompson seminar stated, with no fear of contradiction, 'Communication is not an exact science and advertising is simply communication between people. Mass communication, to be sure. But still, just people talking to people.'[65] The first academic collection on non-verbal communication in advertising managed to overlook entirely the pervasive use of faces as a form of non-verbal endorsement.[66]

Some ads draw the viewer into a more complex web of personal interaction. During the 1950s, the decade of domesticity, family themes abounded. Childhood and its *rites de passage* was another abiding theme, much favoured by Kodak, the film company, and by Hamilton, the watch company.[67] The 1960s added youth bonding. 'The Pepsi Generation' campaign, starting in the early 1960s, identified the soft drink with peer approbation and acceptance. Two young women in bikinis, big smiles, recline on a dinghy in one ad. Two muscular young men cling to the raft in the green water. Two six-packs of Pepsi sweat on the rubber. The campaign struck a chord, and helped Pepsi to catch up with the market leader, Coca-Cola.[68] Romance and sexual attraction are ubiquitous in advertising.

Table 6.2. Faces in magazine display advertisements, c.1946–1966

Periodical	Date	Pages	Ads	Faces	No faces	% Faces
Saturday Evening Post	07-Sep-46	168	129	90	39	70
McCall's	01-May-47	176	135	108	27	80
Better Homes & Gardens	01-Sep-48	262	232	179	53	77
Saturday Evening Post	07-Feb-53	120	68	48	20	71
Ladies' Home Journal	01-Feb-56	178	121	73	48	60
Saturday Evening Post	28-Feb-57	176	127	96	31	76
Ladies' Home Journal	01-Apr-57	134	88	65	23	74
Saturday Evening Post	30-Jan-60	96	43	24	19	56
Ladies' Home Journal	01-Mar-62	138	66	29	37	44
Saturday Evening Post	15-Jan-66	80	27	17	10	63
Life	20-May-66	130	92	60	32	65
TOTAL		1,658	1,128	789	339	67

Source: Convenience sample.

[65] Meads, 'Ads are Like People', fo. 2. (above, n. 50).
[66] Hecker and Stewart, *Nonverbal Communication*.
[67] The family in American advertising, Belk and Pollay, 'Images of Ourselves'.
[68] e.g. Pepsi-Cola, *Life* (20 May 1966); Tedlow, *New and Improved*, 371; the salience of 'person' ads during the 1940s and 1950s, and the subsequent shift to 'lifestyle' ads is documented in Leiss et al., *Social Communication in Advertising*, 274–84.

Fig. 6.2. 'Long lean and packed with punch!' (Automobile advertisement, Nov. 1956.)
Source: Hartman Center Duke University, JWT papers, Wallace Elton Collection, box 3.

They are mocked in a Volkswagen ad, which shows two beauties curled on a car bonnet, and asks 'Why don't they ever sit on a Volkswagen?'[69] In a Ford ad of 1956, a tall cowboy is pointing the way to an adoring woman driver over the slogan 'long, lean and packed with punch' (Fig. 6.2).[70]

From the 1960s onwards television increasingly took over from magazines as the main advertising medium. As the old static formulas began to jade, advertisers increasingly sought novelty and visual surprise. This was the 'creative revolution', originating in London in the late 1960s, in which an inventive and creative post-modern mix of arousal and enticement attempted to capture the fragmentation of experience and values in the 1970s and 1980s.[71] But the theme of interpersonal trust is a hardy

[69] *Design and Art Direction*, 71 (1971), 46.
[70] Ford, *Better Homes and Gardens* (Nov. 1956), ad. no. 1712-A, Wallace Elton papers, outsize box 3, Hartman Center, Duke University.
[71] Goldman, *Reading Ads Socially*; Whitwell, *Making the Market*.

perennial, and a random trawl in current advertising shows no lack of effort to simulate the bonds of interpersonal obligation. An infant is shown sucking at a breast, which is also bisected by a spiralling black telephone cord. The copy says, 'when you breastfeed, you create an important bond with your child; when you talk to First Direct [a telephone-based bank], you're treated as a person, not a number.' A highlighted slogan declares, 'humanity in a bank'.[72]

Advertising tries to simulate the gift relationship in the market economy.[73] A 'gift' is an exchange in which a transfer is not mediated by price, but is rather reciprocated at the discretion of the receiver. It is driven by the pursuit of 'regard', i.e. the quest for approbation, and the intrinsic benefits of social and personal interaction. Gifts are used to personalize the exchange, and to authenticate regard. In contrast, a market transaction is impersonal and is mediated by a money price. Reciprocal gifting gives rise to obligation; the gift survives on a surprisingly large scale in interpersonal exchange. It does so where there are few economies of scale. The market is not a good provider of authentic regard, but when standard commodities have to be sold, prices are an efficient and parsimonious method of coordination and exchange.[74]

Face-to-face relationship cannot be mass produced. But advertising has used the technologies of mass reproduction to simulate (as best it could) the cues of regard. Hence the predominance of interpersonal and obligation cues in advertising, and the normal absence of price information in national media advertising. Where price information is included, it is usually misleading, e.g. the marked-up 'list price'. This allows vendors to escape the market's 'law of one price', and to invite viewers to form their own estimation of 'use value', which individual retailers will attempt to match with a customized 'exchange value'. A slogan of this kind is 'Diamonds are forever', invented by Ayer for De Beers; it captures precisely the subjectivity and obligation implicit in the gift relation.[75] Advertising in the second half of the twentieth century was as much a form of mass production as the commodities it advertised, borne by economies of scale in media communications. As information became cheaper, marketers attempted to narrow their focus, and even to collect information about individual clients, in so-called 'database marketing'. Procter & Gamble sent 'individualized' birthday cards for babies, and reminder letters to move up to the next size of disposable diapers.[76] The goal was to target the

---

[72] First Direct, *The Guardian* (8 Feb. 1995), 9.
[73] Chapter 5 above. Also Schudson, *Advertising*, 135–43.
[74] This is the argument of Chapter 5, above.   [75] 'Ayer at 125', p. A6.
[76] *Economist*, 'Junk Mail into a Goldmine'.

smallest possible market niche—the individual—in order to simulate a personal relationship between sellers and buyers. Customers are increasingly exposed to sales pitches disguised as personal communications.[77] The mass production of advertising described in this chapter is also being undermined by the ability to target consumers precisely over the internet.

Advertising, art, and editorial

Artists also practice deception, and invite us to suspend disbelief, to put ourselves, if only momentarily, in their hands, in the quest for a deeper truth. Art is assumed to possess integrity. Occasionally advertisers make use of well-known artists in their work. A Renault car is parked on the polished wooden floor of an art gallery, while a man (the owner?) contemplates Gainsborough's painting of Mr and Mrs Andrews, sitting under an oak tree framed by their broad acres. The copy says 'A PRIVATE VIEW, A STUDY IN REFINEMENT.'[78] Most commercial art is anonymous, however. It remains art nonetheless, and very distinct from photography (which in advertising has also striven increasingly for artistic effect). The illustrators of Ford car ads in the 1940s were paid upwards of 1,000 dollars for a colour illustration, at a time when a new car cost little more.[79] It is doubtful whether many 'pure' artists could command this kind of fee.

In its quest for credibility, advertising has sought to appropriate credible art. A prime example is Norman Rockwell. Between the 1920s and the 1960s, Rockwell presented a series of images of an idealized small-town America; almost invariably, his illustrations have a charming 'human touch', a sympathetic personal interaction or experience. On the covers of the *Saturday Evening Post* they gave Americans a picture of themselves as a community: they touched on childhood, young love, home and family, the past, Americans in uniform, at work, at play, American faces and the ultimate gifting occasion, Christmas.[80] Rockwell supplied his corny vignettes indiscriminately to editors and advertisers alike.[81] Indeed, he was not always clear in his mind about the distinction between the two. In 1946 and 1947 he wrote to Ford's advertising agents, J. Walter Thompson, proposing to include a Ford automobile in a *Saturday Evening Post* cover, in

[77] Anon., 'Database Marketing'; personal experience. Barclays Insurance Services Company to A. Ofer, April 1993.   [78] Renault, *Independent on Sunday* (20 June 1993), 12–13.
[79] Walter Elton to George Strouse, 11 July 1946, Elton papers, JWT papers, Hartman Center, Duke University; Elton to Strouse, 11 Oct. 1946, ibid.
[80] Based on the chapter headings in Finch, *Norman Rockwell's America*; Marling, *Norman Rockwell*.   [81] Stoltz, *Advertising World of Norman Rockwell*.

return for a Ford station wagon. Cars were scarce at the time, and Ford had no trouble selling them. The offer was turned down.[82]

Advertising's search for credibility is highlighted by its relations with the media, and with the press in particular. The vast bulk of advertising expenditure (typically more than 90 per cent) was on space in editorial media.[83] For its part, most editorial media (both broadcast and printed) depended on advertising. It is a convention that advertising is strictly demarcated from editorial. Advertising is not normally arresting in itself, except for those already contemplating a purchase. For all their acquisitiveness, most people, most of the time, care for their relation to people, for civic, social, political, and cultural affairs, at least as much as for the price and quality of goods. To attract their attention, faith in editorial copy is vital. Editorial material provides the bread of credibility in the advertising sandwich.[84] This boundary is respected by advertisers, because of its value to readers. But the brighter the boundary, the more tempting it is for advertisers to free ride and exploit editorial material for their own purposes.

In 1959 Ford launched the first of its compact cars, the Falcon.[85] It was introduced in response to a buyer revolt against the Detroit 'dinosaurs', the staple cars which had reached a height of extravagance in the previous two years. To underline the message of return to basic values, and especially honesty, the JWT agency signed up Charles Schultz, creator of the 'Peanuts' cartoon series. Charlie Brown, Lucy, Snoopy, and their friends applied their wry homespun 'such is life' wisdom to promoting Ford cars. The account executive explained that 'the Peanuts strip has never been commercialized in an extensive or undesirable way...We have been careful to keep the Peanuts people in character so that references to Ford products will be made in terms of Schultz's philosophy.'[86]

This provoked a debate at the cartoonists association, the 'Newspaper Comics Council', on the intermingling of culture and commerce. Phil Porter's opening presentation was 'How Greedy Can You Get?' Other artists shared his outrage, but found it difficult to support with good

[82] Walter Elton to O'Neill Ryan, 21 Mar. 1946; George Strouse to Elton, 2 Apr. 1946; Walter Elton to Norman Rockwell, 5 Apr. 1946, Walter Elton papers box 5, JWT papers, Hartman Center, Duke University.

[83] Excluding direct mail. In the UK between 1970 and 1992 it averaged 67 per cent on press advertising, and 27 per cent on TV (*Advertising Statistics Yearbook 1993*, table 4.1.2, p. 22). In 1982, direct advertising accounted for about 9 per cent of UK advertising (International Advertising Association, *World Advertising Expenditures 1982*, table 8, pp. 24–5). The American ratio of television to print was rather higher in 1982, standing at 0.6, compared with the British 0.41 (ibid.).   [84] See also Becker, 'Simple Theory of Advertising', 961.

[85] This episode described below, Ch. 10.

[86] W. Elton to Philip Filhaber, 5 Apr. 1960, Wallace W. Elton Papers, JWT papers, Box 10, Hartman Center, Duke University.

reasoning. Two arguments emerged; both of them accused Schultz of free riding. One set of speakers simply objected to breaking the boundary between editorial and advertising. Any sharing of content with advertising was bound to undermine editorial integrity.

The advertisers are buying names, that's all. Just as they buy names of ball players—and faces too—for razor ads, or auto and cigarette ads. Let them buy these testimonials if they wish. We know that many of them are as phoney as a $3 bill, for some of the athletes don't smoke or are too young to shave. But let's not carry this thing into the holy of holies. Isn't there anything left for the reader these days, without a built-in commercial?[87]

An editor chipped in, 'The battle to convince the public that news content is a pure and undefiled area has been made increasingly difficult by TV formats which allow the advertiser to control the content of the show.'[88]

For other speakers what was at stake was not only the public commons of the editorial side of the media, but also a much larger one, the commons of shared culture, in which these cartoon characters stood for emotional integrity.

Let them leave the characters we love alone. Our feelings about 'Peanuts', 'Blondie', 'Beetle Bailey' and 'Dick Tracy' are inextricably tied up with long standing mental associations deep inside each of us. Association with countless happy moments derived from reading our newspapers is what we want, not an association with motor cars, hair tonics, or underarm deodorants. 'Little Lulu' was once a character loveable for traits that certainly weren't related to Kleenex. I can't help but wonder just how much she was hurt by subconscious association with a runny nose.[89]

Another editor said, 'those wonderful kids ought to stay out of the automobile selling racket,'[90] and others spoke in the same vein. But Schultz found some defenders too. One of them argued that editorial integrity was itself merely a marketing vehicle: 'Newspaper publishers are in business for just one reason—to deliver a big, responsive audience to advertisers. This determines whether you remain in business or close your doors.'[91]

Ford also used its own (rather effective) comic strips to convey little homely stories about the purchase decisions of its pick-up trucks. By drawing on common culture, familiar cultural artefacts, and artistic expression, advertising will capture anything that has emotive power.

---

[87] 'Open discussion of secondary rights to comics', Newspaper Comics Council meeting, 5 Feb. 1960, fo. 3. Wallace W. Elton Papers, JWT papers, Box 10.   [88] Ibid., Bill Steven, fo. 6.
[89] Ibid., William Hill, fo. 4.   [90] Ibid., Garry Byrnes, fo. 5.
[91] Ibid., Maurice T. Reilly, fo. 11.

In consequence, the boundary between art and commerce, especially in the United States, has become blurred; commercial products, cars, soft drinks, pervade the country's common culture. Coca-Cola was as much a national symbol as the Stars and Stripes.[92] Art strives to touch the sources of emotion, and finds them in its immediate environment. In a testimony to the power of advertising, by the 1960s artists were returning the compliment. Andy Warhol filled canvasses with cans of Campbell's soup, bottles of Coca-Cola, boxes of Brillo. These banal images excited a surge of recognition, and made him the best known New York artist of the 1960s.[93]

Press and television editors, while no doubt guilty of other forms of excess, take pride in their credibility, which is demarcated from advertising by well-kept fences. No wonder that advertisers yearn to release their cows into the other side. Sometimes a cow will jump the fence on its own: advertisements appear that pretend to be editorial (or sometimes fiction). By convention, they carry a warning.[94] Advertisers sometimes attempt to influence editorial policy.[95] Television, film, even children's books are littered with 'product placements', in which the camera has been paid to linger over commodities and their logos.[96] More important is the practice of public relations. Its purpose is to insinuate the marketing message directly into editorial media. This can be cheaper than buying space, but the greatest attraction is that viewer defences are down when reading editorial material. Public relations is a big enterprise. Unlike advertising, it extends well beyond the commercial world and a good deal of it is undertaken by in-house corporate practitioners.[97]

Costs and benefits

If advertisers choose to play loose with the truth, the effect is primarily harmful to themselves. Advertising has low credibility. Many of its gambits are transparent. American respondents in the 1930s expressed a strong distrust of advertising, repeated in two surveys in 1969 and 1990.[98] In a European Commission survey (1975), 67 per cent of respondents agreed that much of advertising was misleading. In a French government survey

---

[92] Fox, *Madison Avenue Goes to War*, 78.   [93] e.g. Honnef, *Andy Warhol*.

[94] 'Mountain Rescue—A True Short Story . . .' an ad masquerading as a short story, reproduced in Schofield, *100 Top Copy Writers*, 131.

[95] 'Do Advertisers Often Try to Alter Editorial Policy?', *Campaign* (17 Sept. 1993), 17.

[96] Neer, 'Product Placement'.   [97] Ross, *Image Merchants*; Ewen, *PR!*

[98] Borden, *Economic Effects*, ch. 26; Reader's Digest Assocation, *Eurodata*, table 63, pp. 186–7, table 300, 466–9.

in 1979, 66 per cent said that advertising tends to mislead.[99] Even children know that advertising deceives.[100] This is not inconsistent with the repertoire of persuasion and deception described before. At the level of reason, advertising is distrusted. Hence the importance, for advertisers, of bypassing the filter of reason. This accounts for our curious reaction: we know that we are being misled, and yet we find it compelling.

The longest-standing economic arguments both for and against advertising revolve around a single idea. On the one hand, it is said, advertising diffuses information about goods, which makes them attractive to more people. With more people buying, it is possible to achieve economies of scale, and these economies of scale reduce the price of the good. On the other hand, there is no compulsion on successful advertisers to share their efficiency gains with the public; indeed, the more successful they are, the more of the market they capture, the higher the barriers to competition. There has been much research on the subject, and both supporters and critics have been vindicated empirically, but it is only natural to assume that advertising should cost less than its benefits at some times and places, and more at others.

Is advertising, however, a precondition of an affluent society? Is it vital in order to achieve modern levels of income and output? Some clues are provided by comparison of advertising outlays in different countries. The United States spent more than 3 per cent of its GNP on advertising and promotion for most years from the 1900s to the 1930s, and more than 2 per cent since then.[101] Among the advanced industrial countries, the level of outlay on advertising has varied by a factor of three or more. Figure 6.3 compares advertising expenditure since the late 1960s in six industrial countries. The United States was well ahead of the other affluent societies, and spent more than twice as much as any of the others, except for Britain. Nor are the levels negligible. The percentage of national income spent just on advertising in the United States in 1971 was about one-quarter of the outlay on education at all levels.[102]

During this period several of the countries involved closed the income and productivity gap with the United States; at various times Sweden, Japan, and Germany matched or exceeded United States income levels. It was possible for them to catch up with the United States, without laying

[99] Business International SA, *Europe's Consumer Movement*, p. II–69.

[100] Schudson, *Advertising*, 110.

[101] Pease, *Responsibilities of American Advertising*, 13–14; International Research Associates, *Advertising Expenditures around the World* (1960–).

[102] United States Bureau of Census, *Social Indicators III*, table 6/6, p. 290.

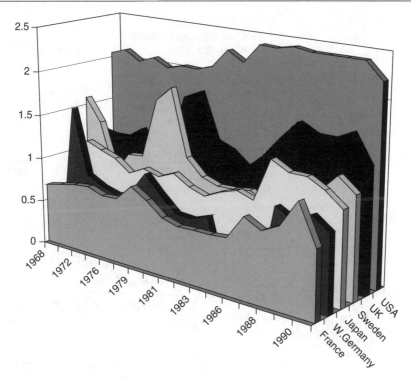

Fig. 6.3. Advertising as percentage of GDP in six different developed countries, 1968–1995

Source: International Advertising Association and Starch Inra Hooper, Inc., *Survey of World Advertising Expenditures* (1968–).

out comparable resources on advertising. Figure 6.4 extends the comparison (at two points in time) to large international samples, in terms of the relation between GNP per head and advertising outlays. Economic activity moves out of the household and into the market as disposable income increases, and as the number of goods and volume of market transactions rise, as literacy and numeracy expand, more market information is required, and mass persuasion becomes more effective. But the now-familiar curvilinear relation between income and social indicators fades away at less than one-third of the maximum income.

In developed economies, economic performance does not depend on advertising. Countries at a comparable level of economic growth devoted different shares of national income to advertising. The United States was an outlier, consistently devoting 2 per cent or more of national income. Other English-speaking countries, Australia, Canada, and the UK

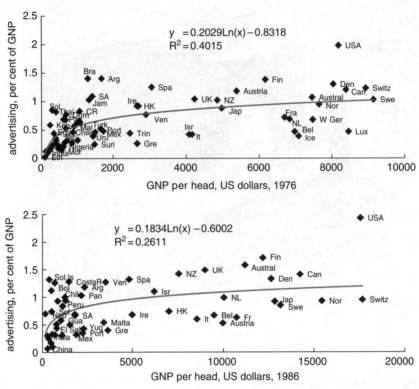

Fig. 6.4. Advertising as a percentage of national income and GNP per head, 1976 and 1986

Sources: International Advertising Association and Inra Hooper, Inc., *Survey of World Advertising Expenditures*; World Bank (International Bank for Reconstruction and Development).

occupied an intermediate position, with approximately 1 per cent. Strong European economies (France, Germany, Netherlands, Belgium) devoted a much lower proportion of GNP to advertising; and the Japanese also kept advertising well below 1 per cent of national income. The proportion of resources devoted to advertising has been relatively constant in the different countries during the post-war years, so that the absolute level of economic activity does not explain the share of advertising. In the 1960s, when the United States was as wealthy as Germany or the UK in the 1990s, it still spent a higher proportion of its resources on advertising. Business culture and the broader cultures of different societies appear to determine different levels of advertising intensity. Given that the United States is both the highest spender in terms of national income, and also the largest economy, advertising is dominantly an American institution.

In 1980, for example, US outlays on advertising formed almost half (47 per cent) of world outlays.[103]

Advertising uses the resources of credibility in order to transmit a message that is often deceptive. In using these resources, does advertising also use them up? Where does credibility come from? Robert Frank suggests that mankind is 'wired' for trust; that there is an innate capacity for trust which is facilitated by the emotions, just as linguists assume an innate capacity for language.[104] If that is the case, then advertising is unlikely to cause permanent damage, since the capacity to form trusting relations is a renewable resource. Another view is that the capacity for trust has to be nurtured and learned. There is some empirical evidence for this. The European Values Survey in 1981–4 presented large samples of people in several countries with the following statement: 'speaking generally, other people can be trusted'. It then invited them to rate this statement as true or untrue. Replies aligned along a clear gradient, interpersonal trust rising with affluence. Three groups can be distinguished: Catholic countries, and poor as well as recently poor countries rate low on interpersonal trust, regardless of income. English-speaking countries occupy an intermediate position. The Nordic countries, on the whole, show the highest levels of trust. The data are shown in Figure 6.5.

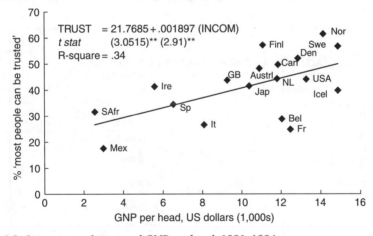

Fig. 6.5. Interpersonal trust and GNP per head, 1981–1984

Notes: Variables in equation: TRUST = percentage replying 'most people can be trusted'. INCOM = GNP per head, 1981.

Source: European Values Survey, 1981–1984; World Bank.

[103] International Research Associates, *Advertising Expenditures around the World, 16th Survey*, table 1, 13–14.   [104] Frank, *Passions within Reason*.

Is it possible, however, that by 'grazing' the commons of interpersonal trust and the common culture, advertising also actively degrades these resources? That it diminishes the value of intangible but valuable public goods, and especially the resources of interpersonal trust? Could it be that by drawing on the resources of interpersonal trust for commercial competition, advertising diminishes the capacity of society to engage in collective action, for both private and public ends?

Figure 6.6 shows that advertising outlay is correlated with interpersonal trust, controlling for income (which is not significant). On the face of it, this suggests that advertising is more effective the higher the level of interpersonal trust: that advertising is exploiting the credibility of inter-personal discourse in order to interpolate its messages, that advertising is less attractive where mistrust is rife. The countries towards the bottom-right corner, which have high levels of trust and low levels of advertising, all operate fairly rigorous controls on advertising, seeking perhaps to protect their gullible citizens.

At the end of the 1950s trust was low in the war-defeated countries, Italy and Germany, lower even than in the poor country, Mexico. Subsequently, as Italian and German societies overcame the trauma of war and experienced rapid economic growth, their social cohesion appears to have improved. Starting at a much higher level, the two English-speaking

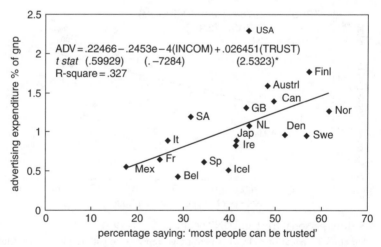

Fig. 6.6. Advertising expenditure and interpersonal trust

Notes: Variables in equation: ADV = advertising expenditure as percentage of GNP; INCOM = income per head in 1981; TRUST = percentage replying 'most people can be trusted'.

Sources: European Values Survey data, 1981–4; International Advertising Association and Starch Inra Hooper, Inc., *Survey of World Advertising Expenditures* (1981).

countries (UK and USA) have experienced quite substantial declines, partly corrected in the latter. A longitudinal survey of interpersonal trust in the United States between 1972 and 1989 found the percentage agreeing that 'most people could be trusted' hovering between 48 and 37 per cent, with a weak downwards trend.[105]

It is tempting to associate the decline of interpersonal trust with massive exposure to television. In both Britain and the United States, the 1960s are the decade in which household television saturation was completed, both in terms of households equipped with television, and in terms of hours spent in front of the box. In terms of time use, television came to dominate leisure hours, with people spending an average of 20 to 35 hours a week in front of the box, depending on social class. Television has a much larger transmission capacity ('bandwidth') than print, and achieved far greater viewer attention.[106]

Robert Putnam has measured the stock of 'social capital' in the United States, using the General Social Survey, for the years 1972–94. He has measured two variables in particular, membership of voluntary groups, and responses to the statement 'most people can be trusted', which we have also used above. He has found a net decline since the early 1970s of voluntary group membership by about 15–20 per cent, and of trust by about 20–25 per cent.[107] The most powerful differentiator (apart from education), was birth cohort. The members of cohorts which turned 18 between the 1920s and the 1950s expressed positive trust at levels of between 50 and 60 per cent. Thereafter, there was a very sharp drop, with the latest cohort ('turned 18 in the 1970s') having a level of trust of between 20 and 30 per cent.[108] Similar patterns (at different levels) were found for voting turnout, newspaper readership, and group membership. The result was controlled for education and life-cycle effects, and is thus quite robust. As Putnam points out, the downturn coincided with 'the television generation', the first cohorts fully exposed to television. Furthermore, voluntary group membership was also found to vary inversely and strongly with hours of television viewing (and positively with education and newspaper readership). As television viewing increased, newspaper readership declined, especially among the younger cohorts. Television viewing is associated with 'materialism', a high ranking for acquisitive preferences. Materialism in its turn is associated with

---

[105] Wood, *American Profile*, 323 ff. I owe this reference to Robert Lane.
[106] The uptake of television is described in detail below, Ch. 8.
[107] Putnam, 'Tuning In', 668.; id., *Bowling Alone*, 140–41.
[108] Putnam, 'Tuning In', 675; also Ch.14, below.

Table 6.3. Confidence in leadership in the United States, 1966–1986 (% stating that they have a great deal of confidence in)

Institution	1986	1973	1966
The military	36	40	61
Higher education	34	44	61
Medicine	33	57	73
Supreme Court	32	33	50
TV news	27	41	
Religion	22	36	41
Congress	21		42
Local govt.	21	28	
The press	19	30	29
White House	19	18	
State govt.	19	24	
Federal govt.	18	19	41
Major companies	16	29	55
Law firms	14	24	
Trade Unions	11	20	22

Source: Harris Polls, cited by Blumberg, *Predatory Society*, table 11.2, p. 204.

frustration and lower well-being.[109] Putnam notes substantial evidence that television viewing is associated with misanthropy, with a 'mean world view'. But he did not consider the corrosive effect of advertising.[110]

Quite separately, there is also considerable evidence of the decline of trust in authority in the United States. Table 6.3 indicates the decline in the reputation of the main sources of social and political authority in American society since the 1960s. Typically the percentage expressing a great deal of confidence in leadership declined by approximately one-half between the 1960s and the 1980s, and both government and politicians are rated low. Other sources have measured similar indicators of decline in authority, much of it taking place from the 1960s to the 1970s.[111] Similar expressions of distrust could be found in the United Kingdom.[112] Recent studies indicate that the decline of trust in government has swept through all developed countries. The trend started during the 1960s, and is strong everywhere, though apparently strongest in the United States. In more detail, the decline is stronger among the young and among the educated. One of the biggest social trends of the post-war period is the rise in education.[113] Another universal trend is the mass diffusion of commercial television all over the developed world. As the level of education has risen, the intelligence of viewers has been increasingly challenged. Educated

[109] Kasser et al., 'Materialistic Values', 17; James, *Britain on the Couch*, 104–7.
[110] Putnam, 'Tuning In', 678–9, amplified in detail in Putnam, *Bowling Alone*, e.g. chs. 8, 13.
[111] e.g. Yankelovich, *New Rules*, 184–6; Abramowitz, 'Political Culture under Stress', 188–96.
[112] Kavanagh, 'Political Culture', 145–7.   [113] Below, Ch. 11, Figs. 11.1, 11.5.

viewers have lower tolerance for television. The decline of trust continues to baffle political scientists.[114] There is a hypothesis waiting to be tested: that disillusion with authority on the part of the young and educated has been driven by the insults to intelligence presented by commercial and political spin on television.

Several developments made leadership a more intractable challenge in the post-1960s period. To mention some of them, the stagnation of real incomes, structural change in the economy, rising crime and social disintegration, and in the United States, the failure in Vietnam. But some of these changes might themselves be regarded as products of the failure of authority (and of social cooperation), rather than as exogenous, independent forces. In all of this, the influence of advertising in undermining general trust cannot be ruled out.

Ever since Dwight Eisenhower's first presidential campaign in 1952, marketing experts have increasingly controlled the format of American electoral campaigns. As David Ogilvy tells it:

In 1952 my old friend Rosser Reeves advertised General Eisenhower as if he were a tube of toothpaste. He created fifty commercials in which the General was made to read out hand-lettered answers to a series of phony questions from imaginary citizens. Like this,

Citizen: 'Mr. Eisenhower, what about the high cost of living?'

General: 'My wife Mamie worries about the same thing. Tell her it's our job to change that on November 14th.'

Between takes the General was heard to say, 'To think that an old soldier should come to this.'[115]

The marketing of politics in the United States was stimulated enormously by the onset of television. Political campaigning adapted to the television commercial format. The high cost of air time has inflated the price of political campaigning in the United States, and has raised the barriers to entry substantially.[116] The campaign itself was constrained by a format of thirty- or sixty-second 'spot' commercials. Political campaigning has thus adopted many of the attributes of commercial advertising: a slick, mass appeal image, the use of jingles and puffs, and short, punchy 'soundbites'.[117]

Jimmy Carter's presidential campaign commercial of 1976 was all faces and authenticity. 'My children will be the sixth generation on the same

[114] Dalton, 'Social Transformation of Trust'.   [115] Ogilvy, *Confessions*, 156–7.

[116] O'Shaughnessy, *Political Marketing*, 47.

[117] Kern, *30-Second Politics*; Biocca, *Television and Political Advertising*; Castleman and Poradzik, *Watching TV*; O'Shaughnessy, *Political Marketing*; Diamond and Bates, *The Spot*.

land'; 'We've always worked for a living. We know what it means to work'; 'I'll never tell a lie. I'll never make a misleading statement.' For all we know, Carter may have believed his lines, but they fall into a common advertising genre, 'the only straight player in the business'.[118] Carter's projected honesty was no match for the radiance of a real actor, Ronald Reagan, whose 'Morning in America' pitch evoked all the homely feel-good themes of margarine pretending to be butter. The Reagan presidency became a 'permanent campaign'.[119]

Political campaigning in America acquired both the benefits and the negative associations of marketing and advertising in general. The main benefit was in compelling attention, by means of a vast amplification of the cues of directness and intimacy. The drawback was that, on the face of it, the credibility of political leaders declined to the low levels associated with commercial advertisers. Clinton, Blair, Bush all have the rugged, sculpted looks of advertising models, and Schwarzenegger was the second movie action man elected as governor of California.

Even some of the greatest stalwarts of advertising have their doubts about its application in politics. John O'Toole, president of the International Association of Advertising, was on the campaign team for Nixon in 1972 and Reagan in 1980. He took a permissive view of advertising as a whole, but regarded political advertising as a violation of an implicit contract with consumers. Towards the end of a campaign, he wrote, the temptation to lie was overwhelming. He advocated limits on the candidates' television time.[120] Another advertising practitioner concluded a book entitled *The Duping of the American Voter* with the statement that political commercials of the 1960s and the 1970s were 'the most deceptive, misleading, unfair and untruthful of all advertising . . . the sky is the limit with regard to what can be said, what can be promised, what accusations can be made, what lies can be told.'[121] David Ogilvy, the best-known advertiser of the 1960s and 1970s, wrote that 'In a period when television commercials are often the decisive factor in deciding who shall be the next President of the United States, dishonest advertising is as evil as stuffing the ballot box.'[122]

These honest advertisers have identified the social issue which arises from mass-media advertising. It is not so much the deception itself, which is widespread in human discourse.[123] Rather advertising in general, and

---

[118] 1976: Ford vs. Carter, in Diamond and Bates, *The Spot*, 238–9.

[119] O'Shaughnessy, *Political Marketing*, ch. 9.

[120] O'Toole, *Trouble with Advertising*, 37–9.

[121] Spero, *Duping*, cited by Ogilvy, *Ogilvy on Advertising*, 211.

[122] Ogilvy, *Ogilvy on Advertising*, 213.   [123] Nyberg, *Varnished Truth*.

political advertising in particular, by legitimizing deception by social authority undermines that very authority, and contaminates the trust that is necessary for compliance. These preceding paragraphs on political advertising were first published in 1996, and have been left here largely unrevised. The analysis was vindicated during the decade that followed. The use of focus groups and of news manipulating 'spin' may have helped to micro-manage political discourse, and reached their spectacular climax in the events surrounding the war in Iraq. Disillusion, indeed disgust with politics and politicians rose higher than it has ever been since the 1960s.[124]

Regulation

Mistrust of advertising is not restricted to social critics. Affluent societies have taken a variety of measures to protect their citizens. These measures provide us with a sense of the guiding values of different business, social, and political cultures.

Advertising is regulated at two different levels. Some is prohibited because the products are recognized as potentially harmful. Narcotics, alcohol, tobacco are all regulated in various ways. Other forms of advertising are implicitly judged to be harmful or intrusive in themselves, and are regulated on these grounds. Billboard advertising in the countryside was withdrawn in the 1920s.[125] Cloudwriting was prohibited by law in Britain in the 1930s. But the central focus of regulation is on the issues of deception and truth.

Three dominant approaches to regulation may be characterized as the American, the British, and the continental patterns. In the United States, advertising is assertive and aggressive. At the national level, it is regulated by a government agency, the Federal Trade Commission (FTC), by means of legal sanctions, which are vigorously contested by the industry. Britain has a variety of restrictive legislation, but active regulation is largely carried out by the industry itself, by means of its own agencies. Compliance is better. Advertisers on the Continent tend to be less assertive, and the state more paternalistic. During the 1970s, the European Commission (now the European Union) embraced some of the critique of advertising, and attempted to formulate a restrictive common policy, and to have it

---

[124] Dalton, 'Social Transformation of Trust'; id., *Democratic Challenges*.
[125] Brown, 'Cultivating a "Green" Image'.

adopted by its members.[126] More recently it has shifted the other way, by lowering barriers of advertising regulation as being inimical to free trade.[127]

The conservative (and professional association) approach to advertising is a desire to trade with as little restriction as possible. Hence conservative parties in the English-speaking countries tended to adopt the advertisers' point of view, and to administer regulation leniently. This is generally supported by conservative economists.[128] In the United States and in Britain, the Democratic and Labour parties respectively used to take a more critical approach, and were more responsive to the social critique of advertising. The European approach used to reflect the more paternalist and prescriptive traditions of European politics, both on the social-democratic and communist left, and on the Christian-democratic right. Hence, European regulators were more willing to identify the disorders of advertising and to act against them. Finally, an important constraint on advertising is the enlightened self-interest of practitioners, of advertisers and their agents seeking to protect themselves against each other.

For many decades that was the motivation of advertising regulation in the United States. A practice code devised by *Printer's Ink*, the industry journal, went on the statute book in thirty-seven states even before the First World War. The Federal Trade Commission was created in 1914 by President Wilson, in the wake of the Progressive anti-trust movement of the turn of the century. Its remit was to monitor unfair competition, in other words, to protect not the consumer, but the market, from predatory actors. A parade of best-selling books during the 1920s and the 1930s exposed advertising as the exploiter of the consumer. The Consumers Union was founded in 1936, and in 1938 the Federal Trade Commission was empowered to regulate advertising.[129]

During the 1950s the FTC continued to focus mainly on anti-competitive behaviour. Towards the end of the decade, in response to the rise of the consumer movement, the FTC shifted its attention to the consumer. In 1958 it began to enforce new guidelines against deceptive pricing. In the 1960s it attacked 'phony mock-ups', used in television commercials. In one case it challenged a television commercial which purported to show Colgate shaving cream being used to shave sandpaper clean. In another

[126] The 'Misleading Advertising Directive' of 1984. See **www.paemen.com/websitecontent/ unfaircompetition/misleadingadvertisingdirconsol.pdf**
[127] The 'Television without Frontiers Directive' of 1989. **http://europa.eu.int/comm/ avpolicy/regul/regul_en.htm#2**.
[128] e.g. Ekelund and Saurman, *Advertising and the Market Process*.
[129] Pease, *Responsibilities of American Advertising*; Wagner, *Federal Trade Commission*; Mulock, *Advertising Regulation*.

case the use of mashed potatoes to represent ice-cream was the subject of a 'cease and desist order'. In the early 1970s the agency began to focus on misleading claims; Listerine and Anacine, two reliefs for sore throats, were required to advertise extensively that they did not cure colds. Other decisions were obtained against Wonder Bread and Geritol Iron Supplement. Cigarette packets were made to carry a health warning and were banned from television ads, automobile ads had to carry certified performance figures, financial advertisements began to carry warnings and to display standardized interest rates.

The FTC relied on court orders to enforce its directives. This method was not very effective. The adversarial method of legal action encouraged defiance. Only on rare occasions were companies actually fined for disregarding directives; directives were resisted in court, and disputes could take years to resolve. By this time, the campaigns had run their course; and a loss in court rarely entailed a serious penalty. By the end of the 1970s, under the influence of the New Right, the FTC retreated from activism. It lost funding and influence in the 1980s, and gave business a respite from regulation. In effect, it has succumbed to 'regulatory capture', in which the industry comes to control its regulators. Despite some pioneering legislative interventions, the United States gives advertisers more freedom than any other affluent country.

Things are different in Britain. Support for advertising is weaker than in the United States; in 1969, for example, 59 per cent in an American Gallup survey supported the view that advertising was essential, but only 46 per cent thought so in Britain.[130] Large areas of the public domain are deliberately kept free of advertising. In the urban and rural environment, advertising is subject to planning regulation that, on the whole, has kept it from defacing natural beauty, though posters do add vitality and colour to urban landscapes. Likewise, much of the broadcasting spectrum was kept free of advertising. Up to 1955 there was no commercial broadcasting except for foreign stations such as Radio Luxembourg. When commercial television was allowed in 1955, the duration and placing of advertising was constrained, with no more than six minutes per hour.[131] Despite eighteen years of Conservative rule, the BBC has survived without advertising.

The contents of advertisements are regulated by a body of statute law, of which the most important is the Trades Description Act of 1968. Some of this legislation corresponds to American law, as e.g. in controlling the advertising of tobacco and alcohol, claims for patent medicine, financial

---

[130] Reader's Digest, *Reader's Digest Eurodata*, table 63, 186–7.
[131] Great Britain, Committee on Broadcasting, *Report*, 71.

advertising, motor car performance etc. Unlike the United States, no single agency is responsible for compliance. Instead, the industry monitors itself, in keeping with a British tradition of self-regulation, which also applies (with mixed results) in the commercial, financial, and legal domains. The Advertising Association, which was founded in 1924, immediately set up a National Vigilance Committee (subsequently the Advertising Investigating Department). In its first seventeen months it dealt with more than 700 complaints, and continued to consider several hundred a year.[132]

American consumerism eventually reached out to Britain. The American Consumers Union extended a loan to set up a British counterpart in 1956. Vance Packard's attack on advertising resonated across the Atlantic.[133] Several forms of public action followed: an official inquiry (the Molony Committee) reported in 1962, and recommended strong controls on advertising.[134] A Royal Commission on the Press examined the influence of advertisers.[135] Another government committee (the Pilkington Committee) looked again at commercial broadcasting, and decided to tighten controls in 1962.[136] In the same year the Labour Party set up a committee of inquiry into advertising under the chairmanship of Lord Reith, legendary founder of the BBC, which took evidence and finally reported in 1965.[137]

In step with this tide of criticism, the Advertising Association set up the Advertising Standards Authority in 1962.[138] This body was nominally independent, with representatives of consumers, labour, and capital, though it was dominated by advertisers. It attempted to strike a balance between the credibility of advertising and creative and commercial freedom for its practitioners. Like the FTC, it accepts puffery, but polices the literal truth of factual claims. Complaints often fail when members of the public do not successfully make these distinctions. These constraints have not necessarily been bad for British advertising. Before the 1960s it was generally considered boring, an impression largely (if subjectively) confirmed by comparing e.g. American and British motor advertising.

---

[132] 'The Story of the Advertising Association' (typescript, 1949), fo. 6; Advertising Association Papers, 12/1–1, History of Advertising Trust.

[133] Box of papers on Motivation Research in the papers of Mark Abrams, copy in possession of the author.   [134] Great Britain, *Report of the Committee on Consumer Protection*.

[135] Royal Commission on the Press, see Institute of Practitioners in Advertising, 'Replies to Questions posed by the Royal Commission on the Press', 4 Aug. 1961, AA 11/17/2, HAT.

[136] Great Britain, *Report of Committee on Broadcasting*.

[137] Reith, *Report of Commission into Advertising*, minutes of evidence and submissions in the Abrams Papers (in possession of the author).

[138] J. S. Williams, 'A Short History of the Advertising Association' (typescript, 16 Nov. 1973), fo. 3; Advertising Association papers, AA 12/3, HAT.

The emergence of more constraining regulation regime has coincided with a 'creative revolution' in British advertising in the 1960s and 1970s, which has already been alluded to.[139] The more vulgar simulations of intimacy have not played a large role; instead, the stress was on entertainment and humour, surprise and wit, though this may be another variant of the same approach: in the more reserved British society, humour is an accepted way of breaking the ice, and the first step for promoting trust.

In the 1970s and 1980s, as the audience became habituated with standard pitches, a more subtle form of advertising began to appropriate post-modern approaches. Advertising will use anything that works. Imaginative agencies surfed on the rising tide of disbelief in advertising, and harnessed it for their commercials.[140] On the whole, my judgement is that professional constraint and public control have between them given Britain a system that provides more of the benefits of advertising, and suffers less from its disorders, than the system of government regulation which is in force in the United States.[141]

In Britain, much of the 1970s and the 1980s were spent in fending off a more earnest approach to regulation, emanating from the European Community, which eventually emerged in 1976 as a draft Community directive on misleading advertising. It took a strong restrictive line.[142]

British advertisers fought every foot of the way. Their objections concentrated on two points. The first was resistance to legislation.[143] The second was the right to puffery. The Community directive placed the locus of deception in the advertisement; the Advertising Association insisted that it was in the consumer's mind. People's preferences were opaque even to themselves:

The thing they object to most in the memorandum, was the assumption that it is possible to define a wrong choice objectively. [sic]

We do not believe it makes sense to describe a man as misled when he has got what he wanted. Choice is not a process which it is possible entirely to encompass in rational terms, and advertising which reflects the consumer's criteria by recognising that there are subjective satisfactions involved in any purchase (as well as objective ones) seems to us neither misleading nor unfair.[144]

---

[139] For a sense of advertising development in Britain since the 1960s, see *Campaign, Silver Jubilee*.

[140] Myers, *Understains*; Whitwell, *Making the Market*; Goldman, *Reading Ads Socially*.

[141] But this may be an expression of the general culture rather than the system of regulation; which may also be true of the system of regulation itself.

[142] Commission of European Communities, 'Second Draft of the First Directive', article 3.

[143] K. C. Hall, Dept of Prices and Consumer Protection, to R. C. G. Hunt-Taylor, Secretary of the Advertising Association, June 1978, AA 17/12/1/1, HAT.

[144] AA, 'Revised comments on the EEC Memorandum', fo. 7.[Dec. 1976], AA 17/12/1/1, HAT.

In 1972 the Labour Party had made a commitment to control false or misleading advertising.[145] In 1978 the Labour minister for consumer affairs, Roy Hattersley, caused some alarm at the Advertising Association when he appeared to be preparing to endorse the Community's draft directive. The AA mobilized political and industrial lobbies, and hinted at more active forms of resistance. These fears were swept away when the Conservatives came into power in 1979. Eventually the draft became a binding directive in 1984. By that time it had been watered down and interpreted so as to satisfy most of the objections of the advertisers, and to leave things, from a legal point of view, essentially unchanged.

Conclusion

Dissimulation is part of all discourse. Few of us have not done so at one time or another, but we do not like to be deceived ourselves. Deception may sometimes be useful, or even necessary, but not as a norm. If truthfulness in discourse declines, it places an additional burden on society, yet another 'transaction cost'. In particular, it inhibits trust and cooperation: interpersonal, social, and political. It makes coordination and leadership more difficult.[146] If some aspect of personal experience or of social performance is genuinely harmful, we can expect individuals to try to do something about it. Initially they may be ridiculed and attacked, but eventually something gets done, often by the perpetrators themselves.

What should society do about misleading advertising? It already does a great deal, more in some countries than in others. An essay like this is part of the flow of comment that keeps society on its toes, that provides the evidence and the concepts to articulate responses to the torrent of marketing. For the historian and social scientist, this should be enough. But perhaps one ought to step a little further into the fray.

To understand the effects of advertising, it is also necessary to understand the psychic impact of goods and services. That is our larger project: the evaluation of advertising and marketing also depends on what we think of the goods it promotes. Should puffs be disallowed? I am in two minds about this. Perhaps they should come (like mortgages and motor cars) with a clear, footnoted health warning. One possibility is a voluntary warranty stamp on the part of advertisers ('Truth in Advertising'?), although that is open to abuse. It is advertisers themselves who have a

---

[145] *Labour's Programme for Britain* (pamphlet, 1972?), 25; AA 11/9/1, HAT.
[146] The same point in James, *Britain on the Couch*, 109.

primary interest in credibility, as they have shown all along. They need assistance from the outside to help them enforce cooperation. There is also a social movement in embryo, led by the (embarrassingly slick) magazine *Adbusters* ('Journal of the Mental Environment'), which campaigns tellingly against advertising in particular, and consumerism in general.

Apart from overgrazing the commons of credibility, there is also the issue of litter. Advertising unrestrained can be a form of pollution. It gives rise to congestion and clutter. Even Ogilvy, the advertising guru, found it all too much. The average household in the United States watched 30,000 commercials a year, on Sundays the *New York Times* carried up to 350 pages of advertising, and some radio stations devoted 40 minutes in the hour to commercials. 'I don't know,' he wrote, 'how all this clutter can ever be brought under control.'[147]

Freedom from advertising is a good, which people are willing to pay for. Unfortunately it is a public good, of which there is not always enough. After six decades of commercial broadcasting, the United States embarked in 1970 on an advertising-free Public Broadcasting system (though advertising has crept back in the form of 'sponsorship'). Boundaries are important: advertising is welcome to do its job, but should be clearly fenced. It should leave enough space free of advertising or 'sponsorship', in the environment, in the media, in the arts, sports, and public domains. How large this space should be is a matter for negotiation and debate. Some people would have it larger, some might be content with less, yet others will require none at all. Finally, research and thinking must continue: it requires sustained attention to alert us to the seductions of intimacy, and to its continued costs.

---

[147] Ogilvy, *Ogilvy on Advertising*, 208.

7

Body Weight and Self-Control

If affluence signifies well-being, then the trends in body weight present an unwelcome paradox. Body weights have been rising above normative levels, first in the United States since the 1960s, and subsequently in Britain. The economic theory of consumer behaviour assumes that consumers are the best judges of their welfare, and that they act consistently and optimally over time.[1] Rising weight can be seen as the outcome of rational consumer choice.[2] Rosemary Green's dilemma presents a challenge for this point of view. In her *Diary of a Fat Housewife*, she wrote,

> I'm starting my diet, tomorrow, that's right
> so let's have that last bite of pizza tonight!

But for many years, tomorrow never came.[3] Like millions of others, despite her best efforts, her weight would not go down. Social norms disparage high body weight on grounds of both health and personal attractiveness. The sustained rise of body weight is the most visible demonstration of how consumers may find it difficult to achieve their objectives. Moving from the individual to society as a whole, the rise of body weight demonstrates how affluence can rise, and yet fail to deliver well-being.

The rise of body weight has generated a vast academic response: in physiology, medicine, and psychology, in anthropology and economics, in history and in cultural studies, and also a lay and expert literature of exhortation and self-help. Detached observers might infer that the volume of publication is inversely related to its efficacy: if rising weight is a problem, there is no reliable knowledge on how to reverse it. Several historical studies are largely written in a socio-cultural, and sometimes explicitly

---

[1] Deaton, *Understanding Consumption*, ch. 1.
[2] Becker and Murphy, 'Rational Addiction'; Philipson and Posner, 'Long-Run Growth'; Lakdawalla and Philipson, 'Growth of Obesity'; Cutler et al., 'Why Have Americans Become More Obese?'   [3] Green, *Diary of a Fat Housewife*, 14.

feminist vein.[4] They are either mostly narrative, or they focus on cultural pressures on women to slim.[5] They do not systematically explain the trends in body weight. Anthropometric historical research on body weight is only just beginning.[6]

Aspirations and reality

The social norms of body weight have reflected two concerns: health and personal attractiveness. Since the 1950s, both appearance and health norms for body weight have been going down. The standard height-adjusted measure is the Body Mass Index (BMI), calculated as weight (kg)/height^2 (m). The World Health Organization defines 'overweight' as starting at a BMI of 25 for women and men, and for all ages, with 'obesity' at BMI 30 and above. American agencies, which had previously used higher thresholds, have now accepted this norm.[7] Large longitudinal studies in the USA indicated that obesity (BMI > 30) doubled mortality risk.[8] Obesity is associated with increased risks of gallbladder diseases, diabetes, heart disease, and hypertension, of eightfold, sixfold, threefold, and one-half respectively.[9] It may account for up to 14 per cent of cancer deaths in men, and 20 per cent in women.[10] That mild overweight is harmful has been disputed,[11] but much work suggests that it is not benign. In a British study of 7,735 men aged 40–59, '[the] risk of cardiovascular death, heart attack, and diabetes increased progressively from an index of <20 even after age, smoking, social class, alcohol consumption, and physical activity were adjusted for.'[12] Similar findings were obtained for American women, aged 30 to 55, on a larger sample.[13] Excess weight is a big health risk.[14] For non-smokers at 40, being overweight reduced life

[4] Recent studies include Schwartz, *Never Satisfied*; Seid, *Never Too Thin*; Stearns, *Fat History*; Hesse-Biber and Janice, *Am I Thin Enough Yet?*; Wolf, *Beauty Myth*.

[5] Stearns, *Fat History*, is the most analytical of these studies.

[6] Rosenbaum, '100 Years of Heights and Weights'; Costa and Steckel, 'Long-Term Trends in Health'; Floud, 'Height, Weight and Body Mass'.

[7] Bray, 'Overweight is Risking Fate'; Kuczmarski et al., 'Varying Body Mass Index'; Flegal et al., 'Overweight and Obesity in the United States', 39.

[8] Bray, 'Overweight'—for example, fig. 3, p. 20.

[9] Wolf and Colditz, 'Social and Economic Effects of Body Weight', table 1, p. 467s.

[10] Calle et al., 'Overweight, Obesity, and Mortality from Cancer'.

[11] Bennet and Gurin, *Dieter's Dilemma*, ch. 5; Seid, *Never Too Thin*, 280–1; Flegal et al., 'Excess Deaths'; Gibbs, 'Overblown Epidemic?'

[12] Shaper et al., 'Body Weight: Implications for the Prevention', 1311.

[13] Manson et al., 'Body Weight and Mortality among Women'.

[14] Ogden et al., 'Epidemiologic Trends'. But see Gibbs, 'Overblown Epidemic?'

expectation by about three years, obesity by about seven.[15] A senior UK scientist has warned that children growing up today could have shorter life expectancies than their parents due to overweight.[16]

The conventions of personal attractiveness place weight norms well below current averages. The overweight were handicapped in personal relations. They were held in low regard, and found it more difficult to make and keep friends and spouses. Attractive persons were more likely to receive help and to elicit cooperation. They had better chances of employment, higher starting salaries, and faster promotions. Simulated juries judged them more leniently. They were favoured in college admissions.[17] Weight norms have followed a long cycle. A long-term record of these norms is provided by the measurement of photographs of models in women's magazines. The bust-to-waist ratios in *Ladies Home Journal* and *Vogue* declined from the turn of the century to a minimum in the 1920s, when weight reduction first came into vogue. They rose to another peak in the late 1940s, a lower peak in the early 1960s, and a particularly sharp decline into the 1980s.[18] *Playboy* centrefolds and Miss America contestants in the 1960s and 1970s fell substantially below normative weights.[19] Such norms were beyond the reach of most women. Feminist writers decried them as oppressive, in titles like *Never too Thin, Unbearable Weight, Am I Thin Enough Yet?, The Beauty Myth,* and *The Tyranny of Slenderness.*[20]

Real consumer spending per head more than doubled in the USA and Britain between 1950 and 1990.[21] In contrast, spending on food, alcohol, and tobacco rose only about one-fifth in the UK, and one-quarter in the United States.[22] In spite of the lag in food consumption, body weights continued to rise while weight norms were going down (Figure 7.1). From

[15] Peeters, 'Obesity in Adulthood'.

[16] Ahmed et al., 'Fat Epidemic Will Cut Life Expectancy'.

[17] Rodin et al., 'Women and Weight', 272; Allon, 'Stigma of Overweight', 136–40; Hatfield and Sprecher, *Mirror, Mirror*.

[18] Silverstein et al., 'Some Correlates of the Thin Standard'; Silverstein et al., 'Possible Causes of the Thin Standard'; Silverstein et al., 'Role of the Mass Media'. On the first slimming vogue for women, *c.*1900–1920s, Levenstein, *Revolution at the Table*, 165–6.

[19] Garner et al., 'Cultural Expectations of Thinness in Women'; Wiseman et al., 'Cultural Expectations of Thinness'. The normative weights were derived from tables published by the Metropolitan Life Insurance Company, New York.

[20] Seid, *Never too Thin*; Bordo, *Unbearable Weight*; Hesse-Biber, *Am I Thin Enough*; Chernin, *Tyranny of Slenderness*; Wolf, *Beauty Myth*.

[21] UK data are in constant 1990 prices, normalized to American 1987 dollars, which are used for American prices. In 1990 purchasing power parity between the pound and the dollar was almost unity. USA: Lebergott, *Pursuing Happiness*, appendix A; UK, ONS, National Income Accounts, downloaded electronically.

[22] Ibid. It declined from 40 to 20 per cent of personal consumption expenditure in the UK, and from 30 per cent to 17 in the USA. Elasticities of food expenditure on consumption were 0.22 in the UK and 0.28 in the USA.

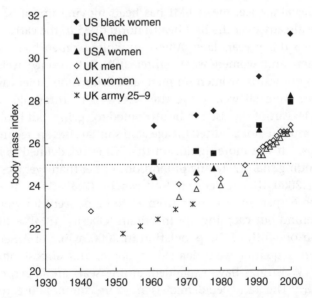

Fig. 7.1. Mean adult Body Mass Index (BMI) in the United States and England and Wales, *c.*1930–2000

Notes: Dotted line = BMI 25, for the USA since 1961 and for the UK since 1980, samples are large and representative, and typical standard errors of the mean are 0.13–0.14 in the USA (1988–91), 0.11–0.14 (E&W 1991), and 0.04–0.06 (E&W 1993–5). (USA adults aged 20 upwards.) The earlier samples were large but were not designed to be encompassing. The dotted line represents the 'overweight' boundary.

Sources: Non-encompassing surveys: (*UK Men, 1929–1932, 1943*)—10,599 men in 1929–32, 27,515 in 1943, civilian manufacturing employees (ages 20–64), Khosla and Lowe, 'Height and Weight', table 1, p. 743. (*UK Men, 1960*)—5,239 employees of a Birmingham electric engineering firm, ibid. (*UK Men, 1968*)—6,168 British Petroleum employees (ages 20–69), Montegriffo, 'Obesity in the United Kingdom', table 1, p. 419. (*UK Men, 1972*)—540 men in London Borough of Richmond, Baird et al., 'Obesity in a London Borough', table 1, p. 707. (*UK Women, 1968*)— 1894 BP employees, Montegriffo, 'Obesity', table 2, p. 419. (*UK Women, 1972*)—794 women in Richmond, in Baird et al., 'Prevalence of Obesity' (*UK Regular Army recruits, age 25–29*)— (1,191–7,192 men), Rosenbaum, '100 Years', table 13, p. 293. Representative national surveys: (*E&W, 1980*) Knight and Eldridge, *Heights and Weights* table 4.5, p. 33 [adults, age 16–64]. (*Great Britain, 1987*) Gregory et al., *Dietary and Nutritional Survey*, tables 15.18–19, p. 246. (*England, 1991–1995*) Great Britain, *Health Survey* (1991–2003). (*USA, 1961–1964—1976–1980*): Kuczmarski, 'Increasing Prevalence', table 4, p. 209. (*USA 1988–1994*) Ogden et al., 'Mean Body Weight'. USA 2000, Fiegal et al., 'Prevalence and Trends', table 4, p. 1726.

around the turn of the century average body weights rose about two BMI units, and may have already reached their 1980 levels in Britain in the 1930s, but were still within the 'optimal' range.[23] Similar magnitudes of increase occurred in the United States, *c.*1894–1961, with most of the increase apparently after 1944.[24] National surveys since the 1960s show

---

[23] Floud, 'Height, Weight and Body Mass', figs. 9–10.
[24] Costa and Steckel, 'Long-Term Trends', fig. 2.4, p. 55. The data are patchy.

that, under affluence, mean BMI has been moving upwards: American men were already over the BMI health norm of 25 in the early 1960s, and rose to 26.5 thirty years later. American white women had lower BMIs, British men and women were lighter still, but average weights were converging upwards, women on men, and Britons on Americans. By the 1990s they were all well above the 'overweight' threshold of 25 BMI (Figure 7.1). Part of the rise can be attributed to ageing, but health-related weight norms are not adjusted for age, and similar rises are recorded *within* age groups.[25] It was more significant that 'Obesity', defined as BMI > 30, was expanding sharply. Taking proportions rather than averages, from the 1970s to *c*.2000, the incidence of 'overweight' (BMI>25) in the USA rose from 51 to 67 per cent for men, from 41 to 62 per cent for women, with Britain behind but catching up. In Britain 'Obesity' (BMI > 30) affected more than one-fifth of the population in 2000, while of American men more than a quarter were defined as obese, and almost one-third of women.[26] Waistlines have expanded, airline seats are larger, coffins are too small.[27] The term 'epidemic' is now in common use to describe these trends.[28]

Self-control

Body weight is regulated individually by the relation between food intake and energy expenditure. The mismatch between weight aspirations and outcomes can be regarded as a problem of self-control. Self-control entails the sacrifice of some immediate reward for the prospect of a superior one. For Norbert Elias, the 'civilizing process' is the rise of self-control over historical time, exemplified in the evolution of table manners, in which the common bowl and greasy fingers gave way to a structured meal.[29]

[25] In Britain, National Food Survey households increased in age from an average 34.1 to 36.6 between 1974–6 and 1992–4. An increase of this magnitude would raise BMI by 0.6–0.8 units, whereas the actual increase was more than twice as large. See Chesher, 'Diet Revealed?', table 1, p. 4; Gregory et al., *Dietary and Nutritional Survey*, table 15.20–2, p. 247.

[26] England: Knight and Eldridge, *Heights and Weights of Adults*, table 4.5, p. 33; Great Britain, *Health Survey for England, 1995*, vol. i, table 8.12, p. 334; *Health Survey for England, 2003*, trends, table 04098915.xls, **www.dh.gov.uk/PublicationsAndStatistics/PublishedSurvey/ HealthSurveyForEngland/HealthSurveyResults/HealthSurveyResultsArticle/fs/ en?CONTENT_ID=4098913&chk=4DPdlh**; USA: Flegal et al., 'Prevalence and Trends', table 4, p. 1726.

[27] Great Britain, House of Commons Health Committee, *Obesity*, p. 8; St John, 'Final Journey'; Picard, 'Childhood Obesity', p. A6.

[28] Björntorp, 'Obesity', 425; Seidell, 'Obesity in Europe'; Laurance, 'Task Force Aims to Halt'; Gardner and Halweil, 'Overfed'; World Health Organization (WHO), 'Obesity and Overweight'.

[29] Elias, *Civilizing Process*, i. 99–113; Wood, *Sociology of the Meal*, 32.

Pierre Bourdieu described the contrast between the coarseness of working-class eating habits in 1960s France and the restrained and decorous procedures of middle-class eating.[30] Both of these were progressive narratives, which linked a rise in affluence to increasing self-control. What they did not anticipate was that self-control might *decline* with abundance, nor did they anticipate the fragmentation of meal patterns and table manners which has been strikingly observed in France itself.[31]

For weights to rise, it was necessary for people to prefer the immediate gratifications of eating, to the delayed ones of normative appearance. It is normal (though not always rational) to discount the future. But when people make choices that imply adverse consequences which they can foresee, and would not have made from a more detached or dispassionate perspective, their choice can be described as 'time inconsistent' or myopic. Such choices have long puzzled social scientists, as confounding the assumptions of rational choice. They are sufficiently common to have motivated several explanatory approaches.[32]

In the rational choice approach there is no such thing as 'overweight'. People gain weight because the benefits outweigh the costs.[33] But, if consumers (such as Mrs Green) are making a sustained effort to *undo* their prior decisions, that suggests that they regret the initial choice, and that compelling, but inferior, preferences pose a genuine difficulty for them. The concept of myopia implies that one can do better by resisting a reward. Self-control, or prudence, the ability to defer gratification, thus becomes an attribute of rationality. The resources and strategies mobilized for self-control are individual and cognitive, involving knowledge, willpower, personal rules, and behavioural 'bright lines'. They also draw for support on commitment devices and social resources such as reputation, interpersonal pledges, contracts, norms, rules, and regulation. The strategies of self-control, both cognitive and social, take time to develop and acquire. When they persist, they form durable clusters of 'culture'. As we have argued in Chapters 3 and 4, if self-control is costly, then the well-off have better access to it than the poor. Partly or wholly, this is because the poor have fewer prospects of remote rewards to look forward to. But self-control does not necessarily increase when society becomes more affluent as a whole. Our hypothesis is that myopic choice

---

[30] Bourdieu, *Distinction*, 194–6; Wood, *Sociology of the Meal*, 20–1; Stearns, *Fat History*, 224.

[31] Seidell, 'Obesity'; Laurier et al., 'Prevalence of Obesity'; Fischler, 'Gastro-nomie et gastro-anomie'; Fischler, *L'homnivore*.   [32] Discussed in detail, Ch. 3 above.

[33] Stigler and Becker, '*De Gustibus Non Est Disputandum*'; Becker and Murphy, 'Rational Addiction'; Viscusi, *Smoking*; Philipson and Posner, 'Long-Run Growth', p. 3; Lakdawalla and Philipson, 'Growth of Obesity'; Cutler et al., 'Why Have Americans Become More Obese?'

is what accounts for the reversal of the historical trend towards greater self-control.[34]

During the post-war period, the bulk of the population finally emerged from under the shadow of indigence (though in the United States, with its extremes of inequality, about one-tenth of households continued to experience hunger and food insecurity).[35] Food prices, which in earlier times had dominated manual incomes, fell sharply as a proportion of income, while supply increased greatly in variety.[36] Affluence may be characterized as a flow of new and inexpensive rewards. If these rewards arrive faster than the disciplines of prudence can form, then self-control will *decline* with affluence: the affluent (with everyone else) will become less prudent. Self-control strategies and commitment devices take time and effort to devise and to learn. Under the impact of affluence, they become obsolete. Overweight and obesity are striking demonstrations: in response to a flood of cheap, available, and appetizing food, the majority of adults in American and British populations have 'let themselves go', and have been unable to prevent their body weights from bloating beyond the bounds of both prudence and self-regard.

More to eat, tastier, available, and cheap

What caused body weights to rise was the shock of easy food availability on existing prudential strategies, interacting with the psychology of food consumption, and the decline in physical activity. Food availability was driven by supply competition. In the 1950s in Britain and America, most eating took place at home on the fixed occasions of three or four set meals. Housewives toiled long over 'the regular unimaginative English meal— meat, potatoes, and sometimes "greens", followed by pudding and helped down by a final cup of coffee or tea'.[37] In the 1950s, six out of every ten men took their main meal at midday and at home. 'To be on the roads in any populated part of the country around mid-day is to see clouds of cyclists and motor cyclists who bear witness to this homeward trek.'[38] American practice was similar. In the early 1950s, the core meal was made

[34] For other recent applications of myopic choice to ingestion, Komlos et al., 'Obesity and the Rate of Time Preference'; Cutler et al., 'Why Have Americans Become More Obese?', 112–16; Gruber, 'Is Addiction Rational?'

[35] Brown, 'Hunger in the U.S.'; Physician Task Force, *Hunger in America*; Nord et al., *Household Food Security*.   [36] See nn 21 and 22, above.

[37] Crawford and Broadley, *People's Food*, 54.

[38] Warren, *Foods We Eat*, 63; see Burnett, *Plenty and Want*, ch. 14.

up of meat, starch (potatoes, corn, rice), and vegetables, but served more usually in the evening; of the ethnic minority cuisines, only the Italian made much headway, with spaghetti and tomato sauce.[39]

Since the 1950s, the 'family-meal' system has been challenged by market competition, which has greatly expanded availability. British multiples increased their shares from one-fifth to three-quarters of the grocery market between 1950 and 1990.[40] American supermarkets increased their share from 15 to 61 per cent in the same period.[41] In the 1950s, they stocked 5,000–8,000 items, rising to more than 25,000 different items by the 1980s. Shops stayed open longer: a median 82 hours a week in the USA in 1975, 108 in 1990, with universal Sunday opening, and almost a third of outlets open for 24 hours a day.[42]

Cautiously, eaters also began to move beyond home cooking in search of variety and convenience.[43] In the 1950s, a fifth of British breakfasts included American-type cereals.[44] French *haute cuisine* had long provided the model for upper-class cooking.[45] Elizabeth David's celebrated recipes introduced Mediterranean rustic flavours and 'slow food', with fresh ingredients, careful preparation, and a relaxed experience of eating. A similar *nouvelle cuisine* appeared in the United States.[46] For those in a hurry, the freezer and chilled sections of the shops carried ready-made food, building on the fish-fingers and frozen peas of the 1950s.[47] At home microwave ovens, introduced in 1973, reached 50 per cent of American and British households by 1985, and more than 80 per cent of British households by 2002.[48] Fridges and freezers made shopping easier.[49] A 1984 British survey found 'convenience' food to account for more than a third of all food outlays.[50]

In Britain, convenience and novelty beckoned in ethnic restaurants and take-aways, Chinese, Indian, Italian and Cypriot, and pizza parlours, burger bars, and fried chicken outlets inspired or franchised from the USA. Still greater culinary variety diffused through the United States, reinforced by an abundance of themed cookbooks.[51] Exotic cuisines entered the

[39] Brown, *American Standards of Living*, 194–5; Levenstein, *Paradox of Plenty*, ch. 8; Neuhaus, *Manly Meals*, ch. 10.   [40] Raven et al., *Off our Trolleys*, 37.
[41] USDA, *U.S. Food Expenditures*, table 16. Sales for Food at Home by Type of Outlet.
[42] Walsh, *Supermarkets Transformed*, 9, 43, 49.   [43] Currie, 'Trends in Food', fos. 22–6.
[44] Collins, 'The "Consumer Revolution" ', 31–43; Crawford, *People's Food*, 39; Warren, *Foods We Eat*, 24.   [45] Driver, *British at Table*, ch. 1.
[46] Ibid. 53; Seid, *Never Too Thin*, 200–1; Levenstein, *Paradox of Plenty*, 220–1; Brenner, *American Appetite*, 143–9.   [47] Åstrom, 'Main Trends of Development', fig. 1, p. 6.
[48] Ch. 8 below, Table 8.1 and Figure 8.2.
[49] Bowden and Offer, 'Household Appliances', table A1, p. 746, and table 8.1 below.
[50] Excluding fast foods and takeaways. Mintel, *Convenience Meals*, table 3, p. 7.
[51] Levenstein, *Paradox of Plenty*, ch. 14; Hess and Hess, *Taste of America*, for a jaundiced view.

domestic cycle as sources of variety and spice, although not yet as staples.[52] 'Alien' cuisines together accounted for about 12 per cent of restaurant turnover in 1975, rising to 27 per cent by 1990, or 36 per cent if 'continental' ones are included.[53]

Eating outside the home claimed less than 10 per cent of food outlays in Britain in 1955. By 1995 eating out had more than doubled its share of food spending, reaching about 25 per cent in the United Kingdom and more than 45 per cent in the United States (Figure 7.2). The appeal was convivial as well as culinary.[54] This is attested by the elasticity of 'eating out' on consumption expenditure, which was 0.93 in America and 0.76 in Britain, i.e. rising much closer in line with consumer expenditures than food outlays.[55]

Fast-food outlets expanded even faster. The per capita number of fast-food outlets in the USA doubled between 1972 and 1997.[56] The calorie-dense, palatable, fat-rich hamburger, pizza, fried chicken, and ethnic take-out cuisines rose from 3 to 16 per cent of US food outlays between 1963 and 1993.[57] Portions also grew, as the conception of a 'normal' helping moved upwards.[58] 'Supersizing' was an effective and profitable sales pitch for fast-food vendors.[59] McDonald's biggest hamburger inflated from 3.7 ounces to almost 9.[60] In a British market survey (1986), three-quarters of adults bought take-away food once a month, rising from about half in 1972.[61] Most readily available were the sweet and salty, energy-heavy, snack or 'junk' foods: crisps, chocolate bars, nuts, cookies, soft drinks, etc. 'The most heavily advertised foods tend to be of dubious nutritional value', and are heavily promoted to children.[62] Defining snacking as 'the consumption of food in-hand, without the use of domestic cutlery or crockery . . . and involving minimal or no immediate preparation', in 1987 in Britain, 'snack foods represent 34 per cent of all food purchases, and snack foods together with all other foods eaten as snacks account for 44 per cent of the total food market'.[63] Adding non-alcoholic drinks would bring the outlay on snacking very close to 50 per cent.[64] A quantitative study of weight gain in the United States between 1984

---

[52] Charles and Kerr, *Women, Food and Families*, 65; DeVault, *Feeding the Family*, 212–14; Marshall, 'Eating at Home', 276–7.

[53] Wardle, *Changing Food*, table 9, p. 38; Key Note Publications, *Restaurants*, table 33, p. 40.

[54] Visser, *Rituals of Dinner*; Finkelstein, *Dining Out*.

[55] For data sources, see n. 21 above, and Figure 7.2.

[56] Chou et al., 'Economic Analysis of Adult Obesity', 5–6.

[57] USDA, *US Food Expenditures*, table 17.   [58] Gardner and Halweil, 'Overfed', 32.

[59] Critser, *Fat Land*, ch. 2.

[60] Fumento, *Fat of the Land*, 44–8; Schlosser, *Fast Fool Nation*, 241.

[61] Mintel Publications, *Snacking*.   [62] Gardner and Halweil, 'Overfed', 29–33.

[63] Mintel Publications, *Snacking*, 11, 19.   [64] USDA, *Expenditures of Food*, table uk.wk1.

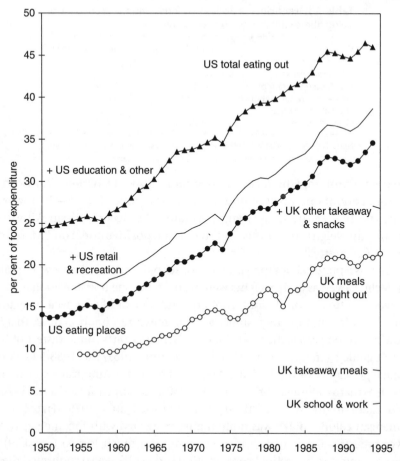

Fig. 7.2. Eating out as percentage of food expenditure, US and UK, 1950–1995 (cumulative)

Sources: United States Department of Agriculture (USDA), *US Food Expenditures*, tables 3, 17; Great Britain, *Family Expenditure Survey* (annual).

and 1999 found that after controlling for a wide range of demographic attributes, the largest impact by far was of the density of fast-food restaurants. The precise findings are shown in Table 7.1. What the table shows is elasticities, i.e. by how much the Body Mass Index (BMI) or the probability of obesity would rise, as a proportion of the rise of the variable in question. For example, if the density of restaurants rose by 10 per cent, BMI would rise by 1.74 per cent.[65] The authors argue, however, that restaurant density has increased in response to time pressure, another

[65] Chou et al., 'Economic Analysis of Adult Obesity'. Other variables held constant.

Table 7.1. Elasticities of Body Mass Index and the probability of being obese with respect to selected variables

Variable	Body Mass Index	Obesity probability
Restaurant density	0.174	0.946
Fast-food restaurant price	−0.05	−0.394
Full-service restaurant price	−0.022	−0.076
Food at home price	−0.035	−0.342
Cigarette price	0.022	0.223

Notes: Dependent variable: Body Mass Index. Computed at sample weighted means.
Source: Chou et al., 'Economic Analysis of Adult Obesity', 50, table 5.

myopic symptom, which is discussed more fully in Chapter 13. Another factor at about one-third of intensity, was the price of food—the lower it was, the higher the body weight. Finally, the decline of smoking has pushed up weight, and this is reflected in the positive effect on BMI of the price of cigarettes.

There is a puzzle about food intake. Household food surveys showed intake in decline, even as body weights were rising.[66] But the British National Food Survey omitted alcohol, confectionery, and soft drinks, as well as eating out.[67] A different, top-down, approach is to measure 'disappearance', that is, how much food *enters* the food chain. This incorporates some waste, but is a better guide to trends. Taking this measure, from 1961/4 to 1988/94 calorie intake per capita in the USA increased 22 per cent.[68] Americans consumed about as many calories as Britons in the 1950s, but surged ahead in the 1970s, and again in the 1980s. Britons only followed after 1979 (Figure 7.3). American calorie intake was quite highly correlated with income per head over time ($r = 0.87$), with British consumption much less so ($r = 0.39$).[69] Recent American household consumption surveys have also confirmed these trends, showing calorie intake rising about 9 per cent since 1977–8.[70]

Decline in physical activity is a residual explanation for the rise in body weight, though there is little research.[71] Bodily exertion at work has declined with manual employment. Britain motorized later than the

[66] Prentice and Jebb, 'Obesity in Britain'; Seid, *Never Too Thin*, 297, n. 49.

[67] Great Britain, *National Food Survey 1994*, fig. 4.28, p. 67; Buss, 'British Diet', 121–32, does not provide calorie estimates; nor does Nelson, 'Social-Class Trends', 101–20. Their analysis of food components is undermined by these omissions, especially for the later periods.

[68] Gortner, 'Nutrition in the United States', table 1, p. 3248; USDA, *Food Consumption, Prices, and Expenditures*, table 40.wk1. There is a large margin of waste. Compare Gregory et al., *Dietary and Nutritional Survey*, table 7.1, p. 53; Kantor et al., 'Estimating and Addressing', 2–12.

[69] 1950–90. The time-series relation is too complicated to explore here.

[70] Lin et al., 'Away-from-home Foods', table 5, p. 7; Cutler et al., 'Why Have Americans become more Obese?', table 2, p. 101.

[71] Prentice and Jebb, 'Obesity in Britain'; Philipson and Posner, 'Long-Run Growth'; Lakdawalla and Philipson, 'Growth of Obesity'.

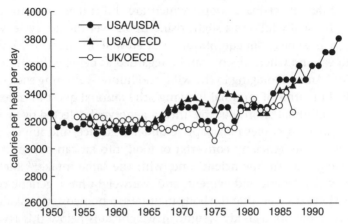

Fig. 7.3. Calories per head per day consumed in the United States and Britain, c.1950–1994

Sources: Office of Economic Cooperation and Development (OECD), *Food Consumption Statistics* (annual); United States Department of Agriculture (USDA), *Food Consumption*, table 42.wkl; USDA, *Agricultural Statistics 1995–6*, table 649.

United States, which may help to explain why Americans were heavier than Britons on the same amount of calories in the 1960s.[72] The fragmentation of dwelling, shopping, and work has required more travel by car. Body weight increased significantly with suburban sprawl, and residents of the lowest-density mid-western suburban county in a large American sample were one BMI point heavier than New Yorkers.[73] It was a far cry from the world in which most men walked or cycled home for lunch. The physical activity that was once a part of daily life now had to be simulated at the gym, and paid for with designated time, space, equipment, and professional advice. But, whatever the contribution of the decline in physical exercise, people have been eating more as well. They have eaten more because more variety has been available more cheaply. But how does food variety undermine self-control?

Psychology of craving

If food availability was the supply shock, on the demand side, the response was mediated by the psychology of satiation. Body weight responds to

---

[72] In 1960 about 75 per cent of American households had motor cars, compared with less than 50 per cent of British ones. See Ch. 8 below, Table 8.1.
[73] Ewing et al., 'Urban Sprawl and Physical Activity', 52.

several different feedback loops, which are difficult to monitor and to control. It usually follows a slight rising trend over the life cycle without varying a great deal, but equilibrium is often well off target. The choice of what to eat and when to stop can be regarded as being either rational or myopic.[74] Animal foraging in the wild, and hunter-gathering societies, are modelled in terms of 'optimal foraging', the rational quest for maximum energy at minimal effort. But the 'thrifty genotype', selected by evolution under scarcity, becomes maladaptive under affluence, and impels people to overeat.[75] An 'efficient' converter of food into fat can put on twice as much weight as an 'inefficient' one, with the same intake.[76] Metabolic efficiency is a genetic endowment, and overweight has a genetic component.[77] There is a view that the body maintains a homeostatic balance that 'defends' a 'set-point' body weight. If weight falls below this level, the body will motivate weight gain.[78] One approach to appetite concentrates on the 'normal' physiological cycle: an empty stomach signals hunger, the subject responds by eating, and a full stomach makes him stop. The feedback is self-contained and physiological, but the cycle is complex and poorly understood.[79]

Once people attempt to restrain eating before satiation, they are easily disinhibited into *excess* eating. The trigger is external stress, which comes in three forms: appetizing food; negative feelings; and the company of other people. Similar results have come out of different research programmes. A robust finding is that eating can restart despite satiation when the subject is newly exposed to palatable food.[80] Rats which maintained a steady weight on monotonous unrestricted 'chow' diets, rose rapidly into obesity when offered a 'supermarket' of appetizing foods.[81] In one research programme, eaters were given a 'preload', in the form of a satiating lunch, and were then presented with a rich milkshake or ice-cream. 'Normal' eaters soon lost interest. 'Restrained eaters' started a new cycle of eating. They could be identified in advance by their concern about body weight and their inclination to diet and binge. Once having overstepped their diets, 'restrained eaters' abandoned restraint altogether. This pattern appears to be pervasive.[82] Although both 'normal' and 'restrained' eating

---

[74] Logue, *Psychology of Eating*, ch. 7.   [75] Blundell, 'Food Intake and Body Weight', 113.

[76] Rodin et al., 'Psychological Features of Obesity', 47, referring to Rose and Williams, 'Metabolic Studies'.   [77] Jebb, 'Aetiology of Obesity'.

[78] Keesey, 'A Set-Point Analysis'; id., 'A Set-Point Theory'; Caterson, 'Group Report', 86–8.

[79] Blundell, 'Food Intake'; Bouchard and Bray, *Regulation, passim*.

[80] Rolls et al., 'Influence of Variety'.   [81] Sclafani, 'Dietary Obesity', 175–8.

[82] Herman and Polivy, 'Restrained Eating', 208–25; id., 'What Does Abnormal Eating Tell Us'; eid., 'Dieting as an Exercise'; Orbach, *Fat is a Feminist Issue*, 16, describes the same syndrome.

habits are found at all weight levels, it seems that weight control is more easily attained by not trying too hard.[83] A survey of thirty-nine animal and human studies finds that food consumption increases when there is more variety in a meal or diet, and that greater dietary variety is associated with increased body weight and fat.[84]

'Restrained' eaters typically turn to food in search of comfort and relief. Food acts as an 'emotional tranquillizer'.[85] Distress is the single most reliable precipitant of a binge. Here again, there is a difference: in response to stress, 'normal' eaters hold intake steady or reduce it, while 'restrained' eaters increase it.[86] In company, people eat more.[87] In everyday settings, a curvilinear power-law relation was observed between the number of eaters and the size of the meal. An increase from one eater to seven increased meal size from 400 to 700 calories. 'Restrained eaters' were more susceptible to disinhibition when in company than unrestrained ones.[88] Food prepared professionally, eaten on a special occasion, is likely to be more appetizing. Restaurant food tends to mimic formal bourgeois eating patterns, only more so.[89] Noise, itself a form of stress, stimulates eating, hence perhaps the ubiquity of background music in restaurants and pubs.[90]

The disinhibiting effect of stress forms the link between the micro-motives of individuals and macro-behavioural patterns. It suggests why Elias and Bourdieu have not been confirmed in their hypothesis that self-control would increase with affluence. The three-meal system was monotonous, regular, predictable, short on stimulation and on novelty. The breakdown of family mealtime routines, expanding food variety and choice, the ubiquity of rich fast foods, and their attendant advertising, exposed increasing numbers to new foods, irregular eating, and eating in public places and in company, thus precipitating a shift from 'normal' to disturbed, or aroused, eating patterns. Eating out, with its large portions, 'standard' three-course meals, and clean plates, has also challenged restraint. In its turn, this has acted to shift body weight upwards, thus

---

[83] That is what some dieting manuals recommend, although the majority stress fairly strict self-control. Among the former are Orbach, *Fat is a Feminist Issue*; Polivy, *Breaking the Diet Habit*; Foreyt and Goodrick, *Living without Dieting*; Tribole and Resch, *Intuitive Eating*; among the latter, Stuart, *Act Thin*.   [84] Raynor and Epstein, 'Dietary Variety'.

[85] Herman and Polivy, 'What Does Abnormal Eating Tell Us', 233; Slochower, *Excessive Eating*, 98; Chernin, *Tyranny of Slenderness*, 11; also Rodin, *Body Traps*, 135–6; Brown, 'The Continuum', 63; Blair et al., 'Does Emotional Eating Interfere'.

[86] Herman and Polivy, 'What Does Abnormal Eating Tell Us', 233–4.

[87] De Castro, 'Social Facilitation'; Clendenen et al., 'Social Facilitation of Eating'; Logue, *Psychology of Eating*, 207.

[88] de Castro and Brewer, 'Amount Eaten in Meals'; Herman and Polivy, 'What Does Abnormal Eating Tell Us', fig. 5.1, p. 212.   [89] Wood, *Sociology of the Meal*, ch. 3.

[90] McCarron and Tierney, 'Effect of Auditory Stimulation'.

increasing the motivation for self-control, and hence for restrained eating. In their turn, 'restrained eaters' found it more difficult to resist arousal and, as their share of the population increased, weight control became collectively more difficult.[91] Dissatisfaction with weight is the most frequently reported hassle in daily life, and small hassles are good predictors of distress,[92] and hence of eating binges.

From physiology on to society: economic and social status also affects desired body weight, both directly, and more importantly through gender. In poor societies, food is scarce, the poor are thin, and the wealthy are fat. Once these societies were exposed to food abundance, they experienced a sharp rise in weights, and rising levels of obesity.[93] In affluent societies, these conditions persist, and the poor tend to fatness, while the well-off are slimmer.[94] Table 7.2 compares the relation between obesity, class, and gender in the USA, Europe, and several developing countries. In poor countries, higher income is associated with obesity, for both women and men. In the developed world, there is a strong inverse relation between income and weight for women. For men there is an inverse relation in Britain and Europe, but an indeterminate one in the United States. Women's obesity is more strongly determined by socio-economic status than men's.[95]

Table 7.3 indicates that, when *average* weights under affluence are considered (rather than obesity), the relation of class and weight is mediated by gender. American weight surveys are coy about social class. There is, however, one representative socio-economic breakdown available, of the national health survey of 1971–4, which is compared

Table 7.2. Relation between socio-economic status and obesity: percentage of studies showing inverse or positive relationship

Relation	Women				Men			
	USA	Britain	Western Europe	Developing countries	USA	Britain	Western Europe	Developing countries
Inverse	93	67	86	0	44	55	55	0
None	7	33	0	9	11	27	9	14
Positive	0	0	14	91	44	18	36	86
N	30	12	7	11	27	22	11	14

Source: Sobal and Stunkard, 'Socioeconomic Status', tables 1, 2, 4.

[91] Presciently observed by Pullar, *Consuming Passions*, 222–4, 233–4.
[92] Argyle, *Social Psychology*, 262–4.
[93] Brown and Konner, 'Anthropological Perspective'; Gardner and Halweil, 'Overfed', 21–8.
[94] Hodge and Zimmet, 'Epidemiology of Obesity'.
[95] Sobal and Stunkard, 'Socioeconomic Status and Obesity', 261–2, 267–8.

Table 7.3. Mean weight, height, BMI, and social class of adults, USA 1971–4, UK 1986–7

Social Category	Men (n)	Women (n)	Men (Height m.)	Men (Weight kgs)	Women (Height m.)	Women (Weight kgs)	Men (BMI)	Women (BMI)
USA Income								
≥$15,000	857	1,215	1.76	79.8	1.62	63.0	25.8	24.0
≤$4,000	1,196	2,072	1.74	74.4	1.61	68.0	24.5	26.2
Probability			<0.001	<0.001	<0.001	<0.001		
USA Education								
≥13 years	1,224	1,714	1.77	78.9	1.63	63.0	25.3	23.7
≤9 years	1,750	1,990	1.72	75.3	1.59	67.6	25.3	26.6
Probability			<0.001	<0.001	<0.001	<0.001		
UK Social Class								
1+2	405	401	1.76	76.2	1.63	62.7	24.7	23.8
4+5	189	235	1.74	74.9	1.60	65.9	24.8	25.8
Probability			>0.5	0.2	>0.5	0.005	>0.5	>0.001

Notes: (1) Ages: 18–74 in the USA, 16–64 for Britain. (2) USA Income: Defined as family income. (3) American BMI is derived from height and weight data. (4) Probability: chance that the difference of the means is equal to 0, using two-tailed t-tests. Tests carried out on aggregate data. Reported data are age adjusted.

Sources: (USA) Fulwood et al., 'Height and Weight of Adults', tables 1, 4, 13, 16. (Great Britain) Gregory, *Dietary and Nutritional Survey of British Adults*, table 15.11.

here with the British one of 1986–7. The gap in time brings the incomes closer together. Table 7.3 describes the two social extremes in the UK and the USA. American and British men at both social extremes differed very little from each other in BMI. In contrast, affluent, educated women were much thinner than poor women and those with little education. The difference in BMI between lower- and upper-class women was between two and three units.[96] These figures largely antedate the big surge in obesity.

These weight norms are consistent with the 'handicap principle' in signalling: it is the scarce and costly which is valued.[97] 'Beauty, if it's to be deemed to have any worth, has to be rare.'[98] Under indigence, girth signals wealth and power. Under affluence, it is slimness that is difficult, and demonstrates a capacity for self-control. If self-control is costly, it is more readily available to the well-off than to the poor.[99]

American research indicates that *economic* rewards to slimness are not in terms of direct levels of pay. There was a small penalty for unattractiveness, and a small premium for attractiveness, but these were gender blind, and the contribution of body weight was not statistically significant.[100] Other

[96] Table 7.3 antedates the surge of obesity. For the impact of various factors including gender since then, see Table 7.6 below. [97] Zahavi and Zahavi, *Handicap Principle*.
[98] Lawson, 'Let's Take a Wider Look'.
[99] Brown and Konner, 'Anthropological Perspective', 42.
[100] Hamermesh and Biddle, 'Beauty and the Labor Market'.

studies show a small wage penalty for obesity, affecting women alone.[101] The rewards for body shape accrued mostly through the competition for mates, a point reluctantly acknowledged by feminist writers.[102] 'Physical attractiveness and weight are still the chief and most wholeheartedly sanctioned domains in which women are encouraged to contend with each other.'[103] Female mating competition is more acute than male competition. Women seek men who are typically older, more educated, and better off than themselves.[104] The age, the income, and the education pyramids taper towards the top, so there are more female seekers than males sought. Women typically marry men who are two to three years older.[105]

But why was it during the period from the 1960s to the 1980s that the 'cult of thinness' re-emerged?[106] There are several reasons why mating competition, especially among middle-class and educated women, might have intensified during this period. These are associated with a reduction in the supply of eligible males. The 1960s–1980s were the decades of massive female entry into higher education and well-paid employment, which reduced the relative number of older males with comparable or superior attributes.[107] Women with high education and occupational achievement are less likely to be married.[108] To make things more difficult, between the 1960s and the 1980s, the sex ratio turned strongly against women in the courting age, and they outnumbered considerably the numbers of men two to three years older.[109] This arose as a result of the 'baby boom' cycle. In a sustained period of rising numbers of marriageable people, the older cohorts will be smaller than the younger ones, thus disadvantaging women seeking older mates. Figure 7.4 shows six different measures of the male/female sex ratio, in a separate cluster for each census year, for the United States and Britain. It shows that, from a level of parity at the 1960–1 censuses, the number of eligible men per 100 women in the 20–9 age groups dropped to around 80, and this ratio persisted in the USA through the 1980 census. It is only by 1990 that parity was restored.

[101] Register and Williams, 'Wage Effects of Obesity'; Dávila and Pagán, 'Obesity, Occupational Attainment, and Earnings'.

[102] Orbach, *Fat is a Feminist Issue*, 31–2; Freedman, *Beauty Bound*, ch. 8; Rodin, *Body Traps*, 104; Mori et al., ' "Eating Lightly" ', 693.   [103] Rodin, *Body Traps*, 95.

[104] Ellis, 'Evolution of Sexual Attraction'; Guttentag and Secord, *Too Many Women*? Harrell, 'Women with MBAs'.

[105] Coleman and Salt, *British Population*, fig. 5.1, p. 181; United States Bureau of Census, *Historical Statistics*, tables A158–9, 19.   [106] Seid, *Never Too Thin*, chs. 7–10.

[107] Goldin, *Understanding the Gender Gap*, 215–17.

[108] Joshi, 'Combining Employment and Child-Rearing', 101, 113; Ermisch, *Fewer Babies*, 9.

[109] As noted by Guttentag and Secord, *Too Many Women*? See also Pedersen, 'Secular Trends', and the references therein.

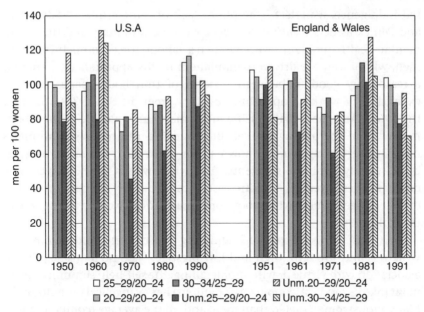

Fig. 7.4. Ratios of eligible men per 100 women, selected age groups, total and unmarried, USA and England and Wales, 1950–1991

Note: Numbers for male 20–9 age group are taken as average for 20–4 and 25–9 age groups.

Sources: US Bureau of Census, *Historical Statistics*; ibid., *Statistical Abstract*; Mitchell, *British Historical Statistics*; Great Britain, Office of Population, Censuses & Surveys, *1991 Census*.

Association is not proof of causation, but the relation is strongly suggestive. During the 1980s and the 1990s, men also began to pay considerable attention to their body weight. This is consistent with the restoration of parity.[110]

In a tightening mating market, body weight was one way for women to compete. The weight target was positioned at the low end of the normal range.[111] American women sought a lower weight for themselves than the level that men found attractive.[112] This is consistent with the view that low weight is not desirable in itself, but is rather a credible signal of self-control and virtue.[113] It also suggests why the media-driven 'cult of thinness' found such ready acceptance among the readers of women's magazines. Overweight was often regarded as an advertisement of moral failure: 'my body remains a visible-to-all-the-world sign that I am not in control of my life', wrote Rosemary Green, 'fat parents are forever a sign of

[110] Pope et al., *Adonis Complex*, chs. 6, 8.   [111] Rodin et al., 'Women and Weight', 281–4.
[112] Fallon and Rozin, 'Sex Differences'; Rodin et al., 'Women and Weight', 87–91.
[113] Stein and Nemeroff, 'Moral Overtones of Food'; Pliner and Chaiken, 'Eating, Social Motives'.

155

self-indulgence, a perfect example of lack of self-control.'[114] Silverstein and Perlick associate eating disorders, extreme slimming, and the rise in mental health problems with women's labour force competition with men, whom they are driven to emulate in bodily appearance.[115] There is a reasonably good fit between a norm of thin body shapes and the expansion of working opportunities for women in the 1920s and after the 1960s. And the signal of self-control may be as valuable in the labour market as in the mating market. But the stick-thin models in women's magazines are not generally shown as power-dressing, but rather as wearing distinctly feminine garments. And while weight norms have come down, women's weights have increased. Anorexia only affects 1–2 per cent of college-age women, while about one-quarter of *all* women were obese in the early 1990s.

Food has symbolic power, signifying masculinity and femininity, weakness and strength, high and low prestige.[116] Some foods acquire an association with virtue or with moral failing: the self-help slimming movement (like its model Alcoholics Anonymous) has evangelical undertones.[117] Many more women dieted than men, and on the average (comparing BMI outcomes), women succeeded better than men, suggesting that more was at stake for women.[118]

Body weight affected the outcomes of courtship. In one American study, women of average weight reported one or two dates per week, overweight women about one per month.[119] Being slim (or tall) has driven social mobility. In Britain, the tallest women were the most likely to raise their social class through marriage, while the shortest were least likely to.[120] Obese women were more likely to be downwardly mobile.[121] In New York in the 1950s, 12 per cent of upwardly mobile women were obese, as compared with 22 per cent of the downwardly mobile, with no comparable trend for men.[122] In a large American study in the 1980s, differences in marriage probabilities and in spouse's earnings accounted for 50 to 95 per cent of the lower economic status of obese women, and visually unattractive women married less educated men: 'the great majority (as much as 96 per cent) of the economic deficit associated with obesity among

[114] Green, *Diary*, 27, 56; see Allon, 'Stigma of Overweight'; Hesse-Biber, *Thin Enough?*, 4 and ch. 2.   [115] Silverstein and Perlick, *Cost of Competence*.
[116] Twigg, 'Vegetarianism and the Meaning of Meat', 18–30.
[117] Stuart and Mitchell, 'Self-Help Groups', 345–54; Sobal, 'Group Dieting'; Goldstein, *Addiction*, 132; Seid, *Never Too Thin*, p. 168.   [118] Horm and Anderson, 'Who in America'.
[119] Stake and Lauer, 'Consequences of Being Overweight', 38.
[120] Knight and Eldridge, *Heights and Weights*, 15, 18.
[121] Braddon et al., 'Onset of Obesity', 301.
[122] Goldblatt et al., 'Social Factors in Obesity'.

women . . . results from differences in the marriage market (especially the probabilities of marriage), not the labor market.'[123] Overweight women were less likely to marry, were poorer, and finished their education earlier than other women, and earlier than men of the same social position.[124] If marital and occupational mobility was restricted for the fat, then consequently the poor had even greater obstacles to overcome than the well-off, and with a lower endowment of resources.[125] In a period of accelerated marriage dissolution, mating competition did not end with marriage.[126] Attractive women reported better sex lives and more faithful husbands and lovers.[127] Figure 7.5 shows that the younger women tended to be thinner than younger men, and how the gap has been closing both with age and over time: women became less competitive as they grew older, and as the sex ratio moved in their favour from the 1960s to the 1990s. Likewise, the convergence of male and female BMIs in the 1990s

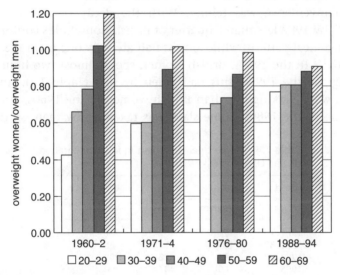

Fig. 7.5. Ratio of proportion of overweight women to proportion of overweight men, USA 1960–1994

Source: Flegal et al., 'Overweight and Obesity', tables 1–3, pp. 41–3.

[123] Averett and Korenman, 'Economic Reality', 327; Hamermesh and Biddle, 'Beauty and the Labor Market', 1189.

[124] Gortmaker et al., 'Social and Economic Consequences of Overweight'. As pointed out elsewhere, poverty is more likely to be a cause than a consequence of weight, and poverty is inversely correlated with education.   [125] Dávila and Pagán, 'Obesity'.

[126] Trent and South, 'Structural Determinants'.

[127] Blumstein and Schwartz, American Couples, 246–9, 266–7; Rodin, Body Traps, 106–7; also Green, Diary, 30–1; Stuart and Jacobson, Weight, Sex and Marriage, 98, 102.

(Figure 7.1) is consistent with the restoration of sex ratio parity during these years.

During courtship, a woman might have struggled to eat as little as possible. In a permanent relationship, she typically aspired to keep her partner and children well fed.[128] 'With cooking you get some appreciation', said a housewife in the 1960s: 'you'll never hear my husband saying the floor looks clean but he'll say he enjoys his food.'[129] Women claimed more satisfaction from cooking than from any other housework.[130] A well-structured 'proper meal' of meat and two veg. for the whole family (or some ethnic variant thereof) has remained the woman's ideal.[131] Several British surveys found 60 to 70 per cent of families eating together on most days in the 1980s.[132] In 1987, 'Family mealtimes are more prevalent among younger people, and in the higher social groups. The presence of children in the family is particularly important.'[133] A serious commitment to cooking survived the pressures towards 'convenience' in about a third of households.[134]

But convenience was telling. With the decay of the 'three-meal system', by 1982 less than a quarter of British households conformed to the three-meal pattern, while almost half ate only one main meal a day by 1982.[135] In the 1960s, British women spent almost two hours a day cooking; by the 1990s, this had fallen by half (Table 7.4). American women were cooking less than British women in the 1960s, and about the same in the 1980s. Some slack was taken up by men, so that the

Table 7.4. Minutes per day spent in food preparation, UK and USA, c.1961–1990

Period	UK		USA	
	Women	Men	Women	Men
1961–70	120	9	106	13
1971–82	103	11	88	12
1983–90	86	26	89	21
1995	60	35		

Source: Provided by Prof. J. Gershuny, University of Essex. Figures are controlled for employment and non-motherhood, both of which reduced time spent cooking, and both of which increased.

[128] Neuhaus, 'Way to a Man's Heart'.   [129] J. Currie, 'Trends in Food', 10–14.

[130] Juster, 'Preferences for Work', table 13.1, p. 336; Gershuny and Halpin, 'Time Use', 200–1.

[131] Charles and Kerr, *Women, Food and Families*, ch. 2; DeVault, *Feeding the Family*, 37–8; Dare, 'Too Many Cooks?'; Murcott, 'Raw, Cooked and Proper Meals', 229.

[132] Dare, 'Too Many Cooks', 150–2; Mintel Publications, *Snacking*, table 11, p. 33; Marshall, 'Eating at Home', 277.   [133] Mintel Publications, *Snacking*, 33.

[134] Davies and Madran, 'Time, Food Shopping, and Food Preparation', 13.

[135] Mintel Publications, *Snacking*, 9.

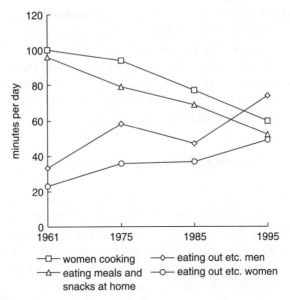

Fig. 7.6. Minutes per day spent in eating-related activities, Great Britain 1961–1995
Note: 'Eating out' includes pubs, cinema, theatre etc.
Source: Gershuny and Fisher, 'UK Leisure'.

overall decline in cooking time was less. By the 1980s about the same time was spent cooking in both countries, with women doing about four-fifths of the work.[136]

With food, women's mating interests diverged from their nurturing ones.[137] For men, the domestic meal restricted their exposure to food; for women, its preparation prolonged this exposure. Children were inimical to maternal slimness. Pregnancy usually had a lasting effect on body weight.[138] Childcare is stressful, and stress disinhibits eating. Children like sweet and salty flavours and energy-dense foods. They also react keenly to television advertising of such foods.[139] Giving way to children, women are exposed more strongly to sweet and savoury snacks.[140] 'Junk food' is an easy way to silence children, and another is to place them in front of

[136] In a 1995 survey, 80 per cent of women prepared every meal, while only 22 per cent of men did the same. Nicolaas, *Cooking: Attitudes and Behaviour*, table 1, p. 2. Robinson and Godbey, *Time for Life*, fig. 8, p. 101, estimate that in 1981 men provided 23 per cent of household cooking, and women 77 per cent. An Australian survey of 1993 found men doing 21 per cent of food preparation (Baxter and Western, 'Satisfaction with Housework', table 2, p. 108).

[137] Charles and Kerr, *Women, Food and Families*, 164; Green, *Diary*, 58.

[138] Rodin, *Body Traps*, 107.

[139] Birch et al., 'Development of Children's Eating Habits', 190, 200; Fumento, *Fat of the Land*, 53–5.   [140] Charles and Kerr, *Women, Food and Families*, 95–104.

the television.[141] When the two practices are combined, the likelihood of obesity in childhood rises.[142] Metabolic rates decline while children are watching TV.[143] When the pressures of home and work mount, one solution is to eat out more, and eating out, as we have seen, is also conducive to more ample eating.[144] The stresses of marriage also disinhibit eating, and body weight can become part of implicit bargaining about sexual exchange, signalling availability or withdrawal.[145]

Reactions: self-control, dieting, denial, defiance

As body weight began to rise, it stimulated an effort to recapture self-control. As in other dimensions of self-control, those with more at stake, and with more access to resources, have been more successful. Women, with more at stake than men, maintained lower weights; the well-off were more successful than the poor. The repertoire of reactions included food choice, exercise, eating disorders, defiance, and acceptance.

If women were driven to slimness by the competition for attractiveness, then, for men, the compelling pressures have been the correlations of animal foods with heart disease. Previously these very foods, red meat in particular, were associated with manliness, while dairy products, fresh, full-fat milk and butter in particular, were regarded as healthy for children.[146] In the 1950s and the 1960s the correlation between cholesterol and heart disease was discovered, and etched in the public mind. Heart disease at that time was the prime cause of death among males. What followed in the 1970s, in both America and Britain, was a shift in eating habits from richer protein and fatty foods, to foods that were perceived as either 'lighter', or as containing vegetable instead of animal fats.[147] A US Senate committee highlighted correlations between food choice and disease in 1977; the Surgeon General urged a lighter diet, and similar British reports followed soon after.[148] Despite some industry resistance,

[141] Dietz and Strasburger, 'Children, Adolescence and Television', 8; Fumento, *Fat of the Land*, 53–5.   [142] Dietz and Strasburger, 'Children, Adolescents and Television', 13–14.
[143] Klesges et al., 'Effects of Television'.
[144] Oropesa, 'Using the Service Economy'; Bonke, 'Economic Influences on Food Choice'. The relation between income and eating out is not straightforward. The convenience of eating out is counteracted by a commitment to family eating among the better-off.
[145] Stuart and Jacobson, *Weight, Sex and Marriage*.
[146] Twigg, 'Vegetarianism'; Levenstein, *Revolution at the Table*, 154–5.
[147] Levenstein, *Paradox of Plenty*, ch. 13.
[148] United States Senate, *Dietary Goals*; Seid, *Never Too Thin*, 176; Great Britain, Dept. of Health and Social Security, *Diet and Cardiovascular Disease*; British Medical Association, *Diet, Nutrition and Health*.

lighter eating became an official health objective.[149] For the United States, some sense of the changes can be gleaned from a list of 'winners' and 'losers', which reflects both the shift to 'lighter' foods (e.g. broccoli, yoghurt), and to more sophisticated ones (e.g. wine, cheese, pasta). Similar changes have occurred in Britain.[150]

Supply-side sources also indicate some shifts within food groups, such as the large shift from butter to margarine in both countries. But for body weight it is *calories* that count, and the rising input of meat, fats, cereals, sugar, and cheese in the United States adds up to a higher calorie intake. Three differences stand out: Americans ate more meat, while the British consumed more vegetables and cereals; and, while Americans were consuming more sugar, the British restrained their sweet tooth.[151] These changes involved some self-deception. There was a shift from 'heavy' meat (beef, pork, mutton) to 'light' meat, but consumption overall increased substantially.[152] Artificial compounds only accounted for about 7 per cent of sweeteners in terms of sugar equivalents.[153] Low-fat 'lite' foods are often almost as high in calories as regular foods.[154] American sales of diet drinks rose from 2 to 12 gallons per year per head, but sugared soft drinks increased from 21 to 40 gallons at the same time (1968–1994).[155]

In both the United States and Britain, improvements in the nutritional quality of food have taken place inside the home.[156] In the stable context of the home, learning took place and prudential eating strategies emerged. But increasingly, as we have seen, food is eaten *outside* the home. The expanding, compelling, novel, and less regular eating environment outside was able to frustrate these strategies. And this food, in the United States, improved much less. It typically contained more of the nutrients overconsumed (fat) and less of those underconsumed (calcium, fibre, and iron).[157] From Britain there is evidence that the prudential task was more difficult

[149] Cannon, *Politics of Food*; Walker and Cannon, *Food Scandal*; Seid, *Never Too Thin*, 191–9; Great Britain, Secretary of State for Health, *Health of the Nation*, 46–64.

[150] Putnam, 'Food Consumption', 2; Ritson and Hutchins, 'Consumption Revolution'. For Britain, Buss, 'British Diet' and Nelson, 'Social-Class Trends', also report these changes. American trends indicate that this improvement will have been partly counteracted by inferior nutritional quality of the growing proportion of food excluded from the National Food Survey, on which these studies are based.

[151] See fig. 5 in the discussion paper version of this chapter, based on OECD, *Food Statistics* (annual).**www.nuff.ox.ac.uk/economics/history/paper25/25offera4.pdf**.

[152] USDA, *Consumption of Red Meat*.

[153] Fine et al., *Consumption in an Age of Affluence*, appendix I, pp. 222–3, and table 6.6, p. 143. The statement applies to the late 1980s.   [154] Fumento, *Fat of the Land*, 80–1.

[155] USDA, *Food Consumption, Prices, and Expenditures*.

[156] The British National Food Survey, which reports these changes, covers only home consumption.   [157] Lin et al., 'Away-from-home Foods'.

for the poor. Specially packaged, palatable 'light foods' tend to be more expensive than the dietary staples, while cheap, low-fat, unsweetened staples such as oatmeal and cabbage take a considerable effort to convert into palatable meals. Poor families found it more difficult to produce balanced diets within their budget constraints.[158] The lower social grades consume 'junk food' more heavily, e.g. 14 per cent of class AB are 'heavy users' of potato crisps, as against 27 and 30 per cent respectively for classes C2 and D.[159] There are large differences in household consumption, and the well-off spend more than the poor on food, especially on high-cost foods.[160] Body weight is implicated in diabetes, cancers, and heart disease. All of them bear more heavily on the lower social classes, and these classes also tend to consume more tobacco, alcohol, and inferior food.[161]

A recent study has attempted to identify the determinants of the rise in body weight in the United States since the 1980s (Table 7.5), with separate explanations for the rise in the Body Mass Index (BMI) and in the percentage 'obese' (BMI > 30). The coefficients each measure the contribution of the particular factor to the total amount of change (2.13 BMI, 12.99 per cent obesity). They add up (roughly) to the total amount of change observed. The interesting columns are (2), which leave out the coefficient for the time trend. By far the largest coefficient is the density of restaurants. All the other coefficients (except food prices) have the right signs. Interestingly, the second largest factor is cigarette prices: this suggests that the decline in smoking (which inhibits appetite) reinforced the rise in weight. Education, income, and ethnicity, all of them proxies for social class, have the right signs, but together add up to only about 10 per cent of the variance. The authors regard the restaurant density as a proxy for the 'time squeeze', another myopic incentive which we discuss in more detail below, and which affects higher earners more than low earners.[162]

An appropriate reaction was to take up exercise: 'Joggers have become an almost familiar sight throughout America in the last year, [1968].'[163]

---

[158] Charles and Kerr, *Women, Food and Families*, 167–78; DeVault, *Feeding the Family*, ch. 7; McKenzie, 'Economic Influences on Food Choice'; Charlton and Quaife, 'Trends in Diet', 105–6. Indications of the relative increase in lower-income group consumption of fats and sugars in the 1970s are also suggestive, but not conclusive in the absence of eating-out data. See Nelson, 'Social-Class Trends', fig. 7.4, p. 109.

[159] Ratcliff, *Snack Foods*, table 20, 46. Similar gradients are found for other 'junk' foods.

[160] McKenzie, 'Economic Influences'; Chesher, 'Household Composition', 57.

[161] Charlton and Quaife, 'Trends in Diet', 97–8, 104–6; Black et al., *Inequalities of Health*, 290–6; Everson et al., 'Epidemiologic Evidence', 892–3.   [162] Below, Ch. 13.

[163] *Chicago Tribune*, 9 July 1968—cited as the first recorded instance in the *Oxford English Dictionary*.

Table 7.5. Impact of selected factors on Body Mass Index and percentage obese, persons 18 years and older, 1984–1999

Factor	BMI Observed Change = 2.13			Obese Observed Change = 12.99 [percentage points]		
	(1)	(2)	(3)	(1)	(2)	(3)
Race/Ethnicity	0.08	0.08	0.08	0.35	0.36	0.35
Schooling	−0.06	−0.06	−0.06	−0.42	−0.42	−0.42
Married	−0.03	−0.03	−0.03	−0.13	−0.13	−0.13
Age	0.23	0.23	0.23	1.13	1.14	1.13
Household income	−0.09	−0.08	−0.08	−0.5	−0.5	−0.5
Trend	2.06		1.73	12.4		9.79
Restaurants		1.46	0.21		8.77	1.54
Fast-food restaurant price		0.09	0.03		0.48	0.17
Full-service restaurant price		0.08	−0.02		0.49	−0.09
Food at home price		0.13	0.06		0.86	0.41
Cigarette price		0.44	0.09		2.96	0.88
Clean indoor air laws		0.09	−0.02		0.57	−0.04
Total predicted change	2.06	2.42	2.23	12.8	14.6	13.09

Note: Based on micro-level data from Behavioral Risk Factor Surveillance System between 1984 and 1999, with a total sample number of 1,111,074.

Source: Chou et al., 'Economic Analysis of Adult Obesity', table 7, p. 52.

Exercise swept the United States in the 1970s and 1980s.[164] Stationary bikes became a spare-bedroom fixture, and younger people spent long hours 'working out'. Fitness clubs were a £1bn industry in the UK by 1998.[165] But exercise requires self-control and resources no less than restrained eating. Table 7.6 is an indicator that exercise (like other forms of self-control) increases with education and income. It also supports the notion that weight control is motivated by courtship. Exercise was as frequent among the never married, as amongst the highest earners and the best educated. In Britain, too, exercise was more of a male activity, and there was a class gradient, with professionals taking exercise more frequently than manual workers (Table 7.5). Both class and gender were converging over time.

Slimming is a repudiation of the prior 'eating decision'. In the 1980s, about 23 per cent of American men and 40 per cent of women were trying to lose weight.[166] In the UK, only 4 per cent of men, and 12 per cent of

[164] Gillick, 'Jogging'; Seid, *Never Too Thin*, 181–6; Yates, 'Running'.
[165] Marks, 'Gym Industry', 8.
[166] Horm and Anderson, 'Who in America', table 2, p. 674; market research places the level much higher (Rodin, *Body Traps*, 166).

Table 7.6. Exercise, drinking, and smoking, USA 1990 (%, age 18 plus)

Characteristic	Exercise or sport regularly	Two plus drinks a day	Current smoker	BMI 27.8 + M 27.3 + F
All persons	40.7	5.5	25.5	27.5
Male	44	9.7	28.4	29.6
Female	37.7	1.7	22.8	25.6
Marital status				
Currently married	39.4	5.3	24.6	29.2
Formerly married	34.3	5.3	30.3	29.1
Never married	51.3	6.6	24.3	19.8
Education				
Less than 12 years	25.9	5.1	31.8	32.7
12 years	37	5.9	29.6	28.6
More than 12 years	52.1	5.4	18.3	23.8
Income				
Less than $10,000	32.9	4.8	31.6	29.3
$10,000 to $19,999	32.3	4.9	29.8	28.5
$20,000 to $34,999	40.5	5.8	26.9	28.2
$35,000 to $49,999	46.1	5.6	23.4	27.8
$50,000 or more	51.7	6.7	19.3	24.9

Source: US Bureau of Census, *Statistical Abstract*, table 221, p. 145.

Table 7.7. Exercise or physical activity of adults within last month in the UK, ages 19–40, by social class and gender (% engaged during last month)

	Professional		Intermediate		Manual	
	Men	Women	Men	Women	Men	Women
All years	55	39	44	29	40	23
1977	50	27	39	20	29	10
1987	59	46	50	36	48	29
1997	57	45	48	42	46	35

Note: Annual, 1977 to 1997.

Source: Great Britain, *General Household Survey*, data extracted by Prof. J. Gershuny.

women were on a slimming diet.[167] Both success and failure were expensive. In 1990, some $8.4bn was being spent in the USA on products for serious dieters, with about $33bn being spent on slimming as a whole.[168] The direct treatment costs of obesity were placed somewhat higher, at $45.8bn.[169]

[167] Gregory et al., *Dietary and Nutritional Survey*, 48.
[168] Armstrong and Mallory, 'Diet Business'; Miller, 'Diets Incorporated'.
[169] Colditz, 'Economic Costs of Obesity'; Hughes and McGuire, 'Economic Analysis of Obesity', 258.

Altogether, what may be termed the money 'regret costs' of eating and drinking came to about 15 per cent of the outlays, comparable to all the increment in annual food and alcohol outlays since 1965.[170] By 1998, about 9 per cent of medical spending in the USA was attributed to over-weight, a level comparable with smoking.[171]

Thousands of diet books attest that losing weight is a major emotional and cognitive undertaking, which often ends in failure.[172] Success is a notable achievement, justifying celebration in a book, and providing credibility for a career as a slimming authority.[173] This was Rosemary Green's motivation to begin her diary, but even the financial incentive was of no avail. After years of yo-yo dieting, she came to see that having come within range of a snack, it was too late to exercise self-control. She finally succeeded by turning over control of household food to her husband, who kept it under lock and key.[174] Nigel Lawson, former British Chancellor of the Exchequer, also wrote a slimming book. Like Mrs Green, he also handed over the keys to his spouse.[175] Both of these successful dieters followed Ainslie's technology of self-control: since food cravings proved impossible to resist, their strategy was to transfer control to a detached but friendly third party, and to follow strict 'bright line' routines.[176]

But self-control can go too far. A rising wave of eating disorders has emerged since the 1970s. Anorexia and bulimia were little known outside the affluent world in the last three decades, although they are not unknown in the western past. They affected young women mainly, especially in college.[177] Clinical diagnosis was infrequent, but in milder forms these disorders affected substantial numbers.[178] The mating hypothesis of female slimming is supported by a 1980s longitudinal study: female student eating disorders were peaking in the early twenties. Seven or eight years later the women were more likely to be married, heavier, and with fewer eating disorders, although still concerned about body weight. Men had fewer disorders initially, gained more weight subsequently, and remained indifferent to it.[179]

The ultimate act of body shaping is cosmetic surgery: in 1996, almost 300,000 fat-sucking operations were carried out in the United States, on

[170] Sources, n. 21 above.   [171] Finkelstein et al., 'National Medical Spending', p. W3–224.
[172] Stuart and Jacobson, *Weight, Sex and Marriage*, 347–9; Stunkard, 'Social Environment', 440–5.   [173] Fumento, *Fat of the Land*, ch. 6.
[174] Green, *Diary*, 336–8.   [175] Lawson, *Nigel Lawson Diet Book*, 63–4.
[176] Ainslie, *Picoeconomics*, 162–70, 296–7, and *passim*. See above, Ch. 3.
[177] Gordon, *Anorexia and Bulimia*, 33–49.
[178] Mitchell and Eckert, 'Scope and Significance', 628–9; Herman and Polivy, 'What does Abnormal Eating Tell Us'; Polivy and Herman, 'Diagnosis and Treatment of Normal Eating'.
[179] Heatherton et al., 'A 10-Year Longitudinal Study'. This is not inconsistent with a labour-force entry interpretation for slimming pressures.

4.4 women for every man.[180] It remains an anomaly that the pursuit of thinness does not seem to have abated, despite the return of sex ratios to parity—but the recent popularity of 'working out' suggests that emphasis has shifted onto 'muscle tone', in which men are more heavily involved than women (Tables 7.6, 7.7).[181]

Black women were the heaviest of all social groups (Figure 7.1). Among the reasons canvassed are fewer educational and financial resources, low physical activity levels, ineffective dieting, and a rejection of non-black weight norms.[182] This research is inconclusive. Many of these factors would apply to black men as well, but black men have similar BMIs to whites, while black women are two BMI units heavier on average than white women.[183] Culture is as likely to be a consequence as an independent cause. The sex-ratio explanation of male–female difference may have some purchase here. For black women, sex ratios were much the worst. Black males were disproportionately absent on military service or in prison, and fell victim excessively to accidents and violence. They achieved less in education than black women. They were more than twice as likely to be married to white women, than black women were likely to be married to white men. Almost half of multi-person black households are now headed by women.[184] In these circumstances, competition for males has become much less compelling, since the likelihood of marital commitment is reduced. The ratio of the percentage of white to black married men was 76 : 67 in 1970, 70 : 55 in 1980, and 66 : 49 in 1990.[185] With marriage prospects so limited for women, there was less to be gained in trying to push body weight below its natural equilibrium.

Three other responses are denial, acceptance, and defiance. As in the case of every public health issue, smoking, AIDS, or climate change, there is a niche for scientific deniers.[186] At the other ideological end, feminist writers of the 1970s and 1980s recommended accepting one's body, and more recently have characterized fat denigration as a form of oppression.[187] They were joined by contrarians and libertarians.[188] The National Association to

---

[180] 292,942 liposuction operations. American Academy of Cosmetic Surgery, 'Statistics', **www.cosmeticsurgeryonline.com/consumer/stats/1996per cent.html**.

[181] Pope et al., *Adonis Complex*, ch. 2.

[182] Riley et al., 'Relation of Self-Image', 1062–3; Hebl and Heatherton, 'Stigma of Obesity in Women'.   [183] Kuczmarski et al., 'Increasing Prevalence of Overweight', table 4, p. 209.

[184] Sollors, *Interracialism*, 461; Guttentag and Secord, *Too Many Women?*, ch. 8; United States, *Statistical Abstract 1998*, table 77, p. 65; see below, Figure 11.4, Ch. 11.

[185] United States, *Statistical Abstract 1992*, table 49, p. 44.

[186] Critser, *Fat Land*, 96–102; Campos, *Obesity Myth*.

[187] Orbach, *Fat*, 14, 31–2; LeBesco, *Revolting Bodies*.

[188] e.g. Klein, *Eat Fat*; Jenkins, 'Nanny Can't Wait'.

Advance Fat Acceptance advocates 'Fat Pride'.[189] Several influences have been acting to relax weight norms. Sex ratios have improved in favour of women (Figure 7.4). Overweight is becoming a majority condition (Figure 7.1).[190] Contrary to much comment, overweight people as a whole are not particularly low in self-esteem, and do not suffer exceptionally from mental disorders.[191]

Conclusion: myopic or rational obesity?

Economists find it difficult to abandon the assumption of rationality, even in the face of choices which are manifestly bad, which even those who make them are unhappy with. A recent example is a review of obesity in a central journal. Like this chapter, it surveys changes in weight, changes in food intake, and changes in physical activity and time use. Like this chapter, it focuses on the reduction in time required for food preparation, due to technological change.[192] If delay is the critical variable, then a model of myopic choice is attractive. When the hurdle of delay is lowered, the myopic consumer will respond with a large increase in consumption. A myopic (hyperbolic discounting) individual,

will always want to begin a diet tomorrow, because the long-term benefits justify the lost utility tomorrow, but not today, because the immediate gratification from food is high. Reductions in the time cost of food preparation may reduce the welfare of this person, by increasing the immediate consumption value of food relative to the long-term health costs.[193]

Having made this leap, the authors hold back. They search for a way to reconcile body-weight gain with the rational consumer. They convert both costs and benefits into the currency of time. The benefits of time saving arise from snacking, eating out, and shorter meal preparation. This point is also made by Chou et al., who regard the density of restaurants (their strongest predictor of weight increase) as a proxy for the demand for time saving.[194] The costs are measured in terms of the time it would have

[189] Millman, *Such a Pretty Face*; NAAFA homepage, **www.naafa.org/** (1998). On the 'Fatlash', Fumento, *Fat of the Land*, 38–43, 115–22.

[190] Polivy and Herman, 'Diagnosis and Treatment'.

[191] Hamermesh and Biddle, 'Beauty and the Labor Market'; Stunkard and Wadden, 'Psychological Aspects of Severe Obesity'.

[192] Cutler et al., 'Why Have Americans become more Obese?'. The present chapter first appeared as a discussion paper in 1998 and as a journal article in 2001.   [193] Ibid. 113.

[194] Chou et al., 'Economic Analysis of Adult Obesity'.

required to exercise off the extra pounds acquired. On balance, it is argued, benefits outweigh the costs, time saved is greater than (potential) working out time lost, ergo the rational consumer is saved. But having already assumed that their consumer is myopic, that she has a self-control problem—it is hardly possible to assume that the exercise-bicycle road to redemption is available costlessly. 'While there is no evidence on the incidence of extreme hyperbolic discounting in the population, we suspect that most people are better off from the technological advances of mass food preparation, even if their weight has increased.'[195]

In fact, as we have seen, the evidence points the other way. As Gruber et al. have shown, smokers welcome the assistance of higher taxes in helping them to exercise self-control.[196] Body weight and healthy behaviours are inversely related to education, income, and gender, the resources of self-control. The massive rise of body weight, whether epidemic or not, is hardly evidence of rationality. Furthermore, it is not clear that the time gained has been such a pure benefit. At the lower end of the income distribution, time saved in housework has largely been devoted to watching television, at the higher end, to spending more time at work—both of these being myopic behaviours in themselves.[197]

Under affluence, the challenge posed by cheap rewards like food is not to maximize consumption, but to pace it down to the rate of optimal reward.[198] Pacing requires self-control, and self-control requires prudential strategies. Knowledge takes time to build up, so that the better-off, who have the resources, are therefore more capable of success. This applies across the board: in women's body weight, in junk food consumption, in taking exercise, in family meals, in smoking.

The example of smoking is suggestive. Society lacks protection from new and cheap rewards, and smoking swept through the United States and Britain until, by 1950, about three-quarters of all American families were buying tobacco.[199] Evidence that smoking was inimical to health emerged before the Second World War. By the early 1960s society was learning to respond. Governments endorsed the medical warnings, and began to regulate advertising. Learning goes on, and tobacco is increasingly restricted and shunned. Consumption peaked in the 1960s, and has been declining ever since. The higher social classes have proved more adept at avoiding

[195] Cutler et al., 'Why have Americans become more Obese', 115–6.
[196] Gruber and Köszegi, 'Is Addiction "Rational"?'; id., Gruber and Mullainathan, 'Do Cigarette Taxes Make Smokers Happier?'; and above, Ch. 3.
[197] Leisure and television, Table 8.2 below; Longer working hours, Ch. 13 below.
[198] Ainslie, *Picoeconomics*, 256–73, 293–300; and Chapter 3 above.
[199] Brown, *American Standards of Living*, 232.

tobacco, and the aversion is spreading. It is the poorest and those least educated who are the most exposed to the reward (Table 7.6).[200] But, as old problems were mastered, new ones appeared. Alcohol is rich in calories, while smoking inhibits appetite. Drinking rose in step with affluence until the 1970s, when it levelled off. Smoking has declined.[201] This pattern is consistent with the rise of body weight. Over a ten-year period in the 1980s, men who quit smoking gained an average 4.4 kg, and women 5.0 kg. They were more than twice as likely to become overweight as non-smokers.[202] More recent evidence also suggests that the decline of smoking has acted to increase body weight. But if a self-control problem persists for long enough, learning will take place. Until the recent Atkins diet fad, the consumption of red meat has also been decreasing. Deaths from heart disease fell by more than half between the 1950s and 2002.[203] The large decline in mortality risk from obesity between the 1970s and the 1990s also suggests a learning process, though its nature is unclear.[204]

New rewards were thrown up by affluence faster than it took to learn to cope with the previous ones, so that overall, despite growing wealth, self-control declined. Obesity shows how abundance, through cheapness, variety, novelty, and choice, could make a mockery of the rational consumer, how it enticed only in order to humiliate. The 'cult of thinness' can be seen as a response to competitive demands on women in mating and the workplace. But its impact on behavioural outcomes was restricted to keeping women's average BMIs below those of men for about two decades; it has not been able to halt the upwards trend of body weight.

---

[200] Ibid., 416; Doll, 'Uncovering the Effects of Smoking'; Doll et al., 'Trends in Mortality', fig. 9.2, p. 132; Flegal et al., 'Influence of Smoking Cessation', table 1, p. 1167.

[201] Sources as n. 18, above.

[202] Flegal et al., 'Influence of Smoking Cessation'; in Britain, male non-smokers were heavier than smokers, but female non-smokers were not. See Gregory, *Dietary and Nutritional Survey*, 229.

[203] US National Center for Health Statistics, *Health, United States 2004*, table 36, p. 169.

[204] Flegal et al., 'Excess Deaths'.

8

Household Appliances and the Use of Time[1]

Cookers, vacuum cleaners, refrigerators, washing machines, radio, television, air conditioning, microwave ovens: a sequence of electrical and mechanical tools has accumulated in American and British households. The outlay on domestic appliances has only claimed a tiny fraction of disposable income, but their impact on experience has been large.[2] Despite the ubiquity of these goods, their diffusion is not well understood. Some kinds of appliances diffuse more rapidly than others. In particular, home entertainment appliances such as radio and television have diffused much faster than household and kitchen machines (e.g. vacuum cleaners, washing machines, and refrigerators). Housework appliances made it possible to put off drudgery and reduce it. They saved time. Entertainment appliances were compelling to impatient consumers. They consumed time. Roughly speaking, the time saved by one set of appliances was consumed by the other.

How appliances diffuse

There are several explanatory approaches to the diffusion of household technology. One is to measure aggregate consumer demand. The national accounts record the annual outlay on clusters of durables. Economists have estimated models which relate consumer outlays to price, income, existing stocks, depreciation, habit, household formation, and other explanatory

[1] A revised version of Bowden and Offer, 'Household Appliances', which was originally written jointly with Sue Bowden.
[2] 0.5 per cent of disposable income in the USA in 1920, up to about 2 per cent in 1980. Olney, *Buy Now, Pay Later*, tables 2.7, 2.8, pp. 41–4, 48–9.

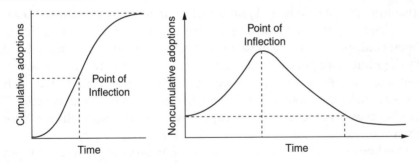

Fig. 8.1. Innovation diffusion curves
Source: Mahajan et al., 'New Product Diffusion Models', fig. 1, p. 4.

variables.[3] Overall, the retrospective fit was generally 'satisfactory to excellent',[4] but they often broke down when applied to household appliances.[5]

Another approach mimics models of the spread of disease in closed populations. The diffusion of appliances follows a rising trend which can be described by a logistic growth curve (Figure 8.1). In such models, the probability and timing of a new purchase are driven by the quantity and pace of previous purchases. The diffusion curve describes the proportion of the target population acquiring the good over time. It is sigmoid (i.e. 's-shaped'), with an inflection point at one-half.[6] Take-up is determined by a learning (or 'contagion') process. Early-movers try out the product. Imitation and publicity spread the word. Diffusion slows down as the target population gets saturated at some level. The sequence of annual sales typically follows a bell-curve shape, rising to a maximum as diffusion accelerates, and declining when most new adoptions have taken place, and a mature market is sustained by replacement purchases and new entrants.[7]

These logistic diffusion models were discovered by economists and marketing experts in the late 1920s, and have been widely used since the 1930s.[8] Such models investigate the rate of diffusion over time,

---

[3] Houthakker and Taylor, *Consumer Demand*; Olney, *Buy Now, Pay Later*.

[4] Houthakker and Taylor, *Consumer Demand*, 3.

[5] For example ibid., 'Kitchen and other household appliances'; also see ibid., fig. 5.2, p. 81; pianos, radios and television see Olney, *Buy Now, Pay Later*, table 3.2, (variable 'MUS'), [music] p. 79.

[6] Pyatt, *Priority Patterns*, 5–6; Rogers, *Diffusion of Innovations*, 244; Mahajan et al., 'New Product Diffusion', 2–5.

[7] This is a simplification, which takes no account of changes in quality, product differentiation, and price. The top of the bell curve is temporally the same as the s-curve inflection point.

[8] Paul T. Cherington, 'The Curve of Progress', presented at the representative's meeting of the J. Walter Thompson advertising agency, New York, 17 May 1927. JWT, Staff Meetings, box 1, Hartman Center, Duke University; Pyatt, *Priority Patterns*, 5–7.

independently of income and price variables. In recent times similar models have been applied by marketing scientists to the diffusion of particular household appliances. The most influential, introduced by Bass, was refined by the addition of price variables, and of variable elasticities, and produces very good fits.[9] But for all their success, both demand and diffusion models are essentially descriptive. Their predictive power is only retrospective.[10] Neither class of model attempts to explain why one appliance diffuses faster than another.

One line of research considers consumer durables indirectly, as an input into household production. This is associated with Gary Becker, and has become familiar as the 'New Home Economics'. It defines 'commodities' created at home by combining housework and market goods, as a source of satisfaction or utility. Allocation of time between domestic and market work depends on marginal productivity in each of the two sectors. In equilibrium, the marginal utility obtained from work at home (including 'leisure') equals the marginal income available from market work. In this approach, household technology is linked to the economics of labour supply, although little work has been done to incorporate household technology into formal models of labour supply and leisure preference.[11]

The question of why some goods diffuse much faster than others, regardless of their relative prices, is broached, in a tentative way, by marketing writers. 'Psychographics', an influential approach to marketing, attempts to explain consumer behaviour in terms of particular needs orientations, which are expressed in different personality types.[12] Preference for particular durables was associated with particular sets of personal values. For example, in one survey, 'consumers who valued security, respect and a sense of belonging (social values) had greater utility for sports, exercise and luxury products. Those who valued fun and excitement (stimulation) had greater utility for home entertainment products, sports and exercise products, and pets.'[13]

Narrative accounts of durables in the household have been inspired by the feminist challenge to the domestic gender division of labour.[14] Some empirical light on the problem is also thrown by time-budget studies, which highlight the many constraints on time allocation, arising

[9] Mahajan et al., 'New Product Diffusion Models'.   [10] Ibid. 9.
[11] Becker, 'Theory of the Allocation of Time', 513, cites Owen, 'Supply of Labor'; Long, *Labor Force*, 120–1 estimates the time saved by household appliances in the USA, 1890–1950.
[12] Gunter and Furnham, *Consumer Profiles*; updated survey, Liu, 'Reading the Minds of Consumers'.   [13] Corfman et al., 'Values, Utility, and Ownership', 201.
[14] Bose, 'Technology and Changes'; Bose et al., 'Household Technology'; Cowan, *More Work for Mother*, 175; Ravetz, 'Modern Technology and an Ancient Occupation', 256–60; Strasser, *Never Done*; Thomas and Zmroczek, 'Household Technology'; Vanek, 'Time Spent in Housework', 83. Summary in Morris, *Workings of the Household*, 80–102.

from social, cultural, and geographical location, from cohort and life-cycle effects.[15] Yet another perspective can be inferred from the *Affluent Worker* studies of the 1960s, where the aspirations of English semi-skilled car workers were found to be focused on standards of domestic life, in which the acquisition of durables loomed large.[16]

The prototype mass-produced consumer durable was the sewing machine, which reached its diffusion inflection point in the USA by the early 1870s (in about fourteen years), and in the UK by 1889.[17] Here, we follow the diffusion trajectories of household appliances in the United States and Britain since the 1920s, and ask why they differ so much from one good to another. The approach is inspired by Becker. What determines the different diffusion rates of different classes of appliances is the effect of such goods on the supply of discretionary time, on its cost, and on the satisfactions it can provide. The flow of new goods has shifted consumers towards a more myopic allocation of time.

Time saving and time using

A simple measure of the speed of adoption of particular durables is the time they take to achieve a certain level of acceptance. This is shown in Table 8.1, which describes the time required for different household appliances to attain household penetration levels of 20, 50, and 75 per cent, in the United States and in Britain. Goods are ranked according to the time they have taken to reach the highest of these three levels of diffusion for which data are available.

Among household goods, the rapid diffusers are quite different from the slow ones. Marketing writers have distinguished between 'time-saving' goods and 'time-using' ones. 'Time-saving' goods reduce the time required to perform a household task. An electric washing machine reduces the time required to clean a tubful of laundry, compared with manual methods. Such goods can release discretionary time, i.e. the time (over and above work and domestic obligations) which can be used according to the person's taste.

The other class of goods, 'time-using' ones, require the allocation of discretionary time for use with the product.[18] Radio and television require

[15] Hartmann, 'The Family as the Locus'; Gershuny, *Changing Times*.
[16] Goldthorpe, *The Affluent Worker*, iii. 8, 22, 164.
[17] Godley, 'Global Diffusion of the Sewing Machine', figures 1, 2, pp. 5, 10.
[18] Engel et al., *Consumer Behavior*, 261–4.

Table 8.1. Diffusion rate of selected household appliances in the United States and Britain

Appliance	Country	Household penetration begins (I%)ᵃ	Additional years to penetration (% households with appliance)			Rankᵇ
			of 20%	of 50%	of 75%	
TV black and white	USA	1948	2	5	7	1
Radioᶜ	USA	1923	3	6	8	2
TV colour	USA	1961	6	6	10	3
TV black and white	E&W	1949	5	9	12	4
TV colour	E&W	1970	4	8	13	5
Video recorder	UK	1979	5	9	15	6
CD player	UK	1984	6	11	16	7
Microwave ovenʰ	USA	1973	9	13	17	8
Radioᵈ	UK	1923	3	10	20	9
Freezer	E&W	1968	9	14	20	10
Refrigerator	USA	1925	7	13	23	11
Microwave oven	UK	1973		18	25	12
Refrigerator	E&W	1946	15	22	27	13
Electric iron	E&W	1909		24	30	14
Electric iron	USA	1910			34	15
Clothes washerᵉ	USA	1916	6	20	34	16
Clothes washer	E&W	1934	23	30	46	17
Vacuum cleaner	E&W	1915	18	40	47	18
Vacuum cleaner	USA	1913		28	48	19
Motor carᶠ	USA	1908		16	52	20
Telephoneᵍ	USA	1890		56	67	21
Motor carⁱ	GB	1908	46	57	94	22
Video recorderʰ	USA	1979	7	9		1
Can opener	USA	1959	5	14		2
Electric blanket	E&W	1955	6	18		3
Personal computer	UK	1981	9	20		4
Personal computer	USA	1981		20		5
Clothes dryer	USA	1950	11	22		6
Electric blanket	USA	1948	11	22		7
Air conditioner	USA	1952	12	22		8
Blender	USA	1948	19	22		9
Water heater	E&W	1934	21	33		10
Dish washer	USA	1922	46	75		11
Clothes dryer	E&W	1950	31	44		13
Dish washer	E&W	1957	39			

Notes:
ᵃ Electrically wired households, unless indicated otherwise below. The early years of innovation, during which the design tended to be unstable, were usually prolonged, so the first year is taken to be the one in which household penetration achieved 1%.
ᵇ Ranking is estimated on basis of (1) length of time taken to achieve 75% penetration level; (2) length of time taken to achieve 50% penetration level; and (3) length of time taken to achieve 20% penetration level, in that order. An appliance which has reached 75% penetration thus ranks higher than an appliance which has failed to reach 75% or 50% and in some cases 20% penetration levels.
For appliances introduced before the First World War, the year of introduction is taken to be the year of first commercial product, with five years added. Sources include Rath, 'Lighting Devices', 20–3; Yarwood, 'The Domestic Interior'. For irons see also Strasser, *Never Done*, 78; Hardyment, *From Mangle to Microwave*, 73; Davidson, *Woman's Work*, 158. For vacuum cleaners seen Hardyment, p. 81; Davidson, p. 58; Yarwood, *British Kitchen*, 136.
ᶜ US Radio: up to 1930, cumulative sales divided by the number of wired households. This overestimates penetration, as some radios were battery models sold to households without electric wiring. There was also some duplication and some scrapping by the end of the period.

^d Radio licences per household as percentage of all households in the UK. *Sources*: Radio licences per 100 persons, Ironmonger, *New Commodities*, table 7.3, p. 143; household size, Great Britain, Office of Population, Census and Surveys, *Britain's Households*, table 1, p. 2.

^e Clothes washers, USA. Saturation levels reported in *Merchandising*, 4/3(Mar. 1979), 46, 48 are set at precisely 20 percentage points below the levels reported in *Merchandising Week*, 28 Feb. 1972. This is lower than England and Wales levels, which suggests a transcription error in the later American data.

^f Motor cars, USA for 1910 and 1960, number of passenger cars as percentage of US households. For 1910, this overstates diffusion at that stage. *Sources*: Cars, US Bureau of Census, *Historical Statistics*, pt. 2, table Q 148, p. 716; households, ibid., pt. 1, table A 288, p. 41. For 1924, cars per 100 households, Society of Motor Manufacturers and Traders, *The Motor Industry of Great Britain*, annual.

^g Telephones, US Bureau of Census, *Historical Statistics*, tables R 1–3, 1920 ratio of telephones to households extrapolated backwards to 1890.

^h Video recorders and microwave ovens, USA. Cumulative shipments as percentage of households, starting with year of 1% penetration. This progressively overstates the diffusion level due to (*a*) scrappings in later years, (*b*) ownership of more than one device, (*c*) ownership by non-household sectors. For example, the household penetration of microwave ovens calculated according to this method was 70 per cent in 1986 and 83 per cent in 1987, while another, independent estimate gives a level of 61 per cent for that year (US Bureau of Census, *Statistical Abstract 1990*, table 1452, p. 843). This is acceptable since it is biased against the hypothesis that time-using appliances diffuse more rapidly: the overstatement is likely to be larger in the case of microwave ovens than video recorders. Last figure taken from USA, *Statistical Abstract 1990*.

ⁱ Great Britain, cars per 100 households. *Sources*: for 1908, Mitchell, *Historical Statistics*, 557, divided by number of households. This overstates diffusion since 'private cars' in business ownership are included. For subsequent years, cars per 100 households, Society of Motor Manufacturers and Traders, *The Motor Industry of Great Britain*, annual.

Sources: USA: 'Fifty Years of Statistics and History', *Merchandising Week*, 27 Feb. 1972; *Merchandising, passim*, 1976–89, esp. Mar. 1978, pp. 46, 48; *Dealerscope Merchandising*, 1991–92; for data after 1980, most of the information is updated from United States, Bureau of Census, *Statistical Abstract* (various edns., online).

England and Wales: Electricity Council (UK), 'Domestic Sector Analysis (England & Wales), 1932/3 to 1978/9', EF 144, July 1980 (this archive has been dispersed, but there is a copy in the possession of the author); Great Britain, Office of Population Censuses and Surveys, Social Survey Division, *General Household Survey Series*, no. 21, (1992) Table 3.17, p. 60. Data after 1980 have been updated using aggregated online micro-data from Great Britain, ONS, *General Household Survey* (acknowledgments to Matthew Polisson for collecting these data).

discretionary time in order to produce satisfaction. Time-saving technology is applied to housework, while radio and television are typical time-using goods. Time-saving goods increase the quantity of discretionary time, whereas time-using goods enhance its quality.

Between the 1920s and the 1970s, these two different classes of goods followed distinctive diffusion trajectories. Figure 8.2 shows the diffusion trajectories of a selected sample of household appliances between the 1920s and 2002.

The vacuum cleaner, refrigerator, and washing machine had all been introduced either shortly before or shortly after the First World War. Each took several decades to diffuse and to enter the majority of households. The same applies to the diffusion of gas and electric cookers.[19] In contrast, 'time-using' appliances entered society at a much steeper trajectory. Three-quarters of American homes had radio within about a decade of its introduction. Black-and-white television was watched in about four-fifths of American homes within ten years of the Second World War, and took only just a little longer to attain the same level in England and Wales.

[19] 'Fifty years', *Merchandising Week*, 28 Feb. 1972; Bowden and Offer, 'Technological Revolution that Never Was'.

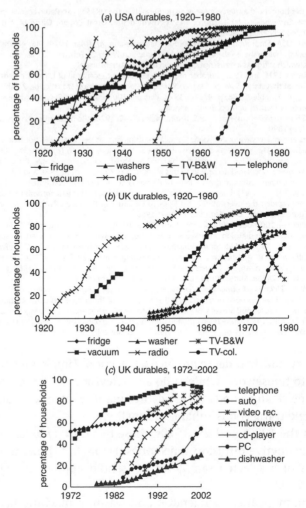

Fig. 8.2. Diffusion of selected household durables in the USA and Britain, 1921–2002

Notes: *US Radio*: up to 1932, cumulative production as percentage of all households; wired households thereafter. *UK Radio*: radio licences per household as percentage of all households in the UK.

Sources: *USA*: Anon., 'Fifty Years of Statistics and History'; Anon., 'Product Saturation Analysis', 46, 48. *Great Britain: Radio licenses per 100 persons*, Ironmonger, *New Commodities*, table 7.3, p. 143; household size, see Great Britain, Office of Population, Census and Surveys, *Britain's Households*, table 1, p. 2; Electricity Council (GB), 'Domestic Sector Analysis'; Great Britain, Office for National Statistics, *General Household Survey* (downloaded electronically). Thanks to Matthew Polisson for his work on this source. For annual series, see Bowden and Offer, 'Household Appliances', Appendix, pp. 745–6.

In contrast, washing machines, first introduced more than three decades before television, had not achieved its level of diffusion by 1970. Refrigerators took more than two decades (excluding the war years) to attain the level of acceptance achieved by television in one.[20]

The same difference between time-saving and time-using appliances is demonstrated in the diffusion lags between the United States and Britain. In the post-war years real income per head in Britain lagged about thirty years behind the United States. In 1960 Britain had just reached the level attained in the United States in 1929, some thirty years before.[21] Consequently the mass diffusion of household appliances which began in the United States in the 1920s only took off in Britain in the 1950s.

The diffusion lag was much longer for time-saving than for time-using appliances. In vacuum cleaners, after an initial lag, Britain closed a large gap quickly in the 1950s. But for both the washing machine and the refrigerator, Britain reached a diffusion level of about 60 per cent of wired households in the 1970s, which is comparable with the United States thirty years before. The diffusion lag of these major time-saving goods appears to match roughly the lag in incomes. The one exception is the microwave oven in the USA, which diffused at almost 'time-using' rates. It reached 75 per cent penetration faster than UK radio more than half a century earlier (though it still diffused more slowly than UK radio initially).[22]

It was very different with time-using durables. Radio and television diffused in Britain with a lag of only five to ten years behind the USA, for articles that were much more expensive in relation to income than in the United States. By the time the video recorder arrived in the 1980s, the gap had closed entirely, and its diffusion in the two countries proceeded at the same frenetic pace, from almost nothing in 1980, to more than 40 per cent penetration in 1986, and more than 60 per cent by 1990.[23]

Why was the diffusion of time-using goods so much faster than that of time-saving goods? It has also been found in Europe: time to take-off 'is four times shorter for entertainment products than for kitchen and laundry appliances'.[24] Our explanation is cast in terms of the cost and benefits of an increment of discretionary time. Consumers have apparently given a

[20] These levels refer to wired homes. Britain overtook the United States in the proportion of wired homes in 1935, at a level of about 65 per cent. Thereafter, the two countries moved very closely together, but did not achieve universal wiring until the mid-1960s.

[21] Bairoch, 'Main Trends in National Economic Disparities', table 1.4, p. 10.

[22] Table 8.1 above, and Figure 8.2 (c).

[23] Gunter and Svennevig, *Behind and in Front of the Screen*, 79; Butsch, 'Home Video', 217; Alvarado, *Video World-Wide*, table 4, p. 23; Klopfenstein, 'Diffusion of the VCR in the United States', table 2.2, p. 25; United States, *Statistical Abstract 1991*, table 919, p. 556.

[24] Tellis et al., 'International Takeoff of New Products', 188.

higher priority to enhancing the quality of discretionary time than to increasing its quantity. This reflects the uneven pace of technological change, which has found it easier to increase the rewards of leisure than to reduce the burden of housework. This argument is developed in the sections that follow.

Time saving

Consumer durables are 'superior goods', and the demand for them typically increases faster than income. Over the post-war period (1947–82), the spending on durable goods in the United States grew at about 1.2 times as much as income (the 'income elasticity of demand'), while consumption as a whole grew slightly less than income, with an income elasticity of 0.94.[25] Income elasticities for 'time-using' goods were much higher. A study of the period 1929 to 1965 found the following long-run income elasticities: spending on cinema grew 3.4 as much as income; radio and television (together with records and musical instruments) 2.9 times.[26] A different study found an income elasticity of 2.73 for radios in the interwar period, with 1.45 for other appliances. For the post-war period income elasticities for kitchen and household appliances are somewhat higher at 1.99, but for time-using durable series the model breaks down altogether, suggesting that neither income nor price provide an adequate explanation for the diffusion of these durables, and that better models are required.[27]

The demand for time-saving durables in the United States has gone through two distinct surges. One is the late 1930s, which seems to be the cumulative effect of several major innovations; the other is the immediate post-war boom, which represents, perhaps, a demand shift associated with post-war restocking, new household formation, and the baby boom. Since then, the income share of time-saving durables has risen very gradually. Time-saving durables have expanded faster than income, but much less rapidly than time-using durables. The income elasticity of demand for appliances over the period 1920–83 (1.36) was found to be lower than the figure for furniture (1.65), and only slightly higher (1.99 : 1.87) for the post-war period.[28] This suggests that the priority for acquiring time-saving durables was similar to that of furnishing a home, and indeed it is likely that the two activities were related. In absolute terms, the outlays were

[25] United States, *National Income and Product Accounts 1929–82*, tables 2.1, 2.3.
[26] Houthakker and Taylor, *Consumer Demand*, 166–7.
[27] Olney, *Buy Now, Pay Later*, table 3.2, variable MUS[music], p. 79.
[28] Ibid., table 3.2, p. 79.

small. In the USA, the outlay on household appliances rose from about 0.6 per cent of disposable income in 1950, to about 0.8 per cent in 1980, while the outlay on durables overall rose to about 10.6 per cent by 1980, from about 9 per cent in 1950.[29]

Housework appliances have limited value for status display, and are normally tucked out of sight. Only one item of a kind is required, and it is kept for long periods of time. The functionality of the sewing machine, cooker, refrigerator, and washing machines was indicated by the stability of their technologies, and the machines were often used in the same household until they were worn out. Although often marketed on superficial styling and feature changes, their functionality changed little over decades.

How has the diffusion of time-saving durables affected the use of time? There is evidence that household appliances had little effect on the time spent in housework.[30] In 1960 American women were spending about as much time in housework as they were in the 1920s.[31] Some writers argue that the reason is cultural and social norms which identified women with housework and specified rising standards of house care. Washing machines did not save time since clothes were washed more often.[32] Vacuum cleaners were used to clean the floors more frequently.[33] New technologies pulled work back from the market and into the home. Domestic washing machines replaced commercial laundries. Tasks assigned to servants, husbands, or children gradually fell to the housewife. Technology did not save women's time because it was not associated with any rearrangement of the gender division of labour at home. In the mid-1970s husbands performed less than 10 per cent of routine domestic work.[34]

Gershuny has analysed time-budget diaries by social-class, marital, and employment status in the UK. He found, like Vanek in the USA, that female housework tended to increase somewhat, from about 400 to about 450 minutes per day (7.5 hours), between 1937 and 1961. But middle-class women had a different experience from those of the working class. For British middle-class women, household workloads almost doubled during these years, from about 250 to 450 minutes a day. For working-class women, after rising from less than 500 minutes in 1937, to more than 500 in 1952, time spent in housework declined to about 450 minutes in 1961, the same level as middle-class women.[35] Since then women's time spent in housework in Britain has declined consistently for both classes at about

---

[29] Ibid., tables A7, C1, pp. 228, 298.   [30] n. 14 above.   [31] Vanek, 'Time spent', 116.
[32] Cowan, *More Work*, 98–9.   [33] Hardyment, *Mangle to Microwave*, 89.
[34] Gershuny, 'Time Budgets as a Social Indicator', table 1, p. 422; Gershuny, 'Are We Running out of Time?', figs. 10, 11, pp. 15, 16.
[35] Gershuny, *Changing Times*, fig. 3.9, and pp. 65–7.

the same pace, down to some 350–75 minutes in 1974/5, but rising somewhat to 1984, and declining again since then. Other countries have followed roughly the same pattern, and employed women have mostly spent less time in housework, at lower levels than full-time housewives.[36] The evidence presented so far indicates no clear link between time-saving appliances and the time spent in housework. It suggests that the decline in housework followed the diffusion of the main household appliances by a considerable lag, and that a decline in housework time only began in the early 1960s.

Time using

Time-using appliances provide sensual arousal. Sensual inactivity is a psychic burden. Sensual deprivation has been used as a form of torture. 'Perfect comfort and lack of stimulation are restful at first, but they soon become boring, then disturbing. At that stage the organism actively seeks stimulation, for ways of increasing its arousal level.'[37] As Lord Byron put it, 'The great object of life is sensation—to feel that we exist, even though in pain.'[38] Utility was perceived as a stream of sensations by the great American economist Irving Fisher, who regarded psychic arousal as the end of economic activity.[39]

Mass producers compete to satisfy this demand for arousal. The printed word was the first mass-produced time-using technology. The Victorian piano became a middle-class necessity, while in working-class neighbourhoods it also provided evidence of respectability and solvency.[40] After the turn of the century, the gramophone provided greater musical variety at a fraction of the cost in money and skill.

Sound, sight, and electricity were blended to create the cinema, providing another substantial reduction in the cost of a unit of arousal. Cinema was the first of the time-using commodities to achieve universal diffusion in the West.[41] Sound continued to evolve through broadcast radio, hi-fi, tape, CD and DVD, the Walkman and the iPod, while cinema was followed by television and video.

[36] American and British data are presented in more detail in Table 8.2. For international comparative data, see Gershuny, *Changing Times*, 186–202.

[37] Scitovsky, *Joyless Economy*, 31.

[38] Howarth, 'Introduction', *Letters of Lord Byron*, p. ix.

[39] Irving Fisher, *Theory of Interest*, 3, 4.

[40] Ehrlich, *The Piano*, ch. 5; Roell, *Piano in America, 1890–1940*, ch. 1.

[41] Gomery, 'Movie Palace'; de Grazia, 'Mass Culture and Sovereignty'; Bakker, 'Entertainment Industrialized.'

The explosive penetration of radio and then television was insensitive to income and price: their possession was imperative, and they diffused through the population with a very short social lag. Class differentials counted for little. By 1958, for example, 57.3 per cent of upper-class households in Britain had television sets, while the level in middle- and lower-class households was 53.4 and 51.1 respectively.[42] A strong skew towards the lower income classes was noted in the diffusion of television in the United States.[43]

Orthodox consumption theory does not aspire to account for tastes. The psychology of myopia, however, provides a series of clues, which together explain the observed behaviour patterns. A myopic consumer ranks immediate arousal much higher than objectively more valuable delayed rewards.[44] TV is instantly available. It is the least demanding source of arousal, the cheapest way of averting boredom. Of all household activities, television requires the lowest level of concentration, alertness, challenge, and skill. In terms of the psychic effort required to stimulate the mind, it requires the lowest input. Activation states while viewing are low, and viewing is experienced as a relaxing release of tension.[45] Children, the most myopic of age groups, are an easy target for television. Metabolic rates appear to plunge while children are watching TV.[46] The marginal cost of viewing in financial terms is also very low. Other activities, like reading, sport, or conversation, might be cheaper, but they are more demanding in terms of psychic effort and perhaps also of prior motivation and ability. Viewing time was inversely related with education, and with income as well.[47] In Britain, for example, in 1986, members of class AB watched an average 19 hours 50 minutes of television a week, compared with 33 hours 35 minutes for class DE.[48] In the USA in 1985, a college education almost halved the hours of television viewing, in comparison with a grade school education (grade school only, 21.3 hours; high school only, 16.6 hours; college only, 11.3 hours).[49]

Television (with radio, video, and listening to recorded music) has come to dominate discretionary time in Britain and the United States, claiming

[42] Needleman, 'Demand for Domestic Appliances', 27.
[43] Graham, 'Class and Conservatism', table 1, p. 94.   [44] On myopia, Ch. 3 above.
[45] Kubey and Czsikszentmihalyi, *Television and the Quality of Life*, 81–3.
[46] Klesges et al., 'Effects of Television on Metabolic Rate'; Ives, 'Childhood Obesity'; Dietz and Strasburger, 'Children, Adolescence and Television'.
[47] United States Department of Commerce, Bureau of the Census, *Social Indicators III*, tables 11/9, p. 557, 11/16, p. 561; Gershuny, 'Time Economy', fig. 'Education Effects', p. 25b.
[48] Great Britain, *Social Trends*, 15 (1985), table 10.7, p. 142. A small-sample study in the United States in the 1990s showed no significant difference by income (Kubey and Csikszentmihalyi, *Television and the Quality of Life*, table 4, p. 72).
[49] Robinson and Godbey, *Time for Life*, table 10, p. 146.

Table 8.2. Domestic work and adult television viewing in the USA and Britain in average minutes per day, c.1961–1985

USA	Activity	1965	1975	1985
Women				
Married housewives	Domestic work	429	380	
All married	Domestic work	271	207	192
Married employed	Domestic work	247	213	
Unmarried	Domestic work	133	147	128
non-employed	Television	96	157	
employed	Television	62	99	
All	Television	80	121	124
Men				
Married	Domestic work	39	58	95
employed	Television	99	131	
All	Television	100	139	135
BRITAIN	Activity	1961	1974–5	1984
Women				
non-employed	Domestic work	432	372	386
part-time employed	Domestic work	335	285	319
Full-time employed	Domestic work	178	180	178
non-employed	Television	125	132	147
part-time employed	Television	98	112	121
Full-time employed	Television	93	103	102
Men				
Full-time employed	Domestic work	78	77	109
Full-time employed	Television	121	126	129

Sources: USA: Sahin and Robinson, 'Beyond the Realm of Necessity', tables 1, 2, pp. 89–90; Robinson, 'Changes in Time Use', table 11.2, p. 301; id., 'Where does the Free Time Go', 6; id., 'Who's Doing the Housework?', 4. *Britain*: Gershuny and Jones, 'The Changing Work/Leisure Balance', tables 3, 5, pp. 24–5, 38–9.

more than two hours a day in both countries after 1960.[50] In general, the viewing trend has been sharply upwards during the years of rapid diffusion. In the United States, viewing time rose by a third (two-thirds for housewives) between 1965 and 1975. It claimed about 40 per cent of the free time of working men and of housewives, and about a third of the free time of employed women.[51]

Despite its compulsive attraction (or perhaps because of it), television rated lower in enjoyment and satisfaction than most voluntary leisure activities, and rather lower than work. The evidence is taken from time-budget studies in the United States in 1975 and 1981. The results are summarized in Tables 8.3 and 8.4. The highest values were placed on

[50] Gershuny, *Changing Times*, table 7.25, p. 208; United States, *Social Indicators III*, table 11/14, p. 559. More detailed breakdowns, Table 8.2 here.
[51] Sahin and Robinson, 'Beyond the Realm of Necessity', 90, 92; comp. United States, *Social Indicators III*, table 11/14, p. 559; Gershuny, *Changing Times*, table 7.25, p. 208.

Table 8.3. Process benefits reported by respondents, US Panel Data, 1975 and 1981 (rising scale from 1 to 10).

Activity	N	1975 data		1981 data	
		Mean score	Std. dev.	Mean score	Std. dev.
Talking with children	312	9.16	1.36	8.98	1.33
Care of children	312	8.87	1.80	8.74	1.53
Trips with children	311	8.87	1.70	8.72	1.63
Games with children	308	8.62	1.96	8.24	2.03
Talking with friends	678	8.38	1.87	8.27	1.78
Going on trips, outings	657	8.24	2.35	8.17	2.12
Job	397	8.02	2.12	7.79	2.01
Home entertainment	662	7.76	2.34	7.54	2.24
Reading books, magazines	668	7.60	2.46	7.49	2.40
Going to church	631	7.23	3.07	7.28	2.85
Reading newspapers	675	7.17	2.46	7.10	2.38
Making things for house	635	6.78	2.96	6.47	2.87
Playing sports	606	6.76	3.17	6.23	3.07
Going to movies, plays	629	6.65	3.03	6.38	2.79
Gardening	642	6.55	3.28	6.27	3.21
Cooking	668	6.17	2.99	6.13	2.74
Television	677	5.93	2.49	6.00	2.43
Other shopping	673	5.69	3.01	5.30	2.90
Housing repairs and alterations	635	5.11	3.03	4.94	2.81
Work, school organizations	587	5.00	3.10	5.13	3.09
Grocery shopping	673	4.57	3.04	4.55	2.77
Cleaning house	672	4.22	3.00	4.18	2.70
Sleeping	610	NA	NA	7.54	2.21
Eating at home	615	NA	NA	7.46	2.06
Personal care	615	NA	NA	7.38	2.14
Eating out	613	NA	NA	7.33	2.46
Taking naps	604	NA	NA	5.20	3.24
Caring for other children	603	NA	NA	4.53	3.14

Source: Juster, 'Preferences for Work', table 13.1, p. 336.

interaction with children and with friends (8–9 out on a scale of 10). Work ranked a little lower at approximately 7.5–8.5. Television viewing (6) was in the same rank as cooking, and somewhat higher than cleaning, where there was a strong difference between men and women. For older women (over 40), and in the earlier survey, cleaning house rated approximately the same as watching television (Table 8.4).[52] Another survey ranked watching television fifteenth out of sixteen activities in terms of its effect on mood.[53]

[52] This may be explained by (*a*) easier cleaning tasks in the absence of small children, and (*b*) habituation.

[53] Kubey and Csikzentmihalyi, *Television and the Quality of Life*, table 8, p. 83, 107 working adults in Chicago, 1996–7. For 'affect' (cheerfulness + friendliness + happiness + sociability) television viewing ranked 15 out of 16, with cooking at 7, and 'chores' at 8. On a 'wish [I was doing] something else' television ranked 6, next to cooking (7), but much higher than 'chores' (16). Evaluation differed on whether it was done before, during, or after viewing,

Table 8.4. Reported process benefits by age and gender, USA 1975–6 (rising scale from 1 to 10)

	15–24	25–29	30–34	35–39	40–44	45–49	50–54	55–59	60–64	65+
MEN	N = 82	N = 109	N = 91	N = 76	N = 63	N = 53	N = 52	N = 53	N = 41	N = 111
Enjoy										
Cleaning house	3.27	3.60	2.89	2.75	3.02	2.52	3.22	3.44	3.32	3.45
Your job	6.89	7.92	7.75	8.22	8.33	8.27	8.31	8.28	9.08	8.79
Talking w/friends	8.38	8.20	8.08	7.67	8.19	8.02	8.33	8.45	8.41	8.31
Home entertainment	7.61	7.68	7.75	6.83	7.37	7.09	7.28	7.24	7.39	7.35
Watching TV	5.74	6.37	6.08	5.48	5.68	6.29	6.37	6.27	7.46	6.48
Playing sports	8.64	7.54	7.87	7.84	6.82	7.00	7.19	5.43	6.10	5.72
Movies and plays	7.96	7.50	7.28	6.88	6.09	6.51	5.92	5.22	5.41	5.09
WOMEN	N = 121	N = 135	N = 121	N = 85	N = 63	N = 65	N = 67	N = 54	N = 70	N = 150
Enjoy										
Cleaning house	4.59	4.83	4.62	4.76	5.25	5.64	5.57	6.04	6.29	5.94
Your job	7.08	7.65	7.71	8.34	7.58	8.37	8.00	9.43	8.10	8.00
Talking w/friends	8.57	8.28	8.25	8.49	8.00	8.19	8.29	8.54	8.27	8.72
Home entertainment	8.27	7.75	7.83	7.73	7.64	7.49	7.56	7.37	7.51	7.79
Watching TV	6.07	5.60	5.76	5.71	5.88	5.65	5.75	6.57	6.79	6.63
Playing sports	7.48	7.27	7.07	6.21	6.79	5.60	5.OS	5.28	3.96	3.44
Movies and plays	8.31	7.66	7.52	7.27	6.36	4.98	5.72	5.13	4.54	4.19

Source: Juster, 'Preferences for Work and Leisure', table 13.4, p. 343.

The substance of these Tables (8.3 and 8.4) is that satisfaction from television was lower than from childcare, social activities, and market work, and, for women, it was in the same range as the combined satisfaction from housework and cooking. Television (like other satisfactions) becomes less rewarding the longer it is viewed.[54] What this suggests is that television-watching expanded to the point where the marginal satisfaction from discretionary time matched the marginal satisfaction from housework. This is consistent with Becker's assumption that time will be allocated so as to equalize utility at the margin.[55] In 1965, 90 per cent of viewers in a USA sample nominated television as the first activity they would forgo.[56] Further, independent evidence from four American surveys suggests that television viewing was well down the list of desirable ways to spend free time.[57]

More time in front of the box was taken from housework. This substitution appears to have taken place in the United States between the mid-1960s and the mid-1970s. In a study of married women, an increase of about five hours in weekly viewing time was matched by a slightly smaller decline in housework for employed housewives, and a slightly larger one for exclusively home-working housewives (see Table 8.2).[58] In the UK the magnitudes were somewhat different: for all categories of women, television viewing increased, but rather less than the decline in housework (Table 8.2). There are no satisfaction scores attached to these activities in the British time-budget surveys. It is notable, however, that the movements are in the same general direction as in the USA.

Compelling contraptions

The decline of housework could have been driven by better technology, lowered standards, harder work, or some combination of the three. What combination? We do not have the evidence. For the time released from housework, the largest single alternative time use was television viewing, in the American case amounting to virtually the whole of the substantial time released between the 1960s and the 1970s. At the margin, housework contracted and television viewing expanded.

(ch. 7), complementing the insights reported by Kahneman and Tversky (Kahneman 'Experienced Utility'). In contrast, a survey of 2,500 American adults in 1985 ranked television at an average 7.8 out of 10, compared with cooking (6.6) and lower scores for various house-work activities (Robinson, 'As We Like It', 46), though there are ambiguities in this report.

[54] Kubey and Czikszentmihalyi, *Television and the Quality of Life*, 172.
[55] Becker, 'Allocation of Time'.   [56] Robinson and Godbey, *Time for Life*, 238–9.
[57] Ibid., 242–3, esp. table 25.   [58] Robinson, 'Changes in Time Use', table 11.2, p. 301.

Television (much like radio before it), was a compelling product. What were the attractions? Vivid experiences of immediate gratification are difficult to resist, even if they involve a disproportionate sacrifice in forgone benefit.[59] Television is second to none in its vivid immediacy. It is often used as a substitute for social interaction and to ward off feelings of loneliness.[60] Viewing can be mildly addictive.[61] Loneliness and negative feelings in the afternoon were followed by heavy viewing later the same evening. Heavier viewers also reported significantly more negative feelings during the week than light viewers. Negative feelings were likely to cause viewing, and not the other way round.[62] One writer concluded that 'if TV has a potential addictive power it arises from the fact that it reduces negative affect'.[63]

Withdrawal from television led to anxiety and suffering. The BBC has found in a recent survey that 15 per cent of those surveyed would not give up television for a million pounds, 20 per cent would not give it up at £500,000, and a third would need a bribe of £100,000. Another third would give it up for £10,000. In the United States and Spain similar surveys showed an even stronger attachment to the box.[64] In 1977 the *Detroit Free Press* offered $500 to 120 families to give up television for one month, before it found five that agreed. Abstainers from television reported increased boredom, nervousness, and depression. Domestic violence, smoking, and the use of tranquillizers increased, anxiety and aggression in families, and boredom and irritation among those who lived alone. One woman reported: 'it was terrible. We did nothing—my husband and I talked.'[65]

As with other addictions, viewers are prone to habituation, desensitization, and satiation.[66] Enjoyment declines with exposure. Television viewing is a typical 'hedonic treadmill', in which an increasing level of arousal is required to maintain a constant level of satisfaction.[67] Music becomes louder, television more violent and more sexually explicit. The visual pace has speeded up, driven by the frantic activity of the commercials, and the accelerating jerkiness promotes a perceptible physiological reaction among viewers, counteracting habituation and grabbing attention.[68]

[59] Above Ch. 3.   [60] Argyle, *Social Psychology of Everyday Life*, 110–11.
[61] Kubey and Csikszentmihalyi, 'Television Addiction'.
[62] Kubey and Czikszentmihalyi, *Television and the Quality of Life*, 172–3.
[63] Singer, 'Power and Limitations of Television', 50, cited in Kubey and Cszikszentmihalyi, *Television and the Quality of Life*, 138.
[64] Toynbee, 'Would you give up TV for £1,000,000?', 14.
[65] Kubey and Cszikszentmihalyi, *Television and the Quality of Life*, 138–9.
[66] Klapp, *Overload and Boredom*.
[67] Kahneman and Varey, 'Notes on the Psychology of Utility', 136–8, 141.
[68] e.g. Arlen, *Thirty Seconds*, 181; Kubey and Cszikszentmihalyi, 'Television Addiction', 65–6.

Commercials absorb resources more than two orders of magnitude greater than ordinary programming: 'programs cost about $4 a second to produce, but commercials cost $2,000 a second.'[69] A TV producer wrote that, 'as commercials got people used to absorb information quickly, I had to change my style to give them more jump cuts or they'd be bored . . . The whole art form has speeded up.' One researcher reports in 1989 that 'virtually everyone in the television industry ardently believes that the audience attention span is growing shorter, and that to hold the audience, television editing must be even faster paced and present more and more exciting visual material.'[70] A longitudinal study of violence in American television showed that the 'index of violence' reached its highest level since 1967 (when the study began) in the 1984–5 television season. Eight out of every ten prime time programmes contained violence. The rate of violent incidents was nearly eight per hour. The nineteen-year average was six per hour.[71]

As media experiences became the staple of everyday discourse, so access to radio, cinema, and television was required in order to avoid social exclusion. Time-using goods were also on public display, and formed part of domestic socializing. Their possession conferred status, their absence a social disadvantage. Antennas signalled the presence of a set, and visibility helped to sell TV in the early days.[72]

Unlike the main housework appliances, 'time-users' delivered satisfactions directly to all members of the household, men and children as well as women. As status goods, they impinged (much more than time-saving goods) on the satisfactions of males, and to the extent that males had more power within households, these goods acquired priority for purchase.[73] All these attributes help to explain their priority in the sequence of acquisition.

Unlike the main housework durables, time-using technology was not stable but innovative, and the product cycle moved fast. As consumers became habituated to the new forms of stimulation, they required an ever-stronger dose. Sound gave way to vision, black and white to colour, broadcasting to the abundance of cable, satellite, videotape, and DVD. Typically, one item of each category is not enough; convenience required as many as could be afforded: a radio in every room, three or four television sets, specialized recording and playing devices for every state of

[69] Ogilvy, *Ogilvy on Advertising*, 112.
[70] Kubey and Csikzsentmihalyi, *Television and the Quality of Life*, 140.
[71] Gerbner and Signorielli, *Violence and Terror*, ch. 2, esp. p. 17.
[72] Packard, *Status Seekers*, 61.   [73] See e.g. Gray, *Video Playtime*, 243–4.

passivity and motion. The number of two-television households in Britain rose from 33 per cent to 56 per cent between 1980 and 1986, while the average reached two sets per household in the United States in 1990.[74] Further economies in housework are not easy to achieve, and the market for housework appliances is largely mature: it is restricted to new households and to replacements. The senses are easy to stimulate in novel ways, and this creates opportunities for innovation and for a spiral of rising stimulation. The product cycles are much more rapid and time-using goods begin to lose their appeal long before they wear out.

Myopic consumers

Prices of time-using appliances have fallen steeply over the period in question, and price has some explanatory power in diffusion, although the effect is difficult to model, due to changes in quality. But this does not seem to distinguish housework appliances from time-using ones. On the whole, rapidly diffusing appliances appear to be less sensitive to price (e.g. they have constant, declining, or zero price elasticities).[75] Despite the steep fall in the cost of time-using goods, the early phase of each successive generation attracted a high premium: television more costly than radio, colour more than black and white, personal computers more than television, etc.

Durable goods can be seen as capital that generates a flow of services over time, and their acquisition may be regarded as a form of saving. But in fact, 'buy now pay later' has long been the rule for durables, so their purchase has usually been financed with borrowed money. A 'general collapse in inhibitions against borrowing' was conspicuous in the 1920s. By the end of the 1920s up to 90 per cent of durable goods were purchased with credit in the USA. Consumer debt as a percentage of income doubled between 1920 and 1930 (from about 4.5 to 9.5 per cent).[76] In the UK in 1938 three-quarters of all radio sets were sold on hire-purchase.[77] During the diffusion phase of television in the UK, its purchase was beyond the means of the average working-class buyer. The most common form of access was rental by the week or month, followed closely by hire-purchase sales.[78]

[74] Gunter and Svennevig, *Behind and in Front*, 78; United States Bureau of Census, *Statistical Abstract 1991*, table 919, p. 556.   [75] Parker, 'Price Elasticity Dynamics', 364–6.
[76] Olney, *Buy Now*, 51–2.   [77] Jefferys, *Distribution of Consumer Goods*, 300.
[78] Bain, *Growth of Television Ownership*, 14–17.

Consumer credit added very considerably to the cost (and in some respects, to the risk) of acquiring the goods. Credit rates tend to be much higher than those for ordinary commercial or real estate loans.[79] In the United States, for example, in the 1920s, typical effective consumer interest rates were on the order of 30 per cent, and ranged between 12 and 98 per cent for radios.[80] In Britain in 1969 the true annual rate of interest charged by a sample of 55 radio and electrical shops ranged between 8 and 63 per cent, with an average of 28 per cent.[81] Retail mark-ups also tended to be much higher in credit sales.[82]

Why did consumers commit themselves to such a costly method of purchase? Hire-purchase may be regarded as a precommitment device, in which consumers bind themselves in advance to follow a course of action which they do not trust themselves to sustain in the absence of external compulsion:[83] 'the discipline of paying, say, five shillings a week to an external creditor is more compelling than saving the same five shillings a week for an eventual cash purchase.'[84] Working-class purchasers, in particular, paid a high premium for this external discipline. Inflated interest and high mark-ups do not capture the whole cost. With limited information, limited contacts, poor understanding of contractual terms, and uncertain prospects, working-class consumers tended to pay much higher premiums than middle-class ones, well beyond the difference suggested by their lower creditworthiness. Ignorant purchasers were easily tricked into unfair contracts, given shoddy goods, and deprived of them at the slightest lapse of payment. Abuses were so extensive that legislation was passed in 1938 and several times afterwards to protect consumers. Although the proportion of bad debts appears to have been small, more than 10 per cent of respondents in one survey (in the 1960s) experienced repayment difficulties, and most defaulters came from low-income groups. A minority found it impossible to cope. The loss of goods already paid for, the anxieties of court proceedings, and court costs should be added on to the heavy premiums paid for consumer credit.[85] What is evident are the high time discount rates, or in other words, the high urgency, represented by borrowing for immediate access to goods that working-class consumers could not otherwise afford. This is typical of myopic

---

[79] Homer and Sylla, *History of Interest*, 424–8.   [80] Olney, *Buy Now*, 115.

[81] Great Britain, Board of Trade, *Report on Consumer Credit*, table 3.4, p. 134. Average overdrafts were charged at 9.2 per cent; ibid., table A139, p. 578.

[82] Vallance, *Hire-Purchase*, 49–50.

[83] Elster, *Ulysses and the Sirens*, ch. 2. Suggested by Charles Feinstein.

[84] Great Britain, Board of Trade, *Report on Consumer Credit*, 149.

[85] Ibid. 132–4, 149–57; Vallance, *Hire-Purchase, passim.*

choice and hyperbolic discounting.[86] These costs and the risks assumed by working-class consumers are an indirect measure of the pressure to acquire the appliances in question.

Children, cars, and telephones

It is sometimes difficult to disentangle the time-saving and time-using attributes of goods. Parents use television as an effective pacifier of demanding children, stimulating the children, but gaining discretionary time for themselves. The bicycle and especially the motor car have dual attributes, time using as well as time saving. The motor car's rapid take-up in the United States in the 1920s occurred at a time when infrastructures were still geared to other forms of transport. Consequently, the most striking impact of the car to contemporary sociologists was its function as a time user, and the inroads it made into discretionary time. In 'Middletown', Indiana, in the 1920s, family and neighbours spent less time on the porch or in the yard together after the advent of the automobile and the movies. The car competed with churchgoing on Sundays, and made leisure-time enjoyment a regular part of every day rather than an occasional event.[87]

Car advertising suggests that the automobile is a vehicle of self-expression, and this is confirmed by its pervasive role in American culture.[88] The demand for cars in the United States rose at a rate three times the rate of increase of income (elasticity 3.01) in 1947–83, almost exactly on a par with television, and only a little less in the interwar period.[89] The car unsettled the habit of saving in some 'Middletown' families. 'I'll go without food before I'll see us give up the car', one woman was quoted as saying, and a large proportion of car owners in one sample there (21 out of 26), had acquired cars but not bathtubs.[90] Robert Lynd noted that by the 1930s cars had achieved near-parity with housing, shelter, and food as a signal of self-respect in Muncie, Indiana. Even those on unemployment relief clung to their motors: 'People give up everything in the world but their car.'[91]

In contrast, the diffusion pattern of the land-line telephone places it firmly in the time-saving cluster. This durable was introduced in England

---

[86] Ch. 3, above.   [87] Lynd and Lynd, *Middletown* (1929), 95, 260.

[88] Mottram, *Blood on the Nash Ambassador*, 75–8; see below, Ch. 9.

[89] Olney, *Buy Now*, 79.   [90] Lynd and Lynd, *Middletown* (1929), 255–6.

[91] Lynd and Lynd, *Middletown in Transition*, 265, 267.

in 1881. Eighty-seven years later (1965) only 21 per cent of households had a telephone, with diffusion levels determined firmly by class (88 per cent upper, 67 per cent middle, 44 per cent lower middle, and 20 per cent working class).[92] The pattern follows the United States. Although ownership grew more quickly than in the UK, by time-using standards growth was slow, and demonstrated distinct class patterns. By 1929 42 per cent of US households had a telephone but it was associated with the middle class. Penetration fell to 32 per cent in 1935.[93] Domestic telephone installations on both sides of the Atlantic grew slowly and varied by income group. As late as 1983 only 77 per cent of households in Britain had acquired a telephone.[94] In the 1980s, the percentage of American households with telephone service stabilized at about 92–3 per cent, a lower level of penetration than television or radio.[95] In contrast, mobile phones have spread like wildfire, reaching 75 per cent penetration levels in the UK in about ten years, which suggests attributes of time using more than time saving.[96]

Conclusion

Time-saving durables have diffused ahead of income. The likely reason is the sheer drudgery of traditional housework. Even if hours remained the same, the workload became easier. Time-using durables have diffused even faster, and somewhat deeper. As household incomes have risen, consumers have given priority to the *quality* of their discretionary time. Entertainment appliances have taken over substantial parts of discretionary time, and now claim the largest single category of leisure time use. They have a larger potential market, providing direct benefits not only to women, but to everyone. But they are also the cheapest method, in economic and psychic terms, of occupying discretionary time. Satisfaction data suggest that the use of these durables has proceeded to the point where they can no longer provide any excess of utility over housework.

Time-using technology has proved to be more innovative than time-saving technology; when one method of arousal began to deliver diminishing

[92] Douglas and Isherwood, *World of Goods*, 100.

[93] Lynd and Lynd, *Middletown* (1929), 173; United States, Bureau of the Census, *Historical Statistics*, 783.

[94] Great Britain, Central Statistical Office, *Social Trends*, 15 (1985) table 6.12, p. 99; (and see Figure 8.2).   [95] United States, *Statistical Abstract 1991*, 556.

[96] 95 per cent of households by 2000. Data from Great Britain, Office for National Statistics, *General Household Survey*.

returns, a new one was ready to repeat the process, with technology that delivered a higher dose of arousal per unit of time, though often at a much higher cost as well, e.g. when television replaced radio and colour television supplanted black and white. Housework technology has not been able to match this achievement over the long term. The task of engaging idle minds has proved more amenable to technology than the challenge of keeping house.

9

The American Automobile Frenzy
of the 1950s

The American passenger car of the mid-1950s was a marvel: a long, low, powerful, chrome-lashed barge on wheels. Its emergence, its popularity, and its crisis, all in the space of seven years, followed a short trajectory which remains engraved in American national memory.[1] Styling competition by car makers, and consumer demand for sensual gratification, combined to generate a *frenzy*, defined here, informally, as a quest or a craving that has run out of control. After ten years of short supply, 6.1 million new cars were sold in 1953, rising to a peak of 7.9 million in 1955, and falling down to 4.2 million in 1958.[2] The 1950s car emerged as the great promise of affluence, and ended up as its first disappointment. Similar cycles of anticipation and habituation have since recurred several times, roughly one for every decade.

Styling competition

In 1953, the industry was concentrated. The 'Big Three', Chrysler (20 per cent), Ford (25 per cent), and General Motors (45 per cent) together supplied about 90 per cent of all new cars sold in the United States. Their oligopoly was uneasy. Its tensions originated in the 1920s. In response to Henry Ford's simple, cheap, and unchanging Model T, which at one point captured more than 50 per cent of the market, General Motors began to

---

[1] Scholarly titles include Armi, *Art of American Car*; Gartman, *Auto-Opium*, ch. 6; car-fan volumes like Mueller, *Fifties Cars*; Morris, *Biography of a Buick*, is a novel; economic analysis includes Fisher et al., 'Model Changes', 433–51, and White, *Automobile Industry*; for cultural impact, F. F. Copolla's film *American Graffiti*. Other references below.

[2] American made. Automobile Manufacturers Association, *Automobile Facts*, 3. Output and sales figures are on a calendar year basis, while the narrative refers to the model year (i.e. 1955 model was introduced in October 1954).

offer variety, in two forms: (*a*) a hierarchy of models designed 'for every purse and purpose', and (*b*) a policy of 'change means progress', an annual 'facelift' which relegated older models to stylistic obsolescence.

Annual redesign was a Faustian bargain, which committed the industry to a quest for eternal youth. Buyers could be cruel. Chrysler, an innovative newcomer in the 1920s, shot up from 10 per cent to 26 per cent of the market in five years. In 1934, it introduced a streamlined 'Airflow' design, but the novelty failed to catch on. The ordeal quenched the company's spirits for two decades. Ford came from behind and overtook Chrysler, with a single styling breakthrough, its 1949 model.[3] The chairman of General Motors wrote in 1941, 'today the appearance of a motor car is a most important factor in the selling end of the business—perhaps the most important single factor.'[4] By 1954, American car makers regarded styling as 'the most significant factor in creating the desire to buy'.[5]

Style change was not a trivial undertaking. In the early 1950s, a design took one to two years to finalize, and tooling another two. Over the model's three-year life cycle, there would be two additional 'facelifts' (Figure 9.1). Early on the cost was modest, but competition drove it up. New tooling costs rose from $19 per car in 1952 to $147 in 1957; or from 1.3 per cent to 7.8 per cent of the average wholesale price.[6] In 1957 an entirely new car model was expected to need prior investment in styling, engineering, tools, and launching (but not production facilities) of about 7.1 per cent of planned life-cycle gross revenues.[7] The sequence of style changes is also shown in Table 9.1.

[3] Ford, Central Marketing Staff, 'Product Philosophy Report' (n.p., summer 1957), Chrysler and Ford 'Lifelines', Ernest Breech Papers, Ford Industrial Archives (henceforth FIA), AR-88-108159. This is a book-length text-and-graphics presentation-format document.

[4] Sloan, *White-Collar Man*, 185, cited Armi, *Art of American Car*, 26.

[5] '1957 Ford Car, Introduction, Merchandising Considerations', n.p. Ford Production Planning Committee no. 128, 2 Dec. 1954, AR-200778-7. The Ford 'Product Philosophy Report' of 1957 (n. 3 above) stressed 'outstanding victories' which were largely attributed to styling. See also e.g. the memo, Henry Jackson, of J. Walter Thompson (Ford Motor Co. advertising agency) to Walter Elton, 20 Dec. 1957, which invoked styling as a buyer motivating factor second only to brand loyalty. Review Board 6/11, J. Walter Thompson papers (henceforth JWT), Hartman Center, Duke University library; JWT, '1959 Ford Car. Review Board Memorandum', 3 Apr. 1958, fos. 2, 4; Review Board 6/10, JWT papers. Survey evidence is mixed. In 1952, 'appearance' was ranked fourth–fifth as a reason for buying; in 1957, in response to a question of what they liked in new cars compared with the previous year's, the largest group of prospective purchasers (32.5 per cent) selected 'Body Styling'. *Look, Automobile Survey*, 21 (1957), 27; 16 (1952), 16–17.

[6] Fisher et al., 'Model Changes', table 3, p. 440; Wholesale price, Automobile Manufacturers Association, *Automobile Facts*, 3.

[7] $51.1 millions at 160,000 units a year over three years, selling wholesale at $1,485. Ford Product Planning Office, 'Economy Car Report', 13 Nov. 1957, fo. 28. FIA Product Planning Committee, 13 Nov. 1957, AR-94-200777-6. The final cost turned out to be $104 million, but was spread over much larger sales. On tooling, White, *Automobile Industry*, 33–41.

Fig. 9.1. Ford sedan facelifts, 1949–1957, front view and side view

Source: Ford Central Marketing Staff, 'Product Philosophy Report' (n.p, summer 1957), Breech Papers, AR-88–108159, Ford Industrial Archives.

Product planners had to anticipate car-buyer preferences three or four years in advance. Some of the smaller companies could not stand the pace. Five 'independent' producers disappeared between 1946 and 1974, and only one (American Motors) remained. Among the Big Three, market shares fluctuated substantially from year to year, in inverse relation to size.

Table 9.1. Style changes and market shares in the 'low-priced' field, 1954–1959

Year	mil cars sold	Chevrolet (GM)		Ford			Plymouth (Chrysler)	
		Style change	Market share (%)	Style change	Market share (%)	Return on assets (%)	Style change	Market share (%)
1954	3.8	1	44.06	1	43.54	19.0	1	12.49
1955	3.9	4	45.41	4	37.31	28.5	4	17.28
1956	3.4	2	44.84	1	40.72	12.4	2	14.44
1957	3.5	3	40.04	4	43.17	16.1	4	16.79
1958	2.6	4	48.59	2	35.96	5.5	1	15.45
1959	3.2	4	44.87	4	42.25	22.3	3	12.88
coeff. of variation			6.2		7.8	46.1		13.3

Notes: Style change legend: 4 = completely new body shell; 3 = all new sheet metal; 2 = some new sheet metal; 1 = grill, tail lamp, trim changes. Market share: 'Big Three' excluding other manufacturers.

Sources: Sherman and Hoffer, 'Does Automobile Style Change Payoff?', 153–65; F. G. Secrest, 'Company-Wide Operating Profits and Returns, 1954–1963', 28 July 1960, Attachment B, no. 4. (Ford car only), McNamara papers, AR-66-12:4, Ford Industrial Archives.

For Chrysler, the coefficient of variation 1946–74 was 24.2 per cent, for Ford it was 12.2 per cent, and even for General Motors, with an average market share of 46 per cent, it was 8.4 per cent.[8] A better measure of risk is the variance of return on assets. Over the period 1954 to 1959, the profit attributed to the Ford car varied almost six times as much as its market share. Motor executives experienced this risk as serious mental strain.[9]

Car use was based firmly on necessity. Ever since the 1920s, American daily life had fragmented, as the territories of home, work, shopping, education, government, and recreation drifted long distances apart, linked together only by a journey at the wheel of a private car.[10] In 1951, 73 per cent of American households owned cars. 59 per cent of workers used their cars to travel to work, and 68 per cent of cars were used for this purpose;[11] 85 per cent of intercity travel was in private cars.[12] Demand for cars came to reflect the demographics and performance of the whole economy. It was determined by income, new and used car prices, existing stocks, interest rates, and consumer demographics. This relation was understood and

[8] i.e. one-third of all observations diverged from the mean by *more* than that percentage. White, *Automobile Industry*, 290–306, tables A.1-6 (for 1953–67); *Ward's Automotive Yearbook 1975*, p. 92, *1980*, p. 47 (for 1968–74).

[9] United States Senate, *Administered Prices Report*, T. Yntema (vice-president for finance, Ford Motor Company), 79–80.

[10] St Clair, *Motorization of Cities*; Whyte, *Exploding Metropolis*; Riesman, 'Suburban Dislocation'; J. Walter Thompson and Yale School of Architecture and Design, 'Interurbia: The Changing Face of America', presentation to Ford Division, 28 June 1957, FIA, J. Wright Papers, AR-75-15565: 18.

[11] *Look, Automobile Survey*, 15 (Oct. 1951), 10; Automobile Manufacturers Association, *Automobile Facts*, 33, has 65 per cent of *families* owning cars in 1951. Both are based on surveys.

[12] Automobile Manufacturers Association, *Automobile Facts*, 46.

applied econometrically by manufacturers to predict the demand for cars.[13] But models of aggregate demand said nothing about market shares for different makes and models. Market share was determined in the dimly perceived areas of consumer motivation, preferences, and satisfactions.[14]

Big Three strategy aimed for two objectives: to prevail in the product design competition, and to contain its risks. Risk was held in check by several different methods. The Big Three avoided competition on price, which could eliminate profits and even drive the weakest out of business.[15] In other words, they strove to maximize joint profits. Exposure to swings in consumer taste was reduced by offering a range of models. Ford had twenty-four in 1952, and projected sixty-five for 1959, while Chrysler had seventy-seven models in 1957, and GM eighty-one.[16] Underneath, however, GM had only three body types for its whole range, while Chrysler used only one.[17] The Big Three signed identical contracts with the United Auto Workers. Company executives sometimes colluded against competition, as when they tried to stop stock car racing in 1957.[18]

The largest stabilizer of market share was consumer brand loyalty. In 1953, 69 per cent of owners intended to buy the same make again.[19] Even a giant company like Ford found them difficult to shake. Despite massive efforts, it never managed to gain mid- or upmarket acceptance in proportion to its total market share, and remained confined largely to the 'low-priced' field.

Advertising was more risk containing than competitive, intended primarily to reassure existing owners, rather than to capture new ones.[20] For the Ford Motor Company as a whole, advertising and sales promotion rose from 1.1 per cent of sales in 1953 to 2.0 per cent in 1957, and 2.6 in 1958. Dealer product advertising added another 30 per cent to company expenditure, and their own-business publicity at least another 30 per cent. At the end of the 1950s, the total level of advertising expenditure was approximately

---

[13] United States Senate, *Administered Prices Report*, ch. 6.

[14] United States Senate, *Administered Prices. Hearings*, Gregory Chow, 30 Apr. 1958, p. 3183.

[15] Price restriction was the ostensible cause of the Senate Hearings. See United States Senate, *Administered Prices. Hearings*, ch. 3; Kefauver, *Monopoly Power*, 89–93; White, *Automobile Industry*, 109–16; Bresnahan, 'Competition and Collusion'; Millner, 'Has Pricing Behaviour Become Competitive?'

[16] In 1957. 'Product Line Comparison, Ford Motor Company 1952 vs. 1959', FIA, Product Planning revised report, 31 Jan. 1957, AR-65-71: 43 (1).

[17] Ford, 'Product Philosophy Report'.   [18] Shapley, *Robert McNamara*, 69.

[19] Cars bought new. *Look, Automobile Survey* (1953), 25; 14 leading brands, standard deviation 9.5. A 1956 survey found 67.2 per cent brand loyalty: 'Why Do People Buy the Cars They Do?', *Popular Mechanics*, 312.

[20] e.g. Henry Flower, 'A Study of Motivation: The Role of Advertising in the Purchase of an Automobile' (revised vers. 16 Dec. 1954), esp. fo. 12; JWT, N. Strouse collection, 1/5, Hartman Center, Duke University library.

3 per cent of retail car values, which was comparable to or a little higher than the share of advertising in GNP.[21] Ford Motor Company's total advertising and promotion expenditure per car (in 1953 prices) was $23 per car in 1953, rising to $51 in 1957 and $72 in 1958.[22] Ford output was weighted towards the low-price end, so its spending would be on the low side. Critics of the styling race depicted advertising as an instrument of consumer manipulation.[23] But advertisers, on the whole, merely communicated styling decisions, and did not create them. They had no role in product planning, and were only shown the models about six months before their release.[24]

When it came to competition, one gambit was to steal a march and to shorten the model cycle (Table 9.1). Ford went down from four years to three in 1952. In 1953 General Motors went down from three years to two. In 1957 Chrysler added soaring fins to its existing 'Forward Look' models, and wrong-footed GM design. In response, GM rushed into a crash revision of its 1959 models, and the 1958 models were consequently offered only for one year. In the space of one decade, General Motors had shortened its model cycle from three years to one, while Ford had taken it from four years to two.

Sherman and Hoffer have identified the main components of styling change, and have estimated their contribution to market share. Styling changes could increase market share (Table 9.1), but in profit terms, even for the mass-produced low-price makes, investment in styling fell just short of breaking even. For the high-priced makes, Cadillac, Lincoln, and Imperial, styling change incurred very big losses, amounting to tens of millions of dollars.[25] Lincoln, acquired by Ford in the 1920s, had never made a profit, and even combined with Mercury (its mid-price car) the joint division made a loss every year between 1956 and 1959.[26] The Big Three styling efforts negated each other and the frenzy of design changes merely allowed them to run faster in order to remain in the same place.

[21] Calculated from Ford, Controller's Office, 'Advertising Promotion and Incentives 1953–1960', 10 Nov. 1959, Marketing Committee Meeting, 12 Nov. 1959, AR-65-71: 36; Additional data from Controller's Office, 'Industry Summary—1949–1963', 24 Feb. 1964, FIA, Yntema papers, AR-93-204131: 2. Advertising and national income, see Economist Intelligence Unit, *Advertising Expenditure 1960*, table 4, p. 30. Compare also White, *Automobile Industry*, 224.
[22] Ibid. (AR-65-71: 36) $45 and $65 and $86 if dealer contributions to product advertising are included. United States Senate, *Administered Prices Report*, estimates the manufacturer's cost per car at $75 in 1958, almost precisely the Ford outlay (p. 103).
[23] Packard, *Hidden Persuaders*, 109–12.
[24] JWT Ford Review Board for 1957 and 1958 models, JWT Review Board 6/11 and 6/12, Duke University library.
[25] Sherman and Hoffer, 'Does Automobile Style Change Payoff?'.
[26] 'Address by Ben D. Mills, 1960 Greenbrier Management Conference', 21 Nov. 1960, Index of Lincoln-Mercury Profits, FIA, McNamara papers, AR-66-12: 5.

The dominance of the stylists

Style could not be quantified, was difficult to explain or even to describe. However constrained by technology and tastes, it remained a matter of creativity and intuition. Paradoxically, the manufacture of cars, a rigid, capital-intensive, tough-minded metal-bashing industry, the largest in America, came to depend on its artistic, romantic, 'right brain' hemisphere. More prosaically, styling was fashion competition, and Detroit made a big commitment to marketing. The chief stylists at GM and Ford were not articulate.[27] Their leadership had an oracular quality, with every new design something of a leap in the dark. They were surrounded by mystique, and reported exclusively to the head of the company.[28]

At GM Harley Earl was approaching the end of a career which stretched back to the 1920s. He controlled a secretive set of studios, where designs were sketched up and transformed into full-scale clay models. The designers' role was enhanced by the adoption of the all-steel body in the late 1930s. The ability to model steel bodies in clay gave the stylists exceptional freedom of expression.[29] They attempted to endow the car with a distinctive 'personality' that would make it recognizable as an individual, but also as a member of a family of ancestors and relatives. A crucial element was the distinctive 'face' of the car, made up of its headlight-eyes and the silver grimace of its grille. The experimental 'Y-Job' of 1936 resonated in the post-war Buicks, with their bulbous curves and chrome-plated 'dollar grin'; it percolated through the whole GM range from the expensive Cadillac to the 'low-price' Chevrolets.[30]

Every decade of cars had a distinctive silhouette. Seen from the back, the 1930s vehicle was a boxy rectangle, standing about as tall as an average man; from the side, it flirted with streamlining, conveyed a thrust of direction and power, and was mounted by way of a running board. It was black, grey, or metalled green. The car of the mid-1950s was more garishly coloured in reds, blues, salmon, and white, often two-toned, and sparkling with chrome. The average woman could look straight over it and had to stoop to enter. Once seated, she found her knees pushing up, and in the

[27] Virgil Exner, at Chrysler, was more garrulous, though still opaque. For a typical presentation, see Ford Styling Department, 'Presentation of Two Models of 195X for Ford Division Product Planning Show', 15 Sept. 1954. FIA, AR-200778-7.

[28] Armi, *Art of American Car*; Gartman, *Auto-Opium*; Ford 'Product Philosophy Report'; and the Edsel Ford oral history project interviews with designers at the Henry Ford Museum, Dearborn, Michigan.

[29] On Earl, Bayley, *Harley Earl*; Armi, *Art of American Car*, ch. 2. Earl's rivals in the 1950s were George Walker at Ford, and Virgil Exner at Chrysler.

[30] Ford, 'Product Philosophy Report'; Armi, *Art of American Car*, 28.

middle rear position, had to straddle a high ridge which contained the driveshaft. Contrary to common assumptions, the 1950s car was not a great deal longer or wider than its predecessors of the 1940s. If it looked sleeker, that was mainly because it had lost up to a foot in height.[31]

'Modern' industrial design was driven by the ideal of bringing form into harmony with function. Modernism was an aesthetic of purity, a rejection of ornament. In the United States, several industrial designers, especially Raymond Loewy, expounded this aesthetic, albeit in adulterated form.[32] In truth, these norms were arbitrary, since pressed steel and extruded plastic were responsive materials, in comparison with iron and wood.[33] But modern movement austerity never really agreed with American popular taste. Loewy had inspired the simple, slab-sided lines of the 1947 Studebaker car, which in turn was the progenitor of the pivotal 1949 Ford.[34] But Loewy never worked for any of the Big Three.

At General Motors, Harley Earl ignored the modern movement. This was not provincial insularity. He visited Europe every year and had an academy of modern design on his doorstep.[35] His cars deliberately *separated* shape from the transport function: they had oversize curves, non-functional grilles, fake portholes; as a subordinate remembered, in Earl's designs, 'everything was like an overstuffed couch'.[36] In the 1950s he added gaudy colours, soaring fins, and more chrome. In fact, these designs were consistent with their true function, which was to express a fantasy of affluence, luxury, sensual delight and power, to enhance their appeal in the showroom. This aesthetic is no easier for me to put into words than it was for Earl, a man who was notoriously incapable of talking about his designs (or for that matter, of drawing them himself). The basic clue, I think, lies in Earl's early origins as a designer of custom car bodies for the Hollywood élite. His cars strive for a glamour akin to that of the Hollywood movies, in which everyone is rich, handsome, and talented; an ambience echoed in automobile advertising. Earl's aesthetic was original, as distinctively American as jazz. He was a postmodernist before his time, reaching promiscuously for inspirations, an artist whose sculptured steel creations poured in their tens of millions onto streets and highways. Blending

---

[31] Stonex, 'Trends of Vehicle Dimensions', was based on data collected by General Motors; White, *Automobile Industry*, table 13.2, p. 217 shows that between 1949 and 1959 the Ford V-8 had grown only 5.7 per cent longer, and 7.1 per cent wider (but 26.8 per cent heavier).

[32] Schönberger, *Raymond Loewy*; Teague, *Design This Day*.

[33] Pye, *Nature of Design*.   [34] Lewis et al., *Ford 1903 to 1984*, 139.

[35] The Cranbrook Academy of Art, which taught Bauhaus-style design, is still located in Bloomfield Hills, where top Detroit executives have their houses.

[36] Garfinkle, in Armi, *Art of American Car*, 173.

well with affluent suburbia, and with 'Main Street' at night, the assertive Detroit car was often incongruous in more workaday or countryside environments. Its natural habitats were the television commercial and the dealer's floor.

The models of 1954–5 had been three years in the making. Appearance-wise, they broke with the simplicity of the post-war models. They were long, low, powerful, colourful. Sales levels were 45 per cent greater than in the two surrounding years, and have challenged econometrics ever since.[37] Chow's model, which predicts new-car sales on the basis of income and price, breaks down for 1955; output rose more than a million units above the predicted level.[38] This reassured the stylists that they were on the right track. In laying down their sketches for the next model cycle (1957–8), they specified more of the same.[39]

That these machines expressed a distinctively American conception of motoring is shown by their poor acceptance abroad. In the 1950s the United States was the largest industrial power, with a big lead in productivity. The industry had large excess capacity. But demand for American cars overseas was limited, about 2 per cent of output. In 1959, America imported almost six times as many cars as it exported (which amounted to 116,520 cars). In the same year, Germany and Britain exported more than five and seven times as much as the United States respectively, around half of their respective outputs.[40]

Consumer satisfaction

The new-car buyer had to pay a big premium. It cost a great deal more to run a new car than a used one. For an average Ford car in 1957, the first year cost in depreciation was $735, vs. $331 in the second year.[41] Assuming that new cars and year-old cars provided transportation of nearly equal quality, what was the premium for? Over and above its value as transport, a new car provided two kinds of satisfaction: it signalled the owner's status, and it provided an increment in sensual gratification. Which of the two

[37] Bresnahan, 'Competition and Collusion', 457.

[38] 16.3 per cent, more than twice the standard error. Chow, 'Statistical Demand Functions', 169.

[39] '1957 Ford Car, Introduction, Merchandising Considerations', n.p., Ford Production Planning Committee no. 128, 2 Dec. 1954, FIA, AR-200778-7, and 'Presentation of Two Models of 195X for Ford Division Product Planning Show', 15 Sept. 1954, ibid.

[40] Automobile Manufacturers Association, *Automobile Facts*, 5, 15.

[41] For a new car costing $2,359. Prices corrected for inflation. Calculated from NADA, *Official Used Car Guide*, Jan. 1957, Feb. 1958.

was paramount? Customer choices indicate a surprisingly clear-cut preference for sensual over status gratification.

New cars are visible. Early in the model year they form a tiny but very distinctive fraction of the total stock. They are expensive, and thus provide a *credible* signifier of status. In American society, where competition was acclaimed, and where other signifiers of social rank were weak, car ownership was an effective way of communicating social standing. Robert McNamara recalled that

Most product offerings could be readily understood or categorised along a simple vertical price or size and status scale . . . Ford and Chevrolet were at the bottom, . . . whether measured by size, price or implied social status. Medium price cars such as Mercury, Buick and Oldsmobile fell in the middle of the scale, and Cadillac and Lincoln were at the top.[42]

Americans understood this hierarchy of cars.[43] With unlimited money to spend, by far the largest group in one survey (35–41 per cent) said they would purchase a Cadillac.[44] Each particular make had its distinctive 'social image'.[45] Ford market research arrayed car models along a sequence which stressed expressive attitudes more than social class. It ran from 'hot rodders', through fast drivers, sporty people, young-minded, show-offs, loud-talkers, economy-minded, and community leaders, to 'dignified people'.[46] A wry advertising man wrote that in comparison with the newly-rich lower-upper class, the upper-middle class (i.e. managers and professionals),

buys for the same driving reasons of prestige and social status, and spends much of its time observing the Joneses and making sure it keeps up with them . . . They would never dream of owning a Cadillac before a prior spell with a Buick. The neighbors and friends might think them 'pushy.' Nor would they drive around in an old Ford and run the risk of being thought a failure.[47]

This focus on the upper-middle class is right. Between 1953 and 1960, 49 per cent of new cars were purchased by the top income quintile; this group also tended to buy the more expensive cars, so that it accounted for a great deal more than half of the *value* of new cars. The top two quintiles

---

[42] 'Address by Robert S. McNamara', 1960 Greenbrier Management Conference, 21 Nov. 1960, fo. 17, FIA AR-66-12: 5.

[43] Social Research Inc., *Automobiles: What they Mean to Americans*.

[44] Anon., 'Why Do People Buy the Cars They Do?', 312.

[45] United States Senate, *Administered Prices Report*, 98–100.

[46] Ford, 'Product Philosophy Report', based on Social Research Inc., *Automobiles: What they Mean to Americans*, and Kenyon and Eckhardt (the Ford Mercury advertising agency) in 1957.

[47] Seldin, *Selling the Good Life*, 79.

purchased 73 per cent of new cars.[48] In American society, a new car was mostly for the better-off, and the ambience of affluence in car advertising is appropriate. It would be easy to conclude that cars were purchased for social distinction. But that does not follow.

The second motive for new car purchase is the expected increment in sensual gratification. There is pleasure in gleaming paintwork, in the smell of new seats, the thunk of a heavy door, the purr of a willing engine. More subtle pleasures need a poet to celebrate. Here is an ode to a Buick –

> As my foot suggests that you leap in the air with your hips of a girl,
> My finger that praises your wheel and announces your voices of song,
> Flouncing your skirts, you blueness of joy, you flirt of politeness,
> You leap, you intelligence, essence of wheelness with silver nose,
> And your platinum clocks of excitement stir like the hairs of a fern.[49]

The 1950s models offered a new appearance, for sure, but also new levels of appointment and performance, and a great surge of energy. Average horsepower of the four Buick models doubled from 138 in 1952, to 283 in 1958 (Figure 9.2).[50] Ford increased its horsepower in the same proportion, from 105 to 214.[51]

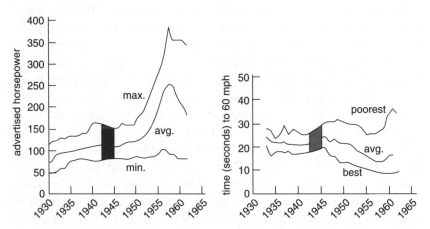

Fig. 9.2. Power and performance indicators, American cars, 1930–1962

Source: Stonex, 'Trends of Vehicle Dimensions and Performance Characteristics', figs. 7, 1: 2, 4. Reprinted with permission, © Society of Automotive Engineers, Inc.

---

[48] Calculated from Smith, *Consumer Demand*, table A.2, p. 90. Each quintile as percentage of sum of the quintiles. [49] Shapiro, 'Buick'.

[50] Norbye and Dunne, *Buick 1946–1978*, Appendix 1, pp. 154–5.

[51] Excluding an optional 300 HP engine. See NADA, *Official Used Car Guide*, Jan. 1957, p. 52; Jan. 1960, p. 66.

Only some of the power was absorbed by additional weight. The Buicks increased in weight only by some ten per cent as power doubled, and that was typical of the average car.[52] The 1950s car followed three other lines of development; effort saving, sensual gratification, and appearance. Effort saving included power steering, power windows, power brakes, power-adjusted seats, retractable roof, and automatic transmission. Sensual comfort was delivered by a heater, tinted glass, air conditioning, radio, and engine options. Appearance was enhanced by whitewall tyres, dual headlamps, two-tone colour schemes, and 'hardtop' and convertible body-type options.[53] Buyers could specify an expensive package of accessories, buy some of them later, or go for a more expensive car, which included them as standard.

List prices rose by about a third during the decade. Griliches has estimated that more than 90 per cent of the price rise could be explained by added features.[54] If one accepts this interpretation, then a simple measure of upwards 'feature drift' is to compare an index of the average wholesale price of a Detroit car with the new car price index of the Bureau of Labor Statistics, which reflected the basic 'low-priced' models. The BLS price index may be regarded as a baseline (itself moving upwards) while the average wholesale price may be regarded as a weighted average price, which takes into account the shifting mix of attributes. The two indices moved together from 1950 to 1954; in 1955 the average price jumped to 114 per cent of the BLS index, rising to a peak of 122 per cent in 1957, before falling back to 115 per cent in 1960. This suggests a shift in the product mix towards better-equipped cars up to 1957. Mid-1950s buyers wanted 'more car per car'.[55] This is also shown in Figure 9.3.

Figure 9.3 might suggest that customers, motivated by status, were moving upmarket. In fact, the movement was the other way, from the mid-price makes, into the low-priced category. But *within* the low-price groups the shift was from the 'stripped' basic models towards the more highly specified ones. Buyers were moving from the Buicks to the Chevrolets, from the Mercury to the Ford; towards a more expensive, more highly appointed 'low-price' model. Both Chevrolet and Ford introduced enhanced model lines alongside the basic ones. The share of the *mid-price* models declined sharply, from 40 per cent of the market in 1955 down to

---

[52] *Official Used Car Guide*; and Stonex, 'Trends of Vehicle Dimensions', fig. 18, p. 9.

[53] See e.g. 'Medium-price Car Buyers Take More Accessories Despite Sales Slump', *Ward's Automotive Yearbook*, 20 (1958), 39.

[54] Griliches, 'Hedonic Price Indexes', table 3.3, p. 65.

[55] T. Yntema, 'Growth in a Changing Market', Greenbrier Management Conference, 22 Nov. 1960, fo. 7, FIA, McNamara Papers, AR-66-12: 5.

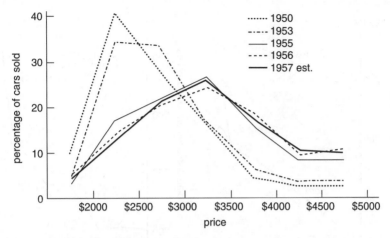

Fig. 9.3. Distribution of new-car expenditures, by price class, 1950–1957

Note: Constant 1957 prices, deflated by Bureau of Labor Statistics New Car Retail Price Index.

Source: Ford Division Programming, 'Economic Factors Related to Industry Volumes and the Medium Price Market' (14 Sept. 1957), exhibit X, Wright papers, AR-75-15565: 23, Ford Industrial Archives.

22 per cent in 1960. In 1957, the 'low-price' Detroit cars captured 60 per cent of the car market.[56]

Buyers chose the high-end low-price car, and not the low-end medium-price car. Expensive cars had lost most of their feature advantage over the cheaper ones. A Ford's engine could be as big as a Cadillac's, and its body almost as large (Figure 9.4). In 1957, Cadillac had no design features that were exclusive to it, and only three trivial items that could not be had on the Ford.[57] All that expensive cars could offer now was *status*, but the buyers' revealed preference was for *features*.

American cars had become remarkably similar. What was the reason? General Motors, which covered the whole price range, had an incentive to differentiate its models clearly. Ford, which made mostly low-price cars, was not constrained that way.[58] It therefore upgraded its models, and forced Chevrolet, its direct GM competitor and the largest-selling brand, to do the same. The more expensive models were constrained from further upgrading as they pushed against the limits of existing infrastructures.

---

[56] Ford Division Programming, 'New Passenger Registrations by Price Class', [June 1960], J. Walter Thompson Creative Review Board, 'Background Memorandum, 1961 Falcon', 9 Aug. 1960, JWT Papers, Review Board 7, Duke University.

[57] Ford Division, 'Economy Car Study: Preliminary Report', 15 July 1957, fo.3, FIA, Product Planning Committee 15 AR-94-200777-5.

[58] Robert McNamara, 'General Product Objectives', 10 Feb. 1953, FIA, AR-66-12: 9.

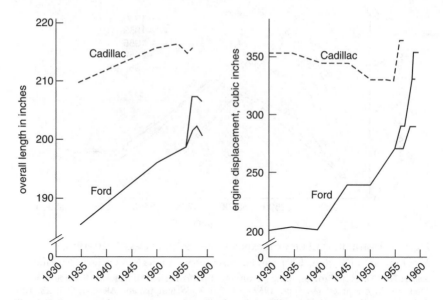

Fig. 9.4. Power and size comparisons, Ford and Cadillac, 1930–1959

Note: Eight-cylinder engines except 1930 Ford, which is four-cylinder.

Source: Ford Product Planning Office, 'Economy Car Study: Preliminary Report' (15 July 1957), fos. 3–4, AR-94-200777-5, Ford Industrial Archives.

Cadillacs took up two parking meter spaces.[59] Some models were too large for home garages built between the wars. And some were getting too wide for the roads. In 1958, several states set a maximum width for cars.[60]

The absence of price competition also weakened the manufacturers' incentives to differentiate. Instead, as suggested by Hotelling's spatial theory of monopolistic competition, they crowded on to the same terrain, and introduced very similar products. The firms wanted to locate their products 'where the demand is', i.e. in the central zone of middle-class American taste. [61]

What buyers wanted, it seems, was not personal distinction, not *status* gratification, but *sensual* gratification. The convergent specification was dubbed 'The Classless Car'.[62] Ford advertised 'A Fine Car at Half the Fine-Car Price'.[63] Unlike the Model T (the previous 'classless car'), its 1950s descendants stressed luxury over utility. But by pushing all cars to

[59] Robert McNamara, 'General Product Objectives', 82.
[60] R. S. McNamara and W. C. Ford, 'Maximum Vehicle Widths', 21 Nov. 1958, and enclosures, FIA, Ford Product Planning Committee, AR-66-12: 9.
[61] Tirole, *Industrial Organization*, 286–7. Thanks to Robin Mason for this reference.
[62] Benedict, 'Era of "Classless" Car'; Ford, 'Product Philosophy Report'.
[63] e.g. memorandum to W. Elton, 18 Apr. 1956, JWT Review Bd. 6/12, Duke University.

the top of the feature range, the Big Three were storing up trouble for themselves.

An insight into their problem is provided by Scitovsky's distinction between 'comfort' and 'pleasure'.[64] Each of these states represents a relationship between an input of stimulation and an output of satisfaction. 'Pleasure' is a *dynamic* state of rising satisfaction. 'Comfort' is an *optimal* state of stimulation, one which cannot be improved upon. Both states are found on different segments of the 'Wundt curve' (Figure 3.3, above).

The two states are not commensurate with each other. 'Comfort' sits higher on the hedonic scale, but is not a stable condition. It is satiated quickly by habituation. Pleasure starts lower on the hedonic scale, but can be sustained by periodic infusions of novelty and uncertainty. It is a state of sustained satisfaction, albeit stopping short of climax. 'Comfort', like a hot bath or the end of a good meal, is a state of immersion and bliss. 'Pleasure', in contrast, is a state of restraint, anticipation, and progression. These are two distinct hedonic ideas. 'Comfort' is being, 'pleasure' is becoming.

Faced by the Wundt curve, consumers aimed for 'comfort': 'Every consumer replies that he has more H.P. than he needs, but then he turns right around and buys a car with yet higher H.P,' the market surveys reported.[65] Scitovsky suggested that this preference for 'comfort' was pervasive in American culture. The American car was designed for 'comfort'. Its steering, suspension, brakes, and noise level were all designed to be 'softer' than European equivalents, and to insulate its driver from the frictions of travel.[66] Americans chose automatic transmission, which was shunned in Europe. The logic of 'change means progress' drove competing manufacturers up the Wundt curve. The feature-rich 'classless car' carried car makers into the 'comfort' zone, with nowhere further to go.

It was assumed that General Motors set the norms in styling, and that everyone followed.[67] In fact, styling permitted genuine competition. American Motors refused to join the weight-and-power race. Chrysler defied it in 1953 and took a beating the following year. It gambled again in 1957, and unsettled Detroit with its soaring fins. Chrysler gained three percentage points of market share while GM lost six. General Motors designers were already too far into the 1958 model designs to make any changes, but chose a completely new line for 1959, which took fins to

---

[64] Scitovsky, *Joyless Economy*, ch. 4. See above, Ch. 3, p. 56.

[65] 'More Horses? Owners say "Nay" ', *Automotive News* (14 Oct. 1954), 2. 'Ford Passenger Car Review Board', 10 Apr. 1957, fo. 1, JWT Ford Review Board, box 6:12; See *Look, Automobile Survey* (1954), 21.   [66] Railton and Sampietro, 'Trends in European Car Design'.

[67] George Romney in United States Senate, *Administered Prices. Hearings*, 29–31; United States Senate, *Administered Prices Report*, 90–2; White, *Automobile Industry*, 206–7.

fantastic extremes.[68] GM designers panicked, ignored established routines, and worked overtime, directly in clay.[69]

[Chrysler] came out with some fins that were a foot and a half over the fender crown lines, and that put fear in the G.M. design staff, so we did wild fins, rockets, and tubes. I often sat back when all of this was happening and wondered where we would go from there, because that was pretty far out.[70]

Each of the Big Three had scores of model variants. All of them had a facelift every year. Trucks, tractors, and overseas cars also needed attention. Each design emerged out of a cluster of false starts. At this pace of styling change, product planning became a big drain on management.[71] At Ford, three product approval committees assembled the company's senior executives with hordes of advisers, all mulling for hours over the shape of the tail lights. Every week or two designers staged a styling extravaganza in which another set of prospective models were presented lifelike in painted clay, often alongside some real cars from the competition.[72] Archive boxes are full of glossy photographs, with endless permutations of indifferent design. A Ford stylist remembered the 'horrendous experience' of feverish proliferation.[73] A junior designer at GM recalled those years,

It wasn't design; it was very superficial, fashion-oriented activity...It is such a transitory kind of industry. When you know that everything is going to be replaced in three years, it is hard to take what you are doing seriously. And we weren't building good products either. I mean that was the era of the '59 Chevrolet....They were constantly searching. It wasn't for something pure or elegant. It was for something attention-getting, unique, and distinctive. But distinctive didn't have to particularly mean quality. It just had to be different. So, in the constant push for something new, it often became bizarre.[74]

Product risk could make or break careers. In 1955, after years of prudent dithering, the careful procedures of planning at Ford broke down, and the

[68] On fins, Gammage and Jones, 'Orgasm in Chrome'.

[69] William B. Mitchell (GM stylist), interview, Aug. 1984, Automotive Design Oral History Project, Edsel B. Ford Design History Center, Henry Ford Museum, Dearborn, Michigan, fos. 25, 57.

[70] Irving Rybicki (GM stylist), interview, 27 June 1985, fo. 48, Automotive Design Oral History Project, Edsel B. Ford Design History Center, Henry Ford Museum, Dearborn, Michigan.

[71] C. L. Goyert (Ford product planner), 1985, Interview, 7 Nov. 1985, fos. 48, 57–8, Automotive Design Oral History Project, Edsel B. Ford Design History Center, Henry Ford Museum, Dearborn, Michigan.

[72] FIA, Product Planning Committee Minutes, e.g. AR-94-200777-5, 15 July 1957. Committee structure, FIA AR-75-15565: 14.

[73] Joseph Oros (Ford stylist), interview, 1985, vol. i, fos. 71–4, Automotive Design Oral History Project, Edsel B. Ford Design History Center, Henry Ford Museum, Dearborn, Michigan.

[74] Gene Garfinkle, in Armi, Art of American Car, 173, 181–2.

company rushed into a massive new product programme. A new Edsel division was set up to launch five models in the mid-price field.[75] Edsel exemplified the movement towards ornamental middle-brow styling excess. It eventually became a byword for folly, the biggest casualty of the new-car frenzy.[76] Jack Reith, one of Ford's high-flying 'Whiz Kids', led the project. He also promoted the premium Mercury 'Turnpike Cruiser'. He failed to see the coming crisis of the mid-priced car, and both models were discontinued in 1958, shortly after their launch. Reith, only 45, left the company, and committed suicide shortly afterwards.[77]

Frequent restyling played havoc with quality. A complex mechanical system takes time to settle down. Styling lurches forced redesigns of engines, transmissions, and suspensions. Engineering was ten to more than twenty times as expensive as styling.[78] Each redesign introduced new faults. There was no time for 'learning by doing'. A product planner recalled,

the engineers want it like they did it last year, because they finally figured out how it worked . . . The stylists, on the other hand in those days, [wanted it] long, low, hot, with fins, looking like it's going eighty miles an hour while it's standing still.[79]

The Edsel acquired a poor reputation for quality; partly because it was a new design, but also because it rolled down the lines intermixed thinly with other Ford cars, and workers never learned to assemble it properly.[80] Warranty costs rose. Survival rates at nine years' age (for all 'low-price' makes) fell from an average 71.6 per cent for 1951 models, to 52.5 per cent for 1958 models.[81] By 1958 a crisis of confidence in Detroit cars was in evidence. To restore confidence, Ford extended the warranty in 1960 from three months to a year, and was quickly emulated by the other two firms.[82]

---

[75] Warnock, *Edsel Affair*, ch. 2, is supported by the poor quality of product planning staffwork reflected in Ford records, e.g. Product Planning Committee meeting no. 24, 28 June 1955, AR-94-200778-8.

[76] Warnock, *Edsel Affair*, pp. v–x. Edsel has spawned its own literature: Brooks, *The Fate of the Edsel*; Deutsch, *Selling the People's Cadillac*.   [77] Byrne, *Whiz Kids*, chs. 22, 24.

[78] e.g. as estimated for the 1958 Ford Custom 300 Tudor 6, $1 per car for styling, $25 for engineering; for the new Falcon 'compact' car, $4 and $41 respectively, Ford Product Planning Office, 'Economy Car Report', 13 Nov. 1957, fo. 28. FIA Product Planning Committee, 13 Nov. 1957, AR-94-200777-6.   [79] Goyert, Oral History, fo. 11 (n. 71 above).

[80] Warnock, *Edsel Affair*, 69–71.

[81] Calculated from White, *Automobile Industry*, table 12.3, p. 197. Arithmetic mean.

[82] e.g. Ben D. Mills to R. McNamara, 14 Mar. 1958; McNamara to Mills, 29 Apr. 1959; McNamara to A. R. Miller, 'Proposed Extension of Warranty and Policy Coverage', 26 Sept. 1960; FIA, McNamara papers, AR-66-12: 8; White, *Automobile Industry*, 220.

10

Driving Prudently: American and European

Consumer experiences

In the 1950s, American car makers followed where new-car buyers seemed to be leading. Feature drift meant that car prices rose faster than income, and faster than prices in general.[1] Buyers paid more for depreciation as car lives shortened. Running costs rose as bigger engines and heavier cars consumed more (and more expensive) high-octane fuel, wore out white-wall tyres, and cost more to repair and insure. Buyers in the mid-1950s surrendered more of their incomes in return for the satisfactions of new-car ownership. Real running costs rose about 9 per cent for a standard low-price three-year-old Ford car between 1954 and 1959. For the more typical shift from a basic Ford Custom 300 to a high-specification Ford Galaxy, the increase in real running costs over these five years was 31 per cent.[2] If new cars were acquired to signal solvency and status, then cost inflation was the outcome of positional competition. Such competition for positional goods is inherently futile, if everyone ends up in the same relative position. If cars were acquired for sensual gratification, that was also bound to disappoint, since there was little scope for further improvement in power and size. Frustration eventually broke out in the form of a strong shift in buyer preferences, away from Detroit's high-powered 'classless car', and towards more austere transport.[3] In Europe, the styling frenzy had

[1] 'Consumer Price Trends 1953 to 1959', in Ford Division Product Planning Office, 'Cost of Ownership Report', 22 June 1959, Product Planning Committee Meeting, FIA AR-94-2000777-9.

[2] Calculated from Ford Division Product Planning Office, 'Cost of Ownership Report', 22 June 1959, Product Planning Committee Meeting, FIA AR-94-2000777-9. Annual running cost assuming 10,000 miles and three years between trade-ins.

[3] On positional competition, see Hirsch, *Social Limits to Growth*; on its futility, see Frank, *Choosing the Right Pond*. Also, Ch. 11 below.

never taken hold. In consequence, European cars and British cars were altered less frequently, and held their prices better than American ones, even British cars of lower quality; likewise the unchanging German Volkswagen sedan which was sold in the United States.

The backlash

In 1958, the sales of Detroit cars slumped. About 2 million new-car buyers either postponed their purchases, or chose imported cars. There are three interpretations: that an economic downturn depressed sales; that there was a shift of tastes among new-car buyers; and that producers had led buyers too far up the Wundt curve.

Intellectuals were the first to argue the futility of styling and horsepower competition, which violated the 'modern movement' principle of austerity. The modernist designer Raymond Loewy described the new models in 1955 as 'a jukebox on wheels'.[4] Walter Teague, a modern-movement purist, wrote that 'this Roman orgy of obsolescence merchandising must come to an end'.[5] Other writers took the styling race as a symptom of deeper malaise, and warned that the public was being conned into overconsumption.[6] Some of these works achieved nationwide impact: Vance Packard followed *The Hidden Persuaders* of 1957 with *The Waste Makers* of 1960. J. K. Galbraith published *The Affluent Society* in 1958. A Berkeley linguist, S. I. Hayakawa, said that American males were uncertain of their virility, and that the car industry had identified an opportunity: 'Let's give them great big cars, glittering all over and pointed at the ends, with 275 h.p. under the hood, so that they can feel like men!'[7] Whatever one thinks of this interpretation (given credence by advertising), Hayakawa perceived correctly that the pursuit of sensual gratification was affecting the shape of the product.

Congress picked up a groundswell of unease, and began to investigate.[8] The hearings are full of discontent. The Automotive Finance Association produced survey responses such as these: 'The present cars have too many gadgets and are too big. The American public today will buy a small sturdy car with less gingerbread and less horsepower.'[9]

---

[4] Loewy, 'A Jukebox on Wheels'.   [5] United States Senate, *Administered Prices Report*, 83.
[6] Other remarkable critiques are Riesman and Larrabee, 'Autos in America', Hayakawa, 'Sexual Fantasy and the 1957 Car', and Keats, *Insolent Chariots*.
[7] Hayakawa, 'Sexual Fantasy and the 1957 Car', 236.
[8] See e.g. United States Senate, *Administered Prices Report and Automobile Price Labeling, Hearings*.
[9] United States Senate, *Administered Prices Report*, 93–4; *Automobile Price Labeling, Hearings*, 57, 61.

Table 10.1. Ford unsolicited correspondence, January 1958–October 1959

	Number	%
Small car	513	32.4
Includes requests to build a smaller car and revive models 'A' and 'T'		
Styling and package	445	28.1
Cars are too low, have too much chrome, difficult to get into, and other styling complaints		
Economy of operation	218	13.8
Purchase price, gasoline consumption, and repair cost complaints		
Horsepower	67	4.2
Other	340	21.5
Total letters received	1,583	100.0

Source: Unsolicited Correspondence reports, 1958–60, FIA; Breech papers, AR-65-71 43 (2). Quote from Report I, 27 May 1958, exhibit II, fo. 10 ibid., Unsolicited Correspondence Summary no. 16, 1959.

Hundreds of letters arrived at the Ford Motor Company, complaining of overdesign and excess features (Table 10.1). The company issued internal reports, monitoring the letters and providing excerpts. Cars had grown too large and powerful. The company was urged to bring back the Model A (first introduced in 1927), and even the ancient Model T.[10]

Customers began to vote with their money. In 1957 the car manufacturers looked forward to another boom year like 1955. Demographics and economics were promising. Instead, buyers stayed at home. New car purchases fell to 4.2 million, the lowest since the end of the Korean war. In 1958, real GNP declined by 0.8 per cent. This recession is a convenient explanation for the collapse of the new-car market. But was the cause from the economy to the new-car market, or possibly the other way? The decline in car output ($12.4 billion) was larger than the decline in GNP ($11.9 billion). Assuming growth at the 1957 level, the decline in car output in 1958 would still account for one-third of the loss of output, net of any multiplier.[11]

As Detroit moved upmarket, it left a gap at the bottom, which did not remain vacant for long. From 1956 onwards, the 'small car' segment began to grow rapidly. It was mostly made up of cars imported from Europe, primarily Volkswagen. The share of imports rose exponentially, from 1 per cent in 1955 to 2 per cent in 1956, 4 per cent in 1957, and 10.5 per cent in 1958. The domestic 'compact car' producer, American Motors, doubled its sales between 1957 and 1958. Its advertising called the competition 'gas guzzlers' that 'rob you blind'.[12]

[10] Unsolicited Correspondence reports, 1958-60, FIA; Breech papers, AR-65-71: 43 (2).

[11] United States President, *Economic Report of the President*, table B-7, p. 295. Car output plus 15 per cent for dealer mark-ups.

[12] Draft of letter to Roy D. Chapin, American Motors, pointing out that these claims were unjustified, 24 June 1958, FIA, Breech papers, AR-65-71:1

In 1958 the spell of styling shattered. Perfection could no longer be perfected. Having promised emotional consummation through comfort and power, Detroit had nothing new to offer. About one-third of potential buyers chose not to pay the new-car premium, and postponed their purchases. The average time new cars were held rose 19 per cent between 1957 and 1959, from 4 years and 5 months in 1955, to 5 years and 3 months.[13]

The American 'classless cars', the high-specification Fords, Chevrolets, Plymouths and some of the cheaper mid-price models, no longer offered genuine 'distinction'.[14] Their styling had filtered down into the lower end of the middle classes, and at second-hand, to working-class owners too. The smart people were now 'Cold Rods', their watchword 'it gets me there and it gets me back'.[15] Sixty per cent of Volkswagen owners had been to college (vs. 13 per cent in the general population), and they were younger and wealthier than the average Ford and Chevrolet buyer.[16]

They had replaced myopia with calculation. Ford market research had discovered in 1956 and 1957 that

a substantial number of economy car buyers have well above average education as well as relatively high income. They appear well able to calculate the true cost of owning and operating a car, and by logical reasoning have decided to purchase a small economy car. These people have established their social positions (education, job, etc.) and are immune to the 'cheap' stigma associated with economy cars in the minds of some people....

Rather than display one's importance and success by buying the largest, most powerful and most expensive car possible, a segment of small economy car buyers appear to be demonstrating their shrewdness by purchasing a unique, small, foreign and economical car. These buyers are proud of their exhibited economy and shrewdness...[17]

Detroit's leaders were not always comfortable with the rule of the stylist. The concept of a basic car appealed to them. Ford had a small-car study every year after the war. It had actually set up a small car division in 1946, but scrapped the project when there seemed to be no demand. So did GM and Chrysler.[18]

[13] *Look, Automobile Survey*. Surveys in July of respective year.
[14] United States senate, *Administered Prices Report*, 100.
[15] Lynes, 'How Do You Rate in the New Leisure?', 89.
[16] Based on Ford, 'Volkswagen Owner Attitude Survey', R. J. Eggert to R. McNamara, 16 July 1956, FIA Wright papers, Market Research, AR-75-15565: 23.
[17] Ford Product Planning Office, 'Economy Car Report', 13 Nov. 1957, fo. 28. FIA Product Planning Committee, 13 Nov. 1957, AR-94-200777-6, fos. 13–14.
[18] Light car file, 1946, E. Breech papers, FIA AR-65-71:35; Lewis et al., *Ford 1903 to 1984*, 130–3; Small Car Studies (1950–3), Henry Ford Museum, Dearborn, Mich., ACC 695, Box 8.

The problem was simple: buyers expected to pay less for a small car, but a small car could not be made for much less. The President of GM stated, 'When you reduce the size of a car, you take value out faster than you can reduce cost.' A small car would also eat into the market share of more profitable models. The independents posed no threat, due to their higher costs.[19] In 1953 Chrysler gambled on a smaller form factor, and suffered a big loss in market share. At Ford small-car studies continued. The Big Three were honest when they said that they only provided what customers wanted.[20] But then, perhaps not entirely. After all, Chrysler found more than a million buyers for its cars in 1953, although they were smaller *and* more expensive than the competition. Likewise, Nash (American Motors) sold 137,000 cars in the same year, mostly of its compact Rambler model, although it was 15 per cent more expensive than the basic Ford.[21]

What forced the hand of the Big Three was Volkswagen's success. The German company had economies of scale in its European markets, and much lower labour costs. Hence, unlike American 'independents', it could sell a small car in America more cheaply than the 'Big Three'. As demand for the Volkswagen soared beyond supply (and also due to its cheaper initial price) it depreciated at almost half the rate of the basic Ford car. Total VW running costs (for a new car over three years) were 60 per cent of those of a basic Ford car, and one-third less even than a two-year-old Ford. Imports were costing Ford $16 million in profits in 1957, and threatened to take $40 million by 1960.[22]

Once this threat crystallized, the Big Three acted quickly. In July 1957 Ford launched an urgent crash programme, which brought a 'compact' car, the Falcon, into the showrooms by October 1959.[23] GM and Chrysler delivered concurrently. Experience with short model cycles allowed Detroit to respond nimbly to a perceived shift in consumer preferences.

When the new Detroit compact cars were introduced in 1959–60, the cars were an enormous hit. The Falcon (with its sister the Comet) sold about 630,000 in 1960, some four times its planning volume.[24] Altogether, the 'small-car category' (imports, and domestic 'compact cars') captured

[19] 'Considerations of a Smaller Ford Car. Outline', 9 Apr. 1953, Henry Ford Museum, Dearborn, Mich., ACC 695, Box 7, n.p.

[20] See discussion in United States Senate, *Administered Prices Report*, 77–81, 90–1.

[21] 'Considerations of a Smaller Ford Car. Outline', 9 Apr. 1953 (prices).

[22] Ford Division, 'Economy Car Study: Preliminary Report', 15 July 1957, FIA, Product Planning Committee 15 AR-94-200777-5, fos. 1–17; costs, fo. 13. Profits, Ford Product Planning Office, 'Economy Car Report', 13 Nov. 1957, fo. 4. FIA Product Planning Committee, 13 Nov. 1957, AR-94-200777-6.   [23] 'Economy car Report', ibid., fo. 3.

[24] Calculated from Controller's Office, 'Industry Summary—1949–1963', 24 Feb. 1964, FIA, Yntema papers, AR-93-204131: 2.

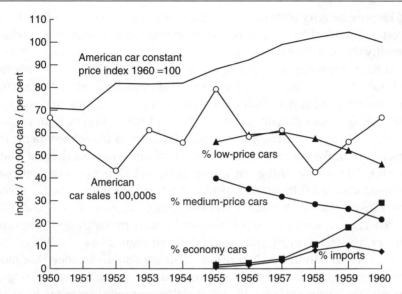

Fig. 10.1. American passenger-car market volume and price indicators, 1950–1960

Sources: Automobile Manufacturers Association, *Automobile Facts and Figures*, 3; Smith, *Consumer Demand*, p. 90; Ford Division Programming, New Passenger Car Registration by Price Class, 'Background Memorandum, 1961 Falcon', 9 Aug. 1960, JWT papers, Hartman Center, Duke University library, J. Walter Thompson Review Board, Box 7/13.

about 20 per cent of the market by 1960 (Figure 10.1), and new car buyers loosened their wallets once again. Popular acceptance is the final clue that the crisis of 1958 was not due to the recession of that year, but indicated a revulsion in consumer tastes, a prudential retreat from the top of the Wundt curve.

Styling competition may be regarded as a non-cooperative reponse to the oligopoly problem of maximizing profit. Without it, cars could have cost less. The cost of model changes, said a Ford economist, 'reflects the struggle between the automobile companies to get customers by changing the product from year to year and trying to get an increase in the volume of business'.[25] A cooperative solution of infrequent model changes would have lowered the cost of new vehicles significantly. From an economic point of view, this failure to cooperate was counter-productive. The price elasticity of demand for cars was estimated variously at the time at about −1.2 to −1.5.[26] A 5 per cent decline in price (made possible by styling restraint) would have increased demand by about 6 to 8 per cent. A method

[25] United States Senate, *Administered Prices. Hearings*, T. Yntema, 5 Feb. 1958, p. 27321.
[26] United States Senate, *Administered Prices Report*, 144; Wykoff's estimates are at the higher end with −1.6: 'A User Cost Approach', table 1, p. 383.

of keeping novelty without costly facelifting was suggested to Ford by its economic adviser: 'develop attractive yet conspicuous monograms... which identify the model-year of each car.'[27]

At Ford, product planning had destroyed Edsel's Jack Reith; it made the Falcon's Robert McNamara. McNamara had been a professor at Harvard, and was a man of austere ethics, and a temperamental rationalist. He shared the intelligentsia's disdain for the products of the styling race, and strove to bring it under control. The compact Falcon was his achievement. For once, Ford broke out of its customer base and captured a big share of a new market: 59 per cent of Big Three compacts, and 42 per cent of American compacts overall.[28] In 1958 he went a step further and launched a project for a smaller car, code-named 'Cardinal', to compete head to head with Volkswagen, a 'world car' to be produced jointly in the United States and Europe, which finally emerged some eighteen years later as the 'Fiesta'.[29]

Much as he detested styling risk, McNamara also understood that most car buyers were still attracted to power and size. In 1958, at a meeting to approve the Falcon compact, he accepted that economy cars were a minority taste, and that Ford had to increase the size of its standard models.[30] His other triumph of 1958 was the four-seat Thunderbird, an expensive, heavy, vanity car.

In April 1958 he asked (with a touch of exasperation),

1. We have eliminated as possible sources of additional buyer appeal in the annual model changes:
     A. Increased acceleration.
     B. Styling changes based on added length, added width, or lower height.
2. In what way may cars be changed to provide added appeal with each new model?
3. What would be the effect of eliminating or minimizing the degree of change in each new model?[31]

In what turned out to be his final statement to the company, he indicated a reversal of policy in the direction of styling restraint and product diversity: more variety with less change.[32]

---

[27] Dean to McNamara, 26 June 1958, FIA, McNamara papers, AR-66-12: 4. This recalls the method used in Britain between the 1960s and 1996 to indicate the model year with a letter on the licence plate.

[28] Controller's Office, 'Industry Summary—1949–1963', 24 Feb. 1964, FIA, Yntema papers, AR-93-204131: 2.

[29] 'Address by Robert S. McNamara', 1960 Greenbrier Management Conference, 21 Nov. 1960, fo. 10, FIA AR-66-12:5; Seidler, *Fiesta*.

[30] Product Planning Committee, 19 Mar. 1958, fo. 7, AR-88-108162: 1, FIA.

[31] McNamara to Goyert, 21 Mar. 1958, FIA AR-66-12: 9.

[32] 'Address by Robert S. McNamara', 1960 Greenbrier Management Conference, 21 Nov. 1960, fos. 19–20, FIA AR-66-12: 5.

The United States and Europe

Recollecting the early days of his romance with the American poet Sylvia Plath in the 1950s, the English poet Ted Hughes invoked their initial impressions of their respective countries' cars. He has Sylvia remember her first responses to Britain:

> '...England
> Was so poor! Was black paint cheaper? Why
> Were English cars all black—to hide the filth?
> Or to stay respectable, like bowlers
> And umbrellas? Every vehicle a hearse.'

Contrast his own,

> I remembered my shock of first sighting
> The revolving edge of Manhattan
> From the deck of the *Queen Elizabeth*—
> The merry-go-round palette of American cars.
> Everywhere the big flower of freedom![33]

The sense here is that British cars in the 1950s were prudential assets, while American ones were short-lived 'flowers'. In the sixties British cars began to swing as well, and with the Austin/Morris Mini, British cars pushed their way briefly into the forefront of fashion. Nevertheless, the prudential evaluation of cars, in a much poorer society, remained typical of Britain, and is captured by respective depreciation curves of cars in the two countries. In Britain, in contrast with the USA, the styling cycle was much slower. Ford renewed their models about every four years, while Morris kept models in production for at least a decade, and sometimes much longer. The novelty signal was a letter on the licence plate, updated once a year. It was uniform and costless. In the United States, novelty had to be signalled expensively for each model by means of annual styling facelifts. Aggressive styling innovation generated higher depreciation rate variance, and depreciated older cars more rapidly, quite apart from any difference in mechanical quality.[34]

Our depreciation curves (Figure 10.3) highlight the more dynamic and competitive styling/innovation regime in the United States, compared with Britain. Apart from year one, British depreciation rates were lower

---

[33] Hughes, 'The Beach', *Birthday Letters*, 154–5.

[34] Purohit, 'Exploring', shows that used car prices could respond positively as well as negatively to car styling changes.

than American ones, despite poor British mechanical quality. Model attrition was faster in the United States.

In the course of styling competition, American producers had moved their models upmarket. Volkswagen, which followed a 'Model T' styling strategy (after Henry Ford's unchanging first mass-production car), was able to fill the gap with a car made in Germany. Its ads promised to improve mechanical quality continuously, without altering the basic design.[35] Sales grew 35 per cent a year between 1955 and 1961, up to 177,000 annual unit sales. Customers were credibly shielded from fashion obsolescence, a point stressed in company advertising.

Volkswagen retail-retail depreciation was exceptionally low. Between 1956 and 1958, one-year-old sedans actually sold for more than the list price of new ones.[36] High retail prices made it possible to combine high mark-ups with low depreciation. Indigenous British manufacturers also followed a 'Model T' policy. The Morris Minor (introduced in 1949) was produced unchanged for 23 years, Morris/Austin Mini (1959) only went out of production in 1991, and the popular Morris/Austin 1100 ran unchanged for ten years.[37] Local cars in Britain and Volkswagen in the United States depreciated much less than comparable American cars (Table 10.2). After five years, a British car in the UK (or Volkswagen in the United States) had kept about 50 per cent more of its initial value than an American one of the same age.

Were British cars more mechanically durable? That is unlikely—they failed in the American market while Volkswagen succeeded. They were built at much lower cost. They had bad quality reputations.[38] If roads in

Table 10.2. Used-car prices as percentage of new prices, American and European makes

	Ford USA	Buick USA	Ford USA	Buick USA	VW USA	VW USA	Ford UK	Morris UK
Year new	1957	1957	1968	1968	1957	1968	1968	1968
New price	100	100	100	100	100	100	100	100
age1	66	63	60	67	81	73	67	66
age2	51	47	43	50	69	62	62	61
age3	40	35	36	43	57	49	51	52
age4	20	20	24	34	35	40	41	42
age5	19		17	23	31	29	31	32

Mean of models in panel. Deflated prices. User's selling price. *Source*: Offer, 'Markup for Lemons', table 5.

[35] www.ciadvertising.org/studies/student/99_spring/interactive/joohwan/bernbach/images/vwad15.gif. Copies in possession of the author.   [36] Calculated from NADA.
[37] Foreman-Peck et al., *British Motor Industry*, 129, 140–2.
[38] Whisler, *British Motor Industry*, 327–49, 358–9.

New England were heavily salted, British roads were salted as well, and the salt affected VW beetles in America too. For both the UK models, and for VW in the USA, there was less uncertainty about fashion durability. In the United States, with its styling race, makers could not credibly commit not to innovate.[39] British producers (and Volkswagen USA) could do so. That was reflected in lower depreciation.

During the build-up of mass-market popular motorization, cheap individual transport was sufficiently compelling for consumers without the additional temptation of frequent styling changes. In developing markets, the 'Model T' styling strategy of Volkswagen, of Morris and Ford in Britain, of Renault and Citroën in France, of Fiat in Italy had the attraction, for car buyers, of avoiding fashion uncertainty and obsolescence, and thus reducing depreciation and transaction costs. Production of VW 'beetles' ended in Europe in 1978, but continued to be viable in a developing country, Mexico, for another twenty-five years. In the 1960s Britain still had the relatively low depreciation of a stable styling regime, and never fully embraced the pace of styling change observed in the United States during the 1950s and 1960s.[40]

Conclusion

The new-car frenzy of the fifties was in some aspects unique to its time. Like first love, it fell into a predetermined pattern, but could never be repeated. Never again would America fall so intensely for the new-model motor car as in 1955. This is revealed in the pattern of within-year depreciation, which was much higher in the fifties than subsequently.[41] Disillusion was also intense. Styling competition threw American car hierarchies into disarray.[42] Brand loyalty, the bedrock of market share, was eroded. From a 69 per cent level of loyalty in buying intentions in 1953, it dipped down to 47 per cent by 1960. Ford fared even worse, falling from 73 per cent to 44 per cent.[43] But the majority had not been won away from the large car. After the first flush of success, imports fell back.

[39] Coase, 'Durability and Monopoly'; Purohit, 'Exploration'.
[40] Sherman and Hoffer, 'Does Automobile Style Change Payoff?'; Hoffer and Reilly, 'Automobile Styling'; Millner and Hoffer, 'Impact of Automotive Styling'.
[41] Pashigian et al., 'Fashion, Styling and the Within-Season Decline'.
[42] 'Address by Robert S. McNamara', 1960 Greenbrier Management Conference, 21 Nov. 1960, fos. 17–19, FIA AR-66-12: 5.　　　　　[43] *Look, Automobile Survey*.

The cycle from simplicity to extravagance was an example of 'the wheel of retailing'. In this model,

new types of retailers usually enter the market as low status, low-margin, low-price operators. Gradually they acquire more elaborate establishments and facilities, with both increased investments and higher operating costs. Finally they mature as high cost, high-price merchants, vulnerable to newer types who, in turn, go through the same pattern.[44]

In automobiles, this cycle has since been repeated several times, and appears to have settled into something of a historical routine. Body sizes and engine power increased to new heights in the 'muscle cars' of the late 1960s, with a resurgence of imports for those who rejected horsepower as a form of self-expression. In 1973, the oil crisis appeared to undermine the large-car concept for good. With its longer product cycles, Detroit now took longer to respond. Japan carved out a permanent slice of the American car market; imports rose to one-third in 1982.[45] But the Japanese understood the logic of the 'wheel of retailing' curve just as well as Detroit, and drove their own cars upmarket, from the lowly Datsuns of the 1960s to the covetable Lexus, which has taken over from Cadillac as a marque of distinction. The gap at the bottom was filled, in turn, by cars from Korea.

In the late 1950s, the American car industry appeared to have reached the limits of physical expansion of the car, and did not know where to go next. But the answer was staring it in the face, in the form of the popular Volkswagen minibus. Instead of expanding lengthwise and sidewise, it could expand vehicles upwards. This idea was explored in the 1970s, and picked up during the 1980s by Chrysler, so that the 1980s became the decade of the minivan, or family carrier.[46] Just as families were declining in America, their needs provided customers with an excuse to buy an even roomier and larger vehicle. In the 1950s, trucks had been a small niche for the Big Three, which met the needs of farmers, small businessmen, and tradesmen. By the 1990s, once the 'people carrier' boom had run its course, small trucks moved to the fore, providing customers with the surge of power and pride, in the form of sports utility vehicles, while providing Detroit with most of its profits.[47] Where to go next? A *New Yorker* cartoon of 2003 shows a wealthy old couple considering a monster 'Hummer'-like SUV in a showroom. The customer says, 'Nice, but my heart's still set on a helicopter gunship.'[48]

---

[44] Hollander, 'Wheel of Retailing', 37. The idea originates with McNair, 'Trends'.
[45] Halberstam, *A Tale of Two Cultures*.   [46] Yates, *Critical Path*, esp. ch. 2.
[47] Bradsher, *High and Mighty*.   [48] *New Yorker*, 16 and 23 June 2003, p. 187

Coming within five years of the end of austerity, the 1958 downturn was the first expression of doubt about affluence as comfort, luxury, and sensual gratification. It can be read as an early stirring of post-material discontent with *mass* consumption, a rejection of the uniformity that it seemed to require, an expression of intelligence, rationality, and prudence in consumption, a quest for more sophisticated forms of distinction and self-expression. It indicated, for the first time in post-war America, that consumption was not a mere quantitative corollary of growth, in which affluence is a reliable proxy for satisfaction. Rather, it presented a more dynamic view of consumption, as a psychic balancing act, which oscillates between comfort and pleasure, between gratification and prudence.

Appendix 10A. Automobile Depreciation Theory

Depreciation was the largest single cost of ownership. Its patterns reveal a good deal about the logic of new car purchase. This subject is shot through with misunderstanding, and it is helpful to correct some misconceptions. The starting point is the fact that cars lose a large share of their value in the first year. There are two standard interpretations of this initial depreciation. One view is that cars lose value at a constant *rate* per year, that is *exponentially*, e.g. 25 or 33 per cent of the value of the previous year. Hence cars would tend to lose much more value, absolutely, in the first year than in subsequent ones.[49] Another view identifies a kink in the depreciation curve during the first year: 'new cars depreciated at almost twice the rate of used cars ... after the first year cars appeared to depreciate at a constant rate.'[50] There has also been an attempt to reconcile the two approaches by fitting the kinked curve to an exponential one.[51] One study regards the initial steep decline as evidence of hyperbolic discounting.[52] Indeed, the kinked depreciation curve is very similar to the approximation of hyperbolic discounting ('quasi-hyperbolic') used in empirical analysis, which assumes a high discount rate in the first period, and a lower discount rate thereafter.[53]

There is something odd about such an exceptional drop in value during the first year, and attempts to explain it require large departures from economic convention. Wykoff posits that new cars are a 'superior good' which commands a special premium for the 'freshness', novelty, and reliability, while Smith treats new and used cars as belonging to quite separate markets.[54] Well known is Akerlof's view (not supported by evidence) that almost-new used cars are more likely to be 'lemons', i.e. are not representative of the underlying population of assets, because only poorer quality units are sold. The immediate large loss of value over new cars is a discount required by buyers to compensate for asymmetric information with the sellers.[55]

But it is possible to explain the course of used-car prices more simply. The error arises from the neglect of transaction costs. Wykoff assumes that cars are sold with negligible transaction costs, and this is implicit in other work.[56] This is a curious assumption to make when comparable

[49] Chow, *Statistical Demand Functions*, 149–50; Mogridge, *The Car Market*, pp. 5–7, 99–103.

[50] Wykoff, 'A User Cost Approach'; see also Wykoff, 'Capital Depreciation'; and Wykoff, 'Economic Depreciation', for substantial empirical tests.

[51] Hulten and Wykoff, 'Issues in the Measurement', 16.

[52] Rachlin and Ranieri, 'Irrationality, Impulsiveness, and Selfishness', 96. On hyperbolic discounting, see Ch. 3 above. [53] Frederick et al., 'Time Discounting', 366.

[54] Wykoff, 'A User Cost Approach', 388; Smith, *Consumer Demand for Cars*, 4–5.

[55] Akerlof, 'Market for Lemons'. See Hulten and Wykoff, 'Issues in the Measurement', 18.

[56] Wykoff, 'Capital Depreciation', 169. Chow, *Demand for Automobiles*, 102–5.

numbers of people (more than 600,000 in 1958) worked to sell cars, and support them, as to make them.[57]

In fact, the initial price decline was not exceptionally steep, but was comparable to (and mostly lower than in) subsequent years. The reason was mundane. Car dealers offered two sets of prices: one is the price at which they sold (the 'retail' price), the other at which they bought (the 'wholesale' one).[58] This applied to new cars and to used cars. There was a big margin between the two prices. When a buyer acquired a new car, she paid the retail price. From that point onwards, its market value to her was its selling price, the 'wholesale' price. Depreciation in the first year included the dealer mark-up, and in subsequent years, it did not. When buying a car, customers paid for the future flow of its intrinsic services, and for the dealer's mark-up as well. Once the car was transferred to the buyer, the value of dealer services was exhausted, and its resale value (the 'wholesale' price at which a dealer would repurchase) only represented its use for conveying passengers, signalling status, and providing sensual pleasure.

If this interpretation is correct, then two findings can be predicted: (a) that *used* cars purchased at retail would show a similar drop in value to wholesale as new cars, and (b) that depreciation would be exponential over time along *both* wholesale prices *and* retail prices, and of approximately the same magnitude, regardless of which of the two measures was used. This is shown schematically in Figure 10.2.

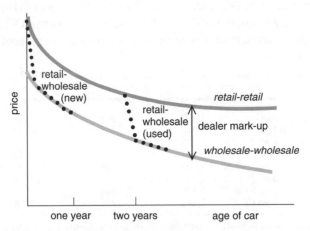

Fig. 10.2. Schematic depreciation schedules of passenger cars

[57] 668,000 worked for dealers (including the proprietors) and 640,000 for manufacturers in 1958. Automobile Manufacturers Association, *Automobile Facts*, 38, 67.

[58] National Automobile Dealers Assocation, *Official Used Car Guide*; Glass's Guide Services Limited, *Glass's Guide to Used Car Values*. New wholesale prices are not reported.

Evidence

This argument is investigated in a study of automobile depreciation in the USA and Britain during the 1950s and the 1960s.[59] Two different sampling frames are used, and each is repeated three times, on different samples. The first frame is a cross-section, sampling the 1957 prices of the four previous model vintages. The second is a panel, which follows the 1957 vintage as it aged over five subsequent years. Our samples are large enough to have some confidence in the results (Table 10.3). The initial United States sample consisted of some 49 Ford and Buick models. The same makes were also sampled again for 1968 (panel) and 1969 (cross-section). Concurrent British samples of 18 Ford and Morris models were also taken (1968 and 1969), as well as United States prices of the Volkswagen 'beetle' sedan (one model, 1964–73). This provides coverage from the early 1950s up to the early 1970s. Ford and Buick sold staple mass-market models, with distinctive positions in the USA status hierarchy, Ford as a 'low price' car, Buick as a 'medium priced' one. In Britain, the ranking was reversed, with Ford making more mid-market models. The total number of depreciation observations is 4,032.

Observations are annual. American ones come from the monthly National Automobile Dealers Association, *Official Used Car Guide*, Eastern edition (henceforth NADA).[60] This was compiled from dealer transaction and auction sales reports. Prices were taken from the January or February issues, and reflect the first quarter of the model year, which began in October.[61] This sampling date maximizes the novelty effect on prices, and reduces ambiguity

Table 10.3. Sample models, new car prices in US dollars (1957 prices)

Year	Make	Mean price	Standard deviation	No. of models
1957	Buick	3,379	508	19
	Ford	2,330	183	35
	VW	1,495		1
1969	Buick	2,727	489	32
	Ford	2,298	394	72
	VW	1,340		1
	Morris UK	1,420	264	10
	Ford UK	1,641	273	8

Sources: see text (derived from NADA and *Glass's Guide*). Prices deflated using United States President, *Economic Report of the President 1991*.

[59] More detail in Offer, 'Markup for Lemons'.

[60] National Automobile Dealers Assocation, *Official Used Car Guide*; Glass's Guide Services Limited, *Glass's Guide to Used Car Values*. New wholesale prices are not reported.

[61] Buick 1969 models, from December 1968. Prices included heater and radio.

about the precise age of year-old cars. The British motor industry was not comparable in the 1950s, when it expanded rapidly after post-war shortages. By the 1960s growth had levelled off, and cycles were similar to American ones.[62] The British source, *Glass's Guide*, is similar to the American one, but covers the whole country. New prices included central taxes. At one-third of the new price, British taxes were about three times as high as American ones. Unlike American cars, British models might be modified at any time, but starting in 1963, the vintage was indicated by means of a letter on the licence plate, which changed every January. In 1967, the new-year letter date was moved to August. *Glass* continued to take its representative car as being 'first registered in the spring', and the sampling month is April throughout.[63]

For new cars, suggested retail prices are used, as quoted in *NADA* and *Glass*. New-car list prices could be discounted substantially, and actual transaction prices are not available.[64] But USA Ford staff calculated in 1958 that customer discounts were offset by delivery costs and state taxes. Hence the list price is a reasonable proxy for the actual transaction price at that time.[65] The dealer mark-up came to 12 per cent of the list price, 13.6 per cent of the factory wholesale price.

Another estimate of new-car mark-ups (for the 1960s) places them higher, but provides no source.[66] NADA reported an average gross dealer mark-up of 14.7 per cent of total sales (standard dev. 0.44) in 1960–6.[67] In 1987, dealer new-car mark-ups before discounts could range between 6 per cent and 14 per cent of list price.[68] List prices placed a ceiling on transaction prices. Using them biases new prices upwards, in favour of Akerlof's argument: any lower actual price means that there is less of an initial discount to explain. A new-car dealer mark-up of 12 per cent is therefore imputed to the 1950s samples, but (in the absence of firm evidence) not to those of the 1960s.

[62] Foreman-Peck et al., *British Motor Industry*, table 4.1, p. 94.

[63] Following practice in the motor trade (*Glass's Guide*, Nov. 1969, pp. 2–4, cited from p. 4, col. 5). Thanks to S. McAndrew for this reference.

[64] Pashigian, *Distribution*, 37, and Ward's, *Ward's Automotive yearbook* (1960), 123, report excess capacity after 1954.

[65] On the basic 1958 Ford car. List price $1,977 from NADA (Feb. 1958); transaction cost ($1,994) calculated from Ford Product Planning Office, 'Economy Car Report', 13 Nov. 1957, fo. 33. FIA Product Planning Committee, 13 Nov. 1957, Ford Archives, AR-94-200777-6. The nominal list price (full dealer mark-up; state taxes and freight excluded) was $1,935. The original figures are adjusted to the NADA bare car price basis by removing optional accessories, and adjusting taxes and the reported dealer mark-up proportionally.

[66] 18 per cent of retail (17–25 per cent of wholesale), increasing in price, and including more expensive cars. White, *Automobile Industry*, 106.

[67] Ward's, *Ward's Automotive Yearbook*, 'Auto Dealers Sales Expense and Operating Profit Before Federal Income Tax' (1961–7).

[68] Harless and Hoffer, 'Do Women Pay More?', 271.

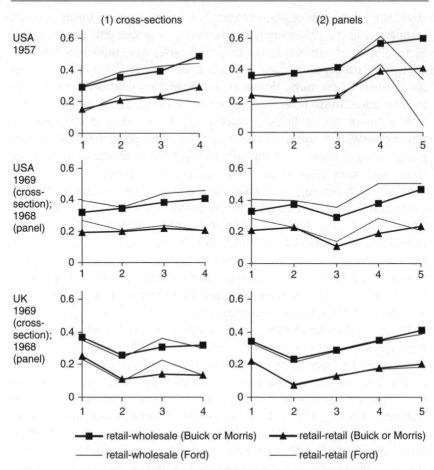

Fig. 10.3. Annual automobile depreciation rates by age, USA and UK
(*Vertical scale* = annual depreciation rate; *Horizontal scale* = age in years)
Source: See text; Offer, 'Markup for Lemons', tables A1–A2.

In studies of automobile depreciation it is customary to estimate the effect of individual ('hedonic') model attributes, but this is redundant here. In common with other studies, most of the variance is explained by age and specific model.[69] In our case, age and manufacturer alone typically explain about 85 to 95 per cent of the depreciation variance.[70] Price trends are estimated and the procedures are described in detail in Offer, 'The Markup for Lemons'. The main set of results are shown in Figure 10.3.

[69] e.g. Purohit, 'Exploring', p. 165.   [70] Offer, 'Markup for Lemons', tables A1–A2.

Figure 10.3 plots the actual mean annual depreciation rate in the six samples, in both cross-section and panel.[71] The vertical scale shows the fraction of value lost compared with the previous year's price. Retail-wholesale is the loss of value from retail price in year $t - 1$, to wholesale price in year t. Retail-retail is the corresponding loss of value on retail prices alone from one year to another. Figure 10.3 shows that at the least, older cars depreciated no less than newer ones, and usually depreciated more.[72] But there is some interesting variation. Taking the American 1957 cross-sections first, Buick retail-wholesale depreciation rate was lowest in the first year, and rose with each additional year, from 0.291 to 0.487 over four years, followed closely by Ford. That is not consistent with the view that initial depreciation was exceptionally high. Increasing depreciation rates with age suggest rising uncertainty about mechanical quality and a decline in the styling desirability of older cars as a whole.

Initial USA 1960s depreciation rate levels were roughly comparable to the 1950s, but rose more slowly over time, suggesting a little mechanical improvement, and/or a weaker styling effect. Ford models (the cheaper make) depreciated about the same as Buick in the 1950s, and more in the 1960s. In Britain first-year depreciation rates were high. The most likely explanation is that list prices were discounted heavily, given the large share of fleet sales in Britain. Genuine adverse selection could also arise if British new-car quality was exceptionally poor, for which there is ample evidence.[73] By year two, a 'lemon' would be fixed, or could not be so easily disguised, and depreciation levels could then fall substantially to their long-run equilibrium. After year one, British depreciation rates were usually lower than American ones during the 1960s. Due to higher taxation, British cars were made at lower cost than price differences between the countries might suggest, and less efficiently as well. Why they held their price so well in comparison with the more solid and desirable American cars is a puzzle we shall return to later.

It is now possible to reconcile the divergent explanations of initial auto price declines, with a single simple one.[74] The car is a normal durable good providing a stream of services. Prices do not usually reflect first-year asymmetric information or opportunism. The findings of constant-rate depreciation are easily explained: they were derived from retail prices series only. The alternative finding of a kinked depreciation curve is also explained: in the first year, prices move from retail (new) to wholesale

[71] Data ibid.
[72] Also observed for 1975–85 cohorts in the USA by Purohit, 'Exploring', 164.
[73] Whisler, *British Motor Industry*, 327–49, 358–9.
[74] Explored in more detail in Offer, 'Markup for Lemons'.

(used).[75] The price of the car in the showroom incorporated the dealer's distribution services. When the buyer took possession, she paid the dealer mark-up, and the car immediately lost that dealer-service element of its value. Now it may be that a good deal of the value of that service for the buyer was derived from the dealer's accountability. But in that case, the same service was also provided by *used* car dealers, and Akerlof's lemon effect is not restricted to new cars. The *used* car buyer also suffered a comparable loss when she bought from a dealer.[76]

For new-car buyers, the most financially prudent course was to keep the car for as long as the saving on dealer mark-ups was greater than the additional cost of repairs. The Ford Motor Company calculated this optimal period as five to six years from new.[77] To buy a new car *every* year cost 26 per cent more in running costs than to keep it for three years.[78] In terms of depreciation, the consumer's choice was not between buying a new or a used car. Both will have lost the same proportion of their value in a year. Rather the choice is whether to buy at all, and pay a dealer mark-up, or to postpone purchase, in which case depreciation would be about one-third lower. The manufacturer's task was to make the new car enticing enough for the buyer to incur the dealer mark-up and the big loss of economic value in the first year. In 1955, new-car buyers were responding to the enticement, and replacing their cars well short of the optimum delay, after an average of four years and five months.[79]

This was facilitated by easier credit. The proportion of cars sold for cash fell from 40 per cent in 1953 to 33 per cent in 1959, and the standard credit contract extended gradually from 12 and 24 months to 36 months.[80] Auto-finance loans were paid for on fixed balance terms, so a longer period, while helping to keep *monthly* payments in check, meant a considerable increase in *total* finance costs. By 1958, about 10–11 per cent of the running cost of a standard car was for finance. Since depreciation was only about 45–50 per cent of these costs, this suggests real interest payments of more than 20 per cent a year, at a time when inflation was 2–3 per cent.[81] If they

---

[75] This is the pattern in Wykoff, 'Economic Depreciation'.
[76] More detail in Offer, 'Markup for Lemons'.
[77] Ford, 'Economy Car Study, Preliminary Report' (15 July 1957), 11.
[78] Ford, 'Cost of Ownership Report', 22 June 1959, PPC Meeting, FIA AR-94-2000777-9.
[79] Calculated from *Look, Automobile Survey* (1955), 18.
[80] United States senate, *Administered Prices Report*, ch. 7; Automobile Manufacturers Association, *Automobile Facts*, 32; *Look, Automobile Survey* (1960), 50. Average number of monthly payments increased from 26 in 1954 to 32 in 1958. See S. Edmunds to J. O. Wright, 'Credit Terms for Passenger Cars', 1 July 1958, FIA, Wright papers, AR-75-15565: 18.
[81] Ford, Product Planning Committee, Cost of Ownership Report, 1959. This is about twice as high as Wykoff's estimate in Wykoff, 'Capital Depreciation', table 2, p. 171.

did not have ready cash, buyers accepted the myopic consumer's very steep discount rates to indulge in their fancy for a new car. In their impatience to buy, borrowers assumed increasingly greater risks. Between 1953 and 1957, repossessions by GMAC, the biggest finance company, rose sixfold.[82]

In conclusion, a study of automobile depreciation rates does not identify a significant initial novelty effect, or alternatively an initial 'lemon' effect, that would act to depress prices exceptionally during the first year. Depreciation rates were normally steady or rising over a car's life. Higher depreciation rates for American cars suggest that consumers responded myopically to the flow of styling changes, while buyers of British cars (and of VW in the USA), in the absence of such rapid changes, evaluated their cars more prudently.

[82] United States senate, *Administered Prices Report*, table 35, p. 167.

Part III

Self and Others

11

Affluence and the Pursuit of Status

Doing better improves the chances of well-being. Higher up the social ladder there are more opportunities, more choice, more satisfying work, better health, longer life. But if everyone is improving *equally*, no one gets ahead. 'When everybody is somebody, then nobody is anybody.'[1] There is no limit to the growth of affluence, but social ranking is capped: room at the top is scarce, whatever the level of affluence. The winners' prizes in social competition are known as 'positional goods'. Their supply does not increase with affluence.[2] For society as a whole, therefore, there might seem to be little benefit in the pursuit of status.[3]

For many people, this relative conception of status is not compelling. They do not perceive the pursuit of social advancement as a 'zero-sum game' with a loser for every winner. In the 'American Dream', the tide raises many boats, while capsizing only a few. And they are not wrong. Post-war affluence has allowed more people to put a larger distance between themselves and the bottom. Up to the 1960s, status was largely something that men strove for: women took it largely from their men. For women, since the 1960s in particular, competition for their own education and workplace advancement has contended with the satisfactions of motherhood. Eventually, however, the pursuit of self-fulfilment converged with another competition, for the sake of the children.

What to measure?

An obvious metric of social standing might seem to be income and wealth. Money is intuitively meaningful, and is objectively measurable. It is a continuous (or cardinal) metric. Every measurement is either higher,

---

[1] Paraphrased from the librettist W. S. Gilbert.   [2] Hirsch, *Social Limits*, ch. 3.
[3] Frank, *Choosing the Right Pond*; id., *Luxury Fever*.

lower, or equal to any other. It is also uniquely fungible—money can buy almost anything.

But money is more reliable as a measure in the aggregate than for individuals. For one thing, personal money stocks and flows are ambiguous and difficult to establish. Many assets (company shares, for example) take the form of uncertain claims on the future. People are coy about their income, and have good motives to under- or over-reveal it.[4] Income is easier to measure than wealth. But the value of money is relative. A loaf of bread is worth more to a homeless person than to a millionaire. Its value is asymmetric: dollars lost are experienced more acutely than dollars gained.[5] Already Adam Smith observed that 'We suffer more . . . when we fall from a better to a worse situation, than we ever enjoy when we rise from a worse to a better.'[6] The measuring rod of money is a little too elastic, and is less reliable than it is convenient.[7]

So money is a means, not an end in itself. 'It is chiefly from this regard to the sentiments of mankind, that we pursue riches and avoid poverty.'[8] And 'regard' (see Chapter 5) can be obtained by other means than money. Soldiers, politicians, teachers, doctors, musicians, officials, managers, are respected for rank and not wealth. Riches do not guarantee regard.[9] Wealthy men of the wrong religion, ethnicity or trade have had to accept the condescension of landowners, priests, or officers. In nineteenth-century Europe, rich Jews were notoriously despised.[10]

But wealth lends credibility to status, by imposing a scarcity on supply. The fortunes that businessmen pay themselves appear to be driven as much by ranking races, as by any craving for commodities. Social standing provides a more encompassing metric of relative reward than money alone, and perhaps gets us closer to the meaning of money as well.

Sociologists are preoccupied with stratification.[11] There are two dominant approaches. One regards society as stratified by 'social classes', i.e. by discrete social clusters determined primarily by economic endowment, or by an occupational role. The binary division into bosses and workers captures the idea that social class is determined by income, wealth, and education. In such stratification schema, up to eleven 'classes' are used. In British

---

[4] e.g. Hauser and Warren, 'Socioeconomic Indexes', 184.

[5] Reviewed in Kahneman and Tversky, *Choices, Values, and Frames*.

[6] Smith, *Moral Sentiments*, Pt. I, sect, ii, ch. 3, p. 50.

[7] For the intractable complexity of economic measurement of inequality, Atkinson, 'Introduction', in Atkinson and Bourguignon, *Handbook of Income Distribution*.

[8] Smith, *Moral Sentiments*, 50.

[9] Or rather, 'esteem' (Brennan and Pettit, *Economy of Esteem*).

[10] Rubinstein, 'Jews in Economic Elites', 18–19.   [11] Grusky, *Social Stratification*.

culture, class is not merely a scientific category, but has been part of ordinary language for almost two centuries.[12] The concept of class still dominates British social research, although the boundaries of 'class' are no longer self-evident, and increasingly have to be determined empirically in terms of the nature of employment relations, autonomy, and control.[13] Similar concepts are often used in American market research, to identify coherent clusters of consumers, though less so in sociology.[14]

In the United States, in contrast to Britain, continuous ranking indices are the rule. American society is more stratified and unequal even than Britain's. But the notion of rigid prescriptive 'classes' is uncongenial. Americans like to think of their societies as fluid and open to ambition.[15] Social prestige is associated with occupations, and there is a rough consensus about how they rank: judges always rank higher than janitors. Prestige rankings have been found to be robust, and have changed very little over long periods of time, whatever the method of measurement.[16] Occupational prestige rankings correlate well internationally too.[17] As new occupations emerge, and as numbers in occupations change, there are slight alterations in prestige rankings, though rarely very large ones.[18]

There are several USA prestige ranking indices to choose from, and they are updated from time to time.[19] The most popular is Duncan's socio-economic index (SEI) and its derivatives. This is an attempt to construct a hierarchy of occupational rankings from the objective determinants of educational qualifications and occupational earnings. The founding project is Duncan's SEI for 1950.[20] Forty-five occupations were ranked for prestige by means of a social survey. A regression model used two variables, education and earnings to 'predict' the prestige ranking. The fit was best when education and income were given approximately equal weights. The coefficients derived were then extrapolated to the majority of American occupations to produce a 'socio-economic index', ranking occupations on a scale from 3 to 96. The study was restricted to men.[21]

This type of exercise was replicated several times between the 1960s and the 1990s, and has also been extended to women, using census data. It was found that when SEI rankings were compared with pure prestige rankings,

[12] e.g. Jones, *Languages of Class*; McKibbin, *Ideologies of Class*; id., *Classes and Cultures*.
[13] Marshall et al., Social *Class*, ch. 8; Marshall et al., *Against the Odds*, 22–8.
[14] e.g. Hawkins et al., *Consumer Behavior*, ch. 4.
[15] Fussell, *Class*, ch. 1; Marshall et al., *Against the Odds*, 38–9; Stokey, 'Shirtsleeves', pp. 210–11.
[16] Nakao and Treas, 'Updating Occupational Prestige', 3, 13, 36.
[17] Treiman's international measure. See ibid. 27.   [18] Ibid. 2.
[19] Ibid.; Hauser and Warren, 'Socioeconomic Indexes'.
[20] Duncan, 'Socioeconomic Index'; Blau et al., *American Occupational Structure*; Hauser and Warren, 'Socioeconomic Indexes'.   [21] Duncan, 'Socioeconomic Index'.

education had to be more heavily weighted than fifty-fifty with income, and for women, education had to be weighted even more than for men, in order to align SEI with prestige rankings.[22] Despite a great deal of tinkering and sniping, SEI measures have gained broad acceptance in the United States as an appropriate measure of social ranking, and have dominated over pure 'prestige' measures and class-based approaches.

The construction of the index tells us what it measures, but not what it means. What exactly is being compared or measured? If it is social status that we are concerned about, it derives its value from vertical social distance.[23] Social distance can be measured from the bottom of the distribution, or from the top, or from the average, or from any other reference point. It can be measured as an ordinal distance, and it can be weighted by the number of people in each ordinal comparison. If the distances measured are the negative ones, they are called 'complaints'.[24] If positive, they might be called 'advantages'. Complaints could be expected to generate dissatisfaction, while advantages give rise to good feeling. There is considerable evidence that complaints and advantages are asymmetric in income. Loss (of employment or partner) was experienced much more strongly than gain (income).[25] This is consistent with Kahneman and Tversky's findings of 'loss aversion', indicating that people will take larger risks to avoid loss than to achieve gain.[26] Adam Smith would have concurred: 'adversity . . . necessarily depresses the mind of the sufferer much more below its natural state, than prosperity can elevate him above it.'[27] In this chapter we focus mainly on the dynamic of 'advantages', the changes in the positive stock of status over time. In the next chapter we consider the effect of 'complaints', the changing stock of negative differences from the top.

Social status is not an abstract category. It is experienced as a relation with other people, more as an emotion than as a fact. It is driven by regard for other people, or by its absence. Positive status can make you flourish, and its absence can make you miserable or even sick. Sen has done more than anybody to question the 'welfarist' notion of well-being, which regards welfare as a matter of access to commodities.[28] But even Sen remains an individualist: what matters are the resources available to individuals, who

[22] Hauser and Warren, 'Socioeconomic Indexes'.
[23] Though in the Erikson-Goldthorpe class system used extensively in Britain and Europe, social distances are regarded as functional, rather than hierarchical (Erikson and Goldthorpe, *Constant Flux*, 30–2).
[24] Temkin, *Inequality*; Cowell and Ebert, 'Complaints and Inequality'; Devooght, 'Counting Complaints'. [25] Above, ch. 2, e.g. Table 2.2.
[26] Kahneman, 'New Challenges', 762–4; and above, Ch. 2.
[27] Smith, *Moral Sentiments*, Pt. I, sect. iii, ch. 1, p. 45. [28] e.g. Sen, 'Social Justice'.

can then find their own way to flourish. The rewards of status are the rewards of regard: our own welfare depends on the reciprocal attentions between ourselves and other people. As Smith argued, nothing is more important to our sense of well-being.[29]

There is no universally valid, linear scale of status or prestige.[30] For most people most of the time, the social differences they experience most acutely are local, not global; not across society (let alone the world) as a whole, but those that enter the field of vision, and those that enter it frequently, e.g. differentials within the family, the workplace, or the community. 'It is not a great disproportion between ourselves and others which produces envy, but on the contrary, a proximity. A common soldier bears no envy for his general compared to what he will feel for his sergeant or corporal...'.[31] None of this is captured by social ranking measures. The social distance that matters is over the short range rather than the long one, between the head nurse and her subordinates, between children and parents, between insiders and outsiders; or beyond the workplace altogether, in voluntary interactions. In small groups, rankings are immediately formed based on observable general characteristics.[32] Semi-skilled workers used skilled ones as their reference groups; colleagues compare rankings within the workplace.[33] Given that social inferiority can damage mental and physical health, this inclination to localize status might be seen as a way of adapting to inequality, by keeping most people insulated from its extremes. It is perhaps no accident that employers rarely divulge information about the relative pay of different workers (it has been argued that wage rank is the most important influence on well-being).[34] People can also escape from the impositions of status into companionship, friendship, collegiality, scholarship, philosophy, art, nature, and religion. Some of the most rewarding of human achievements are insulators from the tyranny of status.[35]

With neither occupation nor income, adolescents count for nothing in conventional status rankings, but they have their own fierce hierarchies. 'Rabbit' Angstrom, the working-class hero of John Updike's Pennsylvania novels, experienced a more exalted sense of status as a high-school

[29] Above, Ch. 5; the social rewards of estimable attributes are discussed theoretically by Brennan and Pettit, *Economy of Esteem*.

[30] Treiman, *Occupational Prestige*, unconvincingly claimed that there was.

[31] Hume, *Treatise of Human Nature*, Bk 2, pt. ii, sect. viii.

[32] Weiss and Fershtman, 'Social Status', 806; also Milgram, *Obedience to Authority*.

[33] Runciman, *Relative Deprivation*; Frank, *Choosing the Right Pond*.

[34] Brown et al., 'Does Wage Rank Affect Employees' Wellbeing?'

[35] Argued engagingly by de Botton, *Status Anxiety*.

basketball star in the 1950s than as the successful owner of a car dealership in the 1970s.[36] Virtually everyone has some positive status. And people are protected from invidious comparison by the 'endowment effect', which leads them to place an optimistic valuation on the assets they possess.[37] More than a hundred studies have shown that people are excessively optimistic in their assessment of their circumstances.[38]

This suggests that social distance might be assigned weights, not only for levels, but also for vertical social distances, applying some inverse square (Weber–Fechner) rule, in which large numbers of people with adjacent status levels should be given more weight than small numbers of comparators whose status is very different.[39] The relation of status to income is not linear, but comparable to the relation of other goods to income, and delivers diminishing returns following the concave (knee-shaped) curve that is seen in such abundance elsewhere.[40] The Royal Family or media celebrities might impinge on ordinary consciousness with a high-status 'weight', but generally the rich and the poor cause little anxiety to each other. Be that as it may, the empirical study of stratification has largely avoided most of these complexities.[41] That means that conventional sociological measures of social standing are still quite far from being truly encompassing or psychologically valid.

Duncan's SEI, in its simplicity, is also a long way from these subtleties. The case for using it as a measure of status is not that it measures status directly, but that it provides some indication of the resources that ultimately determine social standing. Its two components, education and income, are poorly correlated with each other, so on the face of it, appear to be complementary.[42] Since each of them is continuous, their combination also provides a continuous vertical index. This is a simplification and it is not always easy to place a person precisely on a social scale on the basis of occupation and income alone. So SEI is perhaps best thought of as a measure of human capital, i.e. of social worth—which is what status is largely about. It is more a measure of potential than of actual outcomes. It is not deterministic. For any particular individual, this indicator could well be misleading. But measured in the aggregate, it provides a reasonable indicator of social trends.

---

[36] Updike, *Rabbit Omnibus*.   [37] Kahneman et al., 'Endowment Effect'.

[38] James, *Britain on the Couch*, 56–9.

[39] Clark and Oswald, 'Satisfaction and Comparison Income'; Oswald, 'Rank'; Seidel et al., 'Relative Deprivation'. For the range-frequency approach, Poulton, *Bias*.

[40] Coleman et al., *Social Standing*, 33–42, 324–6; van Praag and Fererr-I-Carbonell, *Happiness Quantified*, ch. 2, pp. 34–43.

[41] However, the Cambridge CAMSIN measure of social standing uses social proximity, and weights according to distance within the social circle.

[42] Hauser and Warren, 'Socioeconomic Indexes', figs. 3–5, pp. 205–8.

A drawback of SEI as a measure of social standing is that it takes no account of relative scarcity. Upwards social mobility would reduce the social scarcity of higher positions. If average social ranking rises over time, its value is partly offset by a reduction in the scarcity, or 'positional' value, of social standing.[43] There are four responses. First, so long as the ranking remains intact, the relative position retains its social distance value from the boltom (as 'advantages'), even if the numerical weightings have changed. Secondly, current approaches to social mobility, in all traditions, take very little account of this change in the relative scarcity of status, and focus (whether using financial or other endowments for ranking) on the objective attributes of the assets, as if their value was unchanged by scarcity.[44] Thirdly, occupational status has objective attributes, as a measure of skill, authority, and autonomy, that arise from the nature of the job and change rather slowly. Compare status with other assets: that more people have a washing machine reduces its value for signalling status, but not for cleaning laundry. Having a machine no longer confers distinction, but not having it now invites a stigma. Finally, perceptions of social scarcity are slow to change, so the pleasure of an absolute increase in social ranking from, say, a manual to a supervisory job might linger on even if the number of supervisors in society was rising overall, and no relative change had occurred.

The opportunities for intergenerational social mobility indicate how open a society is to merit, and how just it is, if rewarding 'merit' is taken to be a measure of equity. But if the sources of well-being are immediate and local, then it is not where you come from that matters, but where you are now. In sociology, the intensity of concern about status differences is captured by the preoccupation with social mobility.[45] Social mobility is typically studied by comparing the social position of parents and offspring at a comparable point in life. Comparative research on several countries indicates that social mobility in this sense hardly impinges on subjective experiences of well-being. People who have moved upwards, sideways, and downwards socially from their parents derive the same level of subjective satisfaction as people of similar position who have not.[46] Having done worse or better than Dad appears to make very little difference to life satisfaction, as distinct from the social ranking itself.

---

[43] These issues have been considered by economists, however, e.g. Frank, *Choosing the Right Pond*; Clark and Oswald, 'Satisfaction and Comparison Income'.

[44] e.g. Marshall, *Against the Odds*, ch. 4.   [45] Grusky, *Social Stratification*.

[46] Marshall and Firth, 'Social Mobility'.

Socio-economic status SEI then is a partial and a proxy indicator for social standing, which falls well short of perfection. But no measure captures the essence of social standing, and there may not be a single essence to capture.[47] All measures abstract from reality, and fall short one way or another. For criticism to be effective, it is necessary to show how sensitive the arguments are to the choice of a particular measure, compared not with ideal encompassing measures which do not exist, but with the other ones available. In this respect, Duncan's 1950 SEI has some unique advantages. It is conveniently available in large samples and over a long period. This broad acceptance suggests that it is meaningful. It is highly correlated with any other available or potential measure of social standing. And it is the only one that follows social ranking in the United States consistently over six decades, from 1940 to 2000.

The stock of social standing[48]

The aggregate of individual incomes (GDP), divided by size of population, is the most common measure of affluence. To aggregate individual SEI rankings, and divide them by the size of the working population, is conceptually no different. It would provide a measure of the stock of social ranking per head, or rather of status 'advantages'. Comparing the two provides a measure, albeit crude, of the impact of affluence on status.

Duncan's SEI ranks occupations according to their typical educational requirements, and their typical occupational income, giving similar weights to both. Think of it as measuring not status itself, but the resources of status, not of social standing, but of social standing potential; as economists would put it, not of transitory income, but of permanent income, of human capital, of stable assets or endowments.[49] Given the vagaries of measurement and the volatility of income flows, Amartya Sen has long argued that the appropriate thing to measure is not welfare outcomes, but 'capabilities', i.e. means and not ends. Given the means, similar people will choose differently, and some choices (like the fulfilment of obligations) will not register as 'welfare'.[50] SEI combines the two: it is a measure

---

[47] Sen, 'Social Justice'.

[48] I have benefited here from research carried out by Dr David Engerman, acting as my assistant, and from dissertations by my students: Mullaney, 'Rewards of Status'; Lim, 'Women's Choices'.

[49] Weiss and Fershtman, 'Social Status', p. 806; Hauser and Warren, 'Socioeconomic Indexes', 198.

[50] e.g. Sen and Hawthorn, *Standard of Living*, chs. 1–2; Sen, 'Social Justice'; Dasgupta, *Human Well-Being*, ch. 9, also advocates a wealth-based measure of well-being.

both of input (education) and outcome (income). Sen argues that it is vital to incorporate the heterogeneity of people into assessments of their welfare. A first step in that direction is to take account of a large difference in capabilities and functionings that arises out of gender differences.

SEI raises a familiar index number problem: weights for education and income can be fixed at one point in time (Laspeyres index), or can change over time (Paasche index). The fixed-weight approach provides comparability at the cost of accuracy. But in spite of its disadvantages, is widely used, e.g. in Maddison's international growth comparisons over centuries, which are based on American 1990 prices.[51] The Human Development Index (HDI), which rather arbitrarily combines infant mortality, literacy/education, and income in an index with fixed weights, has also been widely used for comparisons over time. Likewise, SEI has had very broad acceptance in the USA as ranking measure. Every weighting exercise is subject to different errors—perfection is impossible. So SEI is what we use to measure the stock of 'advantages'.

Our data come from the 1 per cent sample of the United States census.[52] This sample assigns a Duncan SEI score to every working individual, itself a token of the acceptance and intuitive validity of SEI as a ranking measure. The census sample uses the Duncan score unchanged, i.e. with similar weights on education and income. As new occupations have come into being, and occupational inventories have changed, new SEI scores have been assigned. This is bound to introduce errors, but so is any other approach. So long as this is kept in mind, SEI remains a meaningful measure over time.

Given the many other sources of error, the Duncan 1950 SEI has the merits of simplicity and, conclusively, of being available. This is therefore the primary indicator we use. But the census 1 per cent samples also make it possible to sample other indicators of status change, including education levels, income, and demographics, which provide additional insights, as well as some measure of control.

Income per head has increased more than threefold between 1940 and 2000 in the United States. What difference has this made to social standing? Table 11.1 records changes in the socio-economic index (Duncan's SEI) in the US labour force since 1940. This is based on the IPUMS 1 per cent census sample. It includes men and women, but only whites, since SEI rankings and other demographics differ considerably between whites and

[51] e.g. Maddison, *World Economy*, 171 ff.

[52] Ruggles et al., *Integrated Public Use Microdata* (henceforth IPUMS). Weighting applied where appropriate (1940, 1950, 1990, 2000).

241

Table 11.1. Mean socio-economic index of white men and women in the labour force, USA, 1940–2000

Year	N	Females %	Male SEI	Coef. of variance	Female SEI	Coef. of variance
1940	465,247	23.0	29.6	0.75	36.3	0.60
1950	544,841	26.8	32.9	0.70	38.6	0.54
1960	596,454	31.0	35.9	0.65	39.8	0.52
1970	729,041	36.5	38.1	0.63	41.5	0.51
1980	917,599	41.2	39.6	0.62	43.5	0.49
1990	1,060,130	44.6	40.8	0.62	46.2	0.47
2000	1,074,934	45.8	43.0	0.57	48.1	0.44

Source: Ruggles et al., *Integrated Public Use Microdata* (IPUMS). 1 per cent USA census sample. Weighting applied where appropriate (1940, 1950, 1990, 2000).

Note: All white persons with occupations, i.e. SEI higher than 0.

blacks. Some racial differences will be considered separately. Figure 11.1 compares SEI to education, income, and labour market participation by gender.

Duncan's SEI ranges between 3 and 96. Average SEI rankings have risen by about 12–13 points over sixty years. In percentage terms, this is about a one-third increase for women, and 45 per cent for men. This increase may be taken to be a measure of the rise in the stock of the determinants of status of working people over sixty years since 1940. This rise is the fundamental reason why the majority of Americans consider themselves 'middle class'.[53] This rise in SEI has also delivered psychic returns. A meta-analysis of the 446 studies of the effect of social standing on self-esteem ($n = 312,940$) has found 'a small but significant relationship', in which higher SEI individuals report higher self-esteem.[54]

This increase in average 'advantages' (distance from the bottom) is a vindication of affluence. It is very large. Overall, jobs are more demanding and more satisfying. Satisfaction at work is one of the most important sources of well-being, and on the whole, it has been remarkably high. In economics, work is regarded as a 'disutility', and wages are 'compensation'. Implicitly, the desirable state is leisure. There is a strong tradition that work is an imposition. From the 'dark satanic mills' to Charlie Chaplin in *Modern Times*, factory work was depicted as dehumanizing.[55] In fact, work is a prime source of well-being, on a variety of dimensions: personal control, using skills, responding to challenge, variety, social context, income, security, supportive supervision, interpersonal contact, and social

[53] Zweig, *Working-Class Majority*, ch. 2.
[54] Twenge and Campbell, 'Self-esteem and Socioeconomic Status', 59.
[55] More recently, Braverman, *Labor and Monopoly Capital*; Gallie, 'Quality of Employment'.

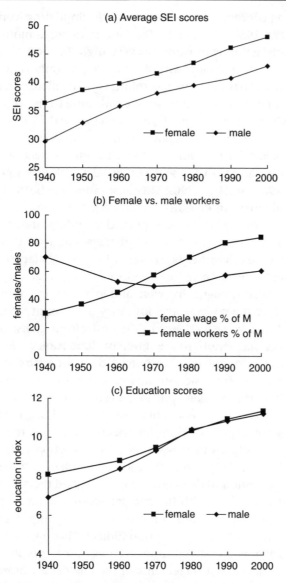

Fig. 11.1. Mean socio-economic index, labour force participation, wages, and education of white men and women in the labour force, USA 1940–2000

Note: White persons with Duncan Socio-Economic Index Score larger than 0. Education scores are based on EDUC99 variable. This ranges from (1) 'no school completed' to (17) 'Doctorate degree'.

Source: IPUMS 1 per cent sample of USA census.

status.[56] Rising education levels implied more stimulating work, and compared with the 1950s, by the 1970s, Americans were more committed to work.[57] Satisfaction with work was very high. In the 1970s more than 50 per cent were 'very happy' with their work, and only 12 to 15 per cent were dissatisfied. That suggests that abilities and challenges remained reasonably well matched.[58] But instead of continuing to rise with education, satisfaction with work entered moderate decline. From the 1970s to the 1990s, the proportion of those 'very happy' about their work in the United States declined to below 50 per cent. In the UK, job satisfaction levels were somewhat lower, and the UK also experienced a decline in job satisfaction between the 1980s and the 1990s. The causes appear to be the same in both countries (and indeed more widely in Europe).

On the one hand, work became more demanding, more challenging, more intrinsically satisfying. On the other, people were driven to work harder. There were minorities of workers whose dissatisfaction arose from being overqualified for their jobs, and increasing insecurity also had a mild effect.[59] Freud thought that work and love were the only things that mattered, and on the positive side, love may have counted for more than work.[60] But losses are experienced differently from gains; positive and negative 'affect' (i.e. emotion) are different dimensions.[61] As a source of ill-being, unemployment is more potent than separation or divorce.[62] In the race between intrinsic satisfaction and stress, on the average the additional effort that workers put in exceeded the psychic satisfactions they received, after taking account of levels of pay. Although the experience of work was generally positive, rising knowledge, effort, and interest delivered diminishing, even slightly negative, returns in satisfaction. If these aggregate choices had been entirely voluntary and independent of other considerations (such as income and demand), we might regard them as myopic.

The comparison of SEI with income per head is telling. While income increases are open-ended, status, on this measure, is capped. Duncan's SEI is linear, but studies of social perception indicate that the relation of status to income, as of most social indicators, is concave (i.e. curvilinear and knee shaped). That means that increments of income deliver more rewarding

---

[56] Warr, 'Well-being in the Workplace'.

[57] Veroff et al., *Inner American*, pp. 278–84, 548.

[58] Blanchflower and Oswald, 'Decline of American Job Satisfaction', table 1, p. 16.

[59] Ibid.; Kallberg, 'Work Quality in the USA'; Green and Gallie, 'High Skills and High Anxiety'.

[60] Veroff et al., *Inner American*, 548.

[61] Bradburn and Noll, *Psychological Well-Being*, chs. 1, 4; Diener and Emmons, 'Positive Affect'; Kahneman et al., *Choice, Values and Frames*, pt. 3.

[62] Above, Ch. 2, Table 2.2; Campbell et al., *Quality of American Life*, fig. 2.5, pp. 52–3.

status at the bottom of the income scale than at the top, and that status cannot increase, as income can, exponentially for everyone over long periods of time. Towards the top, it takes enormous increments of income to move a very small distance upwards.[63] The runaway growth of executive 'compensation' in the last two decades, which has risen from some forty to more than four hundred times average worker salaries in twenty years since 1980, suggests the heavy cost in income that is required to keep ahead, or just stay in the race for status at that level.[64]

Status of women

Women typically earn less than men. Nevertheless, in terms of raw average SEI scores, women have scored substantially higher than men (Figure 11.1). All through the period from 1940 to 2000, women workers have maintained their lead, and consistently score an average SEI that is about 13 per cent higher than men's. This runs entirely counter to conventional expectations.

It could be an artefact of the construction of this particular index. Duncan's 1950 socio-economic index was derived from men's earnings. Since occupations are usually gender segregated, this means that typically female occupations were assigned a score on the basis of male incumbents, e.g. the score of primary schoolteachers or nurses was assigned on the basis of male teachers or nurses. The difference in SEI between women and men has been consistently much smaller than the pay gap between the genders.[65] So the difference in pay between men and women only accounts in part for women's higher scores. This finding is not idiosyncratic. In virtually all early studies, the occupational status of women was found to be the same as or higher than that of men.[66] In 1977 Treiman provided a competing index of occupational rankings, based on perceived prestige alone. Working with me in 1991, David Engerman derived weighted average occupational prestige scores from the US Census for the four census years between 1950 and 1980, separately for men and for women. The average of men and women's occupational prestige score was virtually the same. The ratio of women to men's occupational scores, weighted by the numbers actually in

[63] Coleman et al., *Social Standing*, 33–42, 324–6.
[64] Anderson et al., 'Decade of Excess'; Crystal, *In Search of Excess*; Frank and Cook, *Winner-Takes-All Society*, 67–72; Hartman, 'Part 2. Income Patterns'.
[65] Around 60 per cent of men for full-time earnings between 1960 and 1980, then rising up to about 75 by 1995, and almost to parity (94 per cent) among youngest workers by 1995 (Blau and Kahn, 'Gender Differences in Pay', 75–8).
[66] Boyd, 'Socioeconomic Indices', 458.

the labour force, averaged over the period as a whole, was 1.003, with only a tiny divergence from parity in each census year.[67] In other words, the 'stock of occupational status', for men and women employed, was virtually the same.

One commentator wrote in 1980 that 'the anomalies in the SEI indicate that something badly needs to be fixed'.[68] Careful efforts have gone into separate indices for women, as well as single scales incorporating both male and female occupations. Duncan's SEI (which we use here) might exaggerate the superiority of women somewhat, but even when the determinants are adapted and changed, whether in SEI or in prestige rankings, the results are not reversed: in the aggregate, working women ranked about the same on average as men, sometimes a little more, sometimes a little less. In the census, there is no evidence that women have lower average SEI or prestige rankings than men.[69] Perhaps this is not an anomaly after all—the result needs to be explained, and not fixed.

Several explanations are possible. Women on the whole earn less than men. In order to deliver parity between the genders in the SEI rankings, income has to be weighted less, and education has to be weighted more. Indeed an authoritative study argues that to explain prestige rankings, education alone should count. An economist might then invoke 'compensating wage differentials': higher prestige and more rewarding jobs might be compensating women for lower pay. But Table 11.1 suggests another source of the difference. The dispersion of rankings (captured by the coefficient of variation columns in this table) is smaller for working women than it is for working men. Women's jobs are concentrated in the middle of the prestige hierarchy, while men's jobs vary more widely. Although women are less visible in the highest occupational ranks, they are also relatively absent from the very lowest ones, where men are to be found in abundance, and this finding persists even as women's employment levels have almost converged onto those of men.[70]

Compare this result with the component measures of social ranking, namely education and earnings (Figure 11.1).[71] From the 1940s to the

[67] Carried out at Rutgers University, using scores in Treiman, *Occupational Prestige*. Aggregate results in my possession, but only a few of the detailed tabulations survive.

[68] Huber, 'Ransacking Mobility Tables', 7.

[69] Hauser and Warren, 'Socioeconomic Indexes', 198–9; and see table 4, p. 221. Comparing 'Current or last occupation, 1990 census'. Much smaller samples, from the General Social Survey, indicate a small advantage, 1–2 points, for men. See Nakao and Treas, 'Updating Occupational Prestige', table 4, p. 34.

[70] The same finding in Bose, *Jobs and Gender*, from much smaller samples.

[71] Strictly speaking, social rankings are measured in terms of the proportion of people in an occupation above certain educational and income thresholds.

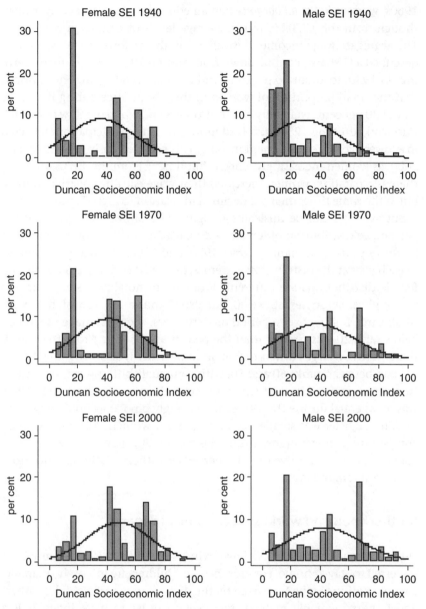

Fig. 11.2. Percentage distribution of female and male Social and Economic Index (SEI) scores, USA 1940, 1970, 2000

Note: White members of the labour force only. Normal distribution superimposed.

Source: IPUMS 1 per cent sample of USA census.

1960s, women *in the labour force* had an educational advantage over men, though from the 1970s onwards, average levels of education converged. The aggregate wage income of women was always lower than men's, and described a U-shape, coming down from around 70 per cent of men's earnings in 1940, to about 50 per cent, and then up to 60 again. The reason is that the small proportion of women in the labour force during the 1940s (about 30 per cent) were mostly in full-time work, while the flow of women into work after the 1950s involved more part-time participation, reflected in a lower average employment income. This changed during the 1990s and 2000, as women increasingly worked full-time.[72] From the 1970s onwards, there is a paradox: women increased their wage earnings relative to men, but at the same time, their SEI declined in relation to men (Figure 11.1).

But averages can be misleading. Figure 11.2 shows histograms of the percentage distribution of female and male SEIs at three points, separated by thirty years each, namely 1940, 1970, and 2000. Compare the genders in each year at the distribution extremes, below 20 and above 80. Male and female distributions are different. Women are notably absent from the very highest SEI scores, above 80, but also from the very lowest, below 15. At all three points, over a period of sixty years, the percentage of women below rank 20 was smaller than the percentage of men. From the outset, there were two large clusters of female employment, between ranks 40 and 60, and between ranks 60 and 80, with a gradual shift upwards over time. In contrast, for men the histogram was skewed towards the bottom in 1940, was more equal during the 1970s, and strongly bipolar again in 2000. The middling cluster was smaller for men than for women. Although women consistently achieve higher mean SEIs than men, they are largely absent above 80. But what drove their higher SEIs was their relative absence from the lowest ranking jobs.

Motherhood and work: an 'economy of regard'

White women avoided these low-paying, unattractive jobs because they preferred to stay at home. For most people, children are intensely desirable: a whole nation can be transfixed by the disappearance of a child. Mothers and fathers incur big material sacrifices in order to have them. It is a paradox, therefore, that lower-income families have more children, on the average, than higher-income ones. In the United States, blacks have more children than whites, although blacks are less well off (Fig. 11.3, below).

---

[72] For wage rates, rather than actual earnings, see Blau, 'Trends in Well-Being', 127–39.

Money is more valuable to the poor than to the rich, so why should poor people have more children? After all, in the post-war United States and Britain, children were only rarely economic assets: they contributed very little to household income, and counted for much less than previously in spreading risk and providing insurance. Economists provide an answer, which resolves the paradox. Although children are desirable, they also involve a sacrifice. The more highly educated the mother, the greater her sacrifice in terms of earnings job and satisfaction. Affluence lowers the cost of many goods, but it raises the cost of children. Much of that cost is 'positional': like their parents, children compete for social position (and future prospects) with other children. Parental competition bids up the cost of their upbringing. Unlike the competition of sellers, which lowers prices, competition among buyers raises them. As a 'positional good' (always scarce), other things being equal, the competitive ranking of particular children is constrained only by the wealth rank of their parents.[73] To succeed in the positional race, it is rational to invest more in each competitor-child, and this is helped by reducing their number.

Such are the intrinsic rewards of parenthood that only a small minority of women have chosen to forgo it altogether. Instead, the response to competitive pressures has been to reduce the number of children. Middle-class parents, in order to compete, tend to have fewer children than the poor, who are squeezed out of the positional race. This is also apparent at the level of society as a whole. In all affluent societies, the birth rate has declined beneath replacement levels. Competing to provide a good start for children has absorbed a good deal of the material rewards of affluence, in the form of more years at school, higher school costs, and competition for better schools. The birth rate has dropped the least in the United States, but that is a consequence of inequality: it has a larger proportion of poor people than any other advanced society.

If the average stock of 'advantages', i.e. of status distance from the bottom, is the same for wage-earning men and women, as we argued above, then perhaps that remains true when housewives are included as well? If income is imputed to housework at a reasonable rate, and equal sharing of income within the household is assumed, then overall, women's effective income per person, and also per hours of work, approximately matched that of men.[74] Young children provided a reason for married women to

[73] Positional goods are defined in this chapter, above.
[74] Though (due to more hours of work for women, and fewer for men), declining from 1.08 of men per hour of work, to 0.92 between 1960 and 1986 (Fuchs, *Women's Quest*, table 5.3, p. 80).

stay out of low-quality work. Women overall were more satisfied than men, and women who stayed at home were just as satisfied as women at work.[75] Poor mothers were poorly educated, and most of the work available to them was unpleasant and badly paid. As a source of approbation and pride, work compared poorly with the satisfactions of motherhood. This was reflected in women's SEI scores. In the United States, in comparison with men, relatively few white women were to be found at work below an SEI of 15, whereas many more men were still to be found there. That level formed a kind of 'minimum reservation price': the rewards of work had to match or improve on the intrinsic satisfactions of motherhood. Despite being poor, such women apparently preferred children over money. And if the children of the poor were destined to be left behind in positional and educational competition, they cost less to raise, so the poor could have more of them.

Work offered fewer rewards to less-educated women, so their children counted for more. This logic does not even require marriage. It is quite compelling even if the poorly educated mother is single, so long as motherhood was fulfilling, and ensured the means of subsistence. Despite the breakdown of marriage and family in black communities, the fertility rate still remained higher than among the whites. Even in the 1940s and 1950s, black marriage was much less secure, levels of education lower, and income much tighter: blacks suffered clear racial discrimination. In consequence, black women did not have the luxury of forgoing the lowest-level occupations. They worked outside the home much more than white women, and mostly in the lowest occupations. Black female labour force participation rates were about 40 per cent in 1950, and the proportion of black working women with SEI below 20 was 89 per cent, compared with only 39 per cent of white working women.[76]

In the 1940s, motherhood was even more compelling. In 1940, more than 60 per cent of white American women aged 22–44 had not achieved a high-school diploma (below, Fig. 11.5(a)). The male single-breadwinner family was the social norm.[77] The Great Depression was over, everyone had a job, incomes were rising fast, and inequalities were declining: not only did absolute income increase, inequalities declined (and 'complaints' fell). For less-educated women, the response to post-war affluence was to avoid low-level work, enter marriage, and embrace motherhood at a young age. The depression and the subsequent years of war had built up a backlog of desire

---

[75] Campbell, *Quality of American Life*, fig. 2.5, pp. 52–3; table 2.2 above.

[76] Mullaney, 'Rewards of Status', fig. 7.1.

[77] Bernard, 'The Good-Provider Role'; Blossfeld and Drobnic, *Careers of Couples*; Crompton, *Restructuring Gender Relations*; Janssens, *Male Breadwinner Family*.

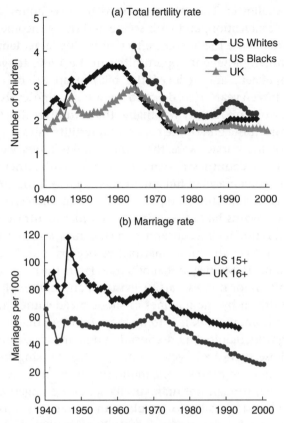

Fig. 11.3. Total fertility rates and marriage rates of women, USA and Britain, *c.*1940–2000

Note: Unmarried women, 15+ in USA, 16+ in UK. Total fertility rate is the average number of children who would be born per woman if women experienced the age-specific fertility rates of the reference period throughout their childbearing lifespan.

Sources: USA—Robert Hauser, *Fertility Tables for Birth Cohorts by Color: United States 1901–1973* (Rockville, Md.: National Center for Health Statistics, 1976). **www.prb.org/Content/ NavigationMenu/Ameristat/Topics1/Fertility/a-FERT_USFertil1.xls** S. J. Ventura (et al.), 'Births: Final Data for [1998–2001]', National Center for Health Statistics (several publications). US Department of Health and Human Services, National Center for Health Statistics, *Vital Statistics of the United States* vol. i, *Natality* (Rockville, Md., 1969). National Vital Statistics Reports 48, no. 3 (2000); 49, no. 1 (2001); 50, no. 5 (2002); 51, no. 2 (2002). UK—UK Office of National Statistics, 'Total period fertility rate, 1924–1998', *Social Trends*, 30; Dataset ST30A3.

for normality. For the first two post-war decades, marriage rates were high, and fertility rose to very high levels, in both the UK and Britain (Figure. 11.3).

Although the British were not so well off as the Americans, the British 'baby boom' still lagged a few years behind the American one, and was shorter and shallower. This is consistent with an economic view that in the absence of education, and with secure and rising incomes, American women would choose the 'income effect' of having larger families. Rising education and employment opportunities in the 1960s triggered off the 'substitution effect', and reduced the relative appeal of motherhood within some fifteen years or so, down to pre-war baseline levels by the mid-1970s. Black women's fertility was higher than white fertility throughout, and it was only at the end of the period that fertility rates converged. But the shapes of the curves were the same. Similar forces were affecting women in the two countries, and in the two races, with rather short lags.

During the 'golden age' of full employment between the 1940s and the 1960s marriage and motherhood provided a 'minimum reservation price', a floor whose rewards had to be bettered, in order to attract women into work. Husbands provided secure and rising incomes, and motherhood was more satisfying than the most unattractive occupations. There was also comfort in numbers. Marriage and motherhood were the norm: competition for consumption, for houses, cars, televisions, and household appliances was initially driven by the incomes of single-breadwinner husbands. To entice young women, work had to be more fulfilling than motherhood, and fulfilling work required more education than most women had.

In 1985, Bose published occupational prestige ranking indices, separately for women and for men. She found that women ranked on average lower than men, though not dramatically so. David Engerman used her occupational ranking scales to calculate an average stock of status for women and men for the censuses of 1970 and 1980, and found that women's weighted average stock of status (over both censuses) was 0.946 of men's. Unlike the majority of occupational rankers, Bose also imputed a prestige ranking for housewives. This was 51, comparable to an office secretary.[78] It was higher than the weighted average status for working women as a whole (44.8 in 1980), which Engerman had calculated independently by applying the Bose prestige ranking scale to the numbers in each occupation. Bose's rankings have come in for criticism and are not entirely credible.[79] But her qualitative conclusion is in line with my own interpretation:

Assuming that they are interested in maximising their status, women can gain more prestige as housewives than they would otherwise obtain in 70 percent of

[78] Bose, *Jobs and Gender*, ch. 4, esp. table 4.2, p. 50. This was a prestige ranking. For comparison with other occupations, she suggests 44 (p. 56).
[79] The sample is very small and questionably representative. And see e.g. Jacobs, 'Review of *Jobs and Gender*'.

other traditional women's jobs. This may explain why working-class women do not denigrate this role, whereas highly educated women with other status alternatives speak of the role as 'only' a housewife.[80]

For women, up to the 1980s, the marriage market offered more opportunities for status enhancement than the labour market, and that was the case in Britain as well.[81]

Gradually, however, from the mid-1960s onwards, education permitted women to aspire to more than the reservation price of motherhood. By 1960, the 1940s pattern was reversed, and more than 60 per cent of women aged 22–42 had achieved a high-school education or better. To those women, work had more to offer, better jobs, with better pay, in comparison with motherhood. The economy needed more middle-ranking workers in offices and shops. In college education, women caught up with men within the space of about twenty years. In 1960, American women took only six-tenths as many first degrees as men, but had reached parity by 1980.[82] By 1984 the number of women graduate students had reached parity with men, and by 1998 their number among graduate students was one-third higher, though they took only 44 per cent of professional degrees.[83] Opportunities in management also started to open up.[84] Education was also a kind of dowry, which increased the prospects of marrying a more educated and better earning mate.[85]

But the positional cost of children also began to rise. The boom babies of the 1940s and 1950s began to compete for education during the 1950s and 1960s. If mothers went out to work, they could help to purchase better homes, neighbourhoods, schools, and college than mothers who remained at home.[86] From the 1970s to the 1990s, working women retained (a narrowing) average occupational lead over men in average SEI scores, and not only increased their presence at work, but also improved their pay rates in relation to men.[87] In the United States, the proportion of dual-earner couples overtook single-earner ones in 1982 (Figure 11.4(a)).

Once this cross-over took place, and a sufficient proportion of married women had gone out to work, two-earner families began to set the norm

[80] Bose, *Jobs and Gender*, 96–7.

[81] Nilson, 'Social Standing'; Hakim, *Work-Lifestyle Choices*, 159–61.

[82] Goldin, *Understanding the Gender Gap*, fig. 8.1.

[83] United States, Dept. of Education, *Digest of Education Statistics 2002*, tables 189, 30; http://nces.ed.gov/programs/digest/d00/dt189.asp; http://nces.ed.gov/pubs2002/ proj2012/ table_30.asp.   [84] Hicks, 'Management Recruitment', ch. 6.

[85] Currie and Moretti, 'Mother's Education', 5, citing Mare, 'Five Decades'; Goldin, 'Career and Family', 39–40; Harrell, 'Women with MBAs'.

[86] Edwards, 'Uncertainty'.   [87] Blau, 'Trends in Well-Being'.

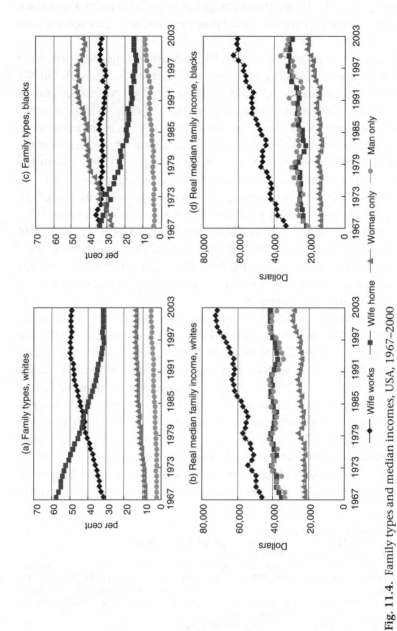

Fig. 11.4. Family types and median incomes, USA, 1967–2000.

Note: Income at year 2000 prices.

Source: United States Census, Historical Income Tables, Table F-7A-B. www.census.gov/hhes/ income/histinc/f07a.html

for household incomes, consumption, and investment in children.[88] But even in 2001, such dual-earner families were only 49 per cent of all households with more than one person. House prices and housing costs were driven up by those two-earner family incomes.[89] The other great positional expense, university tuition, also responded to the rising income of two-earner families. Between the late 1980s and the mid-1990s, college tuition rates increased between 3 and 5 per cent a year (depending on the type of college), while median male earnings stagnated.[90] By *choosing* individually to work, mothers found themselves collectively *compelled* to work, in order to support a college education for their children.

Figure 11.4 shows these different trends for white and black families. From the late 1940s, the proportion of white single-earner 'male-breadwinner' families was in steady decline. Dual-earner families became the majority of couples in 1982, and finally stabilized their share at about half of all families by the early 1990s, while single-earner couples were at about one-third. At the same time, the proportion of single-head families rose to about one-fifth. In terms of income (Figure 11.4(*b*)), it is clear that at median-family level, only two-earner families remained in competition, and that their rising incomes depended on wives' earnings. 'Male-breadwinner' families dropped increasingly behind, until by the end of the period they were earning less than 60 per cent of two-earner families, while woman-headed families earned around 60 per cent as much as 'male-breadwinner' families. To the extent that children imposed comparable costs on childcare, education, clothing, housing and health, then having only one earner pushed families out of the positional race.

For black families (Figure 11.4 (panels *c* and *d*)), the earning power of different types of families was comparable, albeit at lower level. What was different was the composition of families, with two-earner families at about one-third, 'male-breadwinner' couples about 15 per cent, and the largest category, between 40 and 50 per cent, were women-headed families. About two-thirds of black families only had one income, in most cases a woman's income. If a two-earner family was the state of grace, then falling out of it (or perhaps never entering it) was even more dire for blacks than for whites.

The bare majority of households, still made up of single-earner families in middle-ranking jobs, could no longer compete. By the 1980s, about 80 per cent of white mothers had a high-school education or more, and thus potential access to reasonably attractive jobs. As services expanded relative

[88] Oppenheimer, *Work and the Family*, 309–40.   [89] Below, Ch. 12.
[90] Cunningham, *College Costs*, 111–18.

to manufacturing, male muscle was less in demand. To shift the gaze to Britain, the financial industry surged ahead and became the leading sector in the economy. Its workforce almost doubled from 10 to 19 per cent between 1979 and 2000, it paid the highest salaries, and it absorbed a large proportion of the graduates of elite universities. It employed women readily, at all levels.[91]

For women, the choice was for occupational status derived either from motherhood (and indirectly from their partner's occupation), or from work. For the impact of occupation on motherhood, education is a better determinant than occupational status. For one thing, it is argued that education is a better measure of social standing than SEI scores, especially for women.[92] For another, the education measure also captures those women who are not working, and those who have never worked, who are missed by occupational scores. Figure 11.5 shows the relation between education and fertility in the USA (white women). It is a snapshot, showing the number of own children at home for white women (ages 22–42) at each educational level, every ten years, except in 1950.

Look at the panels in Figure 11.5. The top one, panel (a) shows the changing levels of educational endowment among white women of child-bearing age. Starting at age 22 does not exclude women who have had children at a younger age, but excludes most women who have not completed their education. Women with less than complete high-school education declined from more than 60 per cent at the beginning of the period, to about 8 per cent at the end. College graduates, on the other hand, rose from 5 per cent at the outset, to almost 30 per cent at the end.

Panel (b) shows the impact of education on motherhood. In 1940, education inhibited motherhood: the more education, the fewer the children. Between the ages of 22 and 42, women with no high-school education (some 40 per cent) had four times as many children at home as college graduates. Between 1960 and 1980, all women had more children, but the gradient was still there, with a big step reduction in the number of children at home between high-school-plus education and a full college degree. Crossing the degree threshold was the point at which investment in work became decisively more rewarding than investment in children. By the year 2000, poorly educated white women had almost disappeared. Ninety-two per cent of women had a full high-school education or more. In 1990 and 2000 there was convergence, as less-educated women had fewer children,

[91] Offer, *Public Sector*, 26–7.
[92] Hauser and Warren, 'Socioeconomic Indexes', 182, n. 18, p. 195.

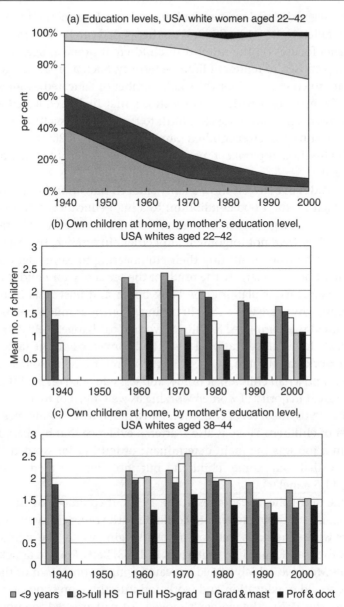

Fig. 11.5. Motherhood and education, white women 22–44, USA

Notes: Before 1990, highest category included women studying for professional and doctoral degrees, as well as those qualified. In 1950, individual educational level was not reported.

Source: IPUMS. Standardized for age structure in 1960 (middle panel).

while college-educated women had more. From four-to-one in 1940, the gap had fallen to 1.5 : 1 by 2000. What happened can be seen in panel (c). This panel focuses on the number of children at home at ages 38–44, an age group chosen to represent lifetime fertility. Such a broad category was necessary to compensate for the small number of educated women at the outset. Comparing it with panel (b) shows that highly educated women had always been postponing childbirth to the later years, although education still resulted in fewer children. But by the census of 2000 most women had a high-school diploma or more, and their work–fertility trade-offs had converged.

The decades in between show a fairly smooth transition from a low education/high motherhood equilibrium to a high education/lower motherhood one. If college graduates were postponing motherhood as much as possible, they were not forgoing it altogether. 'In essence, the baby boom was fuelled by women shifting their childbearing to earlier ages and the subsequent bust was largely the result of the tendency for childbearing to be delayed. Thus, explaining the baby boom and bust rests heavily on explaining why there was a shift in timing of births as much as explaining what caused the completed fertility of women to change.'[93] By 2000 white women at almost all educational levels had converged on the same motherhood/work equilibrium, with educated women having somewhat less than one and a half children at home, and less educated ones a little more, and the great majority of women working as well, most of them full-time.

By the 1990s, the level of education had a much weaker influence on the number of children. There is also scattered evidence that by then, merely being in a job was the main determinant of fertility for women.[94] Work had crowded out some children, but not motherhood altogether (Figure 11.5 panel (c)).

For the new college graduates in the 1950s, it could be cognitively and emotionally stultifying to remain confined with young children in distant suburbs while husbands went out to challenging work. The solution was not another car (Figure 11.6) but a job. In 1963, Betty Friedan attacked *The Feminine Mystique*, which locked educated young women out of the challenging world of education and work and into the repression of motherhood. By the 1970s, the women's movement had affected the normative climate. Within the feminist movement, the liberal wing focused its efforts on removing obstacles in higher education and at work, but also projected

[93] Hotz, 'Economics of Fertility in Developed Countries', 281.
[94] Naz et al., 'Education and Completed Fertility'; Kravdal, 'High Fertility'; Hakim, *Work-Lifestyle Choices*, finds little difference by education in preferences for motherhood.

Stranded in Suburbia...

When suburban fathers go off to work—
as suburban fathers must—their absence
is felt in more ways than one

When the male population leaves Suburbia
each workday morning—millions of housewives are
left virtually prisoners in their own homes.

For, while many harried wives drive Dad to the
station, 11 million others stand and watch Dad go,
taking with him their link with the outside world
—the family car.

In that *left-behind* feeling, Ford finds
a billion-dollar opportunity

Fig. 11.6. Suburban blues. From an advertising agency advertisement, 1956
Source: J. Walter Thompson Newsletters, box 36 [29], Hartman Center, Duke University Library.

a disdain for marriage, motherhood, and men.[95] In the space of two decades, between the 1950s and the 1970s, the occupational term of 'housewife' was transformed from the occupation of most adult women into a derogatory term.[96] For the college-graduate women, aspiring to SEIs at the 70 to 90 levels, the SEI 20-minus 'minimum reservation price' level represented by stay-at-home mothering with low education, or even the average female SEI score of about 40, would have been a crushing retreat. In attacking motherhood in general, feminist writers patronized their less-competitive sisters, less educated, less articulate, excluded from journalism, academia, and the movement. Overall, the normative equilibrium began to shift, from celebrating motherhood, to holding it in disdain.[97]

But the majority of women continued to seek and to value the experience of motherhood. Eighty-five per cent of women continued to have children, a historically high proportion.[98] These are the data for completed fertility.

[95] Roiphe, *Mother's Eye*, ch. 1.   [96] Gavron, *Captive Wife*; Oakley, *Housewife*.
[97] Whitehead, *Divorce Culture*; Coontz, *The Way We Really Are*; Roiphe, *Mother's Eye*; Stacey, *In the Name of the Family*.   [98] Hotz et al., 'Economics of Fertility', fig. 2, p. 280.

About one-fifth of couples have fertility problems, and these increase if the first child is postponed. On the whole, women who were college graduates tended to postpone fertility.[99] If less-educated women insisted on a minimum reservation price to attract them into work in competition with the rewards of motherhood, educated women placed a reservation price on motherhood, in competition with the rewards of high-status work. The financial cost of motherhood includes the direct costs of children, of food, shelter, childcare, and education. It includes the mother's lost wages at work, experience forgone, lower part-time rates, and downwards occupational mobility. Some countries have social policies which compensate mothers.[100] Some costs, such as the premiums paid for living near good schools, are hard to capture, and are not paid by all. If social scientists find the cost of children difficult to unravel, so much more do ordinary people. One attempt to simulate the cost of child-rearing in terms of lifetime earnings between ages in Britain found them to be on the following scale: men 271; women, no children, 185; women, two children, 100. In financial terms, the loss of earnings of a mother of two came to £135,000 during the 1980s, similar to the cost at that time of a detached family house, a comparison replicated again in 2003.[101] Mothers in the USA paid a wage penalty of about 7–13 percentage points per child.[102] In both the USA and Britain in the 1980s, the overall cost of one child was estimated at one-quarter of family income, and for two children around one-third or more.[103]

At the pinnacle of status competition, the rewards of work were more likely to crowd out motherhood altogether. For men, in contrast, effort at work did not have to compete with effort at home. Talent, energy, personality, and luck being equal, the main determinant of success at work is the time invested. As status opportunities opened up for women, the vast majority had to sacrifice potential status gains, in order to achieve the fulfilment of motherhood.

An economist, assuming full information and clearly ranked, stable preferences, would say that for those women who chose it (the vast majority), motherhood counted for more than the opportunities forgone at work. If they chose to pay the cost of motherhood, the benefits must have been

[99] Hotz et al., 'Economics of Fertility', 281 ff.; Rendall and Smallwood, 'Higher Qualifications'; Figure 11.5, panel (c). [100] DiPrete, 'Cross-National Differences'.
[101] Joshi, 'Changing Form', 170–2; see also Joshi et al., 'Wages of Motherhood'; Elliott, 'Saved for the House'—the cost of a single child was calculated at £140,000, more than the average house; Olson, *Costs of Children*, calculated the cost at 37 per cent of the net present value of family income for two children, 51 per cent for three children (p. 3)—rather more than typical mortgage payments.
[102] Budig and England, 'Wage Penalty'; Joshi et al., 'Wages of Motherhood'.
[103] Below, Ch. 13, nn. 109–10.

larger than the cost. This is not meant to justify the extra cost to women (men, after all, suffered no career penalties for parenthood, and in fact enjoyed a substantial 'marriage premium' in pay over unmarried men).[104] But (assuming other things to be equal), the female wage gap (and the other impediments in status competition) can be taken as a measure of the magnitude of the distinctive reward of motherhood, available to women and not to men.[105] Despite the earnings gap, women throughout this period have reported themselves more satisfied with work than men.[106] And stay-at-home women were just as satisfied (on average, in the aggregate) as working ones.[107]

Other things being equal, childless women had more time for competition at work than mothers, and childlessness might thus be higher among high-achieving women. (Or possibly vice versa—high achievement at work may have been more common among childless women.) Marriage and motherhood provide an 'economy of regard', a web of social relations that is supportive in a variety of ways.[108] For high-challenge jobs, the workplace could offer an alternative environment of stimulation and social support.[109] But to excel at work required an investment in time and commitment that only men (or childless women) could make. Marriage is also strongly protective of health. In Britain, among single women, only those in professional jobs had health status comparable to that of mothers with children.[110]

Childlessness might not be intentional. After postponing marriage from their twenties into their early thirties, single women only had a relatively short time to find a suitable mate. At that stage, if they sought older and more qualified men, they faced a harder task than in their twenties, and some might not find an acceptable match.[111] In a large survey of women graduates over 37 in the United States, only 3 per cent reported involuntary infertility, but 16 per cent had never tried to get pregnant at all.[112] In the United States, women of the highest educational categories, as well as women with the highest occupational status, were those most likely to be childless.[113]

---

[104] Waite and Gallagher, *Case for Marriage*, chs. 7–8; Ginther and Zavodny, 'Male Marriage Premium'; Chun, 'Why Do Married Men Earn More?'
[105] Roiphe, *Mother's Eye*; Belkin, 'Opt-out Revolution'.
[106] Blanchflower and Oswald, 'Well-Being, Insecurity', table 3, p. 18, table 6, p. 23.
[107] Campbell et al., *Quality of American Life*, table 2.5, p. 52.
[108] Waite and Gallagher, *Case for Marriage*.   [109] Hochschild, *Time Bind*.
[110] Marmot, *Status Syndrome*, 157–63; Bartley et al., 'Social Position and Women's Health'.
[111] Whitehead, *No Good Men*; Hewlett, *Creating a Life*, ch. 4; Cannold, *What, No Baby?*
[112] Wyshak, 'Infertility'.
[113] Hewlett, *Creating a Life*, ch. 3; Hewlett and Vite-León, 'High-Achieving Women', 11–12.

Figure 11.7 compares childless American white women ('no children at home') by education level, with childless white men, at age 40 for women, and 42 for men, from 1940 to 2000. Level of education is a proxy for status achievement potential. The sample is taken at the end of the reproductive period. The signal is a little noisy—for a few women all children will have already flown the nest, and a very few will not have had children yet; but it is reliable on the whole. Follow the panels, and compare women and men. In panel (*a*), for women between 1940 and 1990, the highest level of education was associated with an exceptionally high level of childlessness. Up to the 1960s, more than half of the most educated women had no children at home. Afterwards, the level came down to between 40 per cent and one-third. Between the 1960s and the 1980s, the level of childlessness for the most highly educated women was about twice as high as for other women, and even in the 1990s, it was still about one-third higher than other educated women (i.e. high school and college; but comparable with those with a poor education).[114] Also, between the 1970s and the 1990s the overall level of childlessness rose by about two-thirds.

The contrast with men (panel (*b*)) is very striking. Men did not sacrifice parenthood for career. On the contrary: education increased their chances of parenthood. From the 1960s onwards, childlessness was highest at low educational levels, and lowest at the highest levels of education. Poorly educated men were the least likely to have children at home, partly due to marriage dissolution, and partly because they had less to offer, when women generally looked to marry equals or upwards. There were many more men in the lowest occupational categories than there were women (above, Figure 11.2).

Once couples decided to have children, the completed family size was similar for all women, regardless of levels of education. The main effect of education on fertility was on whether to have children or not. This is shown in Figure 11.7, panels (*c*) and (*d*). In 1940, the number of children per parent was steeply graded by education, from three children for primary-school parents, down to two children for college educated parents. Men and women were virtually identical. From the 1960s onwards, education levels (except at the lower end) made little difference to the final number of children. The cohort or period effect was the most important one. On average, all people belonging to a particular cohort (those aged 40 in the

---

[114] The convergence of very high and very low education at the same level of childlessness is due to the changing numbers with poor education. Low-education women in the 1990 and 2000 censuses were a very small group, who would either have found it difficult to marry or whose children were often no longer at home.

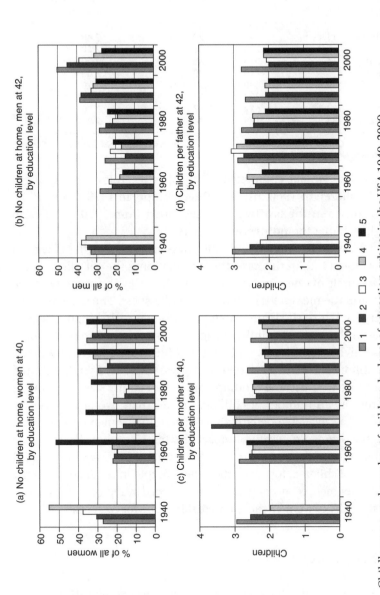

Fig. 11.7. Childlessness, and number of children, by level of education, whites in the USA 1940–2000

Note: Educational levels: (1) less than nine years; (2) more than eight years, less than full high school; (3) full high school or some college; (4) first or master's degrees; (5) professional or doctoral qualification.

Source: IPUMS.

Table 11.2. Number of children by educational qualification, women at 42 in 2000, UK

Highest qualification	% childless	Number	Mean no. of children, for all women	Mean no. of children, excluding childless women
No qualifications	11.1	747	2.20	2.48
CSE Grade 2–5	9.8	754	2.06	2.28
Good 'O' Levels	14.7	2,015	1.88	2.20
AS /one A level	5.3	19	1.89	2.00
A levels	20.4	489	1.75	2.20
Diploma	22.3	273	1.74	2.24
Degree	23.8	652	1.67	2.20
Higher degree	33.9	115	1.34	2.03

Source: Lim, 'Women's Choices', table 4.2, p.25. Sample derived from the National Child Development Survey of the birth cohort of 3–9 March 1958.

census year) had similar completed family size, regardless of education: around 2.5 children in 1960, rising to three or more in 1970, 2.5 in 1980, and down to two in the last two censuses. Apart from 1970, the figures were roughly similar for mothers and fathers.

In the UK as well, women's childlessness increased with education standards (Table 11.2). In this case, the information is the completed birth record of a sample of one week's women born in 1958. The age is 42 in the year 2000, and the measure is of genuine childlessness. The pattern, however, is very similar to the United States. Of women with a higher degree, about one-third remained childless at age 42. One and two steps down, at first-degree/high-school levels, only about a fifth to a quarter of women remained childless, with even lower levels down the scale. As in the United States, for those who became mothers, completed family sizes were much closer, with a mean number of children greater than two at all levels of education. Of all available determinants of fertility, women's educational level had the strongest negative impact in this UK cohort.[115] For male partners, however, social ranking (the measure we have) was *positively* related to the number of children, following the pattern in the United States. As in the United States, for men, economic success was matched by reproductive success; for a large minority of women, the two were substitutes for each other.

What drove status?

Gender provides another take on status. Hakim has argued that women have 'heterogeneous preferences': the majority preferred to combine

[115] Lim, 'Women's Choices'; see Table 11.2.

motherhood with work, while minorities preferred either full-time work or full-time motherhood.[116] The implication is that these 'preferences' are intrinsic and immutable. But preferences for childlessness are not likely to be heritable, and the demographics recorded above show that women respond to social incentives: given the means to compete in the labour market, at times up to half and more have forsaken motherhood in favour of work. The level of childlessness (and the number of children as well) has fluctuated, indicating that it responds to opportunities in society and economy. Women have shown themselves willing to move from motherhood to work, if work is rewarding enough. But women have also had a choice between motherhood and occupational status. As we have seen, they were found more thinly at the bottom and the top of the occupational ladder. Many women never get near the glass ceiling, 'because they are stopped long before by the maternal wall'.[117]

Status is a reward we take for granted, but we should be more surprised, perhaps, by its extraordinary power to motivate. Evolutionary psychology suggests that status is a gendered game, and much more compelling for men than for women.[118] To show this, it seeks for clues that motivation is not constructed on the shifting ground of culture and society, but hardwired, i.e. arises from our inherited human natures. 'Men are from Mars, Women are from Venus', claims the longest-selling self-help book of the last decade.[119] From that point of view, status is perhaps more of a male incentive rather than a female one.[120] If women are less successful at the very top, perhaps it is because they care less? 'Sometimes I worry that we are just a little bit lazier', says one of a group of highly educated 'opt-out women', 'But in my heart of hearts, I think it's really because we're smarter.'[121] Is it just possible that this kind of wisdom is wired in by evolution?

The quest for status is a human universal, but not only human: it is pervasive in animal societies as well. Digging down to the bedrock of motivation, evolution encompasses both animals and humans: status provides a better chance of reproduction, and that is how the drive for status survives so strongly: those who had it reproduced more successfully. Reproduction is gender asymmetric. The number of offspring for women is capped by the potential number of pregnancies. For men, however, the potential number

---

[116] Hakim, *Work-Lifestyle Choices*.

[117] Belkin, 'Opt-out Revolution', citing Williams, *Unbending Gender*.

[118] Browne, 'Sex and Temperament'; Geary, *Male, Female*; Baron-Cohen, *Essential Difference*.

[119] Information from Christine Whelan, author of 'Self-Help Books and the Quest for Self-Control'.

[120] See e.g. Baron-Cohen, *Essential Difference*, 34–58; James, *Britain on the Couch*, 178–206.

[121] Belkin, 'Opt-out Revolution'.

of offspring is a multiple of the women they can have. If status provides better access to women, it is a powerful reward for men in the currency of evolution, which is reproductive 'fitness'.

Male success in status competition is likely to increase their attractiveness to the women available. This is the logic of Darwin's 'sexual selection', of the 'Peacock's tail', grown colourful to impress the females.[122] Human tendencies sometimes find their extreme expression in institutions, and this 'winner-takes-all' relation between male status and mating went to grotesque extremes in the Ottoman Topkapi palace, and in other harems, which provided potentates with unrestricted numbers of women. For women, the evolutionary incentives are reversed. If fulfilment at work requires an investment of time, then 'economic fitness' measured in status or money is purchased at the cost of 'evolutionary fitness', i.e. time withdrawn from motherhood. These differences in strategies are detectable at the aggregate level in American demographics since the 1940s, in which male economic fitness (proxied by education) increased the number of offspring, whereas female economic fitness reduced it (above, Figure 11.5, panels (b) and (c), and Figure 11.7, panels (a) and (b)).

There is considerable overlap between men and women on most attributes: the best-performing women always perform better than some men in almost any sphere: weight, height, strength, speed. On some, like cognitive capacity, they appear to perform better overall.[123] Furthermore, as women entered the workplace, and as they pushed onto higher occupational levels, they had strong incentives to compete for success on male terms.[124]

While one section of the feminist movement has cheered women on to compete, another has stressed the differences. Carol Gilligan notably claims that women interact 'in a different voice'. Deborah Tannen's best-seller *You Don't Understand Me* reveals different gender styles of interaction, the men being more direct, competitive, self-centred; the women more accommodating and non-confrontational. In experimental settings, women have repeatedly been found to strive less hard than men.[125] The initial omission of women from the original American and British status rankings is telling.[126]

That women strive less in competition comes out in several 'natural experiments'. They are safer risks in automobile insurance, and are less involved in traffic accidents. Their participation in crime is a small fraction

---

[122] Ridley, *Red Queen*.   [123] Goldstein, *War and Gender*, ch. 7.

[124] Kohn, *No Contest*, 174–5.

[125] See ibid., ch. 8, nn. 1–4; *The Economist*, 'Be a Man'; Gneezy and Rusticini, 'Gender and Competition'; Babcock and Laschever, *Women Don't Ask*.

[126] Blau, Duncan and Tyree, *American Occupational Structure*; Goldthorpe and Hope, *Social Grading*.

of that of men, especially violent crime. The vast majority of prisoners are male. A prime source of male status is military combat, and women are almost universally absent from the ranks of active combatants in almost all societies. Given the outcomes at stake, if women had been effective combatants, in times of total mobilization this would represent a large sacrifice of fighting power. Even when women have entered the fray, as they have from time to time, their participation in combat remained problematic and peripheral. Young women are less decisive in suicide: they attempt it twice as frequently as young men, but are six times less likely to succeed. Male suicides are three times higher than female ones, and rise even higher after age 65.[127]

Women have now equalled or overtaken men at most levels of educational enrolment. They have better jobs and fewer children than before. A natural experiment is in progress: are women, in the aggregate, less keen for status success, or will they replicate men's status cravings when their ability to compete has been equalized? Is status a matter of nature or of nurture? 'Assertiveness is linked with status and male gender roles,' writes a psychologist who has studied it.[128] In a meta-analysis of studies of assertiveness scores of American college women over time, Twenge has found that men's assertiveness scores, about 0.4 of a standard deviation higher than women's in 1968, had fallen down to parity with women in 1993.[129] On this measure of assertiveness (within American college environments), women had converged on to men. Likewise, the predominance of women among initiators of divorce does not suggest timidity. So even if women may have (in the aggregate) less of an intrinsic appetite for status (which is by no means established), even if motherhood creates a heavy handicap for status competition, it would be wrong to infer that women are indifferent to status or are destined to status inferiority: witness Indira Ghandi, Golda Meir, Margaret Thatcher, strong women who reached the top of democratic politics in different countries during these breakthrough years. Even if women respond more weakly to the incentives of market status, if these incentives become strong and enticing enough, then more women will enter into status competition and more will succeed.

Conclusion

How has affluence affected status? Status is difficult to capture: measured as the aggregate distance from the bottom, the stock of occupational status

---

[127] Cutler et al., 'Youth Suicide', 9.   [128] Twenge, 'Birth Cohort', 208.
[129] Twenge, 'Changes in Women's Assertiveness', 140.

has increased. This can be seen as a success for the commitment technologies of education, which were able to transform the potential rewards of study into effective incentives for women. It is difficult to separate the rise of education from the increasing supply of more demanding and rewarding work. Both education and the experience of work have improved a great deal since the 1940s. Indeed, that may be the greatest single benefit of affluence. For men, the first two post-war decades provided upwards mobility, and full employment. After the 1970s, employment hollowed out, with most of the growth occurring at the lower and upper ends. As demand for labour tightened in the 1970s, more men abandoned work, thus moving out of the occupational status ranking altogether.

For women, the opposite was the case: paid work increased, just as it decreased for men. Women's pay rose, though did not catch up in comparison with men, largely due to the burdens of motherhood. Women entered higher levels of the occupational hierarchy, although, with larger numbers, for older women there was a slight deterioration in their overall relative occupational status position compared to men.[130] For women, education established a new equilibrium between motherhood and work. Between the 1940s and 1960s, with most women at low or lowish educational levels, motherhood was highly attractive. But as education improved, fulfilment in motherhood increasingly had to compete with fulfilment at work. And as baby boom children grew up, the cost of their educational competition, whether in house prices or college fees, encouraged mothers to go out to work even with lower educational qualifications. Younger women postponed marriage, and had fewer babies. Unlike men, at the very highest occupational levels, more than a third of women chose to forgo motherhood completely, although the remainder of highly educated women still had about as many children as other women. For most women, eventually, the commitment to education was followed by commitment to motherhood.

The majority of women chose motherhood and accepted the penalties in earning power and social ranking. We have to assume that the fulfilment of motherhood delivered something more valuable than the sacrifice it required, and that on the whole, this equilibrium has been acceptable to women. That is what the evidence indicates: as education (a proxy for earning power) increased, motherhood was postponed, but (even for the majority of highly educated women), it was not forsaken. As Figure 11.3 shows, equilibrium was established at a level of fertility (less than two

---

[130] SEI, Table 11.1, above. Pay: Blau, 'Trends', table 4, p. 129.

children per woman) that was below society's replacement rate. This contraction in the number of children and young people was storing up serious trouble for the future, when the number of workers for every retired person would be lower than ever. In placing such priority on market rewards, and in giving so little support for mothers, in imposing such sacrifices on women and compensating them so little for their investment in children, both American and British societies, were taking a myopic view of their futures. It has to be said, however, that the societies of Western Europe, with more natalist, mother-friendly, and egalitarian policies, had even lower birth rates. What kept births at higher levels in the United States and Britain was larger inequalities, and the preference of poor people for more children. This new equilibrium, which was broadly acceptable to women, was becoming more fragile, exposed to the rising risks of marriage dissolution, unemployment, and health crises. In the face of these risks, increasing numbers of men and women chose to forgo partnership and parenthood for longer and longer periods, and to plough their furrows alone.[131]

[131] For the experience of love under affluence, Chs. 13–14 below.

12

Inequality Hurts

Money

For economists, income is the prime driver of human action. Like the socio-economic index (SEI) (of which it is a component), the flow of income provides a continuous measure of interpersonal and international comparison over time, which is intuitively clear. But like status, income is also deceptive. It is difficult to measure with complete confidence, and many different measures can be used: per head or per household? Over time or in cross-section? Averaging over the poor and the rich? For all its uniformity, the same amount of money has different value for different people, depending especially on how well off they are, but also on their tastes and expectations. But for broad-brush comparison, simple is not too seriously misleading, at least as a point of departure.[1]

For an individual, if the odds are good, striving to rise is reasonable, even compelling. For society as a whole, it is more ambiguous: the winner's gain is offset by the loser's pain. But even if the stock of status cannot be increased for all, the prospect of rising is an incentive for effort, and therefore a prerequisite of affluence. To have winners, it is necessary to have losers. A lower rank is punished with less autonomy and control, stressful work, more illness, shorter lives, and greater ill-being overall. It can also be a source of mental suffering: 'If we are anguished by the thought of failure, it is because success offers the only reliable incentive for the world to grant us its goodwill.'[2] For society as a whole, the costs of losing need to be set against the benefits of affluence. The previous chapter examined the accumulation of 'advantages' under affluence, the growing stock of positive socio-economic distance from the bottom, and its impact on well-being.

---

[1] Atkinson and Bourguignon, 'Income Distribution and Economics'; Sen, 'Social Justice'.
[2] De Botton, *Status Anxiety*, 104.

Here we turn to 'complaints', the stock of distance from the top, and its impact on ill-being. This will help to judge whether society's gain can offset the individual's pain.

The most popular measure of income inequality is the Gini coefficient, which measures the deviation from a perfectly equal distribution of income within a given population. The range is zero to one. Zero is a completely equal distribution, one is a distribution where one person has everything, and everyone else nothing. A higher figure indicates more inequality. The Gini coefficient can be thought of as an index of 'complaints', i.e. disadvantages relative to the mean. The definition of the Gini coefficient is 'the average, relative to mean income, over all pairs of people in society of the absolute value of their difference in income'.[3] Taking the Gini coefficient for households over time, after 1945, during two decades of full employment and rising incomes, the level of inequality declined in some countries, and stayed level in others. Inequality levels were higher in the United States than in Britain, and comparable in Britain and in Northern Europe. But after the 1970s, inequalities in the United States began to rise quite steeply. These stylized facts are known as 'the Great U-Turn' (see Figure 12.1).[4] The Gini coefficient rose by five decimal points in the USA between 1968 and 1992 up to a level of about 0.43, and continued to rise modestly afterwards. In Britain the rise was even faster: some 10 decimal points between 1978 and 1990, to a level of about 0.34.[5] During the Thatcher years, Britain moved from the 'social-democratic' pattern of low inequality still prevailing in continental Europe, and towards levels of inequality closer to those in the United States. Even as income per head was moving upwards in both countries, so was the intensity of 'complaints', the widening gap from the top downwards. A comparison of sixteen OECD countries found that the strongest explanatory variables for rising inequality were (after excluding the size of the farming sector) declines in union density and in 'decommodification', i.e. in levels of unconditional entitlement.[6] Both of these are social-democratic markers.

How did affluence affect inequality during the post-war years? For most people in the United States and for many in Britain, the question might have been 'what affluence?' For male workers in the United States, real

---

[3] Yitzhaki, 'Relative Deprivation'; Deaton, 'Relative Deprivation', 10; Atkinson and Bourguignon, 'Income Distribution and Economics', 43.

[4] Harrison and Bluestone, *Great U-Turn*.

[5] Atkinson, 'Income Inequality', table 1, p. 33; compare Alderson and Nielsen, 'Globalization and the Great U-Turn', 1290.

[6] Alderson and Nielsen, 'Globalization and the Great U-Turn', table 6, p. 1286.

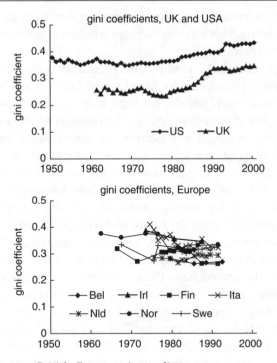

Fig. 12.1. American, British, European inequality

Note: Household Giniless coefficients (family Gini coefficients, USA).

Sources: (UK) Institute of Fiscal Studies, 'Inequality Spreadsheet'/Inequality, before housing costs, **www.ifs.org.uk/inequality/bn19figs.zip.** (USA), US Bureau of Census, **www.census. gov/hhes/income/histinc/f04.html.**
Europe: Deininger and Squire dataset, **www.worldbank.org/research/growth/dddeisqu.htm,** see Deininger and Squire, 'A New Data Set'.

wages hardly increased from *c.*1970 until the mid-1990s. It is only well above the median that any serious increases took place.[7] This should not be taken entirely at face value. For many goods, quality increased and cost fell, so deflation by the standard consumer price index may have understated the full economic value of incomes. The incomes of women rose both absolutely and relative to men, and more of them went out to work.[8] Taken overall, incomes only rose in two-earner families. But to earn that income, hours at work had to rise as well.[9] Women at home were not idle, and as they started working outside, hours spent in housework declined. Given the positive impact of satisfying work on well-being, better work

[7] Blau, 'Trends in Well-Being', table 5, p. 130; Levy, *New Dollars and Dreams,* figures 5-4, 5-6; Wolff, 'Recent Trends', table 1. [8] Blau, 'Trends in Well-Being', table 5, p. 130.
[9] Hout and Hanley, 'Overworked American Family'.

also increased fulfilment overall (though in surveys, housewives did not report themselves any less satisfied than wage-earning women). Finally, in the United States in particular, many of the additional workers at the lower end of the distribution were immigrants, legal and illegal. For immigrants, the appropriate standard of comparison might not be the host society, but the society of origin, in which case the improvements were much larger.[10]

From the early 1980s onwards, inequalities in British and American societies increased sharply, especially in comparison with Europe. Some did much better: highly educated, younger workers in managerial, professional, and highly skilled jobs, women even more than men, pulled well ahead. On top of this came a small layer of the super-affluent. Many standard measures of inequality simply leave these people out. The inequality of wealth was much greater than the inequality of income: a Gini coefficient of around 0.8 for wealth, as opposed to about 0.4 for income. In the United States in 1998, the top 1 per cent, about 1.2 million households, owned almost 40 per cent of net worth in 1998, or about $10.2 millions per household.[11]

Another approach to inequality is to study social mobility, usually from one generation to the next, i.e. differences (usually) from father to son. Up to the 1970s, these accounts were relatively optimistic.[12] If it was easy to move upwards and downwards between the generations, and if the distribution of outcomes reflected a combination of talent, effort, and luck, then the distribution of income was fundamentally just. As we have seen, the general rise in qualifications, and the structural shift to more rewarding jobs, in terms of both income and status, has greatly improved the prospects of younger workers in comparison with older ones.

More recent studies, however, have been less optimistic. For Britain and the USA, Goldthorpe and his collaborators have found little change in mobility regimes. Persistence levels in the same status category have been in the order of about 35 per cent.[13] Given the great importance of the structural change from agriculture to manufacturing, and then to services, in improving distance from the bottom overall, and the fact that educational participation and attainment continues to increase remorselessly, controlling out these effects is open to criticism.[14] More compelling, however, are recent studies in the United States, which have revised previous findings of social mobility, and have shown that persistence at the same level over

---

[10] Lerman, 'U.S. Wage-Inequality Trends'.   [11] Wolff, 'Recent Trends', tables 2–4.

[12] Marshall, *Repositioning Class*; Erikson and Goldthorpe, *Constant Flux*, 3–9.

[13] Erikson and Goldthorpe, *Constant Flux*, fig. 3.3, p. 74; Marshall et al., *Against the Odds*, table 4.2, p. 45.   [14] Noll, 'New Structures', 13.

generations is not on the order of 40 per cent, but that more than 60 per cent stay in their parents' stratum.[15]

Only the top fifth or so have experienced rising incomes since the 1970s. For the majority, as inequality increased, their relative position (in terms of income 'complaints', or distance from the top), now worsened, offsetting some of the 'advantages', the positive improvement in their socio-economic index (SEI). At the lower end of society, the numbers in poverty (measured as a distance from the median) have not fallen, and the quality of their deprivation has 'intensified'.[16] The lowest decile in the United States is much further below the median than in Europe: 'the U.S. poor are really poor'.[17] In the United States in particular, and increasingly in Britain as well, at the bottom of the social distribution there are also ethnic inequalities. The median white person had an order of magnitude (eight to ten times) more wealth than the median black. Average incomes of blacks were less than 60 per cent of white incomes; they suffered more on every measure of deprivation.[18] At the bottom of American society, American affluence was of little avail: 'the wider degree of income inequality found in America offsets its overall wealth to such a degree that low income Americans have a standard of living below those found in almost all other rich nations.'[19]

Absolute and relative income

In standard economic theory, what counts primarily is the absolute level of income. From the point of view of status, however, what counts is not how much you have, but how much more it is than the other person.[20] It has long been suspected that 'relative income', i.e. having more than others, counts more in people's motivation than 'absolute income', i.e. the absolute quantity of goods one can buy.[21] Experiments at Harvard have been suggestive. A small majority of students in an experiment there chose a

[15] Stokey, 'Shirtsleeves to Shirtsleeves'; Bowles and Gintis, 'Inheritance of Inequality'; Mazumder, 'Analyzing Income Mobility'.

[16] Osberg and Sharpe, 'Human Well-being', 44–5, for definition of poverty intensity.

[17] Alesina et al., 'Why Doesn't the United States', 201.

[18] Wealth, Wolff, 'Recent Trends'; Income, US Census Historical Income Tables, Tables P1a–b, **www.census.gov/hhes/income/histinc/p01b.html**; more detail, Oliver and Shapiro, *Black Wealth*; Shapiro, *Hidden Cost*.

[19] Smeeding, 'American Income Inequality', 29.

[20] Hollander, 'Utility Statements'; Frank, *Choosing the Right Pond*.

[21] Duesenberry, *Income, Saving*; Easterlin, 'Does Economic Growth'; id., 'Raising the Incomes of All'.

lower absolute income closer to the top of the income distribution, in preference to a higher absolute income, lower down a different income distribution.[22] At the level of international comparison, in affluent societies, as average incomes have risen over time, they have had little impact on average levels of 'happiness', or more precisely, on reported subjective well-being.[23] Large studies over two or three decades between the 1970s and the 1990s, with controls for attributes such as income, employment situation, education and family condition, have confirmed that subjective well-being in developed countries is at best stagnant, and at worst declining slightly.[24] Within each country, however, a higher income had a strong positive effect on well-being.[25] In the United States, moving from the lowest to the highest quartile could raise satisfaction or subjective well-being about as much as getting married or coming out of unemployment, the most powerful sources of happiness when income is controlled.[26] In Britain, this particular relative income effect was much weaker: only about two-thirds of the divorce/separation effect, and only about a quarter of the unemployment effect. Relative standing counted for less in Europe than in the United States.[27] Relative income was also a source of satisfaction in the United States, with the reference effects stronger upwards ('advantages') than downwards ('complaints').[28]

Relative income is beginning to attract some close attention, and has given rise to interesting methodological conundrums.[29] On the whole, other studies have found that a linear or step-wise measure of well-being is sound, and that *within* countries, income is quite a robust determinant of well-being. In the single study which controls for individual attributes ('personal unobservable fixed effects'), the size of the income effect is reduced almost to nothing—but that is only saying that people differ considerably on how much income matters to them.[30]

One study failed to find an improvement in subjective well-being among the same individuals who had raised their income between two points in time over ten years.[31] This finding, however, is consistent with the work of Easterlin, who finds that people adjust to an increase in

[22] Solnick and Hemenway, 'Is More Always Better?', 378–80; Frank, *Luxury Fever*, chs. 8–9.
[23] Above, Ch. 2.   [24] Blanchflower and Oswald, 'Well-Being over Time'.
[25] Easterlin, 'Does Economic Growth'; id., 'Raising the Incomes of All'.
[26] Above, Ch. 2, Table 2.2.
[27] Blanchflower and Oswald, 'Well-Being over Time', inferred from table 7, p. 1376.
[28] Ibid. 1375–8.
[29] Hollander, 'Utility Statements'; McBride, 'Relative-Income Effects'; Ferrer-I-Carbonell and Frijters, 'How Important is Methodology?'
[30] Ferrer-I-Carbonell and Frijters, 'How Important is Methodology?'
[31] Diener et al., 'Income and Subjective Well-Being', 201–12.

income by raising their aspirations to match, thus remaining on a 'hedonic treadmill'.[32]

Relative and absolute income have been estimated separately within countries.[33] But apart from rough 'eyeballing' estimates this has not been done between countries, on larger numbers.[34] There is one study with negative findings (no relative effect for income), but the population surveyed was college students, a very distinctive and narrow social group, typically outside the workforce, and already enjoying elite status in most countries.[35] It has already been noted that intrinsic attributes of individuals explain most of the variance of well-being,[36] and the same appears to be true of different countries.

This is brought out by our own study of relative and absolute income at the country level. Reported subjective well-being is widely accepted as a robust measure in psychology and sociology, and is gaining ground in economics. Despite the initial doubts of economists about interpersonal comparisons of well-being, treating it as a linear cardinal variable (each interval having the same value), or as an ordinal one (categories can only be greater or smaller than each other), does not seem to matter very much.[37] We have chosen to explain the percentage in each social group that reports itself to be 'very happy'. This provides a continuous measure which allows simple and meaningful estimation with OLS, and also a good deal of variance between different groups domestically, and between countries internationally.

The study confirms that absolute income appears to have had very little effect on subjective well-being, once relative social position was taken into account. We have taken a large sample of countries with large differences in the absolute levels of affluence, but with comparable ordinal social distances, namely being in the bottom third or the top third of the income distribution, relative to the middle third.[38] The comparison is of countries rather than individuals. The results are shown in Table 12.1. The World Values Survey is an international comparative survey which was carried out internationally in four waves between the early 1980s and 2001 and which covered many countries using comparable methods. Using this

[32] Easterlin, 'Income and Happiness'.

[33] Blanchflower and Oswald, 'Well-Being over Time'; McBride, 'Relative-Income Effects'.

[34] Easterlin, 'Does Economic Growth'; Helliwell, 'How's Life?' (2003), uses the World Values Survey to estimate the determinants of well-being, but his categorical measures of income do not capture relative income.   [35] Diener et al., 'Income and Subjective Well-Being', 212–21.

[36] Ferrer-I-Carbonell and Frijters, 'How Important is Methodology?'.

[37] Ibid.; Blanchflower and Oswald, 'Well-Being over Time'.

[38] The analysis was undertaken jointly with Matthew Polisson.

Table 12.1. Effect of relative and absolute income on 'happiness'
Dependent variable: percentage of population describing themselves as 'very happy'

	Coeff.	t-stat	Probability
Income in upper third	1.94	2.15	0.035
Income in lower third	−4.33	−5.55	0.000
Average income	0.0001013	2.54	0.013
Constant	23.18	11.05	0.000
No. of Countries	40		
Adjusted R^2	0.96		
Mean percentage 'very happy'	26.06		

Notes: Omitted country: Israel. Reference income: middle third (percentage very happy, 26.2). This is a comparison of countries, not of individuals within them. A complete table with list of countries can be found in Appendix 12A, Table 12A.1, below. Matthew Polisson has made a valuable contribution to this research.

Sources: Data acquired from 'World Values and European Values Surveys, 1999–2001', through the UK Data Archive (**www.data-archive.ac.uk**). Information about the survey can be found at **http://worldvaluessurvey.org**.

survey, national populations were divided into 'lower', 'moderate', and 'higher' incomes, each group containing about a third of the population surveyed. The average absolute income of each group was calculated from the national surveys in purchasing-power-parity dollars (ppp), as well as the percentage in each group who reported themselves as being 'very happy'. The original questionnaires differ in local detail. A subset of countries was selected whose questionnaires were tractable and where the income data appeared to be robust.[39] The findings reported here are for the wave of 1999–2001. The numbers surveyed were at least 1,000 per country.

The reference observation is the middle third in Israel. The coefficients are to be interpreted as the positive or negative deviation from this reference observation (Israel, middle third of income groups, 26.2 per cent 'very happy'). These coefficients should be taken as comparisons of countries, not of individuals. Absolute levels of income within each group (the variable 'Average Income') had only a very small effect on the proportion reporting that they are 'very happy'. The coefficient was 0.0001013. What this means is that in order to increase the proportion reporting 'very happy' by one percentage point (say from 28 per cent in India to 29 per cent), it would be necessary to increase income by $9,781. At the time, the middle group in India was earning an average of $5,262. Controlling for the level of absolute income, being in the upper third of the income distribution increased the proportion 'very happy' by about 1.9 percentage points, and being in the lower third reduced it by about 4.3 percentage points from the reference point of 26.2 (percentage saying they were 'very happy' in the

[39] The full results are reported in Appendix 12A, below.

'middle third' in Israel). So the difference between the 'lower third' and 'upper third' was about 6.2 percentage points, around a reference of 26.2 percentage points. Once relative and absolute incomes are controlled for, all the other differences among populations are captured by the 'country' variable. This ranges very widely, from 7.6 per cent 'very happy' in Lithuania, to 61.9 in Mexico (the full regression is reported in Appendix 12A, at the end of this chapter). The 'country effect' (where you live) on the proportion 'very happy' was much stronger than the 'relative income' effect (where you are in the social system). In the great majority of cases, the 'country' variable is significant, and overall 96 per cent of the variance is explained. Finally, the 'complaint' of being in the bottom third is more than two times as large as the 'advantage' of being in the top third. Pain was felt twice as strongly as gain.

Consumption and status

Pursuing Happiness is the title of one study of American consumption in the twentieth century. Previous chapters considered in detail the rewards of eating, of household appliances, and of automobiles. Affluence is a flow of ever-cheaper benefits. Something as mundane as artificial light is several orders of magnitude less costly than two centuries ago.[40] Electronic communication is all-pervasive and cheap. Air travel is easy, eating out is very common, clothing is cheaper.[41] Everyone watches television, makes a phone call, listens to recorded music. Leisure is no longer so constrained by indigence. Consumption has risen about threefold in real terms in the United States since 1950, and the cost of living indices probably overstate the cost of many goods. As prices change, consumers change over to other goods and to cheaper outlets. More importantly, quality also changes, usually for the better, new products are introduced, while older ones fade away.

The delights of the pub, the cinema, the ability to eat out occasionally, to make a statement by means of clothing or make-up; the freedom to drive a car, to listen to radio and watch television, to hear and collect recorded music, and to surf the internet, have all worked to equalize everyday experience, and no longer serve so well to provide 'distinction'. But extending supply has also extended desires, and the gap of aspiration remains open.[42]

---

[40] Nordhaus, 'History of Lighting'; though one can have too much lighting.
[41] Majima, 'Fashion and the Mass Consumer Society'.
[42] Easterlin, 'Income and Happiness'.

In the past, for example, high status could be signalled by means of distinctive, expensive, and elaborate clothing. Under affluence, that signal has lost most of its power: it is too easy to fake. Although expensive suits are still used to advantage in local interactions, they cannot be expensive or distinctive enough to demarcate large social boundaries such as those between city dwellers and peasants, or desk workers versus manual workers, as used to be the case in the past and is still the case in poor countries. On state occasions watched by millions on television, the American President and British Prime Minister have discarded expensive formal dress in favour of informality.

To be credible, a good signal needs to be costly. There is a whole world of pseudo-luxury: almost every category of good has a premium brand.[43] Quite apart from any real quality difference, their advertising suggests that they should be used to signal distinction (if only to the purchaser herself). But widely diffused consumer goods confer distinction only temporarily, if at all. In his 1959 classic *The Status Seekers*, Vance Packard devoted only one short chapter (out of twenty-four) to 'shopping for status'. Only at the more costly end of cars and housing is consumption a prime means of signalling status.

As incomes have risen, consumption has moved away from necessities. Brown has investigated American living standards between 1918 and 1988.[44] Her study used consumer expenditure surveys, and investigated the differences between unskilled, skilled, and salaried workers, covering approximately the three middle quintiles of the American income distribution. She divided outlays into 'basic', 'variety', and 'status' categories. 'Basic' expenditures provided a standard quality of subsistence commodities, food, shelter, fuel, etc. 'Variety' extended the quantity and choice of consumption goods at basic quality, whereas 'status' applied to spending on higher-class categories of the same commodity.[45] These distinctions are to some extent arbitrary, but they are consistent throughout. The results are summarized in Figure 12.2. It shows that from the 1930s onwards, 'basic needs' have contracted consistently, and that spending has been becoming increasingly discretionary. As income increased, and people moved up the social scale, ever more expenditure was devoted to 'status', i.e. higher-priced goods in the same category.

What this figure indicates is that in 1973 and 1988, the American 'middle class', skilled workers and salaried ones, were laying out between a

[43] Twitchell, *Living it up*.   [44] Brown, *American Standards*.
[45] The distinction between variety and status is considered in detail above, in Ch. 9, with regard to motor cars.

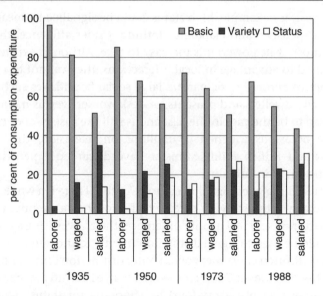

Fig. 12.2. Consumption expenditure, by spending category and occupational status, USA 1935–1988(%)

Source: Calculated from C. Brown, *American Living Standards*, table 8.2, p. 467.

fifth and a third of their expenditures on status signalling. This suggests that status is a 'local', rather than global attribute: these expenditures helped to maintain social standing within a limited social range, and were unlikely to carry any competitive value with higher consumption groups, who spend a larger share of a larger income on maintaining their own status. A salaried worker might buy a new Ford car, and get ahead of Jones, who was running an old one; but he was unlikely to compete for status with a wealthy businessman driving a new BMW or a Porsche. As a higher proportion of consumption was devoted to status display, social standing became more vulnerable to fluctuations in income. This also suggests that at the highest income levels, in the top quintile, not to mention that highest 5 or 1 per cent, a much higher proportion of expenditure was devoted to signalling status.

If one takes the view that status is about competition for top places, then much of this competition is self-defeating, since only a few can win.[46] Another view is that the purpose of status spending is to increase distance from the bottom (increasing 'advantages') or to reduce distance from the top (reduce 'complaints'). Considered this way, the pursuit of status is

---

[46] Hirsch, *Social Limits*; Frank and Cook, *Winner-Takes-All Society*.

psychologically rewarding at all levels, improvements are always within reach, small increments are eminently worthwhile. Status also provides a psychologically credible and rational driver for the pursuit of affluence. But signals need to be scarce and costly in order to confer status credibly. Hence a rising share of resources goes into status signalling as affluence rises, and the expense of signalling status at the very highest levels increases to compete at the very top of the income distribution, Chief Executive Officer 'compensation' as a multiple of average worker pay rose more than tenfold, from 41 in 1960, to 531 in 2000.[47]

If the main purpose of affluence is to provide a sense of social attainment, then it can be done far more efficiently by economizing on the cost of the signals, and by rationing scarcity. The academic world does this with titles and pecking orders (such as the titles of 'Reader' in British universities, or 'Titular Professor' at Oxford, which provide promotion without salary enhancement). British governments do it with medals, knighthoods, and peerages. There is a long-standing tradition of luxury taxes, and a 10 per cent tax on expensive cars, boats, aircraft, furs, and jewellery was introduced in the United States as recently as 1991. Such a tax does nothing to diminish the status value of conspicuous consumption. Robert Frank goes one better with a suggestion of a progressive consumption tax: as the share of luxuries rose in consumption, the tax would only diminish the economic resources used to signal status, without reducing the satisfactions they gave. This is not very different from a progressive income tax, with savings exempted.[48]

When measuring inequality, economists tend to focus on the input, which is income, or on output, the preferences revealed by consumption. The existence of 'premium brands' and luxuries suggest that people are heterogeneous, and that they differ substantially in the benefits that afflu-ence confers on them. For vendors, a great deal is at stake in understanding how people respond to goods, and what needs these goods can fulfil. Since the 1950s there has developed a twilight social science designed to elicit a human hierarchy based on needs, and expressed in lifestyles, and ultimately, in consumption preferences. This activity goes under the name of 'psycho-graphics', and is largely carried out by specialized market research firms. The business is thriving, which is a vindication of sorts. An influential statement of psychographics is Arnold Mitchell's *Nine American Lifestyles* (1983). Its roots are in the therapeutic culture that goes back to Freud, and in the human potential movement which achieved considerable purchase

[47] Hartman, 'Income Patterns'.
[48] Frank, *Luxury Fever*, chs. 13–15; similar ideas, Layard, *Happiness*, 150–6.

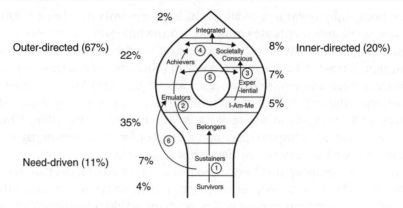

Fig. 12.3. The nine American lifestyles

Note: This diagram conveys the flavour of the psychographic approach, but the precise categories are no longer used by the SRI organization. For changes in analysis and terminology, see Whelan, 'Self-Help Books', ch. 2.

Source: Mitchell, *Nine American Lifestyles*, 46, 63.

in American society by the 1970s and 1980s, which in its self-indulgence and projection of anxiety can also be regarded as a product of affluence.[49]

The American Dream is dynamic, a progressive story of improvement and growth. This is captured in Mitchell's model, which was based on a large survey. Mitchell described a hierarchy of needs orientations, which was neatly expressed in a dynamic diagram, moving upwards from survival and caring, towards emulation, achievement, and personal integration (Figure 12.3). The categories are self-explanatory, the numbers are estimates of population shares.

Psychographics has become a mainstream approach to marketing, and a variety of 'psychographic' schemes are available from commercial vendors.[50] It provides a key to classifying goods and their target customers. It is not hard science: the flux of tastes, preferences, goods, and commercial competition is too complex to be fixed down. But it is suggestive of the range of needs that emerge under affluence.

Housing is the prime example of positional, aspirational goods. The price of such goods does not decline with affluence. Between the 1950s and the 1970s, housing displaced food as the largest single component of consumption expenditure for middling consumers.[51] The phrase 'wrong

[49] Bellah et al., *Habits of the Heart*; Wolfe, 'The Me Decade'; Whelan, 'Self-help Books'.

[50] Gunter and Furnham, *Consumer Profiles*; Kahle and Chiagouris, *Values, Lifestyles and Psychographics*; Liu, 'Reading the Minds of Consumers'.

[51] Brown, *American Standards of Living*.

side of the tracks' conveys this role of housing as a signal of social standing. Housing quality and location is the prime indicator of consumption orientation used by psychographic marketers.[52] Historically, housing is a 'normal', even a 'superior' good, of which more is consumed with higher incomes. But owning a house was not merely a matter of social aspiration.[53] For families with children it was a necessity. With most homes owner occupied, for white people of the working class, gaining access to a reasonable school, and raising children in a safe neighbourhood made it necessary to buy a home.

The actual cost of housing is not easy to measure. It depends on many factors, e.g. housing tenure, house prices, interest rates, demographic composition, location, housing quality, etc. There are two basic approaches: one is to measure spending on rents and to impute a rental value to owner occupation. The other is to measure changes in house prices. Using the rental measure, the share of housing costs as a proportion of total consumption increased by about one-third in the UK between 1963 and 2000, while appearing to remain virtually level in the USA (without controlling for quality).[54] In fact, the cost of housing in the USA increased in real terms between the 1970s and the 1990s, at a time when median male earnings were stagnant. Earnings only kept up with house prices because mothers went out to work. For those who were able to take part and stay the course, this was a considerable success: housing quality rose as well. Taking price as a measure, house *prices* have broadly kept up with income in both the United States and Britain.[55] Both countries, however, have had intense house price frenzies, which were usually localized. The UK, for example, has had three such frenzies, around 1973, 1987–8, and in the late 1990s, all of them focused most intensely on the south-east of the country. Likewise in the United States, house prices have risen in line with incomes, except in a number of 'glamour markets', on the East and West Coast. In these 'hot spots' house price percentage increases could be in two figures for several years running.[56]

With more inequality and with more family breakdowns, as house prices kept up with earnings, or bounded sharply ahead, status became that

[52] Goss, 'We Know Who You Are'.   [53] Ch. 11 above.

[54] United States President, *Economic Report of the President 2000*, table B-16, with virtually no change between 1963 and 2001, at 15.1 per cent; UK, ONS, Housing Consumption Expenditure as Percentage of Total Consumption (Housing, Water, Electricity and Gas), series ADFS. The rise in the share of housing costs in the UK was about 37 per cent, to 18.1 per cent, between 1983 and 2003.

[55] Case and Shiller, 'Is there a Bubble'; Muellbauer and Murphy, 'Booms and Busts'.

[56] Case and Shiller, ibid.; Muellbauer, ibid.

much more precarious. For most of the population, things became worse: the cost of housing rose in real terms, while median incomes levelled off. For the majority, holding on to their housing status became a struggle. For families, this required both parents going to work.[57] Once a sufficient proportion of mothers had gone to work, house prices responded to the rise in family incomes. Stay-at-home parents (mostly mothers) found it difficult to compete for houses against two-earner families. And single-parent households found median-quality housing mostly beyond their reach.

One measure of housing status was whether income was sufficient to cover the cost of a 'standard' thirty-year mortgage. In the United States, most two-earner married couples could afford such a house. But becoming a one-earner family, or a single parent, pushed a median house beyond affordability for the vast majority of such households in the USA (Table 12.2). The table also shows how in Britain the rise in house prices pushed home ownership increasingly out of the reach of new buyers. Between the mid-1980s and 2001, the number of couples unable to buy their first dwelling increased from about one-half, to two-thirds.

Both in Britain and the USA, the shift into two-earner families coincided with liberalization of financial markets. Competing for positional status, for their children and themselves, parents were encouraged to take greater financial risks. Before the 1970s, credit had been rationed, regulated, and tightly controlled. Liberalization made it much easier to borrow and relaxed the upper limits on debt. For example, in the USA, the Equal Credit Opportunity Act of 1974 allowed wives' incomes to be taken into account

Table 12.2. Percentage unable to buy housing, 1980s, 1990s

	USA				UK		
	Cannot afford to buy median house				New households unable to buy		
	Married couple	Male parent	Female parent	All renters	East Midl.	London	Total
1984	40.1	65.8	82.6	91.3			
1986–91					35.4	82.4	54.2
1991	42.2	67.8	83.9	91.2			
1995	42.2	73.2	84.5	93.3			
1997					36.4	77.5	50.4
2001					59.8	79.8	66.4

Note: Affordability 'using conventional, thirty-year, fixed mortgage financing'.

Sources: USA, Census, 'Housing Affordability 1995', Table 4.1, www.census.gov/hhes/www/housing/hsgaffrd/afford95/af95t41.html. UK, Bramley, 'Affordability', table 2, p. 6.

---

[57] Edwards, 'Home Ownership'; Edwards, 'Uncertainty'.

in mortgage lending.[58] In consequence, house prices became much more volatile, at a time when employment became less secure as well. In the 1980s in Britain, real house price increases reached 20 per cent a year during boom years, and then fell sharply in the early 1990s. Liberalization and volatility gave rise to greater uncertainty.[59] During the 1980s housing repossessions began to rise, and the liberalization of mortgage lending gave rise to sharp 'mis-selling' practices on a massive scale, which eventually led government to intervene and require the lenders to compensate many of the borrowers.[60] In south-east England, house prices were driven upwards by the high earnings in this very same liberalized financial industry. In the United States, the relative size of mortgage debts in relation to consumption expenditure rose from 49 to 84 per cent between 1950 and 2000, while personal savings rates have dropped down almost to zero.[61] Housing maintained and indeed improved its position as a tax-free store of value (which exacerbated housing 'bubbles'). However (and apart from bequests), for society as a whole there was little or no gain from rising prices: it was mainly a transfer from the young to the old, since any welfare gains to the sellers were cancelled out by welfare losses to purchasers.[62] For about one-third of households the ladder was out of reach, and they were left ever further behind.

After the Second World War, British governments invested massively in public housing, an investment which drained off the worst of a century's accumulated slums. By the time the project peaked in the mid-1960s, it was moving out of favour, due to high cost, technological problems, and increasing social stigma.[63] Under Thatcher, government stopped the construction of public housing, and sold off the best of the accumulated stock, tearing a big hole in the housing safety net which had started to secure a reasonable quality of housing. It also withdrew the welfare entitlement to mortgage payment support in case of unemployment (though an entitlement to 'housing benefit' for rented housing remained, and local authorities were still obliged to find accommodation for homeless families). By the 1990s, more than half of all new households were unable to buy a house, and some four-fifths in London. Middle-income professionals, including skilled public sector workers, teachers, lecturers, nurses, policemen, could

---

[58] Edwards, 'Home Ownership'.
[59] Compare British and American house price trends, Meen, 'Time-Series Behavior', fig. 1c, p. 4.
[60] Böheim and Taylor, 'My Home was my Castle'.
[61] United States President, *Economic Report of the President, 2000*, table B-16. Housing equity was partly a substitute for savings, but was vulnerable to the high risk of divorce.
[62] Bajari et al., 'House Prices'.   [63] Harold Carter, 'Life and Death of Old Labour'.

no longer afford to buy houses in the most affluent towns and cities in the south-east.[64] Housing market inequalities might have piled up 'advantages' at the top, but they piled up 'complaints' at the bottom.

Status and health

Social ranking is a matter of life and death. The gradient of income is a gradient of health: the higher up the ladder of income, occupation, or status, the longer the expectation of life, and the less the probability of ill-ness. This presents another of the paradoxes of affluence: as affluence has increased overall, health has improved, and life expectation has risen for everyone. But as inequality has risen as well, the differences in health between the best off and the worst off have opened up as well, so that while absolute health has improved overall, health relative to others (i.e. health 'complaints') has worsened.

The relation between mortality and income goes back to the Victorian origins of urbanization. It was observed with renewed force at the end of the demographic and epidemiological transitions to small, long-lived fam-ilies, which took place in the United States and Britain from the end of the nineteenth century up until the 1940s. In the 1960s, it was first noted that life expectancy and health depended strongly on income. In a given year men earning more than $10,000 a year were 77 per cent less likely to die than those earning $2,000. A college education also conferred strong protection.[65] In Britain, the appropriately named 'Black Report' of 1978 showed that an unskilled man was almost twice as likely to die during adulthood (age 15–64) as a professional.[66] By the 1990s, the gap had widened further.[67] Life expectation rose for everyone, but more at the top than at the bottom: social differentials widened. At birth, life expectation for unskilled male workers in 1972–6 was 5.5 years shorter than for male professionals, and 9.5 years shorter thirty years later. Unskilled workers had gained an absolute 'advantage' of about 1.7 years over three decades, but their 'complaint', or disadvantage, increased by four years during the same period compared with professionals and managers.[68] Death and sickness differences could be found in class, income, occupation, and education.[69] English men under 65

---

[64] *Labour Research*, 'Unaffordable Housing'; Böheim and Taylor, 'My Home was my Castle'.
[65] Kitagawa and Hauser, *Differential Mortality*.
[66] Great Britain, Working Group on Inequalities in Health, *Black Report*, e.g. table 7, p. 59.
[67] Acheson, *Report*.   [68] Gordon et al., 'NHS Allocation Review', table 1.3, p. 9.
[69] Wilkinson, *Unhealthy Societies*, 53; Eibner and Evans, 'Relative Deprivation', and refer-ences, 6–7.

who rented their houses from local authorities (about 20 per cent), or, alternatively, had no cars, were more than 50 per cent more likely to die than owners of cars or houses.[70]

The difference was not merely binary, between top and bottom. It was continuous and roughly linear. A large longitudinal study of British civil servants showed a gradient of rising risk of mortality and illness from the top downwards, with a higher risk at every step down the occupational ladder. Such differences are also found in international comparisons. A similar domestic health gradient is almost universally observed in different countries, and even within rather narrow segments in egalitarian countries. It exists, for example, between holders of doctorates, professional degrees, and first-degree graduates in Sweden.[71] Between countries, mortality is curvilinear, (or 'concave') in income: an increment of income at the bottom raises life expectation much more than the same increment at the top.[72] What counts is a percentage change in income, not an absolute increase. Very high levels of life expectation, comparable or better than the richest countries, have been achieved by countries with quite moderate incomes. The United States, the richest country in most years, was recently ranked twenty-eighth in life expectation at birth, while the UK, at 70 per cent of USA income, was one rank higher, below such countries as Israel (53 per cent of USA income per head), Greece (41 per cent), and even Costa Rica (12 per cent).[73] Another implication is that 'income loss appears to have a much stronger effect on health than increases in income'.[74] Whatever causes the gradient of health and mortality in income is largely an internal matter within societies, rather than one of comparison between them.

The inverse relation of health and income is a Big Fact, but there is some disagreement about its source. On the face of it, differences in personal income alone might account for differences in health. Obesity, smoking, risk-taking, accidents, homicide, suicide—the likelihood of all of these increases as income declines.[75] These are all impulsive or addictive behaviours, which place immediate payoffs ahead of any future ones. They reflect the uncertain tomorrows and thin rewards faced by the poor.[76] At age 15, the average American teenager has a three-to-one chance of reaching the age of 65. For a black teenager, it is only one in three.[77] The

---

[70] Gordon et al., 'NHS Allocation Review', table 1.4, p. 10.

[71] Marmot, *Status Syndrome*, chs. 2–3.

[72] Ibid. Also Duleep, 'Mortality and Income Inequality'.   [73] Above, Ch. 2, Figure 2.3.

[74] Judge and Paterson, 'Poverty, Income Inequality', 23.

[75] Eibner and Evans, 'Relative Deprivation', 20.   [76] See above, Ch. 4.

[77] Marmot, *Status Syndrome*, 68.

trade-off between e.g. smoking and lung cancer appears very different to a white teenager than to a black one.

If income alone can explain differences in health, then the increase in inequality is sufficient to 'explain' the rising health gap. It creates more 'poor' people, i.e. people below some normative poverty line, often expressed as some percentage of the median income. Explaining health outcomes in terms of personal income alone is attractive to economists: it is parsimonious, and it privileges the individual decision maker and his incentives, which are at the core of economic theory. And if inequalities are necessary to provide strong incentives, then so be it.[78] But it also follows from the familiar curvilinear (concave) relation between health and income ('diminishing health increments to income') that raising the income of the poorest by taking from the rich (other things being equal) would provide a substantial improvement in public health.

Public health specialists reach for explanations beyond mere income. They assume several layers of causation, starting perhaps with the individual, and extending through family, community, society, and economy.[79] International comparisons immediately suggest that income alone is inadequate as a cause. 'In 1996, black American men had a median income of $26,522 and a life expectancy of only 66.1 years. Men in Costa Rica had a mean income (at purchasing power parity) of only $6,410, yet their life expectancy was 75 years. Four times the real income bought a life expectancy of nine years less.'[80]

This kind of finding has given rise to the 'psychosocial' interpretation of the influence of ranking: what causes the health gradient is not differences in income as such. Income is merely a proxy. It is the pain of inferiority, frustration, lack of autonomy and control which adversely affect the immune system and lead to greater illness, and to shorter lives: that status 'complaints' are sufficiently stressful in themselves to generate ill-health and extra mortality, over and above the effects of income.[81] Animals don't have any 'income', and yet in troops of baboons, social subordination is associated with poor health.[82] Subordinate vervet monkeys are 'unhappier' (have lower Serotonin levels).[83] Closer to home, the 'Whitehall' longitudinal study of the illness records and life expectations of civil servants in the UK has shown that rank is by far the best predictor of ill-being: there were

[78] Quah, 'Growth and Distribution'.   [79] Acheson, *Report*, fig. 1.
[80] Marmot and Wilkinson, 'Psychosocial and Material Pathways', 1235.
[81] Wilkinson, *Unhealthy Societies*, chs. 3–4; Marmot, *Status Syndrome*; Marmot and Wilkinson, 'Psychosocial and Material Pathways'.
[82] Sapolsky, 'Hypercortisolism'.
[83] James, *Britain on the Couch*, 34–6; McGuire and Troisi, *Darwinian Psychiatry*, 92–7, 172–6.

fourfold increases in the incidence of heart disease between senior and junior civil servants, and threefold differences in death rates. Even controlling for lifestyle risks like smoking and body weight, every step down the hierarchy involved a big increase in sickness, and a large shortening of life expectation.[84] None of these workers was indigent: all could satisfy basic needs, and well beyond. What differentiated them was the degree of control and subordination at work.

Within the United States, levels of inequality in American states predict differential mortality between the states.[85] Comparing different societies, what counted for life expectation was not the absolute level of income, it was argued, but the levels of inequality. High levels of inequality posed serious risks to those at the bottom. The causes of death most strongly related to income distribution were social causes such as alcohol-related deaths, homicide, and accidents. More recent work has indicated that 'complaints' or 'relative deprivation' are more important than income in explaining the health gradient:

High relative deprivation increases the probability of dying in all age groups and for those death categories with a high behavioral component. Those with high relative deprivation are more likely to self-report poor health, have high blood pressure or disabilities, and have a host of poor health habits including smoking, not wearing safety belts, high body mass index and not exercising. For nearly all health measures, our results suggest that much of the observed statistical relationship between absolute level of income and health found in previous work is actually measuring the impacts of relative deprivation on health.[86]

But the 'psychosocial' hypothesis that the stresses of inequality are sufficient to generate large health differences has been questioned on the basis of research in advanced countries beyond the United States. After individual differences in income (and sometimes education and initial health states as well) are controlled for statistically (and when income is measured on a comparable basis) then inequality as such is only a weak influence.[87] There is however one large exception to this finding, which is the United States. This is also captured well in gross measures. The United States has for long periods been at the very top of the range for income per head, as well as for medical expenditure per head, both absolutely and in relative terms. It is also the most unequal of the large developed countries. Out of thirteen such countries, the United States ranked an average twelfth

[84] Marmot, 'Social Differences'.
[85] e.g. Kaplan et al., 'Inequality in Income'; Kennedy et al., 'Income Distribution'.
[86] Eibner and Evans, 'Relative Deprivation', 1.
[87] Judge and Patterson, 'Poverty, Income Inequality and Health'.

(one up from the bottom) for sixteen available indicators, ahead only of Germany. This included thirteenth (last) for years of potential lives lost, and tenth for age-adjusted mortality.[88] In 2000, a detailed international comparison of health systems found the USA number one in spending, but only fifteenth in goal attainment ranking; the UK, no. 26 in spending per capita, was ranked ninth in overall goal attainment.[89]

The issue has received close and very expert scrutiny. Using relentlessly statistical approaches it is argued that income inequality as such is not an independent factor in the mortality gradient. For the United States, for example, Deaton has found that income inequality (defined in terms of a relative deprivation model) explains the mortality gradient overall, but does not explain differences between American states. The contradiction is resolved with a finding that the inequality does not affect mortality once regressions are controlled for the proportions of blacks in the population (mortality of whites as well as blacks).[90] This finding conveys the flavour of the argument: 'There is no robust correlation between life expectancy and income inequality among the rich countries, and the correlation across the states and cities of the United States is almost certainly the result of something that is correlated with income inequality, but that is not income inequality itself.' In the United States, it might be noted, black males (at the bottom of the social hierarchy) had a life expectancy at birth 6.8 years shorter than white males. The finding is meant to be statistical rather than substantive. Deaton warns that it does not deny the importance of the social environment for individual health.[91]

The 'income' and 'psychosocial' approaches may be reconciled if it is accepted that low income is correlated with other, unmeasured attributes of society. In Canada, for example, or Sweden, countries almost as affluent as the United States, the relation between inequality and mortality is absent. It is reasonable to deduce that the presence of a welfare state provides a safety net which limits the most extreme afflictions of deprivation, indigence, and despair in the context of an affluent society.[92] The International Labour Organization has ranked countries on an 'Economic Insecurity Index'.[93] The United States, the richest country, ranks far from the top, at number 25, comparable to its rank in life expectation. Advocates of the American model would argue that heightened uncertainty is a

---

[88] Starfield, 'Really the Best', 483.
[89] World Health Organization, *World Health Report 2000*, Annex table 1, pp. 154–5.
[90] Deaton, 'Relative Deprivation'; Deaton, 'Health, Inequality', 149.
[91] Deaton, 'Health, Inequality', 151.
[92] See Lynch, 'Income Inequality and Mortality'.   [93] ILO, *Economic Security*.

Table 12.3. The impact of economic insecurity on life expectation, *c.*2000, ninety countries

Dependent variable = life expectation at birth

		t-stat
Intercept	49.65	24.20
Economic Security Index (1-100)(Coeff.)	0.41	7.56
Real GDP per head (Coeff.)	−0.00	−1.07
Adjusted R^2	0.58	
Observations	90	
Mean Life Expectation	67.8	
Mean ESI	46.6	

Sources: (*a*) Economic Security Index: ILO, *Economic Security*, appendix B8.
(*b*) GDP per head, life expectation at birth, *World Development Indicators*.

condition of prosperity. But John Ruskin has argued 'there is no wealth but life'. The test is not prosperity for some, but prosperity for all. On this test, American prosperity fails to deliver. The economic insecurity index is highly correlated with life expectation ($r = 0.76$). Table 12.3 shows that in a sample of ninety countries around 2000, life expectation at birth was 67.8. With the Economic Security Index (ESI) scaled between 1 and 100, for every increase of the index by 1, life expectation at birth increased by an additional 0.41 of a year. Income per head (what competition is supposed to maximize) had no impact at all on life expectation. Surveys in Europe have shown that job security is by far the largest (positive) influence on job satisfaction,[94] but a separate calculation of the ILO data shows that the Economic Security Index could not explain any of the variance in average subjective well-being ('happiness') among countries, suggesting that insecurity can be a source of stress, but also one of the attributes of the environment that people get used to.

Social capital consists of the non-governmental resources of community and family available to people on the basis of reciprocity: a measure of wealth in the 'economy of regard'. Those states in the USA with a lower proportion of ethnic diversity also appear to have a higher level of social capital, and to be more protective of their citizens, rather like the welfare states of Europe.[95] Consequently, in advanced countries outside the USA, all of whom are more equal in economic outcomes, and all of whom have some form of universal medical coverage, there is no statistical link between mortality and inequality. It is simplistic to use a sample of Swedish communities to test for the effect of inequality on mortality, however

[94] Blanchflower and Oswald, 'Well-being, Insecurity', p. 12 and table 10, p. 29.
[95] Saguaro Seminar, 'Social Capital Community Benchmark', 5–6.

excellent the data.[96] In Sweden, social norms and social policy have converged to remove the kind of inequalities that raise the risk of death.

Falling from grace

If moving upwards in the distribution of income increases subjective well-being, moving down is hard. When status is based on occupation, to lose one's job is to drop below the very bottom. Surveys of well-being show that by far the most potent of general causes of unhappiness is unemployment.[97] Low rank induces misery. The physiological routes have been followed in several studies of primates in the wild. Serotonin is a brain chemical which is associated with positive well-being. Among vervet monkeys, dominant males have much higher levels of serotonin than subordinate ones, and this is an effect, not a cause of high rank. These findings were replicated in (admittedly limited) studies in humans.[98] Another study has shown that in rhesus macaques, the furring of coronary arteries ('atherosclerosis'—the main cause of heart attacks) is inversely related to social rank. A study of baboons in the wild has found that all the biological stress markers follow the social hierarchy, rather like British civil servants.[99] This provides a physiological basis for a type of behaviour observed in both animals and humans, the phenomenon of 'Learned Helplessness': the experience of being boxed in a corner, and faced with intractable dilemmas or choices, with no obvious escape. Numerous studies in both animals and humans show a consistent set of responses: depressed mood, loss of interest, loss of appetite, insomnia, slow thoughts, loss of energy, feelings of worthlessness and guilt, diminished ability to think, and poor concentration.[100] Discursive and qualitative accounts of downwards social mobility in the United States during the 1980s record the intensity of mortification that such experiences can bring about.[101]

Research in Germany has shown that lay-offs and unemployment are likely to permanently lower the sense of subjective well-being, and recovery

[96] Deaton, 'Health Inequality', 140, 147–9; Judge and Paterson, 'Poverty, Income Inequality and Health', 26–7.

[97] Campbell et al., *Quality of American Life*, 52; Ch. 2 above, Table 2.2; Clark and Oswald, 'Unhappiness and Unemployment'.

[98] James, *Britain on the Couch*, 35–6; McGuire and Troisi, *Darwinian Psychiatry*, 92–6, 172–5; Madsen, 'Power Seekers are Different'.

[99] Marmot, *Status Syndrome*, 118–20; Shively, 'Social Status'; Sapolsky, 'Physiology of Unhappiness'.

[100] Peterson, *Learned Helplessness*; James, *Britain on the Couch*, 50–1; Schwartz, *Paradox of Choice*, ch. 10.   [101] Newman, *Falling from Grace*, chs. 3, 4.

in most cases is very difficult. In this respect it is worse than divorce or widowhood.[102] Since the 1970s, the risks have increasingly embraced a growing proportion of the so-called 'middle-class' in the United States, people with families, houses of their own in a safe neighbourhood, and seemingly steady jobs. Once the two-earner family had become the norm, the risks and the stakes rose. In the USA the onset of two-earner families together with rising unemployment made the achievement of social position much less certain. During the two 'golden age' decades of full employment and single breadwinner families, the prospect of improvement was relatively secure. But by the 1980s, two-earner families had ratcheted up the normative levels of hedonic and positional consumption. At the same time, unemployment rose, and structural economic change began to affect in particular the social position of middle-earning semi-skilled males.

After the 1970s, the two-earner family became increasingly vulnerable to three kinds of uncertainty: loss of employment, serious health problems, and family breakdown.[103] The three were related: health insurance was derived from employment, unemployment was stressful to health, and also undermined family stability. For two-earner families, the loss of one earner meant a serious drop from normative levels of living, and thus a loss of social face, of educational provision, of residential safety.[104] The liberalized financial system allowed crises to be postponed by means of credit card and premium mortgage rate debts, but made the final disaster, eviction from the family home, more likely in the end.[105]

A proxy for this experience of 'falling from grace' is provided by the extent of personal bankruptcy. Personal bankruptcy could give some temporary relief from debt, but it did not save the main positional asset, the couple's home. Hence, it provides a measure of increasing status insecurity. Between 1960 and 1980 there were about 2.5 personal bankruptcies per 1,000 households. The number began to rise in the 1980s, up to seven per thousand per year in 1990, and fourteen per thousand per year in 2002.[106] By that year, the number of people affected every year by personal bankruptcy in the United States was close to 2 million, making bankruptcy a greater hazard than divorce or heart attacks.[107] In the space of ten years, more than one-tenth of the adult population could expect to be affected.

---

[102] Clark et al., 'Scarring'; Clark et al., 'Lags and Leads'.
[103] See also Edwards, 'Uncertainty'.
[104] Oppenheimer, 'Women's Employment', 11–12.
[105] Warren and Tyagi, *Two-Income Trap*.
[106] Calculated from Administrative Office of the US Courts, Bankruptcy Statistics, series F-2.
[107] Warren and Tyagi, *Two-Income Trap*, 6, 193–4, n. 7. This includes adult members of affected households. The number of non-business bankruptcies in 2002 was 1.62 million.

Personal bankruptcy was not (on the whole) caused by hedonic reckless-
ness, sustained by easy credit. Its normal cause was the failure of one of the
three pillars of domestic security: health, job, or marriage. To begin with,
about 15 per cent of the population at any given time, more than 40 million
people, had no health insurance at all.[108] Those that did were restricted by
high co-payments or various small print exclusions, most particularly for
'pre-existing conditions'. Even if medical costs were fully covered, if one of
the earners lost their job, the result was a large fall in income, even if other
members of the family did not have to withdraw from work in order to
care for them. From the 1970s onwards, jobs became increasingly insecure.
Official unemployment levels more than doubled in the USA (to 8–9 per
cent) between the mid-1960s and the mid-1980s (and up to 12 per cent in
Britain) and those measures were biased downwards.

Employment in manufacturing was contracting, as much of the
work that had sustained semi-skilled manual worker families migrated
overseas. Much of the new job creation depended either on higher skills
or on location-specific services. The first required an educational endowment that middle-aged and older workers did not have, the second often
paid too little to sustain conventional levels of living. Finally, employment and health stresses increased the pressure on marriages, and
divorce became more likely to remove another pillar of the two-earner
family. With so much committed to the high costs of childcare, education, and especially mortgage payment, the loss of one earner was often a
blow that middle-class status could not survive. The people most likely to
suffer bankruptcy were parents with children at home. 'Having a child
[was] the best single predictor that a woman would end up in financial
collapse.'[109]

In American society, where politics are dominated by the financial
contributions of interests groups, largely from business, where the media
are dominated by corporations, where more is spent on advertising, relatively and absolutely, than anywhere else in the world, and where citizens
are exposed to relentless commodity propaganda, personal wealth and
economic growth are securely positioned as the main private and social
objectives. In a society so committed to positional competition, public
opinion and public discourse are securely in the hands of the successful, in
the media, in business, in politics, in the universities, in the voting system.
Hence the 'culture of contentment', of a majority at any time credibly aspiring to or achieving middle-class lives, in which the virtues of positional

[108] e.g. US Census, Historical Health Insurance Tables, table HI-1, **www.census.gov/hhes/
hlthins/historic/hihistt1.html.** [109] Warren and Tyagi, *Two-Income Trap*, 6.

competition and success are celebrated relentlessly.[110] Hence also the stigma of being a 'loser' in American society and culture.[111]

A world of good schools, happy kids, secure suburban neighbourhoods, two big cars, and long hours at worthwhile jobs for both parents was built up in America since the 1960s, but on fragile foundations. The personal safety net was weak. In America's flexible labour markets, jobs could disappear suddenly, and unemployment has been volatile. For most Americans, personal savings rates, never very high, began to decline in the 1970s, and have gone down close to zero in the 1990s. In a world of expanding opportunities, the diverging aspirations of parents and their different levels of achievement began to encourage early separation, and left children to grow in a one-parent home, overwhelmingly the mother's home. Finally, the decline in the birth rate has begun to build up insecurity for the future, as baby boomers enter retirement, and the ranks of younger workers are diminished. At the personal level, the reciprocal obligations of informal caring and support between old and young have also been undermined by disruption and tension in the family.

Unemployment, illness, divorce affecting two-earner families could easily knock them off the perch of suburban middle-class lifestyles. In the absence of social insurance, failure became common, and its costs were high. At the bottom of the affluent society, the social exclusion of poor men drove them out of the roles of provider and parent, demanding ever more of mothers. In the social ghettos at the bottom of American society, poor schooling, broken families, bad housing, and racial discrimination have generated a cycle of despair and the refuge of alcohol and drugs, and a simmering civil war between young men and the police which is contained at the cost of brutal repression, in the form of high rates of homicide, scores of legal executions, and a gulag of more than 2 million prisoners, a higher rate of incarceration than anywhere else in the world. Another 3 million are ex-convicts with limited civic rights. Almost five million are on probation or parole.[112]

The peril of economic failure is a descent further down towards this social hell. Between the 1970s and the 1990s, the prison population in the United States more than doubled, at almost an order of magnitude more, in relative terms, than in Europe. This is no doubt a good economic discipline for those who are healthy and at work. It might explain the intensity of the American work ethic, the much longer hours, the enduringly high

---

[110] Galbraith, *Culture of Contentment.*   [111] Sandage, *Born Loser.*
[112] Butterfield, 'Correctional Population'; *The Economist,* 'Prison and Beyond'.

absolute levels of productivity won by effort. For the winners, increasing their advantage has become very high priority, and reducing government spending is the prime objective of politics in the American centre and right. The high risks of social insecurity provide support to a lucrative retail finance industry, of liberalized mortgage and consumption lending providing very high returns.

On the face of it, American positional competition might seem to be hedonic.[113] But this is misleading. The quest for position in American society has its imperative in the security of personal well-being.[114] A position at the top defines the prerequisites of well-being, and only a position at the top can guarantee them. But the majority of people cannot be at the top. The cost of losing is awful to contemplate. It is illustrated in the deeply inferior position of single-parent families, captured succinctly in some of its dimensions in Figure 11.4, not to mention the comparative position of blacks. Hence the intensity of positional competition in the United States.

In comparison with the United States and Britain, inequality in Western Europe has remained fairly constant. Hours of work have declined, and are much lower than in the United States. In compensation, productivity per hour in Europe is comparable to that in the United States.[115] The common argument is that European welfare benefits hinder labour market flexibility, and thus sacrifice potential growth. But what is the purpose of growth? Hedonic arousal is stifled by habituation and diminishing returns. In an unequal society, positional success becomes the only guarantee of access to basic needs, to health care, to a competitive educational position, to benign and stable human relations. The costs of education at the top are very large, the costs of illness or divorce potentially very heavy. Hence the earnestness with which Americans pursue the 'American Dream'. This could be defined as sufficient wealth to allow complete freedom of any social ties and obligations. In an unequal society, such aspiration is delusive, since wealth of this magnitude is positional, and only a few can have it. This is also why American primacy in aggregate income and wealth does not buy it a respectable position in the indices of well-being.

During the economic 'golden age' of the post-war decades, in the years of full employment, rising consumption, and declining inequality, conservative and liberal/left parties alternated in power (in both the USA and the UK). Both left- and right-of-centre parties extended the social safety net, promoted education, and established pension and unemployment coverage.

---

[113] Frank, *Luxury Fever*; Schor, *Overspent American*; and Part II above, especially Ch. 9.
[114] Edwards, 'Uncertainty'.   [115] ILO, *Key Indicators*, e.g. fig. 6b, 18c.

Marginal income tax rates peaked at more than 70 per cent in both countries in the late 1960s/early 1970s. Whether it was a cause or an effect, politics were strongly aligned on class lines, with considerable pressure for redistribution downwards.[116] Both societies were social-democratic, in that they strove for greater equality of outcomes, by means of social cooperation and state action.

As the 'great transition' began from the 1970s onwards from social democracy towards market liberalism, from the New Deal to the New Right, the language of class faded out of politics. Former Democrats voted for Reagan; skilled workers for Thatcher. In right-wing papers, editorials condemned attacks on inequality as the language of envy.[117] Despite a large increase in inequality, it was no longer a political issue during the 1980s and the 1990s.[118] No central political party is driven by the demand for redistribution downwards, in the way the British Labour party used to be until the 1970s. Class-based voting is in decline.[119]

But the language of redistribution is not dead, and its pursuit is as vehement as ever, except now it is redistribution upwards rather than downwards that appears to drive political parties. Thatcher led the way in reducing both taxes for the rich, and welfare benefits for the poor during the 1980s, driving a quick and decisive upwards shift in inequality (see Figure 12.1). Even more striking is the vociferous partisanship of American politics, where the Republican party pursues a policy of tax cuts for the rich. Thatcher's policies had at least an economic rationale, and appear to have assisted the process of structural adjustment.[120] But the justification for such policies in the United States is thin, and was widely criticized as being fiscally irresponsible. What is remarkable is the energy and intensity of status pursuit, even when all material needs are satisfied many-fold. This is a powerful demonstration of the driving force of status. It is justified in the name of economic growth, and is an aspiration widely shared in the United States.[121]

The social-democratic (and Christian-democratic) welfare states have mainly striven to lower the cost of losing. They provided a safety net of income which made it more difficult to fall all the way to the bottom. They ensured minimal levels of education, housing, health care, income support, and pensions. In consequence, social inequality did not generate

---

[116] Butler and Stokes, *Political Change in Britain*; Edsall, *Chain Reaction*; Phillips, *Emerging Republican Majority*.

[117] BBC, 'Tories Accuse Labour'; Cohen, 'Jack Welch and "Class Envy"'; Ahier and Beck, 'Politics of Envy', 321–2. [118] Galbraith, *Culture of Contentment*.

[119] Evans (ed.), *End of Class Politics*.

[120] Crafts, *Relative Economic Performance*, ch. 5. But see Florio, *Great Divestiture*.

[121] Harwood Group, *Yearning for Balance*.

such clear differences of outcomes. In the first two post-war decades, prudential restraint led to exceptional levels of economic growth in Europe. This exceptional performance ended in the 1970s, and for the next two decades, Europe and the United States stagnated equally in terms of growth and employment.

The relation between inequality and growth is contested. In the 1950s Kuznets argued for an inverse U-curve: inequality increased in the early stages of industrialization, and then came down again as affluence was achieved. The rise of inequality since the 1970s has suggested a rethink: evidence is beginning to emerge that at the highest levels of affluence, growth is correlated with inequality.[122] If that is the case, then one reason may be that in unequal societies, more is at stake. The longer working hours in the United States have already been noted. Bell and Freeman argue that due to greater inequality, 'the same extra work pays off more in the US, generating more hours worked'.[123] It is just as logical to infer that extra work is driven by fear of loss as by pursuit of gain, and psychologically this is actually more credible.[124] In another finding, however, 'prime males' in e.g. Germany and the United States appeared to work comparable hours. The big difference was that women in the United States worked so much more, in an effort to mitigate the inequality of American households. America would be even more unequal if women there worked fewer hours, and if the gender division of labour was more comparable to Europe. To keep up with the positional race, couples had to invest more working hours. Families with children had a combined 53-hour week working for pay in 1968, and a 64-hour week in 2000.[125]

In this positional game, the losers end up very badly off, even in the context of a rich society. 'Put simply, in the US the relatively poor have to work harder, and still end up poorer, than in other countries.'[126] Britain, standing midway between the United States and Europe, also has a culture of much longer working hours, and has obstructed the European Union Directive for shorter ones.

During the last decade or so, the European choice of prudential restraint appears to have produced lower growth. Europeans work much shorter hours than Americans. If leisure is assigned an economic value, comparable productivity per working hour suggests that even economically Europeans

[122] Barro, 'Inequality and Growth'.
[123] Bell and Freeman, 'Incentive for Working Hard'.
[124] For asymmetries of gain and loss, see e.g. Kahneman et al., 'Loss Aversion'.
[125] Hout and Hanley, 'The Overworked American Family', 11.
[126] Osberg, 'Time, Money and Inequality', 2; also, Alesina et al., 'Why Doesn't the United States', 201.

are no worse off than Americans. In Europe, losing does not pose such an extreme risk to health and well-being. European societies have made a prudential trade-off, which currently appears to produce lower growth against greater security.[127] Why is that the case? Two factors make Europe different from North America. One is a deep racial divide. 'Racial animosity in the US makes redistribution to the poor, who are disproportionately black, unappealing to many voters.' American political institutions, with the great difficulty of registration, also appear biased against the poor.[128] It is easy to make too much of this. The United States is less equal than Europe, but it has a large public sector, and large transfer payments. Some of its programmes, such as social security, have been more generous than those in Britain. Overall, however, in the United States, the response has been to accept positional competition as the only road to success. In Europe, the combination of welfare safety net and rising levels of consumption appears to have taken the sting out of inequality as a political issue. Most voters are no longer interested.[129]

Most indices of economic well-being prioritize income per head.[130] They take no account of inequality or security. As we have seen, the priority given to economic growth is open to question: the very richest society lags behind in health and mortality, and economic growth does very little to increase subjective well-being in countries that are already rich. But there is little doubt about the *costs* of inequality and insecurity: being low down the scale of absolute income is associated with misery: with shorter lives, bad health, discrimination, poor education, incarceration, and many other detriments. GDP per head is a fiction: no one earns GDP per head. And with rising inequality, the volume of 'complaints', of negative differentials, increases.

Placing a money value on non-traded intangibles such as leisure or inequality may be difficult—but ignoring these values is also arbitrary. A recent investigation weights economic performance with measures of saving, economic insecurity, and inequality. The components of economic well-being are taken to be,

(1) current effective per capita consumption flows (a proxy for income);
(2) net societal accumulation of stocks of productive resources (a proxy for assets);
(3) income distribution;
(4) economic security.[131]

---

[127] Alesina and Glaeser, *Fighting Poverty*.
[128] Alesina et al., 'Why Doesn't the United States'.
[129] Galbraith, *Culture of Contentment*.   [130] Ch. 2 above.
[131] Osberg, 'Human Well-Being'.

Table 12.4. Index of economic well-being rankings, 1980–2001: consumption, capital, equality, security

(1) Consumption weighted		(2) Equal weight		(3) GDP per head			(4) Growth rate	
					Index	US$ 1995		
Germany	0.54	Norway	0.68	USA	0.61	26,241	Norway	2.52
UK	0.53	Sweden	0.60	Canada	0.45	22,390	UK	2.24
USA	0.52	Germany	0.59	Norway	0.39	21,130	USA	2.22
Sweden	0.51	USA	0.53	Germany	0.39	20,902	Australia	2.03
Canada	0.50	UK	0.48	Australia	0.35	20,162	Canada	1.48
Norway	0.50	Australia	0.45	Sweden	0.32	19,426	Sweden	1.43
Australia	0.44	Canada	0.45	UK	0.24	17,423	Germany	1.06

Note: Mean of 1980–2001. Index measures change, not levels. Index range is 0–1, over lowest value (−10%) to highest value (+10%) over period as a whole. Consumption weighted: consumption 40, capital 10, inequality 25, insecurity 25. Equal weight: All weighted at 25.

Source: Calculated from Osberg, 'Human Well-Being'.

The index (Table 12.4) is scaled between the minimum and maximum of the ranges for 1980–2001. The number reported and ranked is the mean. Each column's ranking conveys different types of information, and shows how sensitive well-being is to different assumptions. One way of thinking about it is where would a person choose to live, given a position in the lower half, the middle-upper, or the top of the income distribution. The first column weights consumption (40) more heavily than capital stocks (10), but gives high weight to inequality and insecurity (25 each). This type of weighting is myopic in economic resource allocation, and prudent in social arrangements, and is likely to appeal to the broad 'middle classes' in affluent societies. It is the one that minimizes the differences between the different countries with only Australia a fair way behind, suffering from relatively low consumption, and relatively high inequality and insecurity. Allocating equal weights to all four components (col. 2) places European welfare states at the top of the distribution, and English speakers at the bottom, with a combination of low social prudence and low economic prudence. The weighting here would appeal most to those at the bottom of the social distribution, as one that maximizes equality, security, and prudence. That prudence pays is indicated by the position of the welfare states in the middle of the third column (of GDP levels per head), with the United States well in the lead, reaping the benefits of inequality, and the UK at the very bottom. If one regards social policy as causal, then the UK appears to have found a combination of inequality and social insecurity that failed to lift it out of the worst position, although it was second only to Norway during this period in growth rates.

When inequality and insecurity are taken into account (col. 2), the affluence of the years after 1980 is muted. Table 12.4 shows that the United States, the first in levels of GDP per head, and the third in growth rates, was in the middle of the bunch in col. 2. Its follower and imitator, Thatcherite Britain, was even further behind. When the greatest weight is given to consumption, all countries (except Australia) are very close together.

European and American welfare states were largely completed by the late 1960s, and the economic crises of the 1970s and onwards made them difficult to expand, and indeed more difficult to sustain. In the 1980s, Britain (like other English-speaking countries), broke ranks and shifted decisively towards the American equilibrium. This shift may have been instrumental in breaking a long period of relative economic stagnation, but had still not earned it a standard of living and a productivity level comparable with the United States, or even with the most advanced of European welfare states. In consequence, Britain is poised halfway between the two equilibria, with a standard of living and levels of social misery at the bottom of the European league, but (on the whole, and excluding provision for old age), somewhat better social protection than in the United States. But when consumption is weighted highly at the expense of investment, both the UK and the USA rank highly, compensating with high consumption for low security and high inequality.

Competitive economic markets are justified in terms of incentives and efficiency. But competitive status markets have delivered a great deal of dejection, much more so during the recent decades of rising inequality. If increments in GDP per head contribute virtually nothing to subjective well-being, while increases of inequality are strongly and positively harmful (both objectively and subjectively), then the rise in GDP and inequality has left society (in utilitarian terms), clearly worse off. The incentive of status has not paid off. The siren songs of positional competition are in English, and the speakers of English have succumbed to them more readily than others.

Appendix 12A

Table 12A.1. Effect of relative and absolute income on happiness
Dependent variable: percentage of population describing themselves as 'very happy'

	Coeff.	Std. Err.	t-stat	Probability	95 % Intervals	Confidence
upper income third	1.942295	0.904	2.15	0.035	0.141	3.743
lower income third	−4.335323	0.781	−5.55	0.0	−5.890	−2.781
average income	0.0001013	0.000	2.54	0.013	0.000	0.000
Albania	−11.19457	2.775	−4.03	0.0	−16.720	−5.669
Algeria	−5.738542	2.773	−2.07	0.042	−11.259	−0.218
Argentina	8.701584	2.618	3.32	0.001	3.489	13.914
Austria	12.7969	2.606	4.91	0.0	7.607	17.986
Canada	19.11684	2.635	7.25	0.0	13.870	24.364
Chile	12.54603	2.628	4.77	0.0	7.312	17.780
China	−10.55623	2.714	−3.89	0.0	−15.960	−5.152
Croatia	−8.377777	2.770	−3.02	0.003	−13.894	−2.862
Czechoslovakia	−12.86249	2.649	−4.85	0	−18.138	−7.587
Denmark	20.34683	2.764	7.36	0.0	14.843	25.850
Egypt	−4.419954	2.743	−1.61	0.111	−9.883	1.043
Estonia	−16.33422	2.686	−6.08	0.0	−21.682	−10.986
France	9.534764	2.606	3.66	0.0	4.345	14.725
Germany	−4.600285	2.603	−1.77	0.081	−9.784	0.583
India	5.228346	2.675	1.95	0.054	−0.098	10.554
Ireland	18.81886	2.611	7.21	0.0	13.619	24.018
Italy	−6.683715	2.603	−2.57	0.012	−11.868	−1.500
Japan	2.269624	2.696	0.84	0.402	−3.098	7.637
Jordan	−10.97502	2.673	−4.11	0	−16.297	−5.653
Korea	−14.07533	2.603	−5.41	0	−19.259	−8.892
Latvia	−16.15373	2.696	−5.99	0	−21.522	−10.786
Lithuania	−18.66887	2.683	−6.96	0.0	−24.012	−13.326
Macedonia	−1.93473	2.765	−0.7	0.486	−7.441	3.572
Mexico	35.69056	2.707	13.19	0.0	30.301	41.081
Moldova	−15.7715	2.757	−5.72	0.0	−21.261	−10.282
Netherlands	22.40552	2.603	8.61	0.0	17.222	27.589
Peru	7.778542	2.659	2.93	0.005	2.484	13.073
Russia	−17.3834	2.683	−6.48	0	−22.725	−12.042
Singapore	12.02004	2.605	4.61	0	6.833	17.207
Slovakia	−15.15172	2.665	−5.69	0	−20.458	−9.846
Slovenia	−7.502685	2.607	−2.88	0.005	−12.695	−2.311
South Africa	17.06404	2.615	6.52	0.0	11.856	22.272
Spain	−3.965235	2.611	−1.52	0.133	−9.164	1.234
Sweden	11.32458	2.629	4.31	0.0	6.090	16.559
Turkey	11.19214	2.768	4.04	0.0	5.681	16.703
Uganda	9.387794	2.774	3.38	0.001	3.864	14.911
USA	11.97321	2.800	4.28	0.0	6.398	17.549
Venezuela	34.65035	2.694	12.86	0.0	29.286	40.014
Zimbabwe	−2.373418	2.774	−0.86	0.395	−7.898	3.151
Constant	23.18865	2.099	11.05	0.0	19.008	27.369
Observations	120					
Adj. R^2	0.9579					
Countries	40					

Note: Compiled in collaboration with Mathew Polisson. Omitted country is Israel.

Sources: Data acquired from 'World Values and European Values Surveys, 1999–2001', through the UK Data Archive (**www.data-archive.ac.uk**). Information about the survey can be found at **http://worldvaluessurvey.org**.

13

All You Need is Love? Mating since the 1950s

'All you need is love', sang the Beatles in a lyric that lingers, at once compelling and counter-intuitive. Love and sexual intimacy hold out some of the ultimate promises of personal fulfilment, of lifting the veil of reticence, of holding another person, a woman or a man, in an intoxicating bond of mutual regard. This potential of love is a constant preoccupation. In consumer and high cultures alike, it is the theme of popular song, magazine features, advertising, the daily press, but also poetry, fiction, music, dance, painting, and sculpture. Almost every adult has had some experience of love, but until the 1980s, social science was slow to investigate. Scientific knowledge is not particularly helpful to lovers. For guidance, most people still look to intuition, experience, imagination, and conversation, or perhaps to self-help books.

The capacity for love does not depend on income. But well-being is a seamless web, and in spite of the Beatles, love has to compete for attention and time with other opportunities. Under post-war affluence, the quest for love has taken up more of the life cycle. People are single for longer, marry later, divorce more. Abortion, births outside marriage, cohabitation, divorce, single parenthood, infidelity perhaps, have all risen. More intimacy and sexuality is now sought outside the family. The social regulation of sexual arousal has abated. Homosexuality is more salient than ever.

Why have these changes taken place, and what do they mean? They can be understood as the benign outcome of deliberate and rational intentions. Or alternatively as the tentative, short-of-optimal resolutions of the intractable dilemmas of choice, responding fitfully to a changing set of opportunities, seeking for ways to lock in an elusive happiness. As in other dimensions of well-being, the rising tide of novelty has corroded some of the pillars of commitment.

Mating is constrained by conventions, traditions, scripts, rules, and regulations inherited from the past, and is also reinvented constantly. Almost any artefact carries some kind of gendered message, and interest and preoccupation is obsessive. The arts are about little else. Love is easy to perceive as a magical state of grace, but it has always been a market as well, with imputed values for personal attractiveness, social standing, and economic potential, more so perhaps in established pre-industrial cultures than in the romantic fantasies cultivated by the advocates of modern consumerism.[1]

In 1956, the social critic Erich Fromm captured this aspect of mating as a market transaction.

Our whole culture is based on the appetite for buying, on the idea of a mutually favorable exchange.... I am out for a bargain; the object should be desirable from the standpoint of its social value, and at the same time should want me, considering my overt and hidden assets and potentialities. Two persons thus fall in love when they feel they have found the best object available on the market, considering the limitations of their own exchange values. Often, as in buying real estate, the hidden potentialities which can be developed play a considerable role in this bargain.[2]

Shortly afterwards this notion was formalized in Becker's economics of the family.[3] It models mating and parenthood in terms of the preferences of the rational, self-seeking, maximizing consumer.[4] This acute analytical insight (which has not completely lost its power to dismay) was an expression of, perhaps even made possible by, the emerging priority of individual self-seeking as an aspirational norm.[5]

In neoclassical economic models the family is an efficient arrangement for maximizing welfare by means of cooperation and functional specialization. Men, who specialize in market production, cooperate with women, who specialize in reproduction, to maximize their joint satisfaction. Market goods were combined with men and women's time to produce happiness and children at home. But economic growth undermined this bargain: when prices changed, incentives changed as well. Affluence drove down the price of market goods, and made the time devoted to home-making, and to caring for a partner, a child, or a parent, more costly in terms of earning and spending opportunities forgone. Less effort was invested at home, more effort outside. Families might recalculate, split, regroup. But

---

[1] Campbell, *Romantic Ethic*, 69–76; and see Ch. 6 above.   [2] Fromm, *Art of Loving*, 10.
[3] First in the 1960s (e.g. Becker, 'Allocation of Time'). Definitively in Becker, *Treatise on the Family*; recently, Rosenzweig and Stark, *Handbook*; Ermisch, *Economic Analysis*.
[4] Becker, 'Irrational Behavior'.   [5] Veroff et al., *Inner American*, 529–30.

(in the Chicago tradition), since choices were well informed and calculated, everything was always for the best.

Other economic conceptions accepted individual rationality, but queried whether it is always invested for the joint good, and how efficient it was. Family members were not altruistically cooperative, but locked in competition and even conflict. In response to changing incentives, women acquired education, went to work, and earned their own money. As they became more independent, the attractions of marriage declined. From this point of view, the changes in mating were 'rational': at any given point, women and men chose the best for themselves. They bargained from positions of weakness or strength, and implicitly threatened to leave. Outcomes were unstable, unlikely to be optimal or fully efficient, and reflected the elusive equilibria of competing strategies, and bargaining strengths that changed over time.[6]

If, instead, choice is seen as myopic rather than 'rational', the challenge for the partners is different. It is how to impose current desires on a remote future. At the outset, mating is entered in a spirit of high expectations. Dissolution is time inconsistent: at the point of marriage, it is not part of anyone's intentions.[7] The time horizons seem impossibly long—the life-times of couples, children, and parents. In fact, expectations were often disappointed. As successive enticing individual incentives unfolded, the capacity for mutual commitment struggled to keep up. The fallout was often disappointment and failure, as partnership was postponed, or torn apart. For large numbers, however, expectations were not confounded by the challenge of affluence, but by its opposite, economic frustration.

Where does the intensity of craving for love come from? The discipline of evolutionary psychology posits that the preferences for mate selection and bonding are directly rewarded with reproductive success. They are driven by emotions which were hard-wired into the brain in the course of evolution.[8] Sexual desire is intense and volatile. It pulls people together, but it is also easily frustrated and quenched. A more durable emotion is the need for personal attachment. The template for love is assumed to be the bond between mother and infant, which may be seen as an evolutionary adaptation to increase reproductive chances by motivating a protective attitude in the mother.[9]

---

[6] Mahony, *Kidding Ourselves*; Lundberg and Pollak, 'Bargaining and Distribution'; Lundberg and Pollak, 'Efficiency in Marriage'.   [7] Baker and Emery, 'Every Relationship Above Average'.

[8] Buss, *Evolution of Desire*; Fisher, *Anatomy of Love*; Campbell, *Mind of her Own*.

[9] Bowlby, *Attachment and Loss*; Ainsworth, 'Attachments beyond Infancy'.

Evolutionary psychology assumes that mating preferences differ by gender.[10] They are driven by nature's reproductive strategies: for conception, men need minutes, while for women it is a matter of months. Men seek to maximize the frequency of mating encounters, while women seek to maximize their quality. Women prioritize status and earning power in their partners, while men are more concerned with youth and beauty. Mating currencies depreciate with age for women, and appreciate for men. That would explain the age gap at marriage. Women seek men who are somewhat older than themselves. On the other hand, if there is some impatience to mate, then the competition reduces the age gap: 'women of reproductive age are always in much shorter supply than men.'[11] Sexuality is more risky for women than for men. A man can walk away, and leave the woman 'holding the baby'. It gives the woman an incentive to act as the prudent gatekeeper of sexual intimacy.[12] American studies between the 1960s and the 1990s indicated that men were more willing to engage in sexual intercourse, and that women were more wary of casual sex.[13]

Psychologically, the template of love is the non-contingent acceptance of an adoring mother. A child craves physical and emotional closeness. If that need is satisfied, the child develops a secure and stable personality, and is able to receive and bestow emotional and physical closeness in its own turn. If this intimacy is denied or not fully achieved the child is not at ease with itself and the world. At stake is the very sense of self. Identity is validated by the quality of mother's physical and emotional closeness. Her unconditional approbation and acceptance are close to the core of well-being, and convey the consciousness that love is the pinnacle of life's experience.

Secure attachment in infancy builds up the capacity for adult love, sociability, and parenthood. It depends on parental, and especially maternal, investment of time, attention, and love. During the 1960s, parental investment was exposed to competing and compelling demands for self-fulfilment.[14] Attachment may wilt in an environment short of attention and affection, and in a Lamarckian process, this deficit can be transmitted to children and takes on a life of its own. A child who was never secure in her own attachment may not have sufficient confidence to grant it herself. This is a typical outcome of myopic choice, in which an earnest quest for fulfilment produces, in the longer term, a legacy of disappointment.

---

[10] Buss, *Evolution of Desire*, chs. 2–3; Fisher, *Anatomy of Love*; Campbell, *Mind of her Own*.
[11] James, *Britain on the Couch*, 235.   [12] Symons, *Evolution of Human Sexuality*.
[13] Oliver and Hyde, 'Gender Differences in Sexuality'; Campbell, *Mind of her Own*, 42; Tennov, *Love and Limerence*, 72.   [14] Veroff et al., *Inner American*, ch. 5, and p. 529.

Mating

In contrast with the optimizing calculus of economics and of evolutionary psychology, both popular and high culture have traditionally set store on a 'love' which is impulsive, intuitive, and risky. The craving for romantic love appears to fall little short of being a human universal. An ethnographic survey found it in 148 out of 166 cultures sampled (the remainder were not conclusive).[15] Homer, the poems of Sappho, the Song of Songs, the Greek Anthology, the letters of Abelard and Héloïse, the sonnets of Petrarch, have lived on from earlier periods of western civilization, and love is equally celebrated outside it, in Iraq, Persia, India, China, and Japan.[16] Love is a state of heightened arousal, which can be experienced as transcendence or madness. It is linked to state-altering chemicals in the brain, and to intensified activity in specific brain locations.[17] It is a form of intoxication, an experience of being swept away by a larger force, independent of reason and will.[18] The quest for closeness is mixed with erotic attraction. It cannot be turned on and off. The symptoms are common to both genders:

- Intrusive thinking about the love object.
- An acute longing for reciprocation.
- Buoyancy with hope, depression with its absence.
- A physical aching of the chest.
- A general intensification of feeling.
- A heightened appreciation of the loved one.[19]

Emotion overriding calculation is an important part of the experience.

Lovers appear much better to each other than to their other acquaintances. 'Love is the delusion that one woman differs from another.'[20] The authentic lover is the highest bidder in the auction, that rare customer who values your assets more highly than anyone else, perhaps on temporary leave of their senses. Romantic lovers have been found to suppress neural activity associated with critical social assessment of other people and negative emotions as well.[21] They see the world through rose-tinted glasses.[22]

'No sound of clapping comes from one hand without the other hand.'[23] For love, intimacy, mating, and reproduction, individual self-reliance is

[15] Jankowiak and Fisher, 'Cross-Cultural Perspective'; Jankowiak, *Romantic Passion*, 4–5.
[16] Fisher, *Anatomy of Love*, 49–50.   [17] Fisher, *Why We Love*, ch. 3.
[18] Tennov, *Love and Limerence*, 241.   [19] Ibid. 23–4.
[20] Ibid. 208, attributed to H. L. Mencken.   [21] Bartels and Zeki, 'Neural Correlates', 1162.
[22] Hendrick and Hendrick, 'Rose Colored Glasses'.
[23] Jalal-al-Din Rumi and Nicholson, *Rumi*, 122; cited by Fromm, *Art of Loving*, 30.

not enough. Somebody else has to cooperate. 'Assortative mating', the mutual quest for the best possible partner, has tended to produce marriages with reasonably even matches on the scales of physical attractiveness, education, age, social connections, ethnic origins, and earning powers and prospects.[24] Simulation of two-sided mating searches indicates that aspiration levels have to be grounded in one's own mating value to achieve any success.[25]

But intimacy, sexuality, and reproduction are rarely a straightforward market exchange. It is typically an 'economy of regard', a mixed economy of gifts and market goods.[26] In the economy of regard, exchange has an intrinsic value over and above the gains from trade. Given the asymmetry of gender mating strategies, men's motives are open to suspicion. It is well understood that not everyone enters the encounter with the same objectives. A list of love styles includes *eros*, a strong, secure, emotional and erotic attachment; *ludus*—a gamesmanly, shifting, non-committal strategy; *storge*—a slowly maturing affection; *pragma*—a calculating quest; *agape*—an altruistic, self-denying commitment; and *mania*—obsessive, preoccupied, possessive, anxious infatuation. This captures nicely a good deal of what culture and personal experience have to say.[27] Another view collapses these classifications into just three, lust, romantic love, and attachment.[28] Men's promiscuous preferences give them a prima-facie incentive to mislead. To overcome suspicion, they need to establish their good intentions, by means of a credible signal. Honest signals are costly: a credible signal is one that makes it difficult for the sender to cheat. That is why courtship is punctuated by gifting. A successfully personalized gift provides evidence of personal empathy, attention, and resourcefulness. That courtship gifts are good signals is indicated in one study which shows how difficult it is to get them right.[29] As in the gift economy more generally, signalling in courtship involves reciprocity with delay.[30] As in the gift economy, the exchange is intensely rewarding in itself.[31]

Mating-market assets such as family background, education, and looks provide good verifiable signals, and in stable societies they may provide all that is required in order to make a good mating choice. But in fluid, affluent societies, their value is less certain. The pool of those eligible, their capacities and intentions, is imperfectly known, the cues can be ambiguous, and the search has to evaluate every candidate against the probabilities of finding a better one. How potential mates will respond is uncertain. This leaves

[24] Mare, 'Five Decades'. [25] Todd and Miller, 'Pride and Prejudice', 300–6.
[26] Above, Ch. 5. [27] Lee, 'Love Styles'. [28] Fisher, *Why We Love*, 94.
[29] Belk, 'Can't Buy Me Love'. [30] Above, Ch. 5. [31] Belk, 'Gift Giving'.

a good deal of scope for misunderstanding, cross-purposes, and opportunistic or strategic behaviour.

In a gift exchange, the more ardent person is in a position of weakness. If sex is at issue, then the cooler player, with the weaker sex drive, is in control.[32] There is some evidence that men are more prone to 'falling in love' than women.[33] For Willard Waller, who observed American college mating in the 1930s, romantic love (for women) was a matter of calculation:

A girl may pretend to be extremely involved, to be the person wholly dominated by the relationship; this she does in order to lead the young man to fasten his emotions and to prepare for the conventional denouement of marriage, for, in the end, while protesting her love, she makes herself unavailable except in marriage.[34]

On this view, which was common in the sociology of marriage between the 1930s and the 1960s, love was the bait for marriage. That men benefited from marriage was not at issue: the object for women was to get the best possible partner compatible with their own endowments.

At the point of commitment, where reason and foresight might be considered vital, the critical faculties are diminished by the transitory yearnings of love. The trade-off of romantic and sexual consummation in return for commitment is asymmetric. Romantic love is a state of compelling urgency. It exemplifies hyperbolic discounting, in which immediate reward dominates long-term considerations. Since men (typically) are asking for emotional and sexual accommodation, their motives are not above suspicion. True love is scarce, and needs to be authenticated. A contractual commitment in the form of engagement or marriage resolves the ambiguity and constitutes a decisive and credible signal that love is real, enduring, and irreversible.[35] That such a signal is available greatly helps in the search process: potential mates who cannot commit are to be avoided. The commitment to marriage validates the authenticity of love. A religious ceremony confers a transcendental benediction on the vows of marriage, and differentiates them from the ordinary motives of commerce. In the United States, this sanction was underpinned by high levels of attachment to organized religion, which, like marriage, offers a 'haven in a heartless world'.

In the first decade after the Second World War, the exchange of gratification for commitment was relatively clear-cut. Marriage was expected to last. Women's education levels were low, and marriage and motherhood were attractive alternatives to low-paying jobs.[36] On the other hand, sexual

[32] Lasch, *Haven*, 53–4; Allen and Brinig, 'Sex, Property Rights'.
[33] References in Luhmann, *Love as Passion*, 230, n. 6.
[34] Waller, *The Family*, 267; see also Greenfield, 'Love and Marriage', 375–6.
[35] Rowthorn, 'Marriage and Trust'; id., 'Marriage as a Signal'.   [36] Above, Ch. 11.

intercourse outside marriage was not so readily available to men, and for a woman to grant it was a distinctive concession.[37] The signals in both cases were clear. In both the USA and the UK, commitment had to precede sex. On the whole, sexual intercourse was only granted when it was expected to be followed by marriage. Where the order was inadvertently reversed, and pregnancy took place, it was quickly followed by a 'shotgun marriage'. Illegitimacy was very low in both countries.[38] In Britain, up to the 1960s, relaxation of virtue before marriage was even less easily granted, and sex more frequently had to wait until marriage.[39] In interwar USA, high-school and college women would allow sexual foreplay ('petting and necking'—it required the woman's acquiescence) both as an end in itself and in return for temporary commitment.[40] After the war, it became more customary for sexual intercourse to be permitted when 'going steady' with the intended marriage partner. 'Going steady' was less binding than marriage, but was a public commitment none the less, and made quite credible by the notion of romantic love that had a strong currency in popular culture at the time.[41]

Romantic love has two different time horizons. In the short run is the pressing quest for acknowledgement, companionship, and sexual consummation. The other time horizon is open-ended. To mate, marry, and reproduce is the most significant of long-term commitments. On the face of it, there is no contradiction between the two objectives. If closeness is so ardently desired, then to sustain it forever should be no hardship. In fact, a binding commitment entails the sacrifice of subsequent choice. Marriage is a vow of unconditional bonding. The cost and the benefits are weighed once and for all, 'for better or worse'. It extends to the horizons of life, and beyond it. Seen as an exchange, marriage is 'relational' rather than 'transactional'. With a secure lifetime contract, partners did not need to check their balance frequently, to see how well they were doing. They could afford to go into deficit, in the expectation of making up in the future. For couples courting in the 1950s, Irving Berlin's lyrics were believable.

> Days may not be fair Always,
> That's when I'll be there Always.
> Not for just an hour,
> Not for just a day,
> Not for just a year,
> But Always.

[37] Burgess and Wallin, *Engagement and Marriage*, ch. 11.
[38] Akerlof et al., 'Out-of-Wedlock Childbearing'.
[39] Gillis, *For Better, For Worse*, 270–84; Humphries, *Secret World*, ch. 4; Higgins, 'Expectations and Realities', ch. 2.   [40] Waller, 'Dating and Mating Complex'; Bailey, *Front Porch*, 50–6, 95–6.
[41] LeMasters, *Modern Courtship*, ch. 6.

As the prospects for marital endurance have declined in recent decades, wedding displays have gradually become more lavish, compensating for declining expectations of commitment with a costlier signal.[42] Weddings involve large outlays on one-off symbolic goods, like diamond rings, bridesmaids' dresses, flowers, photography, and lavish receptions—an average £16,000–17,000 in the UK today, some $19,000 in the USA; some $40 billion dollars a year overall in the USA. An average wedding dress cost $800 in 2003 and as much again on accessories, and expenditure was growing.[43] Is this an attempt to counter the declining credibility of marriage promises by increasing the solemnity of the occasion?

During the first post-war decade, the currency of romantic exchange was still crisp: as if nature had colluded with culture, and had created a 'commitment trap', in which calculation was disabled by desire. By the late 1950s, the exchange of sexual access for commitment was beginning to fray. For young men, its attraction depended in part on the mystery of sexuality, which, on the whole, women controlled. Sex was still a secret, for which women held the key.[44] From the late 1950s the exchange value of sexuality entered into gradual decline, followed somewhat later by the exchange value of commitment. The number of sexual partners increased.[45] Contemporary accounts suggest an increase in sexual experimentation, at least in colleges, as administrators gave up the pretence of acting *in loco parentis*.[46] For Philip Larkin in Britain, famously, 'sexual intercourse began in nineteen sixty-three', and survey evidence confirms greater laxity at the time.[47] In principle, the birth control pill might have redressed the asymmetry of risk between men and women, but it only disseminated widely from the late 1960s onwards, well after the onset of the sexual revolution.[48] Nor was marriage going out of fashion—yet. The age at marriage declined into the 1960s, and remained low until the mid-1970s. The marriage rate declined somewhat, but that decline can be entirely explained by the decline of the male–female sex ratio.[49] In practice, sexuality was losing some of its value as exchange for commitment.

[42] Whyte, *Dating*, 55–63; Ingraham, *White Weddings*; Mead, 'You're Getting Married'; Peller, 'Wedding Counsel'; *Guardian*, '£1000—to be a Guest'; example of current logistics, **www.hudson2001.com/wedding/history/**.
[43] Cost of dress, Mead, 'You're Getting Married', 78; Ingraham, *White Weddings*, 4–5, ch. 2; Judd, 'Average Wedding "Costs £17,000" '.
[44] Burgess and Wallin, *Engagement and Marriage*, ch. 11.   [45] Whyte, *Dating*, 24–7.
[46] Greene, *Sex and the College Girl*, ch. 5; Kirkendall, 'Premarital Intercourse'; Bailey, *Sex in the Heartland*, ch. 3.   [47] Gorer, *Sex & Marriage*, 39–51.
[48] Marks, *Sexual Chemistry*, 203–7; Goldin and Katz, 'Power of the Pill', 732–8; Cook, *Long Sexual Revolution*, 268–70.   [49] Above, Figure 7.4.

One reason that sexual intimacy was more freely granted was the increasing habituation to sexuality in the market place.[50] This had some parallels with the 'tragedy of the commons' we have already identified in advertising during the same period.[51] In pursuit of effect, every writer or creator had an incentive to evoke the power of sexuality a little further than convention allowed. That gave a temporary advantage, but as everyone followed suit, sexual exposure gradually lost its power to arouse and shock. Consequentially, this gave women less to bargain with. One convenient body of evidence is imaginative literature. In the late 1950s and early 1960s cultural entrepreneurs competed with increasing intensity. Furtive works of erotica became bombshell best-sellers. Both *Ulysses* and *Lady Chatterley's Lover* found publishers in Britain, Nabokov's *Lolita* broke through American conventions, while (a little later) the initial publication of Anaïs Nin's diary began a process of taboo-breaking disclosure which is not over even today. Updike set the seal on Christian sexual morality in his novel *Couples* (1968), while Philip Roth did the same for Jews in *Portnoy's Complaint* (1969). John Updike has an amusing account of the tantalizing emergence of oral sex into literature, and life eventually imitated art in the Starr Report on President Clinton.[52] The strict Hays Code of sexual representation in the cinema was relaxed in the 1960s, and explicit sexual intercourse became increasingly visible on the screen, notably in Brando's *Last Tango in Paris* (1972). As in other areas, colour television combined more permissiveness with a rich broadband colour signal, while video recorders (and later the Internet) made pornography more widely available.

Playboy magazine had emerged as early as 1953, and by the end of the decade was selling more than a million copies a month. It began with airbrushed female breasts, and by the 1980s colour shots of female genitalia could be found at every newsagents. Sex manuals had a long tradition,[53] but Alex Comfort's *The Joy of Sex* (1968) reached a completely new level of explicitness, detail, and circulation. Such publications take years to produce, so the process was well in train by the early 1960s. Sexual explicitness was a kind of 'arms race', in which new weapons rapidly devalue existing ones.[54] In these circumstances the disclosure value of an average woman's sexual intimacy was likely to lose some of its mystery, in comparison with the ideal bodies on show in *The Joy of Sex* or in the cinema. This has been confirmed in a series of experiments: in the most striking one,

[50] Cawallader, 'Marriage'; D'Emilio and Freedman, *Intimate Matters*, ch. 14.
[51] Above, Ch. 6.   [52] Updike, *Picked-up Pieces*, 'An Interesting Emendation', 438–44.
[53] Rusbridger, *Concise History*.   [54] Brown, 'Hey There'.

men exposed to *Playboy* centrefolds rated their partners lower in attractiveness and love than those who were not.[55] The exchange value of sexuality was being devalued by its commodification.

Helen Gurley Brown's *Sex and the Single Girl* (1963) and the *Cosmopolitan* that she edited from 1965 (the leading magazine for women in their twenties) signalled that women were not content to be passive guardians of their own sexuality. Germaine Greer's *The Female Eunuch* (1970) celebrated women's capacity to desire and enjoy their sexuality as intensely as men. Paradoxically, the rising acceptability of sexual enjoyment for women also weakened their bargaining power.[56] In Erica Jong's novel *Fear of Flying* (1972), the heroine Isadora Wing pretends to aspire to the 'zipless fuck', an experience of purely sexual consummation (her actions and emotions rather belie this, and that perhaps is the implicit message). Willard's 'principle of least interest' was that 'the one who cares less can exploit the one who cares more'.[57] Women's pretence of indifference became less credible, thus weakening somewhat their bargaining position.

Simple supply and demand also reduced the allure of female sexuality. From the 1960s, an adverse sex ratio began to affect women. By the census of 1970, there were about 80 eligible men for every 100 eligible women in the USA, and similar shortages affected Britain, with slightly different timings and intensity. By the time the sex ratio for young women began to improve (in the 1980s and 1990s), the ratio of women to men on college campuses (where about half of the cohort arrived) had worsened considerably against them due to their rising enrolments.[58]

The diffusion of the birth control pill also reduced women's sexual bargaining power.[59] *Cosmopolitan* was the barometer of courtship strategies for women in their twenties from the 1960s onwards.

When *Cosmopolitan* magazine discussed men in 1965, almost 90% of the articles centred on marriage and children, with just a few pieces offering first-date advice. By 2000, there had been a complete reversal: Only 5% of articles about men focused on marriage, while the majority of the articles were geared toward short-term dating and sex tips. There was also a marked increase in negative articles about marriage. In 1965, 82% of the articles spoke of marriage in a positive or neutral tone, while in 2000, only 33% of articles viewed marriage in non-negative tones.[60]

---

[55] Kenrick et al., 'Influence of Popular Erotica'. His other experiments described, James, *Britain on the Couch*, 99–101.   [56] Ehrenreich et al., *Feminization of Sex.*
[57] Lasch, *Haven*, 54.
[58] Glenn and Marquardt, 'Hooking Up', 10–11; But Ni Bhrolcháin, 'Flexibility', argues that age preferences adjust to adverse sex ratios. See above, Ch. 7, Figure 7.4.
[59] Akerlof et al., 'Out-of-Wedlock Childbearing'.   [60] Whelan, 'Singles' Magazines', 96.

By the 1990s, *Cosmo* had come to promote uninhibited female sexuality. 'Who says you can't enjoy sex without commitment?', asked one of its articles.[61] Female sexuality has never been more explicit, the number of premarital partners is higher, and the age at first sexual intercourse is lower than in the first half of the twentieth century, for people of comparable education. If love leads into commitment and validates it, and if sexual mystery is conducive to love, then the rise of explicit sexuality has acted to weaken the capacity for commitment.

As women acquired more education and earning potential, as the barriers to exit from marriage came down, their economic dependence declined as well, and with it one of the motives for intense commitment to marriage on the female side. Younger women have experienced a greater variety of dating partners and a higher degree of premarital intimacy.[62] Average age at marriage, especially for the educated and those in managerial and professional work, has risen to the late twenties. The twenties, then, were a time for a sequence of relatively short-term relationships, conditional on a high level of gratification, and weighed in the balance when such expectations were not met. By the early thirties this was combined uneasily with a frustrating quest for commitment. This world is documented in recent British books like *Bridget Jones' Diary*, and Nick Hornby's *High Fidelity*. Slicker, less troubled American versions are the TV series *Friends* and *Sex in the City*.

That is the standard narrative, inasmuch as it exists.[63] In reality this represents just one strand in the unfolding of sexuality, a strand we might call 'permissive' or 'hedonistic'. There is also a countervailing one which we might call 'reticent'. These two strands appear to have persisted throughout the period, albeit with certain modifications of style but less of substance. Serial mating without commitment was already a staple of American college dating scripts in the 1930s, as memorably described in Waller's 'rating and dating complex' of college students in the 1930s, which pushed sexual stimulation just short of intercourse.[64] At the same time, large numbers (about half) continued to abstain entirely from intercourse before marriage.[65] The main change of style is that the intercourse barrier has fallen, and sex has become part of the non-committal and casual practice of serial mating, which is just as prevalent in US campuses today as it was in Waller's time, though on the face of it less ritualized and

---

[61] Kamen, *Her Way*, 223–35; quote, p. 226.   [62] Whyte, *Dating*, 24.

[63] e.g. in Bailey, *Front Porch*.

[64] Waller, 'Rating and Dating'; Kinsey et al., *Male*, see Fig. 3.2(*b*) above; Greene, *Sex and the College Girl*, ch. 5.   [65] Burgess and Wallin, *Engagement and Marriage*, ch. 11.

inhibited. Conservatives are dismayed at this free-wheeling sexual culture of 'hooking up', while liberals profess to be delighted. Testimonies in this area are not completely reliable, and probably reflect norms more than behaviour, but the general impression of a bipolar distribution remains, with a significant minority exploring the boundaries of sexuality without commitment or even affection, women as freely as men, a small minority (about 10 per cent of women) refraining from sex altogether, and a large group in the middle proceeding as warily as before.[66] Men, it seems have increasingly been able to transfer the initiative (and the risk of rejection), to women, and have abandoned the formalities and cost of dining and entertainment. But romantic love has persisted throughout.[67] There is a cluster of strongly bonded couples, and between eight and nine out of ten college women regard marriage as a very important goal.[68] 'The sexual revolution … has cheapened something that isn't cheap', one woman told an investigator in the 1990s.[69] Christian evangelists have promoted a mass absention pledge movement, Wendy Shalit has resonantly called for a *Return to Modesty*. One of the most popular mating self-help books of the 1990s, *The Rules*, recommended a return to withholding and rationing as a female strategy, while stressing how far things had gone the other way.[70]

Just as material and sexual bonds weakened, the yearning for the unconditional, non-contingent factor of 'love' has increased. In the 1960s, when asked about whether they would marry a partner with all desirable qualities, but without love, 40 per cent of women said that they would. But that was changing.[71] By the late 1980s, the figure had fallen to 15 per cent.[72] People increasingly regarded love as a prerequisite of commitment.[73] Given that the intensity of romantic love is a transient state, it was argued by the 1970s that it provided a weak foundation for long-term commitment.

Marriage was not designed as a mechanism for providing friendship, erotic experience, romantic love, personal fulfillment, continuous lay psychotherapy, or recreation. The Western European family was not designed to carry a lifelong load of highly emotional romantic freight.[74]

As people have become more self-regarding, they have more unconditional 'soul-mate' expectations from their marriage partners, at a time when

[66] Glenn and Marquardt, *Hooking Up*; Kamen, *Her Way*, ch. 4.   [67] Fisher, *Why We Love*.
[68] Glenn and Marquardt, *Hooking Up*, 73.   [69] Kamen, *Her Way*, 88.
[70] Bearman and Bruckner, 'Promising the Future'; Shalit, *Return to Modesty*; Fein and Schneider, *The Rules*.   [71] Cawallader, 'Marriage'.
[72] Simpson et al., 'Romantic Love and Marriage'.
[73] Sprecher et al., 'Love: American Style'.
[74] Cawallader, 'Marriage'; also Veroff et al., 'Happiness in Stable Marriages', 154.

marriage is more brittle than ever.[75] A marriage based exclusively on heightened expectations of love was more exposed to dissolution when these expectations were disappointed.[76]

Marriage: the decline of commitment

On conventional measures of well-being and on average, marriage is a superior state. Married people earn more and own more. Marriage protects both physical and mental health, and extends life expectation by several years. It provides a more satisfying and intensive sex life. Married people are happier than those who are separated and divorced (though not happier than singles). They suffer less domestic violence than cohabitators. Children raised by their own married parents do better in almost every respect.[77] It is not merely a selection effect: it is not entirely the case that those who did better were more likely to marry.[78] But even if it was, they must have had good reasons to do so.

After the deprivations of the 1930s depression and the upheaval of the Second World War, the first post-war decade saw a surge of domesticity in both countries. With only limited education, the binding commitments of marriage were attractive to the young women of the post-war cohorts after the dislocations of depression and war. Women's increasing participation in education, work, and sex reduced the urgency of marriage, and the age of marriage rose. In Britain, for example, the median age of marriage (single women) rose by more than six years from a low of 21 in 1967 to more than 27 in 2000. In the USA it rose to 25 in 2000, up from 20 in 1956.[79] Table 13.1 shows the changing marital status of the white population in the United States, and in England and Wales. It records a reduction over five decades of 15–20 per cent in the proportion of adults married, from the mid to high 60s, down to between 50 and 60 per cent.

Marriage is the public affirmation of commitment. As more marriages terminated, it became less reasonable to expect them to last. If marriage is terminable, then commitment is not final, and can be assumed with less deliberation. That in itself is likely to reduce the quality of commitment. By the 1970s, women's increasing access to education, work, sexuality, and

[75] Whitehead and Popenoe, 'Marry a Soul Mate', 11–14.

[76] Eskapa, *Woman versus Woman*.

[77] Waite and Gallagher, *Case for Marriage*; Doherty et al., *Why Marriage Matters*; Wilson and Oswald, 'How Does Marriage'; Waite and Lehrer, 'Benefits from Marriage'.

[78] Wilson and Oswald, 'How Does Marriage'.

[79] USA Census and British Office of National Statistics data.

Table 13.1. Adult marital status, USA and UK, 1950–2000, percent of total

	USA, whites				England & Wales			
	Married	Divorced	Single	Widowed	Married	Divorced	Single	Widowed
1950	67	2	23	8	58	1	34	8
1960	68	2	22	8	67	1	24	9
1970	65	3	24	8	68	1	21	9
1980	63	6	24	7	63	4	24	9
1990	61	8	24	7	58	7	26	9
2000	59	9	26	6	53	9	30	8

Notes: UK year+1, age 15+ up to 1961, then 16+. USA, 14+ up to 1960, then 15+.

Sources: USA: Bureau of Census, Annual Demographic Supplement to the March 2002 Current Population Survey, Current Population Reports, Series P20-547, 'Children's Living Arrangements and Characteristics: March 2002' and earlier reports, table MS-1. Marital Status of the Population 15 Years Old and Over, by Sex and Race: 1950 to Present.
UK: 1951–61, Mitchell, *Historical Statistics*, tables population and vital statistics, 4, 5; 1971–2000, *Health Statistics Quarterly*, 22 (2002), table 1.5.

divorce also lowered the barriers to withdrawal from marriage. By the 1980s, men began to fare less well economically in relation to women, which made them, at the margin, less attractive as partners. If marriage was terminable, if partners could not be certain of the robustness of their investment, they were more likely to hold back, or perhaps to avoid the commitment altogether.[80] Up to the 1960s, divorce procedures, especially in Britain, were demanding, demeaning, and costly. During the 1970s or early 1980s, most jurisdictions adopted no-fault divorce. Free exit further reduced the credibility of commitments made in marriage and exposed every marriage to unilateral withdrawal.

The 'honeymoon' period marked the transition from courtship to marriage. As with any novelty, the initial period of full-time intimacy and sexual intensity was atypical of married life, and was soon followed by a more habituated routine. Marital satisfaction was at its very highest at the outset and declined sharply in the first few years.[81] At this point, time horizons would have shifted. The couple were available to each other, their futures no longer bounded by the uncertainties of the next meeting. To be sure, the force of mutual attraction often ebbs and flows asymmetrically, but that is a private narrative that is more effectively explored in fiction than in a very limited number of social-science studies.[82]

Between the wedding and the birth of the first child was generally the most satisfying period in the life cycle.[83] Bound together securely by the

[80] Cohen, 'Marriage, Divorce', 295; Cohen, 'Marriage: the Long-Term Contract'; Glenn, 'Trend in Marital Success', 269.   [81] Glenn, 'Course of Marital Success', e.g. fig. 1.
[82] But see Allen and Brinig, 'Sex, Property Rights'.
[83] VanLaningham et al., 'Marital Happiness'.

bonds of love, their initial balance hardly yet disturbed, their partnership still fresh, the couple were in a position to enjoy to the full the satisfactions of companionship and intimacy, with very few of the costs. The couple's assets now included their commitment to each other, and over time they would have accumulated common possessions, shared experiences, and social connections. If the woman withdrew partly or completely from the labour force, she had an interest in the man's accumulating property and pension entitlements, and to the extent that ageing devalued her mating and reproductive potential more than her man's, her loss from terminating the marriage was going to be greater than his, and her bargaining power inside the marriage a slightly declining one. Nevertheless, the couple essentially faced the same time horizon. At this stage marriage was 'transactional'—emotional accounts had to be balanced for the partnership to be mutually rewarding. If not, following the Beckerian model, either partner could withdraw at roughly equal cost.

The birth of a child marked the point at which a clear asymmetry emerged between men and women. For all the pleasure that a new child inspired, for most couples the transition was demanding and stressful.[84] In the UK, the arrival of children in a marriage increased the probability of divorce.[85] The child was a new and unfamiliar member of the partnership. Its bond with the mother was intense: a mother shares her body with the child. The frightening, painful, bloody, exhilarating experience of birth was followed by the extended intimacies of nursing. Marriages can be terminated, but parenthood is not. Generalizing, women have bonded more strongly to their children than men. The maternal commitment competed with the spousal one. This reflected prevalent conventions and norms. The evidence is that outside marriage, the vast majority of parental custodians were mothers, not fathers; mothers were also reported to grieve more at the loss of an infant.[86]

A child reduced the woman's capacity to withdraw from the partnership.[87] If there was a shift from lifetime marriage to 'permanent [mating] availability',[88] then with a dependent child (other things being equal) the mother became less attractive to an alternative partner. She had less time and energy for paid work, while needing more resources. Her partner, in addition to being a companion, lover, helpmate, and a source of income, acquired a new role as the other parent, whose presence was desirable for the child's development. With the birth of the child, the mother drew

[84] Cowan and Cowan, *Partners become Parents*; Gottman and Notarius, 'Marital Research'.
[85] Chan and Halpin, 'Union Dissolution in the UK'.   [86] Mahony, *Kidding Ourselves*, 75.
[87] Ibid. 44; Cohen, 'Marriage, Divorce'.   [88] Faber, 'American Family'.

more out of the marriage.[89] She had presented the child, but this was a gift that she could only take back as a last resort, and at a high cost to herself. The child was not a very credible asset to bargain with. The husband gained a bargaining advantage. His ability to defect might have been weakened by the legal obligations of parenthood, and even more so by the emotional and social ones. But these bonds remained (by assumption) weaker than those of the mother. Her dependence on the man had grown.[90]

The unequal division of housework is an abiding puzzle in family studies.[91] Women contribute much more to it than men, even when they work, and even when they earn as much or more than their men. The time ratio is up to six to one, or about four to one if women work full-time.[92] Even high-achieving women are about five times as likely to take prime responsibility for housework and childcare as their partners.[93] Consider the household as a gift economy: goods and services change hands, but no prices are fixed, and when money is transferred, it does not do so as a wage. 'Love makes us generous'—or at least is supposed to.[94] When the balance of bargaining power changed against them after childbirth, women could redress it, by providing the gift of housework and food. In the United States, women with young children increased their core housework ('cooking and cleaning') in comparison with non-mothers by 46 per cent, to 196 minutes of housework a day; men increased it by 28 per cent, to 32 minutes.[95] American mothers of young children increased 'childcare, shopping, and odd jobs' by 83 per cent, to 205 minutes of housework a day; men increased it only by 20 per cent, to 112 minutes a day. British changes were similar.[96] Mothers of young children took on more than two and a half additional hours of domestic work a day in comparison with non-mothers (more than three if the latter were working full-time), an intense labour of love which was truly its own reward.

This asymmetric division of labour in housework is not condoned here: as an interpretation, it has received the support of women writers, both feminist and not-so.[97] It is a matter of motherhood rather than gender, and

---

[89] Cohen, 'Marriage, Divorce'; Allen and Brinig, 'Sex, Property Rights'.

[90] Cohen, 'Marriage, Divorce'.

[91] Brines, 'Exchange Value'; id., 'Economic Dependency'; Baxter and Western, 'Satisfaction with Housework'.

[92] Gershuny, *Changing Times*, table 7.12, p. 186. 6.3 in the UK, 5.5 in the USA; Brines, 'Economic Dependency'.

[93] Hewlett and Vita-León, 'High-Achieving Women', charts 2.3, 3.3, 35–6.

[94] Mahony, *Kidding Ourselves*, 59.

[95] Calculated from Gershuny, *Changing Times*, table 7.12, p. 187.

[96] Ibid., table 7.16, p. 193.

[97] Mahony, *Kidding Ourselves*, 73–128; Grossbard-Schechtman, *Economics of Marriage*, 56.

appears to arise in lesbian households as well.[98] If it is correct, then motherhood has had to be paid for in hard, unglamorous housework. Married women with children spent substantially more time in housework than those without them, and since the 1980s their contribution to housework appears to have fallen less than that of married women without children.[99] Even men who earned less than their wives did not do more housework than other men, suggesting that the 'masculine' gender identity role was at stake.[100] This might be another way of saying that the mother's gift of housework helped to re-establish equilibrium in the reciprocal economy of domestic regard, after the birth of a child.

If we take childbirth as a voluntary decision (which in many cases it clearly was, given access to birth control), then the loss of bargaining power in marriage could be taken as a measure of the intrinsic value of motherhood, and housework as truly 'a labour of love', designed to make the child welcome and to keep the household together. But given the compelling nature of sexual rewards, and the uncertainties of birth control, it is also possible to regard the decision for motherhood as either myopic, or as not a decision for motherhood at all, in which case the burden of housework was unanticipated and unwelcome. Given the different endowments, expectations, and trade-offs newly available to women, the burden of housework could be experienced at either of these extremes, or anywhere in between. In support of this view, that housework reflected the equilibrium of costs and benefits for both spouses, are findings that despite the large imbalance of housework, a large proportion of women responded that they found the division of household labour to be fair.[101]

A central element in the woman's 'gift' was still the provision of food. In terms of time-budgets, preparing food and eating it was the largest single item of housework.[102] It created a direct and daily dependence of the family on the mother. It also made them all the captive recipients of her 'gift' for a set period of time every single day. When meals were cooked at home, from primary ingredients, adapted to the special needs of all members of the family, the 1950s wife provided a service that was difficult to find elsewhere at reasonable cost. Faster food in supermarkets and high streets provided substitutes for the housewife's gift. In the face of this availability, wives strove to maintain the 'proper meal' as the central recurrent ritual of

---

[98] Lewin, *Lesbian Mothers*, 130–4. [99] Gershuny, *Changing Times*, table 7.16, p. 193.
[100] Brines, 'Economic Dependency'.
[101] Baxter and Western, 'Satisfaction with Housework' ('almost half'); Brines, 'Economic Dependency'. Their interpretations differ from mine.
[102] Gershuny, *Changing Times*, table 7.14, p. 189, table 7.15, p. 191; Ch. 7 above, Figure 7.6.

family life. To the extent that they have failed, and that the family meal has declined in importance, so has women's bargaining power, and what they have to offer in the family gift exchange.[103]

The precise balance of obligation was a delicate matter to determine, nor was it static: it changed as the balance of advantage in the marriage shifted, and was easy to misjudge. Some men were certainly inclined to resent their loss of monopoly of attention and affection.[104] Hence, the temptation for men to abuse their bargaining power, by demanding too much, or even by physical violence. Taking a measure of subjective dependency ('wife expects to be hurt more than husband if marriage breaks up'), any level of positive subjective dependency ('low, high, very high') almost tripled the level of vulnerability to 'minor violence', up to about one in eight. Among women who were also 'objectively dependent' (i.e. had a lower income than the husband, and dependent children) the level was even higher. 'Severe violence' rates were likewise about triple those of non-dependent women, and about or higher than one in twenty.[105]

But abuse of bargaining power was not restricted to violence. A common feature of asymmetric marriage was a withdrawal of approbation, intimacy, and respect, and its replacement by denigration and distance.[106] 'Criticism, defensiveness, contempt, and stonewalling' were predictive of subsequent divorce.[107] Cycles of negative reciprocity led to low marital quality and predicted dissolution.[108] To the extent that the perpetrators expected the relationship to continue, this provocation may be regarded as myopic: their partner was currently in a weaker position, and the perpetrator did not look beyond that.

The core of marital expectations remains an emotional exchange. In its most distinctive form, this is experienced as the quality and intensity of the mother–child relationship. Parenting requires presence, concentration, and attention, and takes up a great deal of time. It can be absorbing, satisfying, or disappointing. It also has a 'product', a maturing, well-adjusted parental relationship with a mutual obligation and a commitment to the child that is deeper and more robust than the spousal contract.

[103] Above, Ch. 7.
[104] For a crude expression, Bakeman and Krinbring, *Married to Mommy?*
[105] Kalmuss and Straus, 'Wife's Marital Dependency', esp. pp. 376–7. Other studies on domestic violence suggest that male violence sometimes occurs when there is status inferiority to women. See Anderson, 'Gender, Status, and Domestic Violence'. In terms of intensity and frequency, violence is much more often directed by men at women than vice versa (Johnson and Ferraro, 'Research on Domestic Violence', 952).
[106] Hite, *Women and Love*, ch. 1; Rubin, *Worlds of Pain*, ch. 7; Komarovsky, *Blue-Collar Marriage*, chs. 5–7; Gottman and Notarius, 'Decade Review'; id., 'Marital Research'.
[107] Pinsof, 'Till Death Us Do Part'.   [108] Gottman, *What Predicts Divorce*, 50–2.

This role, and the satisfactions it provides, is primarily available to women. Economists have attempted to quantify the high price paid by women in forgoing full labour force participation, and investing in children. But the cost of children can also be taken as a measure of their value. Since motherhood is voluntary (and assuming that it is), its cost (in market terms) is the magnitude of the disadvantages suffered by mothers in both the labour and spousal markets. The cost is massive: for a two-child family, the lifetime costs are comparable to those of a rather expensive middle-class house; for one child, to a reasonable mortgage. In 1980, the cost was estimated at 37 per cent of family income for two children, and 23 per cent for one.[109] The wage penalty alone for married women was estimated (in the 1980s) to be about 7 per cent per child.[110] The financial benefits that mothers forgo might be taken as a measure of the anticipated benefits of motherhood. This is not meant to imply that these sacrifices are justified: only that the majority of women still chose motherhood in spite of these costs, so it must have been worth more to them than the money and other advantages they lost. That is an economic measure of the value of motherhood. Women valued marriage more than men. About 80 per cent consistently stated that a good marriage was 'extremely important' between the 1970s and the 1990s. Even more were positive about being married.[111] They expressed themselves, on the whole, as satisfied with life as men (Table 2.2, above). Likewise, in more detailed studies of marital success, women were slightly happier with marriage in the years reported (one and eleven), and in any case very similar in satisfaction to men.[112] So one may assume that (at this very high level of generality), the costs that women took on represented an acceptable deal, and that the rewards of motherhood and domestic gift exchange were sufficient to compensate for labour market disadvantages.

This needs to be qualified. The rise in divorce (mostly initiated by women) was not consistent with acquiescence. The maternal trade-off was only satisfactory if the marriage persisted. If the woman was pushed to separate or divorce, then she is suffered even more for her gift of love and care.

If, however, women have invested in motherhood at a level that has left them (in the aggregate) reasonably satisfied, then this level is less than good for society as a whole. The equilibrium between motherhood and

[109] Above, Ch. 11, n. 101; also Olson, *Costs of Children*, 3, 55.
[110] Budig and England, 'Wage Penalty'.
[111] Men were 5 to 10 percentage points lower on both measures. Thornton and Young-DeMarco, 'Trends in Attitudes', table 2, p. 1019.
[112] Glenn, 'Course of Marital Success', fig. 4, p. 573.

work that is currently acceptable for women has driven the birth rate below population replacement levels for North America and most European societies. Motherhood is not attractive enough for women to produce enough children to reproduce existing societies endogenously. If that is a problem, then the heavy cost of motherhood is a case of myopic under-generosity by society as a whole. There is a serious crisis of dependency brewing up, in which the rising proportion of older people in the near future will impose heavy burdens on those who are working. It can be traced directly to the shortfall of children. Substitution of immigrants and their children on a sufficient scale is almost impossible, and raises many new problems of its own.[113]

The competition of family and work

In the economic 'specialization and trading' model, men bring the cash into the family 'firm', because men cannot have children and are less inclined to care for them.[114] As work offered higher wages to women, affluence reduced the cost of market goods, and this increased the relative cost of domestic production, the cost of children, of domestic order, and of time-intensive domestic 'bliss'. In response, more was purchased in the market and less was produced at home. The relative cost of market goods fell partly because of technological change, and partly due to increased demand for women's abilities in the labour markets.[115] The outcomes are indeed largely as described by this theory. But how rational has this shift been, and to what extent has it increased welfare?

Household choices were potentially affected by two biases: one of them is the standard 'social dilemma', in which the pursuit of individual gain proves to be self-defeating. When labour is standardized, then competition among workers is counter-productive. The prospects of promotion are remote. Everyone ends up working harder, with no individual gain. Better for workers to combine and restrict their effort. So compelling is this argument that despite enormous obstacles to collective action, organized labour has repeatedly managed to restrict the hours of labour, which are the chief form of potential competition.[116] Over the long term, since the

[113] Kotlikoff and Burns, *Coming Generational Storm.*
[114] Oppenheimer, 'Women's Employment'. [115] Goldin, *Gender Gap*, ch. 5.
[116] Mill, *Principles*, Bk. 5, ch. 11, sect. 12; Webb and Webb, *Industial Democracy*, ch. 5; Frank, *Choosing the Right Pond*, 90–9. Frank also invokes the status loss involved in competition by effort.

high point during industrialization, the long trend of working hours has been downwards.[117]

But Fordist factory work has diminished. In Britain, at age 35, only 7 per cent of men born before 1900 had been professionals, managers, and administrators in large enterprises, while of those born in 1950–9, almost a quarter were. An additional 35 per cent were self-employed, or managers in small enterprises.[118] Overall, for the youngest UK cohort, almost 60 per cent of males at age 35 fell into these 'status competitive' categories, and stood to gain or lose in workplace competition: competitive ponds in these occupations were much smaller than in Fordist factories. Recent studies in the United States have shown that about one-third of workers have college degrees and a professional or managerial job.[119] Other things (like talent, energy, connections, and temperament) being equal, the only way to compete for status was more time on the job. In some lines of work this was explicit: legal and management firms use 'billable hours' to evaluate effort.[120] The medical and legal professions are both 'greedy institutions' which keep their members on the job or on call for very long hours.

In continental Europe, workers continued to take progressively more of their rewards in leisure, but in the United States and Britain, after the 1970s, the trend for shorter working hours per worker began to reverse.[121] For households the increase has been dramatic, as ever more wives worked for longer hours.[122] A slight reduction in working hours continued for those with limited schooling, but there were fewer of those. College-educated workers put in longer hours. By 1988, the 75th percentile of college-educated white male workers were putting in some 2,600 hours a year, about a quarter more than those with high-school education or lower.[123] As the proportion of managerial and professional workers increased, they also worked for longer hours.[124] By the 1990s such men were working 44.6 hours a week, some 10 per cent longer than other workers. Of these higher-status workers, more than a third were working fifty hours plus a week. Workers were typically satisfied with thirty to fifty hours of work a week, and those with longer hours usually wanted to reduce their time at work by 10 per cent or more.[125] In fact, in the United States in 1997, 46 per cent

[117] Bienefeld, *Working Hours*; Cross, 'Worktime in International Discontinuity'; Huberman, 'Working Hours of the World Unite'; Steinberg, *Wages and Hours*.
[118] Halsey and Webb, *British Social Trends*, 258–60.
[119] Maume and Bellas, 'Overworked American', 1154, n. 3.   [120] Yakura, 'Billables'.
[121] Gershuny, *Changing Times*, 61–2; Costa, 'Wage and Length'; Schor, *Overworked American*.
[122] Hout and Hanley, 'Overworked American Family'; Figure 11.4, above.
[123] Coleman and Pencavel, 'Changes in Work Hours', table 4, p. 268.
[124] Robinson and Godbey, *Time for Life*, 217; Gershuny, *Changing Times*, 175–80.
[125] Jacobs and Gerson, 'Overworked Americans'.

of workers said they would like much more time with their families, and 85 per cent wanted more time. In this international survey, American workers reported the tightest time squeeze, with Britain and France only a short way behind.[126]

More commitment to the job made motherhood harder to sustain. Time on the job was time away from home.[127] Electronic communications made it more difficult to escape the job. If workplace effort delivered higher status and earnings, it also provided the wage-worker with greater domestic leverage at home. The wife's contribution (it was usually the wife) was diminished in comparison, and limited her capacity to reciprocate.[128] For some partners, the workplace became a substitute for home, a less demanding and more accepting environment.[129] Nor was workplace effort optional: once status competition became the norm, it became difficult for a worker to opt out of it, except by accepting immobility, or conscious 'downshifting'.[130] In addition to the financial sacrifice involved, with a more educated workforce, withdrawal from competition might well carry the psychic costs of lower status as well. In the meantime, while both men and women have invested more time in work, 'for most women, in working families, women have shifted away from finding work more satisfying than home towards finding home a haven'.[131]

Even with equal education and talents, women found it more difficult to compete at work. Professional and managerial women worked longer hours than women in other occupations, but fewer hours than similar men, and a smaller proportion put in for fifty-hour-plus working weeks.[132] Since the 1970s, by far the largest increase in joint household working hours has taken in households where both men and women had a college degree.[133] For mothers of young children, workplace competition was an even greater burden: more time on the job was what they found most difficult to provide.[134] Unless they had truly exceptional talents, working mothers fell into 'slow track' status progression, which was reflected in the paucity of women at the highest professional, managerial, and ownership levels. Amongst women graduates from Harvard law, medical, and business

[126] Blanchflower and Oswald, 'Work–Life Balance', 3–4.
[127] Fligstein and Sharone, 'Work in California'; Hochschild, Second Shift.
[128] Case studies in Hochschild, Second Shift.   [129] Hochschild, Time Bind.
[130] Hochschild, Second Shift; Bunting, Willing Slaves, ch. 2.
[131] Kiecolt, 'Satisfaction with Work', 23; similar conclusions, Maume and Bellas, 'Overworked American?', 1151.   [132] Jacobs and Gerson, 'Overworked Americans', 447.
[133] Joint working hours were even longer in households where wives had college degrees and husbands had only completed high school. Hout and Hanley, 'Overworked American Family', tables 4–6.   [134] Graphically portrayed in Pearson, Don't Know How She Does It.

schools during the 1970s, more than two-thirds had reduced their paid hours because of children, and over half had changed jobs to accommodate children.[135] Highest achieving women also had the highest levels of childlessness.[136] Twenty-nine per cent of 'high-achieving women' worked more than fifty hours a week, and more than a third of 'ultra-high' achievers.[137] Women writers have worried over this dilemma, and have advocated statutory limits on men's efforts.[138] In the United States, a majority of women worked full-time. In Britain, the majority preference was for part-time work.[139]

In a positional race which not everyone can win, it was reasonable to redefine the objective away from status and towards domestic satisfactions. Qualified women leaving careers in favour of motherhood is a staple theme in Sunday supplements.[140] 'Downshifting' is a popular aspiration, reflected in the popular British sitcom *The Good Life*. Of two couples sharing the same semi-detached suburban house, one was committed to the workplace and domestic consumption status races, while the other aspired to a simple, self-sufficient lifestyle. The programme poked gentle fun at the inconsistencies in both positions. A recent study of 'downshifting' has found that over a quarter of British adults aged 30–59 have voluntarily made a long-term change in lifestyle that resulted in earning less money. The average reduction in income was 40 per cent.[141] In the United States, between 20 and 30 per cent had made such voluntary lifestyle changes during the 1990s.[142] 'Voluntary Simplicity' has a long tradition in the United States, and disquiet about the work–life balance is rife.[143] The European Union has restricted 'average working hours' to a maximum forty-eight a week, motivated in part by similar family considerations, and France has restricted working hours to thirty-five. Britain has chosen to allow individual workers to opt out, thus negating the purpose of the

[135] Mahony, *Kidding Ourselves*, 139.

[136] Hewlett, *Creating a Life*; Hewlett and Vite-León, 'High-Achieving Women', Table 11.2 and Figure 11.7, above.

[137] Sample sizes of 1,169 and 332 respectively; Hewlett and Vite-León, 'High-Achieving Women', tables 1.1, 1.2, 24–5.

[138] Hewitt, *About Time*; Hochschild, *Second Shift*; Bunting, *Willing Slaves*; Williams, *Unbending Gender*.

[139] Hakim, *Work–Lifestyle Choices*, compare table 4.1, p. 86 and pp. 123–5.

[140] O'Kelly, 'It Beats Working'; Belkin, 'The Opt-Out Revolution'.

[141] Hamilton, 'Downshifting'. For downshifting manuals, see Bull, *Downshifting*; Ghazi and Jones, *Downshifting*. For recent downshifting aspirations, Futures Laboratory, *Shape of Dreams*.

[142] Schor, *Overspent American*, ch. 5–19 per cent voluntary downshifting between 1990 and 1996. Harwood, 'Yearning for Balance' found in 1995 that 28 per cent had voluntarily downshifted; also Meiksins and Whalley, *Work in its Place*. Several downshifting manuals are listed there as well.

[143] Elgin, *Voluntary Simplicity*; Shi, *The Simple Life*; Harwood Group, 'Yearning for Balance'; Etzioni, 'Voluntary Simplicity'.

directive, and expressing a preference for growth over leisure in the balance of well-being.

Another driver of long working hours was competition for the goods which define the conventional level of living. In the affluent society, to be without them was to be poor. Low quantity or quality signified low status. The first priority in this respect was housing, which went a long way to define social position, and which provided access to social goods like security and education for children. Social inclusion required access to consumer durables and services, e.g. radio, television, telephone, washing machine, motor car. When these goods fell in price, new ones came along, which were often still expensive at the stage when they first became socially imperative.[144] On the low incomes of manual workers, one way to acquire these goods was for the wife (in a 'single breadwinner' family) to go out to work, quite often in casual, part-time, and low-paid work. Once a sufficient number of such wives had gone to work, the acceptable 'level of living' rose further. Rising income inequality in American and British societies since the 1970s made this problem worse, since consumption by the rich escalated levels of 'normative' consumption, and the incomes of working professional and managerial couples, often delaying childbirth, raised that threshold (for the 'representative consumer') further still.[145] It is tempting to regard this race as irrational, since only a few could win.[146] That was the position taken by the crusading Canadian magazine *Adbusters*, with its 'buy nothing day', and 'watch no television week'. But the goods in question, however dispensable in other cultures, were truly vital for social participation. In the absence of equal education and of guaranteed safety, a presentable house in a secure neighbourhood, with access to good schools, was no luxury for parents. In the thinly settled expanses of suburbia, a car for every active adult (and often for teenagers too) was a necessity as well. In the United States, employment was insecure, and access to health cover was attached to the workplace. Increasing levels of self-coverage also meant that health care depended increasingly on income. Falling out of the race pushed these necessities out of reach, and constituted a serious threat to life chances and health. It was dangerous, difficult, and costly to shirk the race. But taking part destabilized domestic equilibrium, and constituted a threat to marital stability.[147] With ill-health and unemployment, divorce was one of the 'big three' threats to participation in the 'American Dream'.

[144] Packard, *Status Seekers*, chs. 5–6, 9, 21; Schor, *Overspent American*, chs. 1–4; Ch. 8 above.
[145] Hout, 'Money and Morale'; Frank, *Luxury Fever*; Schor, *Overspent America*, ch. 1.
[146] e.g. Frank, *Luxury Fever*.   [147] Hochschild, *Second Shift*.

Feminism and changing norms

The asymmetry of post-war marriages built up strong pressures of discontent. They burst into public view in Betty Friedan's *Feminine Mystique* (1963). Another outcome was the emergence of no-fault divorce, which diffused through the United States during the 1970s and early 1980s, and appeared in Britain at the same time. The malaise of marriage was confirmed by the large upsurge in divorce during the same period. From around 9 divorces per 1,000 married women in 1960, the rate rose to 22 by 1980, before stabilizing at around 20, and recently declining down to 18 (levels in the UK have been in the range 10–14).[148] A great deal of misery was alleviated: female suicide rates and domestic violence fell significantly.[149] But no-fault divorce seriously weakened the safeguards implicit in the marriage contract for women.[150] For the generation embarking on mating in the 1970s, it signalled that commitment was not as credible as before, and that it could no longer be counted on. Friedan compared the family to a 'comfortable concentration camp'.[151] One strand in the feminist movement sought to discredit the family entirely, and this normative rejection of the family persists.[152] Anne Roiphe describes the dismay of a feminist mother early in the 1970s:

'Just a housewife' became as dirty and derogatory a term as 'spinster' had once been. In certain hip circles 'barren' was replaced by 'cow,' 'old maid' was linguistically lost, children were no longer proof of goodness.[153]

The tide of marriage turned in 1975 when the mean age at marriage began to rise again. The experience of disrupted commitment conventions was described by a woman of that generation:

In the 70's, a time conditioned by the sexual revolution and ambient feminism, there were no rules ... We were free to do as we wished.... so humiliation was more likely to ensue after sleeping with someone who never called back; wasting years in a relationship that didn't become a marriage; becoming pregnant out of wedlock; devoting all of one's energy to a career while expecting family life to fall into place—and winding up alone. Arguably these events lead to a magnitude of emotional devastation far greater than that following any emotional slip that may occur in the realm of chastity....

---

[148] United States Bureau of Census, *Statistical Abstract*; UK, ONS; National Marriage Project, *Unions 2003*, fig. 6, p. 24.   [149] Stevenson and Wolfers, 'Bargaining'.
[150] Rowthorn, 'Marriage and Trust'; Crittenden, *Price of Motherhood*, chs. 7–9.
[151] Friedan, *Feminine Mystique*, ch. 12.
[152] Firestone, *Dialectic of Sex*; Stacey, 'Good Riddance'; Stacey, *In the Name*; Card, 'Against Marriage and Motherhood'.   [153] Roiphe, *Mother's Eye*, 13.

Because we were without useful roadsigns, constraining rules, and even a correct understanding of human nature (that is, male nature), we were doomed to learn little from our mistakes. And we were forced to spend hours in hollow reasoning with our friends, over strategy, tactics, armaments, relations of actions to consequences, likelihood that one's experience was representative or abberational, etc.[154]

While the grandeur of weddings was increasing, their religious authority was diminished. Britain has not been deeply religious since the nineteenth century. But in the United States, secularization has been long in coming, and commitment to religious norms remains high. Inter-faith marriages have increased, and traditional sanctions (if they exist) do not derive equally from both sides of the marriage.[155] The Jews, among the most family-oriented of American ethnic groups, have had intermarriage rates of about 50 per cent. The normative perplexity is captured by Philip Roth, in a passage in his novel *American Pastoral*, in which the old Jewish patriarch spends an afternoon bargaining with his son's Catholic bride (a former Miss New Jersey) about the putative grandchild's religious upbringing.[156] For the daughter that emerges (ironically named 'Merry') this negotiation turns out to be grotesquely irrelevant. She grows up to become a caricature feminist-radical, blows up a post office, and unravels emotionally and physically in a Newark slum, exposing the emptiness of her father's conventional athletic and business success. The novel might be read as a metaphor for normative disorientation.

As the credibility of marriage declined, a time of experiments began. For a while, there was a quest for new contractual forms for marriage. In April 1972 *Life* magazine published a special issue on new forms of marriage, including an article which described a detailed 'contract' allocating tasks to the two partners.[157] Looking back many years later, one of the partners revealed how much of the agreement (and the article) had been wishful thinking and mutual dissimulation.[158] One solution put forward seriously was that of pre-nuptial contracts, as if the marriage contract itself was not solemn enough.[159] Such contracts were intended to lock in the pre-nuptial bargaining equilibrium for the duration of the marriage, which would tilt them in favour of women. Arizona and Louisiana have introduced 'Covenant Marriage' options, which can only be dissolved by demonstrating fault.[160] As a commitment device, the idea has failed to catch on,

---

154 Schiffren, 'Single Minded', 45.
155 Kalmijn, 'Shifting Boundaries'; Heaton and Pratt, 'Religious Homogamy'.
156 Also Chinitz and Brown, 'Religious Homogamy'. 157 *Life*, 'Living by Contract'.
158 Shulman, 'Marriage Disagreement'. 159 Weitzman, *Marriage Contract*.
160 Spaht, 'Louisiana's Covenant Marriage'.

perhaps because premarital ardour is no longer in a position to lock in the married future.[161]

Women responded to new mating conditions by redoubling investment in their own personal capital. Education and work were attractive in themselves, but they had a negative bearing on marital commitment. If well-educated and well-paid women still sought to marry or mate upwards, then they postponed marriage and faced a contracting pool of eligible men, made worse by the adverse sex ratios of the 1970s.[162] At the other end of the social scale, reproduction was being separated from marriage. That is evidence of the decline of the traditional rationale for marriage, namely recruitment of male investment into reproduction. Starting in the 1960s, births out of wedlock began to rise very rapidly. In the lower social end of the black community, marriage seemed to have collapsed almost entirely. Large numbers of black men out of work, in prison, in the military, had few economic resources to invest in child-rearing.[163] The majority of women proceeded into child-rearing on their own, with no contractual reliance and little support from the fathers. About two-thirds of black children are now born out of wedlock, and given the increasing numbers of the black middle class, the standard family among lower-class blacks appears to have contracted drastically.[164]

The next affected group were working-class whites. The large majority of births out of wedlock appeared in this group, and total births out of wedlock rose from less than 5 per cent in the 1960s, to about one-third today. Britain was only a little behind. It is notable that this increase took place almost entirely *after* the emergence of the birth control pill, i.e. of an effective contraceptive controlled by women. The rise of births out of wedlock is a testimony to the rewards of motherhood, even in conditions of material deprivation, and also to the difficulty of recruiting male commitment to the project, or perhaps to the decline in the credibility of the marriage contract. In many cases, the parents of the children remained in touch, and there was some male investment and support: but this support was voluntary, unenforceable, and unreliable. Later in the life course, more single parents were recruited from the separated and divorced. During the 1980s, more than a quarter of white American children were living with a single parent. Nearly half of white children, and two-thirds of black children, were likely to spend part of their childhood in a single-parent family.[165]

---

[161] Lundberg and Pollak, 'Efficiency in Marriage'.

[162] Mahony, *Kidding Ourselves*, 142–6.

[163] Wilson, *Truly Disadvantaged*; id., *When Work Disappears*.   [164] Above, Figure 11.4.

[165] Teachman et al., 'Changing Demography', 1240.

Cohabitation gradually became a routine antecedent of marriage.[166] In the 1990s, some 7 per cent of heterosexual households were cohabiting in the United States, and about one-fifth in Britain.[167] For a large minority of couples, it was also a substitute for marriage. That may have suited some temperaments and attachment styles: it made commitment less certain, and withdrawal easier. Cohabitation therefore required an effort to maintain a high level of gratification, and may have ended up as a way of ensuring it. Cohabitees reported more high-frequency sex than any other group.[168] That was consistent with the position that expectations of gratification have risen. But it also made relationships more fragile. Typically, cohabitation consisted of a period of several months to several years of living together. In the majority of cases, the couple had no common children. Mutual selection was not underpinned by unconditional commitment. The motives might be various: 'dangerous living' which relied on love alone; a concession by one partner to another; or a disbelief in the credibility of marriage. Whatever the cause, the weakness of commitment expressed by cohabitation apparently continued into marriage, when that followed.[169] But cohabitation did not provide the 'protective effect' of marriage in finance, mental health, physical health, and life expectation.[170] Cohabitation was a trial period. More than half of all cohabitations ended in marriage, or in a partnership longer than four years,[171] but these partnerships were less likely to endure, although the two populations (married and cohabiting) probably differed on other dimensions as well.[172] What the rise in cohabitation suggests is that individuals who sought the benefits that a sexual, residential partnership could provide were increasingly rejecting marriage as an effective commitment device, because they refused to be committed themselves, or did not trust it to commit their partners, or both.

A variant of cohabitation is same-sex partnership. Its increasing acceptance is another reason for the decline of heterosexual marriage. The true level of same-sex preferences is not clear, but the proportion of men appears to be higher than that of women, so the withdrawal of male homosexuals from the marriage market reduces women's prospects of marriage.[173] For women, however, as same-sex preferences have become

---

[166] Brown and Booth, 'Cohabitation versus Marriage'; Smock, 'Cohabitation'.

[167] Pinsof, 'Death Us Do Part'.

[168] Michael et al., *Sex in America*, table 8, p. 116; Wellings et al., *Sexual Behaviour in Britain*, table 4.1, p. 140.

[169] DeMaris and Rao, 'Premarital Cohabitation'; Thomson and Colella, 'Cohabitation and Marital Stability'.   [170] Wilson and Oswald, 'How Does Marriage', 7–9.

[171] Smock, 'Cohabitation'.

[172] Teachman, 'Premarital Sex'; Cohan and Kleinbaum, 'Cohabitation Effect'.

[173] Michael et al., *Sex in America*, 171–6.

more socially legitimate, they have also provided an alternative form of companionship and intimacy, and same-sex partnerships are beginning to produce children as well.

In 1990, about a quarter of adults in both countries were living singly, not formally committed, before, between, and outside cohabitation and marriage. These were nominally, from a contractual point of view at least, 'fancy free'. About half of those had no sexual relations or very limited ones, but the other half appeared to match the frequent love-making of married couples.[174]

If evolutionary psychology is correct, then the motives of romantic love should not cease with marriage. Additional partners would confer a reproductive advantage on men (obviously) but also on women.[175] The impulsive 'honey trap' of romantic love could not only lead into marriage, it could also trigger its dissolution. Large absolute numbers (about one-quarter of men in the USA, and 15 per cent of women—similar orders of magnitude in Britain) admit (in confidence) to having pursued love across the boundaries of marriage, and several surveys have reported higher figures.[176] Just as marriage is public, affairs are furtive, and depend on secrecy for survival. They might be seen as an attempt to reactivate the excitable state of romantic love. They are a secret rebellion against the finality of marriage, but unless they come out, their secrecy is an acceptance of that finality. They can generate all the joys and sorrows of romantic love, but are often degraded by the duplicity involved.[177] Such alliances flourish in the shadowlands of moral disapproval, social science neglect, and cognitive dissonance. But in surveys, avowed levels of disapproval are much higher than admitted levels of fidelity.[178] Infidelity exposed is tragic: like many other forms of time inconsistency (or risk-taking), it imposes costs that are out of proportion to the benefits gained. It features extensively in the grown-up genres of fiction, theatre, opera, and biography. Moving between farce, tenderness, and tragedy, from *Così fan tutte* to *Madame Bovary* and *Anna Karenina*, art gets much closer to transgressive love than social science has done so far.[179] It is idle to speculate whether infidelity has risen, though longer hours and more autonomy at work for both

---

[174] Michael et al., *Sex in America*, table 8, p. 116; Wellings et al., *Sexual Behaviour in Britain*, table 4.1, p. 140.   [175] Fisher, *Anatomy*, ch. 4.

[176] Laumann et al., *Sexuality*, 214–16; Wellings et al., *Sexual Behaviour in Britain*, 114. Reported British levels are lower, but cover shorter periods of time. This is not completely out of line with Kinsey et al., *Male*, p. 585 (27–37%), though he assumes considerable underreporting. Both recent surveys were carried out in 1990. Fisher, *Anatomy*, 84–6 cites several other reports.   [177] Taylor, *Affairs*.

[178] Wellings, *Sexual Behaviour in Britain*, table 6.6, p. 258.   [179] Atkins et al., 'Affairs'.

women and men, as well as cheap travel and communications, would all expand the opportunities. Infidelity is usually regarded as a challenge to commitment, but if it makes the boundaries more porous, it may also be protective.

The increasing difficulty of commitment is captured by measures of marital quality. Since the 1950s it had been believed that marital satisfaction began at its highest point, and then declined precipitately, reaching its lowest point when children were young, and rising back again after they left. About two-thirds of newly-weds said that their marriage was very happy, but after twenty years this was down to about a third. The sharp rise of divorce in the 1970s (and the growing insistence on love as a prerequisite for marriage) suggested that surviving marriages ought to be happier.[180] In fact, the recovery of happiness in the third decade of marriage appears to have been a statistical artefact of the use of cross-sections, in which the higher satisfaction rate of earlier cohorts was confounded with a recovery of happiness over the life cycle. The current picture is grim: happiness in marriages falls steeply during the first decade, and continues to decline over the whole life cycle. Older cohorts, married in the 1930s, were substantially happier than younger ones, married in the 1970s.[181] And despite the large increase in divorce, which would have weeded out unhappy marriages, marital quality declined even in the most optimistic and richly specified models.[182]

Conclusion

Monogamous marriage had always been a strain, but up to the 1950s it was normally followed through all the way to sundering by death. Men and women had a strong desire to pair, but permanency was only guaranteed by the economic dependence, sexual exclusivity, and social sanctions of the male breadwinner marriage. Affluence loosened the marital bonds. Sexuality lost some of its mystery as young people in their late teens and early twenties were encouraged by easier contraception and permissive media into more premarital experimentation. Women's education and employment capital allowed them to be more selective before marriage, and more demanding during its course. More opportunities were sacrificed

[180] Glenn, 'Recent Trend', 268.
[181] Glenn, 'Marital Success'; Ono, 'Historical Time'; Rogers and Amato, 'Marital Quality Declining'.
[182] Amato et al., 'Continuity and Change', VanLaningham et al., 'Marital Happiness'.

by committing to motherhood and housekeeping. Market provision of food and clothing undermined the value of traditional domestic skills, even as feminism was actively discrediting them. Rising expectations of love gave more grounds for disappointment. No-fault divorce made withdrawal easier. The workplace drew men and women away from home. And the evidence of failure fed back to make commitment even less credible, obliterated familiar road maps, and threw each individual increasingly on to their own resources. But self-seeking individuals were also less well prepared for the sacrifices that make marriage work. Altruistic families were happier.[183]

For most women, affluence provided a choice: marriage remained the main gate into motherhood. Withdrawal from partnership, whether impulsive or calculated, became easier, and the rewards of interaction and cooperation became more difficult to achieve. Marriage was increasingly postponed, childbirth fell, separation and divorce increased. At the bottom of the social scale, because men's commitment was often neither readily available, nor very credible, and with marriage less durable and less binding, motherhood was also entered more readily without marriage. From the point of view of consumer sovereignty, this was all to the good. It was the consequence of free choices in the market for affection. In the aggregate, people have chosen to invest more directly in themselves, and less in commitment to others, less in companionship, in intimacy, and in the next generation. They demanded that costs and benefits to themselves should balance, and had less patience to wait. 'The new understanding that happiness is not a privilege but a right means that he has a duty to himself to find it.'[184]

Love holds out the promise of bliss. Marriage, more prosaically but durably, locks in the benefits of heterosexual partnership. It gives no guarantees, only a strong likelihood of economic and financial gain. It protects against depression and other psychological problems and promises better health and a longer life. In an affluent market society, the marriage 'economy of regard' can be a beacon of reward if the parties believe in it and its quality is high. Market affluence has not been good for the family. The proportion of adults enjoying the protective effect of marriage has declined by about 15–20 per cent since 1950 (above Table 13.1). Within the family, the pursuit of self-fulfilment has been self-defeating. This choice, between the family and the wider world outside, has been the most salient and intractable challenge presented by affluence in advanced industrial countries.

---

[183] Phelps, 'A Clue'.   [184] Eskapa, *Woman versus Woman*, 129.

14

Women and Children Last:[1] The Retreat from Commitment

Divorce

Since the 1980s, for about one-half of those couples getting married, the disaster or deliverance of divorce waited somewhere down the road.[2] In the dominant economic theory of consumption, individuals follow a consistent strategy which encompasses their whole life cycle.[3] The possibility of divorce is a major dislocation of the life plan of consumption and accumulation. If the probability rises to 50 per cent levels, then a prudent partner will have a contingency plan. The rising costs of divorce partly offset the economic gains of the post-war period. After the 1970s, divorce contributed to the economic stagnation or loss that were experienced by a majority in the United States while the economy continued to grow. It inflicted both temporary and lasting damage, emotional and economic, on the principals and their offspring.

Since the 1960s, the vows of marriage have carried less conviction and the pace of marriage dissolution has picked up. Since the high point of marriage in 1960, the percentage of adults married at any one time has declined from 68 to 59 per cent in the USA, and from 67 to 53 per cent in the UK. Most of this rise in divorce took place between the late 1960s and 1980s. In the USA, the divorce rate per 1,000 adult married women rose from 9.2 in 1960, to 22.6 in 1980, and then declined to 18.8 in 2000.[4] The

---

[1] Chapter title borrowed, with acknowledgement to Sidel, *Women & Children Last.*

[2] Martin and Bumpass, 'Marital Disruption'; Bramlett and Mosher, 'First Marriage Dissolution', tables 3–4; Raley and Bumpass, 'Topography of Divorce'.

[3] Lord, *Household Dynamics.*   [4] National Marriage Project, *Unions 2003*, fig. 6, p. 24.

stock of divorced adults, which stood at about 1–2 per cent in 1950, has risen by an order of magnitude, up to 9–10 per cent by the year 2000 (Table 13.1). In the UK, likewise, the decade of fastest growth in divorce was the 1970s.

There are several explanatory approaches to divorce. The most prominent at the moment is the study of the micro-dynamics of couples by means of close observations of their interactions. It is claimed that these observations allow very accurate predictions of divorce within relatively short time frames of between eighteen months and six years.[5] This may work at the personal level, but not for society as a whole: it does not explain why divorce rates doubled within the 1970s. Likewise, the 'women's independence' hypothesis of family dissolution, which highlights the increasing discretion provided to women by education and work, does not have the right timing: while women's education and work have continued apace, divorce stabilized and even declined a little in the 1990s. And educated women have been catching up on matrimony, rather than abandoning it further.[6] That leaves the shift to no-fault divorce starting in the late 1960s as the most likely candidate.[7] It made separation easier, but was more likely an effect rather than a cause, reflecting a relaxation of the social stigmas of separation. The surge in divorce from the late 1960s until about 1980 may then be regarded as an expression of pent-up demand, arising from the tensions of asymmetric marriage and new opportunities for self-sufficiency, after which divorce rates stabilized at their 'natural' level for the USA, where they have remained ever since (a similar spike of pent-up demand occurred just after the Second World War). Another factor might have been the new welfare benefits, which created a material safety net for women independently of male breadwinner support.

The birth of a child creates an asymmetry of advantage in the marriage and leaves the woman open to exploitation.[8] In the United States, women have initiated about two-thirds of divorces, and this appears to be consistent with avowed preferences elicited by surveys.[9] The dominant reasons reported are a mismatch of emotional expectations.[10] Whereas in the 1940s divorces were initiated for instrumental reasons, by the 1970s, marriage was failing to meet expectations for companionate fulfilment.[11]

[5] Gottman and Notarius, 'Marital Research'.   [6] Lichter et al., 'Race and Retreat'.
[7] Nakonezny, 'No-Fault Divorce'; Friedberg, 'Unilateral Divorce'; Wolfers, 'Unilateral Divorce'.   [8] Above, Ch. 13.
[9] Braver, *Divorced Dads*, 130–6 and references therein; Brinig and Allen, 'Why Most Divorce Filers', table 1, p. 128.   [10] Braver, *Divorced Dads*, 137–45 and references therein.
[11] Kitson, 'Marital Complaints'; Kitson, 'Who Divorces'; James, *Britain on the Couch*, 204–6; Weiss, *To Have and to Hold*, 190–1.

Divorce was often experienced as a release.[12] It was also an escape route from exploitation. The introduction of no-fault divorce was associated with a large, significant drop in married women's suicide, and a large decline in domestic violence for both women and men.[13]

Divorce is a long-drawn out and painful process, rated in the 1960s as only lower than the death of a spouse as source of stress.[14] It continues as second only to unemployment as a source of ill-being.[15] Compared with those in marriage, divorced individuals experienced lower psychological well-being, less happiness, more psychological distress, and poorer self-conception. They had more health problems and a greater risk of mortality, more social isolation, and more negative life events. Their living standards were lower, they possessed less wealth and they experienced more economic hardship. Parenting was more difficult.[16] Divorced people also went for mental health counselling at twice the rate of the population as a whole.[17]

It is well established that married men enjoyed a substantial 'marriage premium' of some 10–30 per cent higher incomes than single ones.[18] But there was an economic marriage premium for women as well (as already suggested in Figure 11.4 above). Women suffered a very substantial drop in standards of living in consequence of divorce, on the order of one-third or higher. Men might do better in comparison, but they suffered too. In the 1970s, men might have hoped to improve their economic position in the aftermath of divorce, but by the 1980s, the majority of men suffered declines in living standards after divorce. The main reason for men's economic divorce penalty was the loss of their share of the wife's income, and of the economies of scale of marriage. Only men who had contributed more than 80 per cent of married income came out any better, and not by a great deal.[19] As we have seen (Figure 11.4 above), such men were in a declining minority during the 1980s, and fared much worse economically than those couples in which both spouses worked.

When family assets were to be divided, and when alimony and child support were calculated, the law usually drew a line on the reciprocal gift economy, ignored the woman's past investment in unpaid care, and

---

[12] Brinig and Allen, 'Why Most Divorce Filers', 129.

[13] Stevenson and Wolfers, 'Bargaining in the Shadow'.

[14] Holmes and Rahe, 'Social Readjustment Rating Scale'.   [15] Above, Ch. 2, Table 2.2.

[16] Amato, 'Consequence of Divorce', 1274.

[17] Olfson et al., 'Outpatient Psychotherapy', table 1, p. 1916.

[18] Waite and Gallagher, *Case for Marriage*, 99–105; Waite and Lehrer, 'Benefits of Marriage'; Ginther and Zavodny, 'Male Marriage Premium'.

[19] McManus and DiPrete, 'Losers and Winners'.

displaced it with a 'market rhetoric' that only took market inputs and assets into account. All the father's assets were regarded, in the first instance, as belonging solely to him, and in post-divorce distribution, only women's out-of-pocket expenses were taken into account. The mother's past and continuing investment of time in care usually did not enter into calculations of her earning capacity.[20] Bessie Smith sang 'how close together love and hate can be'. Separated spouses often put many years of reciprocal altruism behind them, and entered into a hard scrabble for advantage, egged on by their legal advisers.[21] In the political discourse of morality, 'runaway wives' competed with 'deadbeat dads' as figures of calumny. In Britain in the early 1990s, this moral certainty underpinned the determination of government to relieve welfare budgets, and to get more child support from non-custodial fathers. This quest was resisted by many of those affected. Many mothers preferred a clean break and a social entitlement. Men complained of denial of access, and of conflict with obligations to their new families. At stake were two views of parental obligation: government policy reflected the view of fatherhood as a perpetual commitment, while for many men, it appears, once the flow of marital reciprocity had stopped, the sense of obligation ebbed as well. Put more bluntly, they were not willing to pay if they were no longer sleeping with their wives. The British government's Child Support Agency has been a resounding failure.[22] In California, similar attempts to increase the contributions of absent fathers were strongly resisted by their second wives.[23]

If it is women who initiate the majority of divorces, it is possible to frame the decision as a rational one.[24] Not that it necessarily always is rational, in the sense that all foreseeable consequences are taken into account, but, like the decision for childbirth, it is a good way to highlight the considerations involved. For a woman asking for divorce, the cost of divorce might be taken as a measure of the scale of detriment if the marriage is continued. Whatever the costs of divorce, they were less than the anguish of continued marriage. The expected loss represented a 'barrier to exit' that held marriage together.[25] Thus, even with no-fault divorce, marriages persisted even if the balance was negative. For the 'rational' marriage survivor, only when the misery of marriage was greater than the expected economic loss did she move to get a divorce. Starting in the late 1970s, some 2 per cent of all marriages have been dissolved every year. Over two decades, some

---

[20] Crittenden, *Price of Motherhood*, chs. 7–9; Regan, *Alone Together*, chs. 7–8.   [21] Ibid.
[22] Leach, 'Giving from Afar'.   [23] Crittenden, *Price of Motherhood*, 167–76.
[24] Similar reasoning to Brinig and Allen, 'Why Most Divorce Filers'.
[25] Peters, 'Financial Considerations'.

50 per cent of married people would go through this experience at least once. About one in six would experience it twice.[26] As we have seen, personal bankruptcy has risen at a similar rate, and may not be unconnected, both as an effect and as a cause.[27]

On the other hand, in many cases the assumption of rationality and foresight did not apply. Like the decision to marry, the decision to part was often driven by strong emotions, though by anger rather than euphoria. If divorce was myopic, then short-term consequences dominated long-term ones. That is what the evidence suggests.[28] As in other spheres, less education made commitment more difficult. The likelihood of divorce was inversely related to education.[29] Working-class marriages were subject to more material stresses, and to greater insecurity, which, other things being equal, fell more heavily on those in the lower part of society. In the United States, semi-skilled and unskilled male workers have suffered disproportionately since the 1970s. Their relative, and even absolute incomes have declined, their unions have weakened, their pension plans and health coverage have contracted, their relative chances of finding employment were less good than they were before the 1970s, and their relative decline was particularly marked in relation to the improving social and economic position of women at all levels. Relations in working-class marriages in the 1960s and 1970s were depicted by sociologists as full of mutual miscomprehension and pain.[30]

The cost to the kids

While lifelong marital commitment is no longer taken for granted, virtually nobody has called for release from maternal obligations. Maternity may be the last universal sacrament. The maternal bond is taken to be lifelong, and its sundering is intuitively understood as a disaster. Men have given up on fatherhood much more readily, and once departed, their role is seen by society as being more economic than emotional.

The achievement of no-fault divorce and the ability to exit from a bad commitment are celebrated in a good deal of women's writing on marriage.[31] The

[26] Amato, 'Consequence of Divorce', 1269, citing Cherlin, *Marriage, Divorce*.

[27] Above, Ch. 12.

[28] Peters, 'Financial Considerations'. The decision, she argues, focuses on the prospect of immediate financial loss, not on the prospect of emotional liberation.

[29] Sweet and Bumpass, *American Families*, ch. 5; Other references listed in Nakonezny et al., 'Effect of No-Fault Divorce', 478.

[30] Komarovsky, *Blue-Collar Marriage*; Rubin, *Worlds of Pain*.

[31] Coontz, *Way We Really Are*; Stacey, *Name of the Family*; an unfriendly survey in Whitehead, *Divorce Culture*.

retraction of vows may be regretted. But (following Becker), from the point of view of rational self-seeking, it is the voluntary, legitimate choice of informed and willing partners, and is thus calculated (and also guided by the invisible hand) to promote the higher happiness. But in withdrawing from promises to each other, in pursuing their own individual destinies, the partners also withdrew from an implicit contract with their children, whose stake in the partnership had not been a voluntary choice. The partners' quest for self-fulfilment was purchased by discounting the longer-term interests of their kids: by withdrawing some investment from the children, in order to invest in themselves. In the USA, one study found that fifteen years after divorce, four-fifths of divorced mothers felt that separation had been good for them, and one-half of the fathers, but only 10 per cent of the children felt positive about the divorce.[32]

The effect of the withdrawal of parental investment has typically been evaluated in terms of diminished capabilities and functionings of the children, i.e. in terms of their achievements in later life in education, deviance, health, economic success, and the children's own pattern of loving relations. Why this should happen is not discussed so often. Some clues are provided by another body of scholarship, by attachment theory.

Maternal emotions are similar in intensity (and brain location) to romantic love.[33] The attraction of mother and child is likewise mutual. The primal mother–child relation is framed in terms of differing 'attachment styles'.[34] A child craves physical and emotional closeness to its mother. If that need is satisfied, the child develops a secure and stable personality, and is able to receive and to give emotional and physical closeness in its own turn. If this intimacy is denied or not fully achieved the child is unable to feel secure. Infant attachment provides a template for the adult experience of the self. Secure attachment in infancy underpins a general sense of security and well-being, and facilitates secure heterosexual attachment in adulthood. This argument has several implications. It privileges the experience of attachment as a source of well-being, and places it at the core of one's sense of the self. It also suggests that attachment is vulnerable to changes in the environment, in particular to the trade-offs between domestic commitment and market rewards that the economic theory of the family has highlighted.

Attachment is described in several typologies. Ainsworth's early and influential classification was that mother–infant attachments were either

---

[32] Larson et al., *Costly Consequences*, 42.   [33] Bartels and Zeki, 'Neural Correlates'.

[34] Bowlby, *Attachment and Loss*; Ainsworth et al., Patterns of *Attachment*; Ainsworth, 'Attachments beyond Infancy'.

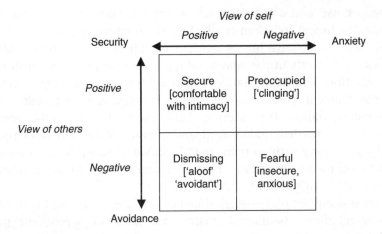

Fig. 14.1. Adult attachment styles

Source: Adapted from Bartholomew and Horowitz, 'Attachment Styles', fig. 1; Brennan et al., 'Self-report Measurement', fig. 3.2.

secure, avoidant, or ambivalent.[35] These infant attachment styles have subsequently been projected into a typology of adult romantic relationships.[36] In one classification, there is a single 'secure' adult attachment style, and two insecure ones, 'avoidant' and 'anxious'.[37] A more intuitive framing of the options makes use of a binary matrix, each dimension signed as either positive and negative. We can view ourselves in a positive light, or in a negative one; likewise with others: we can see them in a positive or a negative light.

This table is a useful heuristic. Instead of three categories, it provides two separate dimensions: security → anxiety, and security → avoidance.[38] It provides one 'secure' attachment style, and three 'insecure' ones.[39] A parent who is aloof, insecure, or preoccupied is unlikely to inculcate a secure attachment style in their infant. The inference is that persons whose attachment style was not secure as infants are less likely to find secure attachments in maturity. In a large survey, the national distribution of adult attachments in the 1990s was similar to that of infants, about 59 per cent secure, 25 per cent avoidant, and 11 per cent anxious. In empirical studies, these attachment styles were significantly correlated with the quality of relationships, personality, depression, social support, religiosity,

[35] Ainsworth et al., *Patterns of Attachment*.
[36] Hazan and Shaver, 'Romantic Love'; Hatfield and Rapson, *Love and Sex*, 73–83; Bartholomew, 'Avoidance of Intimacy'.   [37] Hazan and Shaver, 'Romantic Love'.
[38] Brennan et al., 'Self-Report Measurement'.
[39] Bartholomew and Horowitz, 'Attachment Styles'.

substance use, and domestic violence. There is also some evidence that infant attachment styles can predict later personal outcomes.[40]

In these models, attachment style is related to an environmental effect, namely the quality of parental bonding. This is promising for historical investigation. The circumstances which affect the parental environment are observable in part, especially socio-economic status, education, and parental separation. For example, 'being white, female, well-educated, middle-class, married, middle-aged, and from the Midwest were all associated significantly with an increased likelihood of attachment security'.[41] Risk factors for insecure adult attachment were parental divorce and financial adversity during childhood.[42]

This suggests a link between affluence and the course and quality of gender relations. As marital quality decreased, as investment from children was withdrawn, the positive attachment style became less pervasive, and there were more people with defensive, anxious, or avoidant attachment styles. It is likely that parents with these types of unions would transmit their anxieties to their children, thus generating a rising spiral of unhappiness.

The economic theory of the family regards the declining birth rate as evidence of a preference for fewer children, of higher quality each. The evidence is ambiguous. Taking a sample of sixteen developed countries, women's time spent in childcare declined about one-fifth between 1960 and 1985, and was then wholly restored in the following decade.[43] Couples with higher than secondary education increased their childcare time throughout. Given the falling birth rate, it is likely every child was getting the same or more attention, especially from educated parents.[44] Educated women (high school and higher) spent about one-fifth more time with their children in the 1980s and 1990s, and there were more educated parents (American women spent slightly less than the average 48 minutes a day; British ones about one-tenth more).[45]

If parental education created better emotional outcomes for children, then the large expansion of education was a powerful force for improving childcare outcomes.[46] The formal score of school achievement did not soar, but was not a disaster either. Between the late 1960s and the mid-1990s, American college-entry SAT scores on verbal ability fell from about

---

[40] Mickelson et al., 'Adult Attachment'.   [41] Mickelsen et al., 'Adult Attachment', 1102.
[42] Ibid. 1103.   [43] Gershuny, *Changing Times*, table 7.18, p. 195.
[44] Gershuny, *Changing Times*, 195–6.
[45] Ibid., table 7.19, p. 196. Country coefficients generously provided by Prof. Gershuny.
[46] Above, Ch. 11, Fig. 11.5(a).

540 to 500, before rising modestly again. In maths, they fell from about 516 down to a low of about 492 in the early 1980s, but have risen since to their starting point. This should not be taken as evidence of parental neglect. Academic achievement was imparted in schools, not at home. Participation in college increased considerably during this period, and a widening pool was bound to reduce the quality of measured performance somewhat. The pattern of decline and rise is also consistent with larger baby-boom families in the 1960s and 1970s providing less investment than the smaller ones later.[47] And the tests themselves may not have been a stable measure. 'Intelligence', as measured by IQ, has been rising over the longer term,[48] likewise suggesting an increasing investment in cognitive capability, and consequently an increasing capacity for commitment. So there is no strong evidence of withdrawal of investment from children within marriages, or of neglect by individual parents. Working women have sought to readjust their time-budgets so as to safeguard time with their children even as they increased their participation at work.[49]

What was harmful to children was discord and self-seeking within the family. The long-term consequences of parental discord for children were pervasive and consistently bad. Poor marital quality, as well as declines in marital quality over time, were associated with problematic relationships with mothers and fathers (less affection, less consensus, less perceived support, and less help exchanged); more difficulties in dating among single offspring (fewer dates, more difficulty finding dating partners, and less happiness with current dating partner); lower marital quality among married offspring (less happiness, less interaction, more conflict, more problems, and more divorce proneness); a greater probability of offspring relationship dissolution (cohabiting relationships as well as marriages); lower social integration (less church involvement, smaller networks of close kin and friends, and less community attachment); less education; and poorer psychological well-being (greater psychological distress, lower self-esteem, less happiness, and lower life satisfaction). These results suggest that parents' marital unhappiness and discord had a broad negative impact on virtually every dimension of offspring well-being.[50] If bad marriages were bad for children, then divorce might be considered as a welcome release, not only for parents, but also for the children. Amato and Booth's study confirmed previous findings that divorce had detrimental effects of its own, independently of the level of prior marital discord. In

---

[47] College Board, 'SAT Verbal', table 2, p. 6.   [48] Dickens and Flynn, 'Heritability'.
[49] Yeung and Stafford, 'Intra-Family Child Care'.
[50] Amato and Booth, *Generation at Risk*, 219.

only one-third or so of cases was the level of marital discord so high that children were better off when the parents divorced. More than two-thirds of divorces were preceded by low levels of overt discord. In the absence of prior discord, it was the separation itself that was damaging to children.[51]

The harmful relation between divorce and children is well established. The list is depressing: poor relations with fathers, likelihood of divorce or non-married parenthood, economic hardship and poverty, risk of school failure, lower chance of college graduation and of higher-status jobs, worse physical health (including high infant mortality), higher rates of alcohol and substance abuse, higher rates of psychological distress and of mental illness, a much higher risk of youth suicide, much greater risk of delinquent and criminal behaviour, higher risk of abuse. Such lists are typically compiled by conservative think-tanks.[52] Where divorce is concerned, political postures are reversed. Free-market advocates, usually so strongly supportive of choice, call for restraint; whereas the left-wing supporters of social cooperation and reciprocal norms, are vocal in their support of divorce. Typically this arises from the overlap with a strong liberal feminist position, which is positioned on the left end of the spectrum by convention. Freedom of choice is as much a norm of liberal feminism as it is of Milton Friedman, and is part of the project of gaining women control of their own destinies. But the findings of detriment are also confirmed by reputable academic scholars.[53] In Britain, studies with a more feminist orientation have essentially confirmed the same findings.[54]

While the thrust of these findings is almost uniformly negative and statistically significant, their meaning needs to be qualified. For most outcomes, the effects are not large, i.e. between one-tenth and one-third of a standard deviation. What this means is that the children of separation and divorce are *not destined* to suffer, but they are at greater risk. Some children of intact marriages will show the same detriments, and many children of divorce will not. In the 1980s there was hope that the detrimental effects of divorce were declining over historical time,[55] perhaps due to its shift

[51] Amato and Booth, *Generation at Risk*.

[52] Doherty et al., *Why Marriage Matters*; Fagan and Rector, 'Effects of Divorce'; Morgan, *Farewell to the Family*, ch. 5.

[53] Amato, 'Consequences of Divorce'. Doherty et al., *Why Marriage Matters*, is the work of leading academic writers.

[54] Bhrolcháin et al., 'Parental Divorce'; more pessimistically, Kiernan, 'Legacy of Parental Divorce'; Cherlin et al., 'Parental Divorce'.

[55] Wolfinger, 'Trends in Transmission'; Amato and Booth found that divorce actually benefited children from high-discord families; but as divorce extended to more normal families, this benefit of divorce contracted (*Generation at Risk*, 220).

from being a minority experience to being a common one. But this trend was reversed in the 1990s.[56]

It is important to be clear: children of single parents (whether due to divorce or an absence of marriage in the first place) are not *guaranteed* to suffer from inferior attention or parenting experiences, nor are they doomed to be less mentally healthy, or to achieve less. It is only that in the aggregate, they are *more likely* to display these symptoms. In many cases, dysfunctional parenting is not caused by marital breakdown, but precedes it. The point is important: it implies that merely making divorce more difficult will not necessarily improve the quality of parenting. In other cases, it is the amicable divorce that breaks up an apparently successful household, and delivers a shock to unsuspecting children. It also emphasizes the deeper causes of dysfunctional parenting in withdrawal of commitment, which is driven by myopic preferences under the compelling and competitive pressures of affluence. People seeking the best for themselves, in conditions where commitment was insecure, may have been shifting a cost onto the future, in this case, onto their own children. Opting for the present at the expense of the future is the definition of myopic choice.

The measures of detriment are typically for prevalence, not for intensity. For some serious detriments, a reverse measure is more appropriate: how many of those who suffer come from disrupted families? Here the figures are worrying. One study argues that in the early 1990s, more than two-thirds of the juveniles incarcerated for serious crimes had been raised without fathers; more than two-thirds of out-of-wedlock mothers, more than two-thirds of teenagers who ran away from home.[57] In the last half-century, suicides among teens and young adults have tripled. Living with a divorced parent accounted for as much as two-thirds of the increase.[58] But broken households attract other sources of misery. Divorce can be an effect, and not a cause, and the ultimate causes might be traced back to unobserved factors. Family breakdown is associated with lower income and with black ethnicity. Divorce falls with male income, and rises with female income.[59] The growing inequality of the period since the 1970s has made it more difficult to form enduring relations. Divorce was correlated with poverty, insecurity, and uncertainty. It was not (as perhaps unwittingly implied at some points above) a form of self-indulgence, but yet another aspect of an increasingly harsh, volatile, and risky environment for those below the top 40 per cent or so.

---

[56] Amato, 'Children of Divorce in the 1990s'.
[57] Lykken, 'American Crime Factory', 262. [58] Cutler et al., 'Youth Suicide'.
[59] Cameron, 'Determinants of Divorce', 8.

About a third of children were being born outside marriage. They did not grow up, for long periods of their childhood, in the presence of both parents; and they were likely to be exposed to the trauma of parental separation, and to the presence of step-parents. These children usually lived with their mothers, and suffered disproportionate economic deprivation. Attachment theory posits that such experiences were likely to affect their sense of self, and their ability to form attachments. If that is true, then the process was self-reinforcing: children who experienced insecure childhoods were going to have insecure attachment styles. As more children went through parental breakdown and separation, more of them would be handicapped in their attachment styles, adding to the difficulty and uncertainty of commitment, which was weakened already for the many reasons described.

Evidence is beginning to emerge that attachment styles were also transmitted across the generations.[60] For one thing, parental divorce greatly increased the odds of divorce among children.[61] Aversive attachment styles were similar to parental separation as raising the risk of a wide range of detrimental outcomes.[62] Three longitudinal studies have shown that marital discord is also transmitted from one generation to the next. If the parents' marriage was bad, the children's marriages were likely to be so as well.[63] Parents with unhappy childhoods tended to have more difficulty with each other and with their children. They treated their offspring in a cold, critical, more authoritarian manner.[64]

There is also some indirect, macro-evidence. Attachment styles are related to trust in others. General values surveys in the United States and Britain have found a decline of about 15 per cent in levels of reported interpersonal trust in both populations between the 1950s and the 1990s. Putnam broke this down by cohort. He found a steep decline from the 1960s to the 1990s. Individual cohorts maintained their levels of trust over the life cycle. Of those born before the 1930s, about three-quarters agreed that 'most people can be trusted'. Of those born after 1950, only one-half. Among teenagers in the 1990s, only about one-quarter.[65] Putnam attributed this, speculatively, to the impact of television, but what *is* the impact of television? Chapter 6 above argued that television advertising was likely to undermine interpersonal trust. Television also conveyed strong hedonistic,

---

[60] Waters et al., 'Attachment Security'; Rothbard and Shaver, 'Continuity of Attachment'.
[61] Amato and DeBoer, 'Transmission of Marital Instability'.
[62] Mickelson et al., 'Adult Attachment', 1092.
[63] Amato and Booth, 'Legacy of Parents' Discord'.
[64] Cowan and Cowan, *Partners become Parents*, 205.   [65] Putnam, *Bowling Alone*, 140–1.

materialist, and individualist messages, and these preferences were inimical to commitment. The rising violence content on television (like the rise in explicit sexual content) suggests a desensitization of the kind that has affected mating as well. The implicit message is that violence is acceptable, of no great consequence, a legitimate source of arousal. This is a speculative leap: but the coarsening of personal relations captured by the aggregate decline in trust is of a kind with other trends followed throughout this book. And it accords with the fraying of the family.

Emotional disarray

Affluence, marital breakdown, and mental disorder have risen together, especially since the 1970s. The case for roping them together arises from attachment theory, i.e. from the view that an inadequate infancy leads to a deficient adulthood. If the link is there, then it would explain one of the most striking paradoxes of affluence: that the rise in aggregate wealth has not raised reported subjective well-being, but rather, that it coincided with an epidemic expansion of mental-health disorders and therapies.

In terms of years in disability, mental disorder is the largest public health problem in the world. 'Of the ten leading causes of disability worldwide in 1990, measured in years lived with a disability, five were psychiatric conditions.' In developed societies, it was the largest problem for ages 14–55, and second only to heart disease overall.[66] Figure 14.2 shows the overall incidence of mental conditions within a year, derived from a large uniform international survey carried out in fourteen countries between 2001 and 2003. It shows that clinical-level mental disorder is very common. Mental disorder rises with affluence, or rather, with national income per head.

The exception was of countries with a high level of governance breakdown or strife, such as Colombia, the Lebanon, or the Ukraine. Apart from France, the European countries all had levels of mental disorder that were half or less than in the United States. If the three 'strife' countries are taken out, then income per head provides a strong prediction of mental disorder: some 52 per cent of the variance.

Americans had by far the highest score, with one in four experiencing an episode of mental disorder within twelve months. About one-quarter of these disorders were 'serious'. The ranking is consistent with a previous meta-survey published in 1975, in which median urban rates of 'functional

---

[66] Murray and Lopez, 'Global Burden'.

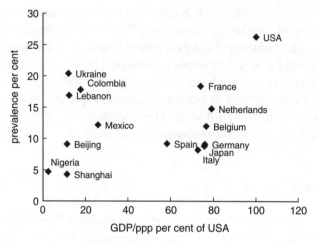

Fig. 14.2. Prevalence of mental disorders within twelve months, 2001–3
Source: Demyttenaere et al., 'Prevalence, Severity', table 3, p. 2585.

psychiatric disorder' prevalence in North America, South America, Europe, Asia, and Australasia were quite similar.[67]

The United States led in mental disorder because it led in competitive market affluence. If the link is valid, then the trend should be detected over time as well: as the country grew in wealth, mental disorder should have increased. The evidence comes from several independent sources. The method is to measure the incidence of mental disorder in successive birth cohorts. A landmark survey of thirteen surveys, published in 1989, estimated the prevalence of depression. This was elicited by means of retrospective questioning. When birth cohorts were divided up by decades, the cumulative probability of major depression increased by cohort throughout the twentieth century. The differences between the oldest cohort (born before 1915) and the youngest (born after 1955) were more than tenfold. Similar increases were found in Sweden, New Zealand, Germany, and Canada. They were not replicated in samples of Puerto Ricans, Mexican-Americans, and Koreans. These low-income groups (like those in Figure 14.2) might be assumed to have a stronger legacy of family bonds. Low income was associated with low levels of depression. The studies also found strong period effects between 1960 and 1975.[68] These findings were confirmed independently by a subsequent study.[69] The method of retrospective recall is open to criticism, but

[67] 21, 18.4, 15.5, 1.8, and 25.9 respectively. Dohrenwend, 'Sociocultural Factors', table 1, p. 367.   [68] Klerman and Weissman, 'Increasing Rates'.
[69] Kessler et al., 'Sex and Depression'; a Canadian local study did not find an increase in serious depression except among young women: Murphy et al., 'A 40-Year Perspective'.

has been robust to subsequent resurvey, and in any case, the sheer scale of change over time (a whole order of magnitude) challenges disbelief.[70] A two to threefold increase appears quite secure.[71]

Other evidence is immune to the criticism of faulty recall. A large study from the first post-war decades was 'Americans View their Mental Health' by Veroff and his associates.[72] It had two nationally representative sweeps, in 1957 and 1976, and was replicated in 1996.[73] The diagnostic question was 'Have you ever felt that you were going to have a nervous breakdown?' Prevalence (adjusted for changing demographics) rose, from 17 per cent in 1957, to 19.6 per cent in 1976, and 24.3 per cent in 1996. In 1996, more than a quarter of these experiences were precipitated by loved ones, divorce, marital strains, marital separation, and troubles with members of the opposite sex, rising from only 10 per cent in 1957. The second group of precipitants (about 17 per cent) were problems at work or at school.

The most compelling evidence of the rise of mental disorder relies on aggregating psychological investigations from the past. Twenge has studied the growth of anxiety and other mental states between the 1950s and the 1990s, making use of 269 contemporary investigations.[74] These studies deployed a small number of instruments, and provide contemporary yardsticks, unaffected by retrospection. Two meta-surveys were carried out, one on studies of college students, the other on studies of children. The method was to correlate anxiety scores with year. The correlations were positive, large, and significant. Overall, over four decades, anxiety scores had shifted upwards by more than one standard deviation. This is a very large shift. What it implied was that the average child of the 1990s would have been regarded as in need of professional attention in the 1950s. There is some confirmation for this in the rising use of psychotropic medications for children and youth in the United States. A large study (more than 900,000 youths) found that total psychotropic medication prevalence for youths had risen two- to threefold over the ten years from 1987.[75] The scale of mental disorder prevalence might have been larger. In another study, only one-fifth of youths treated as outpatients, and 40 per cent treated as inpatients, received drug treatment.[76] In the Netherlands, levels were much lower, but the upwards trend just as fast.[77] At a younger

[70] Warshaw et al., 'An Artifact of Recall'; Seligman, 'Why is There So Much Depression?', 2–4.
[71] Kessler et al., 'Prevalence, Correlates'.
[72] Veroff et al., *Inner American*; Veroff et al., *Mental Health in America*.
[73] Swindle et al., 'Responses to Nervous Breakdowns'.
[74] Twenge, 'Age of Anxiety'; ead., 'Birth Cohort, Social Change'.
[75] Zito et al., 'Psychotropic Practice'.   [76] Safer et al., 'Medication for Youths'.
[77] Schirm et al., 'Psychotropic Medication'.

age, medication treatment for Attention Deficit Disorder in children increased more than threefold between 1987 and 1997, from 0.9 per cent of all children to 3.4 per cent in the USA.[78]

At the extreme, another indicator of mental turmoil is suicide. 'Suicide is generally a complication of a psychiatric disorder.'[79] It is the third largest cause of death among young people in the United States, after homicide and accidents. The rate of youth suicide has increased threefold since the 1960s. There were 200 to 400 attempted suicides for every successful one. Attempted suicide can be seen as a signal of distress.[80] 'About 14 percent of youths report thinking of suicide during one year, and 4 percent report attempting suicide.'[81] Internationally, like mental disorder, suicide is positively and significantly correlated with both the level and the rate of growth of income per head.[82]

The quest for explanation of mental turmoil largely points one way. At a superficial level, what is blamed is 'modernity'.[83] Figure 14.2 indicates that mental disorder increases with affluence, and the argument is clinched by the observation that societies with high social cohesion, and low standards of living, such as the Pennsylvania Amish, a rural sect who adhered to an eighteenth-century lifestyle, had lower levels of mental disorder.[84] What precisely were the mechanisms that generated the rise in mental disorder? Many writers in the 1980s identified it as a shift from social concerns to individual ones, 'a rage for self-fulfilment', an individualism without commitment.[85] In their epidemiological survey of the rise of depression, Klerman et al. also highlight the decline of social connection.[86] At book length, the point has been argued by several writers, including Easterbrook, James, Frank, Kohn, Lane, Lasn, Schwartz, and Schor.[87]

Veroff and his collaborators carried out an immensely detailed comparison of the change in subjective attitudes in the United States at the most crucial turning point, with two surveys, one in 1957, the

[78] Olfson, 'Attention Deficit'.   [79] Mann, 'Current Perspective', 302.
[80] Cutler et al., 'Youth Suicide'.   [81] Ibid. 8.   [82] Jungeilges, 'Economic Welfare'.
[83] Sloan, *Damaged Life*.

[84] Seligman, 'Why is There So Much Depression?', 4–5; Gove and Tudor, 'Adult Sex Roles', 828; but Eaton, *Culture and Mental Disorders*, found a contrary result of relatively high mental disorder among the Hutterite sect members, which they blame on defective survey techniques (ch. 5).

[85] Veroff et al., *Inner American*, e.g. 529–30; Wolfe, 'The Me Decade'; Bellah et al., *Habits of the Heart*, ch. 3. Quote from Yankelovich, *New Rules*, 3, cited Twenge, 'Birth Cohort, Social Change', 205; Seligman, 'Why is There So Much Depression?', 6–9.

[86] See Twenge, 'Birth Cohort, Social Change'.

[87] Easterbrook, *Progress Paradox*; Frank, *Luxury Fever*; James, *Britain on the Couch*; Kohn, *No Contest*; Lane, *Loss of Happiness*; Lasn, *Culture Jam*; Schor, *Overspent American*; Schwartz, *Costs of Living*; on a monthly basis, the Vancouver journal *Adbusters*.

other in 1976. They provide a contemporary testimony of preferences shifting.

There is a clear decrease in the unconditional positive regard that Americans have for parenthood. Fewer people in 1976 thought that parenthood totally enriched people with important positive experiences. The same was true or the way Americans in 1976 saw the changes that marriage brings; they were much more open to the negative facets of the role than people were in 1957.[88]

By 1976, Americans set much more store on aspirations for fulfilment through self-expression and self-direction, had become much more positive about the rewards of work (especially women), and were much more oriented to power than they were in 1956.[89]

One aspect of 'modernity' directly related to unhappiness was 'materialism.' This was defined as giving a high priority to financial success, possessions, projecting a good image, and high status. Extensive research in the 1990s found that those who were highly focused on materialistic values had lower personal well-being and psychological health than those for whom materialistic pursuits were relatively unimportant. Strong materialistic values were associated with a pervasive undermining of well-being, from low life satisfaction and happiness, to depression and anxiety, physical problems such as headaches, personality disorders, narcissism, and antisocial behaviour.[90] The authors who collected this evidence posited two main pathways: from social models that encouraged materialistic values, and from experiences that induced feelings of insecurity.[91] Our chapters on advertising, body weight, consumer durables, and cars are replete with examples of the nature and influence of consumerist advocacy. Materialistic individuals watched a great deal of television, compared themselves unfavourably with those they saw there, were dissatisfied with their standard of living, and had low life satisfaction overall.[92] The abundance of choice in market societies exposed individuals to its fundamental intractability. Some of the symptoms were highly visible, in the form of fat people and fat cars. The 'epidemic of depression' was less visible but no less real. If the market dealt people a losing hand (which it has done increasingly since the 1980s) then none of the choices available was a good one: a dead-end job, ill-health, separation, and divorce could leave the individual in a trap. The response could be a depressive 'learned helplessness', which was only a short way from clinical depression.[93] Twenge found counter-intuitively that (despite the rise in

---

[88] Veroff et al., *Inner American*, 529.   [89] Ibid. 529–30, 544   [90] Kasser, *High Price*.
[91] Kasser et al., 'Materialistic Values', 13.   [92] Kasser, *High Price*, 53–6.
[93] Schwartz, *Paradox of Choice*, ch. 10; Peterson et al., *Learned Helplessness*.

anxiety), there was also a rise in self-esteem scores and in extraversion over the last decades, which she interpreted as an expression of heightened, defensive individualism. Women's assertiveness scores have risen substantially, to the point where they have come to match the assertiveness of males.[94] This is consistent with the previous evidence that women have been less willing to accept unsatisfactory partnerships, and were capable of breaking away when they felt their personal aspirations being thwarted.

The other source of materialism is 'experiences that induce feelings of insecurity'. Kasser and his collaborators suggest that market fulfilment is meant to compensate for doubts about self-worth and general uncertainty. Another source is the denial of basic psychological needs, such as those for autonomy, competence, and relatedness. The source of poor self-confidence and psychological need points to early attachment and to domestic relations. Defective parental styles are associated with increased materialism in children. Late adolescents who craved financial success (as opposed to self-acceptance, affiliation, or community feeling)

were more likely to have mothers who made more negative and fewer positive emotional expressions about the adolescents and who described their own parenting styles as involving less warmth and democracy, along with greater control. Other studies have shown children tend to be more materialistic when they have less frequent communication with their parents...when their parents are over-involved, highly punitive, or quite lax in the structure they provide...and when they perceive their parents as less supportive of their desires for autonomy.[95]

Materialistic young adults were more likely to have divorced parents. A low socio-economic status also predicted materialism.[96] The high correlation between materialism and low economic status links the rise of mental disorders with the rise of inequality and the fraying of the family, in a way that is difficult to disentangle, but leads clearly from clamour of the market to the disturbed and disordered mind.

Economists have also explored the causal routes between self-seeking, familial disruption, and mental distress. Statistically the most important aggregate variable explaining the rise in youth suicide was the increased share of youths living in homes with a divorced parent. Higher female labour force participation predicted higher rates of suicide for males. Divorce rates were highly correlated with youth suicides. Family structure and parental time-budgets also seemed to matter.[97] The hypothesized relation is a

---

[94] Twenge, 'Birth Cohort, Social Change', 207–9.
[95] Kasser et al., 'Materialistic Values', 14.   [96] Ibid. 13–15; also Kasser, *High Price*, ch. 4.
[97] Cutler et al., 'Youth Suicide', 6.

simple one: family connections are important in promoting happiness. Family discord and separation undermines it. The case for 'rational suicide' ('negative expected utility') is forced, but a hyperbolic discounter might regard present pain as obliterating any future gain. In this context, the very high prevalence of attempted suicide can be seen as a signal, interpreted as a plea for attention and a cry for help, by young people with no market power.[98] In a more direct appeal to the Beckerian model of the family, parents allocate time away from childcare and children's well-being and towards market work and more intensive commodified consumption. Higher money income should improve well-being, but the withdrawal of care should reduce it. An empirical investigation found that the protective 'income effect' was larger than the harmful 'substitution effect' of withdrawing time from the household. But as often the case with economists, it regards all outcomes, bad and good, as fungible in dollar terms. The study listed two categories of 'income', wage and non-wage. It was the former which was largely protective of suicide, suggesting that belonging to a wealthy household was the most important protective factor. There were several strong negative confounding factors, such as alcohol and divorce. The presence of other children was a strong protective factor—a proxy for social connectedness within the household?[99] A longitudinal study of young people also identified perceived caring and connectedness to others as important for mental and physical health.[100]

The variance in Figure 14.2 suggests strongly that mental disorder is driven by economic and social factors. Indeed, the very diagnostic instruments, the *Statistical and Diagnostic Manual* used in the surveys, is a very recent artefact which is constantly undergoing revision.[101] Over and above such acute mental illnesses as schizophrenia and bipolar disorder (neither of them diagnosable very precisely), which apparently have some genetic basis and a comparable prevalence worldwide, and of the manifest evidence of suicide, there is also a growing concern with less acute impairments of mental health.[102] Most recently, there is evidence that prior use of cannabis increases the risk of psychosis.[103] Drug use (which has soared since the 1970s) is not an entirely exogenous, external shock—it is another manifestation of myopic choice.

[98] Ibid. 13–15.   [99] Mathur and Freeman, 'Theoretical Model'.
[100] Resnick et al., 'Protecting Adolescents from Harm'.
[101] Kutchins and Kirk, *Making us Crazy*.
[102] Gillon, 'Politics of Deinstitutionalization'; US Dept. of Health, *Mental Health*, 7–9.
[103] Van Os et al., 'Cannabis Use and Psychosis'; Henquet et al., 'Cohort Study of Cannabis Use'.

The quest for relief has extended well beyond the medical profession.[104] Between the 1950s and the 1970s there was a large increase in the willingness to turn to expert mental health advice.[105] The intelligentsia spoke loosely of a 'therapy culture',[106] but the use of psychotherapy services, at about 3.5 per cent of the population every year, did not change much between the 1980s and the 1990s. It was popular with those with postgraduate educations and among the divorced, both groups taking therapy at about twice the average level (around 6–7 per cent).[107] More typically, however, treatment was sought by means of medication.[108] Therapy is the artisan sector of mental health, medication the corporate one. Among therapy patients, the use of medication increased about threefold.[109] Big Pharma is the most profitable sector of the American/British economies.[110] Its most profitable treatments target the fallout of affluence: high cholesterol, ulcers, stress, depression. There is a circularity in this success story. Big Pharma is an engine of economic growth, but as an exemplar of competitive success (albeit protected by patent monopolies) it feeds on the misery that competition generates. And the more misery the market generates, the faster Big Pharma grows.

Individual testimonies are not statistically representative, but they bring us closer to the textures of personal experience. They are also disposed to impute a meaning or to deplore its absence. Elizabeth Wurtzel's best-selling memoir *Prozac Nation* (1994) was a testimony of this kind, of a talented young woman from a disintegrating family just keeping her head above water at ultra-competitive Harvard, with a combination of drugs and therapy, both of them doled out sparingly by her estranged father, whose health insurance was often the only entitlement to treatment that she had. Her illness clearly arose from the 'battlefield on which [her] parents' differences were fought'. In Richard Ford's *Independence Day*, like Roth's *American Pastoral* a Pulitzer Prize best-selling novel of the 1990s, the narrator in his forties was pursuing an enjoyably reflective laid-back life as a small-scale real estate entrepreneur (also in New Jersey), separated from his wife but not quite connecting with his lover. In the meantime his son Paul, shuttling between the two parents, was falling apart emotionally, until (somewhat like Philip Roth's Merry in *American Pastoral*) he was injured in an accident, during a lapse of the father's attention. That the culprit was a

[104] Swindle, 'Responses to Nervous Breakdowns'.
[105] Veroff et al., *Inner American*, 485; Veroff et al., *Mental Health*, ch. 9.
[106] Bellah et al., *Habits of the Heart*, 121–41.
[107] Olfson et al., 'Outpatient Psychotherapy', table 1, p. 1916.
[108] Healy, *Antidepressant Era*.   [109] Olfson et al., 'Outpatient Psychotherapy'.
[110] Angell, *Drug Companies*.

mindless automatic pitching machine, in the Baseball Hall of Fame, on the Fourth of July (Roth's character was a high-school athletic star, as was Updike's 'Rabbit' Angstrom) linked the crisis of the American family with the voiding of the American Dream.

In a therapy session it was possible to buy the undistracted empathy of another person, which previously might have had to be obtained through the commitment of a partner or a friend. On the demand side, the rise of marital breakdown will have generated (according to attachment theory), a sense of anxiety and even pain about childhood experiences and attachments in general. On the supply side, the trained therapist had the expertise to tune in to the client's requirements better than a distracted amateur who might be their partner, or (for divorced people), when there might be no partner at all. The market for therapy provided a substitute for intimacy.

Typically, the subject matter of therapy was the poor state of intimate relations with parents, siblings, or partners. Therapy, divorce, even at the extreme, mental disorder itself, could be regarded, in the aggregate, as types of social 'luxury goods'. The economic definition of this category of goods is that their consumption rises faster than income. Like some other 'luxury goods', they provided substitutes for interpersonal commitment and regard. This interpretation provides a link between affluence, materialism, and mental disorder. It is consistent with our view that the rise of affluence was associated with a decline in the capacity for commitment.[111]

When divorce affects such a high proportion of the population (and even if it affected a smaller one), it is not the historian's business to assign fault. In a turbulent, challenging, competitive environment, in which the majority of people were destined to be survivors, no more, the quest for private self-actualization, held out by the market, may have been self-defeating. Often, however, it was the only choice available. The withdrawal from commitment signalled the loss of security and attachment. It became a cycle, in which anxiously attached parents transmitted alienation to their children through the medium of marital discord. The children then sought solace for psychic distress in materialism (or even drugs), and their frustration eventually infected their own parental priorities and capacity for attachment. Driven by materialism, the cycle of discontent was transmitted from one generation to another even as affluence increased, to form an expanding patch of misery on the pond of abundance.

Affluence acted to increase the expectations from intimacy and passion, while diminishing the ability to satisfy them. The main response was to

[111] Above, Ch. 4.

turn away from stable marriage as a source of arousal, personal validation, and cognitive satisfaction, and to seek these rewards increasingly in the market, or through more temporary and insecure arrangements, at levels of expectations and arousal that were driven up by habituation with the rewards of love. For women, there were substantial losses: the need to compete in mating markets at older ages, when their sexual attraction was reduced, the loss of security in the maternal role, the most gender-specific of rewards, and the harm—quite difficult to pin down and even to acknowledge or admit—to the children, who seem to count more for women than for the men. That the new freedoms were attractive is certain; they opened up new fields of endeavour and accomplishment for women. But in embracing the tide of new rewards, cognitive, occupational, and material, men and women have had to choose, and they have often chosen the shorter view. In particular, they appear to have given a lower priority to the longest of horizons, that which transcends the individual, and extends beyond him and into the future, by means of his or her children.

15

Conclusion

I meant to be diagnostic, not therapeutic. Here is a summary of findings arranged by chapter, and some reflections on the implications.

Findings

Every person can choose their own unique way to self-fulfilment, empowered by family, market, and society. That is the promise of liberal societies. By creating conditions for the pursuit of wealth, markets and governments enlarge the range and quality of choice for every individual. That vision underpins the 'free society' and 'free markets' hailed by politicians and business people as priorities for society. The freedom in question is consistent with the pursuit of corporate objectives. If it also implies a paradise of personal discretion, such a vision of 'freedom' is at odds with common experience. In reality, most lives are hedged in by the prior obligations of work and family, and apart from the supermarket, empowerment and choice (in democratic politics as much as elsewhere) are restricted.

Chapter 2. Affluence has liberated most people (though never all of them) from the anxieties of subsistence, but much more moderate affluence would have sufficed. Since the Second World War, and especially since the 1970s, self-reported 'happiness' has languished at the same levels, or has even declined. That is the 'paradox of happiness'. On any measure used, the rise of aggregate money incomes has done little or nothing to improve the sense of well-being. Levels of life expectation have been similar in rich and in middle-income countries, and higher than the United States even in several poor countries.

Chapter 3. The privileging of individual choice is founded on contestable premises. It assumes that every person has a set of unique and well-ordered preferences, that she is fully informed of all the choices available, that she has good knowledge of herself, and sufficient self-command to achieve her ends. If these assumptions are not satisfied, then individuals would not find it easy to attain their objectives, even if they knew them with any certainty. What people end up choosing cannot be taken as a proper measure of their welfare. Choice is fallible. The main difficulty is in reconciling immediate desires with the commitment required to achieve more remote objectives. Since individual calculation is not reliable, people fall back on social conventions, norms, and institutions. These 'commitment devices' form the fabric of civilization. To achieve a set of desires encompassing the present and the future, it is necessary to ensure the enduring commitment of other people, and also of one's own self. Neither preferences nor logic are sufficient to secure this. It also requires a capacity for social interaction, and for command over the cognitive and emotional resources of self-control. People vary in their capacity for commitment by virtue of upbringing, education, and temperament. But also in their access to the tools of commitment: the heritage and conventions of their social and national cultures, of institutions, law, governance, and commerce.

Chapter 4. In competitive market societies, the flow of novelty and innovation undermines existing conventions, habits, and institutions of commitment. It reinforces a bias for the short term. To secure commitment, people accept a great deal of voluntary restraint and even compulsion. A large trend of the twentieth century has been the growth of active government and regulation. Incrementally, voters have narrowed their own freedom of choice and surrendered control of their futures to social agencies. This trust in government was not always justified, but it has not been forfeited either. The problem of commitment is difficult, and there are no other agents sufficiently accountable or credible to secure it. Government is the commitment agent of last resort, and frequently of first resort as well.

Chapter 5. We rely on others not only in the trivial sense that goods and services come out of the division of labour; but also because our well-being depends on receiving acknowledgement, attention, and approbation, on affirmations, confirmations, and gifts. Positive status, so vital to well-being, is an interpersonal relationship. Even to have people to push around, and to lord over, requires the presence of other people. To the extent that income relative to others is more rewarding than absolute levels of income, even the GNP economy of traded goods is an economy of interpersonal relationships. In the 'economy of regard', the approbation of others is secured by the reciprocal gift of our own. Non-market exchange is pervasive and vital to well-being. In theory at least, for many goods it can allocate resources as efficiently as the impersonal market. It is very large, amounting to a quarter or so of GDP, but has only a shadowy existence in policy and in the National Accounts. The market relation is adversarial, and it is rarely possible to completely relax one's guard. In reciprocal relations, authenticity is vital. The authenticity of friendship, for example, is not something that most people would wish to purchase with money. Merely posting a price can devalue the payoff. The goods in question, like family, friendship, and approbation, rank high among the ultimate rewards.

Chapter 6. If the market is our main source of goods and services, why has it been held in suspicion for so long? An abiding concern is that consumer choice is not entirely autonomous or authentic, due to the influence of marketing and advertising. Is it possible that the language of the market might be generating unwholesome spillovers? Billboard advertising can deface the physical environment. The discourse of marketing can also affect the normative and mental environments. Truth ranks high among personal and social norms, and is strongly associated with several others: with fairness, probity, trustworthiness, authenticity. It becomes difficult to trust and cooperate when social norms are abused. Advertisers are less truthful than even they would like to be, because it is difficult to police transgressors, who 'free-ride' on the others' credibility. Market transactions, even when they benefit both sides, are adversarial and potentially stressful, and advertising attempts to win trust with a simulation of intimacy. Cues of intimacy such as facial communication, testimonial and non-verbal gestures bypass the filter of reason. They are compelling even when consciously disbelieved. By saturating the public domain with false sincerity, advertising makes genuine sincerity more difficult. Trust is emotionally reassuring, from the household and up to the state. When effective, it is remarkably efficient, by saving the cost of monitoring. But when advertising makes use of trust, does it also use it up? Governments have regulated advertising in the interests of market efficiency and the quality of life. But politics has also embraced marketing technique. In political discourse, as in commerce, the cues of sincerity are used to evoke an emotional response. This exploits the social resource of good faith. It lowers the trust between the citizens and leaders, reduces the capacity for commitment and cooperation, and lowers the quality of social interaction overall. Dissimulation and 'spin' have undermined democracy and eroded trust. Puffery may be harmless when soap powders compete. In the service of dissimulating politicians, it can deal out misery, destruction, and death.

Chapter 7. Food abundance has made a mockery of the rational consumer. Body weight has risen in defiance of health and appearance norms. Cheap pre-processed food in supermarkets and sidewalk outlets has driven an excess of both overeating and slimming. Fast food is difficult to resist: restrained eating is easily disinhibited by stress, and more particularly, by the display of food. For men, the rise in body weight has been associated with the decline of family eating and exposure to greater variety. For women, the 'cult of slimming' was associated with mating competition. The costs of abundance fell more heavily on the poor, for whom the benefits of cheaper food were offset by the rising cost of self-control.

Chapter 8. During the post-war years, household appliances were the magic boxes of affluence. Those appliances (like radio and television) that provided sensual arousal diffused very rapidly almost regardless of income, and almost as fast in the USA and Britain. Those that merely lightened the effort of housework diffused at a rate that tracked the growth and levels of income in the two countries. They did not shorten domestic working hours, until the introduction of television made compelling inroads into domestic time. But sensual arousal was eroded by exposure. Television viewing expanded up to the point where it gave little more satisfaction than housework.

Chapters 9–10. Even more than household appliances, motor cars are shiny, expensive, long-lasting durables. Yet in the marketing of motor cars to American society in the 1950s, producers fell over each other in a frenzy of styling novelty. For new-car buyers (always a small minority of car users), the strongest selling point was sensual gratification, rather than status signalling. Eventually, many consumers reacted to styling excess by 'downshifting' to more austere cars. Britain in the 1960s (a comparable period in terms of the diffusion of affluence) had still not fallen for the appeal of constant novelty. In consequence, British cars, though more poorly made, held their prices better than American ones, whose novelty value depreciated rapidly.

Chapter 11. A positive social ranking produces an inner glow that is also matched with a clear advantage in life expectation and health. Status is a personal attribute, but is also affected by the trade-off between the home and market. Status is a male preoccupation, which is rewarded by access to women. For women, motherhood provided a source of self-regard, but it restricted their opportunities for market success. Status is measured here first in terms of occupational status and distance from the bottom, or positive 'advantage'. In the aggregate, this constituted the 'stock' of status. Unexpectedly, though quite consistently, women's average stock of occupational status matched that of men, or even exceeded it. The reason was motherhood. Although women were scarce at the top, they avoided the bottom too: motherhood was preferred over low-status jobs at the bottom, and over childlessness at the top. The stock of status, measured as positive 'advantages', showed a sustained increase in the post-war years, as more education gave access to better jobs in a more sophisticated economy. Much of the payoff, however, was absorbed in positional competition, primarily for the sake of the children's future. The pace was set by two-earner families, who were able to raise their income as more married women worked for longer hours, but more of these families broke up under the strain. Single-earner families (rising in number) fell behind.

Chapter 12. Status produces losers as well as winners and can be measured in terms of negative (downwards) distance, called here 'complaints'. In 'the Great U-Turn', the trend towards greater equality during the post-war 'golden age' was reversed after the 1970s. Britain in particular became more unequal during the Thatcher years. This was justified in terms of higher productivity and economic growth for all, but a more plausible interpretation is that it was driven by positional competition (or less politely, by class conflict)—income growth in itself contributes almost nothing to subjective well-being, but relative income, or rising higher in social rank, delivers a reliable psychic return. As incomes rose and consumption increased, more income flowed into positional consumption. With rising inequality and stagnant productivity, for most people rising incomes could only be earned by the family as a whole (and women in particular) working longer for wages. The price of positional goods responded. House prices followed (or pulled up) the expanding earnings of dual-earner households. In the UK they moved well ahead of incomes, until they priced the majority of new aspirants out of homeownership. In the USA, the crucial two-incomes-per-household were vulnerable to the setbacks of unemployment, divorce, and illness. In the absence of a social safety net, the rising frequency of such disasters was reflected in the rate of personal bankruptcy, which rose almost tenfold between the 1970s and the early 2000s. The largest statistical risk factor for personal bankruptcy was the presence of children.

Status 'complaints' depressed health: lower down the social scale, lives were shorter, and the risk of illness greater. Inequality is the reason why the United States, the wealthiest economy, scores so poorly on the indicators of physiological well-being, and does not lead in subjective well-being either. The high productivity and long working hours in the United States are driven by risks of degradation like that already suffered by the majority of Afro-Americans. Positional conflict extends into politics, with partisan arguments for distribution from the poor to the rich made stridently and effectively by those at the top. At the bottom end, discontent is kept at bay and behind bars with legitimized violence: scores of judicial executions a year, and more than 2 million imprisoned in brutalizing conditions, five to ten times above the levels chosen by more equal societies such as Britain or in Europe.

Chapter 13. Love is a gift, not a market commodity. But love competes in the market for time and attention. Romantic love is an intensely immediate experience. Raising children to maturity is a protracted and patient one. Marriage is the traditional bridge from the one experience to the other. Quite apart from supporting children, the partnership of marriage confers economic, physiological, and mental health. But marriage has fallen into disrepair since the 1970s. Contraception, and the increasing commodification of sexuality, reduced the sexual allure of marriage. With more outsourcing of food preparation, home cooking added less value. Housekeeping could no longer satisfy the aspirations of increasingly educated women. No-fault divorce increased the probability of separation and made investment in marriage less secure. For women, the arrival of children weakened their domestic position. With more education for women, and with better prospects at work, the cost of children increased, and the protection of marriage declined. Hence the large trends of the period: higher divorce, fewer children, fewer marriages, more cohabitation, more births out of wedlock. Despite enhanced abilities and opportunities, mothers were still handicapped in the workplace, and the pace of positional competition drove the more highly educated into increasingly longer working hours. With more to sacrifice and less security, women had fewer children, and had them later. A minority sought escape by means of 'downshifting'. Individually, women appeared (on average) to be satisfied with the bargain, but for society as a whole there are fewer children to replace ageing generations, and a large crisis of dependency in the making. But the argument only carries so far. American fertility remains higher than in Europe. The reasons may be (paradoxically), those very same competitive markets. American birth rates are raised by immigrants and by greater inequality (the poor have more children). Both housing and labour markets are also more flexible in the USA, and thus more accommodating to the needs of mothers.

Chapter 14. As the proportion of those married declined, about one adult in seven lost the protection and benefits that marriage might have conferred. More space for parents to pursue their self-fulfilment (what Sen would call their 'capabilities') has enlarged their freedom. But (to use the same terms), it has cramped some of their 'functionings'. As external market competition became more compelling, it diverted investment away from the household. Attachment theory suggests that a confident and loving self was formed in a secure intimate relationship with the mother. Frustrated attachments as an infant made it more difficult to form secure and loving ones as an adult. The greater ease of separation for parents allowed them to reconsider their options periodically and to respond to life-cycle opportunities. The option of separation alleviated misery, cruelty, and entrapment. But the costs of discretion to leave were also high. For both women and men, divorce was often a disaster. On the average, it led to lower standards of living, worse health, more anxiety and depression, and fewer years of life. These were choices freely made (whether rationally or myopically), by adults. None of their children had signed on to the marriage contract, but they still found themselves paying the costs of separation. For children, parental discord and separation raised the odds against success. Since the 1950s, anxiety in children has increased by more than one standard deviation, and suicide has increased threefold among the young. For every successful adolescent suicide, scores have been attempted, and hundreds contemplated. Overall, mental disorder appears to have increased in line with affluence, both in the cross-section, when different countries are compared, as well as over time. The United States, the wealthiest country, has the largest incidence. The epidemiology is staggering—about one in four within short sampling periods. And unlike physical illness, which attracts money and sympathy, is at the forefront of medical attention, and is tackled aggressively, mental pain is furtive, stigmatized, neglected—unless it can pay off for a drug company. Its prime cause, it appears, is the deficit of interpersonal intimacy and of social connection (though drug abuse may have played a role as well). In their aggressive push for market rewards, affluent societies are pushing against the boundaries of reason.

We have concentrated on individuals, and how their well-being is affected by choices made in the market and at home. There is another dimension which consists of the agencies and agents empowered to manage well-being. The dimension of social choice, in governance and the public domain, is part of the same agenda, although it is largely left out of this volume.[1] The same issues of conflict between immediate and distant horizons, between arousal and commitment, arise in public and social choice. Further investigations might include affluence and crime; suburbanization; free time, culture, and voluntary activities; the social movements of

---

[1] But discussed in Offer, *Public Sector*.

self-control (Green, Consumerist, New Age, Feminist); the politics of myopia, and governments as agents for commitment; and the shift from the New Deal to the New Right, from social democracy to market liberalism. Some issues challenge the capacity for commitment beyond national communities, for example global poverty, and climate change. These are towering challenges that this study, which focuses on the difficulty of personal choice over time, has avoided, perhaps illustrating its own focus on myopia.

Comparable levels of satisfaction can be derived from very different levels of resources. Surveys of satisfaction in the United States and Britain have found the two countries to be roughly level with regard to subjective well-being, although Britain is more than twenty years behind in terms of absolute prosperity. Wherever objective measurement is possible, it suggests that the balance of immediate and delayed rewards is less prudential in the United States than in Britain. America is a less patient society, less capable of self-control. British temperament, culture, and society have evolved strategies of choice that require greater self-control. Given the tendency of hedonic drives to be swamped quickly in conditions of abundance, the British approach has tended to produce similar levels of satisfaction from inferior resources. British material inferiority has provided a better 'pacer' for well-being. This is consistent with our initial hypothesis (Chapter 4), that the capacity for self-control declines with societal affluence over time, even as it rises with individual affluence at any given point in time.

Reality and experience are complex, but averages and central tendencies are still revealing. In the sphere of ingestion, Britain had lower levels of obesity and drug addiction, and a more tolerant attitude to alcohol, tobacco, and drugs. Advertising in the United States was much less restrained than in Britain, while its regulation was more adversarial. Workers worked longer and harder in America, and took fewer holidays. The extremes of wealth and poverty are greater in the United States, but the levels of aspiration there are also higher: the extravagant 'American Dream' was incompatible with British class barriers, and perhaps also with British social solidarity. The reality of stratification, however, was quite similar in the two societies. More education in American produced less status advantages there. British society had a later sexual initiation, and more sexual restraint. Bolder courtship in the United States led to a lower age at marriage; women moved earlier into the labour market, and in larger numbers, after the Second World War. Both the birth rate and divorce have been higher in the United States.

Britain was only a short step behind the United States in the diffusion of broadcast media. But the content of the media was different: a public broadcasting ethos in Britain which extended even to the commercial channels, in comparison with the commercialism, violence, and political partisanship of the American media. The British tend to be spiritually scep-tical, Americans are actively religious. Britain manages the same general level of health with much smaller medical outlays. It has a lower level of violent crime and only one-fifth as many people (pro rata) in prison. The British have expected more from cooperation, from some suppression of individuality, from government, and from the state. Saving rates have fallen in both countries, but more in America than in Britain. Wealth has not been pursued with the same single-minded zeal in Britain, and nor has economic growth.

But there is convergence. The Thatcher project deliberately set out to emulate the American model, and has been pursued with similar ardour by New Labour. If the logic of our interpretation is correct, then it is likely that the culture of restraint inherited from the past should be losing its value as a resource for coping with the permanent flow of novelty.

The 1970s were the decade of transition. Both societies shifted from an agenda of greater social equality, security, and inclusion, towards a socially harsher, more business-friendly regime. At the economic level, it was a period of continued structural change, primarily the decline of older extractive and manufacturing industries (notwithstanding some renewal and organizational change), and the rise of the finance, services, and informa-tion industries. At a personal level, there was a drift towards a more self-regarding individualism, captured by demographic trends such as more divorce, a lower birth rate, later marriages, out of wedlock births; at the normative level by an increased quest for self-fulfilment and an increased assertion of individual entitlements and rights. What is driving what? As an economic historian, my inclination is to explain changes in the pattern of choices by means of changes in the pattern of incentives. I seek the prime driver in technological change and its concomitant, eco-nomic growth. Individuals respond primarily to what is placed before their eyes, by parents, schools, partners, work, markets. They cannot envisage the social consequences of their individual choices, and even if they could, they would not be able to change them. My hypothesis is that the shift from the New Deal to the New Right, from social democracy to market liberalism, the largest historical shift of the last fifty years, has worked up from technologies, to new opportunities and rewards, which unsettled the individual psyche, to consequences both unintended and desired, at the level of society and politics, not only in the English-speaking countries, but spreading outwards to the world as a whole. But that is truly a matter for further research.

Implications

It is tempting to 'do something' with knowledge. It is customary to conclude analytical or descriptive studies with a few limp proposals. What makes them limp is that analysis and action require different skills. Action requires an understanding of what politics can deliver, and the skills of an advocate more than those of a judge. I cannot claim such practical skills for myself. But the temptation is difficult to resist, and some readers may expect prescriptions as part of the package. The suggestions that follow are offered tentatively as options to explore.

If economic growth were the best way to achieve the well-being of society, whose objective would it be to push for it? It might be a role for politicians, but they would do better to target the groups that count the most, those that include the 'median' or marginal voter. If our aim is well-being for society as a whole, then privileging the objective of 'growth', by maximizing average income per head, is counter-productive. It does not follow that growth is 'bad'. But to gain its advantages, in affluent societies, a moderate, regulated level of growth will do. The objective of growth is itself far from self-evident. From the individualistic perspective of market liberalism, it is not even clear *whose* priority the pursuit of growth should be. Under methodological individualism, any claims to espouse the public good need to be treated with suspicion. The working assumption of welfare economics and public finance between the 1930s and the 1950s was that the economist and the civil servant worked for the welfare of all, and that often remains an implicit premiss of policy discourse. This benign view of academic and official mandarins began to be questioned during the 1960s. The public choice school of political economy (Buchanan, Stigler, Tullock, Niskanen) took an individualist view, in which politicians and officials were in it merely for themselves. It follows that similar caution ought to be applied to these theorists' own motives. Although they profess to believe it of others, they never say '*I* am only in it for *myself*.' In affluent societies, the doctrines of economics tend to be aligned with the interests of the powerful. The competition that economists extol is one which the educated, the wealthy, the powerful, are already well placed to win. It strives to exact the greatest efforts from the weakest, to dismantle their securities and defences. In a rich society, the virtue of efficiency appears to be overrated, and also miscalculated. When the benefits of growth are added up, the costs to the losers are often invisible. The winners' prizes are disproportional to the effort invested, and their social value is often questionable: enormous resources are staked and won to secure positional power.

The rational choice criterion of adequacy, Pareto Optimality, simply requires that no one should lose from any intervention without being capable of being compensated. This is a very thin good, and allows massive increments for some, with losses for others. In the theory, compensation only needs to be possible—it is not imperative to provide it. There is a macho appeal to this rhetoric of rugged self-reliance. It legitimizes ego preferences (and property rights) as the only arbiters of desert. As Hume expressed it sarcastically—'It is not contrary to reason to prefer the destruction of the whole world to the scratching of my little finger.' What protects this view from dismissal as mere barbarism is the doctrine of the 'invisible hand', that the self-seeking of individuals adds up to maximize the welfare of society. In this extreme version, the 'invisible hand' doctrine is simply an article of faith. It was not held by Adam Smith himself. Despite more than two centuries of effort, it has never been proved theoretically except under the most stringent and artificial restrictions and qualifications.

Adam Smith actually had a different view. He understood that our well-being depended on the sympathy of others, and suggested a code of conduct that could *earn* their esteem. Each individual earns sympathy by being worthy of sympathy. She follows the guidance of the 'impartial spectator', an inner voice that simulates the norms of society. That is quite similar to my own understanding of how well-being is achieved in the 'economy of regard'. Under reciprocity, the regard of others is earned by providing them with our own regard, directly or indirectly. This view remains individualistic and also empirical: the desire for regard is hard-wired into our psyches, and constitutes the basis of well-being. This is both a more credible and a more ethical basis for policy. It is open to exploitation, but is not a free-rider's charter. The 'warm glow' of positive reciprocity survives, because it is supported by the 'cold glare' of exclusion and punishment.

Choice is fallible, because psychic arousal, which is desirable in itself, can mask out some of the larger opportunities for well-being. Overcoming myopia requires commitment. It requires a blend of cognitive and personal skills, the construction of 'commitment technologies' and access to them, a personal and social repertoire of working traditions and routines. Good choices are not free, and are never 'optimal'—commitment is costly, and uncertain in its results. The rapid pace of innovation under affluence undermines commitment inventories, and generates an excess of arousal, whose rewards are quickly eroded by habituation. Well-being consists of an appropriate dynamic balance, sustained over time, different for each individual, community, society, time, and place, of short-term arousal and long-term prudence. Although best choices are difficult to specify in advance, it might be useful to understand the challenge of well-being in these terms.

If this diagnosis is correct, its main value is not to motivate action, but to underpin judgement. The task is not to launch interventions, but to understand them, to evaluate whether they are constructive or inimical to well-being. In affluent societies, the subjective well-being of the majority is not currently a serious problem. Most people in affluent societies (though not in poor ones) declare themselves to be reasonably happy, and appear to have a natural psychological 'buoyancy' that allows them to disregard objective detriments in their social and personal position, and to find satisfaction with their prospects, with their partners, with work, with their children, and with their leisure.[2] Improving the aggregate level of economic well-being does very little to improve the sense of individual well-being. Hence the priority for raising the standard of living overall in affluent societies is wasteful, and is likely to be counteracted by habituation on the 'hedonic treadmill'.[3] It might be that a constant level of improvement is necessary to maintain this buoyancy, but efforts to raise economic growth must also be evaluated in terms of the unmeasured and invisible costs that they impose. Economic efficiency may be purchased with unemployment, longer hours at work, more stress, family breakdown, poverty, inequality, poor health. We can only know for sure whether we are truly better off, by finding a way to encompass all the costs and benefits, not only those that are traded directly for money. The income gradient of happiness in affluent societies suggests that there is something to be gained from shifting income from the better off to those who are not. There is a stronger argument from global well-being for moving resources from rich countries to poor ones, though even in that context relative income appears to have a larger effect than absolute levels of income, while the largest effects arise from the circumstances that are unique to each individual society: presumably, culture, norms, governance, institutions, the capacity for commitment and trust. Economic growth has a strong positive impact on the quality of life in poor countries. That does

---

[2] Above, Ch. 2, and James, *Britain on the Couch*, 54–9.
[3] Easterlin, 'Income and Happiness'.

not constitute an argument for further enriching the rich in the most affluent ones.

Reported subjective well-being in most affluent societies is remarkably high. It would be very costly to nudge it up much further. A higher priority is to target more precisely the sources of ill-being. In affluent societies, ill-being appears to rise not primarily from absolute destitution, but from two main sources, the social stigma and deprivation associated with low social status and the erosion of intimacy, reciprocity, and regard. It is indicated in the prevalence of physical and mental dysfunction and disability. While life expectation has been increasing (almost regardless of the level of national income), there is an economic gradient of health domestically within each country, with the poor doing much worse than the rich, most notably in the richest and most unequal country, the United States. The blight of mental dysfunction also has an income/social gradient, but appears to be associated with the competitive pressures on families, and the consequent disruption of parental, and especially maternal, attachment, through marital discord and separation. This is highest in rich countries, but affects the poor the most within them.

The task of finding a proper balance between arousal and commitment is not novel: societies already do a great deal, for example, to regulate psychoactive and addictive drugs. In the United States, about a million people are in prison for drug-related offences. On the other hand, the regulation of alcohol is rather lax, and loosening. The serious regulation of tobacco is only beginning. Gambling is increasingly liberalized and accessible, most recently in Britain. Likewise in Britain, the hours in which alcohol is available have been greatly extended, in the name of 'consumer choice', overturning the prudence of previous generations. An emergent problem of substance abuse is associated with pre-processed food, where easy exposure to arousal has altered the body shape of the population, and is beginning to threaten to undo some of the public health achievements of previous decades.

Among policies currently under discussion, one is based on the notion that investing real resources in positional competition is wasteful, since social ranking can be established more efficiently by imposing artificial scarcities on the signals of position. The most developed idea is to tax status signalling, by means of a progressive tax on consumption.[4] This appears to be sound in theory, but requires careful design. It appears to justify more aggressive taxation of luxury goods. But consumption taxes

[4] Frank, 'Frame of Reference'.

are exposed to political bargaining over levels and rates. Experience suggests that a tax of this kind can be captured by the rich, who have shown considerable ability in recent years to shed the burdens of taxation. A tax on consumption is already supported by conservative economists and politicians, and is likely to be applied regressively. If that is the outcome, the proposal might do more harm than good.

Productive interventions might address the sources of unhappiness directly. That means giving a higher priority to mental health.[5] Mental disorder is very widespread, and there is hardly a household that is not touched by it at one time or another. Depression, anxiety, schizophrenia, and the multitude of afflictions set down in the *Diagnostic and Statistical Manual of Mental Disorders* are widespread, increasing, very painful, disabling, and life threatening (through a high incidence of suicide). Effective intervention is available, chemical, psychotherapeutic, and social, but the majority of those who suffer do not receive treatment, and it is difficult to obtain. The healthy and happy find it difficult to imagine that they might ever be afflicted. For a longer view, epidemiological work is necessary to understand both triggers and larger causes. Mental suffering is as insidious, widespread, and growing as obesity, only less visible. Young people are particularly vulnerable.

Choice and freedom for some means constraint for others. The invisible hand doctrine needs to be queried more rigorously. It is a resonant and effective slogan, but it relies on assertion more than on logic. A lower priority for growth means recognition for other priorities, which might have a cost in economic terms, for example by having real choices for fewer hours at work, and more free time. Raising average economic growth does not justify exposing the worst off to greater insecurity, inequality, and exploitation. Rising incomes improve the life of the poor much more than they improve life in the middle or the top, which suggests a case for reducing the standard of living overall, if it improves the lives of the worse off. But measuring capabilities in economic terms alone carries the risk of perverse and unintended consequences. Well-being is much more than market power. Acceptance, autonomy, free expression, control, regard, free time, slack—these are all goods which the national accounts fail to capture. Under affluence, purchasing power is less of a problem—one useful effort would be an audit of well-being that would try to measure what really counts.

The market has strong incentives to provide arousal and novelty, and can be trusted to do so. The resources of commitment require more social

---

[5] Advocated forcefully in Layard, *Happiness*, 181–221.

attention. Here are some priorities in these areas. Families depend on commitment: their rewards are not monetary, and count for little in the calculus of growth. Natalist policies have a bad name—they were associated (in continental Europe in particular) with raising of infantry, and with keeping women at home. But women have not abandoned motherhood, and the balance of advantage needs to shift more in their favour. The current level of rewards has pushed the birth rate below the level of social reproduction, and (contrary to the predictions of Beckerian family theory) has lowered the quality of children as well, by exposing them to marital breakdown and stress. Everything is paid for, but young people, the most vital of resources, are taken by society as free gifts from parents. There is a case for enhancing support for parents, and for mothers in particular. Nor does it have to stop with motherhood. In Britain, for example, after school is over, the convivial and social needs of young people are largely met at the street corner, or (for teenagers) by the pub and alcohol industries. Instead of acquiring the tools of reciprocity and commitment, impressionable young people are exposed to intoxicating, short-term dissipation. There is no commercial profit in offering an alternative, and one role for society and government would be to offer a richer choice, by providing facilities for after-hours conviviality, where young people could meet each other, engage with a variety of challenges, in sport, technology, the arts, public services, adventure, and yes, romance, in a network of youth clubs, which might be housed conveniently within the schools.

At the level of social and cultural norms, the recent privileging of 'choice' can be countered by the traditional counsel of 'moderation'. In the nineteenth century, the rich and powerful in Britain embraced an ideal of self-restraint, the gentlemanly ideal. Some return to greater civility by economic and political elites would enhance everybody's well-being. The idea, for example, that it is vital to fight in order to preserve credibility, to 'punch one's weight' (or with relative decline, 'to punch above one's weight'), has led to terrible disasters in the twentieth century, and continues into the twenty-first. The norms and habits of social and political deference allow the rulers to embark on ruinous wars, to normalize and to moralize destruction and violent death. Instead of the frenzied self-seeking of politics and management, a little 'noblesse oblige', a genuine culture of service to others, a sense of humility and proportion is worth restoring as an ideal to strive for, to delegitimize the destructive (and ultimately self-defeating) pursuit of self-interest, power, dominance, status. The assumption of selfishness in human behaviour is, at best, merely an analytical convenience. If incorporated into personal and policy norms, it becomes self-fulfilling.[6] 'Ha!' I hear my reader say—'wishful thinking, it isn't going to happen.' If it is not, then take it as another example of how impulse and instinct are at odds with the achievement of well-being.

To act effectively, it is necessary to have reasonable grasp of reality. The foundational requirement is respect for the truth. Mutual commitment requires some self-denial by each of the parties. Commitment can only endure if it is honest. For the deceiver, however, that may be long enough. Hence the priority, in the public domain, of investing in and seeking the truth, of aiming for a critical and independent cast of mind, a quest for reality, and an honest discussion. That means more regulation and restriction of marketing (both commercial and political), less puffery and spin, more and better education, more independence and public spirit in the media, as criteria for public policy.

Contracting for the future is difficult. For example, consumer choice finds it difficult to cope with providing support for everyone's old age. The time gap between consumer decisions and their consequences is just too long. It is up to politicians to craft durable commitments for intergenerational transfer, and to acknowledge and engage with the difficult agency problems involved. Selfishness alone is unlikely to produce a solution that will benefit everybody: the strong and wealthy will find a way to defect. The parameters of rational choice do not allow the problem to be solved within prevailing market discount rates. The solutions of the past, which relied on mandatory participation, public management, and an explicit social contract, have done a reasonably good job in their time, and have a good deal to teach us still.

Achieving well-being depends primarily on how (and how well) we understand ourselves. Well-being is more than having more. It is a balance between our own needs, and those of others, on whose goodwill and approbation our own well-being depends. I was not so clear in my mind about this when I set out on this investigation. I present these findings in the hope that they will make our choices appear not simpler and easier, but as complicated and intractable as they really are.

---

[6] Frey, 'A Constitution for Knaves'.

Bibliography

Archival Collections Consulted

Mark Abrams papers. A small collection of papers on marketing and advertising during the late 1950s and early 1960s in Britain, presented on loan by the late Mark Abrams.

Electricity Council Archive, Milbank, London (now dispersed, consulted by Sue Bowden).

Henry Ford Museum and Archives, Dearborn Michigan (older archives of the Ford Motor company, and other archival collections on the motor industry).

John W. Hartman Center for Sales, Advertising and Marketing History, Rare Book, Manuscript, and Special Collections Library, Duke University (large collection of advertising archives, including the papers of J. Walter Thompson, the largest US advertising agency during most of the twentieth century. For long periods they held the Ford Motor company accounts).

History of Advertising Trust, Raveningham, Norfolk (large archival collection of the British advertising and marketing industry, in particular a large deposit of records from J. Walter Thompson, the advertising agency, and the archives of the Advertising Association).

Ford Industrial Archives, Dearborn, Michigan (archives of the Ford Motor company, Dearborn, Michigan).

Published Material and Dissertations

ABRAMOVITZ, MOSES, 'The Retreat from Economic Advance: Changing Ideas about Economic Progress', in Gabriel Almond, Marvin Chodorow, and Roy Harvey (eds.), *Progress and its Discontents* (Berkeley, 1982), 253–79.

ABRAMOWITZ, ALAN I., 'United States: Political Culture under Stress', in Gabriel A. Almond and Sidney Verba (eds.), *The Civic Culture Revisited: An Analytic Study* (Boston, 1980), ch. 6.

ACHESON, DONALD, *Independent Inquiry into Inequalities in Health Report* (London, 1998).

ADVERTISING ASSOCIATION, *Advertising Statistics Yearbook 1989* (Henley, 1989).

AHIER, JOHN, and BECK, JOHN, 'Education and the Politics of Envy', *British Journal of Educational Studies*, 51 (2003), 320–43.

AHMED, KAMAL, REVILL, JO, and HINSLIFF, GABY, 'Official: Fat Epidemic Will Cut Life Expectancy', *Observer*, 9 Nov. 2003.

AHUVIA, AARON C., and FRIEDMAN, DOUGLAS C., 'Income, Consumption, and Subjective Well-Being: Toward a Composite Macromarketing Model', *Journal of Macromarketing*, 18 (1998), 153–68.

AINSLIE, GEORGE, 'Specious Reward: A Behavioral Theory of Impulsiveness and Impulse Control', *Psychological Bulletin*, 82 (1975), 463–96.

—— 'Derivation of "Rational" Economic Behavior from Hyperbolic Discount Curves', *American Economic Review*, 81 (1991), 334–40.

—— *Picoeconomics: The Interaction of Successive Motivational States within the Person* (Cambridge, 1992).

—— *Breakdown of Will* (Cambridge, 2001).

AINSWORTH, MARY D., 'Attachments across the Life Span', *Bulletin of the New York Academy of Medicine*, 61 (1985), 792–812.

—— 'Attachments beyond Infancy', *American Psychologist*, 44 (1989), 709–16.

—— BLEHAR, MARY C., WATERS, EVERETT, and WALL, SALLY, *Patterns of Attachment: A Psychological Study of the Strange Situation* (Hillsdale, NJ, 1978).

AKERLOF, GEORGE, 'The Market for Lemons: Quality Uncertainty and the Market', *Quarterly Journal of Economics*, 84 (1970), 488–500.

—— 'Labor Contracts as Partial Gift Exchange', *Quarterly Journal of Economics*, 87 (1982), 543–69.

—— YELLEN, JANET L., and KATZ, MICHAEL, 'An Analysis of Out-of-Wedlock Childbearing in the United States', *Quarterly Journal of Economics*, 109 (1996), 277–317.

ALDERSON, ARTHUS S., and NIELSEN, FRANÇOIS, 'Globalization and the Great U-Turn: Income Inequality Trends in 16 OECD Countries', *American Journal of Sociology*, 107 (2002), 1244–99.

ALESINA, ALBERTO, and GLAESER, EDWARD L., *Fighting Poverty in the US and Europe: A World of Difference* (Oxford, 2004).

—— —— and SACERDOTE, BRUCE, 'Why Doesn't the United States Have a European-Style Welfare State?' *Brookings Papers on Economic Activity*, 2 (2001), 187–254.

ALLEN, D., and BRINIG, M., 'Sex, Property Rights, and Divorce', *European Journal of Law and Economics*, 5 (1998), 211–34.

ALLEN, DOUGLAS W., and LUECK, DEAN, *The Nature of the Farm: Contracts, Risk, and Organization in Agriculture* (Cambridge, Mass., 2002).

ALLON, N., 'The Stigma of Overweight in Everyday Life', in Benjamin B. Wolman and S. DeBerry, (eds.), *Psychological Aspects of Obesity: A Handbook* (New York, 1982), 130–74.

ALTMAN, IRWIN, 'Reciprocity of Interpersonal Exchange', *Journal for the Theory of Social Behaviour*, 3 (1973), 249–61.

ALVARADO, MANUEL, *Video World-Wide: An International Study* (London, 1988).

AMATO, PAUL R., 'The Consequence of Divorce for Adults and Children', *Journal of Marriage and the Family*, 62 (2000), 1269–87.

—— 'Children of Divorce in the 1990s: An Update of the Amato and Keith (1991) Meta-Analysis', *Journal of Family Psychology*, 15 (2001), 355–70.

—— and BOOTH, ALAN, *A Generation at Risk: Growing up in an Era of Family Upheaval* (Cambridge, Mass., 1997).

—— ——'The Legacy of Parents' Marital Discord: Consequences for Children's Marital Quality', *Journal of Personality and Social Psychology*, 81 (2001), 627–38.

——and DeBoer, Danelle D., 'The Transmission of Marital Instability across Generations: Relationship Skills or Commitment to Marriage?' *Journal of Marriage and the Family*, 63 (2001), 1038–51.

——and Sobolewski, Juliana M., 'The Effects of Divorce and Marital Discord on Adult Children's Psychological Well-Being', *American Sociological Review*, 66 (2001), 900–21.

——Johnson, David R., Booth, Alan, and Rogers, Stacy J., 'Continuity and Change in Marital Quality between 1980 and 2000', *Journal of Marriage and the Family*, 65 (2003), 1–22.

American Bankruptcy Institute, 'U.S. Bankruptcy Filings 1980–2002 (Business, Non-Business, (Total)' (2002), in **www.abiworld.org/stats/1980annual.html**, accessed: 19 Jan. 2004.

Ameriks, John, Caplin, Andrew, Leahy, John, and Tyler, Tom, 'Measuring Self-Control', New York University, Preliminary (New York, 2003).

Anderson, B. L., and Latham, A. J. H. (eds.), *The Market in History: Papers Presented at a Symposium Held 9–13 September 1984 at St. George's House, Windsor Castle, under the Auspices of the Liberty Fund* (London, 1986).

Anderson, Kristin L., 'Gender, Status, and Domestic Violence: An Integration of Feminist and Family Violence Approaches', *Journal of Marriage and the Family*, 59 (1997), 655–69.

Anderson, Sarah, Cavanagh, John, Estes, Ralph, Hartman, Chris, and Collins, Cliff, 'A Decade of Executive Excess: The 1990s Sixth Annual Executive Compensation Survey' (1999), in **www.faireconomy.org/press/archive/1999/Executive_ Excess/decade_of_executive_excess.html**.

—— ——Hartman, Chris, and Klinger, Scott, 'Executive Excess 2003: CEOs Win, Workers and Taxpayers Lose' (2003), in **www.faireconomy.org/press/2003/ EE2003.pdf**.

Angeletos, George-Marios, Laibson, David, Repetto, Andrea, Tobacman, Jeremy, and Weinberg, Stephen, 'The Hyperbolic Consumption Model: Calibration, Simulation, and Emprical Evaluation', in George Loewenstein, Daniel Read, and Roy F. Baumeister (eds.), *Time and Decision: Economic and Psychological Perspectives on Intertemporal Choice* (New York, 2003), 517–43.

Angell, Marcia, *The Truth about the Drug Companies: How They Deceive us and What to Do about It* (New York, 2004).

Anon., 'Why do People Buy the Cars They Do?' *Popular Mechanics* (Feb. 1956), 193–5, 310–12.

——'Fifty Years of Statistics and History', *Merchandising Week* (28 Feb. 1972).

——'Product Saturation Analysis', *Merchandising*, 4 (Mar. 1979), 46, 48.

——'Executive Pay: The Party Ain't over Yet', *Business Week* (26 Apr. 1993), 56–79.

——'Database Marketing', *Business Week* (5 Sept. 1994), 56.

——'Ayer at 125: "Creating Intimacy with Customers"', *Advertising Age* (4 Apr. 1994), A-6.

Bibliography

ARGYLE, MICHAEL, *The Social Psychology of Everyday Life* (London, 1992).

—— 'Subjective Well-Being', in Avner Offer (ed.), *In Pursuit of the Quality of Life* (Oxford, 1996).

—— 'Causes and Correlates of Happiness', in Daniel Kahneman, Ed Diener, and Norbert Schwartz (eds.), *Well-Being: The Foundations of Hedonic Psychology* (New York, 1999), 353–73.

ARIELY, DAN, and CARMON, ZIV, 'Summary Assessment of Experiences: The Whole is Different from the Sum of its Parts', in George Loewenstein, Daniel Read, and Roy F. Baumeister (eds.), *Time and Decision: Economic and Psychological Perspectives on Intertemporal Choice* (New York, 2003), 323–49.

—— and WERTENBROCH, K., 'Procrastination, Deadlines, and Performance: Self-Control by Precommitment', *Psychological Science*, 13 (2002), 219–24.

ARLEN, MICHAEL J., *Thirty Seconds* (New York, 1980).

ARMI, C., *The Art of American Car Design: The Profession and Personalities* (University Park, Pa., 1988).

ARMSTRONG, LARRY, and MALLORY, MARIA, 'The Diet Business Starts Sweating', *Business Week*, 22 (1992), 32–3.

ARROW, KENNETH, DASGUPTA, PARTHA, GOULDER, LAWRENCE, DAILY, GRETCHEN, EHRLICH, PAUL, HEAL, GEOFFREY, LEVIN, SIMON, MALER, K.-G., SCHNEIDER, STEPHEN, STARRETT, DAVID, and WALKER, BRIAN, 'Are We Consuming Too Much?' *Journal of Economic Perspectives*, 18 (2004), 147–72.

ARROWSMITH, J., 'The Struggle over Working Time in Nineteenth- and Twentieth-Century Britain', *Historical Studies in Industrial Relations*, 13 (2002), 83–118.

ÅSTROM, SVERKER, 'Main Trends of Development in the Market for Frozen Foods in Western Europe', in United Nations Food and Agriculture Organization (ed.), *Frozen and Quick-Frozen Food* (Oxford, 1977).

ATKINS, DAVID C., DIMIDJIAN, SONA, and JACOBSON, NEIL S., 'Why Do People Have Affairs? Recent Research and Future Directions about Attributions for Extramarital Involvement', in Valerie Manusov and John H. Harvey (eds.), *Attribution, Communication Behavior, and Close Relationships* (Cambridge, 2001), 305–19.

ATKINSON, A. B., 'On Measurement of Inequality', *Journal of Economic Theory*, 2 (1970), 244–63.

—— 'Income Inequality in OECD Countries: Data and Explanations' paper prepared for the CESifo conference on 'Globalization, Inequality and Well-Being', 8–9 Nov. 2002 (Munich, 2002).

—— and BOURGUIGNON, FRANÇOIS, 'Income Distribution and Economics', in A. B. Atkinson, and François Bourguignon (eds.), *Handbook of Income Distribution*, Handbooks in Economics 16 (Amsterdam, 2000), 1–58.

Automobile Manufacturers Association, *Automobile Facts and Figures*, 1961 edn. (Detroit, 1961).

AVERETT, SUSAN, and KORENMAN, SANDERS, 'The Economic Reality of the Beauty Myth', *Journal of Human Resources*, 31 (1996), 304–30.

AXELROD, ROBERT, *The Evolution of Co-operation* (New York, 1984).

BABCOCK, LINDA, and LASCHEVER, SARA, *Women Don't Ask: Negotiation and the Gender Divide* (Princeton, NJ, 2003).

BAILEY, BETH L., *From Front Porch to Back Seat: Courtship in Twentieth-Century America* (Baltimore, 1988).

—— *Sex in the Heartland* (Cambridge, Mass., 1999).

BAIN, ANDREW D., *The Growth of Television Ownership in the United Kingdom since the War, a Lognormal Model* (Cambridge, 1964).

BAIRD, I. M., SILVERSTONE, J. T., GRIMSHAW, J. J., and ASHWELL, M., 'Prevalence of Obesity in a London Borough', *Practitioner*, 212, 1271 (1974), 706–14.

BAIROCH, PAUL, 'The Main Trends in National Economic Disparities since the Industrial Revolution', in Paul Bairoch and Maurice Lévy-Leboyer (eds.), *Disparities in Economic Development since the Industrial Revolution* (London, 1981), 1–17.

BAJARI, PATRICK, BENKARD, LANIER C., and KRAINER, JOHN, 'House Prices and Consumer Welfare', NBER Working Paper 9783 (2003).

BAKEMAN, JEFF, and KRINBRING, BRIAN, *Married to Mommy? A Survival Guide for Married Guys* (New York, 2002).

BAKER, L. A., and EMERY, R. E., 'When Every Relationship is Above Average: Perceptions and Expectations of Divorce at the Time of Marriage', *Law and Human Behavior*, 17 (1993), 439.

BAKER, SAMM SINCLAIR, *The Permissible Lie: The Inside Truth about Advertising* (London, 1968).

BAKKER, GERBEN, 'Entertainment Industrialized: The Emergence of the International Film Industry, 1890–1940', *Enterprise and Society*, 4 (2003), 579–85.

BARKER, LEWIS M. (ed.), *The Psychobiology of Human Food Selection* (Westport, Conn. 1982).

BARNES, MICHAEL L., and STERNBERG, ROBERT J., *The Psychology of Love* (New Haven, 1988).

BARON-COHEN, SIMON, *The Essential Difference: Men, Women and the Extreme Male Brain* (London, 2003).

BARRO, ROBERT J., 'Inequality and Growth in a Panel of Countries', *Journal of Economic Growth*, 5 (2000), 5–32.

BARTELS, ANDREAS, and ZEKI, SEMIR, 'The Neural Correlates of Maternal and Romantic Love', *Neuroimage*, 21 (2004), 1155–66.

BARTHOLD, THOMAS A., and ITO, TAKATOSHI, *Bequest Taxes and Accumulation of Household Wealth: US-Japan Comparison* (Washington, DC, 1991).

BARTHOLOMEW, KIM, 'Avoidance of Intimacy: An Attachment Perspective', *Journal of Social and Personal Relationships*, 7 (1990), 147–78.

—— and HOROWITZ, LEONARD M., 'Attachment Styles among Young Adults: A Test of a Four-Category Model', *Journal of Personality and Social Psychology*, 61 (1991), 226–44.

BARTLEY, M., SACKER, A., FIRTH, D., and FITZPATRICK, R., 'Social Position, Social Roles and Women's Health in England: Changing Relationships 1984–1993', *Social Science and Medicine*, 48 (1999), 99–116.

BARTOS, RENA, *Marketing to Women around the World* (Boston, 1989).

BAUER, RAYMOND A. (ed.), *Social Indicators* (Cambridge, Mass., 1966).

BAUMEISTER, R. F., and HEATHERTON, T. F., 'Self-Regulation Failure: An Overview', *Pschological Inquiry*, 7 (1996), 1–15.

——and VOHS, KATHLEEN D., 'Willpower, Choice, and Self-Control', in George Loewenstein, Daniel Read, and Roy F. Baumeister (eds.), *Time and Decision: Economic and Psychological Perspectives on Intertemporal Choice* (New York, 2003), 201–16.

BAXTER, JANEEN, 'The Joys and Justice of Housework', *Sociology*, 34 (2000), 609–31.

——and WESTERN, MARK, 'Satisfaction with Housework: Examining the Paradox', *Sociology*, 32 (1998), 101–20.

BAYLEY, S., *Harley Earl and the Dream Machine* (London, 1983).

BAZELON, COLEMAN, and SMETTERS, KENT, 'Discounting inside the Washington D.C. Beltway', *Journal of Economic Perspectives*, 13 (1999), 213–28.

BEARMAN, P. S., and BRUCKNER, H., 'Promising the Future: Virginity Pledges and First Intercourse', *American Journal of Sociology*, 106 (2001), 859–912.

BECKER, GARY S., 'Irrational Behavior and Economic Theory', *Journal of Political Economy*, 70 (1962), 1–13.

——'A Theory of the Allocation of Time', *Economic Journal*, 75 (1965), 493–517.

——*A Treatise on the Family*, enl. edn. (Cambridge, Mass., 1991).

——and MULLIGAN, CASEY B., 'The Endogenous Determination of Time Preference', *Quarterly Journal of Economics*, 112 (1997), 729–58.

——and MURPHY, K., 'A Theory of Rational Addiction', *Journal of Political Economy*, 96 (1988), 675–700.

————'A Simple Theory of Advertising as a Good or Bad', *Quarterly Journal of Economics*, 108 (1993), 941–64.

—— GROSSMAN, MICHAEL, and MURPHY, KEVIN M., 'Rational Addiction and the Effect of Price on Consumption', in Jon Elster, and George Loewenstein, (eds.), *Choice over Time* (New York, 1992), 361–70.

BECKERMAN, W., *In Defence of Economic Growth* (London, 1974).

——'Comparable Growth Rates of "Measureable Economic Welfare": Some Experimental Calculations', in R. C. O. Matthews (ed.), *Economic Growth and Resources*, vol. ii (London, 1980), 36–59.

——'Is Economic Growth Still Desirable?' in Adam Szirmai, Bart van Ark, and Dirk Pilat (eds.), *Explaining Economic Growth: Essays in Honour of Angus Maddison* (Amsterdam, 1993), 77–100.

BELK, RUSSELL W., and COON, GREGORY S., 'Can't Buy Me Love: Dating, Money and Gifts', *Advances in Consumer Research*, 18 (1991), 521–7.

————'Gift Giving as Agapic Love: An Alternative to the Exchange Paradigm Based on Dating Experiences', *Journal of Consumer Research*, 20 (1993), 393–417.

——and POLLAY, RICHARD W., 'Images of Ourselves: The Good Life in Twentieth Century Advertising', *Journal of Consumer Research*, 11 (1985), 887–97.

BELKIN, LISA, 'The Opt-out Revolution', *New York Times Magazine* (26 Oct. 2003), 42.

BELL, LINDA A., and FREEMAN, RICHARD B., 'The Incentive for Working Hard: Explaining Hours Worked Differences in the US and Germany', *Labour Economics*, 8 (2001), 181–202.

BELLAH, ROBERT N, et al., *Habits of the Heart: Individualism and Commitment in American Life* (Berkeley, 1985).

BELLOW, SAUL, *Seize the Day* (London, 1957).

——'The Old System', in Saul Bellow, *Mosby's Memoirs and Other Stories* (Harmondsworth, 1971), 45–81.

BENEDICT, JOHN T., 'Era of "Classless" Car Nears Full Flower', *Automotive News* (25 Oct. 1955).

BENNETT, WILLIAM, and GURIN, JOEL, *The Dieter's Dilemma: Eating Less and Weighing More* (New York, 1982).

BEN-PORATH, YORAM, 'The F-Connection: Families, Friends, and Firms and the Organization of Exchange', *Population and Development Review*, 6 (1980), 1–30.

BERNARD, JESSIE, 'The Good-Provider Role: Its Rise and Fall', in A. Skolnick and J. Skolnick (eds.), *Family in Transition* (Boston 2001).

——SHLEIFER, ANDREW, and SUMMERS, LAWRENCE H., 'The Strategic Bequest Motive', *Journal of Political Economy*, 93 (1985), 1045–76.

BERNHEIM, DOUGLAS B., 'How Strong are Bequest Motives? Evidence Based on Estimates of the Demand for Life Insurance and Annuities', *Journal of Political Economy*, 99 (1991), 899–927.

BERRIDGE, KENT C., 'Irrational Pursuits: Hyper-Incentives from a Visceral Brain', in Isabelle Brocas and Juan Carillo (eds.), *The Psychology of Economic Decisions, i: Rationality and Well-Being* (Oxford, 2003), 17–40.

BERTMAN, STEPHEN, *Hyperculture: The Human Cost of Speed* (Westport, Conn., 1998).

BHROLCHÁIN, MÁIRE NÍ, 'Flexibility in the Marriage Market', *Population*, 55 (2000), 899–940.

——CHAPPELL, ROMA, DIAMOND, IAN, and JAMESON, CATHERINE, 'Parental Divorce and Outcomes for Children: Evidence and Interpretation', *European Sociological Review*, 16, 1 (Mar. 2000), 67–91.

BIENEFELD, MANFRED, *Working Hours in British Industry: An Economic History* (London, 1972).

BIOCCA, FRANK, *Television and Political Advertising* (Hillsdale, N J, 1991).

BIRCH, LEANN L., FISHER, JENNIFER ORLET, and GRIMM-THOMAS, KAREN, 'The Development of Children's Eating Habits', in H. L. Meiselman and H. J. H. MacFie (eds.), *Food Choice, Acceptance and Consumption* (London, 1996), 161–206.

BJÖRNTORP, PER, 'Obesity', *The Lancet*, 350 (1997), 423–6.

BLACK, DOUGLAS, WHITEHEAD, MARGARET, TOWNSEND, PETER, and DAVIDSON, NICK, *Inequalities of Health: The Black Report* (Harmondsworth, 1988).

BLAIR, A. J., LEWIS, V. J., and BOOTH, D. A., 'Does Emotional Eating Interfere with Success in Attempts at Weight Control?', *Appetite*, 15 (1990).

BLANCHFLOWER, DAVID G., and OSWALD, ANDREW, 'Well-Being, Insecurity and the Decline of American Job Satisfaction', unpublished paper, University of Warwick (Coventry, 1999).

BLANCHFLOWER, DAVID G., and OSWALD, ANDREW J., 'Is Something Wrong with Work–Life Balance? A Look at International Data', unpublished paper, University of Warwick June (Coventry, 2000).

————'Well-Being over Time in Britain and the USA', *Journal of Public Economics*, 88 (2004), 1359–86.

————and WARR, PETER B., 'Well-Being over Time in Britain and the USA', unpublished paper (1993).

BLANKSTEIN, KIRK R., and POLIVY, JANET, *Self-Control and Self-Modification of Emotional Behavior* (New York, 1982).

BLAU, FRANCINE D., 'Trends in the Well-Being of American Women, 1970–1995', *Journal of Economic Literature*, 36 (1998), 112–65.

——'The Gender Pay Gap', in Inga Persson and Christina Jonung (eds.), *Women's Work and Wages*, Research in Gender and Society, vol. ii (London, 1998), 15–35.

——and KAHN, LAWRENCE M., 'Gender Differences in Pay', *Journal of Economic Perspectives*, 14 (2000), 75–99.

BLAU, PETER MICHAEL, DUNCAN, OTIS DUDLEY, and TYREE, ANDREA, *The American Occupational Structure* (New York, 1967).

BLOSSFELD, HANS-PETER, and DROBNIC, SONJA (eds.), *Careers of Couples in Contemporary Societies: From Male Breadwinner to Dual Earner Families* (Oxford, 2001).

BLUMBERG, PAUL, *The Predatory Society: Deception in the American Marketplace* (New York, 1989).

BLUMSTEIN, PHILIP, and SCHWARTZ, PEPPER, *American Couples: Money, Work, Sex* (New York, 1983).

BLUNDELL, J. E., 'Food Intake and Body Weight Regulation', in C. Bouchard and G. A. Bray (eds.), *Regulation of Body Weight: Biological and Behavioral Mechanisms* (Chichester, 1996), 111–33.

BODDEWYN, JEAN J., *Global Perspectives on Advertising Self-Regulation: Principles and Practices in Thirty-Eight Countries* (Westport, Conn., 1992).

BÖHEIM, RENÉ, and TAYLOR, MARK, 'My Home was my Castle: Evictions and Repossessions in Britain', University of Essex, 24 February 2000 (Colchester, 2000).

BONKE, JENS, 'Economic Influences on Food Choice—Non-Convenience Versus Convenience Food Consumption', in H. L. Meiselman and H. J. H. MacFie (eds.), *Food Choice, Acceptance and Consumption* (London, 1996), 293–318.

BOOTH, MARTIN, *The Triads: The Chinese Criminal Fraternity* (London, 1990).

BORDEN, NEIL H., *The Economic Effects of Advertising* (Chicago, 1942).

BORDO, SUSAN, *Unbearable Weight: Feminism, Western Culture, and the Body* (Berkeley, 1993).

BORRIE, GORDON, 'Review of the UK Self-Regulatory System of Advertising Control: A Report by the Director General of Fair Trading', Office of Fair Trading, November (London, 1978).

BOSE, C., 'Technology and Changes in the Division of Labour in the American Home', *Women's Studies International Quarterly*, 2 (1979), 295–304.

—— *Jobs and Gender: A Study of Occupational Prestige* (New York, 1985).

—— Bereano, P. L., and Malloy, M., 'Household Technology and the Social Construction of Housework', *Technology and Culture*, 25 (1984), 53–82.

Boswell, James, *Life of Samuel Johnson*, ed. Christopher Hibbert (London, 2003).

Bosworth, Barry, Burtless, Gary, and Sabelhaus, John, 'The Decline in Saving: Evidence from Household Surveys', *Brookings Papers on Economic Activity*, 1 (1991), 183–241.

Bouchard, C., and Bray, G. A. (eds.), *Regulation of Body Weight: Biological and Behavioral Mechanisms* (Chichester, 1996).

Bourdieu, Pierre, 'Les Modes de Domination', *Actes de la Recherche en Sciences Sociales*, 2 (1976), 122–32.

—— *Distinction: A Social Critique of the Judgement of Taste* (London, 1986).

Bowden, Sue, and Offer, Avner, 'Household Appliances and the Use of Time: The United States and Britain since the 1920s', *Economic History Review*, 47 (1994), 725–48.

—— —— 'The Technological Revolution that Never Was: Gender, Class, and the Home Appliance Market in Interwar England', in Victoria de Grazia and Elen Furlough (eds.), *The Sex of Things: Gender and Consumption in Historical Perspective* (Berkeley, 1996), 211–55.

Bowlby, John, *Attachment and Loss*, 2nd edn. (Harmondsworth, 1991).

Bowles, Samuel, and Gintis, Herbert, 'The Inheritance of Inequality', *Journal of Economic Perspectives*, 16 (2002), 3–30.

Boyd, Monica, 'Socioeconomic Indices and Sexual Inequality: A Tale of Scales', *The Canadian Review of Sociology and Anthropology*, 23 (1986), 457–80.

Boyle, David, *Authenticity: Brands, Fakes, Spin and the Lust for Real Life* (London, 2003).

Bradburn, Norman M., and Noll, C. Edward, *The Structure of Psychological Well-Being* (Chicago, 1969).

Braddon, F. E., Rodgers, B., Wadsworth, M. E., and Davies, J. M., 'Onset of Obesity in a 36-Year Birth Cohort Study', *British Medical Journal*, 293 (1986), 299–303.

Bradsher, Keith, *High and Mighty: SUVs—the World's Most Dangerous Vehicles and How They Got That Way* (New York, 2002).

Braithwaite, V. A., and Levi, Margaret, *Trust and Governance* (New York, 1998).

Bramlett, Matthew D., and Mosher, William D., 'First Marriage Dissolution, Divorce, and Remarriage: United States', *Advance Data from Vital and Health Statistics*, 31 May (Hyattsville, Md., 2001).

Bramley, Ken, 'Affordability and the Intermediate Market', Heriot-Watt University, Report to the Barker Inquiry on Housing Supply, October (Edinburgh, 2003).

Braun, John C., 'Unfair Competition and the Regulation Laws in the Common Market Countries', offprint, 28 June 1972 (1972).

Braver, Sanford L., and O'Connell, Diane, *Divorced Dads: Shattering the Myths* (New York, 1998).

BRAVERMAN, HARRY, *Labor and Monopoly Capital: The Degradation of Work in the Twentieth Century* (New York, 1974).

BRAY, G. A., 'Overweight is Risking Fate: Definition, Classification, Prevalence and Risks', *Annals of the New York Academy of Sciences*, 499 (1987), 14–28.

BRENNAN, GEOFFREY, and PETTIT, PHILIP, *The Economy of Esteem: An Essay on Civil and Political Society* (Oxford, 2004).

BRENNAN, KELLY A., CLARK, CATHERINE L., and SHAVER, PHILLIP R., 'Self-Report Measurement of Adult Attachment: An Integrative Overview', in Jeffry A. Simpson and William Steven Rholes (eds.), *Attachment Theory and Close Relationships* (New York, 1998), 46–76.

BRENNER, LESLIE, *American Appetite: The Coming of Age of a Cuisine* (New York, 1999).

BRESNAHAN, T. F., 'Competition and Collusion in the American Automobile Industry: The 1955 Price War', *Journal of Industrial Economics*, 35 (1987), 457–82.

BRINES, JULIE, 'The Exchange Value of Housework', *Rationality and Society*, 5 (1993), 302–340.

——'Economic Dependency, Gender, and the Division of Labor at Home', *American Journal of Sociology*, 100 (1994), 652.

BRINIG, MARGARET F., *From Contract to Covenant: Beyond the Law and Economics of the Family* (Cambridge, Mass., 2000).

——and ALLEN, DOUGLAS W., '"These Boots Are Made for Walking": Why Most Divorce Filers Are Women', *American Law and Economics Review*, 2 (2000), 126–69.

British Broadcasting Corporation, 'Tories Accuse Labour of "Class Envy"' (1999), in **http://news.bbc.co.uk/1/hi/uk_politics/461482.stm**, accessed: 28 Feb., 2004.

British Medical Association, *Diet, Nutrition and Health: Report of the Board of Science and Education* (London, 1986).

BROCAS, ISABELLE, CARRILLO, JUAN D., and DEWATRIPONT, MATHIAS, 'Commitment Devices under Self-Control Problems: An Overview', in Isabelle Brocas and Juan D. Carrillo (eds.), *The Psychology of Economic Decisions, ii: Reasons and Choices* (Oxford, 2004), 49–65.

BROMLEY, DANIEL W., *Environment and Economy: Property Rights and Public Policy* (Oxford, 1991).

BROOKS, JOHN, 'Annals of Business: The Edsel', *New Yorker*, pt. 1, 27 Nov., pt. 2, (3 Dec. 1960), pp. 57–102, 199–224.

——*The Fate of the Edsel and Other Business Adventures* (New York, 1963).

BROWN, CATRINA, 'The Continuum: Anorexia, Bulimia and Weight Preoccupation', in Catrina Brown and Karin Jasper (eds.), *Consuming Passions: Feminist Approaches to Weight Preoccupation and Eating Disorders* (Toronto, 1993), 53–68.

BROWN, CLAIR, *American Standards of Living 1918–1988* (Oxford, 1994).

BROWN, DONALD E., *Human Universals* (New York, 1991).

BROWN, GORDON A., GARDNER, JONATHAN, OSWALD, ANDREW, and QIAN, JING, 'Does Wage Rank Affect Employees' Wellbeing?', unpublished paper, 20 Sept. (Coventry, 2004).

BROWN, J. L., 'Hunger in the U.S.', *Scientific American*, 256 (1987), 37–41.

BROWN, PATRICIA LEIGH, 'Hey There, Couch Potatoes: Hot Enough for You?' *New York Times*, 27 July 2003.

BROWN, PETER J., and KONNER, MELVIN, 'An Anthropological Perspective on Obesity', *Annals of the New York Academy of Sciences*, 499 (1987), 29–46.

BROWN, ROBERT, 'Cultivating a "Green" Image: Oil Companies and Outdoor Publicity in Britain and Europe, 1920–1936', *Journal of European Economic History*, 22 (1993), 347–65.

BROWN, SUSAN L., and BOOTH, ALAN, 'Cohabitation Versus Marriage: A Comparison of Relationship Quality', *Journal of Marriage and the Family*, 58 (1996), 668–78.

BROWNE, K. R., 'Sex and Temperament in Modern Society: A Darwinian View of the Glass Ceiling and the Gender Gap', *Arizona Law Review*, 37 (1995), 971–1106.

BROWNELL, KELLY D., and FOREYT, JOHN P. (eds.), *Handbook of Eating Disorders: Physiology, Psychology and Treatment of Obesity, Anorexia, and Bulimia* (New York, 1986).

BUDIG, M. J., and ENGLAND, P., 'The Wage Penalty for Motherhood', *American Sociological Review*, 66 (2001), 204–25.

BULL, ANDY, *Downshifting: The Ultimate Handbook* (London, 1998).

—— and WATERSON, M. J., *The Advertising Association Handbook* (Eastbourne, 1983).

BULLMORE, JEREMY, 'Advertising, What is It? What is It For?' in Advertising Association (ed.), *Advertising Matters* (London, n.d., c. 1993).

BUNTING, MADELEINE, *Willing Slaves: How the Overwork Culture is Ruling our Lives* (London, 2004).

BURCHINAL, LEE G., HAWKES, GLENN R., and GARDNER, BRUCE, 'Personality Characteristics and Marital Satisfaction', *Social Forces*, 35 (1957), 218–22.

BURGESS, ERNEST WATSON, and WALLIN, PAUL, *Engagement and Marriage* (Philadelphia, 1953).

BURGOYNE, CAROLE B., and ROUTH, DAVID A., 'Constraints on the Use of Money as a Gift at Christmas: The Role of Status and Intimacy', *Journal of Economic Psychology*, 12 (1991), 47–69.

BURNETT, JOHN, *Plenty and Want: A Social History of Diet in England from 1815 to the Present Day*, rev. edn. (London, 1979).

BURROWS, PAUL, 'Patronising Paternalism', *Oxford Economic Papers*, 45 (1993), 542–72.

Business International SA, *Europe's Consumer Movement: Key Issues and Corporate Responses* (Geneva, 1980).

BUSS, DAVID M., *The Evolution of Desire: Strategies of Human Mating* (New York, 1994).

BUSS, D. H., 'Trends in Food Preference in Britain', in Richard Cottrell (ed.), *Food and Health: Now and the Future* (Casterton Hall, 1987), 139–52.

—— 'The British Diet since the End of Food Rationing', in C. Geissler and D. J. Oddy (eds.), *Food, Diet and Economic Change Past and Present* (Leicester, 1994).

BUTLER, DAVID, and STOKES, DONALD E., *Political Change in Britain: The Evolution of Electoral Choice*, 2nd edn. (London, 1974).

BUTSCH, RICHARD, 'Home Video and Corporate Plans: Capital's Limited Power to Manipulate Leisure', in Richard Butsch (ed.), *For Fun and Profit: The Transformation of Leisure into Consumption* (Philadelphia, 1990), 215–35.

BUTTERFIELD, FOX, 'U.S. "Correctional Population" Hits New High', *New York Times*, 26 July 2004.

BYRNE, JOHN A., *The Whiz Kids: The Founding Fathers of American Business—and the Legacy They Left Us* (New York, 1993).

—— BONGIORNO, L., and GROVER, R., 'That Eye-Popping Executive Pay', *Business Week* (25 Apr. 1994), 52–3.

—— FOUST, D., and THERRIEN, L., 'Executive Pay: Compensation at the Top is out of Control. Here's How to Reform It', *Business Week* (30 March 1992), 52–8.

CADWALLADER, MERVYN, 'Marriage as a Wretched Institution', *Atlantic Monthly* (Nov. 1966).

CAIRNS, JOHN A., and VAN DER POL, MARJON M., 'Saving Future Lives: A Comparison of Three Discounting Models', *Health Economics*, 6 (1997), 341–50.

—— —— 'Valuing Future Private and Social Benefits: The Discounted Utility Model Versus Hyperbolic Discounting Models', *Journal of Economic Psychology*, 21 (2000), 191–205.

CALLE, E. E., RODRIGUEZ, C., WALKER-THURMOND, K., and THUN, M. J., 'Overweight, Obesity, and Mortality from Cancer in a Prospectively Studied Cohort of U.S. Adults', *New England Journal of Medicine*, 348 (2003), 1625–38.

CAMERON, SAMUEL, 'The Unacceptability of Money as a Gift and its Status as a Medium of Exchange', *Journal of Economic Psychology*, 10 (1989), 253–5.

—— 'A Review of Economic Research into Determinants of Divorce', *British Review of Economic Issues*, 17 (1995), 1–22.

—— 'The Economic Model of Divorce: The Neglected Role of Search and Specific Capital Formation', *Journal of Socio-Economics*, 32 (2003), 303–16.

Campaign, Silver Jubilee (17 Sept. 1993).

CAMPBELL, ANGUS, CONVERSE, PHILIP E., and RODGERS, WILLARD L., *The Quality of American Life: Perceptions, Evaluations, and Satisfactions* (New York, 1976).

CAMPBELL, ANNE, *A Mind of her Own: The Evolutionary Psychology of Women* (Oxford, 2001).

CAMPBELL, CLIVE, 'Downshifting in Britain: A Sea-Change in the Pursuit of Happiness', The Australian Institute, November (Canberra, 2003).

CAMPBELL, COLIN, *The Romantic Ethic and the Spirit of Modern Consumerism* (Oxford, 1987).

CAMPOS, PAUL F., *The Obesity Myth: Why America's Obsession with Weight is Hazardous to Your Health* (New York, 2004).

CANNOLD, LESLIE, *What, No Baby? Why Women Are Losing the Freedom to Mother, and How They Can Get It Back* (Fremantle, 2005).

CANNON, GEOFFREY, *The Politics of Food* (London, 1987).

CAPLOW, THEODORE, 'Rule Enforcement without Visible Means: Christmas Gift Giving in Middletown', *American Journal of Sociology*, 89 (1984), 1306–23.

CARD, C., 'Against Marriage and Motherhood', *Hypatia*, 11 (1996), 1–23.

CARRIER, JAMES G., *Gifts and Commodities: Exchange and Western Capitalism since 1700* (London, 1995).

CARTER, CHARLES, *Wealth: An Essay on the Purposes of Economics* (London, 1968).

CARTER, HAROLD, 'The Life and Death of Old Labour: Collective Action and Social Cohesion in Sheffield and Southwark, 1945–1997', D.Phil. thesis, University of Oxford, 2005.

CASE, KARL E., and SHILLER, ROBERT J., 'Is There a Bubble in the Housing Market? An Analysis', Paper prepared for Brookings Panel on Economic Activity (Washington, DC, 2003).

CASHDAN, ELIZABETH A., *Risk and Uncertainty in Tribal and Peasant Economies* (Boulder, Colo., 1990).

CASSIDY, JUDE, and SHAVER, PHILLIP R. (eds.), *Handbook of Attachment: Theory, Research, and Clinical Applications* (New York, 1999).

CASTLEMAN, HARRY, and PODRAZIK, WALTER J., *Watching TV: Four Decades of American Television* (New York, 1982).

CATERSON, I. D., 'Group Report: What are the Animal and Human Models for the Study of Regulation of Body Weight and What are their Respective Strengths and Limitations?' in C. Bouchard and G. A. Bray (eds.), *Regulation of Body Weight: Biological and Behavioral Mechanisms* (Chichester, 1996), 85–110.

CHAN, TAK WING, and HALPIN, BRENDAN, 'Union Dissolution in the UK', paper prepared for the volume *Marital and Non-Marital Union Disruption*, ed. Rolf Müller and Hans-Peter Blossfeld, 19 September 2000.

CHAPMAN, GRETCHEN B., 'Time Discounting of Health Outcomes', in George Loewenstein, Daniel Read, and Roy F. Baumeister (eds.), *Time and Decision: Economic and Psychological Perspectives on Intertemporal Choice* (New York, 2003), 395–417.

CHARLES, NICKE, and KERR, MARION, *Women, Food and Families* (Manchester, 1990).

CHARLTON, JOHN, and MURPHY, MIKE, 'Monitoring Health: Data Sources and Methods', in John Charlton and Mike Murphy (eds.), *The Health of Adult Britain, 1841–1994*, vol. i (London, 1997), 2–29.

——and QUAIFE, KAREN, 'Trends in Diet 1841–1993', in John Charlton and Mike Murphy (eds.), *The Health of Adult Britain, 1841–1994*, vol. i (London, 1997), 30–57.

CHASE, STUART, and SCHLINK, FREDERICK J., *Your Money's Worth: A Study in the Waste of the Consumer's Dollar* (New York, 1927).

CHAUNCE, STEPHEN, *Amongst Farm Horses: The Horselads of East Yorkshire* (Stroud, 1991).

CHERLIN, ANDREW J., *Marriage, Divorce Remarriage*, rev. edn. (Cambridge, Mass., 1992).

——KIERNAN, KATHLEEN E., and CHASE LANSDALE, P. LINDSAY, 'Parental Divorce in Childhood and Demographic Outcomes in Young Adulthood', *Demography*, 32 (1995), 299–318.

CHERNIN, KIM, *Womansize: The Tyranny of Slenderness* (London, 1983).

CHESHER, ANDREW, 'Household Composition and Household Food Purchases', in John M. Slater (ed.), *Fifty Years of the National Food Survey, 1940–1990* (London, 1991), 55–86.

CHESHER, ANDREW, 'Diet Revealed? Semiparametric Estimation of Nutrient Intake-Age Relationships', unpublished paper, University of Bristol (Bristol, 1996).

CHINITZ, J. G., and BROWN, R. A., 'Religious Homogamy, Marital Conflict, and Stability in Same-Faith and Interfaith Jewish Marriages', *Journal for the Scientific Study of Religion*, 40 (2001), 723–34.

CHOI, YOUNG BACK, *Paradigms and Conventions: Uncertainty, Decision Making, and Entrepreneurship* (Ann Arbor, 1993).

CHOU, SHIN-YI, SAFFER, HENRY, and GROSSMAN, MICHAEL, 'An Economic Analysis of Adult Obesity: Results from the Behavioral Risk Factor Surveillance System', NBER Working Paper No. 9247 (2003).

CHOW, GREGORY C., *Demand for Automobiles in the United States: A Study in Consumer Durables* (Amsterdam, 1957).

——*Statistical Demand Functions for Automobiles and their Use for Forecasting* (Chicago, 1960).

CHUN, HYUNBAE, and LEE, INJAE, 'Why Do Married Men Earn More: Productivity or Marriage Selection?' *Economic Inquiry*, 39 (2001), 307–19.

CHUNG, SHIN-HO, and HERRNSTEIN, RICHARD J., 'Relative and Absolute Strengths of Response as a Function of Frequency of Reinforcement', *Journal of the Experimental Analysis of Animal Behavior*, 4 (1961), 267–72.

CLARK, ANDREW E., and OSWALD, ANDREW J., 'Unhappiness and Unemployment', *Economic Journal*, 104 (1994), 648–59.

————'Satisfaction and Comparison Income', *Journal of Public Economics*, 61 (1996), 351–89.

——DIENER, ED, GEORGELLIS, YANNIS, and LUCAS, RICHARD E., 'Lags and Leads in Life Satisfaction: A Test of the Baseline Hypothesis', DIW discussion paper no. 371, (Berlin, 2003).

——GEORGELLIS, YANNIS, and SANFEY, PETER, 'Scarring: The Psychological Impact of Past Unemployment', *Economica*, 68 (2001), 221–41.

CLENDENEN, VANESSA, HERMAN, C. PETER, and POLIVY, JANET, 'Social Facilitation of Eating among Friends and Strangers', *Appetite*, 23 (1994), 1–13.

CLIFFORD, CLARKE, and HOLBROOKE, RICHARD C., *Counsel to the President: A Memoir* (New York, 1991).

COASE, RONALD, 'Durability and Monopoly', *Journal of Law and Economics*, 15 (1972), 143–9.

COBB, CLIFFORD, HALSTEAD, TED, and ROWE, JONATHAN, *The Genuine Progress Indicator: Summary of Data and Methodology* (San Francisco, 1995).

COHAN, CATHERINE L., and KLEINBAUM, STACEY, 'Toward a Greater Understanding of the Cohabitation Effect: Premarital Cohabitation and Marital Communication', *Journal of Marriage and Family*, 64 (2002), 180–92.

COHEN, LLOYD, 'Marriage, Divorce, and Quasi Rents; or, "I Gave Him the Best Years of My Life." ', *Journal of Legal Studies*, 26 (1987), 267–303.

——'Marriage: The Long-Term Contract', in Antony Dnes and Robert Rowthorn (eds.), *The Law and Economics of Marriage and Divorce* (Cambridge, 2002), 10–34.

COHEN, RICHARD, 'Jack Welch and "Class Envy" ', *Washington Post*, 17 Sept. 2002, p. A21.

COLDITZ, GRAHAM A., 'Economic Costs of Obesity', *American Journal of Clinical Nutrition*, 55 (1992), 503s–507s.

COLEMAN, DAVID, and SALT, JOHN, *The British Population: Patterns, Trends, and Processes* (Oxford, 1992).

COLEMAN, MARY T., and PENCAVEL, JOHN, 'Changes in Work Hours of Male Employees, 1940–1988', *Industrial and Labor Relations Review*, 46 (1993), 262–83.

————'Trends in Market Work Behavior of Women since 1940', *Industrial and Labor Relations Review*, 46 (1993), 653–76.

COLEMAN, RICHARD PATRICK, RAINWATER, LEE, and MCCLELLAND, KENT A., *Social Standing in America: New Dimensions of Class* (London, 1979).

COLLARD, DAVID, *Altruism and Economy: A Study in Non-Selfish Economics* (Oxford, 1978).

College Board, 'SAT Verbal and Math Scores Up Significantly as a Record-Breaking Number of Students Take the Test' Report N0218 (Washington DC, 2003); http://www.collegeboard.com/prod_downloads/about/news_info/cbsenior/yr2003/pdf/CBS2003Report.pdf, accessed 6 June 2004.

COLLINS, E. J. T., 'The Consumer Revolution and the Growth of Factory Foods: Changing Patterns of Bread and Cereal-Eating in Britain in the 20th Century', in D. S. Oddy and D. S. Miller (eds.), *The Making of the Modern British Diet* (London, 1976).

COLLINS, ROBERT M., *More: The Politics of Economic Growth in Postwar America* (Oxford, 2000).

COOK, HERA, *The Long Sexual Revolution: English Women, Sex, and Contraception, 1800–1975* (Oxford, 2004).

COOK, KAREN S., *Trust in Society* (New York, 2001).

COONTZ, STEPHANIE, *The Way We Really Are: Coming to Terms with America's Changing Families* (New York, 1997).

CORFMAN, KIM P., LEHMANN, DONALD R., and NARAYANAN, SUNDER, 'Values, Utility, and Ownership: Modeling the Relationships for Consumer Durables', *Journal of Retailing*, 67 (1991), 184–204.

COSMIDES, LEDA, and TOOBY, JOHN, 'Cognitive Adaptations for Social Exchange', in James H. Barkow, Leda Cosmides, and John Tooby (eds.), *The Adapted Mind: Evolutionary Psychology and the Generation of Culture* (New York, 1992), 163–228.

COSTA, DORA L., 'The Wage and the Length of the Work Day: From the 1890s to 1991', *Journal of Labor Economics*, 18 (2000), 156–81.

————and STECKEL, RICHARD H., 'Long-Term Trends in Health, Welfare, and Economic Growth in the United States', in Richard H. Steckel and Roderick Floud (eds.), *Health and Welfare During Industrialization* (Chicago, 1997), 47–90.

COWAN, CAROLYN PAPE, and COWAN, PHILIP A., *When Partners become Parents: The Big Life Change for Couples* (Mahwah, NJ, 1999).

COWAN, RUTH S., *More Work for Mother: The Ironies of Household Technology from the Open Hearth to the Microwave* (New York, 1983).

Cowell, Frank A., and Ebert, Udo, 'Complaints and Inequality', London School of Economics, Suntory and Toyota International Centres for Economics and Related Disciplines, Distributional Analysis Research Programme, Toyota Centre, Discussion paper no. 61 (London, 2002).

Coxon, Anthony Peter Macmillan, Davies, Peter, and Jones, Charles L., *Images of Social Stratification: Occupational Structures and Class* (London, 1986).

Crafts, Nicholas F. R., 'Was the Thatcher Experiment Worth It? British Economic Growth in a European Context', in Adam Szirmai, Bart van Ark, and Dirk Pilat (eds.), *Explaining Economic Growth: Essays in Honour of Angus Maddison* (Amsterdam, 1993), 301–26.

——'The Human Development Index and Changes in Standards of Living: Some Historical Comparisons', *European Review of Economic History*, 1 (1997), 299–322.

——*Britain's Relative Economic Decline 1870–1995: A Quantitative Perspective* (London, 1997).

——*Britain's Relative Economic Performance, 1870–1999* (London, 2002).

Crawford, William, and Broadley, Herbert, *The People's Food* (London, 1938).

Critser, Greg, *Fat Land: How Americans Became the Fattest People in the World* (Boston, 2003).

Crittenden, Ann, *The Price of Motherhood: Why the Most Important Job in the World is Still the Least Valued* (New York, 2001).

Crompton, Rosemary (ed.), *Restructuring Gender Relations and Employment: The Decline of the Male Breadwinner* (Oxford, 1999).

Cross, Gary S., 'Worktime in International Discontinuity', in Gary S. Cross (ed.), *Worktime and Industrialization: An International History* (Philadelphia, 1988), 155–81.

——*Quest for Time: Reduction of Work in Britain and France, 1840–1940* (Berkeley, 1989).

Crystal, Graef S., *In Search of Excess: The Overcompensation of American Executives* (New York, 1991).

Cunningham, Alisa F., National Center for Education Statistics, and Educational Resources Information Center (US), *Study of College Costs and Prices, 1988–89 to 1997–98* (Washington, DC, 2001).

Currie, Janet, and Moretti, Enrico, 'Mother's Education and the Intergenerational Transmission of Human Capital: Evidence from College Openings and Longitudinal Data', NBER Working Paper 9360 (2002).

Currie, Jean, 'Trends in Food and Cooking Habits: A Study Based upon Research Undertaken by the British Market Research Bureau on behalf of J. Walter Thompson Company Ltd.' (196?). [JWT papers, History of Advertising Trust; copy in possession of the author]

Curry, Neil, 'Guarding against Hearing Loss: Simple Precautions Can Protect Ears of Music Lovers' (2004), in **http://edition.cnn.com/2004/SHOWBIZ/Music/03/18/hearing.damage/**, accessed: 18 Mar. 2004.

Cutler, D. M., Glaeser, E. L., and Norberg, K. E., 'Explaining the Rise in Youth Suicide', Harvard Institute of Economic Research, Discussion Paper no. 1917 (2001).

—— and SHAPIRO, JESSE M., 'Why Have Americans Become More Obese?' *Journal of Economic Perspectives*, 17 (2003), 93–118.

DALTON, RUSSELL J., *Democratic Challenges, Democratic Choices: The Erosion of Political Support in Advanced Industrial Democracies* (Oxford, 2004).

—— 'The Social Transformation of Trust in Government', *International Review of Sociology*, 15 (2005), 133–54.

DALY, HERMAN E., COBB, JOHN B., and COBB, CLIFFORD W., *For the Common Good: Redirecting the Economy toward Community, the Environment, and a Sustainable Future* (London, 1989).

DARE, S. E., 'Too Many Cooks? Food Acceptability and Women's Work in the Informal Economy', in D. Thomson, (ed.), *Food Acceptability* (London, 1988), 143–53.

DASGUPTA, BILPLAB, *Structural Adjustment, Global Trade and the New Political Economy of Development* (London, 1998).

DASGUPTA, PARTHA, *An Inquiry into Well-Being and Destitution* (Oxford, 1993).

—— *Human Well-Being and the Natural Environment* (Oxford, 2001).

DAVIDSON, CAROLINE, *A Woman's Work is Never Done: A History of Housework in the British Isles 1650–1950* (London, 1982).

DAVIES, GARY, and MADRAN, CANAN, 'Time, Food Shopping, and Food Preparation: Some Attitudinal Linkages', Manchester Business School Working Paper No. 348, Oct. (Manchester, 1996).

DÁVILA, ALBERTO, and PAGÁN, JOSÉ A., 'Obesity, Occupational Attainment, and Earnings', *Social Science Quarterly*, 78 (1997), 756–70.

DAVIS, ALLISON, *Social-Class Influences Upon Learning* (Cambridge, Mass. 1948).

DAVIS, J., 'Gifts and the UK Economy', *Man*, 7 (1972), 408–29.

DEATON, ANGUS, *Understanding Consumption* (Oxford, 1992).

—— 'Relative Deprivation, Inequality, and Mortality', unpublished paper, Center for Health and Wellbeing, Princeton University, January (Princeton, 2001).

—— 'Health, Inequality, and Economic Development', *Journal of Economic Literature*, 41 (2003), 113–58.

DE BOTTON, ALAIN, *Status Anxiety* (London, 2004).

DE CASTRO, JOHN M., 'Social Facilitation of the Spontaneous Meal Size of Humans Occurs Regardless of Time, Place, Alcohol or Snacks', *Appetite*, 15 (1990), 89–101.

—— and BREWER, E. MARIE, 'The Amount Eaten in Meals by Humans is a Power Function of the Number of People Present', *Physiology & Behavior*, 51 (1991), 121–5.

DECI, E. L., KOESTNER, R., and RYAN, R. M., 'A Meta-analytic Review of Experiments Examining the Effects of Extrinsic Rewards on Intrinsic Motivation', *Psychological Bulletin*, 125 (1999), 627–68.

DE GRAAF, JOHN, WANN, DAVID, and NAYLOR, THOMAS H., *Affluenza: The All-Consuming Epidemic* (San Francisco, 2001).

DE GRAZIA, VICTORIA, 'Mass Culture and Sovereignty: The American Challenge to European Cinemas, 1920–1960', *Journal of Modern History*, 61 (1989), 53–87.

Bibliography

DEININGER, KLAUS, and SQUIRE, LYN, 'A New Data Set Measuring Income Inequality', *World Bank Economic Review*, 10 (1996), 565–91.

DEMARIS, ALFRED, and RAO, VANINDHA, 'Premarital Cohabitation and Subsequent Marital Stability in the United States: A Reassessment', *Journal of Marriage and the Family*, 54 (1992), 178–90.

D'EMILIO, JOHN, and FREEDMAN, ESTELLE B., *Intimate Matters: A History of Sexuality in America* (New York, 1988).

DEMYTTENAERE, K., et al., 'Prevalence, Severity, and Unmet Need for Treatment of Mental Disorders in the World Health Organization World Mental Health Surveys', *Journal of the American Medical Association*, 291 (2004), 2581–90.

DESAI, MEGNHAD, 'Human Development: Concepts and Measurement', *European Economic Review*, 35 (1991), 350–7.

DEUTSCH, JAN G., *Selling the People's Cadillac: The Edsel and Corporate Responsiblity* (New Haven, 1976).

DEVAULT, MARJORIE L., *Feeding the Family: The Social Organization of Caring as Gendered Work* (Chicago, 1991).

DEVOOGHT, KURT, 'Measuring Inequality by Counting "Complaints": Theory and Empirics', *Economics and Philosophy*, 19 (2003), 241–63.

DIAMOND, EDWIN, and BATES, STEPHEN, *The Spot: The Rise of Political Advertising on Television*, 3rd edn. (Cambridge, Mass., 1992).

DICKENS, WILLIAM T., and FLYNN, JAMES R., 'Heritability Estimates Versus Large Environmental Effects: The IQ Paradox Resolved', *Psychological Review*, 108 (2001), 346–69.

DIENER, ED, and EMMONS, ROBERT A., 'The Independence of Positive and Negative Affect', *Journal of Personality and Social Psychology*, 47 (1985), 1105–17.

—— and SUH, EUNKOOK, 'Measuring Quality of Life: Economic, Social and Subjective Indicators', *Social Indicators Research*, 40 (1997), 189–216.

—— —— 'National Differences in Subjective Well-Being', in Daniel Kahneman, Ed Diener, and Norbert Schwarz (eds.), *Well-Being: The Foundations of Hedonic Psychology* (New York, 1999), 434–50.

—— DIENER, MARISSA, and DIENER, CAROL, 'Factors Predicting the Subjective Well-Being of Nations', *Journal of Personality and Social Psychology*, 69 (1995), 851–864.

—— SANDVIK, ED, SEIDLITZ, LARRY, and DIENER, MARISSA, 'The Relationship between Income and Subjective Well-Being: Relative or Absolute?' *Social Indicators Research*, 28 (1993), 195–223.

DIETZ, W. H., and STRASBURGER, V. C., 'Children, Adolescence and Television', *Current Problems in Pediatrics*, 28 (1991), 8–31.

DIPRETE, THOMAS A., MORGAN, S. PHILIP, ENGELHARDT, HENRIETTE, and PACALOVA, HANNA, 'Do Cross-National Differences in the Costs of Children Generate Cross-National Differences in Fertility Rates?' Duke University, 16 June (Durham, NC, 2003).

DI TELLA, RAFAEL, MACCULLOCH, ROBERT J., and OSWALD, ANDREW J., 'The Macroeconomics of Happiness', *Review of Economics and Statistics*, 85 (2003), 809–27.

390

DIXIT, VINOD, 'Economics and Sociology of Bride-Price and Dowry in Eastern Rajasthan', *International Journal of the Sociology of Law*, 19 (1991), 341–54.

DOHERTY, WILLIAM J. et al., *Why Marriage Matters: Twenty-One Conclusions from the Social Sciences* (New York, 2002).

DOHRENWEND, BRUCE P., 'Sociocultural and Social-Psychological Factors in the Genesis of Mental Disorders', *Journal of Health and Social Behavior*, 16 (1975), 365–392.

DOLL, RICHARD, 'Uncovering the Effects of Smoking: Historical Perspective', *Statistical Methods in Medical Research*, 7 (1998), 87–117.

——DARBY, SARAH, and WHITLEY, ELISE, 'Trends in Mortality from Smoking-Related Diseases', in John Charlton and Mike Murphy (eds.), *The Health of Adult Britain, 1841–1994* (London, 1997), 128–55.

DONNE, JOHN, *John Donne: A Selection of His Poetry*, ed. John Hayward (London, 1950).

DORSEY, DAVID, *The Force* (London, 1994).

DOUGLAS, MARY, and ISHERWOOD, BARON C., *The World of Goods: Towards an Anthropology of Consumption* (London, 1979).

DOYAL, LEN, and GOUGH, IAN, *A Theory of Human Need* (Basingstoke, 1991).

DRECHSLER, L., 'Problems of Recording Environmental Phenomena in National Accounting Aggregates', *Review of Income and Wealth*, 22 (1976), 239–52.

DRIVER, CHRISTOPHER, *The British at Table, 1940–1980* (London, 1983).

DU BOULAY, JULIET, 'Strangers and Gifts: Hostility and Hospitality in Rural Greece', *Journal of Mediterranean Studies*, 1 (1991), 37–53.

DUESENBERRY, JAMES STEMBLE, *Income, Saving, and the Theory of Consumer Behavior* (Cambridge, Mass., 1949).

DULEEP, HARRIET ORCUTT, 'Mortality and Income Inequality among Economically Developed Countries', *Social Security Bulletin*, 58 (1995), 34–50.

DUNBAR, R. I. M., *Grooming, Gossip and the Evolution of Language* (London, 1996).

DUNCAN, OTIS DUDLEY, 'A Socioeconomic Index for All Occupations', in J. Albert Reiss, Jr. (ed.), *Occupations and Social Status* (New York, 1961).

EASTERBROOK, GREGG, *The Progress Paradox: How Life Gets Better While People Feel Worse* (New York, 2003).

EASTERLIN, RICHARD A., 'Does Economic Growth Improve the Human Lot? Some Empirical Evidence', in Paul David and Melvin W. Reder (eds.), *Nations and Households in Economic Growth: Essays in Honor of Moses Abramowitz* (New York, 1974).

——*Birth and Fortune* (New York, 1980).

——'Will Raising the Incomes of All Increase the Happiness of All?' *Journal of Economic Behavior and Organization*, 27 (1995), 35–47.

——'Income and Happiness: Towards a Unified Theory', *Economic Journal*, 111 (2001), 465–84.

EASTERLY, WILLIAM, 'Life during Growth', unpublished paper, World Bank (1999).

EATON, JOSEPH W., *Culture and Mental Disorders: A Comparative Study of the Hutterites and Other Populations* (Glencoe, Ill., 1955).

Economic Security Planning, Inc. [Kotlikoff, Laurence J., and Gokhale, Jagadeesh], *ESPlanner*^{tm}—*a Revolution in Financial Planning. Tutorial* (2005), in **http://www. esplanner.com/**

Economist, The, 'China: The Numbers Game', *The Economist* (14 October 1995), 96.

—— 'How to Turn Junk Mail into a Goldmine—or Perhaps Not', *The Economist* (1995), 81–2.

—— 'Prison and Beyond: A Stigma That Never Fades', *The Economist* (10 August 2002), 39–41.

—— 'Be a Man', *The Economist* (28 June 2003), 90–1.

—— 'The Amazing Shrinking House', *The Economist* (22 Nov. 2003), 36.

Economist Intelligence Unit, *Advertising Expenditure 1960* (London, 1962).

EDSALL, THOMAS BYRNE, and EDSALL, MARY D., *Chain Reaction: The Impact of Race, Rights, and Taxes on American Politics* (New York, 1991).

EDWARDS, M. E., 'Home Ownership, Affordability, and Mothers' Changing Work and Family Roles', *Social Science Quarterly*, 82 (2001), 369–83.

—— 'Uncertainty and the Rise of the Work-Family Dilemma', *Journal of Marriage and the Family*, 63 (2001), 183–96.

EHRENREICH, BARBARA, HESS, ELIZABETH, and JACOBS, GLORIA, *Re-Making Love: The Feminization of Sex* (London, 1987).

EHRLICH, CYRIL, *The Piano: A History*, rev. edn. (Oxford, 1990).

EIBNER, CHRISTINE E. and EVANS, WILLIAM N., Relative Deprivation, Poor Health Habits, and Mortality (Unpublished paper, University of Maryland 2001).

EISNER, ROBERT, *The Total Incomes System of Accounts* (Chicago, 1989).

EKELUND, ROBERT B., and SAURMAN, DAVID SCOTT, *Advertising and the Market Process: A Modern Economic View* (San Francisco, 1988).

EKMAN, PAUL (ed.), *Emotion in the Human Face* (Cambridge, 1982).

—— *Telling Lies: Clues to Deceit in the Marketplace, Politics and Marriage* (New York, 1985).

—— *Emotions Revealed: Understanding Faces and Feelings* (London, 2003).

Electricity Council (GB), 'Domestic Sector Analysis (England & Wales), 1932/3 to 1978/9', July (1980). [archival source, in possession of the author]

ELGIN, DUANE, *Voluntary Simplicity: Toward a Way of Life that is Outwardly Simple, Inwardly Rich*, rev. edn. (New York, 1993).

ELIAS, NORBERT, *The Civilizing Process: The History of Manners* (New York, 1978).

ELLIOTT, VALERIE, 'You've Saved for the House. Now Save for Your Children. They'll Cost as Much', *The Times*, 21 Nov. 2003.

ELLIS, B. J., 'The Evolution of Sexual Attraction: Evaluative Mechanism in Women', in J. Barkow, L. Cosmides, and R. Tooby (eds.), *The Adapted Mind* (New York, 1991), 267–88.

ELSTER, JON, *Ulysses and the Sirens: Studies in Rationality and Irrationality* (Cambridge, 1979).

—— (ed.), *The Multiple Self* (Cambridge, 1986).

—— (ed.), *Addiction: Entries and Exits* (New York, 1999).

——*Ulysses Unbound: Studies in Rationality, Precommitment, and Constraints* (Cambridge, 2000).

——and LOEWENSTEIN, GEORGE (eds.), *Choice over Time* (New York, 1992).

ENGEL, JAMES F., BLACKWELL, ROGER D., and MINIARD, PAUL W., *Consumer Behavior* (Chicago, 1986).

ENGEN, ERIC M., GALE, WILLIAM G., and UCCELLO, CORI E., 'The Adequacy of Household Saving', *Brookings Papers on Economic Activity*, 2 (1999), 65–165.

ERIKSON, ROBERT, and GOLDTHORPE, JOHN H., *The Constant Flux: A Study of Class Mobility in Industrial Societies* (Oxford, 1992).

ERMISCH, JOHN, *Fewer Babies, Longer Lives: Policy Implications of Current Demographic Trends* (York, 1990).

——*An Economic Analysis of the Family* (Princeton, 2003).

ESKAPA, SHIRLEY, *Woman versus Woman* (London, 1984).

ESTES, RICHARD, *Trends in World Social Development: The Social Progress of Nations, 1970–1987* (New York, 1988).

ETZIONI, AMITAI, 'Voluntary Simplicity: Characterization, Select Psychological Implications, and Societal Consequences', *Journal of Economic Psychology*, 19 (1998), 619–43.

European Communities, Commission of, 'Second Draft of the First Directive Concerning the Approximation of the Laws of Member States on Unfair Trading Practices', Misleading and Unfair advertising. Working Document number 6, Sept. (Brussels, 1976).

EVANS, GEOFFREY (ed.), *The End of Class Politics? Class Voting in Comparative Context* (New York, 1999).

EVERSON, S. A., MATY, S. C., LYNCH, J. W., and KAPLAN, G. A., 'Epidemiologic Evidence for the Relation between Socioeconomic Status and Depression, Obesity, and Diabetes', *Journal of Psychosomatic Research*, 53 (2002), 891–5.

EWEN, STUART, *Captains of Consciousness: Advertising and the Social Roots of the Consumer Culture* (New York, 1976).

——*PR!: A Social History of Spin* (New York, 1996).

EWING, R., SCHMID, T., KILLINGSWORTH, R., ZLOT, A., and RAUDENBUSH, S., 'Relationship between Urban Sprawl and Physical Activity, Obesity, and Morbidity', *American Journal of Health Promotion*, 18 (2003), 47–57.

FABER, BERNARD, 'The Future of the American Family: A Dialectical Account', *Journal of Family Issues*, 8 (1987), 431–3.

FAGAN, PATRICK F., and RECTOR, ROBERT, 'The Effects of Divorce on America', Heritage Foundation Backgrounder no. 1373, June 5 (Washington, DC, 2000).

FALK, ARMIN, and FISCHBACHER, URS, 'A Theory of Reciprocity', Centre for Economic Policy Research, Discussion Paper 3014 (London, 2001).

FALLON, APRIL E., and ROZIN, PAUL, 'Sex Differences in Perceptions of Desirable Body Shape', *Journal of Abnormal Psychology*, 94 (1985), 102–5.

FARBER, BERNARD, 'Limiting Reciprocity among Relatives: Theoretical Implications of a Serendipitous Finding', *Sociological Perspectives*, 32 (1989), 307–30.

393

FARKAS, STEVE, and JOHNSON, JEAN, *Miles to Go: A Status Report on Americans' Plans for Retirement: A Report from Public Agenda* (New York, 1997).

FEHR, ERNST, and FISCHBACHER, URS, 'Why Social Preferences Matter: The Impact of Non-Selfish Motives on Competition, Cooperation and Incentives', *Economic Journal*, 112 (2002), pp. C1–33.

——and GÄCHTER, SIMON, 'Fairness and Retaliation: The Economics of Reciprocity', *Journal of Economic Perspectives*, 14 (2000), 159–81.

FEIN, ELLEN, and SCHNEIDER, SHERRIE, *The Rules: Time-Tested Secrets for Capturing the Heart of Mr. Right* (London, 1995).

FEINSTEIN, CHARLES H., 'Pessimism Perpetuated: Real Wages and the Standard of Living in Britain during and after the Industrial Revolution', *Journal of Economic History*, 58 (1998), 625–58.

FERNANDEZ VILLAVERDE, JESUS, and MUKHERJI, ARIJIT, 'Can We Really Observe Hyperbolic Discounting?' Penn Institute for Economic Research (PIER) [Working Paper 02/008] (2002).

FERRER-I-CARBONELL, A., and FRIJTERS, P., 'How Important is Methodology for the Estimates of the Determinants of Happiness?' *Economic Journal*, 114 (2004), 641–59.

FIELDING, HELEN, *Bridget Jones's Diary: A Novel* (London, 1997).

FINCH, CHRISTOPHER, *Norman Rockwell's America* (New York, 1975).

FINCH, J., 'Responsibilities and the Quality of Relationships in Families', in Avner Offer (ed.), *In Pursuit of the Quality of Life* (Oxford, 1996), 119–39.

——and MASON, JENNIFER, *Negotiating Family Responsiblities* (London, 1993).

FINE, BEN, HEASMAN, MICHAEL, and WRIGHT, JUDITH, *Consumption in an Age of Affluence: The World of Food* (London, 1996).

FINKELSTEIN, E. A., FIEBELKORN, I. C., and WANG, G., 'National Medical Spending Attributable to Overweight and Obesity: How Much, and Who's Paying?', *Health Affairs*, suppl. web exclusives (2003), pp. W3-219–26; **http://content.healthaffairs.org/cgi/reprint/hlthaff.w3.219v1**. accessed 31 Mar. 2005.

FINKELSTEIN, JOANNE, *Dining out: A Sociology of Modern Manners* (Oxford, 1989).

FINLEY, M. I., *The Ancient Economy* (London, 1973).

FIRESTONE, SHULAMITH, *The Dialectic of Sex: The Case for Feminist Revolution* (London, 1971).

FISCHLER, CLAUDE, 'Gastro-Nomie et gastro-anomie: sagesse du corps et crise bioculturelle de l'alimentation moderne', *Communications*, 31 (1979), 189–210.

——*L'Homnivore: le goût, la cuisine et le corps*, 2nd edn. (Paris, 1993).

FISHER, F.M., GRILICHES, Z., and KAYSEN, C., 'The Costs of Automobile Model Changes since 1949', *Journal of Political Economy*, 70 (1962), 433–51.

FISHER, HELEN E., *Anatomy of Love: The Natural History of Monogamy, Adultery, and Divorce* (New York, 1993).

——*Why We Love: The Nature and Chemistry of Romantic Love* (New York, 2004).

FISHER, IRVING, *The Theory of Interest: As Determined by Impatience to Spend Income and Opportunity to Invest It* (New York, 1930).

FISKE, ALAN PAGE, 'Relativity within Moose ("Mossi") Culture: Four Incommensurable Models for Social Relationships', *Ethos*, 18 (1990), 180–204.

FLEGAL, K. M., CARROLL, M. D., KUCZMARSKI, R. J., and JOHNSON, C. L., 'Overweight and Obesity in the United States: Prevalence and Trends, 1960–1994', *International Journal of Obesity*, 22 (1998), 39–47.

—— —— OGDEN, C. L., and JOHNSON, C. L., 'Prevalence and Trends in Obesity among US Adults, 1999–2000', *Journal of the American Medical Association*, 288 (2002), 1723–7.

—— GRAUBARD, B. I., WILLIAMSON, D. F., and GAIL, M. H., 'Excess Deaths Associated with Underweight, Overweight, and Obesity', *JAMA*, 293, 15 (20 April 2005), 1861–7.

—— TROIANO, RICHARD P., PAMUK, ELSIE R., KUCZMARSKI, ROBERT J., and CAMPBELL, STEPHEN M., 'The Influence of Smoking Cessation on the Prevalence of Overweight in the United States', *New England Journal of Medicine*, 333 (1995), 1165–1170.

FLIGSTEIN, NEIL, and SHARONE, OFER, 'Work in the Post Industrial Economy of California', University of California Institute for Labor and Employment, the State of California Labor, 2002 (Berkeley, 2002).

FLORIO, MASSIMO, *The Great Divestiture: Evaluating the Welfare Impact of the British Privatizations, 1979–1997* (Cambridge, Mass., 2004).

FLOUD, R., 'Height, Weight and Body Mass of the British Population since 1820', NBER Historical Paper no. 108, October (Cambridge, Mass., 1998).

—— WACHTER, KENNETH W., and GREGORY, ANNABEL, *Height, Health and History: Nutritional Status in the United Kingdom, 1750–1980* (Cambridge, 1990).

FOGEL, ROBERT W., 'Economic Growth, Population Theory, and Physiology: The Bearing of Long-Term Processes on the Making of Economic Policy', *American Economic Review*, 84 (1994), 369–95.

—— *The Escape from Hunger and Premature Death, 1700–2100: Europe, America, and the Third World* (Cambridge, 2004).

FOREMAN-PECK, JAMES, BOWDEN, SUE, and MCKINLAY, ALAN, *The British Motor Industry* (Manchester, 1995).

FOREYT, JOHN, and GOODRICK, G. KEN, *Living without Dieting* (New York, 1994).

FOX, FRANK W., *Madison Avenue Goes to War: The Strange Military Career of American Advertising, 1941–45* (Provo, Ut., 1975).

FRANK, ROBERT H., *Choosing the Right Pond: Human Behavior and the Quest for Status* (New York, 1985).

—— *Passions within Reason: The Strategic Role of the Emotions* (New York, 1989).

—— 'The Frame of Reference as a Public Good', *Economic Journal*, 107 (1997), 1832–47.

—— *Microeconomics and Behavior* (New York, 1991).

—— *Luxury Fever: Why Money Fails to Satisfy in an Era of Excess* (New York, 1999).

—— and COOK, PHILIP J., *The Winner-Takes-All Society: How More and More Americans Compete for Ever Fewer and Bigger Prizes, Encouraging Economic Waste, Income Inequality, and an Impoverished Cultural Life* (New York, 1995).

395

Bibliography

FRANK, ROBERT H., and HUTCHENS, ROBERT M., 'Wages, Seniority, and the Demand for Rising Consumption Profiles', *Journal of Economic Behavior and Organization*, 21 (1993), 251–76.

FRANKLING, MARK N., *Voter Turnout and the Dynamics of Electoral Competition in Established Democracies since 1945* (Cambridge, 2004).

FREDERICK, SHANE, LOEWENSTEIN, GEORGE, and O'DONOGHUE, TED, 'Time Discounting and Time Preference: A Critical Review', *Journal of Economic Literature*, 40 (2002), 351–401.

FREEDMAN, RITA, *Beauty Bound: Why Women Strive for Physical Perfection* (London, 1988).

FREEMAN, RICHARD B., 'Give to Charity—Well, since You Asked', unpublished paper, LSE conference on the economics and psychology of happiness and fairness, London, 4–5 Nov. 1993.

FREY, BRUNO, 'Economists Favour the Price System—Who Else Does?' *Kyklos*, 39 (1986), 537–63.

—— 'A Constitution for Knaves Crowds out Civic Virtues', *Economic Journal*, 107 (1997), 1043–53.

—— *Not Just for the Money: An Economic Theory of Personal Motivation* (Cheltenham, 1997).

—— and STUTZER, ALOIS, *Happiness and Economics: How the Economy and Institutions Affect Well-Being* (Princeton, 2002).

FRIEDAN, BETTY, *The Feminine Mystique*, 20th anniversary edn. (New York, 1984).

FRIEDBERG, LEORA, 'Did Unilateral Divorce Raise Divorce Rates? Evidence from Panel Data', *American Economic Review*, 88 (1998), 608–27.

FRIEDMAN, DEBRA, HECHTER, MICHAEL, and KANAZAWA, SATOSHI, 'A Theory of the Value of Children', *Demography*, 31 (1994), 375–401.

FRIEDMAN, MILTON, and FRIEDMAN ROSE D., *Capitalism and Freedom* (Chicago, 1963).

FRIEDMAN, WALTER A., *Birth of a Salesman: The Transformation of Selling in America* (Cambridge, Mass., 2004).

Friends of the Earth website, **www.foe.org.uk/progress**.

FRITH, MAXINE, 'Britons Pick Sterilisation as Contraceptive', *Independent*, 28 June 2004.

FROMM, ERICH, *The Art of Loving* (London, 1957).

FRYER, C. D., CARROLL, M. D., and FLEGAL, K. M., 'Mean Body Weight, Height, and Body Mass Index, United States 1960–2002', *Advanced Data from Vital and Health Statistics*, 347 (2004).

FUCHS, VICTOR R., *Women's Quest for Economic Equality* (Cambridge, Mass., 1990).

FUKUYAMA, FRANCIS, *The Great Disruption: Human Nature and the Reconstitution of Social Order* (London, 1999).

FULWOOD, R., ROBINSON, S., ABRAHAM, S., and JOHNSON, C. L., 'Height and Weight of Adults, Ages 18–74 Years by Socioeconomic and Geographic Variables', *Vital and Health Statistics Data*, 224 (1981).

FUMENTO, MICHAEL, *The Fat of the Land: The Obesity Epidemic and How Overweight Americans Can Help Themselves* (New York, 1997).

FUSSELL, PAUL, *Class: A Guide through the American Status System* (New York, 1983).

Futures Laboratory for Standard Life Bank, The, *The Shape of Dreams to Come: Living, Working and Changing Lifestyles in Britain Today* (London, 2004).

GALBRAITH, JOHN KENNETH, *The Affluent Society* (first publ. 1958, Harmondsworth, 1962).

—— *The Culture of Contentment* (Harmondsworth, 1993).

GALE, WILLIAM G., and SABELHAUS, JOHN, 'Perspectives on the Household Saving Rate', *Brookings Papers on Economic Activity*, 1 (1999), 181–214.

GALLIE, DUNCAN, 'The Quality of Employment: Perspectives and Problems', in Avner Offer (ed.), *In Pursuit of the Quality of Life* (Oxford, 1996), 163–87.

GAMBETTA, DIEGO (ed.), *Trust: Making and Breaking Cooperative Relations* (Oxford, 1988).

GAMMAGE, G., and JONES, S. L., 'Orgasm in Chrome: The Rise and Fall of the Automobile Tail-Fin', *Journal of Popular Culture*, 8 (1974), 132–47.

GARDNER, GARY T., and HALWEIL, BRIAN, 'Overfed and Underfed: The Global Epidemic of Malnutrition', Worldwatch Paper 150 (Washington, DC, 2000).

GARNER, D. M., GARFINKEL, P. E., SCHWARTZ, D., and THOMPSON, M., 'Cultural Expectations of Thinness in Women', *Psychological Reports*, 47 (1980), 483–91.

GARTMAN, DAVID, *Auto-Opium: A Social History of American Automobile Design* (London, 1994).

GAVRON, HANNAH, *The Captive Wife: Conflicts of Housebound Mothers* (London, 1966).

GEARY, DAVID C., *Male, Female: The Evolution of Human Sex Differences* (Washington, DC, 1998).

GEISSLER, C., and ODDY, D. J. (eds.), *Food, Diet and Economic Change Past and Present* (Leicester, 1993).

GERBNER, GEORGE, and SIGNORIELLI, NANCY, *Violence and Terror in the Mass Media* (Paris, 1988).

GERSHUNY, JONATHAN, 'Time Budgets as a Social Indicator', *Journal of Public Policy*, 9 (1989), 419–24.

—— 'Are We Running out of Time?' *Futures*, 24 (1992), 3–22.

—— *Changing Times: Work and Leisure in Postindustrial Society* (Oxford, 2000).

—— and FISHER, K., 'UK Leisure in the 20th Century', in A. H. Halsey (ed.), *British Social Trends in the 20th Century* (Basingstoke, 2000).

—— and HALPIN, BRENDAN, 'Time Use, Quality of Life, and Process Benefits', in Avner Offer (ed.), *In Pursuit of the Quality of Life* (Oxford, 1996), 188–210.

—— and JONES, SALLY, 'The Changing Work/Leisure Balance in Britain, 1961–1984', in John Horne, F. Thomas Juster, and Alan Tomlinson (eds.), *Sport, Leisure, and Social Relations* (London, 1987).

—— —— and BAERT, PATRICK, 'The Time Economy or the Economy of Time: An Essay on the Interdependence of Living and Working Conditions', unpublished typescript, Universities of Oxford and Bath (1991).

GHAZI, POLLY, and JONES, JUDY, *Downshifting: The Guide to Happier, Simpler Living* (London, 1997).

GIBBS, W. WAYT, 'Obesity: An Overblown Epidemic?' *Scientific American*, 292, 6 (June 2005), 48–55.

GIBBONS, STEVE, and MACHIN, STEPHEN, 'Valuing English Primary Schools', *Journal of Urban Economics*, 53 (2003), 197–219.

GIFFORD, SHARON, 'The Allocation of Entrepreneurial Attention', *Journal of Economic Behavior and Organization*, 19 (1992), 265–84.

GIGERENZER, GERD, TODD, PETER M., and the ABC Group, *Simple Heuristics that Make Us Smart* (Oxford, 1999).

GILES, MARTIN, 'Indigestion: A Survey of the Food Industry', *The Economist* (4 December 1993), 1–18.

GILLICK, M. R., 'Health Promotion, Jogging, and the Pursuit of the Moral Life', *Journal of Health Politics, Policy and Law*, 9 (1984), 369–87.

GILLIS, JOHN R., *For Better, for Worse: British Marriages, 1600 to the Present* (New York, 1985).

GILLON, STEVEN M., 'The Politics of Deinstitutionalization: The Community Mental Health Act of 1963', in Steven M. Gillon (ed.), *'That's Not What We Meant to Do': Reform and its Unintended Consequences in Twentieth-Century America* (New York, 2000), 87–119.

GINGRICH, ANDRE, 'Is Wa Milh: Brot und Salz. Vom Gastmahl bei den Hawlan bin Amir im Jemen', *Mitteilungen der Anthropologischen Gesellschaft in Wien*, 116 (1986), 41–69.

GINTHER, DONNA K., and ZAVODNY, MADELINE, 'Is the Male Marriage Premium Due to Selection? The Effect of Shotgun Weddings on the Return to Marriage', *Journal of Population Economics*, 14 (2001), 313–28.

GIROUARD, MARK, *Life in the English Country House: A Social and Architectural History* (New Haven, 1978).

Glass's Guide Service Limited, *Glass's Guide to Used Car Values* (Weybridge, 1968–1973) [monthly].

GLENDINNING, CAROLINE, *The Costs of Informal Care: Looking inside the Household* (London, 1992).

GLENN, NORVAL D., 'The Recent Trend in Marital Success in the United States', *Journal of Marriage and the Family*, 53 (1991), 261–70.

——'The Course of Marital Success and Failure in Five American 10-Year Marriage Cohorts', *Journal of Marriage and the Family*, 60 (1998), 569–76.

——and MARQUARDT, ELIZABETH, 'Hooking up, Hanging out, and Hoping for Mr. Right: College Women on Dating and Mating Today', Institute for American Values (New York, 2001).

——and WEAVER, CHARLES N., 'The Contribution of Marital Happiness to Global Happiness', *Journal of Marriage and the Family*, 43 (1981), 161–8.

GMELCH, GEORGE, and GMELCH, SHARON BOHN, 'Begging in Dublin: The Strategies of a Marginal Urban Occupation', *Urban Life*, 6 (1978), 439–54.

GMELCH, WALTER H., and MISKIN, VAL D., *Productivity Teams: Beyond Quality Circles* (New York, 1984).

GNEEZY, URI, and RUSTICHINI, ALDO, 'Pay Enough or Don't Pay at All', *Quarterly Journal of Economics*, 115 (2000), 791–810.

—— 'Gender and Competition at a Young Age', *American Economic Review*, 94 (2004), 377–81.

GODLEY, ANDREW, 'The Global Diffusion of the Sewing Machine, 1850–1914', *Research in Economic History*, 20 (2001), 1–45.

GOKHALE, JAGADEESH, KOTLIKOFF, LAURENCE J., and SABELHAUS, JOHN, 'Understanding the Postwar Decline in U. S. Saving: A Cohort Analysis', *Brookings Papers on Economic Activity*, 1 (1996), 315–90.

GOLD, THOMAS, GUTHRIE, DOUG, and WANK, DAVID L. (eds.), *Social Connections in China: Institutions, Culture, and the Changing Nature of Guanxi* (New York, 2002).

GOLDBLATT, PHILLIP B., MOORE, MARY E., and STUNKARD, ALBERT J., 'Social Factors in Obesity', *Journal of the American Medical Association*, 192 (1965), 97–102.

GOLDIN, CLAUDIA DALE, *Understanding the Gender Gap: An Economic History of American Women* (New York, 1990).

—— 'Career and Family: College Women Look to the Past', in Francine D. Blau and Ronald G. Ehrenberg (eds.), *Gender and Family Issues in the Workplace* (New York, 1997), 20–58.

—— and KATZ, L. F., 'The Power of the Pill: Oral Contraceptives and Women's Career and Marriage Decisions', *Journal of Political Economy*, 110 (2002), 730–70.

GOLDMAN, ROBERT, *Reading Ads Socially* (London, 1992).

GOLDSTEIN, AVRAM, *Addiction: From Biology to Drug Policy* (New York, 1994).

GOLDSTEIN, JOSHUA S., *War and Gender: How Gender Shapes the War System and Vice Versa* (Cambridge, 2001).

GOLDTHORPE, JOHN H., *The Affluent Worker in the Class Structure* (Cambridge, 1969).

—— and HOPE, KEITH, *The Social Grading of Occupations: A New Approach and Scale* (Oxford, 1974).

GOMERY, DOUGLAS, 'The Movie Palace Comes to America's Cities', in Richard Butsch (ed.), *For Fun and Profit: The Transformation of Leisure into Consumption* (Philadelphia, 1990), 36–51.

GONUL, HUSSEIN, 'Is Money an Acceptable Gift in Cyprus?' *Perceptual and Motor Skills*, 61 (1985), 1074.

GORDON, DAVID, LLOYD, ELIZABETH, SENIOR, MARTIN, RIGBY, JAN, SHAW, MARY, and BEN-SHLOMO, YOAV, 'Wales NHS Resource Allocation Review: Independent Report of the Research Team', Universities of Bristol, Cardiff, Lancaster, June (Bristol, 2001).

GORDON, RICHARD A., *Anorexia and Bulimia: Anatomy of a Social Epidemic* (Oxford, 1990).

GORER, GEOFFREY, *Sex & Marriage in England Today: A Study of the Views and Experience of the Under-45s* (London, 1971).

GORTMAKER, S. L., MUST, A., PERRIN, J. M., SOBOL, A. M., and DIETZ, W. H., 'Social and Economic Consequences of Overweight in Adolescence and Young Adulthood', *New England Journal of Medicine*, 329 (1993), 1008–12.

GORTNER, WILLIS A., 'Nutrition in the United States, 1900 to 1974', *Cancer Research*, 35 (1975), 3246–53.

GOSS, JON, ' "We Know Who You Are and We Know Where You Live": The Instrumental Rationality of Geodemographic Systems', *Economic Geography*, 71 (1995), 171–98.

GOTTFREDSON, MICHAEL R., and HIRSCHI, TRAVIS, *A General Theory of Crime* (Stanford, Calif., 1990).

GOTTMAN, JOHN M., *What Predicts Divorce? The Relationship between Marital Processes and Marital Outcomes* (Hillsdale, NJ, 1994).

——and LEVENSON, ROBERT, 'The Social Psychophysiology of Marriage', in Patricia Noller and Mary Anne Fitzpatrick (eds.), *Perspectives on Marital Interaction* (Clevedon, 1988).

——and NOTARIUS, CLIFFORD I., 'Decade Review: Observing Marital Interaction', *Journal of Marriage and the Family*, 62 (2000), 927–47.

————'Marital Research in the 20th Century and a Research Agenda for the 21st Century', *Family Process*, 41 (2002), 159–97.

GOURINCHAS, PIERRE O., and PARKER, JONATHAN A., 'Consumption over the Life Cycle', *Econometrica*, 70 (2002), 47–89.

GOVE, WALTER R., and TUDOR, JEANNETTE F., 'Adult Sex Roles and Mental Illness', *American Journal of Sociology*, 78 (1973), 812–35.

GRAHAM, SAXON, 'Class and Conservatism in the Adoption of Innovations', *Human Relations*, 9 (1956), 91–9.

GRAY, ANNE, *Video Playtime: The Gendering of a Leisure Technology* (London, 1992).

Great Britain, Board of Trade, Committee on Consumer Protection [Molony, J. T., chair], *Final Report of the Committee on Consumer Protection*, P.P. Cmnd 1781 vol. XII (London, 1962).

——Committee on Broadcasting [Pilkington, Lord Harry, Chair], *Report of the Committee on Broadcasting, 1960*, P.P. Cmnd. 1753, vol. x (London, 1962).

——Board of Trade, [Lord Crowther, Chair], *Departmental Committee Report on Consumer Credit*, P.P. Cmnd. 4596 vol. IX (London, 1971).

——HM Treasury, 'The Test Discount Rate and the Required Rate of Return on Investment', Government Economic Service Working Paper no. 22 [Treasury Working Paper no. 9], January (London, 1979).

——Office of Population Censuses and Surveys, *Census 1981, National Report: Great Britain, Part I* (1983).

——Department of Health and Social Security, *Diet and Cardiovascular Disease. Committee on Medical Aspects of Food Policy* (London, 1984).

——Central Statistical Office, *Social Trends* (London, 1970– (annual)).

——Office of Population, Census and Surveys, *Britain's Households* (London, 1986).

——Working Group on Inequalities in Health, Black, Douglas, Townsend, Peter, Davidson, Nick, and Whitehead, Margaret, *Inequalities in Health: The Black Report* (London, 1988).

——Secretary of State for Health, *The Health of the Nation: A Strategy for Health in England* (London, 1992).

—— Office of Population, Censuses and Surveys, Social Survey Division, *General Household Survey Series [Annual]* (1992).

—— Office of Population, Censuses and Surveys, *1991 Census: Sex, Age and Marital Status, Great Britain* (London, 1993).

—— Department of Health, *Health and Personal Social Services Statistics for England, 1994 Edition* (1994).

—— Ministry of Agriculture Fisheries and Food, *National Food Survey: Annual Report on Household Food Consumption and Expenditure* (London, 1994).

—— Dept. of the Environment, and Great Britain. Government Statistical Service, *Indicators of Sustainable Development for the United Kingdom: A Set of Indicators Produced for Discussion and Consultation by an Interdepartmental Working Group, Following a Commitment in the UK's Sustainable Development Strategy of 1994* (London, 1996).

—— Department of Health, *Health Survey for England* (annual, London, 1991–2003).

—— HM Treasury, *The Green Book: Appraisal and Evaluation in Central Government* (London, 1997).

—— Department of the Environment Transport and the Regions, *Sustainability Counts: Consultation Paper on a Set of 'Headline' Indicators of Sustainable Development* (London, 1998).

—— Department of the Environment, Transport and the Regions, *A Better Quality of Life: A Strategy for Sustainable Development for the United Kingdom*, P.P. Cm. 4345 (London, 1999).

—— Office of the Deputy Prime Minister, Department for Transport, and Department of the Environment, Food and Rural Affairs, and OXERA, 'A Social Time Preference Rate for Use in Long-Term Discounting', Discussion Paper (Oxford, 2002).

—— HM Treasury, *The Green Book: Appraisal and Evaluation in Central Government: Treasury Guidance* (London, 2003).

—— Office for National Statistics Social Survey Division, [UK Data Archive], *General Household Survey, 2002–2003 [Computer File]* (Colchester, Essex, UK, 2004), in **www.statistics.gov.uk/ssd/surveys/general_household_survey.asp; www.data-archive.ac.uk/doc/4981/mrdoc/UKDA/UKDA_Study_4981_Information.htm**.

—— House of Commons, Health Committee, *Obesity: Third Report of Session 2003–04, Volume 1, Report, Together with Formal Minutes*, HC23-1 (London, 2004).

GREEN, FRANCIS, 'Work Intensification, Discretion and the Decline in Well-Being at Work', University of Kent, 20–1 Nov. (Canterbury, 2002).

—— 'Why Has Work Effort Become More Intense?', University of Kent (Canterbury, 2003).

—— and GALLIE, DUNCAN, 'High Skills and High Anxiety: Skills, Hard Work and Mental Well-Being', University of Kent, May 2002 (Canterbury, 2002).

GREEN, HAZEL, *Informal Carers* (London, 1988).

GREEN, ROSEMARY, *Diary of a Fat Housewife: A True Story of Humor, Heartbreak, and Hope* (New York, 1995).

GREENE, GAEL, *Sex and the College Girl* (New York, 1964).

GREENFIELD, S., 'Love and Marriage in Modern America: A Functional Analysis', *Sociological Quarterly*, 6 (1956).

GREGORY, C. A., *Gifts and Commodities* (London, 1982).

——'Gifts', in John Eatwell, Murray Milgate, Peter K. Newman, and Robert Harry Inglis Palgrave (eds.), *The New Palgrave: A Dictionary of Economics* (London, 1987).

GREGORY, JAN, Great Britain, Department of Health, Ministry of Agriculture, Fisheries and Food, and Government Social Survey Deptartment, *The Dietary and Nutritional Survey of British Adults: A Survey of the Dietary Behaviour, Nutritional Status and Blood Pressure of Adults Aged 16 to 64 Living in Great Britain* (London, 1990).

GREIF, AVNER, 'Reputation and Coalitions in Medieval Trade: Evidence on the Maghribi Traders', *Journal of Economic History*, 49 (1989), 857–82.

GRILICHES, ZVI, 'Hedonic Price Indexes for Automobiles: An Econometric Analysis of Quality Change', in Zvi Griliches (ed.), *Price Indexes and Quality Change* (Cambridge, Mass., 1971), 55–87.

GROSSBARD-SHECHTMAN, SHOSHANA, *On the Economics of Marriage: A Theory of Marriage, Labor and Divorce* (Boulder, Colo., 1993).

——(ed.), *Marriage and the Economy: Theory and Evidence from Advanced Industrial Societies* (Cambridge, 2003).

GROSSMAN, G., 'The "Second Economy" of the USSR', *Problems in Communism*, 26 (1977), 25–40.

——'The "Shadow Economy" in the Socialist Sector of the USSR', in NATO Economics and Information Directorate, *The CMEA Five-Year Plans (1981–1985) in a New Perspective* (Brussels, 1982).

GRUBER, JONATHAN, and KÖSZEGI, BOTOND, 'Is Addiction "Rational"? Theory and Evidence', *Quarterly Journal of Economics*, 116 (2001), 1261–1303.

——and MULLAINATHAN, SENDHIL, 'Do Cigarette Taxes Make Smokers Happier?' National Bureau of Economic Research, NBER Working Paper 8872, April 2002 (Cambridge, Mass., 2002).

GRUSKY, DAVID B. (ed.), *Social Stratification: Class, Race, and Gender in Sociological Perspective*, 2nd edn. (Boulder, Colo., 2001).

Guardian, 'Weddings Cost £1,000—Just to Be a Guest', *Guardian*, 27 July 2001.

GUL, FARUK, and PESENDORFER, WOLFGANG, 'Temptation and Self-Control', *Econometrica*, 69 (2001), 1403–35.

GUNTER, BARRIE, and FURNHAM, ADRIAN, *Consumer Profiles: An Introduction to Psychographics* (London, 1992).

——and SVENNEVIG, MICHAEL, *Behind and in Front of the Screen: Television's Involvement with Family Life* (London, 1987).

GUTTENTAG, MARCIA, and SECORD, PAUL F., *Too Many Women? The Sex Ratio Question* (Beverly Hills, Calif., 1983).

HAGENAARS, ALDI, DE VOS, KLAAS, and ZAIDI, ASHGAR, 'Patterns of Poverty in Europe', in Jenkins, Stephen P., Keptyn, Arie and van Praag, Bernard M. S. (eds.), *The Distribution of Welfare and Household Production* (Cambridge, 1998), 25–49.

HAKIM, CATHERINE, *Work–Lifestyle Choices in the 21st Century: Preference Theory* (Oxford, 2000).

HALBERSTAM, DAVID, *The Reckoning: A Tale of Two Cultures as Seen through Two Car Companies* (London, 1987).

HALSEY, A. H., and WEBB, JOSEPHINE, *Twentieth-Century British Social Trends* (Basingstoke, 2000).

HAMERMESH, DANIEL S., and BIDDLE, JEFF E., 'Beauty and the Labor Market', *American Economic Review*, 84 (1994), 1174–94.

HAMILTON, CLIVE, 'Downshifting in Britain: A Sea-Change in the Pursuit of Happiness', Australia Institute Discussion Paper no. 58 ([Canberra], Nov. 2003).

HAMPDEN-TURNER, CHARLES, and TOMPENAARS, FONS, *The Seven Cultures of Capitalism* (London, 1994).

HARDYMENT, CHRISTINA, *From Mangle to Microwave: The Mechanization of Household Work* (Cambridge, 1988).

HARLESS, DAVID W., and HOFFER, GEORGE E., 'Do Women Pay More for New Vehicles? Evidence from Transaction Price Data', *American Economic Review*, 92 (2002), 270–9.

HARREL, THOMAS, W., 'Women with MBAs Marry up While Men with MBAs Marry down', *Psychological Reports*, 72 (1993), 1178.

HARRISON, BENNETT, and BLUESTONE, BARRY, *The Great U-Turn: Corporate Restructuring and the Polarizing of America* (New York, 1988).

HARTMAN, CHRIS, 'Part 2. Income Patterns: 2.3. CEO Pay as a Multiple of Average Worker Pay, 1960–2001' (2002), in **www.inequality.org/facts3.html# incomeinequality-org-#2-income.html**, accessed: 1 Sept. 2004.

HARTMANN, HEIDI I., 'The Family as the Locus of Gender, Class and Political Struggle: The Example of Housework', *Signs*, 6 (1981), 366–94.

Harwood Group, 'Yearning for Balance: Views of Americans on Consumption, Materialism, and the Environment', Report for the Merck Foundation (1995) **www.iisd.ca/linkages/consume/harwood.html**.

HATFIELD, ELAINE, and RAPSON, RICHARD L., *Love and Sex: Cross-Cultural Perspectives* (Boston, 1996).

—— and SPRECHER, SUSAN, *Mirror, Mirror: The Importance of Looks in Everyday Life* (Albany, NY, 1986).

HATSOPOULOS, G.N., KRUGMAN, PAUL R., and POTERBA, JAMES M., *Overconsumption: The Challenge to U.S. Economic Policy* (Washington, DC, Waltham, MA, 1989).

HAUG, WOLFGANG FRITZ, *Critique of Commodity Aesthetics: Appearance, Sexuality and Advertising in Capitalist Society* (Cambridge, 1986).

HAUSER, ROBERT M., and WARREN, JOHN ROBERT, 'Socioeconomic Indexes for Occupations: A Review, Update and Critique', *Sociological Methodology*, 27 (1997), 177–298.

HAUSMAN, DANIEL M., *The Inexact and Separate Science of Economics* (Cambridge, 1992).

HAWKINS, DEL I., BEST, ROGER J., and CONEY, KENNETH A., *Consumer Behavior: Building Marketing Strategy*, 9th edn. (Boston, 2004).

HAYAKAWA, S. I., 'Why the Edsel Laid an Egg: Motivational Research vs. The Reality Principle', in S. I. Hayakawa (ed.), *Our Language and Our World: Selections from Etc.: A Review of General Semantics* (New York, 1959).

—— 'Sexual Fantasy and the 1957 Car', in S. I. Hayakawa (ed.), *Our Language and Our World: Selections from Etc.: A Review of General Semantics* (New York, 1959).

HAYEK, F. A., 'The Use of Knowledge in Society', *American Economic Review*, 35 (1945), 519–30.

HAZAN, CINDY, and SHAVER, PHILLIP, 'Romantic Love Conceptualized as an Attachment Process', *Journal of Personality and Social Psychology*, 52 (1987), 511–24.

HEADEY, BRUCE, and WEARING, ALEX, *Understanding Happiness: A Theory of Subjective Well-Being* (Melbourne, 1992).

HEALY, DAVID, *The Antidepressant Era* (Cambridge, Mass, 1997).

HEATH, CHIP, and FENNEMA, M. G., 'Mental Depreciation and Marginal Decision Making', *Organizational Behavior and Human Decision Processes*, 65 (1996), 95–108.

HEATHERTON, TODD F., MAHAMEDI, FARY, STRIEPE, MEG, and FIELD, ALISON E., 'A 10-Year Longitudinal Study of Body Weight, Dieting, and Eating Disorder Symptoms', *Journal of Abnormal Psychology*, 106 (1997), 117–25.

HEATON, TIM B., and PRATT, EDITH L., 'The Effects of Religious Homogamy on Marital Satisfaction and Stability', *Journal of Family Issues*, 11 (1990), 191–207.

HEBL, MICHELLE R., and HEATHERTON, TODD F., 'The Stigma of Obesity in Women: The Difference is Black and White', *Personality and Social Psychology Bulletin*, 24 (1998), 417–26.

HECKER, SIDNEY, and STEWART, DAVID W. (eds.), *Nonverbal Communication in Advertising* (Lexington, Mass., 1988).

HELLIWELL, JOHN F., 'How's Life? Combining Individual and National Variables to Explain Subjective Well-Being', unpublished paper, University of British Columbia (Vancouver, 2000).

—— 'How's Life? Combining Individual and National Variables to Explain Subjective Well-Being', *Economic Modelling*, 20 (2003), 331–60.

HENDERSON, NORMAN, and BATEMAN, IAN, 'Empirical and Public Choice Evidence for Hyperbolic Social Discount Rates and the Implications for Intergenerational Discounting', *Environmental and Resource Economics*, 5 (1995), 413–23.

HENDRICK, CLYDE, and HENDRICK, SUSAN S., 'Lovers Wear Rose Colored Glasses', *Journal of Social and Personal Relationships*, 5 (1988), 161–83.

HENQUET, C., KRABBENDAM, L., SPAUWEN, J., KAPLAN, C., LIEB, R., WITTCHEN, H. U., and VAN OS, J., 'Prospective Cohort Study of Cannabis Use, Predisposition for Psychosis, and Psychotic Symptoms in Young People', *British Medical Journal*, 330 (2005), 11.

HENRY, HARRY, 'Advertising Expenditure in the United Kingdom: Outline of the Statistics', in J. J. D. Bullmore and M. J. Waterson (eds.), *The Advertising Association Handbook* (London, 1983), 7–18.

HEPBURN, CAMERON, 'Hyperbolic Discounting and Resource Collapse', unpublished paper, (Oxford, 2003).

HERMAN, C. PETER, and POLIVY, JANET, 'Restrained Eating', in Albert J. Stunkard (ed.), *Obesity* (Philadelphia, 1980).

————'What Does Abnormal Eating Tell Us about Normal Eating?' in H. L. Meiselman and H. J. H. MacFie (eds.), *Food Choice, Acceptance and Consumption* (London, 1996), 207–38.

————'Dieting as an Exercise in Behavioral Economics', in George, Loewenstein Daniel Read and Roy F. Baumeister (eds.), *Time and Decision: Economic and Psychological Perspectives on Intertemporal Choice* (New York, 2003), 459–89.

HERRNSTEIN, R. J., LOEWENSTEIN, GEORGE F., PRELEC, DRAZEN, and VAUGHAN, WILLIAM, 'Utility Maximization and Melioration: Internalities in Individual Choice', *Journal of Behavioral Decision Making*, 6 (1993), 149–85.

HESS, JOHN L., and HESS, KAREN, *The Taste of America* (Harmondsworth, 1977).

HESSE-BIBER, SHARLENE, *Am I Thin Enough Yet?: The Cult of Thinness and the Commercialization of Identity* (New York 1997).

HEWITT, PATRICIA, *About Time: The Revolution in Work and Family Life* (London, 1993).

HEWLETT, SYLVIA ANN, *Creating a Life: What Every Woman Needs to Know about Having a Baby and a Career*, rev. edn. (New York, 2003).

——and VITE-LEÓN, NORMA, 'High-Achieving Women, 2001', National Parenting Association (New York, 2001).

HICKS, JOHN RICHARD, *Value and Capital: An Inquiry into Some Fundamental Principles of Economic Theory* (Oxford, 1946).

HICKS, MICHAEL E., 'Management Recruitment in Britain, c.1940–2000', D.Phil. thesis, University of Oxford, 2004.

HIGGINS, NATALIE JANE MARIA RUSHTON, 'The Changing Expectations and Realities of Marriage in the English Working Class, 1920–1960', Ph.D. thesis, University of Cambridge, 2003.

HIRSCH, FRED, *Social Limits to Growth* (London, 1976).

HITE, SHERE, *The Hite Report: Women and Love. A Cultural Revolution in Progress* (London, 1987).

HOCH, STEPHEN J., and LOEWENSTEIN, GEORGE F., 'Time-Inconsistent Preferences and Consumer Self-Control', *Journal of Consumer Research*, 17 (1991), 492–507.

HOCHSCHILD, ARLIE RUSSELL, *The Managed Heart: Commercialization of Human Feeling* (Berkeley, Calif., 1983).

——*The Time Bind: When Work Becomes Home and Home Becomes Work* (New York, 1997).

——and MACHUNG, ANNE, *The Second Shift: Working Parents and the Revolution at Home* (London, 1990).

HODGE, ALLISON M., and ZIMMET, PAUL Z., 'The Epidemiology of Obesity', in I.D. Caterson (ed.), *Obesity, Ballières Clinical Endocrinology and Metabolism*, 7, 3 (London, 1994), 577–99.

HOFFER, GEORGE E., and REILLY, ROBERT J., 'Automobile Styling as a Shift Variable: An Investigation by Firm and by Industry', *Applied Economics*, 16 (1984), 291–7.

HOFSTADTER, RICHARD, *The Age of Reform from Bryan to F.D.R.* (New York, 1955).

HOGARTH, ROBIN M., *Judgement and Choice: The Psychology of Decision*, 2nd edn. (Chichester, 1987).

—— and REDER, MELVIN WARREN, *Rational Choice: The Contrast between Economics and Psychology* (Chicago, 1987).

HOLLANDER, HEINZ, 'A Social Exchange Approach to Voluntary Cooperation', *American Economic Review*, 80 (1990), 1157–67.

—— 'On the Validity of Utility Statements: Standard Theory Versus Duesenberry's', *Journal of Economic Behavior and Organization*, 45 (2001), 227–49.

HOLLANDER, STANLEY C., 'The Wheel of Retailing', *Journal of Marketing*, 25, 1 (1960), 37–42.

HOLMES, T. H., and RAHE, R. H., 'The Social Readjustment Rating Scale', *Journal of Psychosomatic Research*, 11 (1967), 213–18.

HOLMSTROM, BENGT, and MILGROM, PAUL, 'Multitask Principal-Agent Analyses: Incentive Contracts, Asset Ownership, and Job Design', *Journal of Law, Economics and Organization*, 7 (1991), 24–52.

HOMER, SIDNEY, and SYLLA, RICHARD, *A History of Interest Rates* (New Brunswick, NJ, 1991).

HONNEF, KLAUS, *Andy Warhol 1928–1987: Commerce into Art* (Cologne, 1990).

HORM, JOHN, and ANDERSON, KAY, 'Who in America is Trying to Lose Weight ?' *Annals of Internal Medicine*, 119 (1993), 672–6.

HOROWITZ, DANIEL, *The Anxieties of Affluence: Critiques of American Consumer Culture, 1939–1979* (Amherst, Mass., 2004).

HOTZ, JOSEPH V., KLERMAN, JACOB A., and WILLIS, ROBERT J., 'The Economics of Fertility in Developed Countries', in Mark R. Rosenzweig and Oded Stark (eds.), *Handbook of Population and Family Economics* (Amsterdam, 1997), 275–345.

HOUT, MICHAEL, 'Money and Morale: What Growing Inequality is Doing to Americans' Views of Themselves and Others', January (Berkeley, 2003).

—— and HANLEY, CAROLINE, 'The Overworked American Family: Trends and Nontrends in Working Hours, 1968–2001', Survey Research Center, University of California, Berkeley, 'A Century of Difference' working paper, June (Berkeley, 2002).

HOUTHAKKER, HENDRIK S., and TAYLOR, LESTER D., *Consumer Demand in the United States: Analyses and Projections*, 2nd edn. (Cambridge, Mass., 1970).

HOWARTH, R. G., 'Introduction', in R. G. Howarth, (ed.), *The Letters of Lord Byron* (London, 1936).

HUBER, JOAN, 'Ransacking Mobility Tables', *Contemporary Sociology*, 9 (1980), 5–8.

HUBERMAN, MICHAEL, 'Working Hours of the World Unite? New International Evidence of Worktime, 1870–1913', *Journal of Economic History*, 64 (2004), 964–1001.

HUGHES, DAVID, and McGUIRE, A., 'A Review of the Economic Analysis of Obesity', *British Medical Bulletin*, 53 (1997), 253–63.

HUGHES, TED, *Birthday Letters* (London, 1998).

HULTEN, CHARLES R., and WYKOFF, FRANK C., 'Issues in the Measurement of Economic Depreciation', *Economic Inquiry*, 34 (1996), 10–23.

HUME, DAVID, *A Treatise of Human Nature*, ed. P. H. Nidditch and L. A. Selby-Bigge, 2nd edn. (Oxford, 1978).

HUMPHRIES, STEVE, *A Secret World of Sex: Forbidden Fruit: The British Experience 1900–1950* (London, 1988).

HWANG, KWANG-KUO, 'Face and Favor: The Chinese Power Game', *American Journal of Sociology*, 92 (1987), 944–74.

INGLEHART, RONALD, *Modernization and Postmodernization: Cultural, Economic, and Political Change in 43 Societies* (Princeton, 1997).

—— BASANEZ, MIGUEL, and MORENO, ALEJANDRO, *Human Values and Beliefs: A Cross-Cultural Sourcebook: Political, Religious, Sexual, and Economic Norms in 43 Societies; Findings from the 1990–1993 World Value Survey* (Ann Arbor, 1998).

INGRAHAM, CHRYS, *White Weddings: Romancing Heterosexuality in Popular Culture* (New York, 1999).

International Advertising Association and Starch Inra Hooper, Inc., *Survey of World Advertising Expenditures* (Mamaroneck, NY, 1960–).

International Labour Organization, *New ILO Study Highlights Labour Trends Worldwide: US Productivity Up, Europe Improves Ability to Create Jobs* (2003), in **www.ilo.org/public/english/bureau/inf/magazine/48/kilm.htm**, accessed: 27 Feb. 2004.

International Labour Organization, *Key Indicators of the Labour Market* (Geneva, 1999–).

—— *Economic Security for a Better World* (Geneva, 2004).

International Research Associates; subsequently Starch Inra Hooper, Inc., *Advertising Expenditures around the World [Bi-Annual]* (1960–).

IRONMONGER, DUNCAN, *New Commodities and Consumer Behaviour* (Cambridge, 1972).

—— *Households Work* (Sydney, 1989).

IVES, NAT, 'A Report on Childhood Obesity', *New York Times*, 25 Feb. 2004.

JACKSON, T., 'Chasing Progress: Beyond Measuring Economic Growth', New Economics Foundation (London, 2004).

—— and MARKS, N., *Measuring Sustainable Economic Welfare: A Pilot Index, 1950–1990* (Stockholm, 1994).

—— —— RALLS, J., and STYMNE, S., *Sustainable Economic Welfare in the UK, 1950–1996* (London, 1997).

JACOBS, JERRY A., 'Review of Christine E. Bose, *Jobs and Gender*', *American Journal of Sociology*, 92 (1988), 481–2.

—— and GERSON, KATHLEEN, 'Who Are the Overworked Americans?' *Review of Social Economy*, 56 (1998), 42–59.

—— —— *The Time Divide: Work, Family, and Gender Inequality* (London, 2004).

JACOBY, JACOB, and HOYER, WAYNE D., 'Viewer Miscomprehension of Televised Communication: Selected Findings', *Journal of Marketing*, 46 (1982), 12–26.

—— —— *The Comprehension and Miscomprehension of Print Communications: An Investigation of Mass Media Magazines* (New York, 1987).

JACOBY, JACOB, and HOYER, WAYNE D., 'The Comprehension/Miscomprehension of Print Communication: Selected Findings', *Journal of Consumer Research*, 15 (1989), 434–43.

————— 'The Miscomprehension of Mass-Media Advertising Claims: A Re-Analysis of Benchmark Data', *Journal of Advertising Research*, 30 (1990), 9–15.

————— and SHELUGA, DAVID A., *Miscomprehension of Televised Communications* (New York, 1980).

JALAL al-DIN RUMI, MAULQNA, and NICHOLSON, REYNOLD ALLEYNE, *Rumi: Poet and Mystic, 1207–1273* (London, 1950).

JAMES, OLIVER, *Britain on the Couch: Why We're Unhappier Compared with 1950, despite Being Richer: A Treatment for the Low-Serotonin Society* (London, 1997).

JANKOWIAK, WILLIAM R., *Romantic Passion: A Universal Experience?* (New York, 1995).

————— and FISHER, E. F., 'A Cross-Cultural Perspective on Romantic Love', *Ethnology*, 31 (1992), 149–55.

JANSSENS, ANGÉLIQUE (ed.), *The Rise and Decline of the Male Breadwinner Family?, International Review of Social History*. Supplement 5 (Cambridge, 1998).

JEBB, SUSAN A., 'Aetiology of Obesity', *British Medical Bulletin*, 53 (1997), 264–85.

JEFFERYS, JAMES B., *The Distribution of Consumer Goods: A Factual Study of Methods and Costs in the United Kingdom in 1938* (Cambridge, 1950).

JEMMOTT, JOHN B., and GONZALEZ, ELIDA, 'Social Status, the Status Distribution, and Performance in Small Groups', *Journal of Applied Social Psychology*, 19 (1989), 584–98.

JENKINS, SIMON, 'Nanny Can't Wait to Slap Our Chubby Wrists', *The Times*, 28 May 2004.

JOHNSON, MICHAEL P., and FERRARO, KATHLEEN J., 'Research on Domestic Violence in the 1990s: Making Distinctions', *Journal of Marriage and the Family*, 62 (2000), pp. 948–963.

JOHNSON, PAUL, *Saving and Spending: The Working-Class Economy in Britain, 1870–1939* (Oxford, 1985).

Joint United Nations Programme on HIV/AIDS, *Report on the Global HIV/AIDS Epidemic,* July (Geneva, 2002).

JONES, GARETH S., *Languages of Class: Studies in English Working Class History, 1832–1982* (Cambridge, 1983).

JOSHI, HEATHER, 'The Changing Form of Women's Economic Dependency', in Heather Joshi (ed.), *The Changing Poplulation of Britain* (Oxford, 1989), 157–76.

————— 'The Cash Opportunity Costs of Childbearing: An Approach to Estimation Using British Data', *Population Studies*, 44 (1990), 41–60.

————— 'The Cost of Caring', in Caroline Glendinning and Jane Millar (eds.), *Women and Poverty in Britain: The 1990s* (London, 1992), pp. 110–25.

————— 'Combining Employment and Child-Rearing: The Story of British Womens' Lives', in Avner Offer (ed.), *In Pursuit of the Quality of Life* (Oxford, 1996), 88–118.

————— PACI, PIERELLA, and WALDFOGEL, JANE, 'The Wages of Motherhood: Better or Worse?' *Cambridge Journal of Economics*, 23 (1999), 543–64.

JUDD, TERRI, 'Average Wedding "Costs £17,000"', *Independent*, 10 Feb. 2005, p. 23.

JUDGE, KEN, and PATERSON, IAN, 'Poverty, Income Inequality and Health', New Zealand Treasury (Wellington, 2001).

JUNGEILGES, JOCHEN, and KIRCHGASSNER, GEBHARD, 'Economic Welfare, Civil Liberty, and Suicide: An Empirical Investigation', *Journal of Socio-Economics*, 31 (2002), 215–31.

JUSTER, F. THOMAS, 'Preferences for Work and Leisure', in F. Thomas Juster and Frank P. Stafford (eds.), *Time, Goods and Well-Being* (Ann Arbor, 1985), 333–51.

—— and STAFFORD, FRANK P. (eds.), *Time, Goods and Well-Being* (Ann Arbor, 1985).

KACELNIK, ALEX, 'The Evolution of Patience', in George Loewenstein, Daniel Read, and Roy F. Baumeister (eds.), *Time and Decision: Economic and Psychological Perspectives on Intertemporal Choice* (New York, 2003), 115–38.

KAHLE, LYNN, and CHIAGOURIS, LARRY (eds.), *Values, Lifestyles, and Psychographics: Advertising and Consumer Psychology* (Mahwa, NJ, 1997).

KAHNEMAN, DANIEL, 'Objective Happiness', in Daniel Kahneman, Ed Diener, and Norbert Schwarz (eds.), *Well-Being: The Foundations of Hedonic Psychology* (New York, 1999), 3–27.

—— 'Experienced Utility and Objective Happiness', in Daniel Kahneman and Amos Tversky (eds.), *Choices, Values and Frames* (New York, 2000), 673–92.

—— 'New Challenges to the Rationality Assumption', in Daniel Kahneman and Amos Tversky (eds.), *Choices, Values, and Frames* (New York, 2000), 758–74.

—— 'A Psychological Perspective on Economics', *American Economic Review*, 93 (2003), 162–8.

—— and VAREY, CAROL, 'Notes on the Psychology of Utility', in Jon Elster and John E. Roemer (eds.), *Interpersonal Comparisons of Well-Being* (Cambridge, 1991), 127–63.

—— DIENER, ED, and SCHWARZ, NORBERT (eds.), *Well-Being: The Foundations of Hedonic Psychology* (New York, 1999).

—— KNETSCH, JACK L., and THALER, RICHARD, 'The Endowment Effect, Loss Aversion, and Status Quo Bias', *Journal of Economic Perspectives*, 5 (1991), 193–206.

—— TVERSKY, AMOS (eds.), *Choices, Values, and Frames* (Cambridge, 2000).

KALDOR, NICHOLAS, 'The Economic Aspects of Advertising', *Review of Economic Studies*, 18 (1950), 1–27.

KALLBERG, ARNE, 'Work Quality in the U.S.A'., Powerpoint presentation (Chapel Hill, NC, 2003) [in possession of the author].

KALMIJN, M., 'Shifting Boundaries—Trends in Religious and Educational Homogamy', *American Sociological Review*, 56 (1991), 786–800.

KALMUSS, D. S., and STRAUS, MURRAY A., 'Wife's Marital Dependency and Wife Abuse', in Murray A. Straus, and Richard J. Gelles (eds.), *Physical Violence in American Families: Risk Factors and Adaptations to Violence in 8,145 Families* (New Brunswick, NJ, 1992), 369–82.

KAMEN, PAULA, *Her Way: Young Women Remake the Sexual Revolution* (New York, 2000).

KANTOR, L. S., LIPTON, K., MANCHESTER, ALDEN, and OLIVEIRA, VICTOR, 'Estimating and Addressing America's Food Losses', *Food Review*, 20 (1997).

KAPLAN, G. A., PAMUK, E. R., LYNCH, J. W., COHEN, R. D., and BALFOUR, J. L., 'Inequality in Income and Mortality in the United States: Analysis of Mortality and Potential Pathways', *British Medical Journal*, 312 (1996), 999–1003.

KAPP, K. W., *The Social Costs of Private Enterprise* (Cambridge, Mass., 1950).

KASSER, TIM, *The High Price of Materialism* (Cambridge, Mass., 2002).

——and KANNER, ALLEN D. (eds.), *Psychology and Consumer Culture: The Struggle for a Good Life in a Materialistic World* (Washington, DC., 2004).

——RYAN, RICHARD M., COUCHMAN, CHARLES E., and SHELDON, KENNON M., 'Materialistic Values: Their Causes and Consequences', in Tim Kasser and Allen D. Kanner (eds.), *Psychology and Consumer Culture: The Struggle for a Good Life in a Materialistic World* (Washington, DC, 2004), 11–28.

KAVANAGH, DENNIS, 'Political Culture in Great Britain: The Decline of the Civic Culture', in Gabriel A. Almond and Sidney Verba (eds.), *The Civic Culture Revisited* (Boston, 1980).

KEATS, JOHN, *The Insolent Chariots* (Philadelphia, 1958).

KEESEY, RICHARD F., 'A Set-Point Analysis of the Regulation of Body Weight', in Albert J. Stunkard (ed.), *Obesity* (Philadelphia, 1980), 144–65.

——'A Set-Point Theory of Obesity', in K. D. Brownell and J. P. Foreyt (eds.), *Handbook of Eating Disorders* (New York, 1986), 63–87.

KEFAUVER, ESTES, *In a Few Hands: Monopoly Power in America* (Baltimore, 1965).

KELLY, ROBERT L., *The Foraging Spectrum: Diversity in Hunter-Gatherer Lifeways* (Washington, DC, 1995).

KENDRICK, JOHN W., 'Studies in the National Income Accounts', *National Bureau of Economic Research, 47th Annual Report*, June (1967).

——LETHEM, YVONNE, and ROWLEY, JENNIFER, *The Formation and Stocks of Total Capital* (New York, 1976).

KENNEDY, B. P., KAWACHI, I., and PROTHROW-STITH, D., 'Income Distribution and Mortality: Cross-Sectional Ecological Study of the Robin Hood Index in the United States', *British Medical Journal*, 312 (1996), 1004–7.

KENRICK, DOUGLAS T., GUTIERRES, SARA E., and GOLDBERG, LAURIE L., 'Influence of Popular Erotica on Judgments of Strangers and Mates', *Journal of Experimental Social Psychology*, 25 (1989), 159–67.

KERN, MONTAGUE, *30-Second Politics: Political Advertising in the Eighties* (New York, 1989).

KESSLER, RONALD C., MCGONAGLE, KATHERINE A., NELSON, CHRISTOPHER B., and HUGHES, MICHAEL, 'Sex and Depression in the National Comorbidity Survey: II. Cohort Effects', *Journal of Affective Disorders*, 30 (1994), 15–26.

——ZHAO, S., BLAZER, D. G., and SWARTZ, M., 'Prevalence, Correlates, and Course of Minor Depression and Major Depression in the National Comorbidity Survey', *Journal of Affective Disorders*, 45 (1997), 19–30.

Key Note Publications, *Restaurants* (Hampton, 1992).

KHARE, R. S., 'Indian Hospitality: Some Cultural Values and Social Dynamics', *Cultural Heritage of the Indian Village*, British Museum Occasional Paper no. 47 (1991), 45–61.

KHOSLA, T., and LOWE, R. C., 'Height and Weight of British Men', *Lancet*, 6 Apr. 1968.

KIECOLT, K. JILL, 'Satisfaction with Work and Family Life: No Evidence of a Cultural Reversal', *Journal of Marriage and the Family*, 65 (2003), 23–35.

KIERNAN, KATHLEEN E., 'The Legacy of Parental Divorce: Social, Economic and Demographic Experiences in Adulthood', Centre for Analysis of Social Exclusion, LSE, CASE Papers no. 1 (London, 1997).

—— and CHERLIN, ANDREW J., 'Parental Divorce and Partnership Dissolution in Adulthood: Evidence from a British Cohort Study', *Population Studies*, 53 (1999), 39–48.

—— and HOBCRAFT, JOHN, 'Parental divorce during Childhood: Age at First Intercourse, Partnership and Parenthood', *Population Studies*, 51 (1997), 41–55.

KING, JAMES, 'No Nest Egg: Research into Attitudes of Younger Consumers to Saving for Retirement', National Consumer Council (London, 2003).

KINSEY, ALFRED C., *Sexual Behavior in the Human Female* (Philadelphia, 1953).

—— POMEROY, WARDELL B., and MARTIN, CLYDE E., *Sexual Behavior in the Human Male* (Philadelphia, 1948).

KIRKENDALL, LESTER A., 'Premarital Intercourse', in Henry Anatole Grunwald (ed.), *Sex in America* (New York, 1964), 40–63.

KITAGAWA, EVELYN M., and HAUSER, PHILIP M., *Differential Mortality in the United States: A Study in Socioeconomic Epidemiology* (Cambridge, Mass., 1973).

KITSON, GAY C., and SUSSMAN, MARVIN B., 'Marital Complaints, Demographic Characteristics, and Symptoms of Mental Distress in Divorce', *Journal of Marriage and the Family*, 44 (1982), 87–101.

—— BABRI, K. B., and ROACH, M. J., 'Who Divorces and Why: A Review', *Journal of Family Issues*, 6 (1985), 255–93.

KLAPP, ORRIN E., *Overload and Boredom: Essays on the Quality of Life in the Information Society* (Westport, Conn., 1986).

KLASSEN, ALBERT D., *Sex and Morality in the US: An Empirical Enquiry under the Auspices of the Kinsey Institute*, ed. Hubert J. O'Gorman (Middletown, Conn., 1989).

KLEIN, RICHARD, *Eat Fat* (London, 1997).

KLERMAN, GERALD L., 'The Current Age of Youthful Melancholia: Evidence for Increase in Depression among Adolescents and Young Adults', *British Journal of Psychiatry*, 152 (1988), 4–14.

—— 'The Changing Rate of Major Depression', *Journal of the American Medical Association*, 268 (1992), 3098–105.

—— and WEISSMAN, M. M., 'Increasing Rates of Depression', *Journal of the American Medical Association*, 261 (1989), 2229–35.

KLESGES, ROBERT C., SHELTEON, MARY L., and KLESGES, LISA M., 'Effects of Television on Metabolic Rate: Potential Implications for Childhood Obesity', *Pediatrics*, 91 (1993).

411

KLESGES, ROBERT C., SHELTEON, MARY L., and KLESGES, LISA M., 'Effects of Television on Metabolic Rate: Potential Implications for Childhood Obesity', *Pediatrics*, 91 (1993), 281–6.

KLOHNEN, EVA C., and BERA, STEPHAN, 'Behavioral and Experiential Patterns of Avoidantly and Securely Attached Women across Adulthood: A 31-Year Longitudinal Perspective', *Journal of Personality and Social Psychology*, 74 (1998), 211–23.

KLOPFENSTEIN, BRUCE C., 'The Diffusion of the VCR in the United States', in Mark R. Levy (ed.), *The VCR Age: Home Video and Mass Communication* (Newbery Park, Calif., 1989), 21–39.

KNEESE, A. V., AYRES, R. Y., and d'ARGE, R. C., *Economics and the Environment: A Material Balances Approach* (Washington, DC, 1970).

KNIGHT, I. B., and ELDRIDGE, JACK, Great Britain, Department of Health and Social Security, and Office of Population, Censuses and Surveys, Social Survey Division, *The Heights and Weights of Adults in Great Britain: Report of a Survey Carried out on behalf of the Department of Health and Social Security Covering Adults Aged 16–64* (London, 1984).

KOHN, ALFIE, *No Contest: The Case against Competition*, rev. edn. (Boston, 1992).

KOMAROVSKY, MIRRA, and PHILIPS, JANE H., *Blue-Collar Marriage*, 2nd edn. (New Haven, 1987).

KOMLOS, J., SMITH, P. K., and BOGIN, B., 'Obesity and the Rate of Time Preference: Is There a Connection?' *Journal of Biosocial Science*, 36 (2004), 209–20.

KONING, NIEK, *The Failure of Agrarian Capitalism: Agrarian Politics in the United Kingdom, Germany, the Netherlands and the USA, 1846–1919* (London, 1994).

KOTLIKOFF, LAURENCE J., 'Intergenerational Transfers and Savings', *Journal of Economic Perspectives*, 77 (1988), 41–58.

—— and BURNS, SCOTT, *The Coming Generational Storm: What You Need to Know About America's Economic Future* (London, 2004).

—— and SPIVAK, A., 'The Family as an Incomplete Annuities Market', *Journal of Political Economy*, 89 (1981), 942–63.

—— and SUMMERS, LAWRENCE H., 'The Role of Integenerational Transfers in Aggregate Capital Accumulation', *Journal of Political Economy*, 89 (1981), 706–32.

KRANTON, RACHEL E., 'Reciprocal Exchange: A Self-Sustaining System', *American Economic Review*, 86 (1996), 830–51

KRAVDAL, ØYSTEIN, 'The Emergence of a Positive Relation between Education and Third Birth Rates in Norway with Supportive Evidence from the United States', *Population Studies*, 46 (1992), 459–75.

—— 'The High Fertility of College Educated Women in Norway: An Artefact of the Separate Modelling of Each Parity Transition', *Demographic Research*, 5 (2001).

KREPS, DAVID M., *A Course in Microeconomic Theory* (New York, 1990).

KRISHNAN, LILA, 'Recipient Need and Anticipation of Reciprocity in Prosocial Exchange', *Journal of Social Psychology*, 128 (1988), 223–31.

KUBEY, ROBERT WILLIAM, and CSIKSZENTMIHALYI, MIHALY, *Television and the Quality of Life: How Viewing Shapes Everyday Experience* (Hillsdale, NJ, 1990).

—— —— 'Television Addiction', *Scientific American*, 286 (2002), 74–81.

KUCZMARSKI, ROBERT J., 'Increasing Prevalence of Overweight among US Adults: The National Health and Nutrition Examination Surveys, 1960 to 1991', *Journal of the American Medical Association*, 272 (1994), 205–11.

—— CARROLL, M. D., FLEGAL, K. M., and TROIANO, R. P., 'Varying Body Mass Index Cutoff Points to Describe Overweight Prevalence among US Adults: NHANES III (1988 to 1994)', *Obesity Research*, 5 (1997), 542–7.

KULIS, STEPHEN S., 'Social Class and the Locus of Reciprocity in Relationships with Adult Children', *Journal of Family Issues*, 13 (1992), 482–504.

KUSSMAUL, ANN, *Servants in Husbandry in Early Modern England* (Cambridge, 1981).

KUTCHINS, HERB, and KIRK, STUART A., *Making us Crazy: DSM: The Psychiatric Bible and the Creation of Mental Disorders* (London, 1999).

Labour Research, 'Unaffordable Housing: Workers Priced out of Housing Market', *Labour Research*, 90 (2001), 9–11.

LAIBSON, DAVID, 'Life-Cycle Consumption and Hyperbolic Discount Functions', *European Economic Review*, 42 (1998), 861–71.

—— REPETTO, ANDREA, and TOBACMAN, JEREMY, 'Self-Control and Saving for Retirement', *Brookings Papers on Economic Activity*, 1 (1998), 91–172.

LAING, WILLIAM, *Financing Long-Term Care: The Crucial Debate* (London, 1993).

LAKDAWALLA, DARIUS, and PHILIPSON, TOMAS, 'The Growth of Obesity and Technological Change: A Theoretical and Empirical Examination', NBER Working Papers 8946 (2002).

LANDA, JANET T., *Trust, Ethnicity, and Identity: Beyond the New Institutional Economics of Ethnic Trading Networks, Contract Law, and Gift-Exchange* (Ann Arbor, 1994).

LANE, ROBERT EDWARDS, *The Loss of Happiness in Market Democracies* (New Haven, 2000).

LARSON, DAVID B., SWYERS, JAMES P., and LARSON, SUSAN S., *The Costly Consequences of Divorce: Assessing the Clinical, Economic, and Public Health Impact of Marital Disruption in the United States. A Research-Based Seminar* (Rockville, Md., 1995).

LASCH, CHRISTOPHER, *Haven in a Heartless World: The Family Besieged* (New York, 1977).

LASN, KALLE, *Culture Jam: How to Reverse America's Suicidal Consumer Binge—and Why We Must* (New York, 2000).

LAUMANN, EDWARD O., GAGNON, JOHN H., MICHAEL, ROBERT T., and STUART, MICHAELS, *The Social Organization of Sexuality: Sexual Practices in the United States* (Chicago, 1994).

LAURANCE, J., 'Task Force Aims to Halt Global Obesity Epidemic', *The Times*, 13 Mar, 1996, p. 10.

LAURIER, D., GUIGUET, M., CHAN, N. P., WELLS, J. A., and WALTERON, A. J., 'Prevalence of Obesity: A Comparative Survey in France, the United Kingdom and the United States', *International Journal of Obesity*, 16 (1992), 565–72.

LAWRANCE, EMILY C., 'Poverty and the Rate of Time Preference: Evidence from Panel Data', *Journal of Political Economy*, 99 (1991), 54–77.

LAWSON, NIGEL, *The Nigel Lawson Diet Book* (London, 1996).

——'Let's Take a Wider Look at the Thin Issue', *The Observer*, 16 Apr. 2000.

LAYARD, RICHARD, *Happiness: Lessons from a New Science* (London, 2005).

LEACH, BRYAN WYKOFF, 'Giving from Afar: The Crisis of Child Support in Post-War Great Britain', M.Phil. Thesis, University of Oxford, 2002.

LEARS, JACKSON, *Fables of Abundance: A Cultural History of Advertising in America* (New York, 1995).

LEBERGOTT, STANLEY, *Pursuing Happiness: American Consumers in the Twentieth Century* (Princeton, 1993).

LEBESCO, KATHLEEN, *Revolting Bodies? The Struggle to Redefine Fat Identity* (Amherst, Mass., 2004).

LEDENEVA, ALENA V., *Russia's Economy of Favours: Blat, Networking and Informal Exchange* (Cambridge, 1998).

LEE, JOHN ALAN, 'Love Styles', in Michael L. Barnes and Robert J. Sternberg (eds.), *The Psychology of Love* (New Haven, 1988), 38–67.

LEECH, DENNIS, and CAMPOS, ERICK, 'Is Comprehensive Education Really Free? A Case-Study of the Effects of Secondary School Admissions Policies on House Prices in One Local Area', *Journal of the Royal Statistical Society: Series A (Statistics in Society)*, 166 (2003), 135–54.

LEISS, WILLIAM, KLINE, STEPHEN, and JHALLY, SUT, *Social Communication in Advertising: Persons, Products and Images of Well-Being* (London, 1990).

LEMASTERS, E. E., *Modern Courtship and Marriage* (New York, 1957).

LEMONICK, MICHAEL D., 'War of the Diapers', *Time* (25 Jan. 1999), 64.

LERMAN, ROBERT I., 'U.S. Wage-Inequality Trends and Recent Immigration', *American Economic Review*, 89 (1999), 23–8.

LEVENSTEIN, HARVEY A., *Revolution at the Table: The Transformation of the American Diet* (New York, 1988).

——*Paradox of Plenty: A Social History of Eating in Modern America* (New York, 1993).

LEVI, ISAAC, *Hard Choices: Decision Making under Unresolved Conflict* (Cambridge, 1986).

LEVITT, TED, *The Marketing Imagination* (New York, 1983).

LEVY, FRANK, *The New Dollars and Dreams: American Incomes and Economic Change* (New York, 1998).

LEVY, KENNETH N., BLATT, SIDNEY J., and SHAVER, PHILLIP R. A, 'Attachment Styles and Parental Representations', *Journal of Personality and Social Psychology*, 74 (1998), 407–19.

LEVY, S., and GUTTMAN, L., 'On the Multivariate Structure of Well-Being', *Social Indicators Research*, 2 (1975), 361–88.

LEWIN, ELLEN, *Lesbian Mothers: Accounts of Gender in American Culture* (Ithaca, NY, 1993).

LEWIS, DAVID L., McCARVILLE, MIKE, and SORENSEN, LORIN, *Ford 1903 to 1984* (New York, 1983).

LIBERMAN, NIRA, and TROPE, YAACOV, 'Construal Level Theory of Intertemporal Judgment and Decision', in George Loewenstein, Daniel Read, and Roy F. Baumeister (eds.), *Time and Decision: Economic and Psychological Perspectives on Intertemporal Choice* (New York, 2003), 277–300.

LICHTER, DANIEL T., MCLAUGHLIN, DIANE K., KEPHART, GEORGE, and LANDRY, DAVID J., 'Race and the Retreat from Marriage: A Shortage of Marriageable Men?' *American Sociological Review*, 57 (1992), 781–99.

Life, 'Living by Contract', *Life*, 72, 16 (28 April 1972), 42–46*b*.

LIM, JOO LEE, 'Women's Choices about Work and Family: A Status Perspective', M.Sc. thesis, University of Oxford, 2003.

LIN, BIING-HWAN, GUTHRIE, JOANNE, and FRAZÃO, ELIZABETH, 'Away-from-home Foods Increasing Important to Quality of American Diet' (Washington, DC, 1999).

LIU, JOYCE, 'Reading the Mind of Consumers: The Development of Psychographic Research in Marketing', M.Sc. thesis, University of Oxford, 2004.

LOAYZA, NORMAN, LOPEZ, HUMBERTO, SCHMIDT-HEBBEL, KLAUS, and SERVEN, LUIS, 'The World Saving Data Base', World Bank, January 1998 (Washington DC, 1998). **www.worldbank.org/research/projects/savings/database.htm**

LOCKE, JOHN, *An Essay Concerning Human Understanding*, ed. P. H. Nidditch (Oxford, 1979).

LOEWENSTEIN, GEORGE, 'The Fall and Rise of Psychological Explanations in the Economics of Intertemporal Choice', in George Loewenstein and Jon Elster (eds.), *Choice over Time* (New York, 1992), 3–34.

—— 'Out of Control: Visceral Influences on Behavior', *Organizational Behavior and Human Decision Processes*, 65 (1996), 272–92.

—— and ELSTER, JON (eds.), *Choice over Time* (New York, 1992).

—— READ, DANIEL, and BAUMEISTER, ROY F. (eds.), *Time and Decision: Economic and Psychological Perspectives on Intertemporal Choice* (New York, 2003).

LOEWY, RAYMOND, 'A Jukebox on Wheels', *Atlantic Monthly*, 195 (1955), 36–8.

LOGUE, A. W., *The Psychology of Eating and Drinking* (New York, 1986).

LOJKINE, JEAN, 'Valeur, valeur d'usage et valeur symbolique', *Cahiers internationaux de sociologie*, 38 (1991), 25–48.

LONG, CLARENCE D., *The Labor Force under Changing Income and Employment* (Princeton, 1958).

LORD, WILLIAM A., *Household Dynamics: Economic Growth and Policy* (New York, 2002).

LOVELL, STEPHEN, LEDENEVA, ALENA V., and ROGACHEVSKI, A. B. (eds.), *Bribery and Blat in Russia: Negotiating Reciprocity from the Middle Ages to the 1990s* (Basingstoke, 2000).

LUCAS, ROBERT E., and STARK, ODED, 'Motivations to Remit: Evidence from Botswana', *Journal of Political Economy*, 93 (1985), 901–18.

LUHMANN, NIKLAS, *Love as Passion: The Codification of Intimacy* (Cambridge, Mass., 1986).

LUNDBERG, SHELLY, and POLLAK, ROBERT A., 'Bargaining and Distribution in Marriage', *Journal of Economic Perspectives*, 10 (1996), 139–58.

415

LUNDBERG, SHELLY, and POLLAK, ROBERT A., 'Efficiency in Marriage', NBER Working Paper No. W8642 (2001).

LYKKEN, DAVID T., 'The American Crime Factory', *Psychological Inquiry*, 8 (1997), 261–70.

——and TELLEGEN, AUKE, 'Happiness is a Stochastic Phenmenon', *Psychological Science*, 7 (1996), 186–9.

LYNCH, J. W., SMITH, G. D., KAPLAN, G. A., and HOUSE, J. S., 'Income Inequality and Mortality: Importance to Health of Individual Income, Psychosocial Environment, or Material Conditions', *British Medical Journal*, 320 (2000), 1200–4.

LYND, ROBERT STAUGHTON, and LYND, HELEN MERRELL, *Middletown: A Study in American Culture* (New York, 1929).

——— *Middletown in Transition: A Study in Cultural Conflicts* (New York, 1937).

LYNES, RUSSELL, 'How Do You Rate in the New Leisure?', *Life* (28 Dec. 1959), 85–9.

LYSGAARD, SVERRE, 'Social Stratification and the Deferred Pattern', presented at the World Congress of Sociology (Liège,1953).

MCBRIDE, MICHAEL, 'Relative-Income Effects on Subjective Well-Being in the Cross-Section', *Journal of Economic Behavior and Organization*, 45 (2001), 251–78.

MCCARRON, ANNE, and TIERNEY, KEVIN J., 'The Effect of Auditory Stimulation on the Consumption of Soft Drinks', *Appetite*, 13 (1989), 155–9.

MCCARTY, NOLAN, POOLE, KEITH T., and ROSENTHAL, HOWARD, 'Political Polarization and Income Inequality', Columbia University, discussion paper (New York, 2001).

MCCLOSKEY, DONALD, '1780–1860: A Survey', in Roderick Floud and D.H. McCloskey (eds.), *The Economic History of Britain since 1799*, 2nd edn. vol. i (Cambridge, 1994), 242–70.

MCGUIRE, MICHAEL T., and TROISI, ALFONSO, *Darwinian Psychiatry* (New York, 1998).

MCKENZIE, JOHN, 'Economic Influences on Food Choice', in M. Turner (ed.), *Nutrition and Lifestyles* (London, 1979), 91–103.

MCKIBBIN, ROSS, *The Ideologies of Class: Social Relations in Britain, 1880–1950* (Oxford, 1990).

——*Classes and Cultures: England 1918–1951* (Oxford, 1998).

MCLANAHAN, SARA, and BUMPASS, LARRY, 'Intergenerational Consequences of Family Disruption', *American Journal of Sociology*, 94 (1988), 130–52.

MCLEAN, IAN, and POULTON, JO, 'Good Blood, Bad Blood, and the Market: The Gift Relationship Revisited', *Journal of Public Policy*, 6 (1987), 431–45.

MCMANUS, PATRICIA A., and DIPRETE, THOMAS A., 'Losers and Winners: The Financial Consequences of Separation and Divorce for Men', *American Sociological Review*, 66 (2001), 246–68.

MCNAIR, MALCOLM P., 'Trends in Large-Scale Retailing', *Harvard Business Review*, 10, 1 (1931), 30–9.

MADDISON, ANGUS, *The World Economy: A Millennial Perspective* (Paris, 2001).

MADSEN, DOUGLAS, 'Power Seekers are Different: Further Biochemical Evidence', *American Political Science Review*, 80 (1986), 261–70.

MAHAJAN, VIJAY, MULLER, Eitan, and BASS, FRANK M., 'New Product Diffusion Models in Marketing: A Review and Directions for Research', *Journal of Marketing*, 54 (1990), 1–26.

MAHONY, RHONA, *Kidding Ourselves: Breadwinning, Babies, and Bargaining Power* (New York, 1995).

MAJIMA, SHINOBU, 'Fashion and the Mass Consumer Society in Britain, c.1950–2000', D.Phil. thesis, Oxford, 2005.

MALINOWSKI, BRONISLAW, *Argonauts of the Western Pacific* (New York, 1922).

MALLABY, SEBASTIAN, *The World's Banker: A Story of Failed States, Financial Crises, and the Wealth and Poverty of Nations* (New York, 2004).

MANN, J. J., 'A Current Perspective of Suicide and Attempted Suicide', *Annals of Internal Medicine*, 136, 4 (2002), 302–11.

MANSON, J. E., WILLETT, W. C., STAMPFER, M. J., COLDITZ, G. A., HUNTER, D. J., and HENKINSON, S. E., 'Body Weight and Mortality among Women', *New England Journal of Medicine*, 333 (1995), 677–84.

MANUCK, STEPHEN B., FLORY, JANINE D., MULDOON, MATTHEW F., and FERRELL, ROBERT E., 'A Neurobiology of Intertemporal Choice', in George Loewenstein, Daniel Read, and Roy F. Baumeister (eds.), *Time and Decision: Economic and Psychological Perspectives on Intertemporal Choice* (New York, 2003), 139–74.

MARCHAND, ROLAND, *Advertising and the American Dream: Making Way for Modernity, 1920–1940* (Berkeley, 1985).

MARE, R. D., 'Five Decades of Educational Assortative Mating', *American Sociological Review*, 56 (1991), 15–32.

MAREMONT, MARK, 'Blind Ambition: How the Pursuit of Results Got out of Hand at Bausch & Lomb', *Business Week*, International Edition (23 Oct. 1995), 46–56.

MARKS, KATHY, 'Gym Industry Now Worth Healthy £1bn', *The Independent*, 21 Aug. 1998, p. 8.

MARKS LARA, *Sexual Chemistry: A History of the Contraceptive Pill* (New Haven, 2001).

MARLING, KARAL ANN, *Norman Rockwell* (New York, 1997).

MARMOT, MICHAEL, 'Social Differences in Health within and between Populations', *Daedalus*, 123 (1994), 197–216.

—— *Status Syndrome: How Your Social Standing Directly Affects Your Health and Life Expectancy* (London, 2004).

—— and WILKINSON, R. G., 'Psychosocial and Material Pathways in the Relation between Income and Health: A Response to Lynch et al', *British Medical Journal*, 322 (2001), pp. 1233–6.

MARSHALL, DAVID WILLIAM (ed.), *Food Choice and the Consumer* (London, 1995).

—— 'Eating at Home: Meals and Food Choice', in David William Marshall (ed.), *Food Choice and the Consumer* (London, 1995), 264–91.

MARSHALL, GORDON, *Repositioning Class: Social Inequality in Industrial Societies* (London, 1997).

MARSHALL, GORDON, and FIRTH, DAVID, 'Social Mobility and Personal Satisfaction: Evidence from Ten Countries', *British Journal of Sociology*, 50 (1999), 28–48.

—— ROSE, DAVID, NEWBY, HOWARD, and VOGLER, CAROL, *Social Class in Modern Britain* (London, 1993).

—— SWIFT, ADAM, and ROBERTS, STEPHEN, *Against the Odds? Social Class and Social Justice in Industrial Societies* (Oxford, 1997).

MARTIN, TERESA CASTRO, and BUMPASS, LARRY L., 'Recent Trends in Marital Disruption', *Demography*, 26 (1989), 37–51.

MATHUR, VIJAY K., and FREEMAN, DONALD G., 'A Theoretical Model of Adolescent Suicide and some Evidence from US Data', *Health Economics*, 11 (2002), 695–708.

MATTHEWS, R. C. O., FEINSTEIN, C. H., and ODLING-SMEE, J. C., *British Economic Growth, 1856–1973* (Stanford, Calif., 1982).

MATTHEWSON, S. B., *Restrictions of Output among Unorganized Workers* (New York, 1931).

MAUME, DAVID J., JR., and BELLAS, MARCIA L., 'The Overworked American or the Time Bind? Assessing Competing Explanations for Time Spent in Paid Labor', *American Behavioral Scientist*, 44, 7 (2001), 1137–56.

MAUSS, MARCEL, *The Gift: The Form and Reason for Exchange in Archaic Societies*, translated by Halls, W. D. (first publ. 1925, London, 1990).

MAZUMDER, BHASH, 'Analyzing Income Mobility over Generations', *Chicago Fed Letter*, 181 (2002).

MEAD, MARGARET, *Male and Female: A Study of the Sexes in a Changing World* (London, 1949).

MEAD, REBECCA, 'You're Getting Married—the Wal-Martization of the Marriage Business', *New Yorker* (21 Apr. 2003), 76–87.

MEEKS, J. G. TULIP, 'Utility in Economics: A Survey of the Literature', in Charles F. Turner and Elizabeth Martin (eds.), *Surveying Subjective Phenomena* (New York, 1984), 41–91.

MEEN, GEOFFREY, 'The Time-Series Behavior of House Prices: A Transatlantic Divide?' *Journal of Housing Economics*, 11 (2002), 1–23.

MEIKSINS, PETER, and WHALLEY, PETER, *Putting Work in its Place: A Quiet Revolution* (Ithaca, NY, 2002).

MEYER, CARRIE A., 'The Greening of National Accounts: The Role of Ideas in a Theory of Institutional Change', unpublished paper, George Mason University (1999).

MICHAEL, ROBERT T., GAGNON, JOHN H., LAUMANN, EDWARD O., and KOLATA, GINA, *Sex in America: A Definitive Survey* (Boston, 1994).

MICKELSON, KRISTIN D., KESSLER, RONALD C., and SHAVER, PHILLIP R., 'Adult Attachment in a Nationally Representative Sample', *Journal of Personality and Social Psychology*, 73 (1997), 1092–106.

MILES, IAN, *Social Indicators for Human Development* (London, 1985).

MILGRAM, STANLEY, *Obedience to Authority: An Experimental View* (London, 1974).

MILL, JOHN STUART, *Principles of Political Economy, with some of their Applications to Social Philosophy* (London, 1848).

MILLER, A., 'Diets Incorporated', *Newsweek* (11 Sept. 1989), 36.

MILLER, ARTHUR, *Death of a Salesman* (London, 1968).

MILLER, DANIEL, *Unwrapping Christmas* (Oxford, 1993).

MILLER, S. M., RIESSMAN, F., and SEAGULL, A. A., 'Poverty and Self-Indulgence: A Critique of the Non-Deferred Gratification Pattern', in L. A. Ferman, J. L. Kornbluh, and A. Haber (eds.), *Poverty in America: A Book of Readings* (Ann Arbor, 1968).

MILLMAN, MARCIA, *Such a Pretty Face: Being Fat in America* (New York, 1980).

MILLNER, EDWARD H., and HOFFER, GEORGE E., 'Has Pricing Behaviour in the US Automobile Industry Become More Competitive?' *Applied Economics*, 21 (1989), 295–304.

——— 'A Re-Examination of the Impact of Automotive Styling on Demand', *Applied Economics*, 25 (1993), 101–10.

Mintel Publications, *Convenience Meals* (London, 1985).

—— *Snacking: An Eating Revolution?* (London, 1987).

MIROWSKI, PHILIP, *Machine Dreams: Economics Becomes a Cyborg Science* (Cambridge, 2002).

MISCHEL, WALTER, AYDUK, OZLEM, and MENDOZA-DENTON, RODOLFO, 'Sustaining Delay of Gratification over Time: A Hot-Cool Systems Perspective', in George Loewenstein, Daniel Read, and Roy F. Baumeister (eds.), *Time and Decision: Economic and Psychological Perspectives on Intertemporal Choice* (New York, 2003), 175–200.

MISHAN, E. J., *The Costs of Economic Growth* (London, 1967).

MITCHELL ARNOLD, *The Nine American Lifestyles: Who We Are and Where We're Going* (New York, 1983).

MITCHELL, B. R., *British Historical Statistics* (Cambridge, 1988).

MITCHELL, JAMES E., and ECKERT, ELKE D., 'Scope and Significance of Eating Disorders', *Journal of Consulting and Clinical Psychology*, 55 (1987), 628–34.

MOGRIDGE, M. J. H., *The Car Market: A Study of the Statistics and Dynamics of Supply-Demand Equilibrium* (London, 1983).

MOLM, LINDA D., *Coercive Power in Social Exchange* (Cambridge, 1997).

MONTEGRIFFO, V. M. E., 'A Survey of the Incidence of Obesity in the United Kingdom', *Postgraduate Medical Journal*, 47, suppl. (1971), 418–22.

MOORE, STEPHEN, and SIMON, JULIAN L., *It's Getting Better All the Time: 100 Greatest Trends of the Last 100 Years* (Washington, DC, 2000).

MORGAN, PATRICIA M., *Farewell to the Family: Public Policy and Family Breakdown in Britain and the USA*, 2nd rev. and updated edn. (London, 1999).

MORGAN, S. PHILIP, 'Characteristic Features of Modern American Fertility', in John B. Casterline, Ronald D. Lee, and Karen A. Foote (eds.), *Fertility in the United States: New Patterns, New Theories* (New York, 1996), 19–63.

MORI, DEANNA, CHAIKEN, SHELLY, and PLINER, PATRICIA, ' "Eating Lightly" and the Self-Presentation of Femininity', *Journal of Personality and Social Psychology*, 53 (1987), 693–702.

MORRIS, BILL, *Biography of a Buick* (London, 1993).

MORRIS, LYDIA, *The Workings of the Household: A US–UK Comparison* (Oxford, 1990).

MORRIS, MORRIS DAVID, *Measuring the Condition of the World's Poor: The Physical Quality of Life Index* (New York, 1979).

MORRIS, MORRIS DAVID, *Measuring the Changing Quality of the World's Poor: The Physical Quality of Life Index* (Providence, RI, 1996).

MORTON, ADAM, *Disasters and Dilemmas: Strategies for Real-Life Decision Making* (Oxford, 1991).

MOTTRAM, ERIC, *Blood on the Nash Ambassador: Investigations in American Culture* (London, 1989).

MUELLBAUER, JOHN, and MURPHY, ANTHONY, 'Booms and Busts in the UK Housing Market', *Economic Journal*, 107 (1997), 1701–27.

MUELLER, MIKE, *Fifties American Cars* (Osceola, Wis., 1994).

MULLANEY, CRAIG, 'The Rewards of Status: Women's Choices about Work and Family, 1950–1990', M.Sc. thesis, University of Oxford, 2002.

MULLIGAN, CASEY B., 'With the Flat Tax, Common Sense is Better than an Economist', *Chicago Sun-Times*, 4 May 1996, p. 14.

——'A Logical Economist's Argument against Hyperbolic Discounting', unpublished paper, University of Chicago (Chicago, 1996). **www.spc.uchicago.edu/~wwwcbm4/.**

MULOCK, BRUCE, 'Advertising Regulation by the Federal Trade Commission', Congressional Research Service Report [79–145-E], 9 July (Washington DC, 1979).

MURCOTT, ANNE, 'Raw, Cooked and Proper Meals at Home', in David William Marshall (ed.), *Food Choice and the Consumer* (London, 1995), 219–35.

MURPHY, JANE M., LAIRD, NAN M., MONSON, RICHARD R., SOBOL, ARTHUR M., and LEIGHTON, ALEXANDER H., 'A 40-Year Perspective on the Prevalence of Depression: The Stirling County Study', *Archives of General Psychiatry*, 57 (2000), 209–215.

MURRAY, CHRISTOPHER J. L., and LOPEZ, ALAN D., *The Global Burden of Disease* (2003), in **www.who.int/msa/mnh/ems/dalys/intro.htm#intro**, accessed: 16 July 2004.

MURRAY, DIAN H., and BAOQI, QIN, *The Origins of the Tiandihui: The Chinese Triads in Legend and History* (Stanford, Calif., 1994).

MYERS, KATHY, *Understains: The Sense and Seduction of Advertising* (London, 1986).

NAKAO, KEIKO, and TREAS, JUDITH, 'Updating Occupational Prestige and Socioeconomic Scores: How the New Measures Measure Up', *Sociological Methodology*, 24 (1994), 1–72.

NAKONEZNY, PAUL A., SHULL, ROBERT D., and RODGERS, JOSEPH LEE, 'The Effect of No-Fault Divorce Law on the Divorce Rate across the 50 States and Its Relation to Income, Education, and Religiosity', *Journal of Marriage and the Family*, 57 (1995), 477–88.

NARAYAN, DEEPA, et al., *Voices of the Poor: Can Anyone Hear Us?* (Oxford, 2000).

National Automobile Dealers' Association [NADA], *Official Used Car Guide* [monthly] (Washington, DC, 1957–73).

National Marriage Project, *The State of Our Unions* [annual] (New Brunswick, NJ, 1999–2004).

NAZ, GHAZALA, NILSEN, OVINID A., and VAGSTAD, STEINER, 'Education and Completed Fertility in Norway', Department of Economics, University of Bergen (Bergen, 2002).

NEAL, LARRY, 'The Finance of Business during the Industrial Revolution', in Roderick Floud and D. H. McCloskey (eds.), *The Economic History of Britain since 1799*, 2nd edn., vol. i (Cambridge, 1994), 151–81.

NEEDLEMAN, L., 'The Demand for Domestic Appliances', *National Institute Economic Review*, 12 (1960), 24–44.

NEELANKAVIL, JAMES P., and STRIDSBERG, ALBERT B., *Advertising Self-Regulation: A Global Perspective* (New York, 1980).

NEER, KATHERINE, 'How Product Placement Works' (2005), in **http://money. howstuffworks.com/product-placement.htm; product-placement.htm**, accessed: 16 March 2005.

NELSON, M., 'Social-Class Trends in Diet in Britain: 1860–1980', in C. Geissler and D. J. Oddy (eds.), *Food, Diet and Economic Change Past and Present* (Leicester, 1994).

NEUHAUS, JESSAMYN, 'The Way to a Man's Heart: Gender Roles, Domestic Ideology, and Cookbooks in the 1950s', *Journal of Social History*, 32 (1999), 529–56.

——*Manly Meals and Mom's Home Cooking: Cookbooks and Gender in Modern America* (Baltimore, 2003).

NEWMAN, KATHERINE S., *Falling from Grace: The Experience of Downward Mobility in the American Middle Class* (New York, 1988).

NICOLAAS, GERRY, *Cooking: Attitudes and Behaviour* (London, 1995).

NICOLAIDES-BOUMAN, ANS, *International Smoking Statistics: A Collection of Historical Data from 22 Economically Developed Countries* (London, 1993).

NILSON, LINDA B., 'The Social Standing of a Housewife', *Journal of Marriage and the Family*, 40, 3 (1978), 541–8.

NOBLE, M., SMITH, G. A. N., PENHALE, B., WRIGHT, G., DIBBEN, C., OWEN, T. and LLOYD, M., 'Measuring Multiple Deprivation at the Small Area Level: The Indices of Deprivation 2000', Department of Transport, Environment and the Regions, *Regeneration Research Summary*, 37 (London, 2000).

NOLL, HEINZ-HERBERT, 'New Structures of Inequality: Some Trends of Social Change in Modernized Societies', Wissenschaftszentrums Berlin für Sozialforschung, Working Paper, February (Berlin, 1999).

NORBYE, JAN P. and DUNNE, JIM, *Buick 1946–1978: The Classic Postwar Years* (Osceola, Wis. 1993).

NORD, MARK, ANDREWS, MARGARET, and CARLSON, STEVEN, 'Household Food Security in the United States, 2003', USDA, Food Assistance and Nutrition Research Report Number 42, October (Washington, DC, 2003).

NORDHAUS, WILLIAM D., 'Reflections on the Concept of Sustainable Economic Growth', in Luigi Pasinetti and Robert M. Solow (eds.), *Economic Growth and the Structure of Long-Term Development* (Basingstoke, 1994), 309–25.

——'Do Real-Output and Real-Wage Measures Capture Reality? The History of Lighting Suggests Not', in Timothy F. Bresnahan and Robert J. Gordon (eds.), *The Economics of New Goods*, National Bureau of Economic Research Studies in Income and Wealth, vol. 58. (Chicago, 1997), 29–66.

NORDHAUS, WILLIAM D., 'The Health of Nations: Irving Fisher and the Contribution of Improved Longevity to Living Standards', Cowles Foundation, Yale University, Cowles Foundation Discussion Papers [1200] (New Haven, 1998).

—— 'New Directions in National Economic Accounting', *American Economic Review*, 90 (2000), 259–63.

—— 'The Health of Nations: The Contribution of Improved Health to Living Standards' (2002).

—— and TOBIN, JAMES, 'Is Growth Obsolete?', in James Tobin, *Essays in Economics*, vol. iii, *Theory and Policy* (Cambridge, Mass., 1982).

NORDIC COUNCIL, *Level of Living and Inequality in the Nordic Countries: A Comparative Analysis of the Nordic Comprehensive Surveys* (Stockholm, 1984).

NYBERG, DAVID, *The Varnished Truth: Truth Telling and Deceiving in Ordinary Life* (Chicago, 1993).

OAKLEY, ANN, *Housewife* (Harmondsworth, 1976).

ODDY, D. S., and MILLER, D. S. (eds.), *The Making of the Modern British Diet* (London, 1976).

O'DONOGHUE, TED, and RABIN, MATTHEW, 'Addiction and Self-Control', in Jon Elster (ed.), *Addiction: Entries and Exits* (New York, 1999), 169–206.

—— —— 'Studying Optimal Paternalism, Illustrated by a Model of Sin Taxes', *American Economic Review*, 93 (2003), 186–91.

—— —— 'Self-Awareness and Self-Control', in George Loewenstein, Daniel Read, and Roy F. Baumeister (eds.), *Time and Decision: Economic and Psychological Perspectives on Intertemporal Choice* (New York, 2003), 217–43.

OFFER, AVNER, *The First World War: An Agrarian Interpretation* (Oxford, 1989).

—— 'Going to War in 1914: A Matter of Honor?' *Politics & Society*, 23 (1995), 213–41.

—— 'The Mask of Intimacy: Advertising and the Quality of Life', in Avner Offer (ed.), *In Pursuit of the Quality of Life* (Oxford, 1996).

—— (ed.), *In Pursuit of the Quality of Life* (Oxford, 1996).

—— 'Between the Gift and the Market: The Economy of Regard', *Economic History Review*, 50 (1997), 450–76.

—— 'The American Automobile Frenzy of the 1950s', in K. Bruland and P. K. O'Brien (eds.), *From Family Firms to Corporate Capitalism* (Oxford, 1998), 315–53.

—— 'Epidemics of Abundance: Overeating and Slimming in the USA and Britain since the 1950s', Oxford University Discussion Papers in Economic and Social History, no. 25 (1998).

—— 'Body Weight and Self-Control in the United States and Britain since the 1950s', *Social History of Medicine*, 14, 1 (2001), 79–106.

—— *Why Has the Public Sector Grown So Large in Market Societies? The Political Economy of Prudence in the UK, c. 1870–2000* (Oxford, 2003); **www.nuff.ox.ac.uk/ Economics/History/Paper44/oup44.pdf**

—— 'The Markup for Lemons: Quality and Uncertainty in American and British Used Car Markets *c.*1953–1973', University of Oxford Discussion Papers in Economic and Social History no. 60 (Oxford, 2005).

OGDEN, C. L., CARROLL, M. D., and FLEGAL, K. M., 'Epidemiologic Trends in Overweight and Obesity', *Endocrinology and Metabolism Clinics of North America*, 32 (2003), 741–60, vii.

—— FRYAR, CHERYL D., CARROLL, MARGARET D., and FLEGAL, KATHERINE M., 'Mean Body Weight, Height, and Body Mass Index, United States, 1960–2002', *Advance Data from Vital and Health Statistics*, 347 (2004), 1–18.

OGILVY, DAVID, *Confessions of an Advertising Man* (New York, 1962).

—— *Ogilvy on Advertising* (New York, 1983).

O'KELLY, LISA, 'It Beats Working', *Observer* (6 June 2004).

OLFSON, MARK, GAMEROFF, MARC J., MARCUS, STEVEN C., and JENSEN, PETER S., 'National Trends in the Treatment of Attention Deficit Hyperactivity Disorder', *American Journal of Psychiatry*, 160 (2003), 1071–77.

—— MARCUS, STEVEN C., DRUSS, BENJAMIN, and PINCUS, HAROLD ALAN, 'National Trends in the Use of Outpatient Psychotherapy', *American Journal of Psychiatry*, 159 (2002), 1914–20.

OLIVER, M. B., and HYDE, J. S., 'Gender Differences in Sexuality: A Meta-Analysis', *Psychological Bulletin*, 114 (1993), 29–51.

OLIVER, MELVIN L., and SHAPIRO, THOMAS M., *Black Wealth/White Wealth: A New Perspective on Racial Inequality* (New York, 1995).

Oliver Wyman & Co., 'The Future Regulation of UK Savings and Investment: Targeting the Savings Gap', commissioned by Association of British Insurers (London, 2001).

OLNEY, MARTHA L., *Buy Now, Pay Later: Advertising, Credit, and Consumer Durables in the 1920s* (Chapel Hill, NC, 1991).

OLSON, LAWRENCE, *Costs of Children* (Lexington, Mass., 1983).

OLSON, MANCUR, *The Rise and Decline of Nations: Economic Growth, Stagflation and Social Rigidities* (New Haven, 1982).

—— and LANDSBERG, HANS H., *The No-Growth Society* (London, 1975).

One Off Media, Inc., 'History of CD Technology' (2005), in **www.oneoffcd.com/ info/historycd.cfm**, accessed: 2 Mar. 2005.

ONO, HIROMI, 'Historical Time and U.S. Marital Dissolution', *Social Forces*, 77 (1999), 969–99.

OPPENHEIMER, VALERIE K., *Work and the Family: A Study in Social Demography* (New York, 1982).

—— 'Women's Employment and the Gain to Marriage: The Specialization and Trading Model', *Annual Review of Sociology*, 23 (1997), 431–53.

ORBACH, SUSIE, *Fat is a Feminist Issue: How to Lose Weight Permanently—without Dieting* (London, 1988).

OROPESA, R. S., 'Using the Service Economy to Relieve the Double Burden: Female Labor Force Participation and Service Purchases', *Journal of Family Issues*, 3 (1993), 438–73.

ORPHANIDES, ATHANASIOS, and ZERVOS, DAVID, 'Rational Addiction with Learning and Regret', *Journal of Political Economy*, 103 (1995), 739–58.

ORPHANIDES, ATHANASIOS, and ZERVOS, DAVID, 'Myopia and Addictive Behaviour', *Economic Journal*, 108 (1998), 75–91.

OSBERG, LARS, 'Time, Money and Inequality in International Perspective', University of Essex, 28 May 2001 (Colchester, 2002).

—— and SHARPE, ANDREW, 'Human Well-Being and Economic Well-Being: What Values are Implicit in Current Indices?' Centre for the Study of Living Standards, CSLS Research Report 2003–4, 28 Aug. (Ottawa, 2003).

OSBORN, RICHARD WARREN, and WILLIAMS, J. IVAN, 'Determining Patterns of Exchanges and Expanded Family Relationships', *International Journal of Sociology of the Family*, 6 (1976), pp. 197–209.

O'SHAUGHNESSY, JOHN, *Why People Buy* (New York, 1987).

—— *Explaining Buyer Behavior: Central Concepts and Philosophy of Science Issues* (New York, 1992).

O'SHAUGHNESSY, NICHOLAS J., *The Phenomenon of Political Marketing* (London, 1990).

OSTROM, ELINOR, *Governing the Commons: The Evolution of Institutions for Collective Action* (Cambridge, 1990).

—— GARDNER, ROY, and WALKER, JAMES, *Rules, Games, and Common-Pool Resources* (Ann Arbor, MI, 1994).

OSWALD, ANDREW, 'Rank is What Matters', discussion paper, Warwick University, August (Warwick, 2003).

O'TOOLE, JOHN E., *The Trouble with Advertising* (New York, 1981).

OWEN, J., 'The Supply of Labor and the Demand for Recreation', Columbia University, Ph.D. thesis, 1964.

PACKARD, VANCE O., *The Status Seekers: An Exploration of Class Behaviour in America* (Harmondsworth, 1959).

—— *The Waste Makers* (New York, 1960).

—— *The Hidden Persuaders* (Harmondsworth, 1960).

PARKER, PHILIP M., 'Price Elasticity Dynamics over the Adoption Life Cycle', *Journal of Marketing Research*, 29 (1992), 358–67.

PARRY, J., 'On the Moral Perils of Exchange', in J. Parry and M. Bloch (eds.), *Money and the Morality of Exchange* (Cambridge, 1989), 64–93.

PASHIGIAN, B. PETER, *The Distribution of Automobiles: An Economic Analysis of the Franchise System* (Englewood Cliffs, NJ, 1961).

—— GOULD, ERIC, and BOWEN, BRIAN, 'Fashion, Styling and the Within-Season Decline in Automobile Prices', *Journal of Law and Economics*, 38 (1995), 281–309.

PEARCE, DAVID W., and ULPH, DAVID, 'A Social Discount Rate for the United Kingdom', in David W. Pearce (ed.), *Economics and Environment: Essays on Ecological Economics and Sustainable Development* (Cheltenham, 1998), 268–85.

PEARSON, ALLISON, *I Don't Know How She Does It: A Comedy about Failure, a Tragedy about Success* (London, 2002).

PEASE, OTIS, *The Responsibilities of American Advertising: Private Control and Public Influence, 1920–1940* (New Haven, 1958).

PEDERSEN, F. A., 'Secular Trends in Human Sex Ratios: Their Influence on Individual and Family Behavior', *Human Nature*, 2 (1991), 271–91.

PEETERS, A., BARENDREGT, J. J., WILLEKENS, F., MACKENBACH, J. P., AL MAMUN, A., and BONNEUX, L., 'Obesity in Adulthood and its Consequences for Life Expectancy: A Life-Table Analysis', *Annals of Internal Medicine*, 138 (2003), 24–32.

PELLER, A. E., 'Wedding Counsel', *The Times*, 28 June 2004.

PETERS, H. ELIZABETH, 'The Importance of Financial Considerations in Divorce Decisions', *Economic Inquiry*, 31 (1993), 71–86.

PETERSON, CHRISTOPHER, MAIER, STEVEN F., and SELIGMAN, MARTIN E. P., *Learned Helplessness: A Theory for the Age of Personal Control* (New York, 1993).

PETERSON, NICOLAS, 'Demand Sharing: Reciprocity and the Pressure for Generosity among Foragers', *American Anthropologist*, 95 (1993), 860–74.

PETERSON, RICHARD R., 'Statistical Errors, Faulty Conclusions, Misguided Policy: Reply to Weitzman', *American Sociological Review*, 61 (1996), 539–40.

——'A Re-evaluation of the Economic Consequences of Divorce', *American Sociological Review*, 61 (1996), 528–36.

PHELPS, C. D., 'A Clue to the Paradox of Happiness', *Journal of Economic Behavior and Organization*, 45 (2001), 293–300.

PHILIPSON, T. J., and POSNER, R. A., 'The Long-Run Growth of Obesity as a Function of Technological Change', NBER Working Paper no. 7423, November (Boston, 1999).

PHILLIPS, KEVIN P., *The Emerging Republican Majority* (New Rochelle, NY, 1969).

Physician Task Force on Hunger in America, *Hunger in America: The Growing Epidemic* (Middletown, Conn., 1985).

PICARD, ANDRÉ, 'Childhood Obesity Accelerating: Study Finds Clothing Manufacturers Adjust by Offering Baggier Styles and Elasticized Waists', *Boston Globe*, 24 Feb. 2004, p. A6.

PIGOU, A. C., *The Economics of Welfare* (London, 1920).

PINKER, STEVEN, *The Language Instinct: The New Science of Language and Mind* (London, 1994).

PINSOF, WILLIAM M., 'The Death of "Till Death Us Do Part": The Transformation of Pair-Bonding in the 20th Century', *Family Process*, 41 (2002), 135–57.

PITT-RIVERS, JULIAN, 'The Stranger, the Guest and the Hostile Host: Introduction to the Study of the Laws of Hospitality', in J. G. Peristiany (ed.), *Contributions to Mediterranean Sociology* (Paris, 1963).

PLINER, P., and CHAIKEN, S., 'Eating, Social Motives and Self-Presentation in Women and Men', *Journal of Experimental Social Psychology*, 26 (1990), 240–54.

POLANYI, KARL, *The Great Transformation* (Boston, 1944).

——'The Economy as Instituted Process', in G. Dalton (ed.), *Primitive, Archaic and Modern Economies: Essays of Karl Polanyi* (Garden City, NJ, 1968), 139–74.

POLIVY, JANET, *Breaking the Diet Habit: The Natural Weight Alternative* (New York, 1983).

——and HERMAN, C. PETER, 'The Diagnosis and Treatment of Normal Eating', *Journal of Consulting and Clinical Psychology*, 55 (1987), 635–44.

425

POLLAY, RICHARD W. (ed.), *Information Sources in Advertising History* (Westport, Conn., 1979).

—— 'The Distorted Mirror: Reflections on the Unintended Consequences of Advertising', *Journal of Marketing*, 50 (1986), 18–36.

—— 'Promotion and Policy for a Pandemic Product: Notes on the History of Cigarette Advertising', University of British Columbia History of Advertising Archives, Working Papers and Research Reprints, January (Vancouver, 1988).

—— 'More Chronological Notes on the Promotion of Cigarettes', University of British Columbia History of Advertising Archives, Working Papers and Research Reprints, August (Vancouver, 1990).

POOLE, KEITH T., *The Polarization of American Politics* (2002), in **http://voteview.uh.edu/default_recpol.htm**.

POPE, HARRISON G., PHILLIPS, KATHARINE A., and OLIVARDIA, ROBERTO, *The Adonis Complex: The Secret Crisis of Male Body Obsession* (New York, 2000).

POTERBA, JAMES M., *International Comparisons of Household Saving* (Chicago, 1994).

—— *Public Policies and Household Saving* (Chicago, 1994).

POULTON, E. C., *Bias in Quantifying Judgements* (Hove, 1989).

PRENTICE, ANDREW M., and JEBB, SUSAN A., 'Obesity in Britain: Gluttony or Sloth?' *British Medical Journal*, 311 (1995), 437–9.

PRESSER, H. B., 'Employment Schedules among Dual-Earner Spouses and the Division of Household Labor by Gender', *American Sociological Review*, 59 (1994), 348.

PRESTON, IVAN L., *The Great American Blow-up: Puffery in Advertising and Selling* (Madison, 1975).

—— *The Tangled Web They Weave: Truth, Falsity and Advertisers* (Madison, 1994).

PRICE, COLIN, *Time, Discounting and Value* (Oxford, 1993).

PULLAR, PHILIPPA, *Consuming Passions: A History of English Food and Appetite* (London, 1970).

PUROHIT, DEVAVRAT, 'Exploring the Relationship between the Markets for New and Used Durable Goods: The Case of Automobiles', *Marketing Science*, 11 (1992), 154–67.

PUTNAM, JUDITH JONES, 'Food Consumption', *National Food Review*, Commodity Economics Division, Economic Research Service, US Department of Agriculture, July–Sept. (1990), 1–9.

PUTNAM, ROBERT D., 'Tuning in, Tuning Out: The Strange Disappearance of Social Capital in America', *Political Science and Politics*, 28 (1995), 664–83.

—— *Bowling Alone: The Collapse and Revival of American Community* (New York, 2000).

PYATT, F. GRAHAM, *Priority Patterns and the Demand for Household Durable Goods* (Cambridge, 1964).

PYE, DAVID, *The Nature of Design* (London, 1964).

QUAH, DANNY, 'The Sir Richard Stone Lectures: Growth and Distribution', 1 (2002), in **http://econ.lse.ac.uk/staff/dquah/**, accessed: 23 Feb. 2003.

RABIN, MATTHEW, 'Moral Preferences, Moral Constraints, and Self-Serving Biases', University of California, Berkeley, Working Paper in Economics (Berkeley, 1995).

—— 'Psychology and Economics', *Journal of Economic Literature*, 36 (1998), 11–46.

—— 'Diminishing Marginal Utility of Wealth Cannot Explain Risk Aversion', in Daniel Kahneman and Amos Tversky (eds.), *Choices, Values, and Frames* (Cambridge, 2000), 202–8.

RACHLIN, HOWARD, and RAINERI, ANDRES, 'Irrationality, Impulsiveness, and Selfishness as Discount Reversal Effects', in George Loewenstein and Jon Elster (eds.), *Choice over Time* (New York, 1992), 93–118.

RAILTON, REID A., and SAMPIETRO, A. O., 'Trends in European Car Design', *Society of Automotive Engineers*, Misc. paper no. 304, 8–10 Mar. 1949.

RALEY, R. KELLY, and BUMPASS, LARRY L., 'The Topography of the Divorce Plateau: Levels and Trends in Union Stability in the United States after 1980', *Demographic Research*, 8 (2003), 245–59.

RATCLIFF, ZOE (ed.), *Snack Foods*, 12th edn. (London, 1997).

RATH, LEE, 'Lighting Devices of All Kinds and Washing Machines Debut', *Merchandising*, 7 (1982), 20–3.

RAVEN, HUGH, LANG, TIM, and DUMONTEIL, CAROLINE, *Off our Trolleys? Food Retailing and the Hypermarket Economy* (London, 1995).

RAVETZ, ALISON, 'Modern Technology and an Ancient Occupation: Housework in Present Day Society', *Technology and Culture*, 6 (1965), 256–60.

RAYNOR, H. A., and EPSTEIN, L. H., 'Dietary Variety, Energy Regulation, and Obesity', *Psychological Bulletin*, 127 (2001), 325–41.

READ, DANIEL, 'Subadditive Intertemporal Choice', in George Loewenstein, Daniel Read, and Roy F. Baumeister (eds.), *Time and Decision: Economic and Psychological Perspectives on Intertemporal Choice* (New York, 2003), 301–22.

Reader's Digest Association, *A Survey of Europe Today: The Peoples and Markets of Sixteen European Countries* (London, 1970).

—— *Reader's Digest Eurodata: A Consumer Survey of 17 European Countries* (London, 1991).

REES, MARTIN J., *Our Final Century: A Scientist's Warning: How Terror, Error, and Environmental Disaster Threaten Humankind's Future in This Century—on Earth and Beyond* (London, 2003).

REGAN, MILTON C., *Alone Together: Law and the Meanings of Marriage* (New York, 1999).

REGISTER, C. A., and WILLIAMS, D. R., 'Wage Effects of Obesity among Young Workers', *Social Science Quarterly*, 71 (1990), 130–41.

REITH, JOHN CHARLES WALSHAM, *Report of a Commission of Enquiry into Advertising* (London, 1966).

RENDALL, MICHAEL, and SMALLWOOD, STEVE, 'Higher Qualifications, First-Birth Timing, and Further Childbearing in England and Wales', *Population Trends*, 111 (2003), 18–26.

RESNICK, MICHAEL D., et al. 'Protecting Adolescents from Harm: Findings from the National Longitudinal Study on Adolescent Health', *Journal of the American Medical Association*, 278 (1997), 823–32.

REYNOLDS, SUSAN, *Kingdoms and Communities in Western Europe, 900–1300* (Oxford, 1984).

RHEINISCH, JUNE, *The Kinsey Institute New Report on Sex* (New York, 1990).

RIDLEY, MATT, *The Red Queen: Sex and the Evolution of Human Nature* (London, 1995).

RIESMAN, DAVID, *Abundance for What? and Other Essays* (London, 1964).

—— *The Suburban Dislocation* (London, 1964 (first published 1957)).

—— and LARRABEE, ERIC, 'Autos in America', in D. Riesman (ed.), *Abundance for What? And Other Essays* (London, 1964), 266–95.

RILEY, N. M., BILD, D. E., COOPER, L., SCHREINER, P., SMITH, D. E., SORLIE, P., and THOMPSON, J. K., 'Relation of Self-Image to Body Size and Weight Loss Attempts in Black Women', *American Journal of Epidemiology*, 148 (1998), 1062–6.

RINDFLEISCH, ARIC, BURROUGHS, JAMES E., and DENTON, FRANK, 'Family Structure, Materialism, and Compulsive Consumption', *Journal of Consumer Research*, 23 (1997), 312–25.

RITSON, CHRISTOPHER, and HUTCHINS, RICHARD, 'The Consumption Revolution', in John Slater (ed.), *Fifty Years of the National Food Survey, 1940–1990* (London, 1991), 35–46.

ROBERTSON, DENNIS H., *What Does the Economist Economize?* (London, 1956).

ROBINSON, JOHN P., 'Changes in Time Use: An Historical Overview', in F. Thomas Juster and Frank P. Stafford (eds.), *Time, Goods and Well-Being* (Ann Arbor, 1985), 289–311.

—— 'Who's Doing the House work,' *American Demographics*, Dec. (1988), 3–6.

—— 'Where does the Free Time Go?' *American Demographics*, Nov. (1990), 5–8.

—— 'As We Like It,' *American Demographics*, Feb. (1993), 44–8.

—— and GODBEY, GEOFFREY, *Time for Life: The Surprising Ways Americans Use their Time* (University Park, Pa., 1997).

RODIN, JUDITH, *Body Traps: How to Overcome Your Body Obsessions—and Liberate the Real You* (London, 1992).

—— SCHANK, DIANE, and STRIEGEL-MOORE, RUTH, 'Psychological Features of Obesity', *Medical Clinics of North America*, 73 (1989), 47–66.

RODIN, J., SILBERSTEIN, L. R., and STREIGEL-MOORE, R. H., 'Women and Weight: A Normative Discontent', in T. B. Sonderegger (ed.), *Nebraska Symposium on Motivation 1984: vol. 32. Psychology and Gender* (Lincoln, Neb., 1985), 267–84.

ROELL, CRAIG H., *The Piano in America, 1890–1940* (Chapel Hill, NC, 1989).

ROGERS, EVERETT M., *Diffusion of Innovations* (New York, 1983).

ROGERS, STACY J., and AMATO, PAUL R., 'Is Marital Quality Declining? The Evidence from Two Generations', *Social Forces*, 75 (1997), 1089–100.

ROIPHE, ANNE RICHARDSON, *A Mother's Eye: Motherhood and Feminism* (London, 1997).

—— *1185 Park Avenue: A Memoir* (New York, 1999).

—— *Married: A Fine Predicament* (London, 2003).

ROLLS, BARBARA, ROLLS, EDMUND T., and ROWE, EDWARD A., 'The Influence of Variety on Human Food Selection and Intake', in Lewis M. Barker (ed.), *The Psychobiology of Human Food Selection* (Westport, Conn., 1982), 101–22.

ROSE, G. A., and WILLIAMS, R. T., 'Metabolic Studies on Large and Small Eaters', *British Journal of Nutrition*, 15 (1961), 1–9.

ROSE-ACKERMAN, SUSAN, 'Altruism, Nonprofits, and Economic Theory', *Journal of Economic Literature*, 34 (1996), 701–28.

ROSENBAUM, S., '100 Years of Heights and Weights', *Journal of the Royal Statistical Society*, ser. A, 151 (1988), 276–309.

ROSENFELD, RICHARD, 'The Case of the Unsolved Crime Decline', *Scientific American*, 290 (2004), 82–90.

ROSENZWEIG, MARK RICHARD, and STARK, ODED (eds.), *Handbook of Population and Family Economics* (Amsterdam, 1997).

ROSS, IRWIN, *The Image Merchants: The Fabulous World of American Public Relations* (London, 1959).

ROSSI, ALICE S., and ROSSI, PETER HENRY, *Of Human Bonding: Parent–Child Relations across the Life Course* (New York, 1990).

ROTH, A. E., 'Bargaining Experiments', in J. H. Kagel and A. E. Roth (eds.), *Handbook of Experimental Economics* (Princeton, 1995), 253–348.

ROTHBARD, JULIE C., and SHAVER, PHILLIP R., 'Continuity of Attachment across the Lifecourse: An Attachment-Theoretical Perspective on Personality', in Michael B. Sperling and William H. Berman (eds.), *Attachment in Adults: Theory, Assessment and Treatment* (New York, 1994), 31–71.

ROWNTREE, B.S., *Poverty: A study of Town Life* (London, 1902).

ROWTHORN, ROBERT, 'Marriage and Trust: Some Lessons from Economics', *Cambridge Journal of Economics*, 23 (1999), 661–91.

—— 'Marriage as a Signal', in Antony W. Dnes and Robert Rowthorn (eds.), *The Law and Economics of Marriage and Divorce* (Cambridge, 2002), 132–56.

RUBIN, LILLIAN B., *Worlds of Pain: Life in the Working-Class Family* (New York, 1976).

RUBIN, ZICK, 'Lovers and Other Strangers: The Development of Intimacy in Encounters and Relationships', *American Scientist*, 62 (1974), 182–90.

RUBINSTEIN, ARIEL, ' "Economics and Psychology"? The Case of Hyperbolic Discounting', *International Economic Review*, 44 (2003), 1207–16.

RUBINSTEIN, WILLIAM D., 'Jews in the Economic Elites of Western Nations and Antisemitism', *Jewish Journal of Sociology*, 42 (2000), 5–35.

RUGGLES, STEVEN, SOBEK, MATTHEW, ALEXANDER, TRENT, FITCH, CATHERINE A., GOEKEN, RONALD, HALL, PATRICIA KELLY, KING, MIRIAM, and RONNANDER, CHAD, *Integrated Public Use Microdata Series: Version 3.0* Minnesota Population Center [producer and distributor], (Minneapolis, MN, 2004). [IPUMS]

RUNCIMAN, W. G., *Relative Deprivation and Social Justice: A Study of Attitudes to Social Inequality in Twentieth-Century England* (London, 1966).

RUSBRIDGER, ALAN, and SIMMONDS, POSY, *A Concise History of the Sex Manual 1886–1986* (London, 1986).

429

SABELHAUS, JOHN, and PENCE, KAREN, 'Household Saving in the '90s: Evidence from Cross-Section Wealth Surveys', *Review of Income and Wealth*, 45 (1999), 435–53.

SAFER, D. J., ZITO, J. M., and DOSREIS, S., 'Concomitant Psychotropic Medication for Youths', *American Journal of Psychiatry*, 160 (2003), 438–49.

SAGUARO SEMINAR, The, 'Social Capital Community Benchmark Survey, Executive Summary', John F. Kennedy School of Government, Harvard University, 1 March 2001 (Cambridge, Mass., 2001).

SAHIN, H, and ROBINSON, JOHN P., 'Beyond the Realm of Necessity: Television and the Colonisation of Leisure', *Media, Culture and Society*, 3 (1980), 85–95.

SAHLINS, MARSHALL, *Stone Age Economics* (London, 1974).

ST CLAIR, DAVID J., *The Motorization of American Cities* (New York, 1986).

ST JOHN, WARREN, 'On the Final Journey, One Size Doesn't Fit All', *New York Times*, 28 Sept. 2003.

SAMETZ, A. W., 'Production of Goods and Services: The Measurement of Economic Growth', in E. B. Sheldon and W. E. Moore (eds.), *Indicators of Social Change: Concepts and Measurements* (New York, 1968).

SANDAGE, SCOTT A., *Born Loser* (Cambridge, Mass., 2005).

SAPOLSKY, ROBERT M., 'The Physiology and Pathophysiology of Unhappiness', in Daniel, Kahneman, Ed Diener, and Norbert Schwartz (eds.), *Well-Being: The Foundations of Hedonic Psychology* (New York, 1999), 453–69.

——ALBERTS, S. C., and ALTMANN, J., 'Hypercortisolism Associated with Social Subordinance or Social Isolation among Wild Baboons', *Archives of General Psychiatry*, 54 (1997), 1137–43.

SCHARLEMANN, J. P., ECKEL, C. C., KACELNIK, A., and WILSON, R. K., 'The Value of a Smile: Game Theory with a Human Face', *Journal of Economic Psychology*, 22 (2001), 617–40.

SCHELLING, THOMAS C., 'The Intimate Contest for Self-Command', *Public Interest*, 60 (1980), 94–118.

——'Self-Command in Practice, in Policy, and in a Theory of Rational Choice', *American Economic Review*, 74 (1984), 1–11.

SCHIFFREN, LISA, 'Single Minded', *National Review* (8 Feb. 1999), 44–5.

SCHIRM, E., TOBI, H., ZITO, J. M., and de JONG-VAN DEN BERG, L. T., 'Psychotropic Medication in Children: A Study from the Netherlands', *Pediatrics*, 108 (2001), e25.

SCHLINK, FREDERICK J., and KALLET, ARTHUR, *100,000,000 Guinea Pigs: Dangers in Everyday Foods, Drugs and Cosmetics* (New York, 1933).

SCHLOSSER, ERIC, *Fast Food Nation* (London, 2001).

SCHOEMAKER, PAUL J. H., 'The Expected Utility Model: Its Variants, Purposes, Evidence and Limitations', *Journal of Economic Literature*, 20 (1982), 529–63.

SCHOFIELD, MICHAEL GEORGE, *The Sexual Behaviour of Young People* (London, 1965).

SCHOFIELD, PERRY, *100 Top Copy Writers and their Favorite Ads* (New York, 1954).

SCHÖNBERGER, ANGELA (ed.), *Raymond Loewy: Pioneer of American Industrial Design* (Munich, 1990).

SCHOR, JULIET B., *The Overworked American: The Unexpected Decline of Leisure* (New York, 1991).

—— *The Overspent American: Why We Want What We Don't Need* (New York, 1999).

SCHUDSON, MICHAEL, *Advertising: The Uneasy Persuasion: Its Dubious Impact on American Society* (New York, 1986).

SCHWARTZ, BARRY, *The Costs of Living: How Market Freedom Erodes the Best Things in Life* (New York, 1994).

—— *The Paradox of Choice: Why More is Less* (New York, 2004).

SCHWARTZ, HILLEL, *Never Satisfied: A Cultural History of Diets, Fantasies, and Fat* (New York, 1986).

SCITOVSKY, TIBOR, *The Joyless Economy: The Psychology of Human Satisfaction*, rev. edn. (first publ. 1976, New York, 1992).

SCLAFANI, ANTHONY, 'Dietary Obesity', in Albert J. Stunkard (ed.), *Obesity* (Philadelphia, 1980), 166–81.

SEID, ROBERTA POLLACK, *Never Too Thin: Why Women Are at War with their Bodies* (New York, 1989).

SEIDEL, CHRISTIAN, TRAUB, STEFAN, and MORONE, ANDREA, 'Relative Deprivation, Personal Income Satisfaction, and Average Well-Being under Different Income Distributions', Christian-Albrecht University, Kiel, Economic Working Paper (Kiel, Germany, 2003).

SEIDELL, J. C., 'Obesity in Europe: Scaling an Epidemic', *International Journal of Obesity*, 19 (1995), pp. s1–s4.

SEIDLER, EDOUARD, *Let's Call It Fiesta: The Autobiography of Ford's Project Bobcat* (Cambridge, 1976).

SELDIN, JOSEPH J., *The Golden Fleece: Selling the Good Life to Americans* (New York, 1963).

SELIGMAN, MARTIN E. P., 'Why is There So Much Depression Today? The Waxing of the Individual and the Waning of the Commons', in Rex Ingram (ed.), *Contemporary Psychological Approaches to Depression* (New York, 1990), 1–9.

SEN, AMARTYA, 'The Welfare Basis of Real Income Comparisons: A Survey', *Journal of Economic Literature*, 17 (1979), 1–45.

—— *The Standard of Living* (Cambridge, 1987).

—— 'Capability and Well-Being', in Martha Nussbaum and Amartya Sen (eds.), *The Quality of Life* (Oxford, 1993), 30–53.

—— 'Social Justice and the Distribution of Income', in A. B. Atkinson and François Bourguignon (eds.), *Handbook of Income Distribution*, Handbooks in Economics 16 (Amsterdam, 2000), 59–86.

—— *Development as Freedom* (Oxford, 2001).

SHAFFER, LEIGH S., 'The Golden Fleece: Anti-Intellectualism and Social Science', *American Psychologist*, 32 (1977), 814–23.

SHALIT, WENDY, *A Return to Modesty: Discovering the Lost Virtue* (New York, 1999).

SHAPER, A. G., WANNAMETHEE, S. G., and WALKER, M., 'Body Weight: Implications for the Prevention of Coronary Heart Disease, Stroke, and Diabetes Mellitus in a Cohort Study of Middle Aged Men', *British Medical Journal*, 314 (1997), 1311–17.

SHAPIRO, KARL, 'Buick,' in *Poems, 1940–1953* (New York, 1953).

SHAPIRO, THOMAS M., *The Hidden Cost of Being African-American: How Wealth Perpetuates Inequality* (New York, 2004).

SHAPLEY, DEBORAH, *Promise and Power: The Life and Times of Robert McNamara* (Boston, 1993).

SHERMAN, R., and HOFFER, G., 'Does Automobile Style Change Payoff?', *Applied Economics*, 3 (1971), 153–65.

SHI, DAVID E., *The Simple Life: Plain Living and High Thinking in American Culture* (New York, 1985).

SHIVELY, C. A., 'Social Status, Stress, and Health in Female Monkeys', in Alvin R. Tarlov and Robert F. St Peter, (eds.), *The Society and Population Health Reader: A State and Community Perspective*, vol. ii (New York, 2000).

SHODA, YUICHI, MISCHEL, WALTER, and PEAKE, PHILIP K., 'Predicting Adolescent Cognitive and Self-Regulatory Competencies from Preschool Delay of Gratification', *Developmental Psychology*, 26 (1990), 978–86.

SHORRIS, EARL, *A Nation of Salesmen: The Tyranny of the Market and the Subversion of Culture* (New York, 1994).

SHULMAN, ALIX, 'A Marriage Disagreement', *Dissent* (Winter 1998), 36–46.

SHYER, KIRBY, 'Microwave Ovens Debut; Ranges Offer Cleaning Features', *Merchandising*, 7 (1982), 64–5.

SIDEL, RUTH, *Women and Children Last: The Plight of Poor Women in Affluent America* (New York, 1987).

SILVERSTEIN, BRETT, and PERLICK, DEBORAH, *The Cost of Competence: Why Inequality Causes Depression, Eating Disorders, and Illness in Women* (New York, 1995).

——PERDUE, L., PETERSON, B., and KELLY, E., 'The Role of the Mass Media in Promoting a Thin Standard of Body Attractiveness for Women', *Sex Roles*, 14 (1986), 512–32.

——————VOGEL, L., and FANTINI, D. A., 'Possible Causes of the Thin Standard of Bodily Attractiveness for Women', *International Journal of Eating Disorders*, 5 (1986), pp. 907–16.

——PETERSON, B., and PERDUE, L., 'Some Correlates of the Thin Standard of Bodily Attractiveness for Women', *International Journal of Eating Disorders*, 5 (1986), 895–905.

SIMPSON, JEFFRY A., and RHOLES, W. STEVEN, *Attachment Theory and Close Relationships* (New York, 1998).

——CAMPBELL, BRUCE, and BERSCHEID, ELLEN, 'The Association between Romantic Love and Marriage: Kephart (1967) Twice Revisited', *Personality and Social Psychology Bulletin*, 12 (1986), 363–72.

SIMPSON-HERBERT, MAYLING, 'Women, Food and Hospitality in Iranian Society', *Canberra Anthropology*, 10 (1987), 24–34.

SINGER, J. L., 'The Power and Limitations of Television: A Cognitive-Affective Analysis', in P. H. Tannenbaum and R. Abeles, (eds.), *The Entertainment Functions of Television* (Hillsdale, NJ, 1980).

SLESNICK, DANIEL T., 'Empirical Approaches to the Measurement of Welfare', *Journal of Economic Literature*, 36 (1998), 2108–65.

SLOAN, ALFRED P., *Adventures of a White-Collar Man* (New York, 1941).

SLOAN, TOD STRATTON, *Damaged Life: The Crisis of the Modern Psyche* (London, 1996).

SLOCHOWER, J. A., *Excessive Eating: The Role of Emotions and the Environment* (New York, 1983).

SLOTTJE, DANIEL J., SCULLY, GERALD W., HIRSCHBERG, JOSEPH G., and HAYES, KATHY J., *Measuring the Quality of Life across Countries: A Multidimensional Analysis* (Boulder, Colo., 1991).

SMART, ALAN, 'Gifts, Bribes, and Guanxi: A Reconsideration of Bourdieu's Social Capital', *Cultural Anthropology*, 8 (1993), 388–408.

SMART, J., and SMART, A., 'Personal Relations and Divergent Economies: A Case-Study of Hong-Kong Investment in South China', *International Journal of Urban and Regional Research*, 15 (1991), 216–33.

SMEEDING, TIMOTHY M., 'American Income Inequality in a Cross-National Perspective: Why are We so Different?' Maxwell School of Citizenship and Public Affairs, Syracuse University, Working Paper No. 157, Apr. 1997 (Syracuse, NY, 1997).

SMITH, ADAM, *An Inquiry into the Nature and Causes of the Wealth of Nations*, ed. R. H. Campbell and Andrew S. Skinner, (Oxford, 1976).

—— *The Theory of Moral Sentiments*, ed. A. L. Macfie and D. D. Raphael (Oxford, 1976).

SMITH, E. A., and BOYD, R., 'Risk and Reciprocity: Hunter-Gatherer Socioecology and the Problem of Collective Action', in E. Cashdan (ed.), *Risk and Uncertainty in Peasant Economies* (Boulder, Colo., 1990), 167–91.

SMITH, JAMES P., 'Healthy Bodies and Thick Wallets: The Dual Relation between Health and Economic Status', *Journal of Economic Perspectives*, 13 (1999), 145–66.

SMITH, RONALD PATRICK, *Consumer Demand for Cars in the USA* (Cambridge, 1975).

SMITH, TOM W., 'American Sexual Behavior: Trends, Socio-Demographic Differences, and Risk Behavior', unpublished paper, National Opinion Research Center, Chicago (1996).

SMOCK, P. J., 'Cohabitation in the United States: An Appraisal of Research Themes, Findings, and Implications', *Annual Review of Sociology*, 26 (2000), 1–82.

SNOOKS, GRAEME D., *Portrait of the Family within the Total Economy: A Study in Longrun Dynamics, Australia 1788–1990* (Cambridge, 1994).

SOBAL, J., 'Group Dieting, the Stigma of Obesity, and Overweight Adolescents: Contributions of Natalie Allon to the Sociology of Obesity', in D. J. Kallen and M. B. Sussman (eds.), *Obesity and the Family* (New York, 1984).

—— and STUNKARD, A. J., 'Socioeconomic Status and Obesity: A Review of the Literature', *Psychological Bulletin*, 105 (1989), 260–75.

Social Research Inc., *Automobiles: What They Mean to Americans* (Chicago, 1953).

SOLLORS, WERNER (ed.) *Interracialism: Black-White Intermarriage in American History, Literature, and Law* (New York, 2000).

SOLNICK, SARA J., and HEMENWAY, DAVID, 'Is More Always Better? A Survey on Positional Concerns', *Journal of Economic Behavior and Organization*, 37 (1998), 373–83.

————'The Deadweight Loss of Christmas: Reply', *American Economic Review*, 90 (2000), 325.

SOLOW, JOHN, 'Is It Really the Thought that Counts? Toward a Rational Theory of Christmas', *Rationality and Society*, 5 (1993), 506–17.

SOMAN, DILIP, 'The Effect of Time Delay on Multi-Attribute Choice', *Journal of Economic Psychology*, 25 (2004), 153–75.

SPACKMAN, MICHAEL, 'Discount Rates and Rates of Return in the Public Sector: Economic Issues', Government Economic Service Working Paper no. 113 (1991).

SPAHT, KATHERINE SHAW, 'Louisiana's Covenant Marriage Law: Recapturing the Meaning of Marriage for the Sake of the Children', in Antony W. Dnes and Robert Rowthorn (eds.), *The Law and Economics of Marriage and Divorce* (Cambridge, 2002), 92–117.

SPERO, ROBERT, *The Duping of the American Voter: Dishonesty and Deception in Presidential Television Advertising* (New York, 1980).

SPITZE, GLENNA, and LOGAN, JOHN R., 'Helping as a Component of Parent–Adult Child Relations', *Research on Aging*, 14 (1992), 291–312.

SPRECHER, SUSAN, ARON, ARTHUR, HATFIELD, ELAINE, CORTESE, ANTHONY, POTAPOVA, ELENA, and LEVITSKAYA, ANNA, 'Love: American Style, Russian Style and Japanese Style', *Personal Relationships*, 1 (1994), 349–69.

STACEY, JUDITH, 'Good Riddance to "the Family": A Response to David Popenoe', *Journal of Marriage and the Family*, 55 (1993), 545–7.

————*In the Name of the Family: Rethinking Family Values in the Postmodern Age* (Boston, 1996).

STAKE, J., and LAUER, M. L., 'The Consequences of Being Overweight', *Sex Roles*, 17 (1987), 31–47.

STANLEY, SHIRLEY C., 'The Relative Deprivation of Husbands in Dual-Earner Households', *Journal of Family Issues*, 7 (1986), 3–20.

STARFIELD, B., 'Is US Health Really the Best in the World?' *Jounal of the American Medical Association*, 284 (2000), 483–5.

STARK, ODED, *Altruism and Beyond: An Economic Analysis of Transfers and Exchanges within Families and Groups* (Cambridge, 1995).

STARR, JENNIFER, and MACMILLAN, IAN C., 'Entrepreneurship, Resource Cooptation, and Social Contracting', in A. Etzioni and Paul R. Lawrence (eds.), *Socio-Economics: Towards a New Synthesis* (Armonk, NY, 1991).

STEARNS, PETER N., *Fat History: Bodies and Beauty in the Modern West* (New York, 1997).

STEIN, R. I., and NEMEROFF, C. J., 'Moral Overtones of Food: Judgments of Others Based on What They Eat', *Personality and Social Psychology*, 21 (1995), 480–90.

STEINBERG, RONNIE, *Wages and Hours: Labor and Reform in Twentieth-Century America* (New Brunswick, NJ, 1982).

STENDHAL, *Love*, ed. Gilbert Sale, Suzanne Sale, Jean Stewart, and B. C. J. G. Knight, (Harmondsworth, 1957).

STERNBERG, ROBERT J., 'Triangulating Love', in Michael L. Barnes and Robert J. Sternberg (eds.), *The Psychology of Love* (New Haven, 1988), 119–38.

STEVENS, DAPHNE, KIGER, GARY, and RILEY, PAMELA J., 'Working Hard and Hardly Working: Domestic Labor and Marital Satisfaction among Dual-Earner Couples', *Journal of Marriage and the Family*, 63 (2001), 514–26.

STEVENSON, BETSEY, and WOLFERS, JUSTIN, 'Bargaining in the Shadow of the Law: Divorce Laws and Family Distress', Stanford Law and Economics Olin Working Paper No. 273; Stanford Law School, Public Law Working Paper No. 73 (2003).

STEWART, JOHN B., 'Planned Obsolescence', *Harvard Business Review*, Sept.–Oct. (1959), 15–28, 169–74.

STIGLER, G. H., and BECKER, G. S., '*De Gustibus Non Est Disputandum*', *American Economic Review*, 67 (1977), 76–90.

STOKEY, NANCY L., 'Shirtsleeves to Shirtsleeves: The Economics of Social Mobility', in Donald P. Jacobs, Ehud Kalai, and Morton I. Kamien (eds.), *Frontiers of Research in Economic Theory: The Nancy L. Schwartz Memorial Lectures, 1983–1997*, Econometric Society Monographs, No. 29 (Cambridge, 1998), 210–41.

STOLTZ, DONALD R., *The Advertising World of Norman Rockwell* (New York, 1985).

STONES, M. J., HADJISTAVROPOULOS, THOMAS, TUUKO, HOLLY, and KOZMA, ALBERT, 'Happiness Has Traitlike and Statelike Properties: A Reply to Veenhoven', *Social Indicators Research*, 36 (1995), 129–44.

STONEX, K. A., 'Trends of Vehicle Dimensions and Performance Characteristics', *Society of Automotive Engineers*, no. 539A, June (1962), 8–11.

STRASSER, SUSAN, *Never Done: A History of American Housework* (New York, 2000).

STROTZ, R. H., 'Myopia and Inconsistency in Dynamic Utility Maximization', *Review of Economic Studies*, 23 (1956), 165–80.

STUART, RICHARD B., *Act Thin, Stay Thin: New Ways to Manage Your Urge to Eat* (London, 1978).

——and JACOBSON, BARBARA, *Weight, Sex and Marriage* (New York, 1987).

——and MITCHELL, CHRISTINE, 'Self-Help Groups in the Control of Body Weight', in Albert J. Stunkard (ed.), *Obesity* (Philadelphia, 1980).

STUDENSKI, PAUL, *The Income of Nations: Theory, Measurement, and Analysis: Past and Present* (New York, 1958).

STUNKARD, ALBERT J., 'The Social Environment and the Control of Obesity', in Albert J. Stunkard (ed.), *Obesity* (Philadelphia, 1980), 439–62.

——(ed.), *Obesity* (Philadelphia, 1980).

——and WADDEN, THOMAS A., 'Psychological Aspects of Severe Obesity', *American Journal of Clinical Nutrition*, 55 (1992), 524s–532s.

SUTTON, JOHN, *Sunk Costs and Market Structure: Price Competition, Advertising, and the Evolution of Concentration* (Cambridge, Mass., 1991).

SWEET, JAMES A., and BUMPASS, LARRY L., *American Families and Households* (New York, 1990).

SWINDLE, RALPH, JR., HELLER, KENNETH, PESCOSOLIDO, BERNICE, and KIKUZAWA, SAEKO, 'Responses to Nervous Breakdowns in America over a 40-Year Period: Mental Health Policy Implications', *American Psychologist*, 55 (2000), 740–9.

Bibliography

Symons, Donald, *The Evolution of Human Sexuality* (New York, 1979).

Szreter, Simon, *Fertility, Class and Gender in Britain, 1860–1940* (Cambridge, 1996).

Taylor, Richard, *Having Love Affairs* (Buffalo, NY, 1982).

Taylor, Michael, *The Possiblity of Cooperation* (Cambridge, 1987).

Teachman, Jay, 'Premarital Sex, Premarital Cohabitation and the Risk of Subsequent Marital Dissolution among Women', *Journal of Marriage and Family*, 65 (2003), 444–55.

——Tedrow, Lucky M., and Crowder, Kyle D., 'The Changing Demography of America's Families', *Journal of Marriage and the Family*, 62 (2000), 1234–46.

Teague, Walter Dorwin, *Design This Day: The Technique of Order in the Machine Age* (New York, 1940).

Tedlow, Richard S., *New and Improved: The Story of Mass Marketing in America* (New York, 1990).

Teixeira, Ruy A., *Why Americans Don't Vote: Turnout Decline in the United States, 1960–1984* (New York, 1987).

Tellis, G. J., Stremersch, S., and Yin, E., 'The International Takeoff of New Products: The Role of Economics, Culture, and Country Innovativeness: Do New Products Take off at Consistently Different Times in Different Countries? Why?' *Marketing Science*, 22 (2003), 188–208.

Temkin, Larry S., *Inequality* (New York, 1993).

Tennov, Dorothy, *Love and Limerence: The Experience of Being in Love* (Chelsea, Mich., 1979).

Terleckyj, Nestor E., *Improvements in the Quality of Life: Estimates of Possibilities in the United States, 1974–1983* (Washington, DC, 1975).

Thaler, Richard H., *The Winner's Curse: Paradoxes and Anomalies of Economic Life* (New York, 1992).

——and Sunstein, Cass R., 'Libertarian Paternalism', *American Economic Review*, 93 (2003), 175–9.

Thomas, G., and Zmroczek, C., 'Household Technology: The Liberation of Women from the Home?' in Paul Close, and Rosemary Collins (eds.), *Family and Economy in Modern Society* (London, 1985), 101–28.

Thompson, Denys, *Voice of Civilisation: An Enquiry into Advertising* (London, 1943).

Thomson, Elizabeth, and Colella, Ugo A., 'Cohabitation and Marital Stability: Quality or Commitment?' *Journal of Marriage and the Family*, 54 (1992), 259–67.

Thornton, Arland, and Young-DeMarco, Linda, 'Four Decades of Trends in Attitudes toward Family Issues in the United States: The 1960s through the 1990s', *Journal of Marriage and the Family*, 63 (2001), 1009–37.

Tirole, Jean, *The Theory of Industrial Organization* (Cambridge, Mass., 1988).

Todd, Peter M., and Miller, Geoffrey F., 'From Pride and Prejudice to Persuasion: Satisficing in Mate Search', in G. Gigerenzer, Peter M. Todd, and the ABC Group, *Simple Heuristics that Make Us Smart* (Oxford, 1999), 287–308.

Toynbee, Polly, 'Would you give up TV for £1,000,000?' *Radio Times* (30 Jan.–5 Feb. 1993), 14.

TREIMAN, DONALD J., *Occupational Prestige in Comparative Perspective* (New York, 1977).

TRENT, K., and SOUTH, S. J., 'Structural Determinants of the Divorce Rate: A Cross-Societal Analysis', *Journal of Marriage and the Family*, 51 (1989), 391–404.

TRIBOLE, EVELYN, and RESCH, ELYSE, *Intuitive Eating* (New York, 1995).

TRIVERS, ROBERT, *Social Evolution* (Menlo Park, Calif., 1985).

TROLLOPE, ANTHONY, *Phineas Finn: The Irish Member* (Oxford, 1999, 1st publ. 1869).

TUFTE, EDWARD R., *The Visual Display of Quantitative Information* (Cheshire, Conn., 1983).

TUNNARD, CHRISTOPHER, and PUSHKAREV, BORIS, *Man-Made America: Chaos or Control? An Inquiry into Selected Problems of Design in the Urbanized Landscape* (New Haven, 1963).

TVERSKY, AMOS, and KAHNEMAN, DANIEL, 'Judgment under Uncertainty: Heuristics and Biases', *Science*, 185 (1974), 1124–31.

TWENGE, J. M., 'The Age of Anxiety? Birth Cohort Change in Anxiety and Neuroticism, 1952–1993', *Journal of Personality and Social Psychology*, 79 (2000), 1007–21.

——'Changes in Women's Assertiveness in Response to Status and Roles: A Cross-Temporal Meta-Analysis, 1931–1993', *Journal of Personality and Social Psychology*, 81 (2001), 133–45.

——'Birth Cohort Changes in Extraversion: A Cross-Temporal Meta-Analysis, 1966–1993', *Personality and Individual Differences*, 30 (2001), 735–48.

——'Birth Cohort, Social Change, and Personality: The Interplay of Dysphoria and Individualism in the 20th Century', in Daniel Cervone, and Walter Mischel (eds.), *Advances in Personality Science* (London, 2002), 196–218.

——and CAMPBELL, W. KEITH, 'Age and Birth Cohort Differences in Self-Esteem: A Cross-Temporal Meta-Analysis', *Personality and Social Psychology Review*, 5 (2001), 321–44.

————'Self-Esteem and Socioeconomic Status: A Meta-Analytic Review', *Personality and Social Psychology Review*, 6 (2002), 59–71.

TWIGG, JULIA, 'Vegetarianism and the Meaning of Meat', in Anne Murcott (ed.), *The Sociology of Food and Eating* (Aldershot, 1983).

——(ed.), *Carers: Research and Practice* (London, 1992).

TWITCHELL, JAMES B., *Living it up: Our Love Affair with Luxury* (New York, 2002).

United Nations, *A System of National Accounts and Supporting Tables*, Studies in Methods, Series F, No. 2 (New York, 1953).

——'Report on International Definition and Measurement of Standards and Levels of Living', UN Publications Sales no. 1954.IV.5 (New York, 1954).

——Social and Economic Council, Working Group on International Statistics and Coordination, 'Social Statistics: The Follow-up to the World Summit for Social Development', unpublished paper (New York, 1996); **www.un.org/Dpets/unsd/social/xgrp2.htm**.

——Development Programme, *Human Development Report 1998* (New York, 1998).

United States, Bureau of Census, *Statistical Abstract of the United States*, [annual] (Washington DC).

United States President, and Council of Economic Advisers, *Economic Report of the President Transmitted to the Congress: Together with the Annual Report of the Council of Economic Advisers* [annual] (Washington, DC).

——Senate Committee on Interstate and Foreign Commerce, *Automobile Price Labeling: Hearings before the Automobile Marketing Subcommittee*, 85 Congress, 2nd sess. Y4.In8/3:Au8/4. (Washington, DC, 1958).

——Senate Subcommittee on Antitrust and Monopoly, *Study of Administered Prices in the Automobile Industry. Report Together with Individual Views, Hearings*; 85 Congress, 2nd Sess. Y4.J89/2:P93/78 (Washington, DC, 1958).

——Department of Commerce, Bureau of the Census, *Historical Statistics of the United States, Colonial Times to 1970* (Washington, DC, 1975, CD edition New York, 1997).

——Department of Commerce, Bureau of Census, *Social Indicators III* (Washington, DC, 1980).

——Senate Select Committee on Nutrition and Human Need, *Dietary Goals for the United States* (Washington, DC, 1977).

——Department of Commerce, *The National Income and Product Accounts of the United States, 1929–82: Statistical Tables* (Washington, DC, 1986).

——Department of Agriculture, *World Per Capita Consumption of Red Meat and Poultry, 1975–91* (Washington, DC, 1994), in **www.mannlib.cornell.edu/data-sets/food/91004/**, accessed: 1998.

——Department of Agriculture, *Expenditures of Food, Beverages and Tobacco, 1970–1988, Table Uk.Wk1* (Washington, DC, 1994), CD-Rom Stock # 93050.

——Department of Agriculture (USDA), *US Food Expenditures* (Washington, DC, 1996), floppy disk stock #91003, in **http://usda.mannlib.cornell.edu/data-sets/food/91003**.

——Department of Agriculture: Economic Research Service, *Food Consumption, Prices, and Expenditures* (Washington, DC, 1996), floppy disk, stock #89015B, in **www.mannlib.cornell.edu/data-sets/food/89015**.

——Department of Agriculture (USDA), *Agricultural Statistics 1995–6* (Washington, DC, 1998).

——Department of Health and Human Services, *Mental Health: A Report of the Surgeon General, Executive Summary* (Rockville, Md., 1999).

——Department of Education, *Digest of Education Statistics* (Washington, DC, 2002), in **http://nces.ed.gov/programs/digest/d00/dt189.asp**.

——Administrative Office of the US Courts, *Bankruptcy Statistics* (Washington, DC, 2003), in **www.uscourts.gov/bnkrpctystats/FY1987–2003.pdf** [1992–2003], table F-2; **www.uscourts.gov/bnkrpctystats/1960–0312-MonthJune.pdf** [1980–1991], p. 5-2; **www.uscourts.gov/bnkrpctystats/1960–0312-MonthJune.pdf** [1960–1979], p. 5-1.

——National Center for Health Statistics, *Health, United States 2004* (Hyatsville, Md., 2004).

UPDIKE, JOHN, *Picked-up Pieces* (London, 1976).

——— *A Rabbit Omnibus: Rabbit, Run; Rabbit Redux; Rabbit is Rich* (London, 1991).

VALLANCE, AYLMER, *Hire-Purchase* (London, 1939).

VANEK, JOANN, 'Time Spent in Housework', in Alice H. Amsden, (ed.), *The Economics of Women and Work* (Harmondsworth, 1980), 82–90.

VANLANINGHAM, JODY, JOHNSON, DAVID R., and AMATO, PAUL, 'Marital Happiness, Marital Duration, and the U-Shaped Curve: Evidence from a Five-Wave Panel Study', *Social Forces*, 79 (2001), 1313–41.

VAN OS, J., BAK, M., HANSSEN, M., BIJL, R. V., DE GRAAF, R., and VERDOUX, H., 'Cannabis Use and Psychosis: A Longitudinal Population-Based Study', *American Journal of Epidemiology*, 156 (2002), 319–27.

VAN PRAAG, BERNARD M. S., and FERRER-I-CARBONELL, ADA, *Happiness Quantified: A Satisfaction Calculus Approach* (Oxford, 2004).

——— and FRIJTERS, PAUL, 'The Measurement of Welfare and Well-Being: The Leyden Approach', in Daniel, Kahneman, Ed Diener, and Norbert Schwarz (eds.), *Well-Being: The Foundations of Hedonic Psychology* (New York, 1999), 413–33.

VARESE, FEDERICO, *The Russian Mafia: Private Protection in a New Market Economy* (Oxford, 2001).

VEENHOVEN, RUUT, 'Is Happiness Relative?' *Social Indicators Research*, 24 (1991), 1–34.

——— 'Developments in Satisfaction Research', *Social Indicators Research*, 37 (1996), 1–46.

——— 'The Study of Life Satisfaction', in Willem E. Saris, Ruut Veenhoven, A. C. Scherpenzeel, and B. Bunting (eds.), *A Comparative Study of Satisfaction with Life in Europe* (Budapest, 1996), 11–48.

——— *World Database of Happiness* (2005), in **www.eur.nl/fsw/research/happiness/**.

VELUPILLAI, KUMARASWAMY, *Computable Economics: The Arne Ryde Memorial Lectures* (Oxford, 2000).

VERMA, SATYENDRA, and LICHTENSTEIN, JULES, 'The Declining Personal Saving Rate: Is There Cause for Alarm?' Public Policy Institute (Washington, DC, 2000).

VEROFF, JOSEPH, DOUVAN, ELIZABETH ANN MALCOLM, and KULKA, RICHARD A., *The Inner American: A Self-Portrait from 1957 to 1976* (New York, 1981).

——— ——— ORBUCH, TERRI L., and ACITELLI, LINDA K., 'Happiness in Stable Marriages: The Early Years', in Thomas N. Bradbury (ed.), *The Developmental Course of Marital Dysfunction* (Cambridge, 1998), 152–79.

——— KULKA, RICHARD, and DOUVAN, ELIZABETH ANN MALCOLM, *Mental Health in America, Patterns for Help-Seeking from 1957 to 1976* (New York, 1981).

VINING, DANIEL R., 'Social Versus Reproductive Success: The Central Theoretical Problem of Human Sociobiology', *Behavioral and Brain Sciences*, 9 (1986), 167–216.

VISCUSI, W. KIP, *Smoking: Making the Risky Decision* (New York, 1992).

VISSER, MARTHA, *The Rituals of Dinner* (London, 1992).

WAGNER, SUSAN, *The Federal Trade Commission* (New York, 1971).

WAITE, LINDA J., and GALLAGHER, MAGGIE, *The Case for Marriage: Why Married People are Happier, Healthier, and Better off Financially* (New York, 2000).

WAITE, LINDA J., and LEHRER, E. L., 'The Benefits from Marriage and Religion in the United States: A Comparative Analysis', *Population and Development Review*, 29 (2003), 255–76.

WALDFOGEL, JOEL, 'The Deadweight Loss of Christmas', *American Economic Review*, 83 (1993), 1328–36.

—— 'The Deadweight Loss of Christmas: Reply', *American Economic Review*, 88 (1998), 1358–9.

WALKER, CAROLINE, and CANNON, GEOFFREY, *The Food Scandal: What's Wrong with the British Diet and How to Put It Right* (London, 1984).

WALLER, WILLARD, 'The Rating and Dating Complex', *American Sociological Review*, 2 (1937), 727–34.

—— *The Family: A Dynamic Interpretation* (New York, 1938).

WALLERSTEIN, JUDITH S., 'The Long-Term Effects of Divorce on Children: A Review', *Journal of the American Academy of Child and Adolescent Psychiatry*, 30 (1991), 349–60.

WALLIS, JOHN J., and NORTH, DOUGLAS, 'Should Transaction Costs Be Subtracted from Gross National Product?' *Journal of Economic History*, 48 (1988), 651–4.

WALSH, JOHN P., *Supermarkets Transformed: Understanding Organizational and Technological Innovations* (New Brunswick, NJ, 1993).

WARDLE, CHRISTOPHER, *Changing Food Habits in the UK* (London, 1977).

Ward's Reports Inc., *Ward's Automotive Yearbook*. vol. 1938–ↄ (Detroit, 1938).

WARING, STEPHEN P., *Taylorism Transformed: Scientific Management Theory since 1945* (Chapel Hill, NC, 1991).

WARNOCK, C. GAYLE, *The Edsel Affair* (Paradise Valley, Ariz., 1980).

WARR, PETER, 'Well-Being and the Workplace', in Daniel, Kahneman Ed Diener, and Norbert Schwartz (eds.), *Well-Being: The Foundations of Hedonic Psychology* (New York, 1999), 392–412.

WARREN, ELIZABETH, and TYAGI, AMELIA W., *The Two-Income Trap: Why Middle-Class Mothers and Fathers are Going Broke* (New York, 2003).

WARREN, GEOFFREY C., *The Foods We Eat: A Survey of Meals, Their Content and Chronology by Season, Day of the Week, Region, Class and Age* (London, 1958).

WARSHAW, M. G., KLERMAN, G. L., and LAVORI, P. W., 'Are Secular Trends in Major Depression an Artifact of Recall?' *Journal of Psychiatric Research*, 25 (1991), 141–51.

WATERS, EVERETT, MERRICK, SUSAN, TREBOUX, DOMINIQUE, CROWELL, JUDITH, and ALBERSHEIM, LEAH, 'Attachment Security in Infancy and Early Adulthood: A Twenty-Year Longitudinal Study', *Child Development*, 71 (2000), 684–9.

WEBB, SIDNEY, and WEBB, BEATRICE P., *Industrial Democracy* (London, 1902).

WEBLEY, P., and LEA, S. E. G., 'The Partial Unacceptability of Money in Repayment for Neighborly Help', *Human Relations*, 46 (1993), 65–76.

———— and PORTALSKA, R., 'The Unacceptability of Money as a Gift', *Journal of Economic Psychology*, 4 (1983), 223–38.

—— and WILSON, RICHENDA, 'Social Relationships and the Unacceptability of Money as a Gift', *Journal of Social Psychology*, 129 (1989), 85–91.

WEISS, JESSICA, *To Have and to Hold: Marriage, the Baby Boom, and Social Change* (Chicago, 2000).

WEISS, YORAM, and FERSHTMAN, CHAIM, 'Social Status and Economic Performance: A Survey', *European Economic Review*, 42 (1998), 801–20.

WEITZMAN, LENORE J., *The Marriage Contract: Spouses, Lovers and the Law* (New York, 1981).

——'The Economic Consequences of Divorce are Still Unequal: Comment on Peterson', *American Sociological Review*, 61 (1996), 537–8.

WEITZMAN, MARTIN L., 'On the Welfare Significance of National Product in a Dynamic Economy', *Quarterly Journal of Economics*, 90 (1976), 156–62.

WELLINGS, KATE, FIELD, JULIA, JOHNSON, ANNE M., and WADSWORTH, JANE, *Sexual Behaviour in Britain: The National Survey of Sexual Attitudes and Lifestyles* (London, 1994).

WELLINS, RICHARD S., BYHAM, WILLIAM C., and WILSON, JEANNE M., *Empowered Teams: Creating Self-Directed Work Groups that Improve Quality, Productivity, and Participation* (San Francisco, 1991).

WERTENBROCH, KLAUS, 'Self-Rationing: Self-Control in Consumer Choice', in George Loewenstein, Daniel Read, and Roy F. Baumeister, (eds.), *Time and Decision: Economic and Psychological Perspectives on Intertemporal Choice* (New York, 2003), 491–516.

WHELAN, CHRISTINE, 'Singles' Magazines and the Rise of Contingent Commitment in the US, 1965–2000', M.Phil. thesis, University of Oxford, 2001.

——'Self-help Books and the Quest for Self-Control in the United States 1950–2000', D.Phil. thesis, University of Oxford, 2004.

WHISLER, TIMOTHY R., *The British Motor Industry, 1945–1994: A Case Study in Industrial Decline* (Oxford, 1999).

WHITE, LAWRENCE J., *The Automobile Industry since 1945* (Cambridge, Mass., 1971).

WHITE, MICHELLE, 'What's Wrong with U.S. Personal Bankruptcy Law and How to Fix It', *Regulation*, 22 (1999).

WHITEHEAD, FRANK, 'Advertising', in Denys Thompson (ed.), *Discrimination and Popular Culture* (Harmondsworth, 1973), 51–77.

WHITEHEAD, BARBARA DAFOE, *The Divorce Culture* (New York, 1997).

——*Why There are No Good Men Left: The Romantic Plight of the New Single Woman* (New York, 2003).

——and POPENOE, DAVID, 'Who Wants to Marry a Soul Mate?' in *The State of our Unions 2001: The Social Health of Marriage in America* (Piscataway, NJ, 2001).

WHITWELL, GREG, *Making the Market: The Rise of Consumer Society* (Melbourne, 1989).

WHYTE, W. H. (ed.), *The Exploding Metropolis* (Garden City, NY, 1958).

WHYTE, MARTIN KING, *Dating, Mating, and Marriage* (New York, 1990).

WIGHT, ROBIN, *The Day the Pigs Refused to Be Driven to Market: Advertising and the Consumer Revolution* (London, 1972).

WILKINSON, RICHARD, 'The Epidemiological Transition: From Material Scarcity to Social Disadvantage?' *Daedalus*, 123 (1994), 61–77.

WILKINSON, RICHARD, *Unhealthy Societies: The Afflictions of Inequality* (London, 1996).

WILLIAMS, JOAN, *Unbending Gender: Why Family and Work Conflict and What to Do about It* (Oxford, 2000).

WILLIAMSON, JUDITH, *Decoding Advertisements: Ideology and Meaning in Advertising* (London, 1987).

WILLIAMSON, OLIVER E., *The Economic Institutions of Capitalism: Firms, Markets, Relational Contracting* (New York, 1985).

WILSON, CHRIS W., and OSWALD, ANDREW J., 'How Does Marriage Affect Physical and Psychological Health? A Survey of the Longitudinal Evidence', University of York and University of Warwick (York, 2002).

WILSON, RICHARD, and MACKLEY, ALAN, *Creating Paradise: The Building of the English Country House, 1660–1880* (London, 2000).

WILSON, WILLIAM J., *The Truly Disadvantaged: The Inner City, the Underclass, and Public Policy* (Chicago, 1987).

—— *When Work Disappears: The World of the New Urban Poor* (New York, 1996).

WISEMAN, C. V., GRAY, J. T., MOSIMANN, J. E., and AHRENS, A. E., 'Cultural Expectations of Thinness in Women: An Update', *International Journal of Eating Disorders*, 11 (1992), 85–9.

WOLF, A. M., and COLDITZ, G. A., 'Social and Economic Effects of Body Weight in the United States', *American Journal of Clinical Nutrition*, 63 (1996), 466–9.

WOLF, NAOMI, *The Beauty Myth: How Images of Beauty Are Used against Women* (London, 1991).

WOLFE, TOM, 'The Me Decade and the Third Great Awakening', in Tom Wolfe (ed.), *The Purple Decades* (Harmondsworth, 1983), 265–96.

WOLFERS, JUSTIN, 'Did Unilateral Divorce Laws Raise Divorce Rates? A Reconciliation and New Results', Stanford Law and Economics Olin Working Paper No. 264; Stanford Law School, Public Law Working Paper No. 68. (2003).

WOLFF, EDWARD N., *Recent Trends in Wealth Ownership, 1983–1998* (2000), in **www.levy.org/docs/wrkpap/papers/300.html**, accessed: 11 Feb. 2004.

—— *Top Heavy: The Increasing Inequality of Wealth in America and What Can Be Done about It* (New York, 2002).

WOLFINGER, NICHOLAS H., 'Trends in the Intergenerational Transmission of Divorce', *Demography*, 36 (1999), 415–20.

WOOD, FLORIS W., *An American Profile: Opinions and Behavior, 1972–1989: Opinion Results on 300 High-Interest Issues Derived from the General Social Survey Conducted by the National Opinion Research Center* (Detroit, 1990).

WOOD, ROY C., *The Sociology of the Meal* (Edinburgh, 1995).

World Bank, *World Tables 1989–1990: Socio-Economic Time-Series Access and Retrieval System* (1990).

—— *Poverty Reduction and the World Bank* (annual, 1993–).

—— *Averting the Old Age Crisis: Policies to Protect the Old and Promote Growth* (New York, 1994).

World Health Organization, 'Obesity and Overweight', World Health Organization (Geneva, 2004).

——*World Health Report 2000: Health Systems: Improving Performance* (Geneva, 2000).

WURTZEL, ELIZABETH, *Prozac Nation: Young and Depressed in America* (London, 1995).

WYKOFF, F. C., 'Capital Depreciation in the Post War Period: Automobiles', *Review of Economics and Statistics*, 52 (1970), 168–72.

——'A User Cost Approach to New Automobile Purchases', *Review of Economic Studies*, 40 (1973), 377–390.

——'Economic Depreciation and the User Cost of Business-Leased Automobiles', in Dale W. Jorgenson, and Ralph Landau, (eds.), *Technology and Capital Formation* (Cambridge, Mass., 1989), 259–92.

WYSHAK, G., 'Infertility in American College Alumnae', *International Journal of Gynecology & Obstetrics*, 73 (2001), 237–42.

YAKURA, ELAINE K., 'Billables: The Valorization of Time in Consulting', *American Behavioral Scientist*, 44 (2001), 1076–96.

YANG, CATHERINE, and STERN, WILLY, 'Maybe They Should Call Them "Scammers": Electronic Checkout Systems May Be Ripping You Off', *Business Week* (16 Jan. 1995), 30–1.

YANG, MAYFAIR MEI-HUI, 'The Gift Economy and State Power in China', *Comparative Studies in Society and History*, 31 (1989), 25–54.

——*Gifts, Favors, and Banquets: The Art of Social Relationships in China* (Ithaca, NY, 1994).

YANKELOVICH, DANIEL, *New Rules, Searching for Self-Fulfillment in a World Turned Upside Down* (New York, 1981).

YARWOOD, DOREEN, *The British Kitchen: Housewifery since Roman Times* (London, 1981).

——*The Domestic Interior: Technology and the Home* (London, 1990).

YATES, A., 'Running: An Analogue of Anorexia?' *New England Journal of Medicine*, 308 (1983), 251–5.

YATES, BROCK W., *The Critical Path: Inventing an Automobile and Reinventing a Corporation*, 1st edn. (Boston, 1996).

YEUNG, W. JEAN, and STAFFORD, FRANK, 'Intra-Family Child Care Time Allocation: Stalled Revolution or Road to Equality?' Center for Advanced Social Science Research, New York University (New York, 2003).

YITZHAKI, SHLOMO, 'Relative Deprivation and the Gini Coefficient', *Quarterly Journal of Economics*, 93 (1979), 321–4.

ZAHAVI, AMOTZ, and ZAHAVI, AVISHAG, *The Handicap Principle: A Missing Piece of Darwin's Puzzle* (Oxford, 1997).

ZAMAGNI, STEFANO (ed.), *The Economics of Altruism* (Aldershot, 1995).

ZELIZER, VIVIANA A. R., *Morals and Markets: The Development of Life Insurance in the United States* (New York, 1979).

——*The Social Meaning of Money* (New York, 1994).

——*Pricing the Priceless Child: The Changing Social Value of Children* (Princeton, 1994).

ZERUBAVEL, EVIATAR, *Hidden Rhythms: Schedules and Calendars in Social Life* (Chicago, 1981).

Zill, Nicholas, Morrison, Donna R., and Coiro, Mary J., 'Long-Term Effects of Parental Divorce on Parent–Child Relationships, Adjustment, and Achievement in Young Adulthood', *Journal of Family Psychology*, 7 (1993), 91–103.

Zito, J. M., Safer, D. J., dosReis, S., Gardner, J. F., Boles, M., and Lynch, F., 'Trends in the Prescribing of Psychotropic Medications to Preschoolers', *Journal of the American Medical Association*, 283 (2000), 1025–30.

———————Magder, L., Soeken, K., Boles, M., Lynch, F., and Riddle, M. A., 'Psychotropic Practice Patterns for Youths: A 10-Year Perspective', *Archives of Pediatrics and Adolescent Medicine*, 157 (2003), pp. 17–25.

Zolotas, Xenophon Euthymiou, *Economic Growth and Declining Social Welfare* (Athens, 1981).

Zweig, Michael, *The Working Class Majority: America's Best Kept Secret* (Ithaca, NY, 2000).

Index

Note: Includes names mentioned in the body of the text, but not those referred to as part of a bibliographical reference in the footnotes.

Index

Index

450

Index